Theoretical and Applied Mathematics in International Business

Bryan Christiansen
Global Research Society, USA

Fatima Shuwaikh
Université Paris Saclay, France

A volume in the Advances in Business Strategy and Competitive Advantage (ABSCA) Book Series

IGI Global
DISSEMINATOR OF KNOWLEDGE

Published in the United States of America by
IGI Global
Business Science Reference (an imprint of IGI Global)
701 E. Chocolate Avenue
Hershey PA, USA 17033
Tel: 717-533-8845
Fax: 717-533-8661
E-mail: cust@igi-global.com
Web site: http://www.igi-global.com

Library of Congress Cataloging-in-Publication Data

Names: Christiansen, Bryan, 1960- editor. | Shuwaikh, Fatima, 1977- editor.
Title: Theoretical and applied mathematics in international business / Bryan Christiansen and Fatima Shuwaikh, editors.
Description: Hershey, PA : Business Science Reference, [2020]
Identifiers: LCCN 2018054604| ISBN 9781522584582 (hardcover) | ISBN 9781522584599 (ebook) | ISBN 9781522585015 (softcover)
Subjects: LCSH: International trade--Mathematics. | International trade--Mathematical models.
Classification: LCC HF1379 .T477 2020 | DDC 338.8/80151--dc23 LC record available at https://lccn.loc.gov/2018054604

This book is published in the IGI Global book series Advances in Business Strategy and Competitive Advantage (ABSCA) (ISSN: 2327-3429; eISSN: 2327-3437)

British Cataloguing in Publication Data
A Cataloguing in Publication record for this book is available from the British Library.

All work contributed to this book is new, previously-unpublished material. The views expressed in this book are those of the authors, but not necessarily of the publisher.

For electronic access to this publication, please contact: eresources@igi-global.com.

Advances in Business Strategy and Competitive Advantage (ABSCA) Book Series

Patricia Ordóñez de Pablos
Universidad de Oviedo, Spain

ISSN:2327-3429
EISSN:2327-3437

Mission

Business entities are constantly seeking new ways through which to gain advantage over their competitors and strengthen their position within the business environment. With competition at an all-time high due to technological advancements allowing for competition on a global scale, firms continue to seek new ways through which to improve and strengthen their business processes, procedures, and profitability.

The **Advances in Business Strategy and Competitive Advantage (ABSCA) Book Series** is a timely series responding to the high demand for state-of-the-art research on how business strategies are created, implemented and re-designed to meet the demands of globalized competitive markets. With a focus on local and global challenges, business opportunities and the needs of society, the **ABSCA** encourages scientific discourse on doing business and managing information technologies for the creation of sustainable competitive advantage.

Coverage

- Ethics and Business Strategy
- Value Creation
- Customer-Orientation Strategy
- Resource-Based Competition
- Adaptive Enterprise
- International Business Strategy
- Small and Medium Enterprises
- Value Chain
- Tacit Knowledge
- Globalization

IGI Global is currently accepting manuscripts for publication within this series. To submit a proposal for a volume in this series, please contact our Acquisition Editors at Acquisitions@igi-global.com or visit: http://www.igi-global.com/publish/.

The Advances in Business Strategy and Competitive Advantage (ABSCA) Book Series (ISSN 2327-3429) is published by IGI Global, 701 E. Chocolate Avenue, Hershey, PA 17033-1240, USA, www.igi-global.com. This series is composed of titles available for purchase individually; each title is edited to be contextually exclusive from any other title within the series. For pricing and ordering information please visit http://www.igi-global.com/book-series/advances-business-strategy-competitive-advantage/73672. Postmaster: Send all address changes to above address.

Titles in this Series

For a list of additional titles in this series, please visit: www.igi-global.com/book-series

Cases on Corporate Social Responsibility and Contemporary Issues in Organizations
Alexandros Antonaras (University of Nicosia, Cyprus) and Paraskevi Dekoulou (University of Nicosia, Cyprus)
Business Science Reference • copyright 2019 • 402pp • H/C (ISBN: 9781522577157) • US $225.00 (our price)

Women Entrepreneurs and Strategic Decision Making in the Global Economy
Florica Tomos (University of South Wales, UK) Naresh Kumar (Universiti Malaysia Kelantan, Malaysia) Nick Clifton (Cardiff Metropolitan University, UK) and Denis Hyams-Ssekasi (University of Bolton, UK)
Business Science Reference • copyright 2019 • 411pp • H/C (ISBN: 9781522574798) • US $215.00 (our price)

Linking Cultural Dimensions and CSR Communication Emerging Research and Opportunities
Maria Palazzo (University of Salerno, Italy)
Business Science Reference • copyright 2019 • 169pp • H/C (ISBN: 9781522579465) • US $165.00 (our price)

Evidence-Based Initiatives for Organizational Change and Development
Robert G. Hamlin (University of Wolverhampton, UK) Andrea D. Ellinger (The University of Texas at Tyler, USA) and Jenni Jones (University of Wolverhampton, UK)
Business Science Reference • copyright 2019 • 850pp • H/C (ISBN: 9781522561552) • US $495.00 (our price)

Environmental, Health, and Business Opportunities in the New Meat Alternatives Market
Diana Bogueva (Curtin University, Australia) Dora Marinova (Curtin University, Australia) Talia Raphaely (Curtin University, Australia) and Kurt Schmidinger (University of Vienna, Austria)
Business Science Reference • copyright 2019 • 395pp • H/C (ISBN: 9781522573500) • US $225.00 (our price)

Handbook of Research on Business Models in Modern Competitive Scenarios
George Leal Jamil (Informações em Rede e Consultoria Ltda., Brazil) Liliane Carvalho Jamil (Independent Researcher, Brazil) Cláudio Roberto Magalhães Pessoa (FUMEC University, Brazil) and Werner Silveira (Philharmonic Orchestra of Minas Gerais, Brazil)
Business Science Reference • copyright 2019 • 537pp • H/C (ISBN: 9781522572657) • US $295.00 (our price)

Strategic Collaborative Innovations in Organizational Systems
Mambo Mupepi (Grand Valley State University, USA) and Robert Costello (Newcastle College, UK)
Business Science Reference • copyright 2019 • 272pp • H/C (ISBN: 9781522573906) • US $195.00 (our price)

IGI Global
DISSEMINATOR OF KNOWLEDGE

701 East Chocolate Avenue, Hershey, PA 17033, USA
Tel: 717-533-8845 x100 • Fax: 717-533-8661
E-Mail: cust@igi-global.com • www.igi-global.com

Editorial Advisory Board

Table of Contents

Detailed Table of Contents

Using an applied mathematics approach, this chapter embeds algorithmic measures into cultural theory in research on international business. The specialized area is concerned with adaptation of multinational enterprise (MNE) cross-borders in which how dynamic functions can strengthen the argument by producing robust models. The chapter contributes to the extant literature by offering a set of mechanisms that can be used by MNEs in adapting to a new or complex environment where culture can be diverse and policy choice is challenging. The mechanism by driving an adaptive approach, in particular, addresses a research issue that is persistent in cultural transition studies. The issue is distinguished from the standard economic model in that individual or rational actors have a fixed set of independent preferences (i.e., decision choice based on price, benefit, or rules of the game), uninfluenced by the behavior of others or the social settings within which they operate. The current study addresses the issue by demonstrating that a range of socio-cultural factors can influence behavior.

Previous research has consistently demonstrated that team work quality plays an important role in predicting the speed of new product development (NPD). However, the examination of the fundamental mechanisms behind this relationship has received less attention than it deserves. Drawing on the resource-based view and internal market orientation theories, this chapter examines mediating effect of internal market orientation in the relationship between teamwork quality and speed of new product development. One hundred and forty-nine team members drawn from the telecom companies in the Kingdom of Saudi Arabia participated in this study. Partial least squares path modelling was employed to test mediating effect of internal market orientation in the relationship between teamwork quality and NPD speed. Findings suggest a positive relationship between teamwork quality and NPD speed. As hypothesized, the findings showed that of internal market orientation mediated the relationship between teamwork quality and NPD speed.

Drug trafficking could be associated with the corrupt structures of governments and any anti-drug enforcement policy would be compromised. At the same time, it is perceived that the flow of foreign direct investment, which is inversely related with drug trafficking, drives the economy and the host government faces a dilemma between encouraging foreign direct investment or allowing drug trafficking. In this chapter, a theoretical model of this stylized fact is made. It is found that the host government sets a strict enforcement policy if the corruption level is low; otherwise, a lax policy would be set. Once the enforcement policy has been set, an increase in the corruption level reduces the enforcement level. Additionally, an increase in the demand for drugs may reduce or increase the enforcement level depending of the size of corruption level compared with the market size for foreign investors. However, with an international specific policy, an increase in demand of drugs reduces unequivocally the optimal enforcement level.

The purpose of this chapter is to build and explain the Gravity Model for the trade flows of Albania and 15 of its trade partners for the period of 2001-2016, both theoretically and empirically. The theoretical development of the subject gives an overview of the economic thought over the years regarding the concept of free trade, its benefits and threats, the Central European Free Trade Agreement (CEFTA), and the Gravity Model in order to be able to explain and interpret the patterns of trade between countries. The econometrical analysis illustrates the impact of gross domestic product (GDP) of partner countries, the distance between them, and CEFTA has on the trade flows of Albania. The Gravity Model built in this study supports the theoretical approach and it shows how GDP has positively affected trade flows, while distance has negatively affected trade flows. The impact of CEFTA is insignificant.

Logistics is a key factor for companies to sustain their businesses, to gain the competitive advantage in the market, and to speed up the transportation process. Companies can perform their own logistic activities using their own core competencies; however, they can face huge logistics costs. To avoid these logistics operating costs, companies need to cooperate with third party logistics service providers (3PL) to perform logistics activities. This chapter proposes an integrated rough MCDM model including Rough

SWARA and Rough COPRAS methods to identify the best 3PL for a Turkish textile company. These two rough methods were not previously utilized in solving any decision-making problems in the extant literature. Thus, the contribution of this study is to develop a new rough integrated model to solve the 3PL service provider selection problem.

In this chapter, the relationship between research and development (R&D) expenditures and economic growth was investigated with both Emirmahmutoğlu and Köse Causality test and the Dimitrescu and Hurlin Panel Causality test based on Rolling Windows Regression for the selected 19 OECD member countries for the period 1996-2015. The results concluded that for all panel there is a causality from economic growth to R&D expenditures. In this study, the relationship between variables was investigated using different mathematical techniques like rolling windows. According to the results of the Dimitrescu and Hurlin Panel Causality Test based on Rolling Window Regression, which is applied differently from other studies in the literature, there was a causality from economic growth to R&D expenditures in 2010. In 2011, there was causality from R&D expenditures to economic growth for all panels.

The purpose of this chapter is to demonstrate how the notion of "proof" can be used to resolve issues of valuation in finance and how the method of simultaneous equations can be applied to determine the value of shares in two firms that hold an investment of shares in one another at the same time. The reader will be introduced to the notion of proof by arbitrage as it is was first pioneered in modern finance by Modigliani and Miller and then its application in providing guidance to practitioners of valuation will be explored.

As the performance of suppliers directly or indirectly affects the performance of the companies with which they engage, working with the most suitable supplier has become the key to success for companies. When solving the supplier selection problem, many different criteria involving qualitative and quantitative criteria are considered. Therefore, the supplier selection problem is considered an MCDM problem. These criteria can include uncertain and imprecise data. Additionally, the judgments of many managers are considered in supplier selection problems. Thus, in this chapter, a fuzzy group integrated model including Fuzzy SWARA (step-wise weight assessment ratio analysis) and Fuzzy ARAS (additive ratio assessment) is proposed to select the best supplier. This study contributes to the extant literature since these two methods were not used in the past to solve any problems together. The proposed model is applied to a Turkish textile company.

The assignment problem (AP) is a particular case of a linear programming problem that deals with the allocation of various resources for various activities on a 1-to-1 basis. It does so in such a manner that the profit or sale involved in the process is maximum and cost or time is minimum. Generally, the profit/sale/cost/time is called the parameter of the AP and this is not a crisp number due to some uncontrollable factors. They can also involve uncertainty and hesitation. Therefore, to solve the AP under an intuitionistic fuzzy environment in this chapter, the author proposes the PSK (P. Senthil Kumar) method. Numerous theorems which are related to intuitionistic fuzzy assignment problem is proposed and is proved by PSK. By using the PSK method, the real-life related fully intuitionistic fuzzy assignment problems are solved. The proposed results are verified by both LINGO 17.0 and TORA software packages. In addition to verifying the efficiency and realism of the proposed method, the computer code based on LINGO 17.0 is presented. Results, discussion, comparative study, and the advantages of the PSK method are given. The chapter ends with the conclusion and future studies.

The Merton Model is the critical model for financial economics to measure the default of a firm. It was the first structural model because it uses the market value of the firm for estimating the default of the firm. The firm will be in default only when the values of the firm goes down to a threshold value (the debt of the firm), and if it occurs, the owner will put the firm to the debt holders. The effects of parameters-asset value V, firms debt D, interest rate r, the volatility σ, and period T on the probability of default was investigated. To estimate the probability of default of a firm, the Black Scholes Model for European call options is used. The aim is to determine which parameter effects more or less on the probability of default. The experiment is based on the orthogonal array L27 in which the five factors (parameters) are varied at three levels. The Taguchi L27 orthogonal method, ANOM, and ANOVA are used to examine the effect of these parameters on the probability of default. It also provides the best combination where the probability of default is minimum.

Firms have experienced extreme competition because of changes in technological and global issues. Globalization of manufacturing has arisen through a faster transfer of materials, complex payment systems, and compression of product life cycle. Eventually, firms need the integration of technologies to meet the increasingly sophisticated customers' needs. Among the technologies, artificial intelligence has attracted much of the attention as it has been foreseen to have a major impact on all industries. Real options approach may be applied to make informed decisions concerning digital technologies investments.

Preface

Mathematics has long played a major role in human history and is at times confused with philosophy. As the only truly universal language, mathematics is found in a wide variety of subjects such as art, business, economics, encryption, music, science, and technology. The field also develops creativity, logic, problem solving, and reasoning which, in turn, spurs development in numerous ways. The laws of mathematics have been discovered and employed over aeons by great thinkers such as Einstein, Euler, Gauss, Nash, Newton, Pythagoras, and Ramanujan who have implemented applied and/or theoretical (pure) mathematics into their different contributions.

Mathematical literacy drives economic growth and international business today is a large component of that growth. In an era of global hypercompetition, the continued development and use of mathematics in international business holds increasing importance at the regional, national, local, and corporate levels. Therefore, the purpose of this publication is to examine some different areas and applications of mathematics within the field of international business that we trust will spur additional research for future benefit to all concerned. Some chapters covered in this book involve unique topics such as drug trafficking and encryption which may not normally be considered in international business; however, the reader will be able to see the connection using a holistic perspective of this publication.

Chapter 1 uses an applied mathematics approach to embed algorithmic measures into cultural theory in research on International Business. The specialized area is concerned with adaptation of multinational enterprise (MNE) cross-borders in which how dynamic functions can strengthen the argument by producing robust models. The chapter contributes to the extant literature by offering a set of mechanisms that can be used by MNEs in adapting to a new or complex environment where culture can be diverse and policy choice is challenging. The mechanism by driving an adaptive approach, in particular, addresses a research issue that is persistent in cultural transition studies. The issue is distinguished from the standard economic model in that individual or rational actors have a fixed set of independent preferences (i.e., decision choice based on price, benefit, or rules of the game), uninfluenced by the behaviour of others or the social settings within which they operate. The current study addresses the issue by demonstrating that a range of socio-cultural factors can influence behavior.

Chapter 2 examines the relationship between team work quality and the speed of new product development (NPD). Previous research has consistently demonstrated that team work quality plays an important role in predicting the speed of NPD. However, the examination of the fundamental mechanisms behind this relationship has received less attention than it deserves. Drawing on the resource-based view and internal market orientation theories, this study examines mediating effect of internal market orientation in the relationship between teamwork quality and speed of NPD. A total of 149 team members drawn from the telecom companies in the Kingdom of Saudi Arabia participated in this study. Partial least squares path modelling was employed to test mediating effect of internal market orientation in the relationship between teamwork quality and NPD speed, and the findings suggest a positive relationship between teamwork quality and NPD speed.

Chapter 3 covers foreign direct investment, corruption, and crime. Drug trafficking could be associated with the corrupt structures of governments and any anti-drug enforcement policy would be compromised. Simultaneously, it is perceived that the flow of foreign direct investment, which is inversely related with drug trafficking, drives the economy and the host government faces a dilemma between encouraging foreign direct investment or allowing drug trafficking. In this work, a theoretical model of this stylized fact is made. It is found that the host government sets a strict enforcement policy if the corruption level is low; otherwise, a lax policy would be set. Once the enforcement policy has been set, an increase in the corruption level reduces the enforcement level. Additionally, an increase in the demand for drugs may reduce or increase the enforcement level depending of the size of corruption level compared with the market size for foreign investors. However, with an international specific policy, an increase in demand of drugs reduces unequivocally the optimal enforcement level.

Chapter 4 builds and explains the Gravity Model for the trade flows of Albania and 15 of its trade partners for the period of 2001-2016, both theoretically and empirically. The theoretical development of the subject gives an overview of the economic thought over the years regarding the concept of free trade, its benefits and threats, the Central European Free Trade Agreement (CEFTA), and the Gravity Model in order to be able to explain and interpret the patterns of trade between countries. The econometrical analysis illustrates the impact of Gross Domestic Product (GDP) of partner countries, the distance between them, and CEFTA has on the trade flows of Albania. The Gravity Model built in this study supports the theoretical approach and shows how GDP has positively affected trade flows, while distance has negatively affected trade flows. The impact of CEFTA is insignificant.

Chapter 5 develops an integrated rough model for third party logistics service provider selection. Logistics is a key factor for companies to sustain their businesses, to gain a competitive advantage in the market, and to speed up the transportation process. Companies can perform their own logistic activities using their own core competencies; however, they can face huge logistics costs. To avoid these logistics operating costs, companies need to cooperate with third party logistics service providers (3PL) to perform logistics activities. This study proposes an integrated rough MCDM model including Rough SWARA and Rough COPRAS methods to identify the best 3PL for a Turkish textile company. These two rough methods were not previously utilised in solving any decision making problems in the extant literature. Thus, the contribution of this study is to develop a new rough integrated model to solve the 3PL service provider selection problem.

Chapter 6 investigates the relationship between research and development (R&D) expenditures and economic growth in 19 OECD countries with both the Emirmahmutoğlu and Köse (2011) Causality test and the Dimitrescu and Hurlin (2012) Panel Causality test based on Rolling Windows Regression for the selected member nations during the period 1996-2015. The results concluded that for all panel there is a causality from economic growth to R&D expenditures. In this study, the relationship between variables was investigated using different mathematical techniques like rolling windows. According to the results of the Dimitrescu and Hurlin Panel Causality Test based on Rolling Window Regression, which is applied differently from other studies in the extant literature, there was a causality from economic growth to R&D expenditures in 2010. In 2011, there was causality from R&D expenditures to economic growth for all panels.

Chapter 7 demonstrates how the notion of 'proof' can be used to resolve issues of valuation in finance and how the method of simultaneous equations can be applied to determine the value of shares in two firms that hold an investment of shares in one another at the same time. The reader will be introduced to the notion of proof by arbitrage as it is was first pioneered in modern finance by Modigliani and Miller (1958) and then its application in providing guidance to practitioners of valuation is explored.

Chapter 8 proposes a model as applied to a Turkish textile company using Fuzzy SWARA (Step-wise Weight Assessment Ratio Analysis) and Fuzzy ARAS (Additive Ratio Assessment) methods to solve the supplier selection problem. As the performance of suppliers directly or indirectly affects the performance of the companies with which they engage, working with the most suitable supplier has become the key to success for companies. When solving the supplier selection problem, many different criteria involving qualitative and quantitative criteria are considered. Therefore, the supplier selection problem is considered an MCDM problem. These criteria can include uncertain and imprecise data. Additionally, the judgments of many managers are considered in supplier selection problems. Thus, in this study, a fuzzy group integrated model including Fuzzy SWARA and Fuzzy ARAS is proposed to select the best supplier. This study contributes to the extant literature since these two methods were not used in the past to solve any problems together.

Chapter 9 introduces the PSK method for solving fully intuitionistic fuzzy assignment problems with some software tools. The Assignment Problem (AP) is a particular case of a linear programming problem which deals with the allocation of various resources for various activities on a 1-to-1 basis. It does so in such a manner that the profit or sale involved in the process is maximum and cost or time is minimum. Generally, the profit/sale/cost/time is called the parameter of the AP and this is not a crisp number due to some uncontrollable factors. They can also involve uncertainty and hesitation. Therefore, to solve the AP under an intuitionistic fuzzy environment in this chapter, the author proposes the PSK (P.Senthil Kumar) method. Numerous theorems which are related to intuitionistic fuzzy assignment problem is proposed and is proved by PSK. By using the PSK method, the real-life related fully intuitionistic fuzzy assignment problems are solved. The proposed results are verified by both LINGO 17.0 and TORA software packages. In addition to verifying the efficiency and realism of the proposed method, the computer code based on LINGO 17.0 is presented. Results, discussion, comparative study and the advantages of the PSK method are given. The chapter ends with the conclusion and future studies.

Chapter 10 estimates the probability of default and its design of experiment via the Merton Model which is the critical model for financial economics to measure the default of a firm. It was the first structural model because it uses the market value of the firm for estimating the default of the firm. The firm will be in default only when the values of the firm goes down to a threshold value (the debt of the firm), and if it occurs the owner will put the firm to the debt holders. The effects of parameters-asset value V, firms debt D, interest rate r, the volatility σ and period T on the probability of default was investigated. To estimate the probability of default of a firm, the Black Scholes Model for European call options is used. The aim is to determine which parameter effects more or less on Probability of Default. The experiment is based on the orthogonal array L27 in which the five factors (parameters) are varied at three levels. The Taguchi L27 orthogonal method, ANOM, and ANOVA are used to examine the effect of these parameters on the probability of default. It also provides the best combination where the probability of default is minimum.

Chapter 11 studies real options and their suitability in assessing international digital investment. Firms have experienced extreme competition because of changes in technological and global issues. Globalization of manufacturing has arisen through a faster transfer of materials, complex payment systems, and compression of product life cycle. Eventually, firms need the integration of technologies to meet the increasingly sophisticated customers' needs. Among the technologies, artificial intelligence has attracted much of the attention as it has been foreseen to have a major impact on all industries. Real options approach may be applied to make informed decisions concerning digital technologies investments. Therefore, firms could decide to defer the option of investing in artificial intelligence for the sake of finding a more favorable future environment. This study provides an adequate tool to reduce uncertainty in deciding whether to implement artificial intelligence in their companies. This tool comprises the strategic perspective of the investment in digital technologies which makes it suitable to be incorporated as a part of the set of strategic tools.

Chapter 12 designs a neural network model for forecasting time series. Artificial neural networks are highly flexible and efficient tools in the approximation of time series patterns. In recent years, more than 5,000 studies oriented to the use of neural networks in the prognosis of time series have been evidenced in the extant literature. However, the methodology used for its specification and construction still involves a lot of trial and error, or is inherited from econometric and statistical procedures that do not fit perfectly to the characteristics of the time series. This is especially true when they present nonlinear behavior; moreover, it is not designed for working with neural networks. The objective of this chapter is to present a five-step guide for the specification, design, and validation of a neural network model for forecasting time series.

Chapter 13 concludes the book by examining encryption techniques. Encryption is the process of converting confidential private data into unreadable form and securing information in the file from unauthorized access using various encryption algorithms. We live in the information age where the exchange of private information has become the integral part of our day-to-day activities. Billions of e-mails and business data are sent throughout the world through Internet daily. The success of the information age is to keep private secure data from unauthorized access and key to access the private and secure data for authorized users. Encryption in this information age plays a vital role in the protecting the confidential data from unauthorized access. In last few decades, the computer network has created a revolution in the use of information. Authorized users access their data or send their private data from anywhere in the world; hence, it has become very important to secure the private data not only where it is stored, but also to maintain high level of confidentiality while transmission of this private data from one machine to another.

As the current century in the new millennium speeds along at an increasingly faster pace, the need for further development of applied and pure mathematics in international business continues to gain importance. We trust this work will assist in that effort and appreciate any constructive feedback on this publication.

Bryan Christiansen
Almaty, Kazakhstan

Fatima Shuwaikh
Paris, France

REFERENCES

Aagaard, A. (2019). *Sustainable Business Models: Innovation, Implementation, and Success*. New York: Palgrave Macmillan. doi:10.1007/978-3-319-93275-0

Celo, S., & Chacar, A. (2015). International Coherence and MNE Performance. *Journal of International Business Studies*, *46*(5), 620–628. doi:10.1057/jibs.2015.4

Colquitt, J. A., & Zapata-Phelan, C. P. (2007). Trends in Theory Building and Theory Testing: A Five-Decade Study of the Academy of Management Journal. *Academy of Management Journal*, *50*(6), 1281–1303. doi:10.5465/amj.2007.28165855

Dadkhah, K. (2011). *Foundations of Mathematical and Computational Economics* (2nd ed.). Berlin: Springer-Verlag. doi:10.1007/978-3-642-13748-8

Karlamova, G., & Vertelieva, O. (2013). The International Competitiveness of Countries: Economic-Mathematical Approach. *Economia e Sociologia (Evora, Portugal)*, *6*(2), 39–52.

Nekrasova, I., Karnaukhova, O., & Christiansen, B. (2018). *Fractal Approaches for Modeling Financial Assets and Predicting Crises*. Hershey, PA: IGI Global. doi:10.4018/978-1-5225-3767-0

Acknowledgment

We wish to thank the editorial board members and chapter authors for their fine contributions to this book. We would also like to thank the numerous reviewers who took the time from their busy schedules to complete the double-blind peer review of each chapter in this publication. Without their input and effort this work would not have been possible.

Chapter 1
Multinational Enterprise Adaptation Dynamics, Mathematical Modelling, and Empirical Analysis

Gzhi Wang
Manchester Metropolitan University, UK

ABSTRACT

Using an applied mathematics approach, this chapter embeds algorithmic measures into cultural theory in research on international business. The specialized area is concerned with adaptation of multinational enterprise (MNE) cross-borders in which how dynamic functions can strengthen the argument by producing robust models. The chapter contributes to the extant literature by offering a set of mechanisms that can be used by MNEs in adapting to a new or complex environment where culture can be diverse and policy choice is challenging. The mechanism by driving an adaptive approach, in particular, addresses a research issue that is persistent in cultural transition studies. The issue is distinguished from the standard economic model in that individual or rational actors have a fixed set of independent preferences (i.e., decision choice based on price, benefit, or rules of the game), uninfluenced by the behavior of others or the social settings within which they operate. The current study addresses the issue by demonstrating that a range of socio-cultural factors can influence behavior.

INTRODUCTION

Using an applied mathematics approach, this chapter embeds algorithmic measures into cultural theory in a specialized area in research on International Business. The area is concerned with adaptation of multinational enterprise (MNE) cross-borders regarding how dynamic functions in mathematical theory can strengthen the argument by producing robust models. The chapter contributes to the extant literature by offering a set of mechanisms that can be used by MNEs in adapting to a new or complex environment where culture can be diverse and policy choice is challenging. The mechanism by driving an adaptive

DOI: 10.4018/978-1-5225-8458-2.ch001

approach, in particular, addresses a research issue that is persistent in cultural transition studies. The issue is distinguished from the standard economic model in that individual or rational actors have a fixed set of independent preferences (i.e., decision choice based on price, benefit, or rules of the game), uninfluenced by the behavior of others or the social settings within which they operate. The current study addresses the issue by demonstrating that a range of socio-cultural factors can influence behavior.

The chapter also contributes to theory advancement in business mathematics and business analytics first by employing general economic productivity function and second by using the dynamic functions with which to compare the results. The techniques by perturbations of measures associated with cultural adaptation, social learning, and organizational fitness enable examination of correlation between the observed variables (exogenous) and organizational replication (endogenous) where robust models have been generated from the dynamic interactive. The empirical analysis draws out results from MNE data and the findings suggest that reproductive success in changing environments resides with MNE adaptation dynamics - adaptations to conformist norms and valuable good practices create evolutionary fitness of MNEs in the given environment.

Globalization with its processes has posed inherited, local, community culture to those multifaceted ones such as culture mutability, malleability and multiplicity (Hong, Morris, Chiu, & Benet-Martínez, 2000; Leung & Morris, 2015). Gen-culture (e.g., native English or native Chinese) coevolutionary processes have led to the emergence of coevolutionary behavioral dispositions, social rules, institutions, learned expectations and beliefs, and common values of communities (Hannan & Freeman, 1989; Cordes et al., 2008; Boyd et al., 2011). Given the coevolution, traditional research becomes less effective in theorizing on how plural, dynamic cultural proficiencies surface situational-based behavior. Unitary and static predispositions are less able to explain the impact of the dynamic cultural environment on the complex of behaviours of humans and societies (Hong et al., 2000; Leung & Morris, 2015). The evolving social context-based behaviour advances the evolutionary societies where the innate aspects on our social norms, tribal psychology, and institutionary theory keep updating, which insist challenge for research, as well as for complex societies.

The organizations of which complex societies are composed in many ways resemble ancestral tribes (Richerson & Boyd, 1999). Resembling the internationalization of business cycles has also brought many non-inherited, non-locally situated (homogenous) cultures, where a diverse range of groups and communities (heterogeneous) norms and cultural traits is evolving. Human culture constitutes socially transmitted information such as attitudes, beliefs, values, practices, and representations capable of affecting behaviours that are not constant between groups (Peysakhovich & Rand, 2016). Culture differences and variant behaviour patterns influence MNEs that are an interesting type of organizations since, in competitive economies, they are free to succeed or fail (Denison & Mishra, 1996; Deal & Kennedy, 2000). Their success and failure crucially depend upon their adaptive cultures and that involve the situation-specific responses.

The argument of the importance of adaptation to a social environment that is continually changing has been consistent researched by several recent studies (e.g., Boyd & Richardson, 1985; Bosworth, Singer, & Snower, 2016; Henrich, 2004; Hoff & Stiglitz, 2016). On Darwin's (1859) thought, adaptation to variation is the key to survival. We see adaptation is a staple of economics and business management successes, inducing replication or reproductive success (of MNEs, global leaders, migrants). Therefore, how MNEs replicate is also explained by how each of the entity acts to create fitness.

Following from the coevolutionary process, we presume that adaptation drives the evolutionary cycles such that primitive social institutions become established in the local populations and, in turn, exert an evolutionary response by a generated social psychology such as a shared cognitive frame and belief to facilitate behavior. When cultural rules that are affectively evaluated in a positive manner are transmitted preferentially, it also means that the evolution consequently becomes dynamic. For instance, the process can make gen-culture (native or ancestral culture) enhanced by dimensional cultural interactions by only a susceptible influence; how a mix of behavioral dispositions is activated depends on a social context. The social context within which people interact then influences behavior.

Consequently, social learning and social interactions drive social psychological adjustment of individuals, migrants, institutions, or business groups (i.e., MNEs) who become better understood in a specific social setting and cultural rules so that individuals generate evolutionary fitness to drive the ongoing efforts of adaptation to a given environment. Regarding this aspect, the chapter studies adaptive behaviour towards the rapid changes of environments, and, in particular, examines how cultural adaptation affects evolutionary fitness and reproductive successes of MNEs. The study in the broader International Business Management area contributes to theory advancement.

The study also contributes to mathematical modelling by demonstrating how algorithmic measures and conjectures can be developed and tested. Through the presentations of analytical results supported by empirical data, the study strengthens the central thesis of the chapter and demonstrates how the adaptive approach informs MNE replication across-borders. While the study uses the mathematical functions to inform the adaptive behavioral approach and organizational practices, in particular it seeks how the dynamic functions based on the analytical results may make a significant difference from the conventional statistical approach (e.g., OLS or linear regression models). More meaningfully, recent research has tended to move from developing pure mathematical model onto business intelligence in the applied field of strategy science; the endeavours undertaken in this chapter should interest researchers in these fields by contributing to research rigor and quality.

THE THEORETICAL FRAMEWORK OF THE ADAPTIVE APPROACH

Following from the conjecture raised earlier, we examine how cultural adaptation relates to evolutionary fitness, leading to MNE replication cross-borders. Sociocultural adaptation in the evolutionary societies aims to meet challenges from an environment wherein diverse cultures coexist. The consequent fitness (cultural fit and behavioral fit) will address the survival challenge from the social context. "Culture"—which following DiMaggio (1997) is the mental models learned from society and cued by the context and on which people draw to conceptualize—has effects like public goods or faults. Culture and social context shape how the individual perceives the world, the lens through which he sees it, and the categories that he uses to understand and interpret it (Hoff & Stiglitz, 2016). This also means culture can give rise to multiple equilibria (e.g., pluralism or societal rigidities). Cultural values and beliefs in a social context give rise to cross-cultural adjustment and adaptation, which are important for the evolutionary origin of humans' social dispositions (e.g., cooperation and fit).

Sociocultural adaptation has important implications for how the MNE can replicate its activities across multiple economic, socio-cultural, environments and in cultural transitions (i.e., an international assignment or international joint venture). It enables values and beliefs to be transmitted between individuals, groups (organization) epigenetically such as through socialization, instantiated through the internalization of norms (Mesoudi, 2009; Gintis, 2014). Adaptation drives MNEs to develop their capacity to fit into the *environment* wherein they by creating 'sense of place' subsequently create cultural dynamics. The dynamics (i.e., cultural diversity and flexibility) enhances social relationships with which they engage and shapes behavior for creating greater competency. The process by raising fitness strengthens the global leadership position of MNEs.

The environments in which MNEs engage and experience vary, which therefore are the reservoirs of cultural representations. Because the adaptive process produces shared social norms and cognitive frameworks, cultural transmission based on social learning plays a crucial role in the formation of these shared cognitive frames. The process of social interaction and social learning increases enlarges the stock of cognitive frameworks that we can draw from to interpret situations, and hence increase our capacity and fit ability to respond to environmental change (see, also DiMaggio & Markus, 2010; Hoff & Stiglitz, 2016). Humans' evolved cognitive apparatus faces constraints that entail a selective processing of sensory information on the basis of discriminative attention processes. Because the change of these frames hinges on processes of intense social interaction, the social interaction and learning update cognitive cues that are employed to discriminate among information and are themselves organized into more complex systems referred to as cognitive frames that guide classificatory and interpretative human activities.

Hitherto, we have highlighted that cultural adaptation allows MNE opportunities to equip themselves with skills and orientation while they are more disposed to changing environments. To adapt to social norms, practices and related behaviors enable representation of specialist knowledge that is deemed as successful local norms, common values, and are practiced and used by most communities in the social context (Boyd & Richerson, 2010; Chudek & Henrich, 2011; Rand & Nowak, 2013). The social context enacts changes that can emanate from influential ideas, practices, and prevailing norms, which constitute changes in self-culture, self-identity, self-schemas of value, bringing out behavior fit to the environment. Importantly, our discussion gives rise to the relationship between cultural adaptation and evolutionary fitness and replication of organizations.

In demonstrating the relationship in practical relevance of mathematical formalism, we next use algorithmic measures to inform the model. The model in producing conjectures of MNE adaptation to an environment, demonstrates the effect of adaptation on replication of the MNE's activities in the environment. Consequently, in adapting to a social environment, individual or firm induced norms and beliefs follow from phenotypic norms (behaviour plasticity) – norm and social learning allow prevailing social norms transmitted in the social context. Crucially, we argue that context-biased cues and valuable practices prevail will increase retention of the organization in the social environment.

Mathematical Formulations of the Adaptive Approach

Following from the argument, we envisage that the resulting *replication,* y_t, of an MNE (or its individual manager) is based on its stationary processes of *adaptation,* a_t, and a disposition of *cultural fit,* c_t, in an environment:

$$y_t = a_t + c_t + \varepsilon_t, \tag{1}$$

From (1), a *replication,* y_t, (or a reproductive success) is dependent on the stationary processes of (*habitual*) *adaptation,* a_t, and *cultural fit,* c_t, expressed, respectively, as:

$$y_t = a_t + \varepsilon_t, \tag{2}$$

and

$$y_t = c_t + \varepsilon_t, \tag{3}$$

The proceeding informs a set of algorithmic measures, which drive the resulting disposition of replication based on (habitual) *adaptation,* a_t, and *cultural fit,* c_t. Thus, their value change can be expressed as

$$a_t = a_{t-1} + \frac{1}{1-p}\varepsilon_t \tag{4}$$

and

$$c_t = c_{t-1} + \frac{1}{1-p}\epsilon_t \tag{5}$$

where a change in a or c, depends on a change in the input component *p* of a, or *p* of c, and ε and ϵ, represents, respectively, other effects (e.g., unobserved exogenous effects).

So,

$$y_t = py_{t-1} + (1-p)a_{t-1} + \varepsilon_t, \tag{6}$$

$$y_t = py_{t-1} + (1-p)c_{t-1} + \epsilon_t, \tag{7}$$

Following from the above, either value change in Δa_t or in Δc_t, or both, can affect a value change in *replication* Δy_t,

$$\Delta a_t = p_a \Delta a_{t-1} + \varepsilon_t, \tag{8}$$

or

$$\Delta c_t = p_a \Delta c_{t-1} + \varepsilon_t, \tag{9}$$

where p_t denotes the two operators functioning in *a* and *c*, respectively.

Presuming both *a* and *c* play a significant role in the process, the joint effect on *replication,* Δy_t, becomes

$$y_t - py_{t-1} = a_t + y_t - p\left(a_{t-1} + c_{t-1}\right) = a_t - py_{t-1} + \varepsilon_t . \tag{11}$$

So that a cointegrating regression is expressed as

$$y_t = \delta y_{t-1} + \left(1 - p\right) + y_{t-1} p_t^{a,c} ,. \tag{12}$$

where *replication,* y_t, as a cointegrating regression resides with the values in *a* and *c* that suggests a value-change in *y* is influenced by the operator p (e.g., coefficients of variables related to adaptation and cultural fit), and a variation in (a_t, or c_t), depending on a variation in (p_t^a, or p_t^c).

We thus far demonstrate how MNEs (or their managers) by adaptation and sociocultural adjustment produce *cultural fit* c_p in a given environment. The extant literature (e.g., Pinker, 2010) explains that individual behavior through communication and coordinating demonstrates the cognitive capacity. That enhanced capacity, for instance, by overcoming more rigid attitudes of cultural self, simple self-defense or self- meanings of culture, enables cultural flexibility and cultural fit. The process increases *cultural intelligence* that, according to DiMaggio (1997), is cognitive schemas, mental models/ideas learned from society and cued by the context and on which people draw to conceptualize. The process raises flexibility that in the cultural transition model (Sussman, 2000) is such that managerial ability makes some necessary modifications by adjusting cultural self and self-schemas identity to the social context. Flexible schemas may discern or emulate the behaviors that would improve the self–environment fit (Sussman, 2002). MNEs, by adjusting their perceptions and behavior in the given situation to align with the social context, develop evolutionary fitness entity meanings and standards.

In strategic management literature, the process of adaptation is exemplified by the concept of dynamic capabilities (e.g., Eisenhardt & Martin, 2000; Teece, Pisano, & Shuen, 1997; Teece, 2007) by which firm successes are characterized as having the capacity and ability to consistently reconfigure their resource base in response to rapidly changing markets. The process suggests that the MNE or its managers through the process have produced behavior which enables them to respond to the environment in more appropriate manners. Therefore, the process enables creation of evolutionary fitness into the sociocultural environment while adaptation through social cultural learning may have influenced norms, cognitions, and actions (Johnsona, Michael, & Van Vugt, 2013).

Following from the illustrations above, explicitly, the first assumption is

$$a_{t-1} + \frac{1}{1-p}\varepsilon_t = 1 \tag{13}$$

and

$$c_{t-1} + \frac{1}{1-p}\varepsilon_t = 1 . \tag{14}$$

Following from (13) and (14), a progressing assumption risen is both *c* and *a* would be correlated with replication (*y*): $c_t = c_{t-1} + p_t$; $b_t = b_{t-1} + p_t$. The assumptions, together, imply that *a* and *c* are correlated:

$$a_t = a_{t-1} + p_t\,;\; c_t = c_{t-1} + p_t\,. \tag{15}$$

Eq. (15) indicates a cointegrating regression; hence, we have

$$\Delta y_t = \left(1-\delta\right)\left(a_{t-1} - c_{t-1}\right) + p_t^{\delta}\,, \tag{16}$$

Then,

$$y_t = py_{t-1} + \left(1-p\right)\delta_{t-1} = 1\,. \tag{17}$$

The mathematical formulation gives rise to the conjecture that *the great magnitude of adaptive mechanisms the higher intensity of cultural fit of the MNE in the given environment, and this will lead to reproductive successes.* Evolutionary fitness emerges from an adaptive process based on the ongoing efforts of the MNE or its managers. Adaptation by addressing issues related to market changes drives MNE cross-border adjustment (i.e., policy, behavior) that by creating fitness in new circumstances or a successful entry consequently induces replication in the new market.

Statistical Data Tests of Correlative Structures in General Productivity Functions

Given the argument in (16) and (17): a value-change in *c* relates to the component efforts, *p*, and a value-change in adaptation, *a*, relates to the component efforts, *p*, that thus directs the analysis towards *replication* y_p by applying a set of behavioral variables, related to a, and $c_{t,i}$, (e.g., adaptation to culturally variant groups, sociocultural learning, knowledge sharing, social and psychological adjustment, etc.) The functions in following from the above formulation is the general economic function. Using the function, the study observes the *adaptive effects* of a_t on $y_{t,i}$. For which the explanatory variables will be associated variables, the coefficients of *adaptive dispositions* (i.e., variable related to social interaction and social learning) where the observation also takes into account the effect of cultural fit, $\delta c_{t,i}$ that can be represented by coefficients of *cultural fitness behavior* (i.e., cultural intelligence, behavioral fit).

The estimates in using such as 2-stage least square will enable a way to obtain estimates, where error terms as uncorrelated effects on the observations of different variables of *a, c,* at data *t.* If the correlating values obtained lend support to the assumptions such that a value change in a affect a value change in cultural fit *c*, it will increase the ability of the MNE to fit into the environment, and hence more likely to induce reproductive successes. Therefore, $\delta y_{t,i}$, will reside with the adaptive mechanisms.

For the statistical analysis, the study draws on a set of empirical data. The tests employed data based primarily on a questionnaire distribution to 250 managers (middle and senior managers, managing directors and CEOs) responsible for major strategic decisions concerned with alliances, research and development (R&D), technical systems, and so forth) who had at least one international assignment and are currently working for MNE with subsidiaries in the United Kingdom, India, China, and African countries. The survey produced 178 usable responses which were accepted for further analysis. The scale measures of the questionnaire, generally, adopted 5-point Likert scales (1= lowest, 5= highest, 3= neutral) based on identification of tendencies, dispositions, and degrees of agreement.

The results of scale data variables test in Table 1 reveal the significant relationship between the *adaptive mechanisms* and *replication* y_p, where (in Row 9) the correlative values of the operator p are: $p = .50$, $t = 2.11$, and VIF>1.51 where the statistical tolerance 0.66 also meets the rules for the required data contingency teats. The estimates suggest that adaptation to a given social environment significantly lend support to the projected functions in $f(y)$, where the proposed *adaptive variables* significantly relate to the enlarged values in $y_{t,i}$. The results also suggest that *cultural fit* c_p is also a set of parameters, including *social learning*, *social norms*, *knowledge sharing*, and *behavioral adjustment*. Higher levels of cultural fit emanates from higher dispositions of *social learning*. The negative coefficients suggest variant mean values for social norms and knowledge sharing behavior and behavioral fit in the environment, where weaker value in adaptation dispositions associates lower value in cultural fit. Significant positive parameter values reinforce cultural fit, thus suggesting transmission and adaptation to prevailing social norms, cultural cues, and available practices contribute to replication.

The Dynamic Functions for the Adaptive Approach

In this session, we continue to develop an approach to dynamic functioning. The aim of the session is to produce an analysis that can be compared to the prior section and is motivated by a dynamic approach to mathematical formalism as a means of demonstrating how different research strategies can enrich our understanding of business practices.

Table 1. Empirical tests of statistical data: cultural fit in relation to proposed adaptive variables

(Constant)	*N*	Mean	Std. Dev.	Std. Error	*t*	Corr.	VIF	Tolerance
Social learning	178	3.33	1.09	0.06	3.80***	0.32**	1.87	0.54
Know. norm sharing /defection	178	3.17	0.73	0.01	-3.04***	-0.42**	4.50	0.22
Relative fit to environ	178	3.20	0.89	0.01	0.63	0.45**	1.72	0.58
Behavioral fit	178	2.93	0.89	0.03	-0.16	-0.26***	1.90	0.53
p (Adaptive disposition)	178	0.69	0.16	0.01	0.19***	0.26**	1.75	0.57
p (Adapt to variances (i.e. cul groups))	178	1.89	0.50	0.03	0.21	0.37*	1.21	0.63
fy (Replication)	178	0.62	0.17	0.03	2.11***	0.50**	1.51	0.66

*significant at 10%, ** significant at 5%, *** significant at 1%.

The approach is also motivated by recent publications in economics and natural science fields. The dynamic matrix data techniques have been also applied in game theory and evolutionary research (e.g., Levinthal & March, 1981; Aumann, 1987; Boyd & Richarson, 1985, 1991; Asano et al., 2011, 2012). Crawford (1995), for instance, proposed a set of dynamic functions that demonstrate the research interest that departs from conventional approach (e.g., linear regression). Biewen (2009) has shown how important variables determining contemporaneous poverty status are likely to be influenced by past poverty outcomes, suggesting that both social and individual feedback effects could compromise outcomes. Pudney (2004) presents estimates using a Poisson process that allowed for a separate dynamic process for initiation of a utility function and the subsequent consumption. With an extended theoretical framework and using the same data sample of their earlier study, Guasch, Laffont, and Strau (2003), and Guasch et al. (2007) estimated a linear probability model by two-stage least squares to show that not only the results are preserved but also a more advanced framework is explained.

In particular, we examine how change in social processes may change people's behavior. According to Peysakhovich and Rand (2016), when biased norms and prestige are successfully copied and spread, they increase the frequency of cooperative encounters in a given social setting. We predict that adaptation produces cultural heterogeneity (i.e., beliefs, preferences, consumption patterns) and creates behavioral shifts to fit into the social context. We let the process be the dynamic interactivity by that both gen-culture (homogeneous culture) transmission, k, and heterogeneous (variant) cultural information transmission, $\hat{k}$, involve the processes. We consider the process of social learning, with respect to adaptation dynamics, so that the modelling articulates the following patterns as

$$k_1 \overset{0_A 1_B}{\leftrightarrows}, k_2 \overset{1_B 1_A}{\leftrightarrows}, \tag{18}$$

$$\hat{k}_3 \overset{1_A 0_C}{\leftrightarrows}, \hat{k}_4 \overset{1_A 1_D}{\leftrightarrows}. \tag{19}$$

where *A*, *B*, *C*, and *D* are adaptation patterns (of individuals or groups, MNEs) involved in the process, $k_{1,2,3,4}$ (or $\hat{k}$) express different states (patterns) of cultural transmission. For example, (1) refers to the transmission that enables *A* through social interactions to transmit her carrying capacity or inherited culture to *B*. And (2) suggests that *A's* through social interactions also enable transmission of *C* and *D* cultures. This would accommodate social learning in the diverse cultural environment, wherein the multiple lens of approach create greater cultural evolutionary effects (i.e. explained by greater statistical collating values)

The evaluation of transmitted cultural information/knowledge, and adaptation to a new or given (i.e. expatriating) environment considers variables related to the behavioural patterns ($k, \hat{k}$) such that take account of different cultural units from different sociocultural groups in social interaction,

$$|k_0|^2 = \frac{|k_1|^2}{|k_2|^2} + \frac{|k_3|^2}{|k_4|^2}, \tag{20}$$

and

$$|\hat{k}_0|^2 = \frac{|k_1|^2}{|\hat{k}_1|^2} + \frac{|\hat{k}_2|^2}{|k_2|^2}, \tag{21}$$

where a higher mean value of coefficient indicates that a greater cultural variant (cultural information) is transmitted, possibly producing a potential benefit from social learning.

As can be seen from the extant literature, cultural transmission is biased – the mechanisms in cultural transmission is the well-studied conformist bias such that people tend to acquire some cultural variants rather than others. This process of cultural transmission is influenced and constrained by humans' evolved psychology that shapes what we learn, how we think, and whom we imitate. The connection between humans' innate psychological predispositions and the organizations in which humans is embedded, so conformist transmission belongs to the class of frequency-dependent biases and has been a simple heuristic that improves the chance of acquiring the locally favored cultural variant (Boyd & Richerson, 1989).

To continue, the approach to dynamic interactivity in the application of a *dynamic operator Q* captures sets of adaptive mechanisms presenting dynamic interactions. In this context, social interaction and cultural adaptation enable MNEs (managers, professionals) to develop a learning process by which to accommodate socio-cultural adjustments more effectively. By the process, MNEs (their managers) develop and present degrees of behavioral (and cultural) flexibility that creates greater assesses to choice available in the situation and make certain role models or reference points into attention. Therefore, we use matrices data of parameter variables (α, β), for the mean value, μ, of dynamic interactivity of cultural information transmission and social learning, which formally are expressed as

$$\mu = \begin{pmatrix} \alpha & 0 \\ 0 & \beta \end{pmatrix}, \text{ with } |\alpha|^2 + |\beta|^2 = 1. \tag{22}$$

where variations drive social interactions such that individuals behave in ways that are the 'best response' to how it expects others to behave (Bicchieri, 2006; Gintis, 2014).

Then the value-change in coefficient means (of *a, b, c,* and *d*) influences the value-change in *replication,* and starts from p_0. Let the parameter variables be represented by means of coefficients of $k_{1,2,3,4}$, and $\tilde{k}_{1,2,3,4}$:

$$\mu_0 \equiv |\alpha|^2 k_1 + |\beta|^2 k_2 + \alpha\beta^* k_3 + \alpha^*\beta k,$$

$$\tilde{\mu}_0 \equiv |\alpha|^2 \tilde{k}_1 + |\beta|^2 \tilde{k}_2 + \alpha\beta^* \tilde{k}_3 + \alpha^*\beta \tilde{k}_4. \tag{23}$$

From (24), by the dynamic interactivity the adaptor, *Q*, drives the function of replication *y*, which can be expressed as

$$p_{y} \to p_{Q} \equiv \frac{Qp_{0}Q^{*}}{tr\left(\mid Q \mid^{2} p_{0}\right)}, \tag{24}$$

And

$$Q = \begin{pmatrix} a & b \\ c & d \end{pmatrix}. \tag{25}$$

where *Q* becomes the determinants of *replication, y,* such that the value-change in terms of coefficient means of μ (*a, b, c,* and *d*) influence the value-change in y. Therefore, *Q* identifies how the MNE fits the environment that is determined by its adaptive effects.

Then, the dynamic interactivity would inform the identification in the correlative values that is expressed as

$$\Delta y_{t} = \left(1 - \delta Q\right)\left(q_{t-1} - \tilde{q}_{t-1}\right) + p_{t}^{Q}. \tag{26}$$

where (26) formally informs the contention that *the greater the magnitude in the dynamic interactivity of adaptation and cultural fit, the greater amplification will bring up the MNE (or its managers) reproductive successes.*

The dynamic formulations in following from Asano et al. (2011, 2012) provide ways of estimating δQ, which exploit the correlation (fitness and replication) in the application of the modelled dynamic algorithmic measures in e.g. (23) and (24).

Empirical Data Results Using the Dynamic Approach

In developing the functions, the above session draws on evolutionary theory explaining how adaptation to variation by meeting the external selection pressures of fitness induces the reproductive success of the MNE. In continually using the same data sets for the analysis, this session seeks to observe the dynamic effects, using dynamic equations. The dynamic functions inform the tests that would generate strong correlative values. If so, the study obtains consistent results that lend support to prior research in relation to applications of dynamic functions. However, if in the case that after different techniques are used in different models where the magnitudes that were expected to change have, in fact, changed, the overall significance of the model remains unchanged and especially the more robust results from the dynamic approach, the study therefore contributes to a more robust model.

In Table 2, the results from using the *dynamic operator Q* show the functions of the model in that selection from the variation in the environment can strengthen adaptive capabilities. The overall results show much large correlating values, compared with those in Table 1. Results in Rows 7-8 are based on matrices data show parameters as we modelled, where higher amplifications rests on parameters of cultural contextual cues and learning benefits. Results in Column 2 reveal coefficients related to adaptive skills, which indicate that when managers with such skills 'sense' movements in the environment and 'seize' any resulting opportunities (Teece, 2007) induce decision-choice in an adaptive fashion.

Results in Column 3 suggest that within groups, the utility of cultural context cues and prevailing norms increase fitness levels in the environment (Row 9). Results in Columns 4-5 show the probability distributions of the pressures and predispositions for adaptation (*a*) to variation, enabling higher amplifications of correlations ($\tilde{\mu}$, μ). The correlating values (Rows 8-9) suggest that external (environmental) selection forces motivate managers to adapt, thus increasing their capabilities for making distinctions between differentiated cultural contexts, such that when (behavioral) fitness levels increase perceived reproductive success also increases (in Column 6).

Results in Table 3 are generated using parameter variables of the *dynamic operator Q,* as explained in Equation 23-26. By examining the variables, high frequency behavior of adaptation to a local group (Q_1) allows managers effectively to embed their experiences in the group activities. When MNEs identify successful local cultural traits and develop competency-acquired skills, their enhanced skills and valuable practices raise their dispositions to cooperate (Column 9). Adaptation to culturally variant groups (Q_2) relates to a greater disposition for behavioral fit (rule following, norm following, adaptation to 'best practice') in the environment which strengthen group (MNE) performance and increase the willingness to cooperate. Replication (reproductive success, Row 3) is explained by coherent norms (sharing common values, valuable practices, norm following). The disposition to replicate is strongly associated with adaptation to prevailing social norms, valuable group practices, learning from high performance groups, and cultural adjustment. Overall, the capacity for replication resides with adaptation, cooperation and coherent social norms (Columns 8-9).

The results suggest that in responses to MNEs' adaptation dynamics, the observed mechanisms have the function and a capacity to contribute to adaptation to the local environment. In the case of adaptation dynamics, different dynamics are used in different models, and the magnitudes that were expected to change have actually done so. However, the overall significance of the model remains unchanged while the dynamic functions, however, yield robust results. The proposed dynamic approach contributes to

Table 2. Tests: Adaptation in the functions of dynamic interactivity of $\mu\tilde{\mu}$

(Q)	$cor(\beta\mu)$	$cor(\alpha\tilde{\mu})$	$P_q(\mu\tilde{\mu}^*)$	$P_q(\mu^*\tilde{\mu})$	P_{rep}
	0.395	0.698	0.300	0.340	
2	0.010	0.505	0.500	0.540	
3	-0.092	0.454	0.550	0.590	
4	-0.030	0.485	0.520	0.560	
5	0.570	0.489	0.510	0.560	
cor(Fitness)	0.530	0.690			0.340
cor(Replication)	0.610	0.680			0.440
N	(178)	(178)	(178)	(178)	(178)

cor for correlative values and *P* for probability distribution.

Table 3. Tests of the functions of the dynamic operator Q

Estimates	$\lvert k \rvert^2$	$\mu\tilde{\mu}^*$	$\lvert \tilde{k} \rvert^2$	$\tilde{\mu}\mu^*$	$P(q_1)$	$P(q_2)$	*Pr (Replicate)*	*Pr (Ada. Dynamics)*
1	0.52	0.01	0.52	0.02	0.51	0.51	0.54	0.53
2	0.54	0.03	0.54	0.04	0.51	0.52	0.56	0.53
3	0.43	0.08	0.62	0.07	0.55	0.53	0.64	0.57
4	0.45	0.02	0.50	0.02	0.48	0.48	0.52	0.52
N	(178)	(178)	(178)	(178)	(178)	(178)	(178)	(178)

Estimations (1, 2, 3, 4) of the probabilities accord with the dynamic operator.

robust model building for generating strong correlating values. As such, the dynamic approach of the study contributes to more rigorous modelling processes and analysis. The dynamic functions produce results which are adherent with multiple regressions, but with strong correlative values, which lending greater support to the conjecture of the study. That is, the greater the dynamic interactivity, the higher dispositions of adaptation dynamics enhance chance of MNE to replicate in the complexity of environment by creating evolutionary fitness.

The findings inform the adaptive approach by suggesting that cultural adaptation can nudge the 'social balance' in a preferred direction, such as inducing social regarding motives, preferences, and behaviors. The adaptive process, therefore, fosters the development of loyalties to wider units (groups and individuals). Adaptation and sociocultural adjustment, in the context of the organizational processes, enable MNEs (and their managers) effectively to serve organizational goals, develop interests to serve group values and confer benefits on others. Social learning, groups at different levels of interaction and the practices strengthen shared common values. Greater benefits derive from MNEs potential to transfer 'best practices' such as when expatriate managers transfer knowledge in expatriating /repatriating MNE setting.

Contribution Highlight and Implications

The chapter considers the consequences of globalization and calls on mechanism that can strengthen the process of culture adaptation that has also an urgent need to study cooperative norms of individuals, organizations, and societies. Cross-culture adaptation with the growing importance, in particular, has crucial implications for international managers/employees in the MNC environment. The chapter contributes to advancements in applying mathematical formalism to organizational analysis using the combination of a general economic productivity function and a dynamic function. The proposed adaptive framework extends theory in dynamic simulation and functioning in economic behavior. The dynamic approach is distinguished from standard economic models. Given the complex environments and social matters, good model building recognizes the analogue of generalized evolutionary systems which is challenging. The dynamic equation functions developed in this chapter help with such analysis by taking advantage of the techniques deployed to develop appropriate observations. Studies in different disciplines stimulate this chapter to help with resolving the problems confronted by prior studies. The implication is concerned with a complex process with analysis of cultural transition involving managers and MNEs in a changeable environment.

The chapter offers multiple techniques to mathematical research and international business studies. In reviewing the modelling sections, the measures of replication draw on multiple parameter variables, including the cogency of knowledge production, performance, and the MNE's general success in the social setting. The indicative variables enable measures of effects on behavioral fit such as the predisposition of adjustment of self-culture, social norms following, and adaptation dynamics which shed light on future research. In using the combined approach to theory advancement and business intelligence, the techniques adapted in this chapter can pervade several analysis where the dynamic operator perturbs cultural adaptive behavior, organizational learning, which by creating fitness benefits, then produce strong correlation, in the dynamic functions, between social learning and social environment and cooperative mechanism. While MNEs may have adopted dynamic interactive patterns, the robustness of the interactive mechanisms shows the functions by bringing up greater probability distribution. The value can change in dynamic interactive that contributes to future research an alternative method.

The findings of the chapter reveal that adaptation enables social learning that through absorbing different cultural cues and salient characteristics increases the likelihood of activating behavior appropriate or well-adjusted to differentiated social contexts. MNEs, through the course of socialization, social targets or role models develop their local knowledge with respect to their social roles and work roles, social learning of culture cues that are common to the local context, that behavior generates fitness. The findings also reveal that adaptation to conformist (or biased) norms (see also Boyd & Richerson, 1982; Chudek, Zhao, & Henrich, 2013; Laland, 2004) drive MNEs to uncover successful traits of social groups and communities and organizational norms within the MNC environment. Generally, the norms enact social learning by adapting to successful traits of culturally variant groups, which not only motivate the adaptation disposition but also contribute to efficacy of the adaptation process.

Adaptation to conformist norms enables MNEs or managers use conformist bias that based on the commonness or rarity of a cultural variant as a basis for choice enhance economic and learning benefit cross-culture. The biased norms, derives based on humans' unique evolved group-regarding social predispositions, and follows successes of desirable behavior of groups that are higher performing groups. MNEs exploit the norms while they develop culture conformity and the ability to comprehend combined appreciations of variant cultures. The conformist bias help MNEs and managers pick the cultural variant that is used mostly in a population (see also Henrich & Boyd, 1998; Richerson & Boyd, 2005; Henrich, 2004).

The chapter makes three contributions to the extant literature. First, the proposed framework contributes to an understanding of how organizations maintain fitness in complex environments, where the study explicating adaptive mechanisms contribute to the MNEs fitness levels. Cultural adaptation is crucial because external pressures will tend to select those variants that match or fit the environment, thus enabling the firm (the MNE) to survive by maintaining resilience as markets shift between system states. The mechanisms drive organizational learning and adaptation to prevailing social norms, which, in turn, increase the preponderance of cooperator types in a group structured population of heterogeneous practices and social norms. The findings suggest that there are some aspects of human nature that are more consistent with the psychologists' concept, and the conjecture of the study is adherent with recent studies of social psychologist and cultural evolutionary economists (e.g., Richerson & Boyd, 1999; Boyd et al., 2011; Peysakhovich & Rand, 2016; Hoff & Stiglitz, 2016). Prior studies of the patterns of group formation and group competition (McElreath et al., 2003) identify that social learning and competition in small-scale societies satisfy the requirements of cultural group selection models (Soltis, Boyd,

& Richerson, 1995; Richerson & Boyd, 2005; Henrich, 2004). If cultural group competition became an appreciable evolutionary force about that time, it would have set in motion a process of gen-culture coevolution.

Second, the chapter reveals that social context affects behavior and strongly influences how individuals act in specific social settings. Actions are also influenced by the mix of dispositional types in a given social setting. A population consisting of a preponderance of co-operator types will behave very different to a situation where competitive types dominate (Bosworth, Singer, & Snower, 2016). How a salient feature of an individual's self-concept of choice primes associates external factors and social context affects behavior and actions. Because endogenous determinants of managers' perceptions and interpretations are subject to external selection, leading to a situation in which fitness levels are positively related to firm performance and where low fitness levels (or misfit) if not addressed can have disastrous consequences for the organization.

Hence, the model further addresses the concern raised in economic research on migrant cultural transition (e.g., Cunha & Heckman, 2009; Bisin & Topa, 2003; Bisin et al., 2008). Prior studies identify a large array social and economic power influences on behavior as cognitive traits of inherited culture is influenced in a complex manner. This chapter suggests that adaptation may lead to structural improvements in social institutions, a variation of a physiological process, a new or modified behavior (e.g., knowledge, cultural traits) and any improvement of the extended phenotype (business strategy, working practices). MNEs with their expectation values by aggregating interests in social learning produce social-regarding concerns.

Third, the study recognizes that long-term international assignments continue to be an integral part of an MNE's strategy so that the challenge of cross-cultural adaptation will remain. Crucially, in diverse business setting, MNEs confront a diverse range of inherited, local, and community situated cultures. Human culture constitutes socially transmitted information such as attitudes, beliefs, values, practices, and representations capable of affecting behaviours and are not constant between groups (Peysakhovich & Rand, 2016). Values and beliefs are transmitted between individuals epigenetically through socialization and are instantiated through the internalization of norms (Mesoudi, 2009; Gintis, 2014). Norms such as the disposition to cooperate vary considerably across organizations (Boyd & Richerson, 2005; Mesoudi, 2009). The plurality of cultures and social norms throws up a challenge for MNEs and managers operating at the international level who encounter situation-specific norms when shifting between national boundaries (Hong et al., 2000; Leung & Morris, 2015). That cross-cultural adaptation poses a challenge is evident from the high attrition rates observed during both expatriation and repatriation reported in several recent studies (Kraimer et al., 2012).

To this end, from two aspects we may develop the arguments. First, it is not just that the social context of the moment of decision influences behavior by making certain norms, role models, or reference points, or other associations focal in attention (see, also Hoff & Stiglitz, 2016). In a sense, prolonged (and sometimes even brief) exposure to a given social context shapes who people are or become. The norms at the intrinsic level are individual norms such that personal knowledge are developed through life experience (Edelman, 1989) and cognitive and heuristic rules (Bingham & Eisenhardt, 2011). Behaviour is activated through stimuli from the social environment (Edelman, 1989) that form a set of intrinsic logics, such as thoughts and philosophies, enacting individual behaviour (Henrich, 2004; Boyd & Richerson, 2009). Norms can be intrinsically (psychologically) developed and extrinsic (socially) held. Norms stablish self in a position in relation to a context.

While the social context within which people interact influences behavior, actors are characterized as self-serving and have a consistent set of preferences unaffected by broader socio-cultural influences (Hoff & Stiglitz, 2016). Social interactions may be as important determinants of economic out comes as the variables upon which economists have traditionally focused. Social determinants of preferences and cognition are increasingly demonstrated in empirical work on individual choice and societal change. The broader perspective expands the explanatory power of economics and the accuracy of economic predictions. Most importantly, this perspective identifies sources of societal rigidity that the standard model takes no account of, and identifies new instruments that can influence behaviorand long-run social change.

Social norms can be developed and influenced through socialization and the internalization, where groups (MNEs) more readily embrace collective cognitive frames (Witt, 2000), acquire commonalities in beliefs and values, making cooperation, a sense of fairness, and tolerance for diversity endogenous social norms (Mengel, 2008; Gintis, 2014). An openness to socialization and the internalization of norms has adaptation enhancing effects for the individual and the group (Mesoudi, 2006; Gintis, 2014). In the complex and new social setting of MNE environment, the implication is also a predilection for norm following. In this form, variations in environmental conditions can be dealt with by an organism that has the capacity to adapt flexibly to a range of circumstances (Gintis, 2014). As such, norm following can explain why individual or group preferences often go beyond self-regarding concerns (Ostrom, 2000).

Indeed, international business is concerned with conducting an integrated set of activities in multiple geographic locations (e.g., MNE subsidiaries, cross-border trade, establishing Joint Ventures (JVs), and engaging in strategic alliances of different types). Understanding these activities will often require mathematical modelling in areas related to financing, real options analysis, cost-benefit analysis, sales & marketing, logistics and global supply chains, decision making, modelling economic growth and distance effects (e.g., gravity models). Feedback from the international business field shows that many challenges relate to cross cultural adaptation of which adaptation to variance in Darwinian evolutionary theory is the key to revival. As such, the evolutionary process of *adaptation-selection-retention* has attracted the attention of many scholars (see Levinthal, 2017).

REFERENCES

Asano, M., Basieva, I., Khrennikov, A., Ohya, M., Tanaka, Y., & Yamato, I. (2012). Quantum-like Model for the Adaptive Dynamics of the Genetic Regulation of E. Coli's Metabolism of Glucose/Lactose. *Systems and Synthetic Biology*, *6*(1-2), 1–7. doi:10.100711693-012-9091-1 PMID:23730359

Asano, M. M., Ohya, Y., Tanaka, I., Basieva, I., & Khrennikov, A. (2011). Quantum-like model of brain's functioning: Decision making from decoherence. *Journal of Theoretical Biology*, *281*(1), 56–64. doi:10.1016/j.jtbi.2011.04.022 PMID:21554890

Aumann, R. J. (1987). Correlated Equilibrium as an Expression of Bayesian Rationality. *Econometrica*, *55*(1), 1–18. doi:10.2307/1911154

Bicchieri, C. (2006). *The Grammar of Society: The Nature and Dynamics of Social Norms*. New York: Cambridge University Press.

Biewen, M. (2009). Measuring state dependence in individual poverty histories when there is feedback to employment status and household composition. *Journal of Applied Econometrics, 24*(7), 1095–1116. doi:10.1002/jae.1081

Bingham, B. C., & Eisenhardt, K. M. (2011). Rational heuristics: The 'simple rules' that strategists learn from process experience. *Strategic Management Journal, 32*(13), 1437–1464. doi:10.1002mj.965

Bisin, A., Eleonora, P., Thierry, V., & Yves, Z. (2008). Are Muslim Immigrants Different in Terms of Cultural Integration? *Journal of the European Economic Association, 6*(2-3), 445–456. doi:10.1162/JEEA.2008.6.2-3.445

Bisin, B., & Topa, G. (2003). Empirical Mode of Cultural Transmission. *Journal of the European Economic Association, 1*(2-3), 363–375. doi:10.1162/154247603322391008

Bosworth, S. J., Singer, T., & Snower, D. J. (2016). Cooperation, motivation and social balance. *Journal of Economic Behavior & Organization, 126*, 72–94. doi:10.1016/j.jebo.2015.12.005

Boyd, R., & Richerson, P. J. (1982). Cultural Transmission and the Evolution of Cooperative Behaviour. *Human Ecology, 10*(3), 325–351. doi:10.1007/BF01531189

Boyd, R., & Richerson, P. J. (1985). *Culture and the Evolutionary Process*. Chicago: University of Chicago Press.

Boyd, R., & Richerson, P. J. (2009). Culture and the Evolution of Human Cooperation. *Philosophical Transactions of the Royal Society of London. Series B, Biological Sciences, 364*(1533), 3281–3288. doi:10.1098/rstb.2009.0134 PMID:19805434

Boyd, R., Richerson, P. J., & Henrich, J. (2011). Rapid cultural adaptation can facilitate the evolution of large-scale cooperation. *Behaviorial Ecology of Social Biology, 65*(3), 431–444. doi:10.100700265-010-1100-3 PMID:21423337

Cordes, C., Richerson, P. J., McElreath, R. S., & Strimling, P. (2008). A Naturalistic Approach to the Theory of the Firm: The Role of Cooperation and Cultural Evolution. *Journal of Economic Behavior & Organization, 68*(1), 125–139. doi:10.1016/j.jebo.2008.03.008

Crawford, V. P. (1995). Adaptive Dynamics in Coordination Games. *Econometrica, 63*(1), 103–143. doi:10.2307/2951699

Cunha, F., & Heckman, J. J. (2009). The economics and psychology of inequality and human development. *Journal of the European Economic Association, 7*(2-3), 320–364. doi:10.1162/JEEA.2009.7.2-3.320 PMID:20209045

Darwin, C. (1859). *On the Origin of the Species by Means of Natural Selection*. London: J. Murray.

Deal, T. E., & Kennedy, A. A. (2000). *Corporate Cultures*. Boston: Addison- Wesley.

Denison, D. R., & Mishra, A. K. (1995). Toward a theory of Organizational Culture and effectiveness. *Organization Science, 6*(2), 204–223. doi:10.1287/orsc.6.2.204

DiMaggio, P. (1997). Culture and cognition. *Annual Review of Sociology*, *23*(1), 263–287. doi:10.1146/annurev.soc.23.1.263

DiMaggio, P., & Markus, H. (2010). Culture and social psychology: Converging perspectives. *Social Psychology Quarterly*, *73*(4), 347–452. doi:10.1177/0190272510389010

Edelman, G. M. (1989). *The remembered present: A biological theory of consciousness.* New York: Basic Books.

Edelman, G. M. (2006). *Second Nature: Brain Science and Human Knowledge*. New Haven, CT: Yale University Press.

Eisenhardt, K. M., & Martin, J. A. (2000). Dynamic capabilities: What are they? *Strategic Management Journal*, *21*(10-11), 1105–1121. doi:10.1002/1097-0266(200010/11)21:10/11<1105::AID-SMJ133>3.0.CO;2-E

Gintis, H. (2014). Inclusive Fitness and the Sociobiology of the Genome. *Biology & Philosophy*, *29*(4), 477–515. doi:10.100710539-013-9404-0

Guasch, J. L., Laffont, J.-J., & Straub, S. (2003). *Renegotiation of concession contracts in Latin America.* World Bank Policy Research Working Paper, 3011.

Guasch, J. L., Laffont, J.-J., & Straub, S. (2007). Concessions of infrastructure in Latin America: Government-led renegotiation. *Journal of Applied Econometrics*, *22*(7), 1267–1294. doi:10.1002/jae.987

Hannan, M. T., & Freeman, J. (1989). *Organizational Ecology*. Cambridge, MA: Harvard University Press.

Henrich, J. (2004). Cultural group selection, coevolutionary processes and large-scale cooperation. *Journal of Economic Behavior & Organization*, *53*, 127–143. doi:10.1016/S0167-2681(03)00117-3

Hoff, K., & Stiglitz, J. E. (2016). Striving for balance in economics: Towards a theory of the social determination of behaviour. *Journal of Economic Behavior & Organization*, *126*, 25–57. doi:10.1016/j.jebo.2016.01.005

Hong, Y., Morris, M. W., Chiu, C., & Benet-Martinez, V. (2000). Multicultural minds: A dynamic constructivist approach to culture and cognition. *The American Psychologist*, *55*(7), 709–720. doi:10.1037/0003-066X.55.7.709 PMID:10916861

Johnsona, D. P., Michael, E. P., & Van Vugt, M. (2013). Darwin's invisible hand: Market competition, evolution and the firm. *Journal of Economic Behavior & Organization*, *90*, 128–140. doi:10.1016/j.jebo.2012.12.016

Kraimer, M. L., Shaffer, M. A., Harrison, D. A., & Ren, H. (2012). No place like home? An identity strain perspective on repatriate turnover. *Academy of Management Journal*, *55*(2), 399–420. doi:10.5465/amj.2009.0644

Leung, K., & Morris, M. W. (2015). Values, schemas, and norms in the culture–behavior nexus: A situated dynamics framework. *Journal of International Business Studies*, *46*(9), 1028–1050. doi:10.1057/jibs.2014.66

Levinthal, D. A. (2017). Mendel in the C-Suite: Design and the Evolution of Strategies. *Strategy Science*, *2*(4), 282–287. doi:10.1287tsc.2017.0047

Levinthal, D. A., & March, J. G. (1981). A model of adaptive organizational search. *Journal of Economic Behavior & Organization*, *2*(4), 307–333. doi:10.1016/0167-2681(81)90012-3

Mayr, E. (1997). The objects of selection. *Proceedings of the National Academy of Sciences of the United States of America*, *94*(6), 2091–2094. doi:10.1073/pnas.94.6.2091 PMID:9122151

McElreath, R., Boyd, R., & Richerson, P. J. (2003). Shared norms and the evolution of ethnic markers. *Current Anthropology*, *44*(1), 122–129. doi:10.1086/345689

Mengel, F. (2008). Matching structure and the cultural transmission of social norms. *Journal of Economic Behavior & Organization*, *67*(3-4), 608–623. doi:10.1016/j.jebo.2008.01.001

Mesoudi, A. (2009). How cultural evolutionary theory can inform social psychology, and vice versa. *Psychological Review*, *116*(4), 929–952. doi:10.1037/a0017062 PMID:19839691

Ostrom, E. (2000). Collective action and the evolution of social norms. *The Journal of Economic Perspectives*, *14*(3), 137–158. doi:10.1257/jep.14.3.137

Peysakhovich, A., & Rand, D. G. (2016). Habits of virtue: Creating norms of cooperation and defection in the laboratory. *Management Science*, *62*(3), 631–647. doi:10.1287/mnsc.2015.2168

Pudney, S. (2004). Keeping off the Grass? An econometric model of cannabis consumption in Britain. *Journal of Applied Econometrics*, *19*(4), 435–453. doi:10.1002/jae.746

Rand, D. G., & Nowak, M. A. (2013). Human cooperation. *Trends in Cognitive Sciences*, *17*(8), 413–425. doi:10.1016/j.tics.2013.06.003 PMID:23856025

Soltis, J., Boyd, R., & Richerson, P. J. (1995). Can Group-Functional Behaviors Evolve by Cultural Group Selection? An Empirical Test. *Current Anthropology*, *63*(3), 473–494. doi:10.1086/204381

Sussman, N. M. (2000). The dynamic nature of cultural identity throughout cultural transitions: Why home is not so sweet. *Personality and Social Psychology Review*, *4*(4), 355–373. doi:10.1207/S15327957PSPR0404_5

Sussman, N. M. (2002). Testing the cultural identity model of the cultural transition cycle: Sojourners return home. *International Journal of Intercultural Relations*, *26*(4), 391–408. doi:10.1016/S0147-1767(02)00013-5

Teece, D. J. (2007). Explicating dynamic capabilities: The nature and microfoundations of (sustainable) enterprise performance. *Strategic Management Journal, 28*(13), 1319–1350. doi:10.1002mj.640

Teece, D. J., Pisano, G. P., & Shuen, A. (1997). Dynamic capabilities and strategic management. *Strategic Management Journal, 18*(7), 119–142. doi:10.1002/(SICI)1097-0266(199708)18:7<509::AID-SMJ882>3.0.CO;2-Z

Witt, U. (2000). Changing cognitive frames --Changing organizational forms: An entrepreneurial theory of organizational development. *Industrial and Corporate Change, 9*(4), 733–745. doi:10.1093/icc/9.4.733

Chapter 2
Re-Examining the Relationship Between Team Work Quality and Speed of New Product Development:
A Test of Mediation Model

Asmat-Nizam Abdul-Talib
Universiti Utara Malaysia, Malaysia

Turki Abdullah Alanazi
Saudi Telecom Company, Saudi Arabia

Hasbullah Ashari
Universiti Teknologi Petronas, Malaysia

Siti Norhasmaedayu Mohd Zamani
Universiti Utara Malaysia, Malaysia

ABSTRACT

Previous research has consistently demonstrated that team work quality plays an important role in predicting the speed of new product development (NPD). However, the examination of the fundamental mechanisms behind this relationship has received less attention than it deserves. Drawing on the resource-based view and internal market orientation theories, this chapter examines mediating effect of internal market orientation in the relationship between teamwork quality and speed of new product development. One hundred and forty-nine team members drawn from the telecom companies in the Kingdom of Saudi Arabia participated in this study. Partial least squares path modelling was employed to test mediating effect of internal market orientation in the relationship between teamwork quality and NPD speed. Findings suggest a positive relationship between teamwork quality and NPD speed. As hypothesized, the findings showed that of internal market orientation mediated the relationship between teamwork quality and NPD speed.

DOI: 10.4018/978-1-5225-8458-2.ch002

INTRODUCTION

In today's fast-changing business environment, the speed of new product development (NPD) is a hallmark of time-based strategy which has become increasingly important for managing innovation (Chen, Damanpour, & Reilly, 2010). Anecdotal and empirical evidence suggests that NPD speed has been a critical factor in achieving a firm's competitiveness (Boston Consulting Group, 2006; Sun, Zhao, & Yau, 2009). Furthermore, for several decades now the extant literature indicates a lack of agreement regarding not only the terminology used, but also the definition offered of what is considered to be a similar construct (Chen et al., 2010). For example, researchers have assigned different names to the NPD speed construct such as time-to-market (Afonso, Nunes, Paisana, & Braga, 2008), innovation speed (Carbonell & Rodríguez-Escudero, 2009; Kessler & Chakrabarti, 1996; Pilar & Ana, 2010), and speed-to-market, among others (McNally, Akdeniz, & Calantone, 2011). Although different terminologies were used and different theoretical perspectives were employed, marketing researchers seem to agree that NPD speed represents how quickly an idea moves from conception to a product in the marketplace (Chen et al., 2010; Zamani, Abdul-Talib & Ashari, 2016).

A theory and a growing body of research over the past two decades has consistently shown that teamwork quality plays a crucial role in predicting the speed of NPD (e.g., Alanazi, Abdul-Talib, Ashari, & Islam, 2015; Barczak & Wilemon, 2003; Dayan & Benedetto, 2009; Hoegl & Gemuenden, 2001; Hoegl & Parboteeah, 2003; Jaworski & Kohli, 1993; Pinto & Pinto, 1990; Sun et al., 2009). Specifically, a study among 145 software development teams in Germany demonstrated a strong positive relationship between teamwork quality and success of innovative projects (Hoegl & Gemuenden, 2001). Similarly, in a sample of 267 firms in the industrial zones of the cities of Ankara and Istanbul in Turkey, Dayan and Benedetto (2009) found that teamwork quality was significantly related to speed-to-market and NPD project success. Furthermore, Sun et al. (2009) showed that teamwork quality, conceptualized in terms of cross-functional teams, training, group decision-making, and the commitment of team members, among others, was significantly and positively related to the speed of new product development.

Despite the well-established relationship between teamwork quality and the NPD cycle time, relatively, only a few studies have examined the fundamental mechanisms through which teamwork quality affects NPD speed (e.g., Alanazi et al., 2015), suggesting that more studies are needed to better understand the antecedents and consequences of NPD speed, particularly in a non-western context. Accordingly, this study proposed internal market orientation as a mediating variable in the teamwork quality-NPD speed relationship. Internal market orientation has been defined as the marketing activities engaged by various departments, geared toward developing an understanding of customers' current and future needs as well as the factors affecting these needs (Jaworski & Kohli, 1993; Kohli & Jaworski, 1990).

The present study proposed internal market orientation as a fundamental mechanism in the relationship between teamwork quality and NPD speed because there is research supporting a strong positive link between teamwork quality and internal market orientation (Resource-based view; Barney, Wright, & Ketchen, 2001; Barney, 2001; Ketchen, Hult, & Slater, 2007; Tokarczyk, Hansen, Green, & Down, 2007) and between internal market orientation and NPD speed (Atuahene-Gima, 1995; Frishammar & Åke Hörte, 2007; Li, Liu, & Zhao, 2006; Wren, Souder, & Berkowitz, 2000). Hence, the present work hypothesized that teamwork quality would be positively associated with internal market orientation, which in turn positively related to NPD speed.

Building upon previous research and theoretical perspective, the present study aimed to test a mediated model of NPD speed graphically depicted in Figure 1. Does internal market orientation mediate the relationship between teamwork quality and NPD speed? Specifically, the model incorporates NPD speed as the criterion variable and teamwork quality as the predictor variable. Figure 1 also assumes internal market orientation as a psychological process through which teamwork quality influences NPD speed.

LITERATURE REVIEW

Teamwork Quality and NPD Speed

Teamwork is the activity of multiple interdependent individuals (Salas, Cooke, & Roosen, 2008). It is a set of interrelated components of performance that are needed to efficiently and successfully facilitate coordinated and adaptive performance (Baker, Gustafson, Beaubien, Salas, & Barach, 2003; Salas et al., 2008; Cannon-Bowers Tannenbaum, Salas, & Volpe, 1995; Parumasur & Govender, 2013; Salas, Bowers, & Cannon-Bowers, 1995). Teamwork quality is a superordinate construct that refers to the degree and quality of team members' interaction (Hoegl & Gemuenden, 2001).

Hoegl and Gemuenden argued that the overall construct of teamwork quality is manifested in six dimensions. The conceptualization of teamwork quality as a 6-dimensional construct is consistent with past research that tends to cluster teamwork into two categories: tasks and interpersonal processes (Bales, 1958). Specifically, task processes include three dimensions: effort, balance of contribution, and coordination. These dimensions are related to the accomplishment of team goals and perform functions that allow teams to provide solutions to the problem that the group is committed to (Gladstein, 1984; Hsu, Shih, Chiang, & Liu, 2012). Interpersonal processes include three other dimensions: mutual support, cohesion, and communication. These dimensions perform maintenance functions (Gladstein, 1984) that are designed to build, strengthen, and regulate group life.

Given that teamwork quality is a higher-order construct represented by six dimensions, it is proposed that a link exists between factors of teamwork quality and NPD cycle time. It is proposed that teamwork quality has a positive influence on the performance of tasks and thus the performance of organizations, represented as NPD cycle time.

Over the past decades, multiple studies on teamwork have been executed. In their literature review, Salas, Stagl, Burke, and Goodwin (2007) reviewed more than 130 models and frameworks of teamwork or a component of it. These include models at different levels of teamwork. Some of the teamwork models in the field are more general models (e.g., Salas et al., 2005), some are more context-specific (e.g., Jeffcott & Mackenzie, 2008, some focus more on specific team processes (e.g., Chow & Cao, 2008), and there are models that focus more on the individual level of teams (e.g., Siau, Tan, & Sheng, 2010).

Nakata and Im (2010) validated a model developed from group effectiveness theory on 206 NPD teams from U.S. high-technology companies. They found that cross-functional integration brought the skills, efforts, and knowledge of differing functions in an NPD team that resulted in producing high-performing new products. Delarue, Hootegem, Proctor, and Burridge (2008) examined the operational and financial teamwork which were direct measures of organizational outcomes performance. They showed that teamwork had a positive impact on all four dimensions of performance. They further observed that performance was further enhanced when teamwork was combined with structural change.

In addition, Katzenbach and Smith (2003) stressed that teams are a curical part of a three part cycle that leads to optimum performance of the organization. These parts include shareholders providing opportunities, employees delivering value, and finally, customers generating returns. In high-performance firms, performance targets have several dimensions that affect all three contributors. The authors demonstrated a team performance curve that relates the effectiveness of the team against their performance impact that results in the organizational path that begins from the working group to pseudo team, potential team, real team and culminates in high-performance team.

Prior studies also concluded that teamwork quality impacts NPD cycle time. According to Dayan and Benedetto (2010), the team members' proximity and team longevity positively associated with the NPD teams' interpersonal trust, while the latter impacts team learning and new product success, but marketing expediency. Similarly, Hoegl, Ernst, and Proserpio (2007) claimed that teamwork quality is more challenging to achieve and more important to team performance with the increase of team dispersion. Ambiguity lies as to the tasks to be achieved and issues that require addressing (Sicotte & Langley, 2000).

Even though combined domain-relevant skills may be sufficient in normal project, highly innovative scenarios call for intensive team members' collaboration to make complete use of domain-relevant skills in dealing with an unstable environment (Ford, 1996; Okhuysen & Eisenhardt, 2002; Taggar, 2002). Additionally, it is not very often that specific individuals have the complex skills set to successfully achieve tasks related with innovative projects. Project success therefore requires collaboration among multiple specialists to integrate their skills in a coherent manner (Sicotte & Langley, 2000) and to reach ideas convergence within the team while adhering to the allocated budget and schedule.

At a fundamental level, teamwork quality elements such as communication, cohesion, sub-tasks coordination, and stress on the team members' contributions to the project enable team members to acknowledge domain-relevant skills possessed by teammates. The awareness of these skills is invaluable as the team will be in a better position to identify the expertise needed in facing uncertain issues. For example, open communication of relevant information (Hauptman & Hirji, 1996; Katz & Allen, 1988), and coordination of individual activities (Adler, 1995; Faraj & Sproull, 2000) enable teams to ensure that every member can contribute their knowledge to the best of their ability (Seers, 1989).

Accordingly, highly communicative teams emphasize every member's contribution and sufficiently coordinate tasks to facilitate team awareness of product information. This makes the teams ready to evaluate problems from various facets and provide an optimum solution (Thompson, 2003; Watson et al., 1991). This collaboration with other teams helps apply the teams' domain-relevant skills in a united project and creates synergy.

The Mediating Effect of Internal Market Orientation (IMO)

In an attempt to examine the influence of a number of organizational factors that are related to teamwork on the performance of some of the large banks, Lancaster and Velden (2004) examined this impact through the mediating influence of internal market orientation. The findings of their study revealed that the market orientation polices mediated the relationship between teamwork characteristics and the performance of the banks. Deshpande and Farley (1998) described market orientation as identical to customer orientation. This is consistent with the contentions of Deshpande and Webster (1989) and Payne (1988) that marketing orientation is aligned with the market.

Wren, Souder, and Berkowitz (2000) argued that products provided by highly market-oriented firms may fit existing customer needs best. As far as NPD cycle time is concerned, Griffin (1997) introduced three components for NPD speed. These components are time to market, concept to customers, and development time. Organizations that have high levels of internal market orientation are expected to have shorter cycle time for their new product development (Saryeddine, 2005). This because these organizations want to reach out to their customers and respond to their needs as fast as possible. In this manner, organizations will not lose their customers to other organizations in a highly competitive market.

Some prior research showed a direct/indirect association between internal market orientation and NPD cycle time. In this context, Subramanian and Gopalakrishna (2001) showed an impact of internal market orientation on new product performance through its direct impact on NPD cycle time. The argument is that the competencies of the market of sensing and responding, indicated by the great degrees of market orientation, leads to high market-oriented firms knowing the desires and needs of their customers and the market offerings. As a result, they react with services/products that satisfy the needs and add value to customers compared to their rivals' offerings.

Internal communication is an important key in the process of IMO according to Gronroos (1990). The proximal distance between the employees and management creates opportunities for this type of communication, and opens up opportunities for the collection of information concerning the employee's wants and needs, as previously explained, and also for information dissemination. The communication process is also crucial in encouraging the identification of organizations (Smidts, Pruyn, & Van Riel, 2001) and the employee subordinate's job outcomes (Keller, 1994), which in turn lead to better organisational performance. Specifically, bi-directional informal communication between management and staff positively impacts front-line staff (Johlke & Duhan, 2001). This is certainly significant in IMO as the relationship between staff and management shows a bi-directional communication that forms a part of workplace behavior. Dissemination of information is, hence, brought forward as the fourth IMO dimension.

A workplace where members of the organization are inclined and have the ability to communicate increases the information exchange frequency. In the context of an open workplace, people readily provide suggestions without having to worry about being taken seriously. Criticisms are expressed freely as it is likely to be accepted and to lead to enhancements. The level of accurate information flow through an organization is imperative as it not only helps steer clear of mistakes but also develops among the many organizational members. On the other hand, communication that is ineffective blocks market-oriented activities and results in conflict due to misunderstandings, erroneous methods and frustrations (Etgar, 1979). Such conflicts and misunderstanding between members could have a negative impact on organisational performance.

Based on the above reasons, the dimensions of information accuracy and general openness influence employee perception of communication as such that employees experience the internal market orientation of the firm (O'Reilly & Roberts, 1976; Price & Mueller, 1986). Workers who feel that their workplace is not conducive to effective communication are more inclined to provide a lower score in the assessment of their company's market orientation which would negatively influence organisational performance.

Responses as an IMO's fifth dimension mentioned in literature entails the reacting to the information produced concerning the employee's wants and needs. In marketing literature, among the top widely recommended uses of IMO information is the development of job products meeting the requirements of employees and satisfying and motivating them (Berry & Parasuraman 1991; Sasser & Arbeit 1976; Stauss & Schultze 1990). According to Sasser and Arbeit (1976), employees often exchange their time, energy and values for money and this is similar to external market exchange where customers primarily provide cash to obtain goods or services.

On the basis of prior internal market orientation literature, action taken is catered to gather favorable customer reaction (Kohli & Jaworski, 1990). However, it is not the action itself that is significant, it is the action drivers. Accordingly, the firm's customer-oriented actions are driven by the expectation of present and potential customers' needs and wants in an attempt to create customer value. An in-depth understanding of customer intelligence and action according to the relevant intelligence is important in using customer orientation approach.

Jaworski and Kholi (1993) conducted a study that attempted to examine the mediating impact of market orientation on the relationships the independent variables of top management, inter-departmental dynamics and organisational system and the dependent variable of business performance. The findings of their study revealed that the construct of market orientation did have a mediating influence on the relationships between the independent variables and the dependent variable.

METHODOLOGY

The present study employed a convenience non-probability sampling method (Keppel, Saufley, & Tokunaga 1992) to examine the effect of teamwork quality on the NPD cycle in the Saudi Arabian telecommunication industry. This sampling method was chosen because of the unfeasibility and impracticality of the situation to select random samples from the teams dedicated to the development of new products in Saudi Arabian telecommunications. Furthermore, this sampling method was appropriate because of the convenience of accessibility and the teams' proximity to the researcher. Numerous studies conducted on technology adoptions had also employed convenience sampling (Al-Hawari, 2011; Cheng, Wang, Lin, & Vivek, 2009; Joseph, McClure, & Joseph, 1999; Kleijnen, Ruyter & Wetzels, 2004), and the present research followed the protocols adopted by past research.

With the use of convenience sampling, the sample was not selected to reflect the opinion of the whole population. To examine the entire population would be ideal, but in some cases the population is just too large and to include the entire population is impossible. In the present study, the sampling frame (postal address) was absent and cultural considerations had to be considered. In addition, data were collected from the telecommunication companies that were willing to participate in the research; the subjects were free to decide whether or not to participate in the research.

Figure 1. Conceptual model

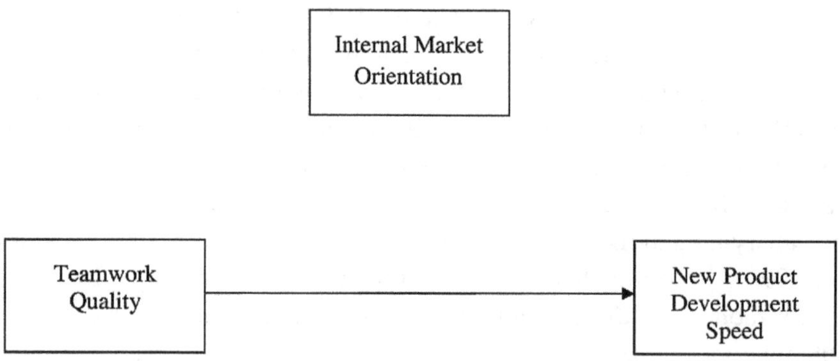

As previously mentioned, participants included 155 team members drawn from telecom companies in the Kingdom of Saudi Arabia. All participants were assured that their participation was confidential and voluntary. To ensure anonymity, the participants were provided a stamped envelope addressed to the researcher so that they could return their responses. Of 155 sets of questionnaires sent out to the participants, a total of 149 were returned with valid responses, accounting for 96% response rate. Of 149 participants, 27.5% were between 36 and 40 years old, 30.2% between 41 and 45 years old, 18.1% 31 and 35, 17.4% 46 and 50, 2.7% 25 and 30, and 4.0% were above 51 years old.

Regarding education qualification, a total of 49% of the participants held a bachelor's degree, a total of 36.9% had a high school diploma, a total of 10.1% had a master's degree, a total of 2.7% completed secondary school, and a total of 1.3% had a doctorate. With regards to job position, a total of 38.9% of the participants were ordinary employees, a total of 21.5% were consultants, a total of 20.1% were division managers, a total of 18.1% were heads of section, and a total of 1.3% were directors or held a higher level position. Finally, a total of 32.2% had between 11 and 15 years of work experience, a total of 21.5% had between 16 and 20 years, a total of 14.5% had between 21 and 25 years, a total of 19.5% had between 5 and 10 years, a total of 10.7% had more than 25 years of work experience, and a total of 2% had work experience less than five years.

Measures

Teamwork Quality

A 12-item short version of the teamwork quality scale developed by Hoegl and Gemuenden (2001) was used to measure teamwork quality. The scale consists of six dimensions; namely, communication, coordination, balance of member contribution, mutual support, effort, and cohesion. For the sake of parsimony, two items were adapted from each of the six dimensions to assess teamwork quality. Sample items included the following: "There is sufficiently frequent, informal, direct, and open communication among our team members," and "Team members help and support each other in carrying out their tasks." The participants were asked to indicate the extent to which they agreed or disagreed with each statement on a 7-point Likert scale (1=strongly disagree to 7 = strongly agree).

Internal Market Orientation

Internal market orientation was assessed using a 10-item short version of the internal market orientation scale, which was developed and validated by Lings and Greenley (2005). Of the 10 items used in the present study, two items were adapted from each of the following five dimensions: informal information generation, formal face-to-face information generation, formally written information generation, information dissemination, and response. Sample items included: "In our company, we have regular staff appraisals in which we discuss what employees want," and "In our company, I regularly meet with all my staff to report about issues relating to the whole organization." Responses of the participants were also measured on a 7-point Likert scale (1=strongly disagree to 7 = strongly agree).

New Product Development (NPD) Speed

Four items adapted from Kessler and Chakrabarti's (1999) NPD cycle time were employed to measure new product development speed. Sample items included: "Top management was pleased with the time it took us from specs to full commercialization," and "This product was developed and launched (fielded) faster than the major competitor for a similar product." The participants were also asked to indicate the extent to which they agreed with each statement on a 7-point Likert scale (1=strongly disagree to 7 = strongly agree).

Analytical Procedure

The partial least square (PLS) path modeling in conjunction with ADANCO software for variance-based structural equation modeling (Henseler & Dijkstra, 2014) was used to test the theoretical model in the present study. PLS path modeling was chosen for data analysis for the following reasons. First, compared with other covariance-based structural equation modelling (SEM) approaches, PLS path modeling has less stringent assumptions on the normal distribution of observations (Hair, Sarstedt, Pieper, & Ringle, 2012a; Henseler, Ringle, & Sinkovics, 2009) Second, PLS path modeling was found to be suitable because the goal of this study was to predict key target constructs (i.e., NPD speed) (Abdul-Latif & Abdul-Talib, 2017). Accordingly, the literature recommends the use of PLS path modelling, mainly if the goal of the researcher is to predict key target constructs and/or identifying key "driver" constructs (Hair, Ringle, & Sarstedt, 2011a, 2011b; Hair et al., 2012a; Hair, Sarstedt, Ringle, & Mena, 2012b).

Finally, PLS path modelling was considered an appropriate technique of data analysis because it has been used successfully in a variety of management disciplines such as strategic management (Hair et al., 2012a), marketing, tourism (Nunkoo, Ramkissoon, & Gursoy, 2013), and operations management, among others (Peng & Lai, 2012). Additionally, to test our mediated-model, Preacher and Hayes' (2008; 2004) bootstrapping technique of estimating indirect effects in simple mediation model was used. In particular, the direct model was evaluated before incorporating the mediating variable in the full model (Klarner, Sarstedt, Hoeck, & Ringle, 2013; Kura, 2016).

Results

Consistent with the recommendations of Henseler et al. (2009), Gnizy, Cadogan, Oliveira, and Nizam (2017), as well as Hair, Hult, Ringle, and Sarstedt (2014), the results of the data analysis are presented in two steps. First, the measurement model was evaluated to ascertain the reliability and validity of the PLS model before testing the structural model (Chin, 1998, 2010). Furthermore, consistent with PLS path modeling literature, a standard bootstrapping procedure with 5000 bootstrap samples were used to assess the significance of the path coefficients (Hair et al., 2014; Hair et al., 2012a; Henseler et al., 2009). The results of the measurement are presented in Table 1.

Results of Measurement Model

The evaluation of a measurement model involves determining individual indicator reliability, internal consistency reliability, convergent validity, as well as discriminant validity. First, indicator reliability was established by checking indicator loading of each construct's measure (Hair et al., 2014; Hair et

Table 1. Result of the measurement model

Constructs/Indicators	Indicator Loadings	Dijkstra-Henseler's Rho (ρa) Composite Reliability	Average Variance Extracted (AVE)
Team Work Quality		*.9372*	*.6515*
AWQ01	.6090		
AWQ02	.6389		
AWQ05	.6763		
AWQ06	.6976		
AWQ07	.5762		
AWQ08	.5606		
AWQ11	.7592		
AWQ12	.6943		
Int. Market Orientation		*.9313*	*.6299*
NPD01	.7315		
NPD02	.7467		
NPD03	.7516		
NPD04	.7089		
New Product Development		*.9172*	*.7347*
BMO03	.6730		
BMO04	.7208		
BMO05	.5630		
BMO06	.6384		
BMO07	.4638		
BMO08	.6129		
BMO09	.6525		
BMO10	.7151		

al., 2011a, 2011b; Henseler, Ringle, & Sarstedt, 2012; Henseler et al., 2009). As a rule of thumb, Hair et al. (2014) recommended retaining items with loadings between .40 and .70. As shown in Table 1, all items used in this study highly and significantly loaded onto their corresponding construct as they were all within the recommended threshold values of between .40 and .70. Regarding internal consistency reliability, it is suggested that the composite reliability of each construct should be at least .70 or higher (Hair et al., 2014).

$$CR = (\Sigma\kappa)^2 / [(\Sigma\kappa)^2 + (\Sigma 1 - \kappa^2)]$$

where κ = factor loading of every item and n = number of items in a model

As expected, Table 1 shows that the composite reliability of each construct was well above the suggested .70 threshold value. Meanwhile, the Average Variance Extracted (AVE) was used to determine the convergent validity. It is also recommended that the AVE of each construct in the model exceeds .50 (Fornell & Bookstein, 1982; Fornell & Larcker, 1981a; Fornell & Larcker, 1981b).

AVE = Σ κ2 / n

where κ = factor loading of every item and n = number of items in a model

As Table 1 shows, all constructs exceeded this threshold; hence, the measurement model suggests adequate convergent reliability.

Finally, discriminant validity was established by ensuring that the square root of the average AVE of each construct exceeded the correlation score of all other constructs (Fornell & Bookstein, 1982; Fornell & Larcker, 1981a; Fornell & Larcker, 1981b). As indicated in Table 2, the square root of the AVEs, shown diagonally, was greater than its correlation with other constructs, suggesting adequate discriminant validity.

Results of Structural Model

The structural model was evaluated to test the mediating effect of internal market orientation in the relationship between teamwork quality and NPD speed. The results of the structural model were presented in two parts following Klarner et al. (2013) as well as Kura (2016). First, the result of the direct effect of the PLS model is depicted in Figure 1. Figure 2 shows a significant and positive relationship between teamwork quality NPD speed, and this model indicated that teamwork quality explained the 28.9% variance in NPD speed.

$$r^2 \text{ (Coefficient of Determination)} = \frac{\sum(y-\bar{y})^2 - \sum(y-\hat{y})^2}{\sum(y-\bar{y})^2}$$

After establishing a significant relationship in the direct effect model, the present study tested the full PLS model, which incorporates the mediating variable. Figure 3 depicts the result of the mediated

Table 2. Discriminant validity

	Construct	1	2	3
1	Teamwork quality	**.6515**		
2	Int. market orientation	.3991	**.6299**	
3	New product development	.2845	.3113	**.7347**

Squared correlations; AVE in the diagonal.

Figure 2. Direct effect model

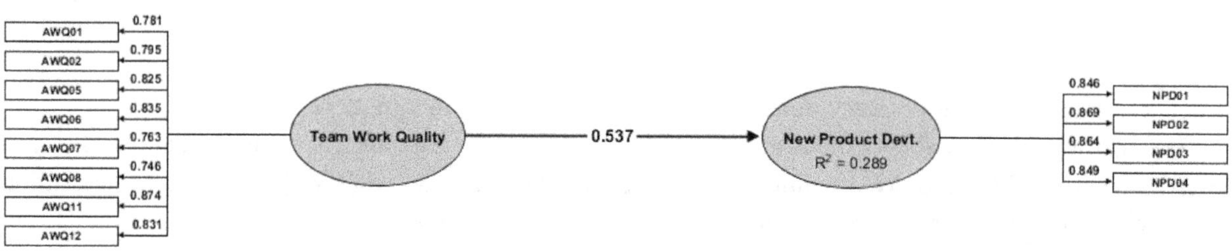

model. Even after incorporating the mediating variable, a significant and positive relationship between teamwork and quality NPD speed was found, but the beta value reduced to .301 from .537. Additionally, the indirect effect of teamwork quality on NPD speed via internal market orientation was also found to be significant (see Table 3; $\beta = .2323$, $t = 3.615$, $p < .01$), as such it can be concluded that the relationship between teamwork quality and NPD speed was mediated by internal market orientation. The mediated model showed that the amount of variance explained in NPD speed was 36.6%.

DISCUSSION AND CONCLUSION

The primary objective of this study was to examine the mediating effect of internal market orientation in the relationship between teamwork and quality NPD speed among team members drawn from telecom companies in the Kingdom of Saudi Arabia. Overall, this study succeeded in advancing the current understanding of the critical determinants of NPD speed by providing an answer to the research question: Does internal market orientation mediate the relationship between teamwork quality and NPD speed? Regarding the direct relationship between the exogenous latent variable and the endogenous latent vari-

Figure 3. Mediating effect model

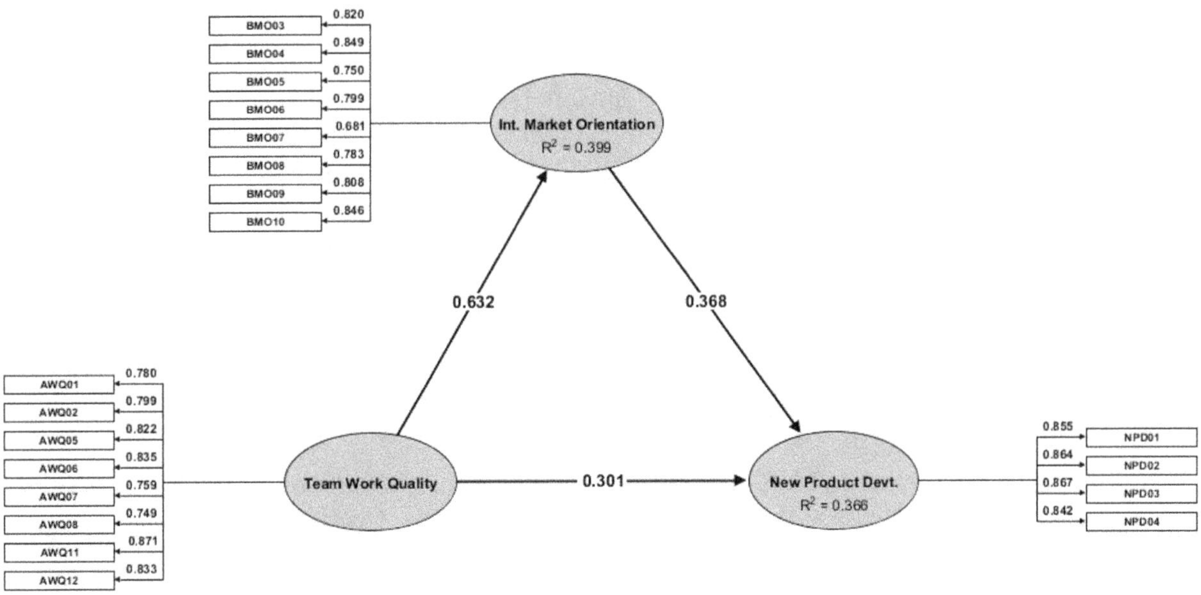

Table 3. Indirect effects inference

Effect	Beta	SE	t-Value	p-Value	Percentile Bootstrap Quantiles	
					.5%	99.5%
Teamwork quality →New product development	.2323	.064	3.615	.000	.0964	.4343

Note: ***Significant at .01 (one-tailed), **Significant at .05 (one-tailed), *Significant at .1 (one-tailed).

ables, the result of the PLS path model showed that teamwork quality was significantly and positively related to NPD speed.

This finding seems to suggest that quality teamwork as reflected by communication, coordination, balance of member contribution, mutual support, effort, and cohesion is likely to contribute to the speed of new product development (e.g., Alanazi et al., 2015; Barczak & Wilemon, 2003; Dayan & Benedetto, 2009; Hoegl & Gemuenden, 2001; Hoegl & Parboteeah, 2003; Pinto & Pinto, 1990; Sun et al., 2009). For internal market orientation (IMO), the result provided empirical support for the mediating role of internal market orientation in the relationship between teamwork quality and NPD speed. The result appears to be congruent with internal market orientation theory (Jaworski & Kohli, 1993; Kohli & Jaworski, 1990), which suggests that internal market orientation is an important mechanism through which teamwork quality affects NPD speed. This finding further suggests that internal market orientation is a mechanism in the relationship between teamwork quality and NPD speed because of the strong positive links between teamwork quality and internal market orientation (Resource-based view; Barney et al., 2001; Barney, 2001; Ketchen et al., 2007; Tokarczyk et al., 2007) and between internal market orientation and NPD speed (Atuahene-Gima, 1995; Frishammar & Åke Hörte, 2007; Li et al., 2006; Wren et al., 2000).

The present study provides additional evidence to the growing body of knowledge concerning the mediating role of internal market orientation in the relationship between teamwork quality and NPD speed. The results of this study lend support our key theoretical propositions. In particular, the current study has successfully answered the research question and met the research objective despite some limitations. Previous research has consistently demonstrated that teamwork quality plays an important role in predicting the speed of new product development. However, the present study has addressed the theoretical gap by incorporating internal market orientation as a fundamental mechanism in this relationship. The theoretical framework of this study has also replicated to the domain of resource-based view and internal market orientation theories by examining the influence of teamwork quality on NPD speed.

REFERENCES

Abdul-Latif, S. A., & Abdul-Talib, A. N. (2017). Consumer racism: A scale modification. *Asia Pacific Journal of Marketing and Logistics*, *29*(3), 616–633. doi:10.1108/APJML-02-2016-0026

Abdul Talib, A. N., & Md Salleh, M. F. (1997). Firm size and export attitudes of Malaysian exporters. In The Proceedings of Second Asian Academy of Manage. Conference: Towards management excellence in the 21st century Asia (pp. 403-408).

Adler, P. S. (1995). Interdepartmental interdependence and coordination: The case of the design/manufacturing interface. *Organization Science*, *6*(2), 7–16. doi:10.1287/orsc.6.2.147

Afonso, P., Nunes, M., Paisana, A., & Braga, A. (2008). The influence of time-to-market and target costing in the new product development success. *International Journal of Production Economics*, *115*(2), 559–568. doi:10.1016/j.ijpe.2008.07.003

Al-Hawari, M. A. (2011). Do online services contribute to establishing brand equity within the retail banking context? *Journal of Relationship Marketing*, *10*(3), 145–166. doi:10.1080/15332667.2011.596466

Alanazi, T. A., Abdul-Talib, A. N., Ashari, H., & Islam, R. (2015). Relationship between teamwork quality and new product development cycle time in Telecom Industry. *Asian Journal of Scientific Research*, *8*(1), 41–53. doi:10.3923/ajsr.2015.41.53

Ashari, H., Yusoff, Y. M., Zamani, S. N. M., & Talib, A. N. A. (2018). A Study of the Effect of Market Orientation on Malaysian Automotive Industry Supply Chain Performance. *International Journal of Technology*, *9*(8), 1651–1657. doi:10.14716/ijtech.v9i8.2749

Atuahene-Gima, K. (1995). An Exploratory Analysis of the Impact of Market Orientation on New Product Performance. *Journal of Product Innovation Management*, *12*(4), 275–293. doi:10.1016/0737-6782(95)00027-Q

Baker, D. P., Gustafson, S., Beaubien, J. M., Salas, E., & Barach, P. (2003). *Medical teamwork and patient safety: The evidence-based relation*. Washington, DC: American Institutes for Research.

Bales, R. F. (1958). Task roles and social roles in problem-solving groups. In E. E. Maccoby, T. M. Newcomb, & E. L. Hartley (Eds.), *Social psychology* (3rd ed.; pp. 437–447). New York: Holt, Rinehart and Winston.

Barczak, G., & Wilemon, D. (2003). Team member experiences in new product development: Views from the trenches. *R & D Management*, *33*(5), 463–479. doi:10.1111/1467-9310.00311

Barney, J., Wright, M., & Ketchen, D. J. Jr. (2001). The resource-based view of the firm: Ten years after 1991. *Journal of Management*, *27*(6), 625–641. doi:10.1177/014920630102700601

Barney, J. B. (2001). Resource-based theories of competitive advantage: A ten-year retrospective on the resource-based view. *Journal of Management*, *27*(6), 643–650. doi:10.1177/014920630102700602

Berry, L. L., & Parasuraman, A. (1991). *Marketing services: Competing through quality*. New York: Free Press.

Boston Consulting Group. (2006, April 24). The world's most innovative companies. *Business Week*. Retrieved from http://www.businessweek.com/magazine/toc/06_17/B39810617innovation.htm

Cannon-Bowers, J. A., Tannenbaum, S. I., Salas, E., & Volpe, C. E. (1995). Defining competencies and establishing team training requirements. In *Team effectiveness and decision making in organizations* (pp. 333–380). San Francisco: Jossey-Bass.

Carbonell, P., & Rodríguez-Escudero, A. I. (2009). Relationships among team's organizational context, innovation speed, and technological uncertainty: An empirical analysis. *Journal of Engineering and Technology Management*, *26*(1–2), 28–45. doi:10.1016/j.jengtecman.2009.03.005

Chen, J., Damanpour, F., & Reilly, R. R. (2010). Understanding antecedents of new product development speed: A meta-analysis. *Journal of Operations Management*, *28*(1), 17–33. doi:10.1016/j.jom.2009.07.001

Chin, W. W. (1998). The partial least squares approach to structural equation modeling. In G. A. Marcoulides (Ed.), *Modern Methods for Business Research* (pp. 295–336). Mahwah, NJ: Laurence Erlbaum Associates.

Chin, W. W. (2010). How to write up and report PLS analyses. In V. E. Vinzi, W. W. Chin, J. Henseler, & H. Wang (Eds.), *Handbook of partial least squares: Concepts, methods and applications in marketing and related fields* (pp. 655–690). Berlin: Springer. doi:10.1007/978-3-540-32827-8_29

Chow, T., & Cao, D. B. (2008). A survey study of critical success factors in agile software projects. *Journal of Systems and Software*, *81*(6), 961–971. doi:10.1016/j.jss.2007.08.020

Dayan, M., & Benedetto, C. A. D. (2009). Antecedents and consequences of teamwork quality in new product development projects. *European Journal of Innovation Management*, *12*(1), 129–155. doi:10.1108/14601060910928201

Dayan, M., & di Benedetto, C. A. (2010). The impact of structural and contextual factors on trust formation in product development teams. *Industrial Marketing Management*, *39*(4), 691–703. doi:10.1016/j.indmarman.2010.01.001

Delarue, A., Hootegem, G. V., Proctor, S., & Burridge, M. (2008). Team working and organizational performance: A review of survey-based research. *International Journal of Management Reviews*, *10*(2), 127–148. doi:10.1111/j.1468-2370.2007.00227.x

Deshpande, R., & Farley, J. U. (1998). Measuring market orientation: Generalization and synthesis. *Journal of Market Focused Management*, *2*, 231–232.

Deshpande, R., & Webster, F. E. Jr. (1989). Organizational culture and marketing: Defining the research agenda. *Journal of Marketing*, *53*(1), 3–15. doi:10.1177/002224298905300102

Etgar, M. (1979). Sources and types of intrachannel conflict. *Journal of Retailing*, *55*, 61–78.

Faraj, S., & Sproull, L. (2000). Coordinating expertise in software development teams. *Management Science*, *46*(12), 1554–1568. doi:10.1287/mnsc.46.12.1554.12072

Fornell, C., & Bookstein, F. L. (1982). Two structural equation models: LISREL and PLS applied to consumer exit-voice theory. *JMR, Journal of Marketing Research*, *19*(4), 440–452. doi:10.1177/002224378201900406

Fornell, C., & Larcker, D. (1981a). Structural equation models with unobservable variables and measurement error: Algebra and statistics. *JMR, Journal of Marketing Research*, *18*(3), 382–388. doi:10.1177/002224378101800313

Fornell, C., & Larcker, D. F. (1981b). Evaluating Structural Equation Models with unobservable variables and measurement error. *JMR, Journal of Marketing Research*, *18*(1), 39–50. doi:10.1177/002224378101800104

Frishammar, J., & Åke Hörte, S. (2007). The Role of Market Orientation and Entrepreneurial Orientation for New Product Development Performance in Manufacturing Firms. *Technology Analysis and Strategic Management*, *19*(6), 765–788. doi:10.1080/09537320701711231

Gladstein, D. L. (1984). Groups in context: A model of task group effectiveness. *Administrative Science Quarterly*, *29*(4), 499–517. doi:10.2307/2392936

Gnizy, I., Cadogan, J. W., Oliveira, J. S., & Nizam, A. (2017). The empirical link between export dispersion and export performance: A contingency-based approach. *International Business Review*, *26*(2), 239–249. doi:10.1016/j.ibusrev.2016.07.002

Griffin, A. (1997). The effect of project and process characteristics on product development cycle time. *JMR, Journal of Marketing Research*, *34*(1), 24–35. doi:10.1177/002224379703400103

Hair, J. F., Hult, G. T. M., Ringle, C. M., & Sarstedt, M. (2014). *A primer on partial least squares structural equation modeling (PLS-SEM)*. Thousand Oaks, CA: Sage Publications.

Hair, J. F., Ringle, C. M., & Sarstedt, M. (2011a). PLS-SEM: Indeed a Silver Bullet. *Journal of Marketing Theory and Practice*, *18*(2), 139–152. doi:10.2753/MTP1069-6679190202

Hair, J. F., Ringle, C. M., & Sarstedt, M. (2011b). The Use of Partial Least Squares (PLS) to Address Marketing Management Topics: From the Special Issue Guest Editors. *Journal of Marketing Theory and Practice*, *18*(2), 135–138. doi:10.1080/10696679.2011.11046435

Hair, J. F., Sarstedt, M., Pieper, T. M., & Ringle, C. M. (2012a). The Use of Partial Least Squares Structural Equation Modeling in Strategic Management Research: A Review of Past Practices and Recommendations for Future Applications. *Long Range Planning*, *45*(5–6), 320–340. doi:10.1016/j.lrp.2012.09.008

Hair, J. F., Sarstedt, M., Ringle, C. M., & Mena, J. A. (2012b). An assessment of the use of partial least squares structural equation modeling in marketing research. *Journal of the Academy of Marketing Science*, *40*(3), 414–433. doi:10.100711747-011-0261-6

Hauptman, O., & Hirji, K. K. (1996). The influence of process concurrency on project outcomes in product development: An empirical study of cross-functional teams. *IEEE Transactions on Engineering Management*, *43*(3), 153–164. doi:10.1109/17.509981

Henseler, J., & Dijkstra, T. K. (2014). *ADANCO 1.0. Kleve: Composite Modeling*. Retrieved on August 13, 2017, from: http://www.compositemodeling.com

Henseler, J., Ringle, C. M., & Sarstedt, M. (2012). Using Partial Least Squares Path Modeling in International Advertising Research: Basic Concepts and Recent Issues. In S. Okazaki (Ed.), *Handbook of Research in International Advertising* (pp. 252–276). Cheltenham, UK: Edward Elgar Publishing. doi:10.4337/9781781001042.00023

Henseler, J., Ringle, C. M., & Sinkovics, R. R. (2009). The Use of Partial Least Squares Path Modeling in International Marketing. In R. R. Sinkovics & P. N. Ghauri (Eds.), *Advances in International Marketing* (Vol. 20, pp. 277–320). Bingley: Emerald. doi:10.1108/S1474-7979(2009)0000020014

Henseler, J., Wilson, B., Götz, O., & Hautvast, C. (2007). Investigating the moderating role of fit on sports sponsoring and brand equity: A structural model. *International Journal of Sports Marketing & Sponsorship*, *8*(4), 321–329. doi:10.1108/IJSMS-08-04-2007-B005

Hoegl, M., Ernst, H., & Proserpio, L. (2007). How teamwork matters more as team member dispersion increases. *Journal of Product Innovation Management*, *24*(2), 156–165. doi:10.1111/j.1540-5885.2007.00240.x

Hoegl, M., & Gemuenden, H. G. (2001). Teamwork quality and the success of innovative projects: A theoretical concept and empirical evidence. *Organization Science*, *12*(4), 435–449. doi:10.1287/orsc.12.4.435.10635

Hoegl, M., & Parboteeah, K. P. (2003). Goal Setting And Team Performance In Innovative Projects: On the Moderating Role of Teamwork Quality. *Small Group Research, 34*(1), 3–19. doi:10.1177/1046496402239575

Hsu, S., Shih, S., Chiang, J. C., & Liu, Y. (2012). The impact of transactive memory systems on IS development teams' coordination, communication, and performance. *International Journal of Project Management, 30*(3), 329–340. doi:10.1016/j.ijproman.2011.08.003

Jaworski, B. J., & Kohli, A. K. (1993). Market orientation: Antecedents and consequences. *Journal of Marketing, 57*(3), 53–70. doi:10.1177/002224299305700304

Jeffcott, S. A., & Mackenzie, C. F. (2008). Measuring team performance in healthcare: Review of research and implications for patient safety. *Journal of Critical Care, 23*(2), 188–196. doi:10.1016/j.jcrc.2007.12.005 PMID:18538211

Johlke, M. C., & Duhan, D. F. (2000). Testing competing models of sales force communication. *Journal of Personal Selling & Sales Management, 21*(4), 265–277.

Joseph, M., McClure, C., & Joseph, B. (1999). Service quality in the banking sector: The impact of technology on service delivery. *International Journal of Bank Marketing, 17*(4), 182–193. doi:10.1108/02652329910278879

Katz, R., & Allen, T. J. (1988). Investigating the not invented here (NIH) syndrome: a look at the performance, tenure, and communication patterns of 50 R&D project groups. In L. Michael, W. L. Tushman, & Moore (Eds.), Readings in the management of innovations (pp. 293–309). Cambridge, MA: Ballinger Publishing.

Katzenbach, J. R., & Smith, D. K. (2003). *The wisdom of teams*. New York: Harper Collins Publishers.

Keller, R. T. (1994). Technology-information processing fit and the performance of R&D project groups: A test of contingency theory. *Academy of Management Journal, 37*(1), 167–179.

Keppel, G., Saufley, W. H., & Tokunaga, H. (1992). *Introduction to design and analysis: A students handbook* (2nd ed.). New York: W.H. Freeman & Company.

Kessler, E. H., & Chakrabarti, A. K. (1996). Innovation speed: A conceptual model of context, antecedents, and outcomes. *Academy of Management Review, 21*(4), 1143–1191. doi:10.5465/amr.1996.9704071866

Kessler, E. H., & Chakrabarti, A. K. (1999). Speeding up the pace of new product development. *Journal of Product Innovation Management, 16*(3), 231–247. doi:10.1016/S0737-6782(98)00048-4

Ketchen, D. J., Hult, G. T. M., & Slater, S. F. (2007). Toward greater understanding of market orientation and the resource-based view. *Strategic Management Journal, 28*(9), 961–964. doi:10.1002mj.620

Klarner, P., Sarstedt, M., Hoeck, M., & Ringle, C. M. (2013). Disentangling the Effects of Team Competences, Team Adaptability, and Client Communication on the Performance of Management Consulting Teams. *Long Range Planning, 46*(3), 258–286. doi:10.1016/j.lrp.2013.03.001

Kleijnen, M., Wetzels, M., & De Ruyter, K. (2004). Consumer acceptance of wireless finance. *Journal of Financial Services Marketing*, *8*(3), 206–217. doi:10.1057/palgrave.fsm.4770120

Kohli, A. K., & Jaworski, B. J. (1990). Market orientation: The construct, research propositions, and managerial implications. *Journal of Marketing*, *54*(2), 1–18. doi:10.1177/002224299005400201

Kura, K. M. (2016). Environmentally-specific transformational leadership and green behaviour at work: Exploring the mediating role of environmental concern. *Global Business Review*, *17*(6), 1S–14S. doi:10.1177/0972150916631069

Lancaster, G., & Van Der Velden, H. (2004). The influence of employee characteristics on market orientation. *International Journal of Bank Marketing*, *22*(5), 343–365. doi:10.1108/02652320410549656

Li, Y., Liu, Y., & Zhao, Y. (2006). The role of market and entrepreneurship orientation and internal control in the new product development activities of Chinese firms. *Industrial Marketing Management*, *35*(3), 336–347. doi:10.1016/j.indmarman.2005.05.016

McNally, R. C., Akdeniz, M. B., & Calantone, R. J. (2011). New Product Development Processes and New Product Profitability: Exploring the Mediating Role of Speed to Market and Product Quality. *Journal of Product Innovation Management*, *28*(s1), 63–77. doi:10.1111/j.1540-5885.2011.00861.x

Ming-Sung Cheng, J., Shih-Tse Wang, E., Ying-Chao Lin, J., & Vivek, S. D. (2009). Why do customers utilize the internet as a retailing platform? A view from consumer perceived value. *Asia Pacific Journal of Marketing and Logistics*, *21*(1), 144–160. doi:10.1108/13555850910926290

Nakata, C., & Im, S. (2010). Spurring cross-functional integration for higher new product performance: A group effectiveness perspective. *Journal of Product Innovation Management*, *27*(4), 554–571. doi:10.1111/j.1540-5885.2010.00735.x

Nunkoo, R., Ramkissoon, H., & Gursoy, D. (2013). Use of Structural Equation Modeling in Tourism Research: Past, Present, and Future. *Journal of Travel Research*, *52*(6), 759–771. doi:10.1177/0047287513478503

O'Reilly, C., & Roberts, K. (1976). *Relationships among components of credibility and communication*. Academic Press.

Parumasur, S. B., & Govender, P. (2013). The Importance of Teamwork, Continuous Top Management Support and Training in Bringing About TQM. *Journal of Economics and Behavioral Studies*, *9*(5), 639–651.

Payne, A. F. (1988). Developing a marketing-oriented organization. *Business Horizons*, *31*(3), 46–53. doi:10.1016/0007-6813(88)90008-0

Peng, D. X., & Lai, F. (2012). Using partial least squares in operations management research: A practical guideline and summary of past research. *Journal of Operations Management*, *30*(6), 467–480. doi:10.1016/j.jom.2012.06.002

Pilar, C., & Ana, I. R. E. (2010). The effect of market orientation on innovation speed and new product performance. *Journal of Business and Industrial Marketing*, *25*(7), 501–513. doi:10.1108/08858621011077736

Pinto, M. B., & Pinto, J. K. (1990). Project Team Communication and Cross-Functional Cooperation in New Program Development. *Journal of Product Innovation Management*, *7*(3), 200–212. doi:10.1016/0737-6782(90)90004-X

Preacher, K. J., & Hayes, A. (2008). Asymptotic and resampling strategies for assessing and comparing indirect effects in multiple mediator models. *Behavior Research Methods*, *40*(3), 879–891. doi:10.3758/BRM.40.3.879 PMID:18697684

Preacher, K. J., & Hayes, A. F. (2004). SPSS and SAS procedures for estimating indirect effects in simple mediation models. *Behavior Research Methods, Instruments, & Computers*, *36*(4), 717–731. doi:10.3758/BF03206553 PMID:15641418

Price, J., & Mueller, C. (1986). *Handbook of organizational measurement*. Marshfield, MA: Pitman Publishing.

Salas, E., Bowers, C. A., & Cannon-Bowers, J. A. (1995). Military team research: 10 years of progress. *Military Psychology*, *7*(2), 55–75. doi:10.120715327876mp0702_2

Salas, E., Sims, D. E., & Burke, C. S. (2005). Is there a "Big Five" in teamwork? *Small Group Research*, *36*(5), 555–599. doi:10.1177/1046496405277134

Salas, E., Stagle, K. C., Burke, C. S., & Goodwin, G. F. (2007). Fostering team effectiveness in organizations: Toward an integrative theoretical framework of team performance. In R. A. Dienstbier, J. W. Shuart, W. Spaulding, & J. Poland (Eds.), Modeling complex systems: Motivation, cognition and social processes. Academic Press.

Sasser, E. W., & Arbeit, S. P. (1976). Selling jobs in the services sector. *Business Horizons*, *19*(3), 61–65. doi:10.1016/0007-6813(76)90053-7

Seers, A. (1989). Team-member exchange quality: A new construct for role-making research. *Organizational Behavior and Human Decision Processes*, *43*(1), 118–135. doi:10.1016/0749-5978(89)90060-5

Siau, K., Tan, X., & Sheng, H. (2010). Important characteristics of software development team members: An empirical investigation using Repertory Grid. *Information Systems Journal*, *20*(6), 563–580. doi:10.1111/j.1365-2575.2007.00254.x

Smidts, A., Pruyn, A. T. H., & van Riel, C. B. M. (2001). The impact of employee communication and perceived external prestige on organizational identification. *Academy of Management Journal*, *44*, 1051–1062.

Stauss, V. B., & Schultze, H. S. (1990). Internet marketing. *Journal of Marketing*, *3*(3), 149–158.

Subramanian, R., & Gopalakrishna, P. (2001). The market orientation-performance relationship in the context of a developing economy: An empirical analysis. *Journal of Business Research*, *53*(1), 1–13. doi:10.1016/S0148-2963(99)00109-5

Sun, H., Zhao, Y., & Yau, H. K. (2009). The relationship between quality management and the speed of new product development. *The TQM Journal*, *21*(6), 576–588. doi:10.1108/17542730910995855

Tokarczyk, J., Hansen, E., Green, M., & Down, J. (2007). A Resource-Based View and Market Orientation Theory Examination of the Role of "Familiness" in Family Business Success. *Family Business Review*, *20*(1), 17–31. doi:10.1111/j.1741-6248.2007.00081.x

Wren, B. M., Souder, W. E., & Berkowitz, D. (2000). Market Orientation and New Product Development in Global Industrial Firms. *Industrial Marketing Management*, *29*(6), 601–611. doi:10.1016/S0019-8501(00)00120-6

Zamani, S. N. M., Abdul-Talib, A. N., & Ashari, H. (2016). Strategic orientations and new product success: The mediating impact of innovation speed. International Information Institute (Tokyo) Information, 19(7B), 2785.

Chapter 3
Foreign Direct Investment, Corruption, and Crime:
A Theoretical Analysis of Drug Trafficking

Rafael Salvador Espinosa Ramirez
https://orcid.org/0000-0002-5049-9175
University of Guadalajara, Mexico

ABSTRACT

Drug trafficking could be associated with the corrupt structures of governments and any anti-drug enforcement policy would be compromised. At the same time, it is perceived that the flow of foreign direct investment, which is inversely related with drug trafficking, drives the economy and the host government faces a dilemma between encouraging foreign direct investment or allowing drug trafficking. In this chapter, a theoretical model of this stylized fact is made. It is found that the host government sets a strict enforcement policy if the corruption level is low; otherwise, a lax policy would be set. Once the enforcement policy has been set, an increase in the corruption level reduces the enforcement level. Additionally, an increase in the demand for drugs may reduce or increase the enforcement level depending of the size of corruption level compared with the market size for foreign investors. However, with an international specific policy, an increase in demand of drugs reduces unequivocally the optimal enforcement level.

INTRODUCTION

The need to explain the location of multinationals and the flow of investment all over the world is given by the increasing globalization process and the inherent integration among the economies. International trade is not the only reason to integrate economies, but several positive externalities derived from the attraction of foreign capital such as employment, transfer of technology, and clustering with local firms. All these externalities are believed to promote growth and development (Cortez Yactayo & Espinosa Ramirez, 2011). Foreign Direct Investment (FDI) is one of the most desired foreign investments. FDI is understood as long-term capital in which foreign firms and multinationals assume risk to locate in foreign markets to obtain a higher rate of return and to enter foreign and local markets. It is a strategy

DOI: 10.4018/978-1-5225-8458-2.ch003

game between foreign investors and receiving developing countries in order to determine the location of foreign investment.

On one hand, foreign investors evaluate the conditions and treaties to locate in developing countries (Salacuse, 2017). On the other hand, it is crucial for host countries to identify the determinant factors in order to attract foreign direct investment. Even when it is quite important to know the reasons for FDI location for emerging economies, there is not a consensus about the patter of localization of foreign investment (Singh & Jun, 1995). In the report on World Investment 2018 made by UNCTAD, between 2016 and 2017 FDI flows to developed economies fell by one-third to US$712 billion, while FDI inflows to developing economies remained close to their 2016 level at US$671 billion (UNCTAD, 2018, p. 2). Despite the last year general decline in FDI worldwide, emphasis is given to the growing flow of investment addressed to developing economies after 2015.

However, despite the stable scenario for developing economies, UNCTAD warns to keep healthy institutional policies as the investment law and institutional reforms (UNCTAD, 2018, p. 106). International investors seem to be sensitive to the institutional health of a country to invest; in particular, the investment made in emerging economies. Hernandez and Guillen (2018) reviewed the classic theory of Multinational Enterprises (MNE) and past attempts to use it to understand the internationalization of firms from emerging markets. They found that emerging markets offer the opportunity to observe the origin of the capabilities of MNEs in general and the development of the institutional ecosystem that supports internationalization.

Jude and Levieuge (2017) investigated the effect of FDI on economic growth conditions on the institutional quality of host countries. They show that FDI has a positive effect on growth only beyond a certain threshold of institutional quality. Smith and Thomas (2017) argue the importance of institutional change and FDI, and specifically, the social impact of this relationship in Russia. Shi, Sun, Yan, and Zhu (2017) develop the concept of institutional fragility to investigate the outward foreign direct investment behavior of firms from emerging economies, and specifically in China.

Corruption is one of the most important concerns for foreign investors with regards to institutional factors. Corruption in many developing economies is a well-established institution as it is supported socially and individuals engage in the practice to reduce transaction costs. Corruption in developing economies guarantees stability in the social order (Della Porta & Vannucci, 2016). With this argument, Huang (2017), using a sample of 13 Asia-Pacific countries, does not support the common perception that corruption is bad for economic growth. In this work, corruption may encourage growth as in the case of Korea and China.

However, it is believed that corruption undermines the social structures and inhibits economic growth. For instance, Aghion, Akcigit, Cage, and Kerr (2016) analyze the relationships between taxation, corruption, and economic growth. They found that reducing corruption provides the largest potential impact for welfare gain through its impact on the uses of tax revenues. D'Agostino, Dunne, and Pieroni (2016) show the negative effect of corruption and military spending in Africa, but also show that corruption interacts with the military burden through indirect and complementary effects to further increase its negative effect. In summary, even when corruption is morally condemned, there is no consensus on the impact of corruption on economic growth (Farrag & Ezzat, 2016).

There is no robust evidence of political interest to eradicate due to its social place (Dzhumashev, 2014). On the other hand, it seems foreign investors have an ambiguous perception about corruption (Belasen & Toma, 2016). Therefore, the impact of corruption on foreign investment flows is contradictory (Cuervo-

Cazurra, 2016). Corruption is spread all over the world, and the thesis of an inverse correlation between corruption and economic and political development has been frequently and convincingly challenged (Della Porta, 2017). The extant literature is divided into two approaches: The first approach is called the "Sand the Wheels" in which the corrupted governments are institutionally weak and investors are not willing to enter these economies (Campos, Lien, & Pradhan, 1999). The second approach is called "Grease the Wheels" in which corruption is useful to avoid government inefficiencies encouraging the flows of foreign investment (Leff, 1964; Bardhan, 1997).

For this work, it is definitely assumed the first approach. However corruption itself is not the barrier for incoming foreign investment, but the illegal activities related to corruption like crime. Among criminal activities, drug trafficking is relevant for developed governments and foreign companies. Global drug trafficking has been a growing problem in the last few decades. According to the United Nation Office on Drugs and Crime (UNODC) in its 2018 World Drug Report (UNODC, 2018), about 275 million people worldwide, representing a total of 5.6 percent of the global population aged 15–64 years, used drugs at least once during 2016. The actual number of people using drugs increased by 20 million people between the period 2015-2016. Some 31 million people who use drugs suffer from disorders, meaning their drug use is harmful to the point where they require proper treatment.

The World Health Organization (WHO) estimated that approximately 450,000 people died as a result of drug use in 2015. Of those deaths, a total of 167,750 were directly associated with drug use disorders while the remainder were indirectly attributable to drug use itself (UNODC, 2018, p. 7). From the UNODC, the illegal trafficked drugs are the marijuana (the most consumed drug), hashish, heroin, cocaine, ecstasy, opium, amphetamine, and methamphetamine. Therefore, drug use is widely blamed for a broad range of personal and social ills. The market in illegal drugs promotes crime, destroys inner cities, spread AIDS, corrupts law enforcement officials and politicians, produces and exacerbates poverty, and erodes the moral fabric of society.

According to the Office of National Drug Control Policy (ONDCP) of the White House in his National Drug Control Strategy (NDCS) 2016, the most common response to these facts is a belief that governments should prohibit the production, traffic, sale, and consumption of illegal drugs. This is not an easy task as governments in developed countries, which are generally the drug recipients, have failed to eradicate the problem, and they blame the weak policy efforts made by the drug senders in developing countries to decrease their drug production. However, it is recognized that the demand for drugs should be considered as an engine for drug trafficking as well (ONDCP, 2016).

For drug producing countries such as Afghanistan, Pakistan, Myanmar, Bahamas, Belize, Bolivia, Colombia, Costa Rica, Dominican Republic, Ecuador, El Salvador, Guatemala, Haiti, Honduras, India, Jamaica, Laos, Mexico, Nicaragua, Panama, Peru, and Venezuela, the production of illicit narcotics and the narcotics trade provide a reasonable and attainable level of income for the poorest sectors in those countries. In the short term, drug trafficking is a very profitable business (UNODC, 2016). According to the United Nations Office on Drugs and Crime, the illegal trade in organized crime adds annual profits of over US$2 trillion dollars.

This figure is equivalent to 3.6% of everything produced and consumed by the planet in a year, or from a Latin American perspective, four times the Gross Domestic Product (GDP) of Argentina or almost 10 times that of Colombia, two countries with high average income in the world. Taking into account money laundering, the benefits of the final seller and related criminal activities, profits can reach US$3 trillion dollars, which are distributed between developed and developing countries (UNODC, 2016).

There are two options to fight drug trafficking: 1) promote a reduction of demand for illicit drugs; and 2) a reduction of supply. According to 2016 NDCS, in 2017 a total of US$31.1 US billion was requested by the President to support National Drug Control Strategy efforts to reduce drug use and its consequences in the United States. The President's Budget includes a request for US$1.1 billion dollars in new funding to address the misuse of opioid medications and the use of heroin. The 2017 President's Budget includes increased funding of more than US$500 million dollars (1.7 percent) over the enacted 2016 level. However, according to UNODC (2018), this strategy has produced a poor result in the fight against drug production and traffic.

In previous decades, the most common policies used by developed economies to force developing economies to eradicate the production and traffic of drugs is the Sanctions/Economic Assistance[1]. This policy involves the threat or application of sanctions against drug producer or trafficker nations. These range from suspension of foreign assistance to curtailment of air transportation. Who is subject to be included in this policy strategy? Enacted by the U.S. Congress in 1986, the certification policy adopted by the U.S. government mainly for the Latin America countries was a policy used by the U.S. to urge for a tough policy against drug production and trafficking (ONDCP, 2012). This policy originally consisted of a set of penalties and incentives for the Latin America Countries (LACs) and later to the rest of Low Development Countries (LDCs) involved in the drug business. The certification policy was determined to consider the efforts made in each country. A strong effort was rewarded with more foreign aid, reasonable loans and a well-reputed image for private investors. A weak effort means less foreign aid, closed financial markets, and a high-risk country label.

Even when this certification policy has been eliminated from the U.S. Government Drug Policy, indirectly there exists a signaling policy affecting the reputation of these countries. One of the most important effects of this policy has been on the flow of FDI into LDCs. American FDI plays a vital role in these countries; however, a bad signal discourages multinational firms to invest in those LDCs, which have a poor record in combating drug production and trafficking.

This discouragement sometimes takes the form of a cost for the foreign investment located in those LDCs. The cost is produced by a bad reputation among producers-consumers or by security reasons or even by the delay in administrative and financial procedures inside the corrupted drug producers LDCs. In previous years, there was surprisingly no negative relationship between FDI and drug trafficking. According to the statistics of Economic Commission for Latin American and Caribbean (ECLAC), in his FDI in Latin America and the Caribbean 2018 report, before 2015 the flow of FDI to the main drug-producing countries remained relatively high (ECLAC, 2018). Drug production did not seem to affect FDI flows. Different studies have analyzed the relationship between economic development and drug trafficking; or rather, the economic consequences of drug trafficking (Loret de Mola, 2001). These studies identify this activity's costs, which derive fundamentally from violence, corruption, and local drug use (Correa-Cabrera, 2013).

During the last five years, the scenery changed dramatically as violence generates important losses in FDI. The violence generated by drug trafficking in producing countries, rather than the drug trafficking itself, increase significantly and FDI flows began to decline in several sectors. According to ECLAC (2018), the main drug producers and trafficking countries have been a net reduction in the flow of FDI since 2015 until 2017: Mexico -8.8%, Colombia -0.1% and Peru -1.4%. Garriga and Phillips (2015) analyze the case of Mexico and found that measures of criminal violence and organized crime as drug trafficking are not directly associate to FDI. However, they found a conditional dissuasive effect: criminal violence and organized crime affect negatively democracy, economic growth, and human capital, all key factors to attract FDI. The alarming increase in violence in countries that send drugs due to, or related to, drug trafficking activity is beginning to reduce the flow of FDI into their economies.

Wolf (2016) states it is expected those developing countries play in favor of a reduction in the drug production and trafficking in order to attract foreign firms and receive economic incentives. However, this situation is complicated by the fact that in many LDCs, drug barons have significant political influence and make political contributions to protect their interests. The government in these LDCs has to weigh the benefit (from FDI) and costs (loss of political contribution) in deciding the level of enforcement of domestic drugs levels (Wolf, 2016).

THEORETICAL BACKGROUND

This chapter develops a mathematical political-economic model capturing the above-stylized facts. It has developed a partial equilibrium model in which two goods are produced in the recipient country of FDI. FDI produces a legal good, and the drug is produced by a particular important domestic private sector. FDI creates employment for unemployed factors. The drug barons lobby the government not to enforce laws restricting drugs production and trafficking. On the other hand, because of the policies in the sending country of FDI, the number of foreign firms entering the country is inversely related to the drug reaching the home country of FDI.

Lobbying occurs in the host country which determines the level of enforcement on drug markets. The authors' model lobbies by following the political contribution approach. That is to say the lobbyists make political contributions to the political party in power, and the amount they contribute is contingent upon the policy that the government adopts. The political contributions approach, derived from the common agency problem analyzed by Bernheim and Whinston (1986), was first introduced by Grossman and Helpman (1994) in modeling the political economy of trade protection with quasi-linear preferences.[2] Dixit, Grossman, and Helpman (1997) generalized the Bernheim-Whinston framework to allow for general preferences and therefore variability in marginal utilities of income. Given that our framework is a partial equilibrium effort, it shall be followed the original Grossman-Helpman approach but it is set the problem according to Dixit et al. (1997) approach.

The intention of this chapter is to construct a mathematical model in which the reasons for a particular enforcement level is found not only in the sanction imposed by the FDI sending country, but also in the way the domestic political equilibrium is determined. The authors shall focus on the determination of the optimal enforcement level and how it is affected by the changes in corruption parameter and the demand for drugs. The model is spelled in detail in the following section. Later, the authors determine the optimal enforcement policy under the normal assumptions of a negative relation between drugs and the number of incoming firms and make some comparative static respect to the change in the enforcement policy. The subsequent section analyzes the case of a specific enforcement policy set by drug recipients countries to eradicate the drug trafficking and the explicit determination of the number of foreign firms. Here the comparative statictics made in the previous section provided. Finally, the conclusions complete the chapter.

THE MODEL

The model is focused on a country which hosts n foreign owned firms or multinationals. These firms come from another country called the source country and produce a homogeneous good x. There are two types of individuals in the host country: honest (labeled σ) and dishonest (labeled ς). They are homogeneous within their own type. Dishonest people work and obtain their income from illegal activities, specifically from the production of drugs which is sold to the source country. In this model, the existence of a single type of drug is assumed to be marketed and consumed (e.g., marijuana or cocaine) instead of different types of drugs. With this assumption, it will be defined amount of drug instead of a number of drugs. We shall assume the drug dealers behave as a monopoly in the drug market so it will be referred to as drug dealer[3].

It is assumed, as in Brander and Spencer (1987), that there is unemployment in the host country. In particular, the variable input cost of the n multinational firms is taken to be the income of honest nationals of the host country[4]. In this case, multinationals repatriate profits to the source country.

The authors assume that drug consumption imposes a negative externality on the people living in the source country. The number of multinationals is determined by the amount of drug exported by the host country (D), i.e. $n = n(D)$. It is assumed that $n(D)$ is a linear and decreasing function such that $n'(D) = n_D < 0$ and $n''(D) = n_{DD} < 0$. That is, the flow of firms to the host country decreases when drug export increases. This can be seen as a reduced form of a more general model for the source country which the authors do not model to start with. However, the authors shall specify this functional form in a later section and it shall be seen that the results are similar.

The host country government can apply enforcement policies to reduce drug production by choosing a level of enforcement (ε) used to catch a drug dealer[5]. The level of enforcement affects the probability of being successful (not being caught) in the production and trafficking of the drug. $\theta = \theta(\varepsilon)$ is the probability of success, which is a linear and decreasing function of ε such that $\theta'(\varepsilon) < 0$, $\theta''(\varepsilon) = 0$, $\theta(\bar{\varepsilon}) = 0$ and $\theta(0) = 1$.

Taking into account the considerations mentioned above, the authors shall specify the utility function of the honest people, drug dealer, and the government, and using these functions to determine the optimal enforcement level. Assuming quasi-linear preferences the indirect utility of honest people can be defined as:

$$I^{\sigma} = nxc_x - \varepsilon + CS \tag{1}$$

where c_x is the average and marginal costs in the production of the legal good x. In expression (1), the first term is the income of employed factors in the production of the legal good, the second term is the cost of enforcement, which is levied by the host government and financed by taxing the honest people; the third term is the consumer surplus which satisfies:

$$dCS = -Qdp \tag{2}$$

where $Q = nx$ is the total consumption of x, and p is its price.

The indirect utility of drug producer is given by the expected income:

$$I^{\varsigma} = \theta\left[p_D - c_D\right]D + \left(1-\theta\right)\left[-c_D\right]D \tag{3}$$

where p_D is the price of the drug and c_D is the average and marginal costs in the production of drug D. This expression states that the income of drug baron is equal to the profit $\left[p_D - c_D\right]$ that he would obtain if he is not detected multiplied by the probability θ, plus the cost $\left[-c_D\right]$ that he would pay if he is detected multiplied by the probability $(1-\theta)$. It is assumed that the drug producer do not consume x^5.

The enforcement parameter ε is a policy instrument for the government of the host country, and this instrument is determined politically in a political equilibrium. It is followed closely by Dixit et al. (1997) in specifying this equilibrium.

The honest people do not lobby the government, but the drug dealer makes political contributions to influence the government's decisions. The political contribution schedule for the drug dealer is denoted by $c\left(\varepsilon\right)$. The host government's objective function is given by:

$$G = \rho c + I^{\sigma} \tag{4}$$

where $\rho > 0$ is a constant parameter. (4) states that the government considers the total welfare of its nationals, as well as the total amount of political contribution that it receives from drug barons.

The political equilibrium is the outcome of a 2-stage game. In stage one of the game, the drug dealer chooses his contribution schedule. The government then sets its enforcement policy in the second stage. A political equilibrium is given by *(i)* a political contribution function $c^{*}\left(\varepsilon\right)$, such that it maximizes the welfare the drug dealer given the anticipated political optimization by the government, and *(ii)* a policy variable, ε^{*}, that maximizes the government's objective function given by (4), taking the contribution schedule as given.

Dixit et al. (1997) develop a refinement known as truthful equilibria that implement Pareto efficient outcomes. Stated formally, let $\left(c^{\circ}\left(\varepsilon^{\circ}, I^{\varsigma\circ}\right), \varepsilon^{\circ}\right)$ be a truthful equilibrium in which $I^{\varsigma\circ}$ is the equilibrium per-capita utility level of the drug dealer. Then $\left(c^{\circ}\left(\varepsilon^{\circ}, I^{\varsigma\circ}\right), \varepsilon^{\circ}, I^{\varsigma\circ}\right)$ is characterized by:

$$c\left(\varepsilon, I^{\varsigma\circ}\right) = Max\left(0, \delta\right) \tag{5}$$

$$\varepsilon^{\circ} = Argmax_{\varepsilon}\left\{\rho c\left(\varepsilon, I^{\varsigma\circ}\right) + I^{\sigma}\left(\varepsilon\right)\right\} \tag{6}$$

$$I^{\sigma}\left(\varepsilon_1\right) = \rho c\left(\varepsilon^{\circ}, I^{\varsigma\circ}\right) + \left(I^{\sigma}\left(\varepsilon^{\circ}\right)\right) \tag{7}$$

where δ is defined in

$$I^{\varsigma o} = \left(I^{\varsigma} - \delta\right) \tag{8}$$

and

$$\varepsilon_1 = Argmax_{\varepsilon}\left(I^{\sigma}\left(\varepsilon\right)\right) \tag{9}$$

Equation (5) (together with (8) state that the truthful contribution schedule is set to the level of compensating variation relative to the equilibrium utility level of the drug dealers. The definition of δ is the basic concept of the compensating variations. Under a truthful equilibrium payment function, for any change in ε, the change in the contribution received by the government will exactly equal the change in the dealer's welfare, provided that the payment both before and after the change is strictly positive. Equation (6) is self-explanatory: the government takes the utility level of the drug dealer as given and chooses the enforcement level so as to maximize its objective function.

Equation (7) (together with (9) complete the characterization of the truthful equilibrium and tie down the equilibrium utility level of the drug dealer, which is derived from the premise that the drug dealer would pay the lowest possible contribution to induce the government of pursue the equilibrium policy given in (6). For this to be the case, the government must be indifferent between *(i)* implementing the equilibrium policy and receiving contributions from the drug dealer, and *(ii)* implementing a policy by accepting no contribution. Equation (7) states precisely that.[7]

According to Grossman and Helpman (1994, pp. 845-846), in the case of one lobby group, there is no opposition from competing interests, and the lobby group captures all of the surpluses from its political relationship with the government. In this political equilibrium, the government derives exactly the same utility as they would have achieved by allowing no contribution.

As the drug dealer behaves as a monopolist, the first order condition of his profit maximization is:

$$\theta D p_D' + \theta p_D = c_D \tag{10}$$

From (10) it is obtained:

$$D'\left(\varepsilon\right) = D_{\varepsilon} = -\frac{\theta'\left(\varepsilon\right)c_D}{2\theta^2 p_D'} < 0 \tag{11}$$

An increase in enforcement reduces the amount of drug produced. The foreign firms behave as Cournot oligopolist so that the first order condition is:

$$p'\left(Q\right)x + p\left(Q\right) = c_x \tag{12}$$

where $p(Q)$ is the inverse demand function for the legal good. It is assumed $p(Q)$ to be a linear function. From (12) it can be found that:

$$x'(n) = x_n = -\frac{x}{n+1} < 0 \tag{13}$$

An increase in the number of firms reduces the optimal output produced by each firm given by the increasing competition. In the next sections, the authors determine the optimal policy and the comparative static.

OPTIMAL ENFORCEMENT POLICY

Having described the properties of the political equilibrium, the authors shall analyze the comparative statics of the case in which legal goods are exported and consumer surplus is not considered in this case. It is examined how the enforcement level is affected by three parameters: the degree of corruption in the host country, the autonomous consumption of drugs, and the marginal cost of production of the legal good x. Starting from the equilibrium enforcement level, it is also analyzed the effect of an increase in the enforcement on the utility of both the drug dealer and honest people.

The first step in this exercise is to obtain the first order condition for the optimization problem given in (6). From derivation of (1), (3), and (4) it is obtained the first order condition of the maximization problem as:

$$\frac{dG}{d\varepsilon} = G_\varepsilon = \rho p_D D\theta'(\varepsilon) + \frac{nxn_D D_\varepsilon}{n+1}\left[c_x - p'(Q)\right] - 1 = 0 \tag{14}$$

Implicitly from (14), it can be seen clearly that an increase in the enforcement level reduces the political contribution made by drug barons, increases the consumer surplus and the income paid to employed factors and increases the amount of taxes paid to set the enforcement level. The optimal enforcement level depends on the corruption parameter and the market size of the good produced by multinationals. With a corruption parameter (ρ) sufficiently larger makes than the market size (nx), (14) becomes negative and the optimal enforcement level is zero ($\varepsilon^* = 0$). On the other hand, with a sufficiently larger market size (nx) and a small corruption parameter, the optimal policy would be to set the strictest enforcement level. Formally,

Proposition 1: When the drug dealer lobbies the government, the optimal enforcement level will be zero if the corruption is sufficiently larger than the market size, and it will be positive if the corruption parameter is sufficiently smaller than the market size.

Intuitively speaking, a larger corruption parameter makes a political contribution more valuable than the benefit obtained in consumer surplus and employment offered by multinationals and the government is willing to set a lax enforcement policy. However, when the government does not accept political contributions and the market for multinational goods is large enough, the optimal policy is a strict enforcement policy.

Once the optimal policy is set, it is analyzed the impact of some change in parameters on the optimal enforcement policy. The impact of variation in corruption on enforcement policy could be analyzed by taking the implicit derivative of (14) as:

$$\frac{d\varepsilon}{d\rho} = -\frac{G_{\varepsilon\rho}}{G_{\varepsilon\varepsilon}} \tag{15}$$

where $dG_{\varepsilon} / d\rho = G_{\varepsilon\rho} = p_D D\theta'(\varepsilon) < 0$. Combining this result with the assumption that the government's objective function is concave in ε ($dG_{\varepsilon} / d\varepsilon = G_{\varepsilon\varepsilon} < 0$), it is obtained:

$$\frac{d\varepsilon}{d\rho} < 0.$$

An increase in the corruption parameter increases the impact of the contribution on the government's objective function. Intuitively, the increase in the corruption parameter gives greater weight to the bribe offered by the drug dealer. The government is willing to reduce the enforcement level encouraging an increase in the amount of drug produced. The benefit of an increase in the drug traffic comes from the increase in the payment made by the drug dealer and the reduction of taxes paid by honest people. These gains exceed the losses due to a reduction in the number of foreign firms affecting negatively the employment and consumer surplus. Formally,

Proposition 2: When the drug dealer lobbies the government, an increase in the degree of corruption reduces the level of drug enforcement.

The authors next consider the effect of a shift in the demand for the drug in the source country on the level of enforcement. For this, it is considered a linear form of the demand for the drug, $p_D = a - bD$. In such a case a shift in demand can be seen as a change in the parameter a. In this case:

$$\frac{d\varepsilon}{da} = -\frac{G_{\varepsilon a}}{G_{\varepsilon\varepsilon}} \tag{16}$$

where

$$\frac{dG_{\varepsilon}}{da} = G_{\varepsilon a} = \rho\frac{c_D\theta'(\varepsilon)}{\theta b} - c_x A_1 \tag{17}$$

and

$$A_1 = \frac{2x\left(n_D\right)^2 D_\varepsilon}{b\left(n+1\right)^2} < 0$$

An increase in the demand for drugs decreases the enforcement level when the corruption parameter ρ is sufficiently large. On the other hand, when the corruption parameter ρ is sufficiently small, the optimal enforcement movement depends on the income received by employed workers and on consumer surplus. In particular, from (16) and (17) it is obtained:

$$\frac{d\varepsilon}{da} = \begin{cases} < 0 \; if \; \rho \gg 1 \\ > 0 \; if \; \rho \to 0 \end{cases} \tag{18}$$

An increase in the demand for drugs encourages the drug dealer to produce more D increasing the total contribution to the government. On the other hand, an increase in D reduces the incoming number of firms and consequently the consumer surplus and the income received by the honest people working for multinationals. When the corruption parameter is large, the former effect dominates the latter. In the case in which there is not corruption, there is not benefit for any political contribution and the benefit given by multinationals on employment and consumer surplus is larger. Formally,

Proposition 3: When the drug dealer lobbies the government, an increase in the demand for drug increases (decreases) the enforcement level if the corruption parameter is sufficiently small (big).

Intuitively, when the corruption parameter is small the effect of a bribe on the government's objective function is negligible. An increase in the consumption of the drug increases the enforcement level since the rise in the welfare from the increased contribution is smaller than the loss in the welfare given by the reduction in the income provided by the multinationals to the honest people. When the corruption parameter is large, an increase in the consumption of drug reduces the enforcement level since political contributions have a significant weight on the government's objective function. An increase in the consumption of drug reduces the enforcement level since the effects of the increase in the contribution outweigh the loss due to the reduction in the income provided by the multinationals to the honest people in the form of employment and consumer surplus.

Finally, starting from the equilibrium set in (14), it shall be analyzed the effect of an increase in the enforcement level on the utility of the honest and dishonest people. From (1) and (3) it is obtained:

$$\left.\frac{dI^\sigma}{d\varepsilon}\right|_{\varepsilon = \varepsilon^\circ} = -\rho p_D D\theta'\left(\varepsilon\right) > 0 \tag{19}$$

$$\left.\frac{dI^{s}}{d\varepsilon}\right|_{\varepsilon=\varepsilon^{\circ}} = p_{D} D\theta'\left(\varepsilon\right) < 0 \tag{20}$$

Starting from the equilibrium level ε° it is clear that an increase in the enforcement level benefits the honest people and harms the drug dealer. Formally,

Proposition 4: Starting from the enforcement's equilibrium level, an increase in the level of enforcement will benefit the honest people and will harm the drug dealer.

Intuitively an increase in the enforcement level reduces the probability of success for the drug dealer and consequently reduces the amount of drug produced. In this sense, the profit obtained by the drug dealer, and consequently their utility, decreases. On the other hand, the reduction in drug production increases the number of incoming firms. The utility of honest people is affected by two factors: First, there is a positive effect due to the increase in income from working for the multinationals and increase in consumer surplus. Second, the utility of the honest people decreases by the increase in the tax levied by the government in order to obtain resources to finance drug enforcement. At equilibrium, the positive effect is greater than the negative effect and the increase in the level of enforcement benefits honest people.

ENFORCEMENT POLICY: FOREIGN PRESSURE

In the previous sections, the number of firms in the host economy has been given as a linear function of the amount of drug produced. There was no consideration of how this function was determined. In this section, the number of incoming firms is determined endogenously as the last section. Having set up the model, It shall be analyzed the effect of a change in the corruption parameter and demand for the drug on the optimal enforcement level, as well as the effect of a change in the enforcement level on the equilibrium utility levels of the various parties.

One possible policy option for the authorities in the countries affected by the drug is to levy a tax on all firms that invest in the sending drug country. In the extreme, the authorities could transfer to the multinational firms the entire social cost of the drug trade. This can be written as:

$$nT = kD \tag{21}$$

where k is the marginal disutility of drug consumption (in terms of the numeraire good) and T is the lump-sum tax levied by the source government on each firm. This expression can be re-written as:

$$T = kD \,/\, n \tag{22}$$

It is assumed that the host country is small in the market for multinationals (i.e., firms would move into (out of) the host country if the profits they make in the host country is larger (smaller) than the reservation profits $\bar{\pi}$ it can make in the rest of the world). Assuming a linear demand function for the output produced by multinationals such that $p = \alpha - \beta nx$, the FDI equilibrium condition is given by:

$$\pi = \left(p - c_x\right)x - T = \bar{\pi} \tag{23}$$

With linear demand function, at profit-maximizing equilibrium in (12), it is obtained:

$$\beta x^2 - T = \bar{\pi} \tag{24}$$

and

$$x = \frac{\alpha - c_x}{\beta\left(n+1\right)} = S_x / \left(n+1\right)$$

Therefore, the number of firms is a function of α, c_x, k, D and $\bar{\pi}$ such that from (23) it is deduced the following comparative static:

$$n_D = -\frac{n}{D} < 0 \tag{25}$$

$$n_\alpha = -\frac{2}{\left(n+1\right)\pi_n} > 0 \tag{26}$$

$$n_{\bar{\pi}} = \frac{1}{\pi_n} < 0 \tag{27}$$

$$n_a = -\frac{\left(n+1\right)k}{2nxb} < 0 \tag{28}$$

where

$$\pi_n = -\frac{1}{n}\left(\beta x^2 + \bar{\pi}\right) = -\frac{T}{n} < 0 \tag{29}$$

According to (25), (26), (27) y (28), an increase in the production of drug reduces the number of incoming firms as assumed before; an increase in the size of the market of multinationals attracts more firms into market; an increase in the profits made by foreign firms outside reduces the flow of incoming firms into the host market; and, an increase in the drug market reduces the number of foreign firms into the host country. At the same time that in this section the results are explicitly derived, in the previous section, they are assumed. On the other hand, from (25) and (11) it is obtained:

$$n_{\varepsilon} = -\frac{n\theta'(\varepsilon)c_D}{2\theta^2 bD} > 0 \tag{29}$$

An increase in enforcement increases the number of incoming firms into host country as assumed before. Considering the lobby problem from the last section, from (4), (1), (3), and (21)-(28) it is obtained the first order condition:

$$G_{\varepsilon} = \rho D p_D \theta'(\varepsilon) + \frac{nS_x n_{\varepsilon}}{(n+1)^2}[c_x + \beta] - 1 = 0 \tag{30}$$

From (30) it is confirmed explicitly Proposition 1 in which the optimal enforcement level would be positive with a sufficiently larger market size compared to corruption parameter ($S_x \gg \rho$), since the benefit by consumer surplus and employment is larger than the loss in political contribution and tax payment. The government is willing to set a strict enforcement in order to benefit the honest people; the firms are willing to enter in the host country because of the large benefits they may obtain in. If the host market is not attractive for foreign firms ($S_x \to 0$), the host government privileges the political contribution over the benefit on honest citizens.

On the other hand, differentiating (30) it obtains the following results:

$$\frac{d\varepsilon}{d\rho} = -\frac{G_{\varepsilon\rho}}{G_{\varepsilon\varepsilon}} \tag{31}$$

where $G_{\varepsilon\rho} = Dp_D\theta'(\varepsilon) < 0$. Combining this result with the assumption that the government's objective function in ε is concave ($G_{\varepsilon\varepsilon} < 0$), it is obtained:

$$\frac{d\varepsilon}{d\rho} < 0 \tag{32}$$

When the number of firms is endogenously determined the result is the same that in Proposition 2 in which an increase in corruption reduces the incentives to set a strict enforcement policy. With this specific policy, the authors can analyze the impact on the enforcement level with an increase in the amount of drug demanded. From (30),

$$\frac{d\varepsilon}{da} = -\frac{G_{\varepsilon a}}{G_{\varepsilon\varepsilon}} \tag{33}$$

where

$$G_{\varepsilon a} = \frac{\rho\theta'\left(\varepsilon\right)a}{2b} + A_2\left[2Dn_a - n\left(n+1\right)/2b\right] < 0 \tag{34}$$

and

$$A_2 = \frac{S_x\left(c_x + \beta\right)n_\varepsilon}{\left(n+1\right)^3} > 0$$

Combining (34) with (28) and the assumption that the government's objective function in ε is concave ($G_{\varepsilon\varepsilon} < 0$), it is obtained:

$$\frac{d\varepsilon}{da} < 0 \tag{35}$$

Different to Proposition 3, with this specific enforcement policy an increase in the consumption of drug reduces the enforcement level. This policy may be not enough to inhibit the negative externality in investment and employment given by the increase in drug consumption. Formally,

Proposition 5: When only the drug dealer lobbies the government and n are explicitly determined, an increase in the demand for drug decreases the enforcement level.

Intuitively this result may be contra-intuitive. At first, an increase in drug consumption has a significant impact on the number of incoming firms. This decrease in the number of firms may affect negatively both consumer surplus and employment. It may be suspected that the benefit obtained by political contribution is larger than the loss in consumer surplus and employment.

However, even in the case in which there is no corruption at all ($\rho = 0$), and the political contribution is negligible, amazingly an increase in drug consumption reduces the enforcement level. The question is why? Basically, this policy is not enough to overcome the trafficking of the drug. Actually, the reduction in the number of incoming firms may produce some monopolistic distortions, and the optimal output produced by the remaining firms may be so large that the benefit in employment may be larger than in the case of more foreign firms. This effect on employment plus the benefit for the reduction in tax payment made by honest people may be a good reason to reduce the enforcement level made by the government. This result supports the initiative for increasing investment to overcome the benefit of drug production in emerging economies.

Some interesting extensions can be made for further research. It is not taking into account domestic firms' oligopolistic competition in which may inhibit the incentives to set a strict enforcement policy as the employment and consumer surplus may be provided by local firms. Additionally, it is possible to consider not foreign profits repatriation. On the other hand, local consumption of the drug is not assumed and its disutility which may encourage strict enforcement policies. Finally, it is considered an exogenous level of government corruption; however, it may be endogenous as the foreign political pressure may affect this parameter.

CONCLUSION

The competition for FDI is fundamental for developing countries. There is fierce competition among emerging economies because investment is a source of employment, technology, and benefits in consumption. However, this competition is affected by economic, social and institutional variables. It is assumed that drug trafficking has a significant impact on the flow of foreign direct investment flowing into a country.

The immense effort to stop drug traffic going to some developed countries has had disappointing results. Misunderstanding the action of the drug producers on society's interests may lead to unsuccessful enforcement policies. The production and traffic of drug is not a typical criminal activity like murders, burglary, kidnap or rape, which are widely rejected by the community. Drug production is more complicated. Historically, in many developing countries, drug use is part of their culture, their identity and, sometimes, their religion. Today drug trade represents a source of income for people and governments of these countries. Drug producers are important players in the political process.

This work attempted to explain why some sanctions made by the international community on the producers' countries have failed and how the FDI has been affected by such policies. Corruption in the government and the benefit that the drug trade gives to the inhabitants of the producing countries can inhibit any action carried out by the international community. Bribes are the origin and the consequences of the corruption; the drug dealer makes payments to the party in power to guarantee the level of enforcement according to their needs. Likewise, governments must consider the benefits of its citizens and a part of the benefits come from drug production and trafficking. The drug dealer lobbies the government taking into account their interests, and the government considers both the interest of the drug producers and their nationals.

Lobbying is modeled following the common agency problem as developed by Grossman and Helpman (1994). In this framework the government accepts political contributions from the lobbyists and the level of contribution depends on the policy that the government pursues. On the other hand, the sanctions applied by the international community is reflected in the reduction in the number of firms going to the producer country (producing a legal good) and consequently the reduction in its employment and consumers surplus. It is analyzed the effect of the corruption parameter and demand for the drug on the optimal drug enforcement and the flow of incoming firms.

This work presented the case in which only the drug producer makes political contributions. The optimal enforcement level is given by the difference between the corruption level and the market for the legal good consumer in the host country. If the corruption parameter is sufficiently larger than the market share, then the optimal enforcement policy is zero. On the other hand, with a sufficiently larger market share than the corruption parameter, the optimal enforcement policy is positive.

In the former, the weight attached to political contribution is oversized by the high level of corruption and the government considers setting the laxest enforcement policy despite the loss in employment and consumer surplus. In the latter, the government in the host country is willing to fight against drug trafficking since the benefit in employment and consumer surplus is relevant for the social welfare, at least more relevant than the benefit in political contributions.

Starting from the optimal enforcement policy, an increase in corruption reduces the enforcement policy. The weight given to the payment is large and the government finds more profitable reduce the enforcement policy. More corruption increases the weight attached to bribe and there are incentives to augment the level of enforcement. On the other hand, an increase in the demand for drug reduces the enforcement if the corruption parameter is sufficiently small, otherwise the enforcement level increases. In the first case, the benefit of honest people is greater than the political contribution made by the drug dealer. A small corruption parameter inhibits the effect of a bribe, and the response of the government is an increase in the enforcement level. In the second case in which the corruption parameter is large enough, an increase in the demand of drug reduces the enforcement level since the government overvalues the political contribution despite the loss in employment and consumer surplus.

When a specific policy is set and the number of firms is determined endogenously, the affected country transfers the social cost of the drug to the multinational firms. In this case, an increase in the corruption parameter reduces the enforcement level. On the other hand, an increase in the demand for drug remarkable reduces the enforcement level. The political pressure on developing economies in order to stop the traffic of drug may produce ambiguous results. In this work corruption and unemployment play a significant role in the final policy decision. Political corruption may magnify or inhibit any political action of the local agents and produce some unexpected results in the fights against drug traffic. Actually, corruption may play in favor of enforcement policies as long as the honest agents get involved in the lobby game.

Fighting corruption seems to be a more suitable strategy than trying to the stop drugs from the source countries. It is seen that the policy addressed to stop the production and traffic of drug may generate more incentives to produce and traffic drug because the economic temptation offered by drug dealers and the social acceptance of drug activities is larger than the economic incentives to obtain for stopping drug traffic. It seems an institutional reform joint with an economic incentives program addressed to substitute the place of drug dealers on society is the best way to eradicate the drug problem. Under this view, the worst option is a penalty strategy.

As another option, the receiving drug countries may play (and sometimes they do) with the same rules played by drug dealers. It is called "learning from corruption" and it is a very common practice in everyday life for millions of people living in developing economies. Corruption reduces the transaction costs in the short term making easy the life. The formal and legal institutions lack an efficient structure and process on those developing countries and corruption emerges as a cheaper and efficient option.

The limitations of this research are based on the nature of a mathematical model. Strictly speaking, a mathematical model is a simplification of reality and the number of variables to analyze is very small. This simplification is analytically powerful, but empirically it must be tested to validate the findings. Of course, a mathematical model must precede an empirical model, but the limitation is given by the absence of available data on the problem analyzed. A mathematical model will always be a limited abstraction of reality.

REFERENCES

Aghion, P., Akcigit, U., Cagé, J., & Kerr, W. R. (2016). Taxation, corruption, and growth. *European Economic Review*, *86*, 24–51. doi:10.1016/j.euroecorev.2016.01.012

Agosin, M., & French-Davis, R. (1993). La liberalización comercial en América Latina. *Revista de la CEPAL*, *50*, 41–62. doi:10.18356/b4d728f4-en

Asako, K. (1979). Environmental pollution in an open economy. *The Economic Record*, *55*(151), 359–367. doi:10.1111/j.1475-4932.1979.tb02241.x

Bardhan, P. (1997). Corruption and Development: A Review of Issues. *Journal of Economic Literature, 35*(3), 1320–1346.

Belasen, A. T., & Toma, R. (2016). *Confronting Corruption in Business. Trusted Leadership, Civic Engagement*. New York: Routledge.

Bernheim, B., & Whinston, M. (1986). Common agency. *Econometrica, 54*(4), 923–942. doi:10.2307/1912844

Brander, J. A., & Spencer, B. J. (1987). Foreign direct investment with unemployment and endogenous taxes and tariffs. *Journal of International Economics, 22*(3-4), 257–279. doi:10.1016/S0022-1996(87)80023-5

Campos, J. E., Lien, D., & Pradhan, S. (1999). The Impact of Corruption on Investment: Predictability Matters. *World Development, 27*(6), 1059–1067. doi:10.1016/S0305-750X(99)00040-6

Correa-Cabrera, G. (2013). Violence and FDI in Mexico. The Economic Impact of the "War against Drugs". *Voices of Mexico, 96*(1), 17–22.

Cortez Yactayo, W. W., & Espinosa Ramirez, R. S. (2011). Reentendiendo la inversión extranjera directa vertical: Una aproximación a la evidencia latinoamericana actual. *Carta Economica Regional, 107*, 129–144.

Cuervo-Cazurra, A. (2016). Corruption in international business. *Journal of World Business, 51*(1), 35–49. doi:10.1016/j.jwb.2015.08.015

D'Agostino, G., Dunne, J. P., & Pieroni, L. (2016). Corruption and growth in Africa. *European Journal of Political Economy, 43*, 71–88. doi:10.1016/j.ejpoleco.2016.03.002

Della Porta, D. (2017). *Corrupt Exchanges. Actors, Resources, and Mechanisms of Political Corruption*. New York: Routledge. doi:10.4324/9781315080284

Della Porta, D., & Vannucci, A. (2016). *The Hidden Order of Corruption. An Institutional Approach*. London: Routledge. doi:10.4324/9781315557267

Dixit, A. K. (1996). Special-interest Lobbying and endogenous Commodity taxation. *Eastern Economic Journal, 22*(4), 375–388.

Dixit, A. K., Grossman, G. M., & Helpman, E. (1997). Common agency and coordination: General theory and application to policy making. *Journal of Political Economy, 105*(4), 752–769. doi:10.1086/262092

Dzhumashev, R. (2014). Corruption and growth: The role of governance, public spending, and economic development. *Economic Modelling, 37*, 202–215. doi:10.1016/j.econmod.2013.11.007

ECLAC. (2018). *Foreign Direct Investment in Latin America and the Caribbean 2018*. Retrieved on August 24, 2018, from: https://repositorio.cepal.org/bitstream/handle/11362/43690/7/S1800683_en.pdf

Farrag, N. A., & Ezzat, A. M. (2016). The Impact of Corruption on Economic Growth: A Comparative Analysis between Europe and MENA Countries. In M. M. Erdoğdu & B. Christiansen (Eds.), *Handbook of Research on Comparative Economic Development Perspectives on Europe and the MENA Region* (pp. 74–97). Hershey, PA: IGI Global. doi:10.4018/978-1-4666-9548-1.ch005

Findlay, R., & Wellisz, S. (1982). Endogenous tariffs, the political economy of trade restrictions, and welfare. In J. N. Bhagwati (Ed.), *Import competition and response* (pp. 223–234). Chicago: University of Chicago Press.

Garriga, A. N., & Phillips, B. J. (2015). *Criminal Violence and the Subnational Distribution of Foreign Direct Investment* (Documentos de Trabajo CIDE No. 279). Retrieved from The CIDE website: http://repositorio-digital.cide.edu/handle/11651/1377

Grossman, G. M., & Helpman, E. (1994). Protection for Sale. *The American Economic Review*, *84*(4), 833–854.

Hernandez, E., & Guillen, M. F. (2018). What's theoretically novel about emerging-market multinationals? *Journal of International Business Studies*, *49*(1), 24–33. doi:10.105741267-017-0131-7

Huang, C.-J. (2017). Is corruption bad for economic growth? Evidence from Asia-Pacific countries. *The North American Journal of Economics and Finance*, *35*, 247–256. doi:10.1016/j.najef.2015.10.013

Jude, C., & Levieuge, G. (2017). Growth Effect of Foreign Direct Investment in Developing Economies: The Role of Institutional Quality. *World Economy*, *40*(4), 715–742. doi:10.1111/twec.12402

Leff, N. H. (1964). Economic development through bureaucratic corruption. *The American Behavioral Scientist*, *8*(3), 8–14. doi:10.1177/000276426400800303

Loret de Mola, C. (2001). *El Negocio: LA Economía De México Atrapada Por El Narcotráfico*. DF, Mexico: Grijalbo Mondadori.

Magee, S. P., Brock, W. A., & Young, L. (1989). *Black hole tariffs and endogenous policy theory*. Cambridge, UK: Cambridge University Press.

Mayer, W. (1984). Endogenous tariff formation. *The American Economic Review*, *74*(5), 970–985.

ONDCP. (2012). *National Control Drug Strategy*. Retrieved on April 22, 2018, from: https://obamawhitehouse.archives.gov/sites/default/files/ondcp/2012_ndcs.pdf

ONDCP. (2016). *2016 National Control Drug Strategy*. Retrieved on April 22, 2018, from: https://obamawhitehouse.archives.gov/sites/default/files/ondcp/policy-and-research/2016_ndcs_final_report.pdf

Salacuse, J. W. (2017). BIT by BIT: The Growth of Bilateral Investment Treaties and Their Impact on Foreign Investment in Developing Countries. In F. Beveridge (Ed.), *Globalization and International Investment* (pp. 655–676). London: Routledge.

Shi, W., Sun, S. L., Yan, D., & Zhu, Z. (2017). Institutional fragility and outward foreign direct investment from China. *Journal of International Business Studies*, *48*(4), 452–476. doi:10.105741267-016-0050-z

Singh, H., & Jun, K. W. (1995). *Some New Evidence on Determinants of Foreign Direct Investment in Developing Countries* (Policy Research Working Paper No. WPS 1531). Retrieved on September 22, 2017, from: https://elibrary.worldbank.org/doi/abs/10.1596/1813-9450-1531

Smith, M., & Thomas, E. (2017). Exploring the Social Impact of Foreign Direct Investment on Institutional Change: The case of Russia. In M. A. Khan (Ed.), *Multinational Enterprise Management Strategies in Developing Countries* (pp. 198–214). Hershey, PA: IGI Global.

UNCTAD. (2018). *World Investment Report 2015*. Retrieved on April 22, 2018, from: https://unctad.org/en/PublicationsLibrary/wir2018_en.pdf

UNODC. (2018). *2018 World Drug Report*. Retrieved on April 22, 2018, from: https://www.unodc.org/wdr2018/

Wolf, S. (2016). Drugs, Violence, and Corruption: Perspectives from Mexico and Central America. *Latin American Politics and Society*, *58*(1), 146–155. doi:10.1111/j.1548-2456.2016.00298.x

ENDNOTES

1 According to the ONDCP (2012), international narcotics control policy is implemented by multifaceted strategy that includes the followings: (1) eradication of narcotics crops, (2) interdiction and law enforcement activities in drug-producing and drug-transiting countries, (3) international cooperation, (4) sanctions/economic assistance, and (5) institutions development.

2 The importance of political process in economic decision making in general and international policy issues in particular is well recognized (see Dixit, 1996). The particular aspect of lobbying by interest group has derived a lot of attention from international economists. The alternatives approaches in modeling political equilibrium include the tariff-formation approach (Findlay & Wellisz, 1982), the political support function approach (Hilman, 1989), median voter approach (Mayer, 1984), the campaign contribution approach (Magee, Brock, & Young, 1989), and the political contribution approach (Grossman & Helpman, 1994).

3 The ambition for power creates wars between the drug dealers in order to gain a larger market share. It is common that dealers dominate entire regions nationally or internationally.

4 Implicitly, it is assumed that there is a competitive sector in the background. This sector uses labor and a specific factor (say land) under constant returns to scale. The imperfectly competitive sector uses labor and constant returns to scale technology. The wage rate of labor (in terms of the numeraire competitive good) is exogenously given at a level higher than the market clearing one. With these assumptions, the total amount of labor used in the competitive sector and the rental rate of land would not depend on any of the policy parameters. Any policy induced change in employment in the non-competitive sector would be the total change in employment in the economy.

5 The enforcement is specified as the legal, political and judicial instruments addressed to stop the production and trade of illegal drugs. In this case, these instruments mean a cost for the government in order to finance them. As seen later, this cost is attached as a lump sum tax to the honest people.

6 The dealer consumes the numeraire good.

7 See Dixit et al. (1997, pp. 756-759).

Chapter 4
Free Trade and Gravity Model:
Albania as Part of Central European Free Trade Agreement (CEFTA)

Nerajda Feruni
Epoka University, Albania

Eglantina Hysa
https://orcid.org/0000-0002-3429-5738
Epoka University, Albania

ABSTRACT

The purpose of this chapter is to build and explain the Gravity Model for the trade flows of Albania and 15 of its trade partners for the period of 2001-2016, both theoretically and empirically. The theoretical development of the subject gives an overview of the economic thought over the years regarding the concept of free trade, its benefits and threats, the Central European Free Trade Agreement (CEFTA), and the Gravity Model in order to be able to explain and interpret the patterns of trade between countries. The econometrical analysis illustrates the impact of gross domestic product (GDP) of partner countries, the distance between them, and CEFTA has on the trade flows of Albania. The Gravity Model built in this study supports the theoretical approach and it shows how GDP has positively affected trade flows, while distance has negatively affected trade flows. The impact of CEFTA is insignificant.

INTRODUCTION

In contemporary globalization, the interaction of people and countries exchanging ideas, values, money, and resources has rapidly grown over the last few decades. The concept of going global shows that our world and society have become borderless, meaning that countries must face various changes such as free trade agreements, trade liberalization theories, and comparative advantage policies. Trade barriers continue to be broken down and economies are opening up to the free flow of labour, capital, goods, and services between countries. Thus, countries have signed different free trade agreements among each other such as European Free Trade Association (EFTA), the ASEAN Free Trade Area (AFTA), the North

DOI: 10.4018/978-1-5225-8458-2.ch004

American Free Trade Agreement (NAFTA), the Central European Free Trade Agreement (CEFTA) the South Asian Free Trade Area (SAFTA), the East African Community (EAC), the Pacific Alliance Free Trade Area (PAFTA), and the Trans-Pacific Partnership (TPP) among others.

Albania embraced the free market economy in 1990 and passed from a centralized economy in which all assets were publicly owned into an open market, which led to liberalization in foreign direct investment (FDI) and trade. Albania has become part of many trade agreements during the years, being they bilateral or multilateral and today it applies a liberal trade regime under the supervision of the European Union (EU) and the World Trade Organization (WTO). The most known trade agreements that Albania has signed are the free trade agreement with Turkey, the Stabilization and Association Agreement (SAA) with the EU, the FTA signed between the Republic of Albania and EFTA countries and CEFTA, and each one of them has had its impact on the patters of trade of the country.

One of the objectives of the chapter is to define the concept of free trade and the benefits and threats associated with it based on economic thought. Another objective is to analyze the trade relations of Albania with its Intra-CEFTA trade partners and other main trade partners, focusing on the last few years. The extant literature review on the Gravity Model used for the estimation of trade flows has been analyzed to be able to identify the explanatory and explained variables needed to build such a model. In addition, based on the literature review, the aim of the chapter is to estimate the Gravity Model for Albania's trade flows by deriving quantitative conclusions on the effect of the selected explanatory variables and in particular, the impact of the trade agreement of CEFTA on the trade flows of Albania.

In the latest decades, the Gravity Model has been widely used by many authors in order to rate the potential of trade between countries. Even Albanian researchers have used the Gravity Model to measure the trade flow of Albania, but these researchers are limited in number (Agolli & Xhepa, 2003; Kastrati, 2015; Kraja & Sejdini 2014; Mitaj & Osmani, 2017; Pllaha, 2011). The first part of the chapter explains the concept of free trade and makes an analysis of benefits and threats as two contradictory approaches based on the economic thought over the years. In addition, it provides background information on CEFTA agreement and the manner in which Albania finds itself under such an agreement as well as its main trade partners. The second part includes the Literature Review and provides an overview of the Gravity Model and the variables used in similar work. The literature review serves as a starting point for presenting basic theory concepts and research methodologies and it leads the path toward the third part of the study, that of data and the Gravity Model.

The Gravity Model applied to the case of Albania considers 15 partner countries such as Bosnia and Herzegovina, Macedonia, Montenegro, Serbia, Kosovo, Croatia, Bulgaria, Germany, Greece, Italy, Poland, Romania, Spain, Austria and Holland. The last part of the study provides the conclusions derived by combining both the theoretical development of the subject and the empirical results.

BACKGROUND

Free trade is an economic policy which allows buyers and sellers of different nations and countries to freely trade without government interventions in forms of quotas, tariffs, or restrictions on their goods and services (Collins, 2018). Some studies refer to free trade agreements as an easy way to enter and a country can adopt such policies unilaterally or on a bilateral basis by joining a free-trade area (Black, 2009). Some other studies refer to free trade as a way of relaxing from previous government interventions and restrictions on the economic policies of countries involved (Melnikas, 2008). However, the main argument and the most important point of view regarding trade liberalization is that of increasing the efficiency of a country by exposing the economy of a country to international competition (Black, 2009).

Free trade has existed since the earliest recorded history of humankind back in the times of ancient Egypt and slaveholders. However, the economic connotation of free trade policies dates back to the father of modern economics, Adam Smith, in the 18th century who believed that free trade gives opportunities for countries to go beyond their scope of capabilities. He argued that every man is left perfectly free to pursue his own interest in his own way without trade restriction (Smith, 1776). Today, two centuries later, some economists argue in the favour of free trade according to the ideas of Smith while others opposing it.

Trade would have not been possible in some cases if it were not for trade liberalization and free trade agreements which create trade opportunities. Ricardo (1817) was the individual who made case for free trade based on comparative advantage, by putting great emphasis on the specialization of the production process. He focused on the idea that countries should specialize in the production of that good in which they have comparative advantage in order to be able to produce in a more efficient and effective manner with the lowest opportunity cost. By taking advantage of lower opportunity costs, countries can achieve an increase in economic welfare and in their standards of living (Edge, 2010; Krugman, Obstfeld, & Melitz, 2012).

Since there are no limited barriers such as quotas or tariffs between countries that are involved in free trade agreements, on one hand suppliers offer their goods and services at lower prices while, on the other hand, consumers take advantage of such prices. As prices fall due to the lack of tariffs, consumer purchasing power increases as well as the consumer surplus and as a result, new job positions are available (EC, 2006). At the same time, free trade is likely to create employment opportunities, especially for exporting nations, because of market expansion; hence, the demand for goods and services increases (Lattimore, 2009). More labour force is required to deal with this expansion; thus, more jobs are available.

Being exposed to foreign competition, domestic industries find themselves in a difficult position of becoming more competitive and efficient (EC, 2006). If a country uses its resources efficiently, it will have a higher productivity level and the amount of domestic goods and services produced will be higher. With the usage of new technology, the country will produce new and differentiated products due to the increased competition. Standards of living will rise as well due to the higher efficiency and productivity level. It appears there are many benefits associated with the freely flowing of goods and services between free-trade area countries; however, there are even quite threats or disadvantages against free trade. Specializing in a production of a certain good in which a country has comparative advantage, leads to a focus on a precise area of activities and skills as well as knowledge. It means that in cases of high competition, the country will not be flexible enough to adapt to the new changes of technology and to the production of innovative goods and services.

Due to trade liberalization, two other concepts appear known as outsourcing and job off shoring. Many firms relocate their industries and factories in other countries to take advantage of cheaper labour forces, so many native workers are threatened of job loss. According to Edge (2010), the increase of imports in one country reduces employment as the demand for domestic goods and services falls and, in cases of free trade, structural unemployment may occur in short-term. Another point to consider is the quality of products. Quality standards are not same for all the countries as they differ among different countries.

Hence, liberalizing trade with so-called "Third World" nations may bring much ambiguity and doubt regarding the quality of their production and, in such cases, the domestic market requires some protection against low quality products. Overall, benefits and threats of free trade can be considered as the "Yin and

Yang"[1] duality, so that they are intervened together. Once a trade agreement enters into force, there will be both sides of the medal and countries involved will deal with benefits and threats at the same time.

Historical Background of CEFTA

The Central European Free Trade Agreement (CEFTA) is an arrangement between non-EU member states. Signed on 21 December 1992 in Krakow, Poland by the former Soviet block countries of Poland, Hungary and Czechoslovakia, it aimed to integrate these countries into western Europe's economic and political organizations. The agreement entered into force in 1994. CEFTA experiences a serious of changes in the late 1990s and early 2000s to keep up with political changes and economic development of that time. Since the day CEFTA entered into force, it has had a rule for the member states: once they become part of the EU, they should surrender their respective membership. The founding countries of this agreement became part of the EU by the end of 2004; thus, in 2005 a meeting held in the city of Zagreb produced some decisions for the continuation of the agreement. The meeting produced the criteria that in order to obtain member state status, countries should be part of the WTO and the country should have other free trade agreements with CEFTA member-states (Kiprop, 2018).

In December 2006, membership expanded to Southeastern Europe thus creating CEFTA 2006 which signed by Albania, Bosnia and Herzegovina, Croatia, Macedonia, Moldova, Montenegro, Serbia, and United Nations Interim Administration Mission in Kosovo (UNMIK), which entered into force in November, 2007. The current members under the agreement are all the above mentioned with the exception of Croatia, which become part of the EU in 2013 (CEFTAsecretariat, 2017).

Albania and Its Intra-CEFTA Trade Partners

The Central European Free Trade Agreement is one of highly importance for trade partners in both economical and political fields. The export of goods and services of CEFTA countries have increased among themselves from 12% to 17% in recent years (CEFTAsecretariat, 2017). With regards to Albania, Kosovo has always been the main Intra-CEFTA trade partner comprising more than 60% of the total amount of exports of Albania over the years. It reached a peak in 2012 when Kosovo comprised 69% of the total amount of exports, while in the previous two years the amount had declined up to 50%. Exports toward Macedonia, which is the second one after Kosovo, have not varied much over the years. It faced a decline in 2015 when it reached 14% of the total amount and later reached around 20% in the following years.

Montenegro comprised a constant percentage of 7% for two years in a row in 2011 and 2012 and a constant percentage of 12% for 2013 and 2014, resulting in an increase of 5% in total. Lately, it has experienced a slight decrease of 1% from 13% in 2016 to 12% in 2017. Regarding the exports of goods and services in Serbia, fluctuations have been present from 2010 to 2017. It reached a peak in 2011 and comprised approximately 15% of the total amount while the minimum in 2010 reached 5%. Exports with Bosnia and Herzegovina have varied between 1% and 2% over the years and the largest percentage was in 2016 and 2017 which amounted to 3% for these years. Exports toward Moldova are so small that it is insignificant (INSTAT, 2017).

In terms of imports, Serbia is the main Intra-CEFTA trade partner of Albania comprising more than 50% of the total amount of imports during most years. It reached a peak in 2012 when Serbia comprised 56% of the total amount. In 2016, imports of goods and services from Serbia comprised 48% of the total amount while in 2017 there was an increase of 3% thus reaching 51%. After Serbia, Macedonia is the nation from which Albania mostly imports. In general, the amount of imports from Macedonia has been around 20% and higher with the exception of 2017 when it comprised 17% of the total amount of imports.

Likewise, Kosovo comprised 17% of the total amount in 2017 and it faced an increase of 2% over the previous year. Besides an increase of 5% from 2012 to 2013, when it reached 17%, Albanian imports from Kosovo have not varied much over the years. Taking in consideration Bosnia and Herzegovina, Albania imports more from this country than the amount that exports to it. It reached the peak in 2011 with an amount that comprised 14% of the total amount of imports. In 2012 and 2013, Albania imported from Bosnia and Herzegovina an amount that comprised 9% of the total and in the following years of 2014-2015, it faced a slight decrease of 1%. The lowest amount reached is that of 2017 which consisted in 7% of the total. The imports of Albania from Montenegro reached the peak in 2015, when they constituted 8% of the total amount. From 2010 to 2012, the amount counted for 3% of the total and in the consecutive years of 2013 and 2014, there was an increase of 2%. In the last two years, the amount has been stable at 7%. Regarding the amount of imports toward Moldova, the amount is trivial.

In general, with Intra-CEFTA countries, Albania traded mostly manufactured goods classified by material, crude materials and mineral fuels (INSTAT, 2017).

Albania's Primary Trade Partners

Albania is the 131st largest exporter and 124th largest importer economy in the world (OEC, 2016). Albania has trade relations with many countries such as Italy, Greece, Germany, France, Switzerland, Hungary, Bulgaria, and Turkey. However, with a few of them it has close relations. In terms of exports, Albania exports more than 93% of the amount of goods and services toward European countries, a total of 4% toward Asia and a very small percentage to North America. Albania exports many goods and services; however, it exports mostly mineral products, textiles, footwear and metals. In 2017, Italy, Kosovo, Greece, Serbia, and Spain were the main five export destinations of Albania. Italy was on top of the list comprising 72% of the amount of exports, followed by Kosovo, which counted for 10%. There was a small difference of 1% between the other countries. Germany comprised 5% of the total amount,

Figure 1. Albania and its intra-CEFTA exports
Source: Authors

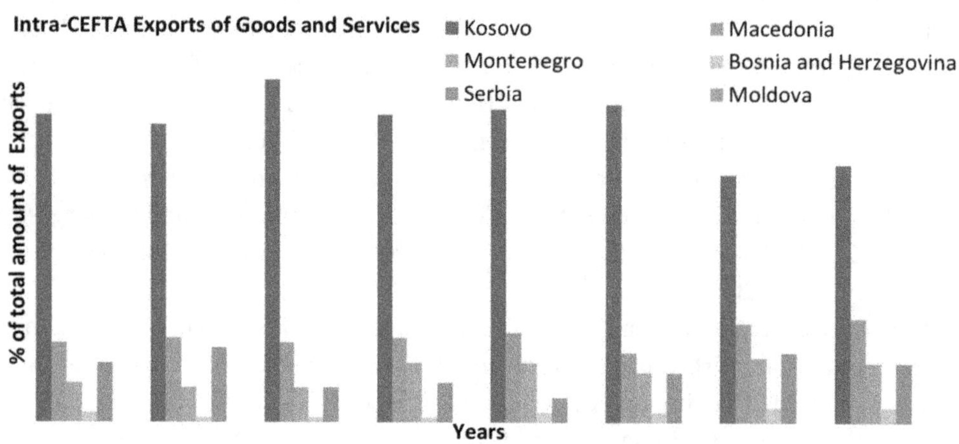

Figure 2. Intra-CEFTA imports of goods and services
Source: Authors

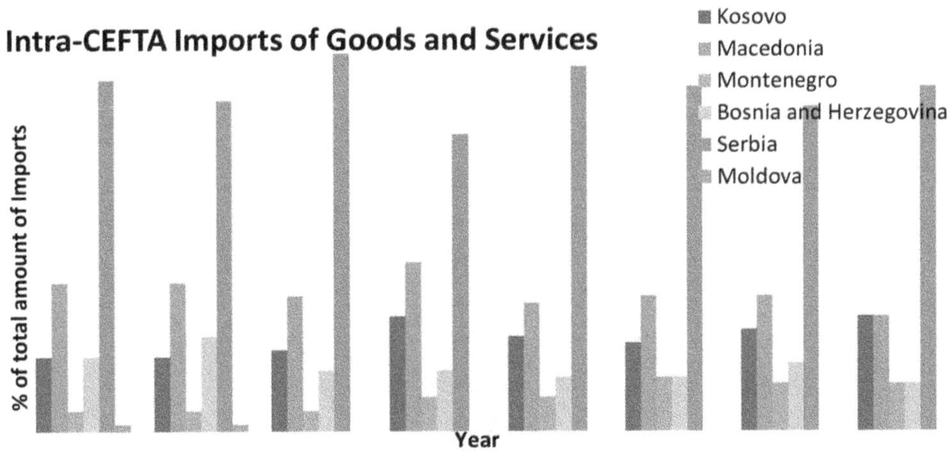

Greece 6% and Spain 7% (INSTAT, 2017). Albania exports many goods and services however; it exports mostly mineral products, textiles, footwear and metals.

In terms of imports, Albania imports approximately 83% from European countries, around 12% from Asia and a small portion from North America. It imports mostly machines, refined petroleum, textiles and a large amount of unspecified goods. In 2017, the top five import destinations were Italy, Germany, Greece, Turkey and Serbia. Imports from Italy comprised more than half of the total amount, specifically 51%. The amounts of imports from Serbia counted for 7% of the total amount, while imports from Germany, Greece and Turkey comprised 42% all together. Separately, each one of these countries comprised around 14% of the total amount of goods and services imported (INSTAT, 2017).

Figure 3. Top export destination of Albania in 2017
Source: Authors

Figure 4. Top import destinations of Albania in 2017[2]
Source: Authors

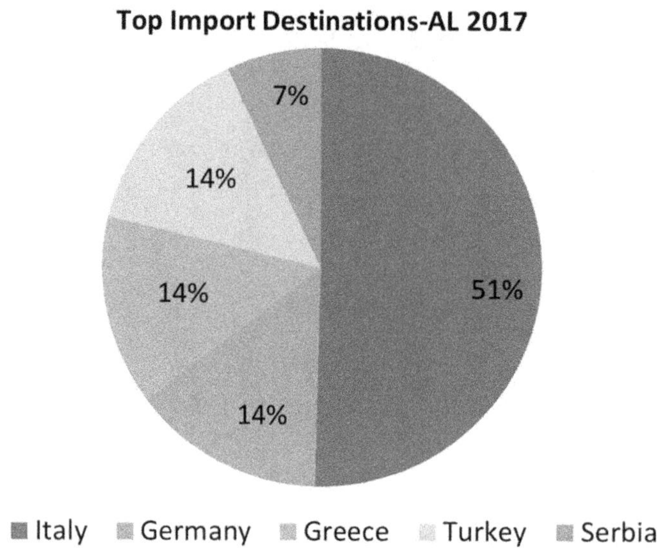

LITERATURE REVIEW

Trade models have been widely used over the past decades with a focus on understanding the potential effects of trade between bilateral or multilateral partners. For more than half century, a model known as the Gravity Model has been used to identify the effects that factors like borders among partner countries, foreign investments, cost of transportation, common language, free trade agreements, distance between places, and size of countries as measured by the influence of Gross Domestic Product (GDP) on trade flows.

The Gravity Model shows the relationship between trade flows, economic size of two trading countries as measured by their GDP or Gross National Product (GNP) and the distance between them. It is based on Newton's universal law of gravitation which measures the attraction between two objects based on their mass and distance. Newton (1687) mentioned that this attraction is directly proportional to the product of their masses and reversely proportional to the square of distance between the objects. Similarly, the Gravity Model shows that the bilateral trade between two countries is in direct relationship with GNP and GDP and in inverse relationship with the distance between them.

The Gravity Model assumes identical preferences of Cobb-Douglas cases of consumers among partner countries. It was first applied by Tinbergen (1962) and later on by Linnemann (1966) and Isard (1975). It is based on international trade theory models 1) Ricardian Model, which is based on technological differences among countries that are partners in trade; 2) Hecksher-Ohlin Model, which predicts patterns of commerce and production based on the factor endowments of a trading region and 3) Modern Theories. which take in consideration the economies of scale in an enterprise.

Anderson (1979) took further steps in developing the model by supposing specialisation in production and identical preferences of consumers in partner countries. Anderson and Wincoop (2004) developed a model of the overall international equilibrium, which takes in considerate the exogenous costs of bilateral trade, such as costs of transactions and custom costs, which have a negative impact on bilateral trade flows. Deardoff (1998) and Anderson and Wincoop (2003) argue that the Gravity Model does not prove the validity of any theory, but it serves as a formal tool to empirically test trade theories.

Among measuring trade flows between countries, authors have used the Gravity Model for other purposes as well. Ramos and Surinach (2013) introduced their paper under the name: "A Gravity Model of Migration between ENC and EU". They divided their analysis in two different empirical studies. They estimated a Gravity Model by taking in consideration 200 countries for the period 1960-2010 and later on, they focused on within EU migration flows, before and after the enlargement. They derived the conclusion that there is an increase in migratory pressure from ENC to EU.

In the last few decades, the Gravity Model has been widely used by many authors in order to rate the potential of trade between countries. It is found that the Gravity Model has also been used from Albanian researchers to measure the trade flow of Albania but the number of these researchers is limited (Agolli & Xhepa, 2003; Kastrati, 2015; Kraja & Sejdini 2014; Mitaj & Osmani, 2017; Pllaha, 2011). Xhepa and Agolli (2003) used the Gravity Model to study the imports and exports of Albania for the period of 1994-2002 by taking in account 21 main partner countries. Their model showed that the amount of imports and exports relates positively to the countries' economic size and negatively to the distance and nominal exchange rate.

Pllaha (2012) considered nine Southeast European countries to study their trade flows and found out that most of them traded below their potentials. Kraja and Sejdini (2014) used the Gravity Model to study the imports and exports of Albania with 27 partner countries from 1993-2012. The empirical results show that both imports and exports are sustainable. They are negatively correlated to distance between countries, while there is a positive correlation between trade flows and GDP of countries involved, common borders and same free trade agreements.

Kastrati (2015) used the Gravity Model for the case of Albania by taking in consideration 22 partner countries, from 2001-2015. After calculations, she found out that there is a positive correlation between trade flows and GDP, common borders, and the population of countries involved, while there is a negative correlation between trade and distance. Mitaj and Osmani (2017) used the Gravity Model to analyze the possible effects of trade creation and trade diversion of Albania by taking in account 21 partner countries and by using both fixed effect models and random effects models. They discovered that countries involved did not trade at any level beyond what is considered as normal.

Econometric Analysis

This section illustrates the Gravity Model for Albania case by examining 15 trade partners: Bosnia and Herzegovina, Macedonia, Montenegro, Serbia, Kosovo, Croatia, Bulgaria, Germany, Greece, Italy, Poland, Romania, Spain, Austria and Holland.

Methodology and Data

This part of the study focuses on the Gravity Model by taking imports (Mij) and exports (Xij) between Albania and partner countries as dependent variables in two separate equations and GDPi(Gross Domestic Product of Albania), GDPj(Gross Domestic Product of partner country), Dij(Distance between Albania and partner country), and CEFTA as independent variables. Mij, Xij, GDPi, GDPj and Dij are quantitative data, while CEFTA is qualitative data and it is considered as dummy variable since it can take values of only 0 and 1. The program used is E-views, while the data gathered is from different sources and it is in terms of billions of US dollars. Distance is in miles. GDPi and GDPj are taken from World Bank, Mij, Xij are taken from Comtrade, and Dij is taken from DistanceCalculator.net. Years taken in consideration include 2001-2016 and there are 240 observations in total chosen randomly. The model deals with panel data and the method used is the Panel Estimated Generalized Least Square.

Modelling and Hypotheses

The model used to explain trade flows between Albania and partner countries is the Gravity Model. Gravity Model shows that the bilateral trade between two countries is in direct relationship with GNP and GDP and in inverse relationship with the distance between them. Based on Newton's gravitational rule, it is expressed as follow:

$$Fij = G\frac{GDPi\,GDPj}{Dij}$$

In the above equation, Fij is the trade flow between Albania and partner country and G is a constant. I expect my estimated equations to have the following form:

$$\log(Xij) = \beta_0 + \beta_1 \log(GDPi) + \beta_2 \log(GDPj) - \beta_3 \log(Dij) + \beta_4 \, CEFTA$$

$$\log(Mij) = \beta_0 + \beta_1 \log(GDPi) + \beta_2 \log(GDPj) - \beta_3 \log(Dij) + \beta_4 \, CEFTA$$

Two hypotheses arise based on main objectives stated at the beginning:
First Hypothesis:

H_0: Gravity Model in the case of Albania does not follow Newton's gravitational rule
H_1: Gravity Model in the case of Albania follows Newton's gravitational rule

Second Hypothesis:

H_0: CEFTA agreement does not have a positive significant impact on trade flows
H_1: CEFTA agreement does have a positive significant impact on trade flows

Unit Root Test

Before running the above-mentioned equations by using E-views, it is important to run firstly some tests that are necessary for the validity of the model. The Unit Root Test is a type of test used to identify whether each one of the dependent and independent variables (except dummies) is stationary or not. Another exception from such a test is the variable of distance since the distance between countries is constant and do not change over time. The hypothesis for unit root test is H_0: Data is non-stationary and H_1: Data is stationary. Level of significance taken in account for such a test is 5%. After conducting Unit Root Test, p-values for log GDPi, log GDPj, log (Mij) and log (Xij) are less than 0.005, resulting in a rejection of null hypothesis concluding that data used for the Gravity Model is stationary as shown in Appendix C.

Gravity Model

The model provides two regression equations, one with the amount of exports as the dependent variable and another one with the amount of imports as the dependent variable

Exports Equation

The first equation under the Gravity Model is that of exports.

First Hypothesis:

H_0: Gravity Model in the case of Albania does not follow Newton's gravitational rule
H_1: Gravity Model in the case of Albania follows Newton's gravitational rule

Second Hypothesis:

H_0: CEFTA agreement does not have a positive significant impact on exports ($\beta_4 \leq 0$)
H_1: CEFTA agreement does have a positive significant impact on exports ($\beta_4 > 0$)

The level of significance for testing the hypothesis is 5%. The estimated regression equation is log (XIJ) = -30.30 + 1.84 log (GDPi) + 0.96 log (GDPj) - 1.24 log (Dij) +0.24 CEFTA. 1% increase in GDPi, ceteris paribus, will tend to increase Xij by 1.84% and since its p-value=0 and 0.00<0.05, the impact of GDPi is significant. 1% increase in GDPj, ceteris paribus, will tend to increase Xij by 0.96%. Its p-value = 0, making GDPj significant at 5%. 1% increase in Dij, ceteris paribus, will tend to decrease Xij by 1.24%. Distance is significant at 5% because its p-value <0.05. Considering all these three variables, which are highly significant at 5%, we reject the null hypothesis, concluding that the Gravity Model for Albania case is in accordance to Newton's gravitational rule. Regarding the dummy variable of CEFTA, its impact appears positive however its p-value = 0.485, which makes the variable not significant at 5%. Thus, we fail to reject the null hypothesis, concluding that CEFTA does not have a significant positive impact on the amount of exports in the case of Albania.

Imports Equation

The second equation under the Gravity Model is that of imports. The level of significance to test the hypotheses is 5%.

First Hypothesis:

H_0: Gravity Model in the case of Albania does not follow Newton's gravitational rule
H_1: Gravity Model in the case of Albania follows Newton's gravitational rule

Second Hypothesis:

H_0: CEFTA agreement does not have a positive significant impact on imports ($\beta_4 \leq 0$)
H_1: CEFTA agreement does have a positive significant impact on imports ($\beta_4 > 0$)

Table 1. Gravity model for exports of Albania

Dependent Variable: LOG(XIJ)				
Method: Panel EGLS (Period random effects)				
Sample: 2001 2016				
Periods included: 16				
Cross-sections included: 15				
Total panel (balanced) observations: 240				
Swamy and Arora estimator of component variances				
Variable	**Coefficient**	**Std. Error**	**t-Statistic**	**Prob.**
LOG(GDPI)	1.845504	0.326912	5.645255	0
LOG(GDPJ)	0.960265	0.054625	17.5793	0
LOG(DIJ)	-1.243469	0.167424	-7.427084	0
CEFTA	0.243288	0.347859	0.699388	0.485
C	-30.30809	5.030685	-6.024645	0
Effects Specification				
	S.D.			Rho
Period random	0			0
Idiosyncratic random	1.724015			1
Weighted Statistics				
R-squared	0.641838	Mean dependent var		9.862386
Adjusted R-squared	0.635742	S.D. dependent var		2.813063
S.E. of regression	1.69779	Sum squared resid		677.3853
F-statistic	105.2821	Durbin-Watson stat		0.143399
Prob(F-statistic)	0			
Unweighted Statistics				
R-squared	0.641838	Mean dependent var		9.862386
Sum squared resid	677.3853	Durbin-Watson stat		0.143399

Source: Authors

The estimated regression equation is log (MIJ) = -17.32+ 1.18 log (GDPi) + 0.67 log (GDPj) – 0.55 log (Dij) + 0.50 CEFTA. 1% increase in GDPi, ceteris paribus, will tend to increase Mij by 1.18% and since its p-value=0 and 0.00<0.05, the impact of GDPi is significant. 1% increase in GDPj, ceteris paribus, will tend to increase Mij by 0.67%.

Its p-value=0, making GDPj significant at 5%. 1% increase in Dij, ceteris paribus, will tend to decrease Mij by 0.55%. Distance is significant at 5% because its p-value <0.05. Considering all these three variables, which are highly significant at 5%, we reject the null hypothesis, concluding that the Gravity Model for Albania case is in accordance to Newton's gravitational rule. Regarding the dummy variable of CEFTA, its impact appears positive; however, its p-value= 0.485, which makes the variable not significant at 5%. Thus, we fail to reject the null hypothesis, concluding that CEFTA does not have a significant positive impact on the amount of imports in the case of Albania.

Table 2. Gravity model for imports of Albania

Dependent Variable: LOG(MIJ)				
Method: Panel EGLS (Period random effects)				
Sample: 2001 2016				
Periods included: 16				
Cross-sections included: 15				
Total panel (balanced) observations: 240				
Swamy and Arora estimator of component variances				
Variable	**Coefficient**	**Std. Error**	**t-Statistic**	**Prob.**
LOG(GDPJ)	0.67631	0.059295	11.40577	0
LOG(GDPI)	1.183954	0.354865	3.336349	0.001
LOG(DIJ)	-0.553595	0.181739	-3.046098	0.0026
CEFTA	0.508141	0.377603	1.345703	0.1797
C	-17.32053	5.460834	-3.171774	0.0017
Effects Specification				
	S.D.			Rho
Period random	0			0
Idiosyncratic random	1.871427			1
Weighted Statistics				
R-squared	0.436458	Mean dependent var		11.29992
Adjusted R-squared	0.426866	S.D. dependent var		2.40687
S.E. of regression	1.822136	Sum squared resid		780.2423
F-statistic	45.50129	Durbin-Watson stat		0.112325
Prob(F-statistic)	0			
Unweighted Statistics				
R-squared	0.436458	Mean dependent var		11.29992
Sum squared resid	780.2423	Durbin-Watson stat		0.112325

Source: Authors

Overall, in both cases, the Gravity Model applied for Albania is in direct relationship to the GDP of partner countries and in inverse relationship to the distance between them. The impact of respective GDPs and distance is highly significant at 5%, while the dummy variable of CEFTA it is significant neither for imports, nor for exports. [3]

SOLUTIONS AND RECOMMENDATIONS

Through the years, countries have signed different trade agreements between them and each one of them has had its impact on countries involved. Based on the economic thought over the years, these trade agreements have been associated with many benefits and threats. Even Albania is part of such trade agreements and CEFTA, which entered into force in 2007, is one of them. Among Intra-CEFTA countries, Albania mostly trades with Kosovo and rarely with Moldova. On one hand, by entering into trade agreements countries can take advantages of lower opportunity costs by specializing in the production of that good in which they have comparative advantage.

Furthermore, by being exposure to foreign competition, countries become more competitive, they tend to use resources more effectively and as a result, they have a higher productivity level. Moreover, the removal of trade barriers gives to consumers the opportunity to find products at lower prices and it creates employment opportunities especially for the exporting country. On the other hand, due to trade liberalization, many native workers lose their jobs, as firms tend to relocate their industries to take advantage of cheaper labour force. In addition, liberalizing trade with third world countries would bring much ambiguity and doubts regarding the quality of their products, so in such cases the domestic market needs some protection against low quality products.

Since trade barriers are being torn down and trade patterns are changing, many authors and economists have used different models to predict trade flows. The Gravity Model, which states that trade flows the bilateral trade between two countries is in direct relationship with GDP and in inverse relationship with the distance between them, is widely used by many researchers.

FUTURE RESEARCH DIRECTIONS

Researchers interested in the same topic can use the high significance of the base equation of the Gravity Model in this study as a guideline for their own work. However, despite the high significance, there is room for improvements. In further studies, authors can use a higher number of observations or new independent variables. Increasing the sample size by adding more partner countries or taking in account variables such as common borders, common language, exchange rates or the number of population may lead to interesting results.

CONCLUSION

This study appears to be important since it gives some crucial insights and future direction when discussing the position of Albania in the international economy. The Republic of Albania has been an official candidate for accession to the European Union since June, 2014 and is on the current agenda for future enlargement of the EU. Even though Albania is part of the CEFTA agreement, this country is mostly oriented toward the EU especially in the trade of goods and services. The Gravity Model used for the case of Albania turned out to be in accordance with the literature review and highly significant at 5% level of significance, however the variable of CEFTA appears to be positive but not significant. This may come as a result that Albania exports and imports mostly from countries that are not part of the CEFTA agreement such as Italy, Greece, Germany, Turkey and Spain and these countries together with Bulgaria, Poland, Romania, Austria and Holland comprise the majority of the sample size.

REFERENCES

Anderson, J. (1979). A Theoritical Foundation for the Gravity Equation. *The American Economic Review*, 106–116.

Anderson, J., & Wincoop, V. (2004). Trade Costs. *Journal of Economic Literature*, *42*(3), 691–751. doi:10.1257/0022051042177649

Black, J. (2009). *A Dictionary of Economics*. Oxford, UK: Oxford University Press. doi:10.1093/acref/9780199237043.001.0001

CEFTA. (2017). *CEFTA Parties*. Retrieved April 25, 2018, from: http://cefta.int/cefta-parties-2/

Collins, C. (2018). Retrieved on April 2018, 23, from: https://www.collinsdictionary.com/dictionary/english/free-trade

Deardorff, A. (1998). *Determinants of Bilateral Trade: Does Gravity Work in a Neoclassical World?* Chicago: University of Chicago Press.

EC. (2006, April 3). *European Comission: Trade*. Retrieved on April 23, 2018, from: http://trade.ec.europa.eu/doclib/docs/2006/september/tradoc_129992.pdf

Edge, K. (2010). *Free Trade and Protection: Advantages and Disadvantages of Free Trade*. Cardiff, UK: Cardiff High School.

INSTAT. (2017). *Institute of Statistics: International Trade*. Retrieved on April 25, 2018, from: http://instat.gov.al/en/themes/international-trade/international-trade-in-goods

Isard, W. (1975). A Simple Rationale for Gravity-Model-Type Behavior. *Papers in Regional Science*, *35*(1), 25–30. doi:10.1007/BF01947465

Karlgren, B. (1923). Analytic Dictionary of Chinese and Sino-Japanese. Taipei: CH'ENG-WEN Publishing Company.

Kastrati, P. (2015, September 25). *University of Tirana*. Retrieved on May 4, 2018, from: http://www.doktoratura.unitir.edu.al/2015/09/doktoratura-pranvera-kastrati-fakulteti-ekonomik-departamenti-i-manaxhimit/

Kiprop, J. (2018, February 6). *Economics: What is CEFTA*. Retrieved on April 25, 2018, from: https://www.worldatlas.com/articles/what-is-the-central-european-free-trade-agreement.html

Kraja, I., & Sejdini, A. (2014). International Trade of Albania. Gravity model. *European Journal of Social Sciences Education and Research*, 219-227.

Krugman, P., Obstfeld, M., & Melitz, M. (2012). *International Economics*. Boston: Pearson Education.

Lattimore, R. (2009). *OECD*. Retrieved on January 2018, from: Free, Fair and Open: http://www.oecd.org/

Linnemann, H. (1966). *An Econometric Study of International Trade Flows*. Amsterdam: North-Holland.

Melnikas, B. (2008). Transformation Processes in Central and Eastern Europe: Liberalization Integral Cultural Space and Social Environment for Economic Development. *Ekonomika (Nis)*, 63–80.

Mitaj, A., & Osmani, M. (2017). Trade Creation and Trade Diversion Effects for Albania. *International Journal of Economics, Commerce and Management*, 569-588.

Newton, I. (1687). *Principia*. London: Pepys Press.

OEC. (2016). *The Observatory of Economic Complexity: Albania Indicators*. Retrieved on April 22, 2017, from: https://atlas.media.mit.edu/en/profile/country/alb/

Olivier, J., Thoenig, M., & Verdier, T. (2008). Globalization and the Dynamics of Cultural Identity. *Journal of International Economics*, *76*(2), 356–370. doi:10.1016/j.jinteco.2008.06.009

Pllaha, A. (2012). *Free Trade Agreements and Trade Integration among South Eastern European Countries: Gravity Model Estimations*. Tirana: Bank of Albania.

Ramos, R., & Suriñach, J. (2013). *A Gravity Model of Migration Between ENC and EU*. Barcelona: Research Institute of Applied Economics.

Ricardo, D. (1817). *On the Principles of Political Economy and Taxation*. London: John Murrey.

Smith, A. (1776). *The Wealth of Nations*. London: Methuen and Co., Ltd.

Tinbergen, J. (1962). *Shaping the World Economy; Suggestions for an International Economic Policy*. New York: Twentieth Century Fund.

Xhepa, S., & Agolli, M. (2003). *Albania's Foreign Trade Through a Gravity Model*. Tirana: Trade and Economic Integration of the Western Balkan Countries in the European Union.

KEY TERMS AND DEFINITIONS

ASEAN Free Trade Area: A trade bloc agreement by the Association of Southeast Asian Nations supporting local manufacturing in all ASEAN countries. The AFTA agreement was signed on 28 January 1992 in Singapore.

Central European Free Trade Agreement (CEFTA): An agreement originally signed by the countries of the Visegrad group (the Czech Republic, Hungary, Poland, and the Slovak Republic) on 21 December 1992 and effective since July 1994. Later on, Slovenia (1996), Romania (1997), Bulgaria (1999), and Croatia (2003) joined CEFTA. When those countries became members of the EU they subsequently left the CEFTA.

East African Community (EAC): An intergovernmental organization composed of six countries in the African Great Lakes region in eastern Africa: Burundi, Kenya, Rwanda, South Sudan, Tanzania, and Uganda.

European Free Trade Association (EFTA): An intergovernmental organization working to promote free trade and economic integration for its member states. It was founded in 1960 by Austria, Denmark, Norway, Portugal, Sweden, Switzerland, and the United Kingdom, and later joined by Finland, Iceland, and Liechtenstein.

Gravity Model of International Trade: A model that, in its traditional form, predicts bilateral trade flows based on the economic sizes (often using GDP measurements) and distance between two units.

South Asian Free Trade Area (SAFTA): An agreement reached on January 6, 2004, at the 12th SAARC summit in Islamabad, Pakistan. It created a free trade area of 1.6 billion people in n Afghanistan, Bangladesh, Bhutan, India, Maldives, Nepal, Pakistan, and Sri Lanka.

ENDNOTES

1. In Chinese philosophy, yin and yang describes how seemingly opposite or contrary forces may actually be complementary Karlgren (1923).
2. The data used to build the charts in 2.3 and 2.4 is on Appendix 4.
3. The data used for the Gravity Model can be found in Appendix 5.

APPENDIX 1

Table 3. Intra-CEFTA exports of goods and services

Countries	2010	2011	2012	2013	2014	2015	2016	2017
Kosovo	62%	60%	69%	62%	63%	64%	50%	52%
Macedonia	16%	17%	16%	17%	18%	14%	20%	21%
Montenegro	8%	7%	7%	12%	12%	10%	13%	12%
BIH	2%	1%	1%	1%	2%	2%	3%	3%
Serbia	12%	15%	7%	8%	5%	10%	14%	12%
Moldova	0%	0%	0%	0%	0%	0%	0%	0%

Source: INSTAT

APPENDIX 2

Table 4. Intra-Cefta imports of goods and services

Countries	2010	2011	2012	2013	2014	2015	2016	2017
Kosovo	11%	11%	12%	17%	14%	13%	15%	17%
Macedonia	22%	22%	20%	25%	19%	20%	20%	17%
Montenegro	3%	3%	3%	5%	5%	8%	7%	7%
BIH	11%	14%	9%	9%	8%	8%	10%	7%
Serbia	52%	49%	56%	44%	54%	51%	48%	51%
Moldova	1%	1%	0%	0%	0%	0%	0%	0%

APPENDIX 3

Table 5. Top exports destinations of Albania in 2017

Countries	Exports in 2017
Greece	6%
Italy	72%
Kosovo	10%
Germany	5%
Spain	7%

Source: INSTAT

APPENDIX 4

Table 6. Top imports destinations of Albania in 2017

Countries	Imports in 2017
Italy	51%
Germany	14%
Greece	14%
Turkey	14%
Serbia	7%

Source: INSTAT

APPENDIX 5

Table 7. Data used for the gravity model

Year	Pairs	Xij*	Mij*	GDPi**	GDPj**	Dij***	Fta
2001	BIH	7.4	71.2	4,091,020	5,748,991	304	0
2002	BIH	73.8	660.0	4,449,373	6,651,226	304	0
2003	BIH	269.0	1,500.0	5,652,325	8,370,020	304	0
2004	BIH	491.0	2,190.0	7,464,447	10,022,841	304	0
2005	BIH	1,670.0	4,090.0	8,376,484	10,948,051	304	0
2006	BIH	5,520.0	7,750.0	9,132,562	12,400,103	304	0
2007	BIH	5,530.0	12,500.0	10,704,662	15,280,616	304	1
2008	BIH	2,840.0	14,500.0	12,968,653	18,543,289	304	1
2009	BIH	1,320.0	10,700.0	12,118,581	17,082,889	304	1
2010	BIH	3,690.0	34,200.0	11,858,166	16,775,470	304	1
2011	BIH	3,140.0	52,300.0	12,959,564	18,252,422	304	1
2012	BIH	3,230.0	33,600.0	12,648,096	17,465,959	304	1
2013	BIH	3,750.0	33,000.0	12,923,000	17,851,000	304	1
2014	BIH	5,230.0	27,900.0	13,278,000	15,995,392	304	1
2015	BIH	5,148.3	25,686.3	11,455,596	18,521,000	304	1
2016	BIH	7,420	29,239	11,863,866	16910277	304	1
2001	XK	2,163.0	1,893.5	4,091,020	2535333632	251	0
2002	XK	3,671.6	2,153.5	4,449,373	2702427047	251	0
2003	XK	7,643.0	2,400.3	5,652,325	3355083117	251	0
2004	XK	27,672.1	3,405.5	7,464,447	3639935348	251	0
2005	XK	27,138.0	9,613.5	8,376,484	3736599925	251	0
2006	XK	29,765.5	14,261.0	9,132,562	4078158324	251	0
2007	XK	51,404.9	23,971.2	10,704,662	4833561456	251	1
2008	XK	87,900.8	31,136.0	12,968,653	5687488209	251	1
2009	XK	75,817.6	31,238.5	12,118,581	5653792720	251	1
2010	XK	96,290.0	36,557.8	11,858,166	5829933775	251	1
2011	XK	145,346.6	44,722.1	12,959,564	6649291076	251	1
2012	XK	160,476.6	47,173.7	12,648,096	6473724785	251	1
2013	XK	373,622.4	82,149.2	12,923,000	7072092406	251	1
2014	XK	162,925.0	51,859.4	13,278,000	7386891336	251	1
2015	XK	166,315.4	43,587.2	11,455,596	6440501275	251	1
2016	XK	167,890.0	46,987.0	11,863,866	6649888889	251	1
2001	FYR	6,408,644.0	15,295,224.0	4,091,020	3709637830	292	0
2002	FYR	4,969,178.0	16,562,931.0	4,449,373	4018365247	292	0

continued on following page

Table 7. Continued

Year	Pairs	Xij*	Mij*	GDPi**	GDPj**	Dij***	Fta
2003	FYR	3,039,411.0	5,477,800.0	5,652,325	4946292775	292	0
2004	FYR	7,453,216.0	23,789,750.0	7,464,447	5682719260	292	0
2005	FYR	10,308,094	31,991,386.0	8,376,484	6258600714	292	0
2006	FYR	12,653,021.0	48,809,382.0	9,132,562	6861222332	292	0
2007	FYR	24,391,725.0	81,368,277.0	10,704,662	8336478142	292	1
2008	FYR	38,811,610	115,606,777	12,968,653	9909548411	292	1
2009	FYR	30,266,687	82,799,872.0	12,118,58	9401731496	292	1
2010	FYR	25,958,571	72,575,791.0	11,858,16	9407168702	292	1
2011	FYR	41,096,495	88,043,728.0	12,959,56	9414632699	292	1
2012	FYR	38,353,097	77,276,274.0	12,648,09	9745251126	292	1
2013	FYR	41,612,152	81,529,751.0	12,923,00	1081771213	292	1
2014	FYR	50,376,407	79,014,955.0	13,278,00	1136227283	292	1
2015	FYR	50,893,790	68,045,204.0	11,455,59	1005165916	292	1
2016	FYR	51,740,214	62,675,476	11,863,86	1089958315	292	1
2001	FYR	859.5	539.2	4,091,020	1,159,892	153	0
2002	FYR	673.6	1,165.9	4,449,373	1,284,505	153	0
2003	FYR	260.7	762.9	5,652,325	1,707,663	153	0
2004	FYR	215.4	1,185.7	7,464,447	2,073,256	153	0
2005	FYR	497.5	1,472.7	8,376,484	2,257,182	153	0
2006	FYR	966.1	2,442.2	9,132,562	2,696,021	153	0
2007	FYR	2,312.4	11,214.6	10,704,66	3,668,857	153	1
2008	FYR	24,085.2	9,310.6	12,968,65	4,519,732	153	1
2009	FYR	14,367.2	8,146.3	12,118,58	4,157,853	153	1
2010	FYR	18,770.2	8,896.9	11,858,16	4,114,781	153	1
2011	FYR	35,670.2	13,698.2	12,959,56	4,501,812	153	1
2012	FYR	16,569.4	10,033.8	12,648,09	4,373,171	153	1
2013	FYR	47,379.8	37,057.2	12,923,00	4,416,000	153	1
2014	FYR	30,544.0	20,052.3	13,278,00	3,992,640	153	1
2015	FYR	26,830.0	24,383.3	11,455,59	4,588,000	153	1
2016	FYR	35,275	21,913	11,863,86	4374122.32	153	1
2001	RS	8,690.4	5,451.5	4,091,020	11,390,469	735	0
2002	RS	6,810.4	11,789.0	4,449,373	15,102,568	735	0
2003	RS	2,636.1	7,714.0	5,652,325	19,550,782	735	0
2004	RS	2,178.2	11,988.7	7,464,447	23,649,854	735	0
2005	RS	5,030.2	14,890.2	8,376,484	25,234,409	735	0
2006	RS	9,767.9	24,693.4	9,132,562	29,221,082	735	0
2007	RS	23,380.5	113,391.7	10,704,66	38,952,094	735	1
2008	RS	27,805.7	212,933.1	12,968,65	47,760,580	735	1

continued on following page

Table 7. Continued

Year	Pairs	Xij*	Mij*	GDPi**	GDPj**	Dij***	Fta
2009	RS	8,606.4	120,609.1	12,118,58	40,249,480	735	1
2010	RS	12,005.4	170,355.9	11,858,16	36,990,001	735	1
2011	RS	16,694.5	194,423.4	12,959,56	43,291,846	735	1
2012	RS	15,218.5	215,467.9	12,648,09	37,488,935	735	1
2013	RS	22,891.7	162,001.9	12,923,00	45,520,000	735	1
2014	RS	13,956.4	205,362.9	13,278,00	36,513,027	735	1
2015	RS	25,474.6	164,965.7	11,455,59	44,211,000	735	1
2016	RS	27,168	192,752,429	11,863,86	38299854.69	735	1
2001	HR	935.0	12,900.0	4,091,020	23,052,045	264	0
2002	HR	326.0	23,100.0	4,449,373	26,524,896	264	0
2003	HR	849.0	34,700.0	5,652,325	34,143,409	264	0
2004	HR	1,010.0	33,700.0	7,464,447	41,003,559	264	0
2005	HR	1,380.0	34,400.0	8,376,484	44,821,409	264	0
2006	HR	2,800.0	49,400.0	9,132,562	49,855,079	264	0
2007	HR	3,040.0	52,500.0	10,704,66	59,335,977	264	1
2008	HR	5,030.0	65,000.0	12,968,65	69,595,272	264	1
2009	HR	3,240.0	47,600.0	12,118,58	62,244,203	264	1
2010	HR	5,740.0	90,400.0	11,858,16	58,873,839	264	1
2011	HR	4,870.0	73,500.0	12,959,56	61,789,184	264	1
2012	HR	5,580.0	90,000.0	12,648,09	59,228,247	264	1
2013	HR	3,680.0	81,600.0	12,923,00	57,869,000	264	0
2014	HR	3,720.0	74,500.0	13,278,00	48,732,004	264	0
2015	HR	3,876.2	59,234.2	11,455,59	57,136,000	264	0
2016	HR	7,595	35,560	11,863,86	58,458,713	264	0
2001	BG	135.0	25,200.0	4,091,020	13,868,601	543	0
2002	BG	219.0	26,600.0	4,449,373	15,979,195	543	0
2003	BG	337.0	34,200.0	5,652,325	20,668,177	543	0
2004	BG	1,930.0	49,700.0	7,464,447	25,283,228	543	0
2005	BG	3,840.0	81,900.0	8,376,484	28,895,084	543	0
2006	BG	4,230.0	85,000.0	9,132,562	33,209,189	543	0
2007	BG	10,600.0	76,000.0	10,704,66	42,113,656	543	0
2008	BG	11,400.0	90,500.0	12,968,65	51,824,893	543	0
2009	BG	12,460.0	87,800.0	12,118,58	48,568,714	543	0
2010	BG	16,800.0	79,700.0	11,858,16	47,727,326	543	0
2011	BG	24,500.0	70,500.0	12,959,56	53,544,649	543	0
2012	BG	24,900.0	66,300.0	12,648,09	50,972,110	543	0
2013	BG	24,400.0	83,700.0	12,923,00	54,480,000	543	0
2014	BG	25,000.0	78,800.0	13,278,00	48,952,959	543	0

continued on following page

Table 7. Continued

Year	Pairs	Xij*	Mij*	GDPi**	GDPj**	Dij***	Fta
2015	BG	25,116.6	59,451.7	11,455,59	56,717,000	543	0
2016	BG	26,146.9	60,542.0	11,863,86	55,237,882	543	0
2001	DE	22,800.0	82,800.0	4,091,020	1,880,894,85	1977	0
2002	DE	24,400.0	90,200.0	4,449,373	2,006,587,61	1977	0
2003	DE	25,100.0	112,000.0	5,652,325	2,423,814,89	1977	0
2004	DE	27,400.0	143,000.0	7,464,447	2,726,341,47	1977	0
2005	DE	34,000.0	149,000.0	8,376,484	2,766,253,79	1977	0
2006	DE	43,100.0	182,000.0	9,132,562	2,902,748,69	1977	0
2007	DE	53,900.0	233,000.0	10,704,66	3,323,807,41	1977	0
2008	DE	53,400.0	322,000.0	12,968,65	3,623,686,23	1977	0
2009	DE	53,900.0	298,000.0	12,118,58	3,298,219,19	1977	0
2010	DE	60,900.0	256,000.0	11,858,16	3,282,894,73	1977	0
2011	DE	84,500.0	302,000.0	12,959,56	3,624,861,11	1977	0
2012	DE	102,000.0	291,000.0	12,648,09	3,428,130,62	1977	0
2013	DE	112,000.0	282,000.0	12,923,00	3,730,261,00	1977	0
2014	DE	77,800.0	235,000.0	13,278,00	3,355,772,43	1977	0
2015	DE	60,165.0	288,967.0	11,455,59	3,868,000,00	1977	0
2016	DE	61,154.0	290,875.0	11,863,86	3,911,327,65	1977	0
2001	GR	70,700.0	335,000.0	4,091,020	129,841,697	705	0
2002	GR	31,800.0	319,000.0	4,449,373	146,050,256	705	0
2003	GR	43,900.0	375,000.0	5,652,325	192,850,219	705	0
2004	GR	55,100.0	418,000.0	7,464,447	227,950,420	705	0
2005	GR	55,900.0	431,000.0	8,376,484	240,075,690	705	0
2006	GR	73,600.0	482,000.0	9,132,562	261,713,233	705	0
2007	GR	107,000.0	618,000.0	10,704,66	305,431,771	705	0
2008	GR	164,000.0	511,000.0	12,968,65	341,593,976	705	0
2009	GR	106,000.0	693,000.0	12,118,58	321,016,155	705	0
2010	GR	122,000.5	598,000.0	11,858,16	292,304,603	705	0
2011	GR	115,000.0	556,000.0	12,959,56	289,627,363	705	0
2012	GR	107,000.0	452,000.0	12,648,09	249,098,684	705	0
2013	GR	87,200.0	434,000.0	12,923,00	242,230,000	705	0
2014	GR	65,200.0	414,000.0	13,278,00	195,212,006	705	0
2015	GR	75,611.0	339,598.0	11,455,59	235,574,000	705	0
2016	GR	80,473.0	421,178.0	11,863,86	241,867,001	705	0
2001	IT	170,000.0	415,000.0	4,091,020	1,123,702,69	757	0
2002	IT	292,000.0	509,000.0	4,449,373	1,225,176,96	757	0
2003	IT	310,000.0	607,000.0	5,652,325	1,514,503,53	757	0
2004	IT	453,000.0	690,000.0	7,464,447	1,735,521,50	757	0

continued on following page

Table 7. Continued

Year	Pairs	Xij*	Mij*	GDPi**	GDPj**	Dij***	Fta
2005	IT	470,000.0	736,000.0	8,376,484	1,786,275,01	757	0
2006	IT	466,000.0	832,000.0	9,132,562	1,872,982,70	757	0
2007	IT	674,000.0	1,070,000.0	10,704,66	2,127,180,49	757	0
2008	IT	663,000.0	1,280,000.0	12,968,65	2,307,311,49	757	0
2009	IT	662,000.0	1,100,000.0	12,118,58	2,111,148,00	757	0
2010	IT	796,000.0	1,180,000.0	11,858,16	2,041,954,74	757	0
2011	IT	924,000.0	1,640,000.0	12,959,56	2,195,014,08	757	0
2012	IT	956,000.0	1,560,000.0	12,648,09	2,014,669,58	757	0
2013	IT	1,060,000.0	1,600,000.0	12,923,00	2,149,485,00	757	0
2014	IT	1,154,612.6	1,380,000.0	13,278,00	1,814,762,86	757	0
2015	IT	1,383,408.2	1,311,630.9	11,455,59	2,139,000,00	757	0
2016	IT	1,456,983.0	1,360,852.0	11,863,86	2,436,739,21	757	0
2001	PL	54.8	918.0	4,091,020	190,420,870	1971	0
2002	PL	63.3	1,870.0	4,449,373	198,179,425	1971	0
2003	PL	89.2	4,790.0	5,652,325	216,800,889	1971	0
2004	PL	693.0	7,150.0	7,464,447	252,768,999	1971	0
2005	PL	215.0	8,950.0	8,376,484	303,912,248	1971	0
2006	PL	1,060.0	16,500.0	9,132,562	341,669,944	1971	0
2007	PL	1,620.0	28,900.0	10,704,66	425,321,502	1971	0
2008	PL	2,380.0	38,200.0	12,968,65	529,432,301	1971	0
2009	PL	1,630.0	48,800.0	12,118,58	430,917,310	1971	0
2010	PL	2,520.0	58,000.0	11,858,16	469,736,811	1971	0
2011	PL	3,510.0	56,600.0	12,959,56	515,666,869	1971	0
2012	PL	3,280.0	61,100.0	12,648,09	489,795,487	1971	0
2013	PL	6,950.0	69,900.0	12,923,00	525,866,000	1971	0
2014	PL	7,200.0	54,900.0	13,278,00	474,783,393	1971	0
2015	PL	9,564.8	66,070.1	11,455,59	524,059,000	1971	0
2016	PL	10,367.0	69,376.0	11,863,86	514,758,112	1971	0
2001	RO	853.0	12,800.0	4,091,020	40,180,746	904	0
2002	RO	63.3	17,400.0	4,449,373	45,824,530	904	0
2003	RO	88.9	16,100.0	5,652,325	59,507,346	904	0
2004	RO	376.0	12,000.0	7,464,447	75,489,440	904	0
2005	RO	2,450.0	15,800.0	8,376,484	98,913,392	904	0
2006	RO	1,550.0	51,900.0	9,132,562	122,641,509	904	0
2007	RO	6,210.0	18,600.0	10,704,66	169,282,492	904	0
2008	RO	3,450.0	33,800.0	12,968,65	204,335,226	904	0
2009	RO	7,400.0	40,200.0	12,118,58	164,345,719	904	0
2010	RO	1,500.0	60,000.0	11,858,16	164,435,980	904	0

continued on following page

Table 7. Continued

Year	Pairs	Xij*	Mij*	GDPi**	GDPj**	Dij***	Fta
2011	RO	3,300.0	47,200.0	12,959,56	189,775,739	904	0
2012	RO	4,480.0	56,400.0	12,648,09	192,710,685	904	0
2013	RO	4,980.0	35,200.0	12,923,00	189,638,000	904	0
2014	RO	7,980.0	49,400.0	13,278,00	177,954,490	904	0
2015	RO	10,626.1	48,364.6	11,455,59	199,324,000	904	0
2016	RO	11,834.0	50,167.0	11,863,86	201,412,311	904	0
2001	ES	1,490.0	16,400.0	4,091,020	608,856,376	2703	0
2002	ES	1,450.0	21,000.0	4,449,373	686,295,878	2703	0
2003	ES	7,460.0	32,800.0	5,652,325	883,839,729	2703	0
2004	ES	2,700.0	33,700.0	7,464,447	1,044,612,07	2703	0
2005	ES	1,910.0	44,700.0	8,376,484	1,130,798,88	2703	0
2006	ES	3,810.0	51,100.0	9,132,562	1,236,352,16	2703	0
2007	ES	4,810.0	55,000.0	10,704,66	1,441,426,53	2703	0
2008	ES	25,200.0	56,900.0	12,968,65	1,593,420,00	2703	0
2009	ES	36,300.0	76,500.0	12,118,58	1,454,336,57	2703	0
2010	ES	124,000.0	39,900.0	11,858,16	1,375,815,78	2703	0
2011	ES	113,000.0	62,300.0	12,959,56	1,453,231,94	2703	0
2012	ES	190,000.0	78,700.0	12,648,09	1,322,964,77	2703	0
2013	ES	239,000.0	76,600.0	12,923,00	1,393,040,00	2703	0
2014	ES	168,000.0	79,800.0	13,278,00	1,199,057,34	2703	0
2015	ES	100,224.3	69,282.6	11,455,59	1,381,000,00	2703	0
2016	ES	123,643.0	73,568.0	11,863,86	1,419,451,12	2703	0
2001	AT	2,550.0	11,800.0	4,091,020	196,953,629	1222	0
2002	AT	3,500.0	23,100.0	4,449,373	212,970,685	1222	0
2003	AT	5,340.0	32,000.0	5,652,325	260,721,479	1222	0
2004	AT	6,500.0	30,300.0	7,464,447	299,870,270	1222	0
2005	AT	5,810.0	50,500.0	8,376,484	314,641,161	1222	0
2006	AT	6,490.0	38,900.0	9,132,562	334,292,247	1222	0
2007	AT	6,760.0	60,700.0	10,704,66	386,439,117	1222	0
2008	AT	14,100.0	74,400.0	12,968,65	427,627,368	1222	0
2009	AT	76,600.0	62,800.0	12,118,58	397,570,327	1222	0
2010	AT	42,200.0	76,800.0	11,858,16	389,656,072	1222	0
2011	AT	43,700.0	103,000.0	12,959,56	429,099,514	1222	0
2012	AT	38,200.0	66,000.0	12,648,09	407,575,161	1222	0
2013	AT	27,500.0	61,500.0	12,923,00	428,322,000	1222	0
2014	AT	23,600.0	47,000.0	13,278,00	374,055,872	1222	0
2015	AT	23,655.8	58,098.7	11,455,59	436,888,000	1222	0
2016	AT	25,718.0	60,934.0	11,863,86	442,714,514	1222	0

continued on following page

Table 7. Continued

Year	Pairs	Xij*	Mij*	GDPi**	GDPj**	Dij***	Fta
2001	NL	1,970.0	11,500.0	4,091,020	426,091,275	2177	0
2002	NL	2,700.0	9,510.0	4,449,373	464,478,637	2177	0
2003	NL	1,190.0	14,600.0	5,652,325	570,917,607	2177	0
2004	NL	3,270.0	20,200.0	7,464,447	646,069,794	2177	0
2005	NL	1,810.0	27,800.0	8,376,484	672,357,360	2177	0
2006	NL	2,200.0	18,200.0	9,132,562	719,376,020	2177	0
2007	NL	35,600.0	27,600.0	10,704,66	833,147,765	2177	0
2008	NL	33,800.0	44,900.0	12,968,65	931,327,892	2177	0
2009	NL	4,710.0	48,400.0	12,118,58	858,033,893	2177	0
2010	NL	7,230.0	51,200.0	11,858,16	836,389,937	2177	0
2011	NL	10,600.0	48,600.0	12,959,56	893,757,287	2177	0
2012	NL	20,400.0	31,000.0	12,648,09	823,139,235	2177	0
2013	NL	13,200.0	39,600.0	12,923,00	853,539,352	2177	0
2014	NL	16,250.0	42,200.0	13,278,00	752,547,410	2177	0
2015	NL	16,360.3	28,548.6	11,455,59	879,319,000	2177	0
2016	NL	20,328.0	34,829.0	11,863,86	880,176,211	2177	0

Source: *Comtrade, **World Bank, *** DistanceCalculator.net

APPENDIX 6

Table 8. Unit root test for Log(GDPI)

Method	Statistic	Prob.**	Cross-Sections	Obs
Null: Unit Root (Assumes Common Unit Root Process)				
Levin, Lin & Chu t*	-15.2077	0.0000	15	210
Null: Unit Root (Assumes Individual Unit Root Process)				
Im, Pesaran and Shin W-stat	-9.53632	0.0000	15	210
ADF - Fisher Chi-square	139.777	0.0000	15	210
PP - Fisher Chi-square	215.112	0.0000	15	225

** $p<0.05$, log (GDPi) is stationary

APPENDIX 7

Table 9. Unit root test for Log (GDPJ)

Method	Statistic	Prob.**	Cross-Sections	Obs
Null: Unit Root (Assumes Common Unit Root Process)				
Levin, Lin & Chu t*	-10.7736	0.0000	15	210
Null: Unit Root (Assumes Individual Unit Root Process)				
Im, Pesaran and Shin W-stat	-6.61503	0.0000	15	210
ADF - Fisher Chi-square	98.5649	0.0000	15	210
PP - Fisher Chi-square	159.921	0.0000	15	225

** $p<0.05$, log (GDPj) is stationary

APPENDIX 8

Table 10. Unit root test for Log (MIJ)

Method	Statistic	Prob.**	Cross-sections	Obs
Null: Unit Root (Assumes Common Unit Root Process)				
Levin, Lin & Chu t*	-5.97872	0.0000	15	210
Null: Unit Root (Assumes Individual Unit Root Process)				
Im, Pesaran and Shin W-stat	-2.43744	0.0074	15	210
ADF - Fisher Chi-square	51.9568	0.0077	15	210
PP - Fisher Chi-square	114.635	0.0000	15	225

** $p<0.05$, log (Mij) is stationary

APPENDIX 9

Table 11. Unit root test for Log(XIJ)

Method	Statistic	Prob.**	Cross-Sections	Obs
Null: Unit Root (Assumes Common Unit Root Process)				
Levin, Lin & Chu t*	-5.30467	0.0000	15	210
Null: Unit Root (Assumes Individual Unit Root Process)				
Im, Pesaran and Shin W-stat	-1.85439	0.0318	15	210
ADF - Fisher Chi-square	41.5758	0.0778	15	210
PP - Fisher Chi-square	83.7955	0.0000	15	225

** $p<0.05$, log (Xij) is stationary

Chapter 5
An Integrated Rough Model for Third Party Logistics Service Provider Selection

Alptekin Ulutas
https://orcid.org/0000-0002-8130-1301
Cumhuriyet University, Turkey

ABSTRACT

Logistics is a key factor for companies to sustain their businesses, to gain the competitive advantage in the market, and to speed up the transportation process. Companies can perform their own logistic activities using their own core competencies; however, they can face huge logistics costs. To avoid these logistics operating costs, companies need to cooperate with third party logistics service providers (3PL) to perform logistics activities. This chapter proposes an integrated rough MCDM model including Rough SWARA and Rough COPRAS methods to identify the best 3PL for a Turkish textile company. These two rough methods were not previously utilized in solving any decision-making problems in the extant literature. Thus, the contribution of this study is to develop a new rough integrated model to solve the 3PL service provider selection problem.

INTRODUCTION

Today, as a result of rapid changes in technology, companies are forced to manufacture better quality products at a lower price to be able to sustain their businesses and to gain competitive advantage in the marketplace as well as to speed up the transportation process. In order to achieve all these objectives and to adapt to the quick changes in the market, it can be said the most effective tool to be used is "logistics" as competition between businesses depends on the realization of successful logistics activities.

Logistics can be briefly defined as delivering the right product in accurate quantity from the source point to the accurate final consumption point at the right time. Logistics plays a key role in unifying the supply chain of an industry and there is a strong impact of logistics on the productivity and whole supply chain's cost (Li et al., 2012; Govindan et al., 2016). If companies perform their logistics activities

DOI: 10.4018/978-1-5225-8458-2.ch005

with their own core competencies, this can bring high costs to the companies. Therefore, firms fulfil their logistics activities through working with an outsourcing company; namely, third party logistics (3PL) service providers.

The use of 3PL service providers in logistics has become a conventional activity because of the experience and expertise of 3PL service providers in supporting customers (Govindan et al., 2016).

The main benefits of working with logistics providers allows more focus on the company's core competencies, increased company productivity and performance, reduced transportation costs, and restructured supply chain (Li et al., 2012). The 3PL service provider presents the following services; consolidation of freight and distribution, stock management, storage, transportation, and cross-docking (Govindan et al., 2016). As a result, 3PL service providers have become an indispensable and important part of logistics activities for companies which choose to outsource.

Aguezzoul (2014) identified and listed 11 main criteria commonly used in selecting 3PL service providers in the extant literature. These criteria are as follows: relationship, cost, quality, flexibility, information and equipment systems, location, delivery, services, financial position, professionalism, and reputation. Therefore, it can be said that the choice of 3PL service provider is a complicated process as many qualitative and quantitative criteria, which generally conflict each other, influence this process. Hence, the choice of 3PL service provider can be classified as a multi-criteria decision making (MCDM) problem comprising various types of uncertainty.

There are many methods and models in literature to choose the right 3PL service provider. Most of the models used fuzzy set theory and small number of models used grey set theory to solve 3PL service provider selection problem. However, any rough integrated model has not been proposed before to solve this problem. In addition to the fuzzy theory, rough set theory is an appropriate tool to treat uncertainty without any effect of subjectivism (Vasiljević et al., 2018). Additionally, using rough set theory can bring some benefits such as easy collection of data and simple and quick calculation.

In this study, a new rough integrated model including rough SWARA (Step-wise Weight Assessment Ratio Analysis) method and rough COPRAS (Complex Proportional Assessment) method is used to handle uncertainty in selecting a 3PL service provider. The benefits of using rough SWARA are the reduction of the uncertainty, the decreasing of decision maker's subjectivity, consisting of small number of steps, the collection of data easily and simplicity in access creation (Zavadskas et al., 2018). The benefits of rough COPRAS can be small number of steps to go through and quick computation. Rough SWARA was introduced by Zavadskas et al. (2018) and rough COPRAS was developed by Stević et al. (2017a).

These two rough methods were not utilised together before in solving any decision making problem in the existing literature. Thus, the contribution of this study is to develop a new rough integrated model to solve the 3PL service provider selection problem. This rough integrated model is applied into a Turkish textile company, which would like to work with a 3PL service provider to deliver its products to local shops.

THE IMPORTANCE OF THIRD PARTY LOGISTICS SERVICE PROVIDER SELECTION

Logistics has generally played a supporting role for business functions such as marketing and production and transportation. In recent years, the role of logistics has begun to change in a significant way and its importance level has started to be seen as a critical factor that has become more prominent in competitive advantage in enterprises. The concept of logistics was initially thought to be limited to storage and transportation. However, other business functions such as purchasing, inventory management, distribution, order management, packaging, returns, demand forecasting, parts and service support, recycling, production programming and disposal of waste, and even customer service can be added to this concept.

One of the biggest benefits of outsourcing in logistics service is the reduction of the costs arising from the above-mentioned business functions. A 3PL logistics provider with high coordination capabilities can enable the companies to effectively manage the flow of goods between the companies to the customer. Effective material flow can strengthen the bond between the customer and the company and increase customer loyalty. It will also aid to regulate the flow of activities in/out the company. If the company does not work with a 3PL firm that provides such benefits, it must organize and implement all the required steps by itself. This can lead to increased costs and time loss for the company. In addition, the company can not be able to focus on its core competencies, which can cause the company to lose its competitive advantage in the market.

Companies in many countries have begun working in coordination with third party logistics service providers. In recent years, about 70% of corporations in Japan and about 42% of corporations in the US have been conducting their logistics activities through 3PL service providers (Li et al., 2012; Govindan et al., 2016). Working with such firms that is suitable for the business targets of the company will bring many benefits mentioned above. Therefore, companies should choose the most appropriate provider. Working with an inappropriate service provider may lead to the failure of the company to attain its objectives and to increase the costs of function as well as lead to the loss of customers. Therefore, the selection process of the correct 3PL service provider is critical.

BACKGROUND

Several articles have recently been published about the selection of 3PL service providers. Most of these articles proposed MCDM methods to assess the performance of 3PL service providers under criteria. For example, Yayla et al. (2015) integrated Fuzzy Analytic Hierarchy Process (AHP) and Fuzzy TOPSIS to evaluate the performance of 3PL service providers and select the best one for a confectionary company. Sahu et al. (2015) developed a fuzzy based appraisement platform including interval-valued fuzzy numbers to select the most appropriate 3PL provider for a company locating in an Indian automobile part manufacturing industry.

Binici et al. (2015) proposed Fuzzy Analytic Network Process (ANP) under Benefits, Opportunities, Costs and Risks criteria. Bali et al. (2015) developed dynamic intuitionistic fuzzy TOPSIS model to select 3PL provider for a company manufacturing heat systems. Zhang and Li (2015) developed a fuzzy integrated model including fuzzy ANP and fuzzy TOPSIS to evaluate the performance of 3PL providers in agricultural products. Aguezzoul and Pires (2016) proposed ELECTRE I to solve 3PL provider selection problem. Gürcan et al. (2016) proposed AHP to choose the best 3PL for a company operating in İstanbul. Prakash and Barua (2016) developed a model consisting of fuzzy AHP and VIKOR to select the best third party reverse logistics firm for an Indian electronics company.

Govindan et al. (2016) proposed Grey DEMATEL to identify significant criteria for 3PL provider selection and evaluation. Govindan and Chaudhuri (2016) proposed DEMATEL to analyse interrelationships between risks faced by 3PL service providers in relation to one of its customers. Ghorabaee et al. (2017) integrated the CRITIC and WASPAS method under interval type-2 to evaluate the performance of 3PL providers. Mavi et al. (2017) combined fuzzy SWARA and fuzzy MOORA to evaluate the performance of third party reverse logistics providers in plastic industry. Awasthi and Baležentis (2017) integrated BOCR and fuzzy MULTIMOORA methods to select the best logistics service provider.

Senturk et al. (2017) proposed interval type 2 fuzzy ANP to identify the best 3PL provider company. Singh et al. (2017) combined fuzzy AHP and fuzzy TOPSIS to determine the best 3PL service provider for cold chain management. Zarbakhshnia et al. (2018) integrated fuzzy SWARA and fuzzy COPRAS to identify the best sustainable third party reverse logistics provider for a company from automotive industry. Ecer (2018) combined fuzzy AHP and EDAS methods to determine the best 3PL service provider for a marble company. Many studies in the literature have solved the 3PL selection problem by using MCDM methods. However, in this study an integrated rough model consisting of Rough SWARA and Rough COPRAS methods will be used. The following section will present the methodology of the proposed model.

METHODOLOGY

Rough Numbers

K can be defined as the universe including all of the objects, T can be defined as an arbitrary object of K, R covering all the objects in K consists of a set of k classes and $R = \{H_1, H_2, ..., H_k\}$. These classes are ranked as $H_1 < H_2 < ... < H_k$, then $\forall T \in K, H_q \in R, 1 \le q \le k$, by $R(T)$ meaning the class to which object belongs. The upper approximation ($\overline{Apr}(H_q)$), the lower approximation ($\underline{Apr}(H_q)$), and boundary region ($\overline{Bnd}(H_q)$) of class H_q are defined as (Zavadskas et al.,2018):

$$\underline{Apr}(H_q) = \{T \in K \,/\, R(T) \le H_q\} \tag{1}$$

$$\overline{Apr}(H_q) = \{T \in K \,/\, R(T) \ge H_q\} \tag{2}$$

$$Bnd(H_q) = \{T \in K \,/\, R(T) \ne H_q\} = \{T \in K \,/\, R(T) > H_q\} \cup \{T \in K \,/\, R(T) < H_q\} \tag{3}$$

Then H_q can be indicated as a rough number ($RN(H_q)$), which is identified by its corresponding lower limit ($\underline{Lim}(H_q)$) and upper limit ($\overline{Lim}(H_q)$) where:

$$\underline{Lim}(H_q) = \frac{1}{M_L} \sum_{T \in \underline{Apr}(H_q)} R(T) \tag{4}$$

$$\overline{Lim}(H_q) = \frac{1}{M_U} \sum_{T \in \overline{Apr}(H_q)} R(T) \tag{5}$$

$$RN(H_q) = \left[\underline{Lim}(H_q), \overline{Lim}(H_q)\right] \tag{6}$$

where M_L and M_U are the numbers of objects contained in $\overline{Apr}(H_q)$ and $\overline{Apr}(H_q)$ respectively.

The basic operation for two rough numbers ($RN(D)$ and $RN(G)$);

Addition: $RN(D) + RN(G) = \left[\underline{Lim}(D) + \underline{Lim}(G), \overline{Lim}(D) + \overline{Lim}(G)\right]$ (7)

Subtraction: $RN(D) - RN(G) = \left[\underline{Lim}(D) - \overline{Lim}(G), \overline{Lim}(D) - \underline{Lim}(G)\right]$ (8)

Multiplication: $RN(D) \times RN(G) = \left[\underline{Lim}(D) \times \underline{Lim}(G), \overline{Lim}(D) \times \overline{Lim}(G)\right]$ (9)

Division: $RN(D) / RN(G) = \left[\underline{Lim}(D) / \overline{Lim}(G), \overline{Lim}(D) / \underline{Lim}(G)\right]$ (10)

Rough SWARA

In the extant literature, the SWARA (Step-wise Weight Assessment Ratio Analysis) method, which was developed by Keršuliene et al. (2010), is used to obtain the weights of criteria. The steps of Rough SWARA can be described as following (Zavadskas et al. (2018)):

Step 1: Criteria list is structured.

Step 2: Expert team is formed. First, these experts will rank the criteria with respect to their importance degree. Then, s_j is identified in such a way, starting from the second criterion, to compare importance degree of criterion c_1 and criterion c_{1-n} .

Step 3: A group rough matrix is structured by combining individual responses of experts using equations 1-6.

$$RN(C_j) = \left[c_j^L, c_j^U\right]_{1 \times m} \tag{11}$$

Step 4: Rough group matrix is normalised to determine the matrix ($RN(S_j)$).

$$RN(S_j) = \left[s_j^L, s_j^U\right]_{1\times m} \tag{12}$$

where,

$$RN(S_j) = \frac{\left[c_j^L, c_j^U\right]}{\max\limits_r \left[c_r^L, c_r^U\right]} \tag{13}$$

If $j = 1, \left[s_j^L, s_j^U\right] = \left[1,1\right]$. For others ($j > 1$), the equation 13 can be computed using the equation (14):

$$RN(S_j) = \left[\frac{c_j^L}{\max\limits_r \left(c_r^L\right)}; \frac{c_j^U}{\max\limits_r \left(c_r^U\right)}\right]_{1\times m} \tag{14}$$

Step 5: The matrix $RN(K_j)$ can be computed as following equation:

$$RN(K_j) = \left[k_j^L, k_j^U\right]_{1\times m} \tag{15}$$

by using following equation:

$$RN(K_j) = \left[s_j^L + 1, s_j^U + 1\right]_{1\times m} \tag{16}$$

Step 6: Recalculated weights' matrix $RN(Q_j)$ is computed as:

$$RN(Q_j) = \left[q_j^L, q_j^U\right]_{1\times m} \tag{17}$$

The members of $RN(Q_j)$ are calculated by following equation:

$$RN(Q_j) = \left[q_j^L = \begin{cases} 1.00 & j=1 \\ \dfrac{q_{j-1}^L}{k_j^U} & j>1 \end{cases}, q_j^U = \begin{cases} 1.00 & j=1 \\ \dfrac{q_{j-1}^U}{k_j^L} & j>1 \end{cases} \right]_{1\times m} \tag{18}$$

Step 7: Criteria weights' matrix $RN(W_j)$ is calculated as:

$$RN(W_j) = \left[w_j^L, w_j^U\right]_{1\times m} \tag{19}$$

where

$$\left[w_j^L, w_j^U\right] = \left[\frac{\left[q_j^L, q_j^U\right]}{\sum_{j=1}^{m}\left[q_j^L, q_j^U\right]} \right] \tag{20}$$

The matrix of criteria weights is transferred into Rough COPRAS.

Rough COPRAS

In this study, COPRAS (Complex Proportional Assessment) method is used to rank 3PL service providers with respect to their overall performance against criteria. The steps of Rough COPRAS are as follows:

Step 1: A group decision rough matrix is developed by integrating individual responses of experts using equations 1-6. Group decision rough matrix $RN(D_i)$ is shown in equation 21.

$$RN(D_i) = \left[d_i^L, d_i^U\right]_{n\times m} \tag{21}$$

Step 2: Equation 23 is used to obtain normalized rough matrix $RN(F_i)$.

$$RN(F_i) = \left[f_i^L, f_i^U\right]_{n\times m} \tag{22}$$

where,

$$RN(F_i) = \left[\frac{d_i^L}{\sum_{i=1}^{n} d_i^U}, \frac{d_i^U}{\sum_{i=1}^{n} d_i^L} \right]_{n \times m} \tag{23}$$

Step 3: By using equation 25, weighted normalized rough matrix $RN(B_i)$ is computed as:

$$RN(B_i) = \left[b_i^L, b_i^U \right]_{n \times m} \tag{24}$$

where,

$$RN(B_i) = \left[f_i^L \times w_j^L, f_i^U \times w_j^U \right] \tag{25}$$

Step 4: Rough sum matrixes $RN(V_i^+)$ and $RN(V_i^-)$ of performance values under beneficial (equation 26) and non-beneficial (equation 27) criteria are computed as following equations.

$$RN(V_i^+) = \sum_{i=1}^{o} \left[b_i^L, b_i^U \right] \tag{26}$$

$$RN(V_i^-) = \sum_{i=o+1}^{n} \left[b_i^L, b_i^U \right] \tag{27}$$

Step 5: Rough relative importance matrix $RN(E_i)$ is computed as follows.

$$RN(E_i) = \left[e_i^L, e_i^U \right] \tag{28}$$

where,

$$RN(E_i) = RN(V_i^+) + \frac{\sum_{i=1}^{n} RN(V_i^-)}{RN(V_i^-) \times \sum_{i=1}^{n} \frac{1}{RN(V_i^-)}} \tag{29}$$

Step 6: Rough overall performance matrix $RN(U_i)$ can be calculated as follows.

$$RN(U_i) = \left[u_i^L, u_i^U\right] = \left[\frac{e_i^L}{\max e_i^U}, \frac{e_i^U}{\max e_i^L}\right] \tag{30}$$

Step 7: Crisp overall performance score (u_i) can be calculated by using equation 31.

$$u_i = \frac{u_i^L + u_i^U}{2} \tag{31}$$

3PL service providers are ranked with respect to crisp overall performance scores and 3PL service provider having the highest score is determined as the best alternative.

APPLICATION

This rough integrated model including Rough SWARA and Rough COPRAS is applied into a Turkish textile company which wanted to work with a 3PL service provider to deliver its products to local shops. The performance of five 3PL service providers is evaluated with respect to five criteria which were determined after consultation with managers of the textile company. These criteria include the following: cost of transportation (C), service quality (SQ), technological capability (TC), financial health (FH), and provider reputation (PR). Among these criteria, only cost is non-beneficial criterion and others are beneficial criteria.

The managers consulted in this study are factory manager (FM), customer relationship manager (CRM), planning manager (PM) and factory assistant manager (FAM). The Rough SWARA method is utilised to obtain the weights of identified criteria and rough COPRAS is utilised to evaluate the performance of 3PL service providers with respect to identified criteria and to determine overall score to rank 3PL service providers. In the Rough SWARA method, managers ranked the criteria with respect to importance. Table 1 indicates the evaluation of criteria by managers.

Individual responses of managers are combined by using equations 1-6 to obtain group rough matrix. The elements of this matrix are as follows.

$RN(c_1)$=[1,1]

$RN(c_2)$=[1.563,1.938]

$RN(c_3)$=[3.750,4.625]

$RN(c_4)$=[3.584,4.417]

Table 1. The evaluation of criteria by managers

Criteria	Managers			
	FM	CRM	PM	FAM
C	1	1	2	1
SQ	2	2	1	2
TC	5	3	5	4
FH	4	5	4	3
PR	3	4	3	5

$RN(c_5)$ =[3.271,4.250]

These values are normalized by using equation 13. The normalized values are as follows:

$RN(s_1)$ =[1,1]

$RN(s_2)$ =[0.338,0.517]

$RN(s_3)$ =[0.811,1.233]

$RN(s_4)$ =[0.775,1.178]

$RN(s_5)$ =[0.707,1.133]

By adding each rough number except $RN(s_1)$, $RN(k_j)$ value for each criterion can be calculated. These values are as follows:

$RN(k_1)$ =[1,1]

$RN(k_2)$ =[1.338,1.517]

$RN(k_5)$ =[1.707,2.133]

$RN(k_4)$ =[1.775,2.178]

$RN(k_3)$ =[1.811,2.233]

Recalculated weights and criteria weights are indicated in Table 2.

After calculating of criteria weights, Rough COPRAS is used to rank 3PL service providers. In this process, managers assigned 1-9 score for the performance of each alternative under each criterion. For beneficial criteria, 1 is the lowest score and 9 is the highest score; on the other hand, for non-beneficial criteria 1 is highest score and 9 is the lowest score. The assessment of alternatives by managers is indicated in Table 3.

These values are combined by using equations 1-6 to structure a group decision rough matrix. Table 4 indicates the group decision rough matrix.

These values are normalized by using equation 23. Normalized Rough matrix $RN(F_i)$ is indicated in Table 5.

These normalized rough values are multiplied by rough criteria weights (found in Rough SWARA) to structure weighted normalized rough matrix. Table 6 shows the weighted normalized rough matrix.

Rough sum matrixes ($RN(V_i^+)$ and $RN(V_i^-)$), rough relative importance matrix ($RN(E_i)$), rough overall performance matrix ($RN(U_i)$) and crisp overall performance score (u_i) are calculated by using equations 26-31. The results of Rough COPRAS are indicated in Table 7.

The 3PL service providers are ranked with respect to the rough COPRAS results as follows; A5 > A3 > A1 > A2 > A4. As a result, the best 3PL service provider is determined as A5.

DISCUSSION

The proposed model was compared with other rough MCDM methods. Rough weights obtained in SWARA were not changed, and these weights were also used for other Rough MCDM methods. Rough ARAS (Radović et al., 2018), Rough MOORA, and Rough SAW (Stević et al., 2017b) methods were used to compare with the Rough COPRAS method. Table 8 indicates the comparison of rough methods.

As can be seen from Table 8, the order of alternatives is the same as the proposed rough method. Thus, the proposed rough model has reached the correct result.

Table 2. The weights of criteria

Criteria	Results	
	$RN(Q_j)$	$RN(W_j)$
C	[1,1]	[0.389,0.460]
SQ	[0.659,0.747]	[0.257,0.344]
TC	[0.064,0.136]	[0.025,0.063]
FH	[0.142,0.247]	[0.055,0.114]
PR	[0.309,0.438]	[0.120,0.201]

Table 3. The assessment of alternatives by managers

Alternatives	Criteria				
	C	SQ	TC	FH	PR
Factory Manager					
A1	6	5	7	6	7
A2	7	6	5	6	6
A3	5	7	8	4	5
A4	7	5	6	6	7
A5	5	7	7	7	5
Customer Relationship Manager					
A1	7	6	6	5	7
A2	6	6	4	5	6
A3	6	7	8	4	5
A4	8	6	5	7	7
A5	6	6	7	6	6
Planning Manager					
A1	6	5	6	6	7
A2	6	6	5	5	7
A3	5	6	7	5	5
A4	8	5	4	7	6
A5	5	7	6	7	6
Factory Assistant Manager					
A1	6	6	7	5	8
A2	7	7	4	5	7
A3	6	6	8	5	6
A4	8	5	5	8	7
A5	6	7	7	6	6

Table 4. The group decision rough matrix

Alternatives	Criteria				
	C	SQ	TC	FH	PR
A1	[6.063,6.438]	[5.250,5.750]	[6.250,6.750]	[5.250,5.750]	[7.063,7.438]
A2	[6.250,6.750]	[6.063,6.438]	[4.250,4.750]	[5.063,5.438]	[6.250,6.750]
A3	[5.250,5.750]	[6.250,6.750]	[7.563,7.938]	[4.250,4.750]	[5.063,5.438]
A4	[7.563,7.938]	[5.063,5.438]	[4.584,5.417]	[6.584,7.417]	[6.563,6.938]
A5	[5.250,5.750]	[6.563,6.938]	[6.563,6.938]	[6.250,6.750]	[5.563,5.938]

Table 5. The normalized rough matrix

Alternatives	Criteria				
	C	SQ	TC	FH	PR
A1	[0.186,0.212]	[0.168,0.197]	[0.197,0.231]	[0.174,0.210]	[0.217,0.244]
A2	[0.192,0.222]	[0.194,0.221]	[0.134,0.163]	[0.168,0.198]	[0.192,0.221]
A3	[0.161,0.189]	[0.200,0.231]	[0.238,0.272]	[0.141,0.173]	[0.156,0.178]
A4	[0.232,0.261]	[0.162,0.186]	[0.144,0.185]	[0.219,0.271]	[0.202,0.227]
A5	[0.161,0.189]	[0.210,0.238]	[0.206,0.238]	[0.208,0.246]	[0.171,0.195]

Table 6. The weighted normalized rough matrix

Alternatives	Criteria				
	C	SQ	TC	FH	PR
A1	[0.072,0.098]	[0.043,0.068]	[0.005,0.015]	[0.010,0.024]	[0.026,0.049]
A2	[0.075,0.102]	[0.050,0.076]	[0.003,0.010]	[0.009,0.023]	[0.023,0.044]
A3	[0.063,0.087]	[0.051,0.079]	[0.006,0.017]	[0.008,0.020]	[0.019,0.036]
A4	[0.090,0.120]	[0.042,0.064]	[0.004,0.012]	[0.012,0.031]	[0.024,0.046]
A5	[0.063,0.087]	[0.054,0.082]	[0.005,0.015]	[0.011,0.028]	[0.021,0.039]

Table 7. The results of rough COPRAS

Alternatives	Results					
	$RN(V_i^+)$	$RN(V_i^-)$	$RN(E_i)$	$RN(U_i)$	u_i	Rank
A1	[0.084,0.156]	[0.072,0.098]	[0.137,0.290]	[0.432,1.921]	1.177	3
A2	[0.085,0.153]	[0.075,0.102]	[0.136,0.281]	[0.429,1.861]	1.145	4
A3	[0.084,0.152]	[0.063,0.087]	[0.144,0.305]	[0.454,2.020]	1.237	2
A4	[0.082,0.153]	[0.090,0.120]	[0.125,0.260]	[0.394,1.722]	1.058	5
A5	[0.091,0.164]	[0.063,0.087]	[0.151,0.317]	[0.476,2.099]	1.288	1

Table 8. The results of rough methods

Rough Methods	Rough ARAS		Rough MOORA		Rough SAW	
Alternatives	Results					
	Values	Rank	Values	Rank	Values	Rank
A1	[0.534,1.411]	3	[0.026,0.129]	3	[0.685,1.105]	3
A2	[0.529,1.377]	4	[0.024,0.114]	4	[0.680,1.086]	4
A3	[0.563,1.479]	2	[0.047,0.145]	2	[0.725,1.161]	2
A4	[0.483,1.281]	5	[-0.018,0.073]	5	[0.614,1.005]	5
A5	[0.581,1.548]	1	[0.063,0.171]	1	[0.755,1.212]	1

CONCLUSION

Logistics is a key factor for companies to sustain their businesses, to gain the competitive advantage in the market, and to speed up the transportation process. Companies can perform their own logistics activities using their own core competencies; however, they can face huge logistics costs. To avoid these costs, companies must cooperate with 3PL service providers to perform logistics activities. For companies which outsource, 3PL service provider has become an indispensable part and a significant member of logistics activities. Therefore, choosing the 3PL service provider is an important decision-making problem. As both qualitative and quantitative criteria are involved in the choosing the 3PL service provider process, this problem can be referred to as the MCDM problem.

In the extant literature, there are many MCDM models proposed to select the best 3PL service provider. In this study, a rough integrated model including Rough SWARA and Rough COPRAS is proposed to determine the best 3PL service provider for a Turkish textile company. It is the first time that this study combines these two rough methods to solve 3PL service provider selection problem. This is the contribution of this study to the literature. Future studies may use different rough methods to solve same problem or they can use the proposed model to solve other MCDM problems.

REFERENCES

Aguezzoul, A. (2014). Third-party logistics selection problem: A literature review on criteria and methods. *Omega, 49*, 69–78. doi:10.1016/j.omega.2014.05.009

Aguezzoul, A., & Pires, S. (2016). 3PL performance evaluation and selection: a MCDM method. *Supply Chain Forum: An International Journal, 17*(2), 87-94.

Awasthi, A., & Balezentis, T. (2017). A hybrid approach based on BOCR and fuzzy MULTIMOORA for logistics service provider selection. *International Journal of Logistics Systems and Management, 27*(3), 261–282. doi:10.1504/IJLSM.2017.084466

Bali, Ö., Gümüş, S., & Kaya, I. (2015). A Multi-Period Decision Making Procedure Based on Intuitionistic Fuzzy Sets for Selection Among Third-Party Logistics Providers. *Journal of Multiple-Valued Logic & Soft Computing, 24*(5).

Binici, Y., Senturk, S., & Ozdemir, O. (2015). Selection of the Best Third-Party Logistics (3PL) Company with Fuzzy Analytic Network Process (FANP). *The 4th International Fuzzy Systems Symposium (FUZZYSS'15).*

Ecer, F. (2018). Third-party logistics (3PLs) provider selection via Fuzzy AHP and EDAS integrated model. *Technological and Economic Development of Economy, 24*(2), 615–634. doi:10.3846/20294913.2016.1213207

Ghorabaee, M. K., Amiri, M., Kazimieras Zavadskas, E., & Antuchevičienė, J. (2017). Assessment of third-party logistics providers using a CRITIC–WASPAS approach with interval type-2 fuzzy sets. *Transport, 32*(1), 66–78. doi:10.3846/16484142.2017.1282381

Govindan, K., & Chaudhuri, A. (2016). Interrelationships of risks faced by third party logistics service providers: A DEMATEL based approach. *Transportation Research Part E, Logistics and Transportation Review*, *90*, 177–195. doi:10.1016/j.tre.2015.11.010

Govindan, K., Khodaverdi, R., & Vafadarnikjoo, A. (2016). A grey DEMATEL approach to develop third-party logistics provider selection criteria. *Industrial Management & Data Systems*, *116*(4), 690–722. doi:10.1108/IMDS-05-2015-0180

Gürcan, Ö. F., Yazıcı, İ., Beyca, Ö. F., Arslan, Ç. Y., & Eldemir, F. (2016). Third party logistics (3PL) provider selection with AHP application. *Procedia: Social and Behavioral Sciences*, *235*, 226–234. doi:10.1016/j.sbspro.2016.11.018

Keršuliene, V., Zavadskas, E. K., & Turskis, Z. (2010). Selection of rational dispute resolution method by applying new step-wise weight assessment ratio analysis (SWARA). *Journal of business economics and management*, *11*(2), 243–258. doi:10.3846/jbem.2010.12

Li, F., Li, L., Jin, C., Wang, R., Wang, H., & Yang, L. (2012). A 3PL supplier selection model based on fuzzy sets. *Computers & Operations Research*, *39*(8), 1879–1884. doi:10.1016/j.cor.2011.06.022

Mavi, R. K., Goh, M., & Zarbakhshnia, N. (2017). Sustainable third-party reverse logistic provider selection with fuzzy SWARA and fuzzy MOORA in plastic industry. *International Journal of Advanced Manufacturing Technology*, *91*(5-8), 2401–2418. doi:10.100700170-016-9880-x

Prakash, C., & Barua, M. K. (2016). A combined MCDM approach for evaluation and selection of third-party reverse logistics partner for Indian electronics industry. *Sustainable Production and Consumption*, *7*, 66–78. doi:10.1016/j.spc.2016.04.001

Radović, D., Stević, Ž., Pamučar, D., Zavadskas, E., Badi, I., Antuchevičiene, J., & Turskis, Z. (2018). Measuring performance in transportation companies in developing countries: A novel rough ARAS model. *Symmetry*, *10*(10), 434. doi:10.3390ym10100434

Sahu, N. K., Datta, S., & Mahapatra, S. S. (2015). Fuzzy based appraisement module for 3PL evaluation and selection. *Benchmarking: An International Journal*, *22*(3), 354–392. doi:10.1108/BIJ-01-2013-0002

Senturk, S., Erginel, N., & Binici, Y. (2017). Interval Type-2 Fuzzy Analytic Network Process for Modelling a Third-party Logistics (3PL) Company. *Journal of Multiple-Valued Logic & Soft Computing, 28*.

Singh, R. K., Gunasekaran, A., & Kumar, P. (2017). Third party logistics (3PL) selection for cold chain management: A fuzzy AHP and fuzzy TOPSIS approach. *Annals of Operations Research*, 1–23.

Stević, Ž., Pamučar, D., Kazimieras Zavadskas, E., Ćirović, G., & Prentkovskis, O. (2017b). The selection of wagons for the internal transport of a logistics company: A novel approach based on rough BWM and rough SAW methods. *Symmetry*, *9*(11), 264. doi:10.3390ym9110264

Stević, Ž., Pamučar, D., Vasiljević, M., Stojić, G., & Korica, S. (2017a). Novel Integrated Multi-Criteria Model for Supplier Selection: Case Study Construction Company. *Symmetry*, *9*(11), 279. doi:10.3390ym9110279

Vasiljević, M., Fazlollahtabar, H., Stević, Ž., & Vesković, S. (2018). A rough multicriteria approach for evaluation of supplier criteria in automotive industry. *Decision Making: Applications in Management and Engineering*, *1*(1), 82–96.

Yayla, A. Y., Oztekin, A., Gumus, A. T., & Gunasekaran, A. (2015). A hybrid data analytic methodology for 3PL transportation provider evaluation using fuzzy multi-criteria decision making. *International Journal of Production Research*, *53*(20), 6097–6113. doi:10.1080/00207543.2015.1022266

Zarbakhshnia, N., Soleimani, H., & Ghaderi, H. (2018). Sustainable third-party reverse logistics provider evaluation and selection using fuzzy SWARA and developed fuzzy COPRAS in the presence of risk criteria. *Applied Soft Computing*, *65*, 307–319. doi:10.1016/j.asoc.2018.01.023

Zavadskas, E. K., Stević, Ž., Tanackov, I., & Prentkovskis, O. (2018). A Novel Multicriteria Approach–Rough Step-Wise Weight Assessment Ratio Analysis Method (R-SWARA) and Its Application in Logistics. *Studies in Informatics and Control*, *27*(1), 97–106. doi:10.24846/v27i1y201810

Zhang, S., & Li, X. (2015). A hybrid performance evaluation model of TPL providers in agricultural products based on fuzzy ANP-TOPSIS. *Custos E Agronegocio On Line*, *11*(3), 144–165.

Chapter 6
The Relationship Between R&D Expenditures and Economic Growth in OECD Countries With Different Causality Tests

Gökhan Karhan
Batman University, Turkey

ABSTRACT

In this chapter, the relationship between research and development (R&D) expenditures and economic growth was investigated with both Emirmahmutoğlu and Köse Causality test and the Dimitrescu and Hurlin Panel Causality test based on Rolling Windows Regression for the selected 19 OECD member countries for the period 1996-2015. The results concluded that for all panel there is a causality from economic growth to R&D expenditures. In this study, the relationship between variables was investigated using different mathematical techniques like rolling windows. According to the results of the Dimitrescu and Hurlin Panel Causality Test based on Rolling Window Regression, which is applied differently from other studies in the literature, there was a causality from economic growth to R&D expenditures in 2010. In 2011, there was causality from R&D expenditures to economic growth for all panels.

INTRODUCTION

Most of the increase in living standards is due to innovation. Today, innovative performance is an important factor for determining competitiveness and national progress. In addition, innovation is important to find solutions for specific problems such as climate change and sustainable development (OECD, 2007). Humanity has managed to develop itself as a result of coincidence for many years. As of the recent past, development has begun to occur by resorting to more systematic means to reach today's level of civilization. Today, no national economy or business has grown to the point where it can be left to chance. Therefore, every business and national economy must pay attention to investments in research and development (R&D) within its financial capabilities (Zerenler, Turker, & Sahin, 2007).

DOI: 10.4018/978-1-5225-8458-2.ch006

Today, the productivity levels of national economies and production structures have attained great importance in terms of achieving stable economic growth and increasing social welfare. In this framework, the tendency towards R&D and innovation activities are gaining momentum globally, and countries are creating added value with fewer resources. Research shows that innovation has a positive impact on labor and total factor productivity (TFP) and contributes to an increase in welfare. R&D expenditures are considered among the inputs required for innovation (Erkiletlioglu, 2013). Therefore, national R&D expenditures are considered as a demonstration of the innovation cultures of those countries.

The increase in R&D activities contributes to the raise in the level of innovative products which, in turns, brings an increase in economic growth via the transfer mechanism. In this context, the importance that countries give to R&D activities has become an indispensable element of sustainable economic growth. As Aghion et al., (2010) highlights, market competition in the market is caused by the entry of new innovations into the market and the exclusion of old technologies, thus increasing economic growth.

THEORETICAL BACKGROUND

Until the emergence of endogenous Growth Models, classical economists such as the Neoclassical economists and the Evolutionary approach failed to fully explain the relationship between technological growth and economic growth. These deficiencies have been addressed with the studies of Romer (1986) and Lucas (1988), whose investigated economic growth model that includes knowledge referred to as Endogenous Growth Models.

The ''endogenous'' term refers to innovations that arise from conscious activities realized by companies or consumers to maximize their profits or benefits (Dinopoulos & Şener, 2003).

The Endogenous growth theories emphasize that the main driving force to ensure the sustainability of growth are R&D activities and that the inputs related to these activities should be supported. Although there are many studies that attempt to explain the impact of R&D activities on growth, there are two main approaches.

In the first group of models (Romer, 1986; Lucas, 1988; Rebelo, 1991; and Barro 1990), technological development is indirectly caused by economic activities which are related to some other factors. The common feature of these group models is that they are based on competitive market conditions. Rebelo's model (1991) which shows in the simplest way that per capita growth can be sustained even in the absence of external technological development by abolishing the assumption of the diminishing marginal return of capital.

$$Y = AK$$

In the model, Y represents output of economy, A represents level of technology and K represents capital. In this function, it is assumed there is a linear relationship between the capital and the output of the economy. A general feature of the model is the broad evaluation of the capital factor which is shows by K. In other words, there are human capital factors within the capital. The distinguishing feature of the second group of models (Romer, 1990; Grossman & Helpman, 1989; Aghion & Howitt, 1992) is that technological development can be achieved via direct investment to technology by a separate sector and based on non-competitive markets. In the extant literature the second group of models are also referred to as R&D or Schumpeterian models. Romer (1990) states growth is due to technological development through the investments made by the companies which are want to maximize their profits.

Technology is non-rival and partly excludable. Technological development encourages economic units to accumulate more capital, and this situation increase the production per labor force. However, technological development is revealed by the initiatives of the firms that closely follow up the market incentives. The interiority of technology also stems from these initiatives.For both approaches, technological developments are among the determinants of growth. The first group indicates technological development indirectly affects the growth and for the second group this relation is direct. In the next part of the study, the relationship between technological development and growth will be examined empirically for the 19 OECD member countries.

LITERATURE REVIEW

The relationship between economic growth and R&D presents a great interest for researchers. As a result, this issue has been well discussed in the extant literature. The selected literature on the subject is listed below. Aghion and Howitt (1992) have tested the models of economic growth on the basis of R&D in their work and thus stated that it would be beneficial to allocate R&D share from Gross Domestic Product (GDP). In the study for the USA, it is stated that even though the increase in R&D expenditures in GDP is not a direct effect to economic growth, it does not contradict with the internal growth models on the basis of research and development.

Lichtenberg (1993) analyzed the effect of R&D expenditures on the economic growth in the private and public sectors for 74 countries during the period 1964-1989 with a causality test. The effect of R&D expenditures on economic growth in the private sector was found to be positive. In the public sector, no positive or negative effect was found. The study conducted by Landesmann and Pfaffermayr (1997) for the OECD countries from 1967 to 1987 showed that exports in the USA, the United Kingdom (UK) and Japan were positively affected by R&D expenditures. In Germany and France, the effect of R&D expenditures on exports was found to be negative. This situation is explained as follows, "constantly increasing R&D expenditures are causing the decrease in the economy."

Bassanini and Scarpetta (2001) examined the relationship between R&D and economic growth in the 21 OECD countries by panel data method which use a dynamic fixed-effect estimator (DFE) and found that the relationship between R&D and economic growth is positive. According to the findings of the study, a 1% increase in R&D expenditures increases economic growth by 0.3% - 0.4%. Ulku (2004) examined the data of 20 OECD countries and 10 non-OECD countries for the period 1981-1997 by panel data analysis. Findings shows that the relationship between innovation and GDP per capita is statistically significant in both groups of countries. However, it concluded that there is a positive relationship between R&D expenditures and innovation in OECD countries. Wu et al. (2007), has investigated relationship between R&D and economic growth between 1953-2004 for China by using cointegration and causality tests. According to the study, it has been found that in long-run, there is a two-way causality relationship between R&D spending and GDP.

Pessoa (2007) stated the relationship between economic growth and research and development expenditures in the case of Sweden and Ireland. The findings suggest there is not a relationship between research and development expenditures and economic growth. Altin and Kaya (2009) examined the connection between R&D and economic growth during the period 1990-2005. In this study R&D expenditures – growth relation has been analyzed by using VEC (Vector Error Correction) model. results are shown, in the short-run there is no relationship between R&D expenditures and economic growth however, in the long-run results shown that R&D expenditures causes economic growth.

Guloglu and Tekin (2012) investigated the causality relationship between R&D, innovation, and economic growth between 1991-2007 using the data from 13 OECD countries. The findings show there is a bi-directional causality relationship between R&D and economic growth. At the same time, the same result has been achieved between innovation and economic growth. Eid (2012) examined the effect of R&D expenditure on efficiency during the period 1981-2006 for 17 OECD member countries which showed there has been a significant increase in efficiency in R&D expenditures. Gülmez and Yardımcıoğlu (2012) examined 21 OECD countries for the period 1990-2010 which showed a 1% increase in R&D expenditure that provided a 0.77% contribution to economic growth over the long-term. Özcan and Arı (2014) stated that R&D expenditures affect the economic growth positively in their study for 15 OECD countries by using panel data analysis method between the years 1990-2011.

Dam and Yildiz (2016) conducted a study using panel data analysis for the period 2000-2012 period which demonstrated the impact of R&D and innovation on economic growth in the BRICS-TM countries (Brazil, Russia, India, China, South Africa, Turkey and Mexico). According to results of the panel data, the impact of R&D and innovation are statistically positively related to economic growth. According to Sezgin (2017), the contribution of R&D to economic growth for developing countries was 5.7%. In developed countries this rate was determined as 10.7%. Yıldırım and Kantarcı (2018) examined the contribution of R&D expenditures to economic growth in 15 developing countries using the panel data analysis method. Empirical results show there is no positive or negative effect.

As the extant literature shows, even if the country group is the same different results are obtained with different methods. This is due to the structural differences of the tests used in the selected period for selected countries. For example, some tests consider structural breaks in crisis periods while others do not consider this situation.

DATA SET AND ECONOMETRIC MODEL

Research and development (R&D) includes systematic work undertaken to increase knowledge and use it to develop new applications. R&D includes three activities: basic research, applied research, and experimental development. The main aggregate used for international comparisons is gross domestic expenditure on R&D. This consists of the total expenditure (*current and capital*) on R&D carried out by all resident companies, research institutes, universities, and government laboratories (OECD, 2016).

In this study, the relationship between the per capita income and R&D intensity (*ratio of R&D expenditures to GDP)* of the 19 OECD member countries with anual data for the 1996-2015 period was investigated with the latest panel data analysis techniques. The logarithms of the variables are taken and the model is included. The data was taken from the World Data Bank data distribution system. Table 1 shows the variables used in the study.

The estimated econometric model (1) in this framework is shown in equality.

$$\ln GDP_{it} = \alpha_i + \beta_{1i} \ln RD_{it} + \varepsilon_{it}$$

Table 1. Variables used in study

Variable Name	Acronym	Calculation	Database	Period
Per capita income	GDP	GDP / Population	World Bank	1996-2015
R&D Intensity	RD	R&D Expenditures / GNP	World Bank	1996-2015

(1) The variables in the model are respectively the national income per capita(GDP_{it}), R&D intensity (the share of R&D expenditure in national income(RD_{it})) and the error term (ε_{it}).

EMPIRICAL RESULTS

In selected OECD countries it is necessary to conduct some preliminary tests for the countries involved in the panel before starting the econometric analysis to determine the causality relationship between R&D expenditure and economic growth. Therefore, primarily the homogeneity test developed by Pesaran and Yamagata (2008) was used to test whether the slope coefficients are homogeneously distributed for the countries included in the panel.

According to the homogeneity test results developed by Pesaran and Yamagata (2008), the null hypothesis, which accepts the assumption of slope homogeneity, is rejected and the alternative hypothesis is accepted which accepts heterogeneity. Subsequently, cross-section dependency tests, which test the interdependence between countries within the scope of the research, were applied. It was decided whether the unit root test to be performed according to the result of this test will be the 1st Generation or the 2nd Generation unit root test. If there is no cross section dependency, it is appropriate to use the 1st Generation unit root tests and if there is cross section dependency, it is appropriate to use the 2nd Generation unit root tests. Peseran (2004) CD_{LM}, Breusch-Pagan CD_{LM1}, Peseran (2004) CD_{LM2} tests were used to test cross-sectional dependence in the study. CD_{LM1} and CD_{LM2} tests are performed when the time dimension is larger than the cross section size, and the CD_{LM} test results are taken into account when the time dimension is small.

In the cross section dependency tests, the hypotheses are as follows:

Table 2. Homogeneity tests

Regression Model		
$\ln GDP_{it} = \alpha_i + \beta_{1i} \ln RD_{it} + \varepsilon_{it}$		
Homogeneity Tests		
	Statistic	p-Value
$\tilde{\Delta}$	11.548	0.000***
$\tilde{\Delta}_{adj}$	13.156	0.000***

H_0: Does not have cross section dependency.
H_1: Has cross-section dependency.

In the present research, the CD_{LM1} and CD_{LM2} test results were taken into consideration due to the fact that time dimension was greater than the cross section size and the alternative hypothesis (H1) that cross-section dependence included in both variables is accepted. This result expresses that an effect that would occur in one of the panel-constituting countries will affect the others as well. Through the assumption of the cross section dependency, which is also assigned to the mutually interdependent among the panel-constituting countries, the stationarity of the variables will be investigated by 2nd Generation unit root tests. The CADF test within the Generation 2 unit root tests allows for stability testing both for the entire panel and also for each country in the panel separately. On the other hand, another privilege provided by the CADF test is that it can be used in both T> N and N> T. The hypothesis in the CADF test is as follows:

H_0: Serial has a unit root so it is not stationary.
H_1: Serial has no unit root so it is stationary.

The CADF test statistic is compared with the critical values given by Peseran (2007). If the CADF critical values are larger than the CADF statistics, the alternative hypothesis is accepted and it is assumed that the country has no unit root so it is stationary.

When the results of the CADF test are examined, while Austria and Belgium have a unit root for national income per capita, Austria, Belgium, Canada, France, Germany, Netherlands, Slovakia, Spain, Turkey and the UK have a unit root for R&D intensity. It is noteworthy that the majority of the countries possessing a unit root are EU member countries. Furthermore, according to the results of the CIPS test which is calculated by averaging the unit root test statistics of each cross section and gives the unit root test statistic for the panel (Pesaran, 2007), it was seen for the whole of the panel that the per capita income variable does not possess a unit root, while the R&D intensity does.

Table 3. Cross-section dependency tests

Constant Model	GDPPC		R&D	
	Statistic	p-Value	Statistic	p-Value
CD_{lm} (BP,1980)	835.665	0.00***	852.975	0.00***
CD_{lm} (Pesaran, 2004)	35.941	0.00***	36.877	0.00***
CD (Pesaran, 2004)	-1.858	0.08*	-2.160	0.01**
LM_{adj} (PUY, 2008)	17.607	0.00***	29474	0.00***

$$\Delta y_{i,t} = d_i + \delta_i y_{i,t-1} + \sum_{j=1}^{p_i} \lambda_{i,j} \Delta y_{i,t-j} + u_{i,t}$$

The number of lag (pi) is taken ‘ 1’ i n model.

Table 4. CADF Unit Root Test Results

Country	GDPPC				R&D			
	Constant		Constant and Trend		Constant		Constant and Trend	
	Lags	CADF stat	Lags	CADF stat	Lags	CADF stat	Lags	CADF stat
Austria	1	-4.390***	1	-4.621**	1	-3.289*	1	-4.333**
Belgium	1	-4.485***	1	-4.359**	1	-5.588***	1	-5.417***
Canada	1	-3.207*	1	-3.047	1	-3.792**	1	-3.716*
Czech Republic	1	-0.758	1	-0.242	1	-2.397	1	-2.719
Finland	1	-0.626	1	-0.306	1	-2.947	1	-3.002
France	1	-0.265	1	-0.410	1	-3.873**	1	-4.098**
Germany	1	-0.341	1	-0.453	1	-4.442***	1	-4.706**
Ireland	1	-1.241	1	-2.057	1	-1.117	1	-1.400
Italy	1	-1.374	1	-1.569	1	-0.688	1	-1.001
Japan	1	-1.418	1	-1.516	1	-1.330	1	-1.707
Israel	1	-2.677	1	-2.551	1	-2.392	1	-3.059
Netherlands	1	-2.606	1	-2.495	1	-4.996***	1	-4.725***
Poland	1	-2.254	1	-2.476	1	-2.872	1	-3.095
Portugal	1	-2.088	1	-2.383	1	-2.719	1	-3.247
Slovak Republic	1	-1.235	1	-1.413	1	-3.562**	1	-4.006**
Spain	1	-1.149	1	-1.326	1	-3.958**	1	-4.353**
Turkey	1	-2.003	1	-2.591	1	--3.199*	1	-4.513**
United States	1	-1.276	1	-1.219	1	-2.132	1	-3.163
United Kingdom	1	-1.340	1	-1.908	1	-2.922	1	-5.081***
Panel CIPS		-1.828		-1.944		-3.117***		-3.544***

Notes: Maximum lag length is considered as four and determined according to Schwarz Information Criteria. CADF test statistics values for constant model are as follows: -4.11 (%1), -3.36 (%5) and -2.97 (%10) (Pesaran 2007, table I(b), p:275) ; for constant and trend -4.67 (%1), -3.87 (%5) and -3.49 (%10) (Pesaran 2007, table I(c), p:276). Panel statistics critical values for constant model; -2.57 (%1), -2.33 (%5) and -2.21 (%10) (Pesaran 2007, table II(b), p:280) ; for constant and trend model -3.10 (%1), -2.86 (%5) and -2.73 (%10) (Pesaran 2007, table II(c), p:281). Panel statistics are average of CADF statistics. The figures which is ***, ** and * show 1%, 5% and 10% levels, respectively.

Based on the cross section dependency and homogeneity test findings, it is understood that cross section dependency and causality tests that consider heterogeneity should be used. For this reason, the causality relationship between the variables were investigated primarily with the Emirmahmutoglu and Kose (2011) causality tests, which can be used in situations where there is no cointegration long-term relationship between variables and allows cross section dependency and heterogeneity. It has been investigated by the Panel Causality Test of Dimitrescu and Hurlin (2012) based on Rolling Window Regression, which is one of the current causality tests, can be used in similar situations.

According to panel results of Emirmahmutoglu and Kose (2011) panel causality test, a causality from GDP per capita to R&D intensity was revealed for the countries including Austria, Germany, Ireland, Japan, Netherlands, Poland, Spain, and the USA. The results show that the R&D intensity increases together with the GDP per capita increase in these countries. Therefore, it is possible to state that the

Table 5. Emirmahmutoğlu and Köse (2011) panel causality test

Country	Lag	GDPPC≠>R&D		R&D ≠> GDPPC	
		Wald	p-Value	Wald	p-Value
Austria	3	6.706	0.081*	1.973	0.577
Belgium	1	0.760	0.383	0.997	0.317
Canada	1	1.833	0.175	0.045	0.831
Czech Republic	3	4.657	0.198	2.780	0.426
Finland	2	4.353	0.113	0.853	0.652
France	1	0.756	0.384	0.073	0.786
Germany	1	4.620	0.031**	0.029	0.863
Ireland	2	14.766	0.00***	4.673	0.096*
Italy	1	0.056	0.812	0.519	0.471
Japan	1	13.729	0.00***	0.284	0.594
Israel	3	3.531	0.316	7.752	0.051*
Netherlands	3	10.801	0.012**	0.194	0.978
Poland	1	5.874	0.015**	0.095	0.756
Portugal	1	1.784	0.409	1.933	0.380
Slovak Republic	2	0.424	0.808	0.179	0.914
Spain	2	10.183	0.017**	2.459	0.482
Turkey	3	0.009	0.922	3.139	0.076*
United States	1	17.503	0.00***	1.779	0.619
United Kingdom	3	0.211	0.645	0.111	0.738
Fisher		**104.649**	**0.00*****	**31.199**	**0.777**

increase rate in R&D spending in these countries is higher than the increase rate in per capita income. However, R&D spending shows there is causality to the per capita income at low level of significance (10%) in Ireland, Israel, and Turkey. For the entire panel, it was concluded that the raise in per capita income is the casual of increase in R&D intensity.

As mentioned earlier, the causality test developed by Dimitrescu and Hurlin (2012) is preferred to take into account the cross section dependency between panel-forming countries, when the cross section size is smaller than the time dimension and to be used on unbalanced panels. However, this test is being applied based on an analysis method known as a rolling window, which is different from the studies in the literature and is used to see during which periods the causality is concentrated. In this scope, this econometric method is being applied for the first time in the extant literature for this topic.

In the rolling windows method, a window is created by taking a certain number of observations and a test statistic is calculated for the observations included in this window. Then, each time leaving an observation from the beginning, adding a last observation, the window is moved along the time dimension, and so other test statistics are generated. Because of this working mechanism, this test is also called "Causality Test in Rolling Windows" (Gocer & Gerede, 2015).

Structural changes can be pre-defined and included in the estimation using a variety of techniques, such as sample splitting and use of dummy variables. But these techniques bring about the disadvantage of pre-test bias (Yang & Wu, 2015). To defeat the non-constancy parameter and to avoid pre-test bias, this study was proposed using the Dimitrescu and Hurlin (2012) The Panel Causality test was based on the modified bootstrap prediction for the first time in the extant literature which investigated the relationship between GDP and R&D intensity.

Two important reasons make it necessary to use the Rolling windows estimation. First, the rolling window agrees with the fact that the causal relationship between variables changes over time. Second, the rolling estimation can observe instability across different sub-samples due to the presence of structural changes (Yang & Wu, 2015). In this study, the first nine observations were used for the rolling windows regression from the beginning of the analysis period. Afterwards, the unit root test was performed for each data interval according to the same procedure and the causality test developed by Dimitrescu and Hurlin (2012) was applied to take the lag length as one.

According to the results of the Panel Causality Test by Dimitrescu and Hurlin (2012) based on Rolling Window Regression, there is causality towards R&D intensity from a per capita income for whole countries that constituted the panel in 2010. This results show an increase in national income in 2010 which causes raising R&D expenditures in national income. In 2011, it is understood there is a causality from R&D intensity to per capita income.

CONCLUSION

With the penetration of technology into every aspect of life, the prosperity of R&D and innovation-based development process has increased steadily. Essentially, academic studies dealing with the effects of technological novelty/change on economic processes are not unique. Many researchers and academics, beginning from Marx and Schumpeter, have studied technological change, production efficiency, profitability, capital accumulation, and most of the positive effects on national income and they have contributed to the literature (Akbey, 2014). In the vast majority of previous empirical studies, it has been concluded that there was a strong relationship between R&D and economic growth.

Table 6. Dimitrescu and Hurlin (2012) panel causality test based on rolling windows

Date	Lag	GDPPC≠>R&D		R&D ≠> GDPPC	
		W Stat	p-Value	W Stat	p-Value
2005	1	2.547	0.415	2.482	0.450
2006	1	2.377	0.253	1.449	0.947
2007	1	2.130	0.412	1.721	0.773
2008	1	2.673	0.127	1.400	0.897
2009	1	1.794	0.701	2.263	0.321
2010	1	2.910	0.066*	2.001	0.514
2011	1	2.358	0.264	2.950	0.059*
2012	1	2.455	0.214	1.132	0.632
2013	1	2.015	0.502	0.913	0.445
2014	1	1.918	0.586	0.656	0.272
2015	1	1.693	0.801	0.725	0.313

R&D activities could be accepted as the most important prerequisites for innovation, which have vital priorities in many aspects such as raising living standards, increasing productivity and ensuring economic growth. Therefore, the share of national income to be used in R&D activities is regarded as a sign of innovativeness culture. In this study, the causality relation between R&D expenditures and economic growth was investigated using the variables "per capita income and R&D intensity (share of R&D expenditures to national income)" for 19 OECD countries with data for the period 1996-2015.

First, the causality relation was investigated in the study by the panel causality test of Emirmahmutoğlu and Köse (2011), which is widely used in the extant literature. According to the results, there is a right causality from per capita income to R&D expenditures in Austria, Germany, Ireland, Japan, Netherlands, Poland, Spain, and USA and it is seen there is causality from R&D expenditures to the national income per capita at the low level of significance (10%) in Ireland, Israel and Turkey. However, it was reached to causality from per capita income to R&D expenditures for all of the panels. This subject shows that the increase in the per capita income leads to an increase in the share of the income to research and development activities expenditures.

In the final part of the study, R&D expenditures and economic growth relation are examined by Dimitrescu and Hurlin (2012) Panel Causality Test based on Rolling Window Regression method which is different from other studies in the literature. According to the results of Panel Causality Test of Dimitrescu and Hurlin (2012) based on Rolling Window Regression, there is a causality from economic growth to R&D expenditures for all of the countries that constitute the panel in 2010. This results are shown; an increases national income leads to the increases the R&D expenditures in gross domestic product for 2010. And in 2011 there is a casuality from R&D expenditures to economic growth.

As can be understood from this study, the concepts R&D and economic growth variables are mutually influenced by each other. However, in countries which possess high technology there is a causality from R&D to economic growth, whereas in countries which has lower technology relatively other countries there is causality from economic growth to R&D. This results can be interpreted as R&D expenditures have raises economic growth after a certain period of time.

REFERENCES

Aghion, P., Harmgart, H., & Weisshaar, N. (2010). *Fostering growth in CEE countries: a country-tailored approach to growth policy.* European Bank for Reconstruction and Development, Working Paper, No. 118/2010.

Aghion, P., & Howitt, P. (1990). *A model of growth through creative destruction (No. w3223).* National Bureau of Economic Research. doi:10.3386/w3223

Akbey, F. (2014). Ar-Ge, İnovasyon ve Kalkınma İlişkisine Yönelik Bir Literatür Taraması: Kuramsal Özet. *Maliye Dergisi, 166*, 1–16.

Altin, O., & Kaya A. (2009). Türkiye'de Ar-Ge Harcamalari Ve Ekonomik Büyüme Arasindaki Nedensel İlişkinin Analizi. *Ege Akademik Bakış*, 250-260.

Barro R.J. (1990). Goverment Spending in a Simple Model of Endogenous Growth. *Journal of Political Economy, 98*(5), 103-125.

Bassanini, A., & Scarpetta, S. (2001). *Does human capital matter for growth in OECD countries? Evidence from pooled mean-group estimates*. Academic Press.

Breusch, T. S., & Pagan, A. R. (1980). The Lagrange Multiplier Test and Its Applications to Model Specification in Econometrics. *The Review of Economic Studies*, *47*(1), 239–253. doi:10.2307/2297111

Dam, M. M., & Yıldız, B. (2016). BRICS-TM Ülkelerinde AR-GE ve İnovasyonun Ekonomik Büyüme Üzerine Etkisi: Ekonometrik Bir Analiz. *Akdeniz Üniversitesi İktisadi ve İdari Bilimler Fakültesi Dergisi*, (33), 220-236.

Dinopoulos, E., & Şener, F. (2003). New Directions in Schumpeterian Growth Theory. *Erişim Tarihi.*

Dumitrescu, E., & Hurlin, C. (2012). Testing for Granger Non-causality in Heterogeneous Panels. *Economic Modelling*, *29*(4), 1450–1460. doi:10.1016/j.econmod.2012.02.014

Eid, A. (2012). Higher education R&D and productivity growth: An empirical study on high-income OECD countries. *Education Economics*, *20*(1), 53–68. doi:10.1080/09645291003726855

Emirmahmutoğlu, F., & Köse, N. (2011). Testing for Granger Causality in Heterogeneous Mixed Panels. *Economic Modelling*, *28*(3), 870–876. doi:10.1016/j.econmod.2010.10.018

Erkiletlioğlu, H. (2013). *Dünyada ve Türkiye'de Ar-Ge Faaliyetleri. Türkiye İş Bankası İktisadi Araştırmalar Bölümü*. Retrieved on August 19, 2018, from: https://ekonomi. isbank. com.tr/UserFiles/pdf/ar_07_2013.pdf

Freeman, C., & Soete, L. (2003). *Yenilik İktisadı*. Ankara: Tübitak Yayını.

Göçer, İ., & Gerede, A. G. C. (2016). *Dış Ticaretin Enflasyon Üzerindeki Etkileri: Türkiye İçin Zaman İçinde Değişen Birim Kök ve Nedensellik Testler.i* Eskişehir Osmangazi Üniversitesi IIBF Dergisi.

Grossman, G. M., & Elhanan Helpman, E. (1989). *Quality Ladders in the Growth Theory*. NBER Working Paper No. 3099.

Gülmez, A., & Yardımcıoğlu, F. (2012). OECD Ülkelerinde Ar-Ge Harcamaları ve Ekonomik Büyüme İlişkisi: Panel Eşbütünleşme ve Panel Nedensellik Analizi (1990-2010). *Maliye Dergisi*, *163*(1), 335–353.

Guloglu, B., & Tekin, R. B. (2012). A panel causality analysis of the relationship among research and development, innovation, and economic growth in high-income OECD countries. *Eurasian Economic Review*, *2*(1), 32–47.

Landesmann, M., & Pfaffermayr, M. (1997). Technological competition and trade performance. *Applied Economics*, *29*(2), 179–196. doi:10.1080/000368497327254

Lichtenberg, F. R. (1992). *R&D investment and international productivity differences (No. w4161)*. National Bureau of Economic Research.

Lucas, R. E. Jr. (1988). On The Mechanics of Economic Development. *Journal of Monetary Economics*, *22*(1), 25–50. doi:10.1016/0304-3932(88)90168-7

Ming-Hsien, Y., & Chih-She, W.U. (2015). Revisit Export and GDP Nexus in China and Taiwan: A Rolling Window Granger Causality Test. *Theoretical & Applied Economics, 22*(3).

OECD. (2007). *Innovations and growth: Rational for an innovation strategy*. OECD.

OECD. (2016). *OECD Science, Technology and Innovation Outlook 2016*. Paris: OECD Publishing.

Özcan, B., & Arı, A. (2014). Araştırma-Geliştirme Harcamaları ve Ekonomik Büyüme İlişkisi: *Panel Veri Analizi. Maliye Dergisi*, *166*(1), 39–55.

Pesaran, M. H. (2004). *General Diagnostic Tests for Cross Section Dependence in Panels*. Cambridge Working Papers in Economics, No: 0435. Retrieved on June 2, 2018, from: http://www.econ.cam.ac.uk/dae/repec/cam/pdf/cwpe0435.pdf

Pesaran, M. H. (2007). A Simple Panel Unit Root Test in the Presence of Cross-Section Dependence. *Journal of Applied Econometrics*, *22*(2), 265–312. doi:10.1002/jae.951

Pesaran, M. H., & Yamagata, T. (2008). Testing Slope Homogeneity in Large Panels. *Journal of Econometrics*, *142*(1), 50–93. doi:10.1016/j.jeconom.2007.05.010

Pessoa, A. (2007). *Innovation and Economic Growth: What is the actual importance of R&D?* University of Porto, FEP Working Papers, no. 254.

Rebelo, S. T. (1991). Long-Run Policy Analysis and Long-Run Growth. *Journal of Political Economy*, *99*(3), 500–521. doi:10.1086/261764

Romer, P. M. (1986). Increasing Returns and Long-Run Growth. *Journal of Political Economy*, *94*(5), 1002–1037. doi:10.1086/261420

Romer, P.M. (1990). Endogenous Technical Change. *Journal of Political Economy*, *98*(5).

Sezgin, F. H. (2017, October). AR-GE Harcamalarının Büyüme ile İlişkisinin Analizi: Gelişmiş ve Gelişmekte Ülkeler Karşılaştırması. *3rd International Conference on Economic and Social Impacts of Globalization*, 69.

Ulku, H. (2004). R&D, innovation, and Economic Growth: An Empirical Analysis (No. 4-185). International Monetary Fund.

World Data Bank. (2018). Retrieved on July 8, 2018, from: http://databank.worldbank.org/data/source/world-development-indicators

Wu, Y., Zhou, L., & Li, J. X. (2007). Cointegration and causality between R&D expenditure and economic growth in China: 1953-2004. *International Conference on Public Administration*, 76.

Yıldırım, D. Ç., & Kantarcı, T. (2014). Araştırma Geliştirme Harcamaları ve Ekonomik Büyüme İlişkisi Üzerine Bir Panel Veri Analizi. *Anemon Muş Alparslan Üniversitesi Sosyal Bilimler Dergisi*, *6*(5), 661–670.

Zerenler, M., Türker, N., & Şahin, E. (2007). Küresel Teknoloji, Araştırma-Geliştirme (Ar-Ge) Ve Yenilik İlişkisi. *Selçuk Üniversitesi Sosyal Bilimler Enstitüsü Dergisi*, *1*(17), 653–667.

Chapter 7
The Application of Proof and Simultaneous Equations in Valuation:
The Valuation of Shares When a Firm Acquires Shares in Other Firms or From Its Own Shareholders

Graeme Paul Gould
University of Adelaide, Australia

ABSTRACT

The purpose of this chapter is to demonstrate how the notion of "proof" can be used to resolve issues of valuation in finance and how the method of simultaneous equations can be applied to determine the value of shares in two firms that hold an investment of shares in one another at the same time. The reader will be introduced to the notion of proof by arbitrage as it is was first pioneered in modern finance by Modigliani and Miller and then its application in providing guidance to practitioners of valuation will be explored.

INTRODUCTION

Valuation is a branch of finance concerned with the estimation of an asset's value. In particular, it is the intrinsic value of an asset defined as the value of an asset given a hypothetically complete understanding of the asset's investment characteristics that is of interest. Although models that are used in valuation are quantitative, valuation can be thought of as both an art and a science since inputs are often the result of subjective judgements. As a result, for "any particular investor, an estimate of the intrinsic value reflects his or her view of the "true" or "real" value of an asset" (Pinto, Henry, Robinson, & Stowe, 2010, p. 2). A basic challenge for the investor is therefore to reduce the level of subjectivity involved and replace it with an objective rigour that assists in making financial decisions. This chapter is concerned with how

DOI: 10.4018/978-1-5225-8458-2.ch007

mathematical reasoning can help reduce the level of subjectivity in valuation by providing a framework in which to analyse a problem and offer direction in which to solve it. In particular the role of proof in finance will be examined and how it can be utilised to resolve issues in valuation.

This chapter will begin with an introduction to the method of 'arbitrage' as a formal proof to propositions in finance and then explore its application for the purpose of establishing the equity value of a firm in instances where it acquires shares in another firm or from its own shareholders. Before examining the case in which two or more firms hold shares in each other at the same time the more common situation in which a firm acquires shares in another firm as a form of investment will be explored. Finally, the outcome of a share repurchase will be investigated and concluding remarks will be discussed.

BACKGROUND

"A postulate of sound investing is that an investor does not pay more than for an asset than it's worth" (Damodaran, 2002, p.1). The price paid should reflect the future cash flows that are expected to be generated from holding the asset. The source of these cash flows are the expected earnings stream that is generated from the operating assets employed by the firm for which the asset has a claim over and, as such when appraising the price, investors should consider these along with the obligations that a firm has to other security holders. A sound methodology in which to evaluate a firm and its securities is therefore required and a wide array of models and techniques are used in practice.

These range from the simple to the complex and each relies on a range of assumptions which lead to outcomes that may vary significantly. For example, the discounted cash flow model relies on estimates of expected future cash flows that are then discounted to a present value. A simple approach to model cash flows is to assume the current level of cash flows will occur in perpetuity, whereas a more complex approach will entail a detailed analyst in which individual items of cash flow together with their sources are considered and then aggregated on an annual basis. In other approaches, such as relative valuation models, estimates of future performance are not required and a value is determined from observation of the price of a comparable asset and its relationship with an accounting variable, such as earnings per share.

As such, the choice of model type and the underlying assumptions will determine the outcome and employing more than one model will lead to a disparity in values. Wishing to avoid paying a price for a security that is more than it is worth, practitioners may adopt techniques that minimise this variation and to provide a verification that the outcome is reasonable.

One approach is to employ a number of these methodologies to be used to act as a cross-check but ultimately the determination of value is a matter of judgement. A framework which enables the user to reconcile the outcome of one method against another and provide a justification for implementing a preferred method or set of assumptions is more useful to investors than comparing the outcomes from a set of disparate assumptions or models. As such this chapter is interested in how mathematics assists in this endeavour.

THE NOTION OF PROOF IN FINANCE

Proof is used by mathematicians to determine which statements of mathematics are true. In finance, proof of whether a firm's financing decisions can affect its market value can be established by way of appeal to 'arbitrage'. Arbitrage refers to the ability to exploit an investment opportunity without risk. The method of establishing proof by way of arbitrage was first introduced to modern finance by Modigliani and Miller in their seminal paper of 1958 (MM hereafter) to prove that the market value of any firm is independent of the capital structure (the ratio of debt to equity) that it employs (Proposition I).

In the 1950's corporate finance theory was undergoing a fundamental shift from being normative orientated to adopting the analytical methods and techniques traditional to economics (Smith, 1990). MM is considered to be the first attempt to convert the discipline of corporate finance from a case-study approach which had been taught in business schools for almost a century into a more systematic and scientific discipline (Chew, 2001; Barclay & Smith, 2001). Modigliani and Miller were awarded the Nobel Prize in Economic Sciences in 1985 and 1990 respectively and are famous for their propositions on capital structure and dividend policy of firms.

It is considered for capital markets to be in equilibrium the presence of riskless arbitrage opportunities cannot be possible. In equilibrium, it is expected that market prices be set so that supply equals demand for each security and that two securities with the same expected payoffs be priced identically (law of one price). For if this were not the case, then profit-seeking investors will buy the security at the lower price and sell the security at the higher price whilst maintaining their expected payoffs and making an arbitrage profit. By extension of logic, if the financing decisions of a firm affect its market value, there are arbitrage opportunities that can be exploited by investors and since such opportunities is inconsistent with equilibrium in a perfect capital market, one can conclude that the market value of a firm is unaffected by its financing decisions (Fama, 1978).

Therefore if it can be shown that mispricing of an asset can be exploited by profit-seeking investors a formal proof by way of arbitrage has been established. Although novel at the time, MM's approach to proof by arbitrage is now common to other areas of finance (Miller, 2001). For example, for a state preference, complete- markets proof (Hirshleifer, 1965, 1966); on the pricing of options (Black & Scholes, 1973); showing that individual wealth and consumption opportunities are unaffected by capital structures (Stiglitz, 1974); and on the structure of capital asset prices generally (Ross, 1976) as well as others.

Under the assumptions of no taxes or market imperfections, the MM proposition is formally stated as:

$$V_j = S_j + D_j = X_j / r_k, \text{ for any firm } j \text{ in class } k. \quad (1)$$

where

V_j = the total market value of the firm j
S_j = the market value of common shares of firm j
D_j = the market value of debt of firm j
X_j = the expected earnings stream from the assets owned by firm j before the deduction of interest on debt.
r_k = the average cost of capital of any firm in class k, of which firm j belongs.

Equation (1) states that the total market value of a firm is equal to the combined market value of its shares and debt which in turn is equal to the capitalisation of the expected earnings stream derived from its assets. MM alternatively express their proposition in terms of the firm's average cost of capital as:

$$X_j / (S_j + D_j) = X_j / V_j = r_k, \text{ for any firm } j \text{ in class } k. \quad (2)$$

Equation (2) states that '*the average cost of capital to any firm is completely independent of its capital structure and is equal to the capitalisation rate of a pure equity stream of its class*' (pp. 268-269). MM appeal to the notion of arbitrage to prove their proposition and argue that as long as the relations in (1) and (2) do not hold between any pair of firms of the same class, arbitrage will take place and restore the stated equalities. This will be achieved by investors buying and selling shares and bonds in such a way as to exchange one income stream for another that is identical in all respects but selling at a lower price.

By exploiting these arbitrage opportunities, the price of the overpriced shares will fall and that of the underpriced shares will rise until the discrepancy between their values is eliminated and equilibrium is re-established. By way of proof, MM consider two firms in the same class and enjoying the same expected earnings stream, X. Company 1 is financed entirely by equity while company 2 has some debt in its capital structure. Suppose the value of the levered firm, V_2, to be larger than that of the unlevered firm, V_1; and that an investor holds a fraction α of the total outstanding shares of company 2 and therefore the market of shares of company 2, S_2.

The return to the individual investor's holding in company 2, denoted by Y_2, will be a fraction α of the income available to shareholders of company 2, which is equal to the earnings from assets, X, less the interest charge on debt, $r_d D_2$, where r_d represents the required return to debtholders of company 2. Hence, MM identify the return to the individual investor as:

$$Y_2 = \alpha\,(X - r_d\,D_2) \tag{3}$$

Now consider the investor sold his αS_2 worth of company 2 shares and acquires an amount $\alpha(S_2 + D_2)$ of the shares of company 1. This will be achieved by utilising the amount αS_2 realised from the sale of their shares in company 2 and borrowing an additional amount αD_2 on credit. As such, the investor would secure themselves a fraction $\alpha(S_2 + D_2)/S_1$ of the shares in company 1 and therefore the earnings stream of company 1. The return to the investor from their new portfolio consisting of shares in company 1 and personal debt is given by:

$$Y_1 = \{[\alpha\,(S_2 + D_2)]/S_1\}\,X - r_d\,\alpha\,D_2 = \alpha\,(V_2/V_1)\,X - r_d\,\alpha\,D_2 \tag{4}$$

Comparing equations (3) with (4), as long as $V_2 > V_1$ we must have $Y_1 > Y_2$ since the investor is able to have a larger portion of the earnings stream, X, of company 1. Recognising this profitable opportunity, other shareholders of company 2 will sell their holdings, thereby depressing S_2 and hence V_2; and acquire shares of company 1, thereby raising S_1 and V_1. This will continue until in equilibrium, investors will be indifferent between holding shares in either company 1 or company 2. MM conclude therefore that levered companies cannot command a premium over unlevered companies because investors can replicate the capital structure of firms themselves by borrowing on their personal account.

To provide an illustration of MM's proposition and application of proof consider two companies, Omega and Pi, that are equivalent in all respects except that Omega is an all equity firm and that Pi has equal portions of shares and debt in its capital structure. Both firms are expected to earn \$3m in perpetuity from their assets and have an average cost of capital, r, of 15%. According to equation (1) the total market value of both firms, V, is 3/.15 = \$20m. Since Omega is an all equity firm, $S_{Omega} = V_{Omega}$ = \$20m, and since Pi has equal portions of debt and equity in its capital structure $S_{Pi} = D_{Pi}$ = \$10m.

Consider also that Pi pays a 10% interest charge on its debt so that the earnings stream of Pi after the deduction of interest, $X - r_d D_{Pi}$, is 3 – 0.1(10) = \$2m. Suppose also that an individual investor holds 5% of the shares in Pi so that the value of their wealth, αS_{Pi}, is equal to 5% (10) = \$0.5m, and according to equation (3) will enjoy an expected earnings stream, *Y*, equal to 5% [3 -10% (10)] = \$0.1m.

Now consider the investor wishes to sell their 5% stake in the shares of Pi and acquire a value of $\alpha (S_{Pi} + D_{Pi})$, equal to 5% (10 +10) = \$1m in shares of Omega. This can be achieved from the proceeds of selling their \$0.5m shareholding in Pi and then borrowing an amount, αD_{Pi}, equal to 5% (10) = \$0.5m on credit. From this arrangement the investor will acquire a fraction, α, equal to 1/ 20 = 5%, in the market value of shares and therefore earnings stream of Omega. The return to the investor from their new portfolio as measured by equation (4) will be:

$$Y_{Omega} = \{[5\% \ (10+10)]/\ 20\}3 - 10\% \ (5\%) \ 10 = 0.15 - 0.05 = \$0.1\text{m}$$

As such, the earnings stream from both portfolios is equivalent and therefore the investor will be indifferent between holding shares in Pi or selling their shares and borrowing on their personal account an equivalent amount and using the proceeds to acquire shares in Omega. Thus the market value of a levered and unlevered firm of the same class must be the same, that is, $V_{Omega} = V_{Pi}$.

Suppose instead that S_{Pi} = \$15m so that we have the condition $V_{Pi} > V_{Omega}$. Under these circumstances the investor will still have an earnings stream, $\alpha (X_{Pi} - r_d D_{Pi})$, according to equation (3) equal to 5% [3 – 10% (2)] = \$0.1m from their investment in Pi. If the investor sells their fraction of the shareholding, αS_{Pi}, for 5% (15) = \$0.75m and borrow an amount, αD_{Pi}, equal to 5% (10) = \$0.5m on personal account and acquire \$1.25m worth of shares in Omega they will acquire a fraction, α, equal to 1.25/ 20 = 6.25% of the market value of shares in Omega which will entitle them to a 6.25% fraction in the earnings stream of Omega, αX_{Omega}, equal to 6.25% (3) = \$0.1875m. The return of this portfolio to the investor after deducting the interest charge, $\alpha (r_d D_{Pi})$, as measured by equation (4) of will be:

$$Y_{Omega} = \{[5\% \ (15+10)]/\ 20\}3 - 10\% \ (5\%) \ 10 = \$0.1375\text{m}$$

Comparing the two earnings streams, the investor will profit 0.1375m – 0.10 = \$0.0375m from selling their shareholding in Pi. Other investors recognising this opportunity will replicate the strategy, thereby depressing the price of shares in Pi and raising the price of shares in Omega until $V_{Pi} = V_{Omega}$. Thus, by way of proof and using the logic of arbitrage it is established that the proposition of MM is correct. More importantly, it means that this technique can be applied in other situations that will be explored forthwith.

The Acquisition of Shares in Other Firms

It is not unusual for a firm to hold an investment of shares in another firm as an alternative to holding surplus cash in the bank or other form of financial securities and in some cases may be for the purpose of gaining an active or controlling interest in another firm. In such instances, the market value of a firm's shares should include a proportional interest in the market value of the shares in which it has a shareholding as well as the present value associated with the expected earnings stream derived from its own operating assets. Such investments are regarded as non-operating and should be reflected at their current market value (Pinto, Henry, Robinson, & Stowe, 2010, p. 194).

The value of such investments is easily ascertained if the shares are listed on a stock exchange but require a valuation using a suitable model if they are not. A particular problem arises when two or more firms hold shares in each other at the same time, referred to as a cross-shareholding. Such associations present a unique problem since the equity of each firm involved in a cross-shareholding derives value indirectly from the ownership interest that a firm has in itself and, therefore, following an approach that does not consider this will understate the true worth of shares for each firm involved. It is therefore critical that a correct methodology of valuation can be established in each situation for practitioners of financial markets to follow.

Before examining a cross-shareholding an approach to valuing investments in other firms will be considered and then its application to more complex situations will be explored. To begin, denote S_j as the market value of shares in firm *j*; Op_j as the market value of the earnings stream that firm *j* derives from its operating assets; and S_i as the market value of shares in firm *i*, of which firm *j* holds a fraction, α. Dispensing with the notion of debt the total value of a firm, *V*, will be equal to the total market value of its shares, *S*, which can be represented as follows:

$$V_j = S_j = Op_j + \alpha\, S_i \tag{5}$$

Equation (5) states that if company *j* has an investment interest in the shares of company *i*, then the market value of its shares, S_j, is equal to the market value derived from its operating assets, Op_j; plus a fraction, α, in the market value of shares in firm *i*, expressed as αS_i. Alternatively, S_j, can be represented as the capitalisation of its expected earnings stream, X_j, as follows:

$$S_j = X_j / r_j = (Xop_j + \alpha\, Xop_i)/ r_j \tag{6}$$

Where $X_j = Xop_j + \alpha Xop_i$, Xop_j represents the expected earnings stream derived from the operating assets of firm *j* and αXop_i represents the proportional interest held by firm *j* in the expected earnings stream derived from the operating assets of firm *i*. To illustrate, consider we have two firms, Alpha and Beta, whose expected earnings stream from operating assets and average cost of capital are as follows.

We can represent the market value of the earnings stream from Alpha's operations as $Op_{Alpha} = Xop_{Alpha} / r_{Alpha} = 3/0.1 = \$30$m, and for Beta, $Op_{Beta} = Xop_{Beta} / r_{Beta} = 4/0.2 = \$20$m. Suppose that Alpha also holds 30% of the shares in Beta so that its market value comprises not only the capitalisation of the expected earnings derived from its own operating assets but also a proportional share in the capitalised earnings stream of Beta. Consider Beta does not hold an ownership interest in another firm so that $S_{Beta} = Op_{Beta}$. What is the result of this investment on the value of shares in Alpha? Consistent with equation (5) the market value of shares in Alpha, S_{Alpha}, can be represented as the combination of its market value derived from its operations, Xop_{Alpha} / r_{Alpha}, plus a proportion, $\alpha = 30\%$, in the market value of shares in Beta, S_{Beta}, as follows:

Table 1.

	Alpha	Beta
Expected earnings stream from operating assets (*Xop*)	\$3m	\$4m
Average cost of capital (*r*)	0.10	0.20

$S_{Alpha} = Xop_{Alpha} / r_{Alpha} + \alpha S_{Beta} = 30 + 30\% \ (20) = \$36m$

Alternatively, from equation (6) this can be represented as the capitalised earnings stream of Alpha, where earnings are derived from its own operating assets, Xop_{Alpha}, plus a fraction, α, of the earnings stream earned from the assets of Beta, X_{Beta}, measured as:

$Xop_{Alpha} + \alpha X_{Beta} = \$3m + 30\% \ (4) = \$4.2m$

A question arises as to the appropriate measure of the average cost of capital for Alpha, r_{Alpha}, given its investment in firm i. If we assume a cost of capital appropriate for its own operating assets, $r = 10\%$, then market value of its shares, S_{Alpha}, becomes 4.2/ 0.1 = \$42m, which is inconsistent with the answer derived under equation (5) above. In a competitive capital market, such as discrepancy in share price should not exist since it can easily be exploited by investors buying at the lower price and selling at a higher price until any mispricing is eliminated.

More importantly from a methodology perspective, which of the two valuations is correct? Following the approach provided in Lonergan for valuing cross-shareholdings (2000, pp. 242-243), a verification can be established by way of a simple proof that can also be applied in more complex structures. Consider an investor who does not hold shares in either Alpha or Beta but has the means to acquire the entire shareholding of both firms. To this investor, the investment of shares held by one firm in the other is of no consequence since they will be the sole shareholder of both firms and as such, the combined value of Alpha and Beta for which this investor is willing to pay must be equal to the combined capitalised earnings stream that each firm generates from its own operating assets. This can be formally represented as follows:

$$S_{j+i} = (Xop_j / r_j) + (Xop_i / r_i) \tag{7}$$

Equation (7) states the combined value of two firms, j and i, where firm j has an ownership interest, α, in the shares of i, is the equivalent to acquiring both firms absent of the intercompany investment and is therefore equal the earnings stream derived from each firms' assets capitalised at their respective cost of capital. In turn this value must be equal to the cost that the investor is willing to pay for the acquisitions which can be represented as the cost of acquiring the entire shareholding in firm j and firm i absent of the shares held by firm j as follows:

$$S_{j+i} = S_j + (1 - \alpha) \, S_i \tag{8}$$

As such the equality between equations (7) and (8) must hold. Consistent with equation (7) the cost of acquiring Alpha and Beta is therefore equal to:

$S_{Alpha+Beta} = (Xop_{Alpha} / r_{Alpha}) + (Xop_{Beta} / r_{Beta}) = 3/.1 + 4/.2 = \$50m.$

Applying equation (8) and recognising $S_j = \$36m$ derived from above using equation (5) the investor will achieve the acquisition of both Alpha and Beta as follows:

$S_{Alpha + Beta} = S_{Alpha} + (1\text{-}30\%) \, S_{Beta} = 36 + 70\% \ (20) = \$50m$

If we substitute S_{Alpha} = \$42m derived from equation (6) into equation (8) the outcome will result in the value, $S_{Alpha + Beta}$, being equal to 42 + 70% (20) = \$56m, which is inconsistent with that derived under equation (7) and is therefore incorrect. If this were not the case then an arbitrage opportunity would present itself. For example, if we assume that an individual investor holds a 5% interest in the shares of Alpha they will be entitled to an expected earnings stream, $Xop_{Alpha} + \alpha X_{Beta}$, of 5% (4.2m) = \$0.21m.

Suppose the investor decides to sell their shareholding in Alpha, S_{Alpha}, measured as 5% (42) = \$2.1m, and replicate the investment portfolio of Alpha. This can be achieved by using a fraction of their proceeds, {30/ [30 +30% (20)]} 2.1= 83.33%, to acquire a value, 83.33% (2.1m) = \$1.75m, in the shares of a firm belonging to the same risk class as Alpha and use the remainder of the proceeds, {[30% (20)]/ [30 +30% (20)]} 2.1m =\$0.35m, to acquire shares in Beta. This will entitle the investor to an expected earnings stream, Y, consisting of the fraction, α, (1.75/ 30) = 5.833% of the expected earnings stream in a firm equivalent to that of Alpha, represented as 5.833% (3) = \$0.175m; and the fraction, α, (0.35/ 20) = 1.75% of the expected earnings stream of Beta, equal to 1.75% (4) = \$0.07m.

In total, the investor will be entitled to an expected earnings stream of 0.175 + 0.07 = \$0.245m from their portfolio compared to \$2.1m from holding onto their shares in Alpha and therefore will realise a net profit of \$0.035m. Other investors recognising the profitable opportunity will replicate the strategy until the arbitrage opportunity is eliminated and equilibrium is established. As such it can be confirmed that the market value of shares in Alpha must be equal to \$36m and not \$42m and from this we can infer the correct method is provided by equation (5) and not equation (6).

The error illustrated in this example can be attributed to the earnings stream received from the investment in Beta being matched with the cost of capital of Alpha which does not correctly reflect the risk class of Beta. As such, given the valuation established by proof it can be recognised that the appropriate cost of capital for a firm that has an investment interest in another should represent a weighted average of each firm's cost of capital attributable to the riskiness of their operations and in proportion to their market values. Formally, this can be represented as:

$$r_j = [Op_j / (S_j)]\, r'_j + [\alpha Op_i / (S_j)]\, r'_i \tag{9}$$

where r'_j and r'_i represent the cost of capital appropriate for the operating assets of firm j and firm i. The cost of capital from equation (9) for Alpha is therefore:

$$\mathrm{r}_{\mathrm{Alpha}} = [\mathrm{Op}_{\mathrm{Alpha}} / (\mathrm{S}_{\mathrm{Alpha}})]\, \mathrm{r'}_{\mathrm{Alpha}} + [\alpha \mathrm{S}_{\mathrm{Beta}} / (\mathrm{S}_{\mathrm{Alpha}})]\, \mathrm{r'}_{\mathrm{Beta}}$$

$$= [30 / (30 + 6)]\ 0.1 + [6 / (30 + 6)]\ 0.2 = 0.1167$$

The value, S_{Alpha}, according to equation (6) is therefore 4.2/ .1167 = \$36m; which is consistent with that derived under equation (5) and reconciles with the proof established from equations (7) and (8). This example demonstrates how the application of proof can be used to eliminate inconsistencies and establish a correct approach to valuation for firms which have an investment of shares in another, and provides a foundation for more complex inter-company investment structures such as in a cross-shareholding.

Cross-Shareholding and the Method of Simultaneous Equations

A cross-shareholding occurs when two or more firms hold an investment of shares in each other at the same time. Although the practice of cross-shareholding is best associated with the "main bank system" and "*keiretsu*" business structures of Japan since World War II, cross-shareholding is common in other countries, such as Germany and China, but is thought to be uncommon in the US and the UK. A notable cross-shareholding occurred in the automotive industry between Renault and Nissan during the period 1999-2001, in which Renault acquired a 36.8% (later increased to 44.4%) stake in Nissan and Nissan acquired a 15% stake in Renault (Nissan Press release 2009).

The structure of a cross-shareholding may be comparatively simple, involving only two firms such as in the Renault – Nissan case, but may be quite complex involving several firms. A two-firm cross shareholding is illustrated in Diagram A below. Both x and y have an investment of shares in each other, giving rise to each firm having an indirect ownership interest in itself. For example, if x holds a 30% interest in the shareholding of y which in turn holds a 30% interest in the shareholding of x, then both x and y will have an ownership interest of (30%) (30%) = 9% in itself.

The ownership interest arises from x and y having a direct investment in each other but in more complex structures the connection between them may be indirect as in the case of a cross-shareholding involving three firms illustrated in Diagram B. Here *x* has a direct investment in *y* but y's investment in *x* is indirect via its investment in *z* which in turn has an investment in *x*. Furthermore, this relation applies to each member of the cross-shareholding. Assuming that x holds a 30% interest in y and y in turn holds a 30% interest in z and z in turn holds a 30% interest in x, then each firm will have an interest of (30%) (30%)(30%) = 2.7% in itself.

From a valuation perspective the indirect interest that a firm has in itself is of interest because it effectively increases the market value of a share. To illustrate, consider now that firms Alpha and Beta are part of a cross-shareholding in which Beta has a 20% shareholding in Alpha at the same time that Alpha holds a 30% interest in the shareholding of Beta. As a result each firm as an ownership interest of (30%) (20%) = 6% in itself. Applying equation (5) we can represent the market value of shares in Alpha and Beta as follows:

Figure 1.

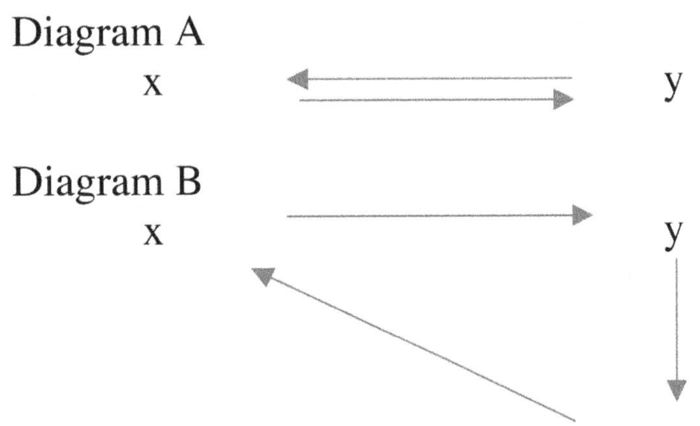

$S_{Alpha} = Op_{Alpha} + \alpha S_{Beta} = 30 + 30\% \ (20) = \$36m$

$S_{Beta} = Op_{Beta} + \alpha S_{Alpha} = 20 + 20\% \ (30) = \$26m$

Equivalently, from equation (6) we can represent the market value as the capitalisation of the expected earnings stream from the operating assets for each firm, including the proportional interest from each firm's investment. The expected earnings stream for each firm is:

$X_{Alpha} = Xop_{Alpha} + \alpha Xop_{Beta} = 3 + 30\% \ (4) = \$4.2m$

$X_{Beta} = Xop_{Beta} + \alpha Xop_{Alpha} = 4 + 20\% \ (3) = \$4.6m$

Recognising from equation (9) that the appropriate cost of capital for each firm represents a weighted average as follows:

$r_{Alpha} = [S_{Alpha} / (S_{Alpha} + \alpha S_{Beta})]r_{Alpha} + [\alpha S_{Beta} / (S_{Alpha} + \alpha S_{Beta})]r_{Beta}$

$= [30/ (30+6)] \ 10\% + [6/ (30 +6)] \ 20\% = 11.67\%$

$r_{Beta} = [S_{Beta} / (S_{Beta} + \alpha S_{Alpha})] \ r_{Beta} + [\alpha S_{Alpha} / (S_{Beta} + \alpha S_{Alpha})]r_{Alpha}$

$= [20/ (20 +6)] \ 20\% + [6/ (20+6) \ 10\% = 17.69\%$

Substituting the expected earnings stream and cost of capital derived from equation (9) into equation (6) we can represent the market value of shares for each firm as follows:

$S_{Alpha} = 4.2 / .11667 = \$36m$

$S_{Beta} = 4.6 / .1767 = \$26m$

Importantly, the value derived for each firm under either method yields a consistent outcome. As in the previous section, this solution can be verified by invoking the notion of an independent investor who is only prepared to pay \$50m to acquire both firms, equal to the capitalisation of the expected earnings stream from the operating assets of each firm determined from equation (7). If the above market values for Alpha and Beta are correct, then the cost of acquiring both firms according to equation (8) should reconcile with this value as follows:

$S_{Alpha+Beta} = (1- \alpha) \ S_{Alpha} + (1- \alpha) \ S_{Beta} = (1\text{- } 20\%) \ 36 + (1\text{-}30\%) \ 26 = \$47m$

This outcome demonstrates that although appropriate for valuing a firm with an investment of shares in another, this methodology is not appropriate under an arrangement where a cross-shareholding exists. If Alpha and Beta can be acquired for \$47m, then it would pay the investor to sell each firm individually for a total of \$50m and make a profit of \$3m in the process. In a competitive capital market such arbitrage opportunities should not exist in equilibrium. More importantly this example demonstrates that an alternative approach to valuing shares is needed in the case of a cross-shareholding (Lonergan, 2002, pp. 241-243). Let us begin by stating the market value of shares in each firm according to equation (5) as follows:

$$S_{Alpha} = Op_{Alpha} + \alpha S_{Beta} = 30 + 30\%\ S_{Beta} \tag{1}$$

$$S_{Beta} = Op_{Beta} + \alpha S_{Alpha} = 20 + 20\%\ S_{Alpha} \tag{2}$$

Since we have two equations and two unknowns, a solution can be achieved by method of simultaneous equations. Substituting (2) into (1):

$$S_{Alpha} = 30 + 30\%\ [20 + 20\%\ S_{Alpha}] \tag{1}$$

This simplifies to:

$$S_{Alpha} = 36 + 6\%\ S_{Alpha} \tag{1}$$

Re-arranging:

$$S_{Alpha} = 36 / 0.94 = \$38.3m \tag{1}$$

Substituting (1) into (2):

$$S_{Beta} = 20 + 20\%\ (38.3) = \$27.66m \tag{2}$$

The combined equity value of Alpha and Beta for which the outside investor will acquire according to equation (8) is as follows:

$$(1\text{- } 20\%)\ S_{Alpha} + (1 - 30\%)\ S_{Beta} = (80\%)\ 38.3 + (70\%)\ 27.66 = \$50m$$

Since the outcome of equation (8) agrees with that of equation (7), the methodology applied must be correct also and demonstrates the importance of proof to validate the application of a theoretical model. Without this verification investors may enter into share transactions at prices that do not represent their true value. This example demonstrates that while one methodology is appropriate in some cases it may not be appropriate in all circumstances and therefore validation is crucial.

The method of simultaneous equations can be extended to consider structures where more than two companies are involved in a cross-shareholding. For example, consider a structure involving three firms in which, as before Alpha owns a 30% interest in Beta but Beta has a 10% ownership interest in a third entity, Delta, which in turn has a 50% ownership interest in Delta. The ownership structure between the three firms is demonstrated by following diagram.

Assume also that Delta generates an expected earnings stream of $6m from its operating assets and has a cost of capital of 15% so that the value of its operations, Op_{Delta} is 6/ .15 =$40m. Representing

Figure 2.

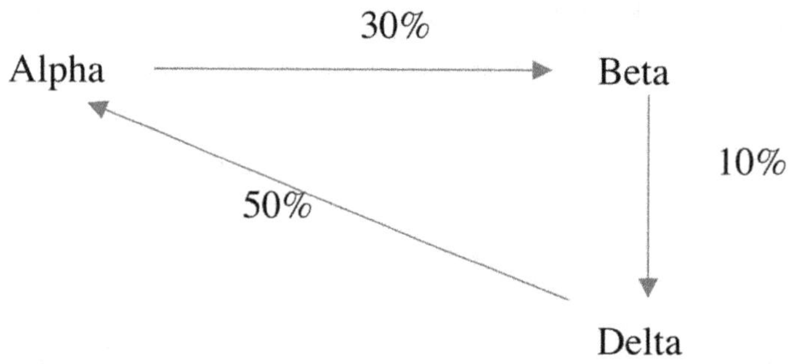

the market value of shares in each firm as an equation and solving for three unknowns by method of simultaneous equations as follows:

$$S_{Alpha} = 30 + 30\% \, S_{Beta} \quad (1)$$

$$S_{Beta} = 20 + 10\% \, S_{Delta} \quad (2)$$

$$S_{Delta} = 40 + 50\% \, S_{Beta} \quad (3)$$

Substituting (3) into (2)

$$S_{Beta} = 20 + 10\% \, [40 + 50\% \, S_{Alpha}] \quad (2)$$

This simplifies to:

$$S_{Beta} = 24 + 5\% \, S_{Alpha} \quad (2)$$

Substituting (2) in (1):

$$S_{Alpha} = 30 + 30\% \, [24 + 5\% \, S_{Alpha}] \quad (1)$$

This simplifies to:

$$S_{Alpha} = 37.2 + 1.5\% \, S_{Alpha} \quad (1)$$

Re-arranging:

$$S_{Alpha} = 37.2 / 0.985 = \$37.77\text{m} \quad (1)$$

Substituting (1) into (3):

$S_{Delta} = 40 + 50\% \, (37.77) = \$58.88m$ (3)

Substituting (3) into (2):

$S_{Beta} = 20 + 10\% \, (58.88) = \$25.89m$ (2)

To the outside investor who acquires all three firms, the combined value is equal to the combined capitalised expected earnings stream of each firm according to equation (7) is as follows:

$S_{(Alpha + Beta + Delta)} = 30 + 20 + 40 = \$90m$

Which is the equivalent value to the cost determined under equation (8) as follows:

$S_{(Alpha + Beta + Delta)} = (1\text{-}50\%) \, S_{Alpha} + (1\text{-} 30\%) \, S_{Beta} + (1\text{-}10\%) \, S_{Delta}$

$= 50\% \, (37.77) + 70\% \, (25.89) + 90\% \, (58.88) = \$90m$

Whilst the method of simultaneous equations can be applied to cross-shareholdings involving many companies rather than just two or three as demonstrated here it would involve a complex web of equations to solve. Fortunately a pattern emerges that will allow a simpler approach to be applied. A key element of cross-shareholding is the interest that each firm holds in itself. In this example we can recognise that each firm has an ownership interest in itself equal to the product of each firm's investment interest as 30% (10%) (50%) = 1.5%. As such, the market value of shares for a firm involved in a cross-shareholding can be expressed as a function of this self-interest as follows:

$S_j = (Op_j + \alpha \, Op_i)/\, (1\text{-} \alpha\alpha))$ (10)

where $\alpha\alpha$ signifies the fraction of shares held by firm j in itself and is the product of the fraction of shares held by firm j in firm i and firm i in firm j. Therefore, the value of shares in Alpha, Beta and Delta according to equation (10) can be expressed as follows:

$S_{Alpha} = [30 + 30\% \, (20) + 30\% \, (10\%) \, 40]/ \, (1 \text{-}.015) = \$37.77m$ (1)

$S_{Beta} = [20 + 10\% \, (40) + 10\% \, (50\%) \, 30)]/ \, (1 \text{-}.015) = \$25.89m$ (2)

$S_{Delta} = [40 + 50\% \, (30) + 50\% \, (30\%) \, 20]/ \, (1 \text{-}.015) = \$58.89m$ (3)

This example demonstrates that with the aid of a proof from which a correct outcome can be verified an alternative, more practical approach in which to solve more complex problems can be identified.

Share Repurchases

Share repurchases, otherwise known as share buy-backs, are a common method for firms to disburse cash to shareholders, first became a focus of attention in the literature due to the increasing repurchase activity in the USA, especially during the 1980s and 1990s (Ikenberry, Lakonishok, & Vermaelen, 1995; Grullon & Ikenberry, 2000). In a share repurchase transaction, a firm acquires shares from its own shareholders. Although share repurchases come in a variety of forms, on-market share repurchases are of particular interest since firms are not obligated to follow thru with their intentions and they acquire shares on the open market in the normal course of trading on the stock exchange at market price.

On-market share repurchases are commonly interpreted in the literature as a means for a firm to convey a signal to the market of the undervaluation of its shares (see, for example, Vermaelen, 1981; Comment & Jarrell, 1991; Ikenberry, Lakonishok, & Vermaelen, 1995; and Stephens & Weisbach, 1998). At the same time, management of firms have also expressed their desire to repurchase shares in order to increase the earnings per share of their firm (Brav, Graham, Harvey, & Michaely, 2005) or to offset its potential dilution (Bens, Nagar, Skinner, & Wong, 2003; Hribar, Jenkins, & Johnson, 2006) and to the extent that the market sets prices by mechanically capitalising reported earnings per share at industry-wide multiples, then stock prices will go up when EPS increase also.

As such, given the inherent flexibility of on-market share repurchases and the potential impact on share price, they are seen as providing firms with the ability of transferring wealth from participating shareholders to non-participating shareholders (Dann, 1992). It is therefore a question whether firms are motivated to conduct these transactions for the benefit of their shareholders and whether a shareholder is better off participating in a repurchase program or not.

This issue can be approached in a similar way to that provided in MM's capital structure irrelevance argument. To begin, assume that we have two firms, firm j and firm i, that belong to the same class and enjoy the same expected earnings stream from assets so that from equation (1) $X = X_j = X_i$; $r = rj = ri$; $V_j = X/r = V_i = X/r$ and so on. Also assume that both firms are debt free so that $S_j = V_j = S_i = V_i$; and that firm j executes a share repurchase program whereas firm i does not. Let Sbb_j represent the market value of firm j at the completion of the repurchase program and bb represent the fraction of shares that is acquired. The market value of shares in firm j at the completion of the program can be represented as follows:

$$Sbb_j = (1 - bb)\, S = (1 - bb)\, X/r \tag{11}$$

Equation (11) states that if firm j repurchases a fraction bb of its shares then the market value of its shares, Sbb_j, will be equal to the fraction, $1 - bb$, of the share value, S_j, and the capitalisation of the expected earnings stream, X, before the program. Although $Sbb_j < S_j$ can it be concluded that shareholders of firm j are better or worse off as a result of the repurchase and does it make a difference whether they participate or not? Suppose that an investor holds a fraction, α, of the shares in firm j so that their fraction of wealth prior to the repurchase program is αS_j and their expected earnings stream from equation (3) is, $Y = \alpha X_j$. If the investor decides not to participate in the program then their fraction of the market value in firm j becomes:

$$\alpha Sbb_j = [\alpha/(1 - bb)]\,(1 - bb)\, S = \alpha S \tag{12}$$

Alternatively, this can be expressed in terms of the capitalised earnings stream as:

$$\alpha Sbb_j = [\alpha/(1-bb)]\,(1-bb)\,X/r = \alpha X/r \tag{13}$$

Equations (12) and (13) recognise if the investor does not sell their shares to the firm during the repurchase program their fraction of the shareholding in firm j will increase from α to $\alpha/(1-bb)$, thereby maintaining their share of wealth, $\alpha Sbb_j = \alpha S$, and expected earnings stream αX. Now assume instead, that the investor sells their shareholding, αSj, in firm j and with the proceeds acquires a shareholding in firm i to the same value so that $\alpha Sj = \alpha Si = \alpha S$ which will therefore entitle them to the same expected earnings stream in firm i, αX. Under these conditions, the investor should be indifferent between participating in the repurchase program or not.

Suppose instead that $Sbb_j > (1-bb)\,S_j$. If the investor decides not to participate in the program then their personal wealth, αSbb_j, will increase whilst their fraction of the expected earnings stream, αX, will be maintained. If the investor instead sells their shareholding in firm j for consideration αSbb_j and acquires a fraction, α, of the shareholding in firm i equal to $\alpha Sbb_j/Si$ then the investor will acquire a greater fraction of the shareholding in firm i, since $\alpha Sbb_j/Si > \alpha\,Si$ and therefore enjoy a greater fraction of the earnings stream of firm i, $(\alpha Sbb_j/Si)\,X > \alpha X$.

Other investors recognising this arbitrage opportunity will also participate in the repurchase program thereby depressing the market value of shares in firm j, Sbb_j, and increasing the market value of shares in firm i, S_i. This will continue until market equilibrium is restored and investors will be indifferent between participating in the repurchase program or not. By application of proof it can be established that in equilibrium the market value of a firm's shares cannot be increased from a repurchase program.

To illustrate this point, consider that we have two companies, Omega and Pi, that are equivalent in all respects; each having the same expected earnings stream of \$3m, the same cost of capital, $r = 15\%$, and having no outstanding debt. According to equation (1) the market values, V and S, of both firms are equal to 3/.15 = \$20m. Consider an investor who holds fraction, α, equal to 5% of the shareholding in Omega. The personal wealth of the investor's shareholding in Omega, αS_{Omega}, is therefore equal to 5% (20) = \$1m and their fraction of the expected earnings stream, Y_{Omega}, is equal to 5% (3) = \$0.15m.

Now consider that Omega repurchases fraction, bb, which is equal to 10% of its outstanding shares at market value. The market value of shares in Omega at the completion of the program, Sbb_j, according to equation (11) will be equal to (1-10%) 20 = \$18m. If the investor decides not to sell their shares then their fraction of wealth in Omega, α, will be equal to 5% /(1-10%) = 5.556%, but their share of wealth in Omega, αSbb_{Omega}, remains unchanged and equal to 5.556% (18) = \$1m.

Similarly, their fraction of the expected earnings stream derived from the assets of Omega after the repurchase program, $\alpha\,(1-bb)\,X_{Omega}$, will be equal to 5.556% (1-10%) 3 = \$0.15m. If, on the other hand the investor sells their shares in Omega for \$1m and acquires a fraction, α, equal to 1/ 20 = 5%, of the shares in Pi they will be entitled to an expected earnings stream of 5% (3) = \$0.15m, equivalent to that before. Under these conditions the investor will be indifferent between selling or holding on to their shares.

Consider now instead that market value of shares, Sbb_{Omega}, is \$20m so that the condition, $Sbb_{Omega} > (1-bb)\,S_{Omega}$, now holds. If the investor does not sell their shares then their wealth increases from \$1m to 5.556% (20) = \$1.11m but their expected earnings stream of \$0.15m will be maintained. If on the other hand the investor sells their shareholding for \$1.11m and then acquires a fraction, α, equal to 1.11/20 = 5.556% of the shareholding in Pi they will be entitled to a fraction of the expected earnings stream generated from the assets of Pi equal to 5.556% (3) = \$0.167m.

As such, the investor will increase their expected earnings stream from \$0.15m to \$0.167m if they participate in the program and use the proceeds to buy shares in Pi. Other investors recognising the profitable opportunity will also participate in the repurchase program and buy shares in Pi, thereby decreasing the price of shares in Omega and increasing the price of shares in Pi until investors become indifferent between participating and not participating in the repurchase program. As such, it can be proved by the logic of arbitrage that shareholders are not worse off if they sell their shares in a repurchase program.

CONCLUSION

This chapter is concerned with how the logic of mathematics is applied in the finance discipline for the purpose of determining the value of an asset. Proof by method of arbitrage as it was first introduced to the discipline is examined and then applied in instances where a firm acquires the shares of another firm and from itself. A key theme to this chapter is formulating a framework in which a theory or proposition can be examined and verified assists in identifying a correct approach to valuation.

It is established with the aid of proof that the technique required to determine the value of a shareholding for a firm that has an investment of shares in another firm that is part of a cross-shareholding is different to that where a cross-shareholding is not involved. It is established that the value of shares for a firm involved in a cross-shareholding can be determined by method of simultaneous equations. Another finding of this chapter is that establishing a proof also assists in identifying whether share repurchases benefit shareholders and whether a shareholder is better off participating in a repurchase program or not.

REFERENCES

Barclay, M. J., & Smith, C. W. Jr. (2001). The capital structure puzzle: Another look at the evidence. In D. H. Chew (Ed.), *Corporate finance: Where theory meets practice* (3rd ed.; pp. 197–209). Singapore: McGraw-Hill.

Bens, D. A., Nagar, V., Skinner, D. J., & Wong, M. H. F. (2003). Employee stock options, EPS dilution, and stock repurchases. *Journal of Accounting and Economics*, *36*(1-3), 51–90. doi:10.1016/j.jacceco.2003.10.006

Black, F., & Scholes, M. (1973). The pricing of options and corporate liabilities. *Journal of Political Economy*, *81*(3), 637–654. doi:10.1086/260062

Brav, A., Graham, J., Harvey, C., & Michaely, R. (2005). Payout policy in the 21st century. *Journal of Financial Economics*, *77*(3), 483–527. doi:10.1016/j.jfineco.2004.07.004

Chew, D. H. (2001). Introduction: Financial innovation in the 1980s and 1990s. In D. H. Chew (Ed.), *Corporate finance: Where theory meets practice* (3rd ed.; pp. xiii–xxii). Singapore: McGraw-Hill.

Comment, R., & Jarrell, G. A. (1991). The relative signalling power of Dutch-Auctionand fixed-price self-tender offers and open-market share repurchases. *The Journal of Finance*, *46*(4), 1243–1271. doi:10.1111/j.1540-6261.1991.tb04617.x

Damodaran, A. (2002). *Investment valuation: Tools and techniques for determining the value of any asset* (2nd ed.). New York: John Wiley and Sons.

Dann, L. Y. (1992). Common stock repurchases: What do they really accomplish? In J. M. Stern & D. H. Chew (Eds.), *The revolution in corporate finance*. Cambridge, MA: Basil Blackwell.

Fama, E. F. (1978). The effects of a firm's investment and financing decisions on the welfare of its security holders. *The American Economic Review*, *68*, 272–284.

Grullon, G., & Ikenberry, D. L. (2000). What do we know about stock repurchases? *Journal of Applied Corporate Finance*, *13*(1), 31–51. doi:10.1111/j.1745-6622.2000.tb00040.x

Hirshleifer, J. (1965). Investment decisions under uncertainty: Choice theoretic approaches. *The Quarterly Journal of Economics*, *79*(4), 509–536. doi:10.2307/1880650

Hirshleifer, J. (1966). Investment decisions under uncertainty: Applications of the state preference approach. *The Quarterly Journal of Economics*, *80*(2), 611–617. doi:10.2307/1880692

Hribar, P., Jenkins, N. T., & Johnson, W. B. (2006). Stock repurchases as an earnings management device. *Journal of Accounting and Economics*, *41*(1-2), 3–27. doi:10.1016/j.jacceco.2005.10.002

Ikenberry, D., Lakonishok, J., & Vermaelen, T. (1995). Market underreaction to open market share repurchases. *Journal of Financial Economics*, *39*(2-3), 161–180. doi:10.1016/0304-405X(95)00826-Z

Lonergan, W. (2000). *The valuation of businesses, shares and other equity* (3rd ed.). Warriewood, NSW, Australia: Business and Professional Publishing.

Miller, M. H. (2001). The Modigliani-Miller propositions after thirty years. In D. H. Chew (Ed.), *Corporate finance: Where theory meets practice* (3rd ed.; pp. 184–196). Singapore: McGraw-Hill.

Modigliani, F., & Miller, M. H. (1958, June). The cost of capital, corporation finance, and the theory of investment. *The American Economic Review*, 261–297.

Pinto, J. E., Henry, E., Robinson, T. R., & Stowe, J. D. (2010). *Equity asset valuation* (2nd ed.). Hoboken, NJ: John Wiley & Sons.

Ross, S. (1976). Return, risk and arbitrage. In I. Friend & J. Bicksler (Eds.), *Risk and return in finance* (Vol. 1, pp. 189–219). Cambridge, MA: Ballinger.

Smith, C. W. Jr. (1990). The theory of corporate finance: A historical overview. In C. W. Smith Jr., (Ed.), *The modern theory of corporate finance* (2nd ed.; pp. 3–24). New York: McGraw-Hill.

Stephens, C. P., & Weisbach, M. S. (1998). Actual share reacquisitions in open-market repurchase programs. *The Journal of Finance*, *53*(1), 313–333. doi:10.1111/0022-1082.115194

Stiglitz, J. (1974, December). On the irrelevance of corporate financial policy. *The American Economic Review*, 851–866.

Vermaelen, T. (1981). Common stock repurchases and market signalling: An empirical study. *Journal of Financial Economics*, *9*(2), 139–183. doi:10.1016/0304-405X(81)90011-8

Chapter 8
Using of Fuzzy SWARA and Fuzzy ARAS Methods to Solve Supplier Selection Problem

Alptekin Ulutas
https://orcid.org/0000-0002-8130-1301
Cumhuriyet University, Turkey

ABSTRACT

As the performance of suppliers directly or indirectly affects the performance of the companies with which they engage, working with the most suitable supplier has become the key to success for companies. When solving the supplier selection problem, many different criteria involving qualitative and quantitative criteria are considered. Therefore, the supplier selection problem is considered an MCDM problem. These criteria can include uncertain and imprecise data. Additionally, the judgments of many managers are considered in supplier selection problems. Thus, in this chapter, a fuzzy group integrated model including Fuzzy SWARA (step-wise weight assessment ratio analysis) and Fuzzy ARAS (additive ratio assessment) is proposed to select the best supplier. This study contributes to the extant literature since these two methods were not used in the past to solve any problems together. The proposed model is applied to a Turkish textile company.

INTRODUCTION

In today's competitive environment, the aim of companies is to use all their resources efficiently and productively. The efficient use of these resources will enable companies to meet demands of their customers in a timely and complete manner. Companies must ensure their products or services are accepted by their customers to ensure increased profitability is achieved over time. Therefore, firms must strike a balance among certain elements such as speed, flexibility, quality, technological adaptability and so forth. It is not sufficient for the companies simply to assess only their processes in order to ensure the balance of these elements. Simultaneously, the firm's alliances (e.g., suppliers) must collaborate well to build a solid structure of the company.

DOI: 10.4018/978-1-5225-8458-2.ch008

Over time, supply chain alliances and agreements have become increasingly critical in order to reduce costs, to capture market opportunities, and to increase profitability. Efficient and strong supply chains are the creation of a network that includes suppliers, producers, warehouses, customers, and transportation links, among others. In a supply chain where relationships are not structured well, it is unlikely to be successful and productive in terms of information, product and material flow. Hence, cooperation and collaboration among the members of the supply chain are indispensable key factors.

Manufacturing companies in the supply chain environment have noticed in recent years that they will not be able to optimize performance factors such as low price, high quality products, on-time delivery and so forth by themselves. Therefore, outsourcing has become an inevitable activity for such organizations. Purchasing is one of the most important aspects of outsourcing and suppliers are a key factor. For most industries, approximately 70% of the cost of a product consists of the costs of raw materials and parts (Ghobadian et al.,1993). Therefore, the selection of the supplier, which is the key member of the supply chain in purchasing and outsourcing, is a very important decision.

As long as the companies are operating, they are faced with decision-making problems at every stage of operation and supplier selection is one of these major challenges. This is a well-known multi-criteria decision making (MCDM) problem where a number of different criteria including qualitative and quantitative criteria are considered. Generally, there are conflicting criteria in supplier selection problems. For example, when the delivery time of the material requested by the supplier is shortened, extra costs can be incurred in transportation costs. Conversely, when cheap transportation is selected, product quality may be reduced. As supplier selection has both critical value and conflicting criteria, detailed and advanced methods need to be used instead of using traditional methods to solve this problem.

Information related to real-world problems is not usually precisely known and this ambiguity makes the decision-making process much more complicated (Ghorabaee et al., 2016).

The supplier selection problem also includes uncertain and imprecise information due to human judgement. To overcome this uncertainty, there are many methods including fuzzy set theory (FST), grey theory, and rough set theory as proposed in the extant literature. FST was developed by Zadeh (1965) to handle imprecise and uncertain information. Additionally, the judgements of many managers are considered in supplier selection problems. Therefore, in this study, a fuzzy group integrated model including fuzzy SWARA (Step-wise Weight Assessment Ratio Analysis) and fuzzy ARAS (Additive Ratio Assessment) are used to solve the supplier selection problem.

Fuzzy SWARA and fuzzy ARAS methods are preferred since they are easy to use and provide quick data collection. These two methods (fuzzy SWARA and fuzzy ARAS) were not previously used to solve any problem simultaneously. Therefore, the contribution of this study to the extant literature is to develop a new fuzzy group integrated model to solve supplier selection problem. To identify criteria weights, fuzzy SWARA is used, while fuzzy ARAS is employed to assess suppliers' performance and to rank the suppliers respecting their performance.

BACKGROUND

Suppliers are one of the most crucial members of the supply chain as they can affect the performance of the entire supply chain. Problems caused by suppliers, such as delays in delivery, delivery of defective products, delivery of products with low-quality standards, and purchase of high-cost components or raw materials, adversely affect the performance of an entire supply chain, especially the manufacturer. The selection of the appropriate upstream suppliers is an important factor that will considerably decrease the cost of purchase, improve satisfaction of the downstream customer and increase competitiveness (Liao & Kao, 2010).The rising demands of customers push companies to concentrate on their core competencies and allow suppliers to achieve a larger portion of the work than before (Jain et al., 2018).This will force companies to work more in partnership with their suppliers, which will allow the supply chain to become more coordinated. Therefore, to achieve the desired performance results for the company located in such partnerships, it is essential to review the performance of the suppliers which are directly or indirectly involved in the company's processes and to work with the suppliers that are the most appropriate for corporate goals.

In addition, working with the right supplier has an important role in securing and consolidating competitive power in a competitive market. Supplier selection is a key decision that companies make to determine the best ones offering high-value materials and services as a result of their performance evaluations. Accordingly, the supplier selection is a vital process for the company to achieve business targets. Today, the selection of a supplier requires more than only scanning a number of price lists (Jain et al., 2018). Today, more criteria or attributes are considered for the selection of supplier which makes supplier selection much more complex. These criteria weights vary according to the needs, priorities, and objectives of the company. Even the identification of criteria can vary from sector to sector, so the identification of criteria is a significant step in the process.

The criteria used in supplier selection may include verbal or numerical data. Therefore, the MCDM approach is proposed for the solution of this problem by considering all these sub-issues in supplier selection. Criteria often contains both ambiguous and uncertain data, so to eliminate this uncertainty a number of methods have been proposed in the literature and FST is one of them. This theory is useful to handle uncertain data in any MCDM problem. There are many fuzzy integrated models proposed to handle uncertainty in selecting supplier in the extant literature (Ho et al., 2010; Chai et al., 2013; Ghorabaee et al., 2017).Unlike fuzzy models, other models (grey and rough) have also been used to solve supplier selection.

LITERATURE REVIEW

In recent years, many academic publications related to the supplier selection have been released as Table 1 shows.

As can be seen from Table 1, many publications attempted to solve supplier selection using MCDM methods. An MCDM model will also be used in this study. This study proposes an integrated fuzzy MCDM model including fuzzy SWARA and fuzzy ARAS to solve supplier selection challenges.

METHODOLOGY

Fuzzy Numbers

$\tilde{K} = \left(l_K, m_K, u_K\right)$ and $\tilde{L} = \left(l_L, m_L, u_L\right)$ are fuzzy numbers. Following equations 1-4 indicate thebasic operations on these numbers (Van Laarhoven & Pedrycz, 1983):

Table 1. The recent publications on the supplier selection

Authors	Methods	Year
Hashemi et al.	ANP (Analytic Network Process) and GRA (Grey Relational Analysis)	2015
You et al.	Interval 2-tuple linguistic VIKOR	2015
Kannan et al.	Fuzzy Axiomatic Design	2015
Rajesh and Ravi	GRA	2015
Chen et al.	Fuzzy AHP and Fuzzy TOPSIS	2016
Dweiri et al.	AHP	2016
Wu et al.	Extended VIKOR	2016
Sang and Liu	TODIM under Interval type-2 fuzzy sets	2016
Fahmi et al.	ELECTRE I with Hesitant Linguistic Term Set	2016
Ulutas et al.	Fuzzy AHP, Fuzzy COPRAS and Fuzzy Linear Programming	2016
Büyüközkan and Göçer	Intuitionistic Fuzzy AHP and Fuzzy Axiomatic Design	2017
Wan et al.	ANP and ELECTRE II under interval 2-tuple linguistic environment	2017
Qin et al.	Interval type-2 fuzzy TODIM	2017
Wang et al.	Building Information Modelling, Geographic Information System, AHP and GRA	2017
Ahmadi et al.	AHP and GRA	2017
Stević et al.	Rough DEMATEL and Rough EDAS	2017
Banaeian et al.	Fuzzy TOPSIS, Fuzzy VIKOR and Fuzzy GRA	2018
Wang and Tsai	Fuzzy AHP and Data Envelopment Analysis	2018
Jain et al.	Fuzzy AHP and TOPSIS	2018

$$\tilde{K} + \tilde{L} = (l_K + l_L, m_K + m_L, u_K + u_L) \quad (1)$$

$$\tilde{K} - \tilde{L} = (l_K - u_L, m_K - m_L, u_K - l_L) \quad (2)$$

$$\tilde{K} \times \tilde{L} = (l_K \times l_L, m_K \times m_L, u_K \times u_L) \quad (3)$$

$$\tilde{K} / \tilde{L} = (l_K / u_L, m_K / m_L, u_K / l_L) \quad (4)$$

Fuzzy SWARA

Fuzzy SWARA is utilised to identify the weights of supplier selection criteria and the required steps are shown below (Mavi et al., 2017):

Step 1: Determined criteria are listed in descending order in order of importance with respect to expert opinion.

Step 2: To obtain $\tilde{c}_j$ (the comparative importance of average value), j th criterion is compared with $j+1$ th criterion by using linguistic values indicated in Table 2. These linguistic values are converted into fuzzy values by using Table 2.

Step 3: Equation 5 is used to compute $\tilde{b}_j$ (coefficient).

$$\tilde{b}_j = \begin{cases} \tilde{1} & j=1 \\ \tilde{c}_j + \tilde{1} & j>1 \end{cases} \tag{5}$$

Step 4: By using equation 6, $\tilde{s}_j$ (recalculated weight) is determined.

$$\tilde{s}_j = \begin{cases} \tilde{1} & j=1 \\ \dfrac{\tilde{s}_{j-1}}{\tilde{b}_j} & j>1 \end{cases} \tag{6}$$

Step 5: The weight ($\tilde{w}_j$) of each criterion can be computed by utilising of equation 7. Weights of criteria are calculated for each decision maker separately. Then, weights of criteria are combined by using equation 9. As these weights will be used in the Fuzzy ARAS method, these are transferred into Fuzzy ARAS.

$$\tilde{w}_j = \frac{\tilde{s}_j}{\sum_{k=1}^{n} \tilde{s}_k} \tag{7}$$

Table 2. Linguistic and fuzzy values for ranking criteria

Linguistic Values	Fuzzy Values
Equally Significant	(1,1,1)
Moderately Less Significant	(2/3,1,3/2)
Less Significant	(2/5,1/2,2/3)
Very Less Significant	(2/7,1/3,2/5)
Much Less Significant	(2/9,1/4,2/7)

(Chang, 1996)

Fuzzy ARAS

Fuzzy ARAS is used to rank suppliers respecting their performances under selection criteria and the steps involved are as follows (Zamani et al., 2014):

Step 1: Decision makers assign the linguistic ratings indicated in Table 3 for the performance of suppliers under selection criteria. These linguistic ratings are converted into fuzzy ratings by using Table 3.

Step 2: The fuzzy ratings obtained from decision makers are aggregated to structure fuzzy decision matrix ($\tilde{X}$) (equation 10) by using equation 9.

$$\tilde{x}_{ij} = \left(l_{x_{ij}}, m_{x_{ij}}, u_{x_{ij}}\right); t = 1, 2, \ldots, T \tag{8}$$

$$l_{x_{ij}} = \frac{\sum_{t=1}^{T} l_{x_{ijt}}}{T}, m_{x_{ij}} = \frac{\sum_{t=1}^{T} m_{x_{ijt}}}{T}, u_{x_{ij}} = \frac{\sum_{t=1}^{T} u_{x_{ijt}}}{T} \tag{9}$$

$$\tilde{X} = \begin{bmatrix} \tilde{x}_{01} & \cdots & \tilde{x}_{0j} & \cdots & \tilde{x}_{0n} \\ \vdots & \ddots & \vdots & \ddots & \vdots \\ \tilde{x}_{i1} & \cdots & \tilde{x}_{ij} & \cdots & \tilde{x}_{in} \\ \vdots & \ddots & \vdots & \ddots & \vdots \\ \tilde{x}_{m1} & \cdots & \tilde{x}_{mj} & \cdots & \tilde{x}_{mn} \end{bmatrix} \tag{10}$$

Step 3: The fuzzy optimal value of each criterion ($\tilde{x}_{0j}$) is computed as following equations.

$$\tilde{x}_{0j} = \max_i \tilde{x}_{ij} \text{ (for beneficial criteria)} \tag{11}$$

Table 3. Linguistic and fuzzy ratings

Linguistic Ratings	Fuzzy Ratings
Very High	(0.7,0.85,1)
High	(0.5,0.65,0.8)
Medium	(0.4,0.5,0.6)
Low	(0.2,0.35,0.5)
Very Low	(0,0.15,0.30)

$$\tilde{x}_{0j} = \min_i \tilde{x}_{ij} \text{ (for non-beneficial criteria)} \tag{12}$$

Step 4: Each fuzzy element in the fuzzy decision matrix are normalised by using equations to structure the fuzzy normalized decision matrix.

$$\tilde{\bar{x}}_{ij} = \frac{\tilde{x}_{ij}}{\sum_{i=0}^{m} \tilde{x}_{ij}} \text{ (for beneficial criteria)} \tag{13}$$

$$\tilde{x}_{ij}^{*} = \frac{1}{\tilde{x}_{ij}}; \tilde{\bar{x}}_{ij} = \frac{\tilde{x}_{ij}^{*}}{\sum_{i=0}^{m} \tilde{x}_{ij}^{*}} \text{ (for non-beneficial criteria)} \tag{14}$$

Step 5: Fuzzy normalized values are multiplied by their fuzzy weights (determined in Fuzzy SWARA) to find fuzzy weighted normalized matrix.

$$\tilde{\hat{x}}_{ij} = \tilde{\bar{x}}_{ij} \times \tilde{w}_j \tag{15}$$

Step 6: The fuzzy optimality function of each alternative can be computed as:

$$\tilde{A}_i = \sum_{j=1}^{n} \tilde{\hat{x}}_{ij} \tag{16}$$

Step 7: The fuzzy optimality function ($\tilde{A}_i = \left(l_{A_i}, m_{A_i}, u_{A_i}\right)$) of each alternative can be defuzzified by using equation 17to obtain crisp optimality function (A_i).

$$A_i = \left(\frac{l_{A_i} + m_{A_i} + u_{A_i}}{3}\right) \tag{17}$$

Step 8: The utility function for each alternative can be calculated as:

$$U_i = \frac{A_i}{A_0} \tag{18}$$

In equation 18, A_0 is the optimality function of optimum value.

APPLICATION

The fuzzy group integrated model is applied to a Turkish textile company in which six suppliers of the company's are evaluated considering their performance with respect to eight criteria: cost (C), quality (Q), late delivery ratio (LDR), technological capability (TC), volume flexibility (VF), reputation (R), financial capability (FC), and communication capability (CC) which were identified by the company's managers. Cost and late delivery ratio are identified as non-beneficial criteria and the remainder are identified as beneficial criteria. Four managers of the company including purchasing manager, quality control manager, factory manager and human resource manager participated in this study. Fuzzy SWARA is utilized to obtain criteria weights. Data obtained from the purchasing manager is analysed by using Fuzzy SWARA. Table 4 presents the results of these data.

Criteria weights are calculated in the same manner for other managers. The calculated criteria weights according to all managers are aggregated by using equation 9. Table 5 indicates the aggregated criteria weights.

After calculation of criteria weights, Fuzzy ARAS is used to rank suppliers. Fuzzy ratings, which are obtained from managers, are aggregated by using equation 9 in the same time the fuzzy optimal value of each criterion is calculated by using equations 11-12. Table 6 presents the fuzzy decision matrix.

By using equations 13 and 14, the fuzzy decision matrix is normalized. Table 7 indicates the fuzzy normalized decision matrix.

After the normalization process, the fuzzy normalized values are multiplied by fuzzy criteria weights to obtain the fuzzy weighted normalized matrix. Table 8 shows the fuzzy weighted normalized matrix.

By using equations 16-18, the results of Fuzzy ARAS are obtained. Table 9 indicates the results of the proposed model.

According to Table 9, suppliers are listed as follows: Supplier 3, Supplier 5, Supplier 2, Supplier 4, Supplier 1 and Supplier 6.

Table 4. Fuzzy SWARA results of purchasing manager

Criteria	Ranking	Criteria	$\tilde{c}_j$	$\tilde{b}_j$	$\tilde{s}_j$	$\tilde{w}_j$
C	1	C		(1,1,1)	(1,1,1)	(0.341,0.411,0.498)
Q	2	Q	(0.667,1,1.5)	(1.667,2,2.5)	(0.4,0.5,0.6)	(0.137,0.205,0.299)
LDR	3	LDR	(0.4,0.5,0.667)	(1.4,1.5,1.667)	(0.24,0.333,0.429)	(0.082,0.137,0.213)
TC	6	FC	(0.286,0.333,0.4)	(1.286,1.333,1.4)	(0.171,0.25,0.334)	(0.058,0.103,0.166)
VF	7	R	(0.286,0.333,0.4)	(1.286,1.333,1.4)	(0.122,0.188,0.26)	(0.042,0.077,0.129)
R	5	TC	(0.667,1,1.5)	(1.667,2,2.5)	(0.049,0.094,0.156)	(0.017,0.039,0.078)
FC	4	VF	(0.667,1,1.5)	(1.667,2,2.5)	(0.02,0.047,0.094)	(0.007,0.019,0.047)
CC	8	CC	(0.667,1,1.5)	(1.667,2,2.5)	(0.008,0.024,0.056)	(0.003,0.01,0.028)

Table 5. Aggregated criteria weights

Criteria	$\tilde{w}_j$
C	(0.333,0.395,0.470)
Q	(0.198,0.254,0.327)
LDR	(0.116,0.161,0.224)
FC	(0.032,0.062,0.109)
R	(0.023,0.041,0.069)
TC	(0.040,0.064,0.100)
VF	(0.004,0.011,0.025)
CC	(0.006,0.014,0.031)

Table 6. Fuzzy decision matrix

Suppliers	Criteria			
	C	**LDR**	**Q**	**TC**
Optimal Value	(0.2,0.35,0.5)	(0.3,0.425,0.55)	(0.65,0.8,0.95)	(0.6,0.75,0.9)
S1	(0.4,0.5,0.6)	(0.45,0.575,0.7)	(0.6,0.75,0.9)	(0.6,0.75,0.9)
S2	(0.3,0.425,0.55)	(0.3,0.425,0.55)	(0.65,0.8,0.95)	(0.55,0.7,0.85)
S3	(0.25,0.388,0.525)	(0.3,0.425,0.55)	(0.55,0.7,0.85)	(0.6,0.75,0.9)
S4	(0.3,0.425,0.55)	(0.4,0.5,0.6)	(0.6,0.75,0.9)	(0.6,0.75,0.9)
S5	(0.2,0.35,0.5)	(0.45,0.575,0.7)	(0.5,0.65,0.8)	(0.45,0.575,0.7)
S6	(0.425,0.538,0.65)	(0.5,0.65,0.8)	(0.65,0.8,0.95)	(0.6,0.75,0.9)
	VF	**R**	**FC**	**CC**
Optimal Value	(0.6,0.75,0.9)	(0.7,0.85,1)	(0.6,0.75,0.9)	(0.5,0.65,0.8)
S1	(0.6,0.75,0.9)	(0.65,0.8,0.95)	(0.6,0.75,0.9)	(0.5,0.65,0.8)
S2	(0.5,0.65,0.8)	(0.4,0.5,0.6)	(0.425,0.538,0.65)	(0.45,0.575,0.7)
S3	(0.6,0.75,0.9)	(0.425,0.538,0.65)	(0.45,0.575,0.7)	(0.5,0.65,0.8)
S4	(0.6,0.75,0.9)	(0.5,0.65,0.8)	(0.5,0.65,0.8)	(0.475,0.613,0.75)
S5	(0.45,0.575,0.7)	(0.45,0.575,0.7)	(0.425,0.538,0.65)	(0.475,0.613,0.75)
S6	(0.4,0.5,0.6)	(0.7,0.85,1)	(0.6,0.75,0.9)	(0.45,0.575,0.7)

CONCLUSION

As supplier performance directly or indirectly affects the performance of the companies with which they work, choosing the most suitable supplier has become key to success for companies. Supplier selection is an MCDM challenge in which many different criteria are considered in the selection process. As these criteria can include uncertain and imprecise data, there are many methods including fuzzy set theory, grey theory and rough set theory, and so forth. proposed in the extant literature. Additionally, the judgements of many managers are considered in the supplier selection problems.

Table 7. Fuzzy normalized decision matrix

Suppliers	Criteria			
	C	LDR	Q	TC
Optimal Value	(0.078,0.169,0.392)	(0.096,0.167,0.297)	(0.103,0.152,0.226)	(0.099,0.149,0.225)
S1	(0.065,0.119,0.196)	(0.075,0.124,0.198)	(0.095,0.143,0.214)	(0.099,0.149,0.225)
S2	(0.071,0.140,0.261)	(0.096,0.167,0.297)	(0.103,0.152,0.226)	(0.091,0.139,0.213)
S3	(0.075,0.153,0.314)	(0.096,0.167,0.297)	(0.087,0.133,0.202)	(0.099,0.149,0.225)
S4	(0.071,0.140,0.261)	(0.088,0.142,0.223)	(0.095,0.143,0.214)	(0.099,0.149,0.225)
S5	(0.078,0.169,0.392)	(0.075,0.124,0.198)	(0.079,0.124,0.190)	(0.074,0.114,0.175)
S6	(0.060,0.110,0.185)	(0.066,0.109,0.178)	(0.103,0.152,0.226)	(0.099,0.149,0.225)
	VF	R	FC	CC
Optimal Value	(0.105,0.159,0.240)	(0.123,0.178,0.261)	(0.109,0.165,0.250)	(0.094,0.150,0.239)
S1	(0.105,0.159,0.240)	(0.114,0.168,0.248)	(0.109,0.165,0.250)	(0.094,0.150,0.239)
S2	(0.088,0.138,0.213)	(0.070,0.105,0.157)	(0.077,0.118,0.181)	(0.085,0.133,0.209)
S3	(0.105,0.159,0.240)	(0.075,0.113,0.170)	(0.082,0.126,0.194)	(0.094,0.150,0.239)
S4	(0.105,0.159,0.240)	(0.088,0.136,0.209)	(0.091,0.143,0.222)	(0.090,0.142,0.224)
S5	(0.079,0.122,0.187)	(0.079,0.121,0.183)	(0.077,0.118,0.181)	(0.090,0.142,0.224)
S6	(0.070,0.106,0.160)	(0.123,0.178,0.261)	(0.109,0.165,0.250)	(0.085,0.133,0.209)

Table 8. Fuzzy weighted normalized decision matrix

Suppliers	Criteria			
	C	LDR	Q	TC
Optimal Value	(0.026,0.067,0.184)	(0.011,0.027,0.067)	(0.020,0.039,0.074)	(0.004,0.010,0.023)
S1	(0.022,0.047,0.092)	(0.009,0.020,0.044)	(0.019,0.036,0.070)	(0.004,0.010,0.023)
S2	(0.024,0.055,0.123)	(0.011,0.027,0.067)	(0.020,0.039,0.074)	(0.004,0.009,0.021)
S3	(0.025,0.060,0.148)	(0.011,0.027,0.067)	(0.017,0.034,0.066)	(0.004,0.010,0.023)
S4	(0.024,0.055,0.123)	(0.010,0.023,0.050)	(0.019,0.036,0.070)	(0.004,0.010,0.023)
S5	(0.026,0.067,0.184)	(0.009,0.020,0.044)	(0.016,0.031,0.062)	(0.003,0.007,0.018)
S6	(0.020,0.043,0.087)	(0.008,0.018,0.040)	(0.020,0.039,0.074)	(0.004,0.010,0.023)
	VF	R	FC	CC
Optimal Value	(0.0004,0.002,0.006)	(0.003,0.007,0.018)	(0.003,0.010,0.027)	(0.001,0.002,0.007)
S1	(0.0004,0.002,0.006)	(0.003,0.007,0.017)	(0.003,0.010,0.027)	(0.001,0.002,0.007)
S2	(0.0004,0.002,0.005)	(0.002,0.004,0.011)	(0.002,0.007,0.020)	(0.001,0.002,0.006)
S3	(0.0004,0.002,0.006)	(0.002,0.005,0.012)	(0.003,0.008,0.021)	(0.001,0.002,0.007)
S4	(0.0004,0.002,0.006)	(0.002,0.006,0.014)	(0.003,0.009,0.024)	(0.001,0.002,0.007)
S5	(0.0003,0.001,0.005)	(0.002,0.005,0.013)	(0.002,0.007,0.020)	(0.001,0.002,0.007)
S6	(0.0003,0.001,0.004)	(0.003,0.007,0.018)	(0.003,0.010,0.027)	(0.001,0.002,0.006)

Table 9. The Results

Suppliers	Results			
	$\tilde{A}_i$	A_i	U_i	Ranking
Optimal Value	(0.0684,0.164,0.406)	0.213	1	-
S1	(0.0614,0.134,0.286)	0.160	0.751	5
S2	(0.0644,0.145,0.327)	0.179	0.840	3
S3	(0.0634,0.148,0.350)	0.187	0.878	1
S4	(0.0634,0.143,0.317)	0.174	0.817	4
S5	(0.0593,0.140,0.353)	0.184	0.864	2
S6	(0.0593,0.130,0.279)	0.156	0.732	6

Thus, in this study a fuzzy group integrated model including Fuzzy SWARA (Step-wise Weight Assessment Ratio Analysis) and Fuzzy ARAS (Additive Ratio Assessment) is proposed to select the best supplier. This study contributes to the extant literature since these two methods were not previously used to solve any problem together. The proposed model is applied to a Turkish textile company. Future research can extend this fuzzy integrated model to solve other decision making issues. Additionally, future research may use other fuzzy methods to solve supplier selection problem for other industries.

REFERENCES

Ahmadi, H. B., Petrudi, S. H. H., & Wang, X. (2017). Integrating sustainability into supplier selection with analytical hierarchy process and improved grey relational analysis: A case of telecom industry. *International Journal of Advanced Manufacturing Technology*, *90*(9-12), 2413–2427. doi:10.100700170-016-9518-z

Banaeian, N., Mobli, H., Fahimnia, B., Nielsen, I. E., & Omid, M. (2018). Green supplier selection using fuzzy group decision making methods: A case study from the agri-food industry. *Computers & Operations Research*, *89*, 337–347. doi:10.1016/j.cor.2016.02.015

Büyüközkan, G., & Göçer, F. (2017). Application of a new combined intuitionistic fuzzy MCDM approach based on axiomatic design methodology for the supplier selection problem. *Applied Soft Computing*, *52*, 1222–1238. doi:10.1016/j.asoc.2016.08.051

Chai, J., Liu, J. N., & Ngai, E. W. (2013). Application of decision-making techniques in supplier selection: A systematic review of literature. *Expert Systems with Applications*, *40*(10), 3872–3885. doi:10.1016/j.eswa.2012.12.040

Chang, D. Y. (1996). Applications of the extent analysis method on fuzzy AHP. *European Journal of Operational Research*, *95*(3), 649–655. doi:10.1016/0377-2217(95)00300-2

Chen, H. M. W., Chou, S. Y., Luu, Q. D., & Yu, T. H. K. (2016). A fuzzy MCDM approach for green supplier selection from the economic and environmental aspects. *Mathematical Problems in Engineering*.

Dweiri, F., Kumar, S., Khan, S. A., & Jain, V. (2016). Designing an integrated AHP based decision support system for supplier selection in automotive industry. *Expert Systems with Applications*, *62*, 273–283. doi:10.1016/j.eswa.2016.06.030

Fahmi, A., Kahraman, C., & Bilen, Ü. (2016). ELECTRE I method using hesitant linguistic term sets: An application to supplier selection. *International Journal of Computational Intelligence Systems*, *9*(1), 153–167. doi:10.1080/18756891.2016.1146532

Ghobadian, A., Stainer, A., & Kiss, T. (1993). A computerized vendor rating system. In *Proceedings of the first international symposium on logistics*. The University of Nottingham.

Ghorabaee, M. K., Amiri, M., Zavadskas, E. K., & Antucheviciene, J. (2017). Supplier evaluation and selection in fuzzy environments: A review of MADM approaches. *Economic research-. Ekonomska Istrazivanja*, *30*(1), 1073–1118. doi:10.1080/1331677X.2017.1314828

Ghorabaee, M. K., Zavadskas, E. K., Amiri, M., & Turskis, Z. (2016). Extended EDAS method for fuzzy multi-criteria decision-making: An application to supplier selection. *International Journal of Computers, Communications & Control*, *11*(3), 358–371. doi:10.15837/ijccc.2016.3.2557

Hashemi, S. H., Karimi, A., & Tavana, M. (2015). An integrated green supplier selection approach with analytic network process and improved Grey relational analysis. *International Journal of Production Economics*, *159*, 178–191. doi:10.1016/j.ijpe.2014.09.027

Ho, W., Xu, X., & Dey, P. K. (2010). Multi-criteria decision making approaches for supplier evaluation and selection: A literature review. *European Journal of Operational Research*, *202*(1), 16–24. doi:10.1016/j.ejor.2009.05.009

Jain, V., Sangaiah, A. K., Sakhuja, S., Thoduka, N., & Aggarwal, R. (2018). Supplier selection using fuzzy AHP and TOPSIS: A case study in the Indian automotive industry. *Neural Computing & Applications*, *29*(7), 555–564. doi:10.100700521-016-2533-z

Kannan, D., Govindan, K., & Rajendran, S. (2015). Fuzzy Axiomatic Design approach based green supplier selection: A case study from Singapore. *Journal of Cleaner Production*, *96*, 194–208. doi:10.1016/j.jclepro.2013.12.076

Liao, C. N., & Kao, H. P. (2010). Supplier selection model using Taguchi loss function, analytical hierarchy process and multi-choice goal programming. *Computers & Industrial Engineering*, *58*(4), 571–577. doi:10.1016/j.cie.2009.12.004

Mavi, R. K., Goh, M., & Zarbakhshnia, N. (2017). Sustainable third-party reverse logistic provider selection with fuzzy SWARA and fuzzy MOORA in plastic industry. *International Journal of Advanced Manufacturing Technology*, *91*(5-8), 2401–2418. doi:10.100700170-016-9880-x

Qin, J., Liu, X., & Pedrycz, W. (2017). An extended TODIM multi-criteria group decision making method for green supplier selection in interval type-2 fuzzy environment. *European Journal of Operational Research*, *258*(2), 626–638. doi:10.1016/j.ejor.2016.09.059

Rajesh, R., & Ravi, V. (2015). Supplier selection in resilient supply chains: A grey relational analysis approach. *Journal of Cleaner Production*, *86*, 343–359. doi:10.1016/j.jclepro.2014.08.054

Sang, X., & Liu, X. (2016). An interval type-2 fuzzy sets-based TODIM method and its application to green supplier selection. *The Journal of the Operational Research Society*, *67*(5), 722–734. doi:10.1057/jors.2015.86

Stević, Ž., Pamučar, D., Vasiljević, M., Stojić, G., & Korica, S. (2017). Novel integrated multi-criteria model for supplier selection: Case study construction company. *Symmetry*, *9*(11), 279. doi:10.3390ym9110279

Ulutas, A., Shukla, N., Kiridena, S., & Gibson, P. (2016). A utility-driven approach to supplier evaluation and selection: Empirical validation of an integrated solution framework. *International Journal of Production Research*, *54*(5), 1554–1567. doi:10.1080/00207543.2015.1098787

Van Laarhoven, P. J. M., & Pedrycz, W. (1983). A fuzzy extension of Saaty's priority theory. *Fuzzy Sets and Systems*, *11*(1-3), 229–241. doi:10.1016/S0165-0114(83)80082-7

Wan, S. P., Xu, G. L., & Dong, J. Y. (2017). Supplier selection using ANP and ELECTRE II in interval 2-tuple linguistic environment. *Information Sciences*, *385*, 19–38. doi:10.1016/j.ins.2016.12.032

Wang, T. C., & Tsai, S. Y. (2018). Solar panel supplier selection for the photovoltaic system design by using fuzzy multi-criteria decision making (MCDM) approaches. *Energies*, *11*(8), 1989. doi:10.3390/en11081989

Wang, T. K., Zhang, Q., Chong, H. Y., & Wang, X. (2017). Integrated supplier selection framework in a resilient construction supply chain: An approach via analytic hierarchy process (AHP) and grey relational analysis (GRA). *Sustainability*, *9*(2), 289. doi:10.3390u9020289

Wu, Y., Chen, K., Zeng, B., Xu, H., & Yang, Y. (2016). Supplier selection in nuclear power industry with extended VIKOR method under linguistic information. *Applied Soft Computing*, *48*, 444–457. doi:10.1016/j.asoc.2016.07.023

You, X. Y., You, J. X., Liu, H. C., & Zhen, L. (2015). Group multi-criteria supplier selection using an extended VIKOR method with interval 2-tuple linguistic information. *Expert Systems with Applications*, *42*(4), 1906–1916. doi:10.1016/j.eswa.2014.10.004

Zadeh, L. A. (1965). Fuzzy sets. *Information and Control*, *8*(3), 338–353. doi:10.1016/S0019-9958(65)90241-X

Zamani, M., Rabbani, A., Yazdani-Chamzini, A., & Turskis, Z. (2014). An integrated model for extending brand based on fuzzy ARAS and ANP methods. *Journal of Business Economics and Management*, *15*(3), 403–423. doi:10.3846/16111699.2014.923929

Chapter 9
The PSK Method for Solving Fully Intuitionistic Fuzzy Assignment Problems With Some Software Tools

P. Senthil Kumar
Navodaya Institute of Technology, India

ABSTRACT

The assignment problem (AP) is a particular case of a linear programming problem that deals with the allocation of various resources for various activities on a 1-to-1 basis. It does so in such a manner that the profit or sale involved in the process is maximum and cost or time is minimum. Generally, the profit/sale/cost/time is called the parameter of the AP and this is not a crisp number due to some uncontrollable factors. They can also involve uncertainty and hesitation. Therefore, to solve the AP under an intuitionistic fuzzy environment in this chapter, the author proposes the PSK (P. Senthil Kumar) method. Numerous theorems which are related to intuitionistic fuzzy assignment problem is proposed and is proved by PSK. By using the PSK method, the real-life related fully intuitionistic fuzzy assignment problems are solved. The proposed results are verified by both LINGO 17.0 and TORA software packages. In addition to verifying the efficiency and realism of the proposed method, the computer code based on LINGO 17.0 is presented. Results, discussion, comparative study, and the advantages of the PSK method are given. The chapter ends with the conclusion and future studies.

INTRODUCTION AND LITERATURE REVIEW

The Assignment Problem (AP) is used worldwide in solving real-world problems. An AP plays an important role in assigning drivers to trucks, trucks to routes, persons to jobs, operators to machines, or problems to research teams. The AP is a special case of the linear programming problem (LPP) in which the aim of the decision maker (DM) is to assign n number of jobs to n number of machines (persons) at a minimum cost/minimum time/maximum profit. To find the solution to APs in the extant literature,

DOI: 10.4018/978-1-5225-8458-2.ch009

Kuhn (1955) proposed the Hungarian method while Thompson (1981) discussed a recursive method for solving the AP. Avis and Devroye (1985) presented an analysis of a decomposition heuristic for the AP and Balinski (1986) developed a competitive (dual) simplex method. Paparrizos (1991) created an efficient exterior point simplex type algorithm for the AP. Barr et al. (1977) gave the alternating basis algorithm for assignment problems.

Ping et al. (1997) discussed a new algorithm for the AP which they also called an alternative to the Hungarian Method. Their assignment algorithm is based on a $2n*2n$ matrix in which operators performed on the matrix until an optimal solution is found. Lin and Wen (2004) proposed an efficient algorithm based on a labeling method for solving the linear fractional programming case. Singh (2012) discussed note on assignment algorithms with easy method of drawing lines to cover all zeros. However, in real-life situations, the parameter of the AP is in imprecise instead of fixed real numbers because the time/cost/profit for completing a job by a facility (machine/person) might vary due to different situations.

To deal quantitatively with imprecise information in making decisions, Zadeh (1965) introduced the fuzzy set theory and has applied it successfully in various fields. The use of fuzzy set theory increased dramatically in the field of optimization after the pioneering work by Bellman and Zadeh (1970). The fuzzy set deals with the degree of membership (belongingness) of an element in the set, but it does not consider the non-membership (non-belongingness) of an element in the set. In a fuzzy set, the membership value (level of acceptance or level of satisfaction) lies between 0 and 1, whereas in a crisp set the element belongs to the set that represents 1 and the element not in the set that represents 0.

Therefore, the applications of fuzzy set theory enabled many practitioners to solve assignment, transportation, and LPPs by using fuzzy representation for data. Kumar et al. (2009) proposed a method for solving fully fuzzy assignment problems by using triangular fuzzy numbers. Mohideen and Kumar (2010) presented a comparative study on transportation problem in fuzzy environments. Mukherjee and Basu (2010) presented an application of fuzzy ranking method for solving assignment problems with fuzzy costs. Kumar and Gupta (2012) investigated assignment and travelling salesman problems with cost coefficients as LR fuzzy parameters.

De and Yadav (2012) evolved a general approach for solving APs involving fuzzy costs coefficients. Thorani and Shankar (2013) completed the fuzzy AP with generalized fuzzy numbers. Palanivel et al. (2014) discussed fuzzy APs of trapezoidal membership functions within the sort of alpha optimal solution using a ranking principle. Kumar and Kaur (2011) presented methods for solving fully fuzzy transportation problems based on classical transportation methods. Ebrahimnejad et al. (2011) proposed bounded primal simplex algorithm for bounded linear programming with fuzzy cost coefficients. Nasseri and Ebrahimnejad (2011) conducted sensitivity analysis on LPPs with trapezoidal fuzzy variables. Pattnaik (2015) presented a decision making approach to fuzzy LLPs with post optimal analysis.

Kumar (2016a) developed a simple method for solving Type-2 and Type-4 fuzzy transportation problems. Gotmare and Khot (2016) presented a solution of a fuzzy assignment problem by using the Branch-and-Bound technique with the application of linguistic variables. Kumar and Shukla (2016) studied resource management through fuzzy APs in a cloud computing environment. Malini and Ananthanarayanan (2016) solved fuzzy APs using the ranking of generalized trapezoidal fuzzy numbers. Kumar (2016b, 2017b) developed the PSK method for solving type-1 and type-3 fuzzy transportation problems. *Fuzzy systems: Concepts, methodologies, tools, and applications* (Management Association, 2017) discuss the transportation problem under imprecise environments.

Muralidaran and Venkateswarlu (2017) developed a method for solving equally spread symmetric fuzzy APs using the Branch-and-Bound technique. Muruganandam and Hema (2017) developed an optimal solution to fuzzy APs using ones suffix and improved ones suffix method. Kumar (2018a) presented the search for an optimal solution to vague traffic problems using the PSK method. The *Handbook of Research on Investigations in Artificial Life Research and Development* (Habib, 2018) deals with the transportation problem under uncertain environment.

In the AP, the timing of each job to the workers is not known exactly. This may be due to lack of experience, interest, capacity, understanding, and so forth. In such situations, the DM cannot predict performing time exactly; hence, the DM may hesitate. The fuzzy set deals with the belongingness of an element in the set, but it does not consider the non-belongingness (rejections level) of an element in the set.

Therefore, to counter these uncertainties with hesitation, Atanassov (1983) proposed the intuitionistic fuzzy set (IFS) which is more reliable than the fuzzy set proposed by Zadeh (1965). The major advantage of intuitionistic fuzzy sets over fuzzy sets is that the IFS separates the degree of membership (belongingness) and the degree of non-membership (non belongingness) of an element in the set. With the help of IFS theory, DMs can decide about the degree of acceptance, the degree of non-acceptance and the degree of hesitation for some quantity. In APs, the DM can decide about the level of acceptance and non-acceptance for the assignment cost/profit/time. Therefore, the application of IFS theory becomes very popular in project schedules, medical diagnosis, transportation problems, image processing, modelling, planning, manufacturing, and decision making theory and network flow problems.

In the extant literature, due to the lack of uncertainty of the parameter of the fuzzy assignment problem, many practitioners and academics have solved the AP via the intuitionistic fuzzy version. Mukherjee and Basu (2012) presented the solution of a class of intuitionistic fuzzy APs by using similarity measures. Jose and Kuriakose (2013) discussed algorithms for solving an assignment model within an intuitionistic fuzzy context. Kumar and Hussain (2014a) developed a new algorithm for solving mixed intuitionistic fuzzy assignment problems (MIFAP). Kumar and Hussain (2014c) presented a method for finding an optimal solution of an AP under mixed intuitionistic fuzzy environments. Kumar and Bajaj (2014) evolved a solution of interval valued intuitionistic fuzzy APs using similarity measure and score functions. Kumar and Hussain (2014d) did a method for solving balanced intuitionistic fuzzy assignment problem (BIFAP). Dinagar and Thiripurasundari (2014) found a new method for finding the cost of fuzzy APs using a genetic algorithm of artificial intelligence. Prabakaran and Ganesan (2014) presented the fuzzy Hungarian method for solving intuitionistic fuzzy APs.

Srinivas and Ganesan (2015) proposed a method for solving intuitionistic fuzzy assignment problem using the Branch-and-Bound method. Kumar and Hussain (2016a) studied an algorithm for solving unbalanced intuitionistic fuzzy APs using triangular intuitionistic fuzzy number (TIFN). Nagoorgani et al. (2016) developed a labelling algorithm for solving intuitionistic fuzzy optimal APs. Kumar and Hussain (2016c) proposed a simple method for solving fully intuitionistic fuzzy real life APs. Pothiraj and Rajaram (2017) investigated intuitionistic fuzzy APs with replacement based on intuitionistic fuzzy aggregation. Jinshuai et al. (2017) proposed optimization of weapon-target assignment problem by intuitionistic fuzzy genetic algorithm. Kumar (2017a) introduced the algorithmic approach for solving allocation problems under intuitionistic fuzzy environment. Lone et al. (2017) presented an intuitionistic fuzzy AP via an application in agriculture.

The intuitionistic fuzzy travelling salesman problem is one of the special cases within the intuitionistic fuzzy AP. With the help of the Hungarian method, Prabakaran and Ganesan (2018) developed the fuzzy Hungarian method for solving intuitionistic fuzzy travelling salesman problems. Intuitionistic fuzzy assignment problem is one of the special case of the intuitionistic fuzzy transportation problem. Due to this, with the help of linear programming approach, Kumar (2018b) presented linear programming approach for solving balanced and unbalanced intuitionistic fuzzy transportation problems. Kumar (2018c) developed a simple and efficient algorithm for solving type-1 intuitionistic fuzzy solid transportation problems. Kumar (2018d) discussed a note on 'a new approach for solving intuitionistic fuzzy transportation problems of Type-2'. Kumar (2018e) proposed intuitionistic fuzzy zero point method for solving type-2 intuitionistic fuzzy transportation problem. Kumar (2018f) developed the PSK method for solving intuitionistic fuzzy solid transportation problems. Recently, Kumar (2018g, h; 2019a,b,c) developed new methods for solving solid transportation problems and solid APs in three different environments.

An AP is a special case of transportation problem where the sources are assignees and the destinations are tasks. Furthermore, every source has a supply of 1 (since each assignee is to be assigned to exactly one task) and every destination has a demand of 1 (since each task is to be performed by exactly one assignee). Also, the objective is to minimize the total cost or to maximize the total profit of allocation. Hence, every intuitionistic fuzzy assignment problem can be represented by intuitionistic fuzzy transportation problem if their supply of sources and demand of destinations should be exactly one.

Hussain and Kumar (2012a) discussed the transportation problem in an intuitionistic fuzzy environment. Gani and Abbas (2012) investigated a method for solving transportation problem in which all the parameters except transportation cost are represented by TIFN. Hussain and Kumar (2012b) proposed an algorithmic approach for solving intuitionistic fuzzy transportation problems. Hussain and Kumar (2012c) developed the transportation problem with the aid of triangular intuitionistic fuzzy numbers (IFNs). Hussain and Kumar (2013) proposed an optimal more-for-less solution of mixed constraints intuitionistic fuzzy transportation problems. Antony et al. (2014) discussed the transportation problem using triangular fuzzy number. They considered triangular fuzzy number as triangular intuitionistic fuzzy number by using only the format but they are always triangular fuzzy numbers.

Kumar and Hussain (2014b) introduced a systematic approach for solving mixed intuitionistic fuzzy transportation problems. Dinagar and Thiripurasundari (2014) solved transportation problem by taking all the parameters that are trapezoidal intuitionistic fuzzy numbers. Singh and Yadav (2014) developed an efficient approach for solving Type-1 intuitionistic fuzzy transportation problems where the supply and demand are TIFNs and the cost is a fixed crisp number. Aggarwal and Gupta (2014) have proposed an algorithm for solving intuitionistic fuzzy transportation problems with generalized trapezoidal intuitionistic fuzzy numbers via a new ranking method. Chakraborty et al. (2015) presented a new approach to solve multi-objective multi-choice multi-item Atanassov's intuitionistic fuzzy transportation problems using a chance operator.

Kumar and Hussain (2015) developed a method for solving unbalanced intuitionistic fuzzy transportation problems. Srinivas and Ganesan (2015) presented optimal solution for intuitionistic fuzzy transportation problem via Revised Distribution Method. Kumar and Hussain (2016b) proposed computationally simple approach for solving fully intuitionistic fuzzy real life transportation problems. Kumar (2019d,e,f, 2020) developed different methods to solve the various kinds of fuzzy and intuitionistic fuzzy optimization problems.

Ranking of alternatives in intuitionistic fuzzy environment plays a major role in decision making. Burillo et al. (1994) proposed a definition of intuitionistic fuzzy numbers and studied its properties. Various researchers such as Grzegorzewski (2003), Mitchell (2004), Nehi et al. (2005), Ban (2008), Nayagam et al. (2008), Guha and Chakraborty (2010), Deng Feng Li et al. (2010), Nehi (2010), Das and Guha (2013), Kumar and Kaur (2013), and Shabani and Jamkhaneh (2014) studied IFNs and analyzed their properties. Corresponding to every intuitionistic fuzzy number, Varghese and Kuriakose (2012) have proposed its crisp equivalent using its membership and non-membership function. Mahapatra and Roy (2009), Shaw and Roy (2012), Mahapatra and Roy (2013) have proposed some arithmetic operations on triangular intuitionistic fuzzy number.

In this chapter, we investigate a more realistic problem; namely, the fully intuitionistic fuzzy AP. Let $\tilde{c}_{ij}^{I}$ be the intuitionistic fuzzy time of assigning the jth job to the ith machine. We assume that one machine can be assigned exactly one job; in addition, each machine can do at most one job. The problem is to find an optimal assignment so the total intuitionistic fuzzy performing time of all jobs is a minimum. The objective function is considered also a fully intuitionistic fuzzy number.

The method is to rank the intuitionistic fuzzy objective values of the objective function by some ranking method for intuitionistic fuzzy numbers to find the best alternative. The ranking procedure of Varghese and Kuriakose (2012) is used to transform the fully intuitionistic fuzzy AP to a crisp one so the Hungarian method may be applied to solve the AP. The assigned (occupied) cells of the crisp AP that is obtained are as same as the assigned cells of the fully intuitionistic fuzzy assignment problem (FIFAP), but the time of assigned cells of an optimum FIFAT is intuitionistic fuzzy zeros. On the basis of this idea, the optimal solution (optimal assignment) of crisp AP and FIFAP both are the same but the optimum objective time of FIFAP is the sum of the costs of the assigned cells which corresponds to the original problem. Hence, the new method called the PSK method is proposed to find the optimal solution and optimum objective time in terms of TIFNs. We have proved a theorem, which states that every assignment obtained by PSK method to fully intuitionistic fuzzy assignment problem is optimal.

The remainder of this chapter is organized as follows. Section 2 provides some initial concepts and definitions of intuitionistic fuzzy numbers from the extant literature. Section 3 presents the ranking method of the triangular intuitionistic fuzzy number. Section 4 introduces the fully intuitionistic fuzzy assignment problem (FIFAP) and its mathematical model. The tabular representation of FIFAP and some important definitions are also presented in the same section. The proposed solution approach and some new and important theorems are presented in Section 5. To examine the effectiveness and the realism of the PSK method, four different numerical examples are presented in Section 6. The chapter concludes with Section 7.

PRELIMINARIES

Some preliminaries of fuzzy set theory and fuzzy number theory, especially the intuitionistic fuzzy sets and intuitionistic fuzzy numbers, are mentioned in this section.

Definition: Intuitionistic Fuzzy Set (Atanassov, 1999)

Let X be a finite universal set. An intuitionistic fuzzy set A in X is an object having the form

$$A = \left\{ \left\langle x, \mu_A\left(x\right), \vartheta_A\left(x\right) \right\rangle : x \in X \right\},$$

where the functions

$$\mu_A\left(x\right), \vartheta_A\left(x\right) : X \to \left[0,1\right]$$

define, respectively, the degree of membership and degree of non-membership of the element $x \in X$ to the set A, which is a subset of X, and for every element $x \in X$,

$$0 \leq \mu_A\left(x\right) + \vartheta_A\left(x\right) \leq 1.$$

Furthermore, we have

$$\pi_A\left(x\right) = 1 - \mu_A\left(x\right) - \vartheta_A\left(x\right)$$

called the intuitionistic fuzzy set index or hesitation margin of x in A. $\pi_A\left(x\right)$ is the degree of indeterminacy of $x \in X$ to the IFS A and $\pi_A\left(x\right) \in \left[0,1\right]$ i.e., $\pi_A\left(x\right) : X \to \left[0,1\right]$ and $0 \leq \pi_A\left(x\right) \leq 1$ for every $x \in X$. $\pi_A\left(x\right)$ expresses the lack of knowledge of whether x belongs to IFS A or not.

For example, let A be an intuitionistic fuzzy set with $\mu_A\left(x\right) = 0.5$ and

$$\vartheta_A\left(x\right) = 0.4 \Rightarrow \pi_A\left(x\right) = 1 - 0.5 - 0.4 = 0.1.$$

It can be interpreted as "the degree that the object x belongs to IFS A is 0.5, the degree that the object x does not belongs to IFS A is 0.4 and the degree of hesitancy is 0.1".

Definition: Intuitionistic Fuzzy Number

An Intuitionistic fuzzy subset A = {<x, $\mu_A(x)$, $\vartheta_A(x)$>: $x \in$ X} of the real line R is called an intuitionistic fuzzy number (IFN) if the following holds:

1. There exists $m \in$ R such that $\mu_A(m) = 1$ and $\vartheta_A(m) = 0$, (m is called the mean value of A).
2. μ_A is a continuous mapping from R to the closed interval [0,1] and $\forall x \in R$, the relation $0 \leq \mu_A\left(x\right) + \vartheta_A\left(x\right) \leq 1$ holds.

The membership and non – membership function of A is of the following form:

$$\mu_A(x) = \begin{cases} 0, & for -\infty < x \le m-\alpha \\ f_1(x), & for\, x \in [m-\alpha, m] \\ 1, & for\, x = m \\ h_1(x), & for\, x \in [m, m+\beta] \\ 0, & for\, m+\beta \le x < \infty \end{cases}$$

where $f_1(x)$ and $h_1(x)$ are strictly increasing and decreasing function in $[m-\alpha, m]$ and $[m, m+\beta]$. respectively.

$$\vartheta_A(x) = \begin{cases} 1, & for -\infty < x \le m-\alpha' \\ f_2(x), & for\, x \in [m-\alpha', m]; 0 \le f_1(x) + f_2(x) \le 1 \\ 0, & for\, x = m \\ h_2(x), & for\, x \in [m, m+\beta']; 0 \le h_1(x) + h_2(x) \le 1 \\ 1, & for\, m+\beta' \le x < \infty \end{cases}$$

Here m is the mean value of A. α, β are called left and right spreads of membership function $\mu_A(x)$, respectively. α', β' are represents left and right spreads of non-membership function $\vartheta_A(x)$, respectively. Symbolically, the intuitionistic fuzzy number $\tilde{A}^I$ is represented as $A_{IFN} = (m; \alpha, \beta; \alpha', \beta')$.

Definition: Triangular Fuzzy Number

A fuzzy number A is defined to be a triangular fuzzy number if its membership functions $\mu_A : R \to [0, 1]$ is equal to

$$\mu_A(x) = \begin{cases} \frac{x-a_1}{a_2-a_1} & if\, x \in [a_1, a_2] \\ \frac{a_3-x}{a_3-a_2} & if\, x \in [a_2, a_3] \\ 0 & otherwise \end{cases}$$

The graphical representation of a membership function $\mu_{\tilde{a}}(x) = (a_1, a_2, a_3)$ is given in Figure 1.

Definition: Triangular Intuitionistic Fuzzy Number

A Triangular Intuitionistic Fuzzy Number (A is an intuitionistic fuzzy set in R with the following membership function $\mu_A(x)$ and non-membership function $\vartheta_A(x)$):

Figure 1. Graphical representation of TFN

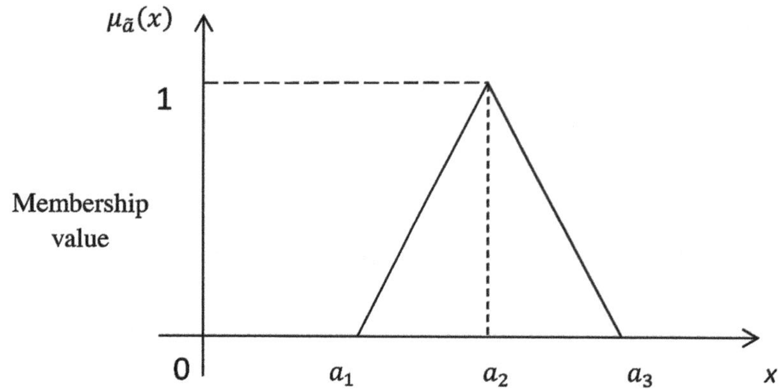

$$\mu_A(x)=\begin{cases}0, & for\ x<a_1\\ \dfrac{x-a_1}{a_2-a_1}, & for\ a_1\le x\le a_2\\ 1, & for\ x=a_2\\ \dfrac{a_3-x}{a_3-a_2}, & for\ a_2\le x\le a_3\\ 0, & for\ x>a_3\end{cases}$$

$$\vartheta_A(x)=\begin{cases}1, & for\ x<a_1^{'}\\ \dfrac{a_2-x}{a_2-a_1^{'}}, & for\ a_1^{'}\le x\le a_2\\ 0, & for\ x=a_2\\ \dfrac{x-a_2}{a_3^{'}-a_2}, & for\ a_2\le x\le a_3^{'}\\ 1, & for\ x>a_3^{'}\end{cases}$$

where $a_1^{'}\le a_1\le a_2\le a_3\le a_3^{'}$ and $\mu_A(x),\vartheta_A(x)\le 0.5$ for $\mu_A(x)=\vartheta_A(x)\ \forall x\in R$. This TIFN is denoted by $\tilde{A}^I=(a_1,a_2,a_3)(a_1^{'},a_2,a_3^{'})$.

The membership and non-membership functions of TIFN are shown in Figure 2.

Particular Cases

Let $\tilde{A}^I=(a_1,a_2,a_3)(a_1^{'},a_2,a_3^{'})$ be a TIFN. Then the following cases arise

Case 1: If $a_1^{'}=a_1$, $a_3^{'}=a_3$ then $\tilde{A}^I$ represents a Triangular Fuzzy Number (TFN).

Figure 2. Membership and non-membership functions for a TIFN.

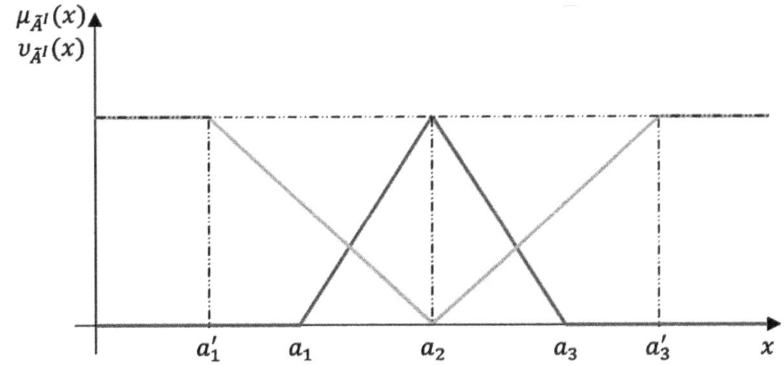

It is denoted by $\tilde{A} = (a_1, a_2, a_3)$.

Case 2: If $a_1' = a_1 = a_2 = a_3 = a_3' = m$ then $\tilde{A}^I$ represent a real number m.

Definition: Arithmetic Operations on TIFN

Let $\tilde{A}^I = (a_1, a_2, a_3)(a_1', a_2, a_3')$ and $\tilde{B}^I = (b_1, b_2, b_3)(b_1', b_2, b_3')$ be any two TIFNs then the arithmetic operations are as follows:

Addition:

$$\tilde{A}^I \oplus \tilde{B}^I = (a_1 + b_1, a_2 + b_2, a_3 + b_3)(a_1' + b_1', a_2 + b_2, a_3' + b_3')$$

Multiplication:

$$\tilde{A}^I \otimes \tilde{B}^I = (a_1(\tilde{B}^I), a_2(\tilde{B}^I), a_3(\tilde{B}^I))(a_1'(\tilde{B}^I), a_2(\tilde{B}^I), a_3'(\tilde{B}^I))$$

if $(\tilde{A}^I), (\tilde{B}^I) \geq 0$

Subtraction:

$$\tilde{A}^I \ominus \tilde{B}^I = (a_1 - b_3, a_2 - b_2, a_3 - b_1)(a_1' - b_3', a_2 - b_2, a_3' - b_1')$$

COMPARISON OF TIFN

This section presents some basic and important definitions and centroid (ranking) of TIFNs.

Definition

Let $\tilde{A}^I = (a_1, a_2, a_3)(a_1^{'}, a_2, a_3^{'})$ and $\tilde{B}^I = (b_1, b_2, b_3)(b_1^{'}, b_2, b_3^{'})$ be two TIFNs. Then the set of TIFNs is defined as follows:

1. $\Re(\tilde{A}^I) > \Re(\tilde{B}^I)$ iff $\tilde{A}^I \succ \tilde{B}^I$
2. $\Re(\tilde{A}^I) < \Re(\tilde{B}^I)$ iff $\tilde{A}^I \prec \tilde{B}^I$
3. $\Re(\tilde{A}^I) = \Re(\tilde{B}^I)$ iff $\tilde{A}^I \approx \tilde{B}^I$

where,

$$\Re(\tilde{A}^I) = \frac{1}{3}\left[\frac{(a_3^{'} - a_1^{'})(a_2 - 2a_3^{'} - 2a_1^{'}) + (a_3 - a_1)(a_1 + a_2 + a_3) + 3(a_3^{'2} - a_1^{'2})}{a_3^{'} - a_1^{'} + a_3 - a_1}\right]$$

$$\Re(\tilde{B}^I) = \frac{1}{3}\left[\frac{(b_3^{'} - b_1^{'})(b_2 - 2b_3^{'} - 2b_1^{'}) + (b_3 - b_1)(b_1 + b_2 + b_3) + 3(b_3^{'2} - b_1^{'2})}{b_3^{'} - b_1^{'} + b_3 - b_1}\right]$$

Whenever the above formula does not provide finite value, then we can make use of the following formula. The score function for the membership function $\mu_A(x)$ is denoted by $S(\mu_A(x))$ and is defined by $S(\mu_A(x)) = \frac{a_1 + 2a_2 + a_3}{4}$. The score function for the non-membership function $\vartheta_A(x)$ is denoted by $S(\vartheta_A(x))$ and is defined by $S(\vartheta_A(x)) = \frac{a_1^{'} + 2a_2 + a_3^{'}}{4}$. The accuracy function of $\tilde{A}^I$ is denoted by $f(\tilde{A}^I)$ and is defined by

$$f(\tilde{A}^I) = \frac{S(\mu_A(x)) + S(\vartheta_A(x))}{2} = \frac{(a_1 + 2a_2 + a_3) + (a_1^{'} + 2a_2 + a_3^{'})}{8}$$

From the accuracy function, we have

1. $f(\tilde{A}^I) > f(\tilde{B}^I)$ iff $\tilde{A}^I \succ \tilde{B}^I$
2. $f(\tilde{A}^I) < f(\tilde{B}^I)$ iff $\tilde{A}^I \prec \tilde{B}^I$
3. $f(\tilde{A}^I) = f(\tilde{B}^I)$ iff $\tilde{A}^I \approx \tilde{B}^I$

Definition

The ordering $\succeq$ and $\preccurlyeq$ between any two TIFNs $\tilde{A}^I$ and $\tilde{B}^I$ are defined as follows:

1. $\tilde{A}^I \succeq \tilde{B}^I$ iff $\tilde{A}^I \succ \tilde{B}^I$ or $\tilde{A}^I \approx \tilde{B}^I$
2. $\tilde{A}^I \preceq \tilde{B}^I$ iff $\tilde{A}^I \prec \tilde{B}^I$ or $\tilde{A}^I \approx \tilde{B}^I$

Definition

Let $\{\tilde{A}_i^I, i = 1,2,\ldots,n\}$ be a set of TIFNs. If $\Re(\tilde{A}_k^I) \leq \Re(\tilde{A}_i^I)$ for all *i*, then the TIFN $\tilde{A}_k^I$ is the minimum of $\{\tilde{A}_i^I, i = 1,2,\ldots,n\}$.

Definition

Let $\{\tilde{A}_i^I, i = 1,2,\ldots,n\}$ be a set of TIFNs. If $\Re(\tilde{A}_t^I) \geq \Re(\tilde{A}_i^I)$ for all *i*, then the TIFN $\tilde{A}_t^I$ is the maximum of $\{\tilde{A}_i^I, i = 1,2,\ldots,n\}$.

FULLY INTUITIONISTIC FUZZY ASSIGNMENT PROBLEM AND ITS MATHEMATICAL FORMULATION

This section shows that the mathematical formulation of the fully intuitionistic fuzzy assignment problem. This section also shows that the tabular representation of the FIFAP, and its related definitions. Consider the situation of assigning *n* machines to *n* jobs (or *n* jobs to *n* machines) and each machine is capable of doing any job at different costs. Let c_{ij} be the cost of assigning the jth job to the ith machine. Let x_{ij} be the decision variable that denotes the assignment of the machine *i* to the job *j*. The objective is to minimize the total cost of assigning all the jobs to the available machines (one job per machine) at the least total cost. This situation is known as balanced assignment problem (BAP).

Mathematically the AP can be stated as:

(Model 1) (Problem P) Minimize $Z = \sum_{i=1}^{n}\sum_{j=1}^{n} c_{ij} x_{ij}$ (objective function)

subject to the constraints:

$$\sum_{j=1}^{n} x_{ij} = 1, for\ i = 1,2,\ldots,n \text{ (Machine or row restriction)} \quad (1)$$

$$\sum_{i=1}^{n} x_{ij} = 1, for\ j = 1,2,\ldots,n \text{ (Job or column restriction)} \quad (2)$$

$$x_{ij} \in \{0,1\} \tag{3}$$

where

$$x_{ij} = \begin{cases} 0, & if\ i^{th}\ machine\ is\ not\ assigned\ to\ j^{th}\ job \\ 1, & if\ i^{th}\ machine\ is\ assigned\ to\ j^{th}\ job \end{cases}$$

When the costs $\tilde{c}_{ij}^{I}$ are intuitionistic fuzzy numbers, then the total cost becomes an intuitionistic fuzzy number $\tilde{Z}^{I} \approx \sum_{i=1}^{n}\sum_{j=1}^{n}\tilde{c}_{ij}^{I}x_{ij}$. Therefore, it cannot be minimized directly. For solving the problem we convert an intuitionistic fuzzy cost coefficient into crisp ones by an intuitionistic fuzzy number ranking method of Varghese and Kuriakose (2012).

Consider the situation of assigning *n* machines to *n* jobs (or *n* jobs to *n* machines) and each machine is capable of doing any job at different costs. Let $\tilde{c}_{ij}^{I}$ be an intuitionistic fuzzy cost of assigning the jth job to the ith machine. Let x_{ij} be the decision variable that denotes the assignment of the machine *i* to the job *j*. The objective is to minimize the total intuitionistic fuzzy cost of assigning all the jobs to the available machines (one job per machine) at the least total cost. This situation is known as the balanced intuitionistic fuzzy assignment problem (BIFAP).

(Model 2) (Problem P*) Minimize $\Re\left(\tilde{Z}^{I^*}\right) = \sum_{i=1}^{n}\sum_{j=1}^{n}\Re\left(\tilde{c}_{ij}^{I}\right)x_{ij}$ (objective function)

subject to the constraints:

$$\sum_{j=1}^{n} x_{ij} = 1, for\ i = 1,2,\ldots,n \text{ (Machine or row restriction)} \tag{4}$$

$$\sum_{i=1}^{n} x_{ij} = 1, for\ j = 1,2,\ldots,n \text{ (Job or column restriction)} \tag{5}$$

$$x_{ij} \in \{0,1\} \tag{6}$$

where

$$x_{ij} = \begin{cases} 0, & if\ i^{th}\ machine\ is\ not\ assigned\ to\ j^{th}\ job \\ 1, & if\ i^{th}\ machine\ is\ assigned\ to\ j^{th}\ job \end{cases}$$

Since $\Re(\tilde{c}_{ij}^{I})$ are crisp values, this problem (P*) is obviously the crisp assignment problem of the form (P) which can be solved by the conventional method namely the Hungarian Method .Once the optimal solution x^* of Model (2) is found, the optimal intuitionistic fuzzy objective value $\tilde{Z}^{I*}$ of the original problem can be calculated as:

$$\tilde{Z}^{I*} \approx \sum_{i=1}^{n}\sum_{j=1}^{n}\tilde{c}_{ij}^{I}x_{ij}^{*}$$

where $\tilde{c}_{ij}^{I} \approx \left(c_{ij}^{1}, c_{ij}^{2}, c_{ij}^{3}\right)\left(c_{ij}^{1'}, c_{ij}^{2}, c_{ij}^{3'}\right)$ (intuitionistic fuzzy cost is represented by a TIFN)

Mathematically, the intuitionistic fuzzy assignment problem can be modeled as follows:

Minimize $\tilde{Z}^{I} = \sum_{i=1}^{n}\sum_{j=1}^{n}\tilde{c}_{ij}^{I}x_{ij}$ (objective function)

subject to (1) to (3) are satisfied.

The above IFAP and its equivalent crisp AP both are can be stated in the tabular form, which are shown in the following Tables 1 and 2.

The IFAT (Table 1) and its equivalent crisp AT (Table 2) both are can be further represented as a transportation model, which is shown in the following Tables 3 and 4.

Table 1. $n \times n$ intuitionistic fuzzy assignment problem

	1	**2**	**...**	j	**...**	n
1	$\tilde{c}_{11}^{I}$	$\tilde{c}_{12}^{I}$	...	$\tilde{c}_{1j}^{I}$		$\tilde{c}_{1n}^{I}$
2	$\tilde{c}_{21}^{I}$	$\tilde{c}_{22}^{I}$	...	$\tilde{c}_{2j}^{I}$.	...	$\tilde{c}_{2n}^{I}$
. . .	. . .	. . .	. . .	. . .	. . .	. . .
i	$\tilde{c}_{i1}^{I}$	$\tilde{c}_{i2}^{I}$	...	$\tilde{c}_{ij}^{I}$	...	$\tilde{c}_{in}^{I}$
. . .	. . .	. . .	. . .	. . .	. . .	. . .
n	$\tilde{c}_{n1}^{I}$	$\tilde{c}_{n2}^{I}$	...	$\tilde{c}_{nj}^{I}$	...	$\tilde{c}_{nn}^{I}$

Table 2. Crisp version of $n \times n$ *intuitionistic fuzzy assignment problem*

	1	**2**	**...**	j	**...**	n
1	$\Re\left(\tilde{c}_{11}^{I}\right)$	$\Re\left(\tilde{c}_{12}^{I}\right)$	...	$\Re\left(\tilde{c}_{1j}^{I}\right)$		$\Re\left(\tilde{c}_{1n}^{I}\right)$
2	$\Re\left(\tilde{c}_{21}^{I}\right)$	$\Re\left(\tilde{c}_{22}^{I}\right)$	...	$\Re\left(\tilde{c}_{2j}^{I}\right)$	...	$\Re\left(\tilde{c}_{2n}^{I}\right)$
⋮	⋮	⋮	⋮	⋮	⋮	⋮
i	$\Re\left(\tilde{c}_{i1}^{I}\right)$	$\Re\left(\tilde{c}_{i2}^{I}\right)$	...	$\Re\left(\tilde{c}_{ij}^{I}\right)$	...	$\Re\left(\tilde{c}_{in}^{I}\right)$
⋮	⋮	⋮	⋮	⋮	⋮	⋮
n	$\Re\left(\tilde{c}_{n1}^{I}\right)$	$\Re\left(\tilde{c}_{n2}^{I}\right)$	...	$\Re\left(\tilde{c}_{nj}^{I}\right)$	...	$\Re\left(\tilde{c}_{nn}^{I}\right)$

Table 3. Transportation representation of IFAC

	1	**2**	**...**	j	**...**	n	**Supply**
1	$\tilde{c}_{11}^{I}$	$\tilde{c}_{12}^{I}$	...	$\tilde{c}_{1j}^{I}$		$\tilde{c}_{1n}^{I}$	1
2	$\tilde{c}_{21}^{I}$	$\tilde{c}_{22}^{I}$	...	$\tilde{c}_{2j}^{I}$	...	$\tilde{c}_{2n}^{I}$	1
⋮	⋮	⋮	⋮	⋮	⋮	⋮	⋮
i	$\tilde{c}_{i1}^{I}$	$\tilde{c}_{i2}^{I}$	...	$\tilde{c}_{ij}^{I}$	...	$\tilde{c}_{in}^{I}$	1
⋮	⋮	⋮	⋮	⋮	⋮	⋮	⋮
n	$\tilde{c}_{n1}^{I}$	$\tilde{c}_{n2}^{I}$	...	$\tilde{c}_{nj}^{I}$	...	$\tilde{c}_{nn}^{I}$	1
Demand	1	1	...	1	...	1	n

Definition: The AP is said to be FIFAP or IFAP if all the cost/time/profit of the AP must be in IFNs.

Definition: If the AP having all the cost/time/profit are in the mixture of crisp numbers, TIFNs and TrIFNs then the problem is called mixed intuitionistic fuzzy assignment problem (MIFAP).

Definition: If the total number of machines (say m rows) is equal to the total number of jobs (say n columns) in IFAP then the problem is called balanced intuitionistic fuzzy assignment problem (BIFAP) (i.e., total number of rows = total number of columns).

Table 4. Transportation representation of crisp assignment cost

	1	2	…	j	…	n	Supply
1	$\Re\left(\tilde{c}^I_{11}\right)$	$\Re\left(\tilde{c}^I_{12}\right)$	…	$\Re\left(\tilde{c}^I_{1j}\right)$		$\Re\left(\tilde{c}^I_{1n}\right)$	1
2	$\Re\left(\tilde{c}^I_{21}\right)$	$\Re\left(\tilde{c}^I_{22}\right)$	…	$\Re\left(\tilde{c}^I_{2j}\right)$	…	$\Re\left(\tilde{c}^I_{2n}\right)$	1
⋮	⋮	⋮	⋮	⋮	⋮	⋮	⋮
i	$\Re\left(\tilde{c}^I_{i1}\right)$	$\Re\left(\tilde{c}^I_{i2}\right)$	…	$\Re\left(\tilde{c}^I_{ij}\right)$	…	$\Re\left(\tilde{c}^I_{in}\right)$	1
⋮	⋮	⋮	⋮	⋮	⋮	⋮	⋮
n	$\Re\left(\tilde{c}^I_{n1}\right)$	$\Re\left(\tilde{c}^I_{n2}\right)$	…	$\Re\left(\tilde{c}^I_{nj}\right)$	…	$\Re\left(\tilde{c}^I_{nn}\right)$	1
Demand	1	1	…	1	…	1	n

Definition: If the total number of machines (say m rows) is not equal to the total number of jobs (say n columns) in IFAP then the problem is called unbalanced intuitionistic fuzzy assignment problem (UBIFAP) (i.e., total number of rows $\neq$ total number of columns).

The next section presents PSK method, new theorem and corollary and then its proof.

THE PSK METHOD

The proposed PSK method follows the steps below.

Step 1: Construct the balanced fully intuitionistic fuzzy assignment table (BFIFAT) for the given intuitionistic fuzzy assignment problem with rows representing machines and columns representing the jobs.

Step 2: Next, transform the BFIFAP into its equivalent crisp AP, using the ranking procedure of Varghese and Kuriakose (2012).

Step 3: After using Step 2 of the proposed method, now solve the crisp AP by using the Hungarian method or software packages such as LINGO 17.0, TORA, and so forth. This step yields the optimum objective value and optimum assignment for the crisp AP.

Step 4: Next, construct the new FIFAT whose assigned cells cost are intuitionistic fuzzy zeros and the remaining cells cost are its original cost. Then, subtract each row's entries for the current table from the row minimum and subtract each column's entries of the reduced table from the column minimum. Clearly, each row and each column of the resulting table has exactly one intuitionistic fuzzy zero. Thus, the current resulting table is called the optimal/optimum table.

Step 5: Now, assign the ith machine to j^{th} job if the intersection of the cost (occupied cells cost) of the ith row and j^{th} column is intuitionistic fuzzy zero. Furthermore, let it be noted that the value of the decision variable in this occupied cell

$$x_{ij} = 1\left(i = 1, 2, \ldots, n \; and \; j = 1, 2, \ldots n\right).$$

If not, $(\tilde{c}_{ij}^I \Theta \tilde{u}_i^I \Theta v_j^I) \succ \tilde{0}^I$ then we put

$$x_{ij} = 0\left(i = 1, 2, \ldots, n \; and \; j = 1, 2, \ldots n\right)$$

for all these cells in such a way that assign all the machines to all the jobs (or all the jobs to all the machines). Finally, calculate the total intuitionistic fuzzy assignment cost by using the relation $\tilde{Z}^I \approx \sum_{i=1}^{n}\sum_{j=1}^{n} \tilde{c}_{ij}^I x_{ij}$.

Next, we prove the following theorems which are used to derive the assignment to the FIFAP obtained by the PSK method is an optimal assignment to the FIFAP.

Theorem

Any optimal assignment to the fully intuitionistic fuzzy assignment problem (P_1) where

$$(P_1) \text{ Minimize } \tilde{Z}^{I*} \approx \sum_{i=1}^{n}\sum_{j=1}^{n} (\tilde{c}_{ij}^I \Theta \tilde{u}_i^I \Theta \tilde{v}_j^I) x_{ij}$$

Subject to (1) to (3) are satisfied, where $\tilde{u}_i^I$ (minimum of ith row of the newly constructed assignment table $\tilde{c}_{ij}^I$) and $\tilde{v}_j^I$ (minimum of jth column of the resulting assignment table $[\tilde{c}_{ij}^I \Theta \tilde{u}_i^I]$) are some real TIFNs, is an optimal assignment to the problem (P) where (P) Minimize $\tilde{Z}^I \approx \sum_{i=1}^{n}\sum_{j=1}^{n} \tilde{c}_{ij}^I \otimes x_{ij}$

Subject to (1) to (3) are satisfied.

Proof

Let $\tilde{u}_i^I$ be the minimum of ith row of the newly constructed assignment table [$\tilde{c}_{ij}^I$]. Now, we subtract $\tilde{u}_i^I$ from the ith row entries so that the resulting table is [$\tilde{c}_{ij}^I \Theta \tilde{u}_i^I$]. Let $\tilde{v}_j^I$ be the minimum of jth column of the resulting table $[\tilde{c}_{ij}^I \Theta \tilde{u}_i^I]$. Now, we subtract $\tilde{v}_j^I$ from the jth column entries so that the resulting table is $\left(\tilde{c}_{ij}^I \Theta \tilde{u}_i^I \Theta \tilde{v}_j^I\right)$. It may be noted that $\left(\tilde{c}_{ij}^I \Theta \tilde{u}_i^I \Theta \tilde{v}_j^I\right) \succ \tilde{0}^I$, for all *i* and *j*. Further, each column and each row having exactly one intuitionistic fuzzy zero.

Now,

$$\tilde{Z}^{I*} \approx \sum_{i=1}^{n}\sum_{j=1}^{n}(\tilde{c}_{ij}^{I}\Theta\tilde{u}_{i}^{I}\Theta\tilde{v}_{j}^{I})x_{ij}$$

$$\approx \sum_{i=1}^{n}\sum_{j=1}^{n}\tilde{c}_{ij}^{I}\otimes x_{ij}\Theta\sum_{i=1}^{n}\sum_{j=1}^{n}\tilde{u}_{i}^{I}\otimes x_{ij}\Theta\sum_{i=1}^{n}\sum_{j=1}^{n}\tilde{v}_{j}^{I}\otimes x_{ij}$$

Now problem () is an optimal solution the fully intuitionistic fuzzy transportation problem.

$$\approx \tilde{Z}^{I}\Theta\sum_{i=1}^{n}\tilde{u}_{i}^{I}\sum_{j=1}^{n}x_{ij}\Theta\sum_{j=1}^{n}\tilde{v}_{j}^{I}\sum_{i=1}^{n}x_{ij}$$

$$\tilde{Z}^{I*} \approx \tilde{Z}^{I}\Theta\sum_{i=1}^{n}\tilde{u}_{i}^{I}\Theta\sum_{j=1}^{n}\tilde{v}_{j}^{I}$$

Since $\sum_{i=1}^{n}\tilde{u}_{i}^{I}$ and $\sum_{j=1}^{n}\tilde{v}_{j}^{I}$ are independent of x_{ij}, for all *i* and *j*, we can conclude that any optimal assignment to the problem (P_1) is also an optimal assignment to the problem (P). Hence the theorem.

Corollary

If

$$\left\{x_{ij}^{oI}, i = 1,2,\ldots,n \; and \; j = 1,2,\ldots n\right\}$$

is a feasible assignment/solution to the problem (P) and $\left(\tilde{c}_{ij}^{I}\Theta\tilde{u}_{i}^{I}\Theta v_{j}^{I}\right) \succ \tilde{0}^{I}$, for all *i* and *j* where $\tilde{u}_{i}^{I}$ and $\tilde{v}_{j}^{I}$ are some real TIFNs, such that the minimum $\sum_{i=1}^{n}\sum_{j=1}^{n}(\tilde{c}_{ij}^{I}\Theta\tilde{u}_{i}^{I}\Theta\tilde{v}_{j}^{I})x_{ij}$ subject to (1) to (3) are satisfied, is intuitionistic fuzzy zero, then

$$\left\{x_{ij}^{oI}, i = 1,2,\ldots,n \; and \; j = 1,2,\ldots n\right\}$$

is an optimal assignment/solution to the problem (P).

Proof

Let

$$\left\{\tilde{x}_{ij}^{oI}, i = 1,2,\ldots,m \; and \; j = 1,2,\ldots,n\right\}$$

be the feasible assignment/solution to the problem (P). Now, consider the problem (P) with $\left(\tilde{c}_{ij}^{I}\Theta\tilde{u}_{i}^{I}\Theta\tilde{v}_{j}^{I}\right) \succ \tilde{0}^{I}$, for all *i* and *j* denoted by problem (P_1). From Theorem 5.1, clearly (P) is a original problem and (P_1) is a reduced problem of problem (P). Moreover, in problem (P_1) there is no possibility to minimize the cost below intuitionistic fuzzy zero. Hence, if

$$\left\{x_{ij}^{oI}, i = 1,2,\ldots,n \; and \; j = 1,2,\ldots n\right\}$$

is a feasible assignment/solution to the problem (P) and $\left(\tilde{c}_{ij}^{I}\Theta\tilde{u}_{i}^{I}\Theta v_{j}^{I}\right) \succ \tilde{0}^{I}$, for all *i* and *j* where $\tilde{u}_{i}^{I}$ and $\tilde{v}_{j}^{I}$ are some real TIFNs, such that the minimum $\sum_{i=1}^{n}\sum_{j=1}^{n}(\tilde{c}_{ij}^{I}\Theta\tilde{u}_{i}^{I}\Theta\tilde{v}_{j}^{I})x_{ij}$ subject to (1) to (3) are satisfied, is intuitionistic fuzzy zero, then

$$\left\{x_{ij}^{oI}, i = 1,2,\ldots,n \; and \; j = 1,2,\ldots n\right\}$$

is an optimal assignment/solution to the problem (P).

Theorem (PSK Theorem)

The assignment obtained by the PSK method for a fully intuitionistic fuzzy assignment problem (P) is an optimal assignment for the fully intuitionistic fuzzy assignment problem (P).

Proof

Let us now describe the PSK method in detail.

Construct the balanced fully intuitionistic fuzzy assignment table (BFIFAT) for the given intuitionistic fuzzy assignment problem (IFAP) with rows representing machines and columns representing the jobs. Next, transform the BFIFAP into its equivalent crisp AP, using the ranking procedure of Varghese and Kuriakose (2012). Now, solve the crisp AP by using the Hungarian method or software packages such as LINGO 17.0, TORA. This process will yield the optimum objective value and optimum assignment for the crisp AP (The optimal assigned cells in crisp assignment table are referred as assigned cells. The remaining cells are called unassigned cells. The total number of assigned cells in *n*x*n* crisp AP which are exactly *n* and all have zero cost. Similarly, in the FIFAP also have the same *n* number of assigned cells but its corresponding costs are intuitionistic fuzzy zeros. Furthermore, the crisp AP has exactly one assigned cells in each row and each column. According to the definitions 3.1 to 3.4 the FIFAP also has exactly only one assigned cell in each row and each column).

Now, construct the new fully intuitionistic fuzzy assignment table (FIFAT) whose assigned cells cost are intuitionistic fuzzy zeros and the remaining cells cost are its original cost. Let $\tilde{u}_{i}^{I}$ be the minimum of ith row of the current table [$\tilde{c}_{ij}^{I}$]. Now, we subtract $\tilde{u}_{i}^{I}$ from the ith row entries so that the resulting table is [$\tilde{c}_{ij}^{I}\Theta\tilde{u}_{i}^{I}$]. Let $\tilde{v}_{j}^{I}$ be the minimum of jth column of the resulting table [$\tilde{c}_{ij}^{I}\Theta\tilde{u}_{i}^{I}$]. Now, we subtract $\tilde{v}_{j}^{I}$ from the jth column entries so that the resulting table is $\left(\tilde{c}_{ij}^{I}\Theta\tilde{u}_{i}^{I}\Theta\tilde{v}_{j}^{I}\right)$. It may be noted that $\left(\tilde{c}_{ij}^{I}\Theta\tilde{u}_{i}^{I}\Theta\tilde{v}_{j}^{I}\right)\succ\tilde{0}^{I}$, for all *i* and *j*. Clearly, each row and each column has exactly one intuitionistic fuzzy zero. The current resulting table is referred to as the optimal assignment table.

Finally, we have a solution (assignment)

$$\left\{x_{ij}, i = 1,2,\ldots,n \text{ and } j = 1,2,\ldots n\right\}$$

for the FIFAP whose cost matrix is [$\tilde{c}_{ij}^{I}\Theta\tilde{u}_{i}^{I}\Theta\tilde{v}_{j}^{I}$] such that $x_{ij}=0$ for ($\tilde{c}_{ij}^{I}\Theta\tilde{u}_{i}^{I}\Theta\tilde{v}_{j}^{I}$) $\succ\tilde{0}^{I}$ and $x_{ij}=1$ for ($\tilde{c}_{ij}^{I}\Theta\tilde{u}_{i}^{I}\Theta\tilde{v}_{j}^{I}$) $\approx\tilde{0}^{I}$. Therefore, the minimum $\sum_{i=1}^{n}\sum_{j=1}^{n}(\tilde{c}_{ij}^{I}\Theta\tilde{u}_{i}^{I}\Theta\tilde{v}_{j}^{I})x_{ij}$ subject to (1) to (3) are satisfied, is intuitionistic fuzzy zero. Thus, by the Corollary 5.1, the assignment

$$\left\{x_{ij}, i = 1,2,\ldots,n\ and\ j = 1,2,\ldots n\right\}$$

is obtained by the PSK method for a fully intuitionistic fuzzy assignment problem is an optimal assignment (solution) for the fully intuitionistic fuzzy assignment problem. Hence the theorem.

Theorem

If some/all of the IFNs in the FIFAP/IFAP (intuitionistic fuzzy assignment costs) are replaced by equivalent IFNs (their ranking values, for instance), then the new FIFAP/IFAP has the same set of optimal assignments/solutions.

Proof

Generally, FIFAP/IFAP is an AP in which only the assignment costs are represented in terms of IFNs. We notice that, in a FIFAP/IFAP the decision variables are all in crisp numbers. In a FIFAP/IFAP, the decision variables depends on its constraints (i.e., machine (see eqn. 1), job (see eqn. 2), and feasible restriction (refer to eqn. 3)). However, the constraints all have crisp decision variables. From the above discussion, the optimal solution/assignment of FIFAP is always crisp numbers. The optimal solution/assignment is always unchanged if all the costs of the assignment problem is unchanged.

Furthermore, our assumption is to replace equivalent IFNs in the FIFAPs/IFAPs. Therefore, the costs is unchanged in a new FIFAP and only the existing assignment costs are replaced by its equivalent IFNs. This implies that, if some/all of the IFNs in the FIFAP/IFAP (intuitionistic fuzzy assignment costs) are replaced by equivalent IFNs (their ranking values, for instance), then the new FIFAP/IFAP has the same set of optimal solutions/assignments. Hence the theorem.

Theorem

Every optimal solution/assignment to the fully fuzzy assignment problem (FFAP) is also an optimal solution/assignment to its equivalent crisp AP.

Proof

The proof is similar to that of Theorem 5.3.

Theorem

Every optimal solution/assignment to the mixed fuzzy assignment problem (MFAP) is also an optimal solution/assignment to its equivalent crisp AP.

Proof

The proof is similar to that of Theorem 5.4.

Theorem

Every optimal solution/assignment to the FIFAP is also an optimal solution/assignment to its equivalent crisp AP.

Proof

The proof is similar to that of Theorem 5.5.

Theorem

Every optimal solution/assignment to the mixed intuitionistic fuzzy assignment problem (MIFAP) is also an optimal solution/assignment to its equivalent crisp AP.

Proof

The proof is similar to that of Theorem 5.6.

ILLUSTRATIVE EXAMPLE

To examine the effectiveness and the realism of the proposed PSK method, four examples are given in this section which is implemented in both LINGO 17.0 and TORA working platforms.

Example 1

A TV manufacturing company has three jobs; namely, assembling, testing, and packing. These three jobs can be done by three workers; namely, X, Y, and Z. All three workers are capable of doing all three jobs, but a single person can undertake only one job at a time. The performing time of each job is not known exactly due to lack of experience, interest, capacity, understanding, and so forth. Therefore, the time consumption for all the jobs are not known exactly, which are given in terms of TIFNs. From past experience, the time (in hours) that each man takes to do each job is given in Table 5.

Find the assignment of men to jobs that will minimize the total time taken.

Solution

Let x_{11}, x_{12}, x_{13}, x_{21}, x_{22}, x_{23}, x_{31}, x_{32}, x_{33} be the decision variables. To find out the values of x_{11}, x_{12}, x_{13}, x_{21}, x_{22}, x_{23}, x_{31}, x_{32}, x_{33}. Now using Step 2 of the proposed method, transform the BFIFAP into its equivalent crisp AP is as follows:

$$\text{Min } \tilde{Z}^I = \mathfrak{R}(7,21,29)(2,21,34)\,x_{11} + \mathfrak{R}(7,20,57)(3,20,61)\,x_{12}$$

$$+\mathfrak{R}(12,25,56)(8,25,60)\,x_{13} + \mathfrak{R}(8,9,16)(2,9,22)\,x_{21} + \mathfrak{R}(4,12,35)(1,12,38)\,x_{22}$$

$$+\mathfrak{R}(6,14,28)(3,14,31)\,x_{23} + \mathfrak{R}(5,9,22)(2,9,25)\,x_{31} + \mathfrak{R}(10,15,20)(5,15,25)\,x_{32}$$

$$+\mathfrak{R}(4,16,19)(1,16,22)\,x_{33} \text{ (objective function)}$$

Subject to the constraints

$$x_{11} + x_{12} + x_{13} = 1,$$

$$x_{21} + x_{22} + x_{23} = 1, \text{Machines (X, Y, Z) constraint}$$

$$x_{31} + x_{32} + x_{33} = 1,$$

Table 5. IFAP (Example 1)

	Assembling	Testing	Packing
X	(7,21,29)(2,21,34)	(7,20,57)(3,20,61)	(12,25,56)(8,25,60)
Y	(8,9,16)(2,9,22)	(4,12,35)(1,12,38)	(6,14,28)(3,14,31)
Z	(5,9,22)(2,9,25)	(10,15,20)(5,15,25)	(4,16,19)(1,16,22)

$x_{11} + x_{21} + x_{31} = 1,$

$x_{12} + x_{22} + x_{32} = 1,$ Jobs (Assembling, Testing, Packing) constraint

$x_{13} + x_{23} + x_{33} = 1,$

$x_{ij} \in \{0,1\}.$

(possible values of x_{ij} i.e., this is the non-negative and feasible restriction)

Using the ranking method of Varghese and Kuriakose (2012), the above problem can be transformed into the crisp version of the assignment problem is presented in Table 6.

We can write the above problem (see Table 6) as an LPP, which is as follows:

$$\text{Min } Z = \text{Min } \Re\left(\tilde{Z}^I\right) = 19x_{11} + 28x_{12} + 31x_{13} + 11x_{21} + 17x_{22} + 16x_{23} + 12x_{31} + 15x_{32} + 13x_{33}$$

Subject to the constraints

$x_{11} + x_{12} + x_{13} = 1,$

$x_{11} + x_{21} + x_{31} = 1,$

$x_{21} + x_{22} + x_{23} = 1,$

$x_{12} + x_{22} + x_{32} = 1,$

$x_{31} + x_{32} + x_{33} = 1,$

$x_{13} + x_{23} + x_{33} = 1,$

Table 6. Crisp version of IFAP (Example 1)

	Assembling	Testing	Packing
X	19	28	31
Y	11	17	16
Z	12	15	13

$x_{ij} \in \{0,1\}$.

By using Step 3 of the proposed method, now solve the crisp AP by using the Hungarian method or software packages such as LINGO 17.0, TORA, and so forth. This step yields the optimum objective value and optimum assignment for the crisp AP.

Therefore, the optimal solution is

$$x_{11} = x_{22} = x_{33} = 1,\ x_{12} = x_{13} = x_{21} = x_{23} = x_{31} = x_{32} = 0,$$

With the optimal objective value $\Re\left(\tilde{Z}^I\right) = 49$ (in hours) which represents the optimal total time. In other words, the optimal assignment is:

Worker $X \rightarrow$ Assembling, Worker $Y \rightarrow$ Testing, Worker $Z \rightarrow$ Packing

The intuitionistic fuzzy minimum total time is calculated as

$$\tilde{c}_{11}^I + \tilde{c}_{22}^I + \tilde{c}_{33}^I = (7,21,29)(2,21,34) + (4,12,35)(1,12,38) + (4,16,19)(1,16,22)$$

$$\text{Min } \tilde{Z}^I = (15,49,83)(4,49,94) \tag{7}$$

Also we find that $\Re\left(\tilde{Z}^I\right) = \Re(15,49,83)(4,49,94) = 49$ (in hours)

In the above example, it has been shown that the total optimal time obtained by our method remains same as that obtained by converting the total intuitionistic fuzzy time by applying the ranking method of Varghese and Kuriakose (2012).

Solution by LINGO 17.0

Now, by applying the ranking method to the given FIFAP, then we obtain the following crisp AP (see Table 6):

We can write the above problem (see Table 6) as a pure integer linear programming (PILP), which is as follows:

$$\text{Min Z} = 19x_{11} + 28x_{12} + 31x_{13} + 11x_{21} + 17x_{22} + 16x_{23} + 12x_{31} + 15x_{32} + 13x_{33}$$

Subject to

$$x_{11} + x_{12} + x_{13} = 1,$$

$$x_{11} + x_{21} + x_{31} = 1,$$

$x_{21} + x_{22} + x_{23} = 1,$

$x_{12} + x_{22} + x_{32} = 1,$

$x_{31} + x_{32} + x_{33} = 1,$

$x_{13} + x_{23} + x_{33} = 1,$

$x_{ij} \in \{0,1\}.$

We can write the computer code for the above PILP in LINGO 17.0 tool, which is as follows:

```
!Objective function;
Min = 19 * x11 + 28 * x12 + 31 * x13 + 11 * x21 + 17 * x22 + 16 * x23 + 12 *
x31 + 15 * x32 + 13 * x33;
!Subject to the constraints;
@BIN(x11);
@BIN(x12);
@BIN(x13);
@BIN(x21);
@BIN(x22);
@BIN(x23);
@BIN(x31);
@BIN(x32);
@BIN(x33);
x11 + x12 + x13 = 1;
x21 + x22 + x23 = 1;
x31 + x32 + x33 = 1;
x11 + x21 + x31 = 1;
x12 + x22 + x32 = 1;
x13 + x23 + x33 = 1;
```

Using the above code in LINGO 17.0 tool, we get the following optimal solution and optimal objective value, to the reduced problem in Table 6.

The optimal solution and the total assignment time are:

$x_{11} = x_{22} = x_{33} = 1,\ x_{12} = x_{13} = x_{21} = x_{23} = x_{31} = x_{32} = 0$ and Min Z = 49 (in hours)

From the obtained solution, we can write the optimal objective value for the given FIFAP as follows:

Min $\tilde{Z}^{I} = (15, 49, 83)(4, 49, 94)$ (minimum intuitionistic fuzzy objective time)

From the obtained objective value of the given FIFAP, we can write the optimal objective value for the crisp AP as follows:

$$\text{Min Z} = \text{Min } \Re(\tilde{Z}) = \Re(15, 49, 83)(4, 49, 94)$$

$$= \frac{1}{3}\left[\frac{(94-4)(49-2(94)-2(4)) + (83-15)(15+49+83) + 3(94^2-4^2)}{94-4+83-15}\right]$$

$$= 49$$

Figure 3 shows the optimal solution and optimal objective value of the given FIFAP and its crisp AP. From Figure 3, the optimal solution and optimal objective value of the given FIFAP and its crisp AP have been verified by using both the proposed method and the existing method.

Figure 4 shows the lingo matrix picture for the crisp AP corresponding to the given FIFAP.

Solution by TORA

Consider the above integer programming problem (IPP). By applying TORA software to this problem (see Table 6), we get the following optimal solution and optimal objective value.

Figure 3. Output summary for FIFAP and its crisp AP: PILP approach (LINGO 17.0)

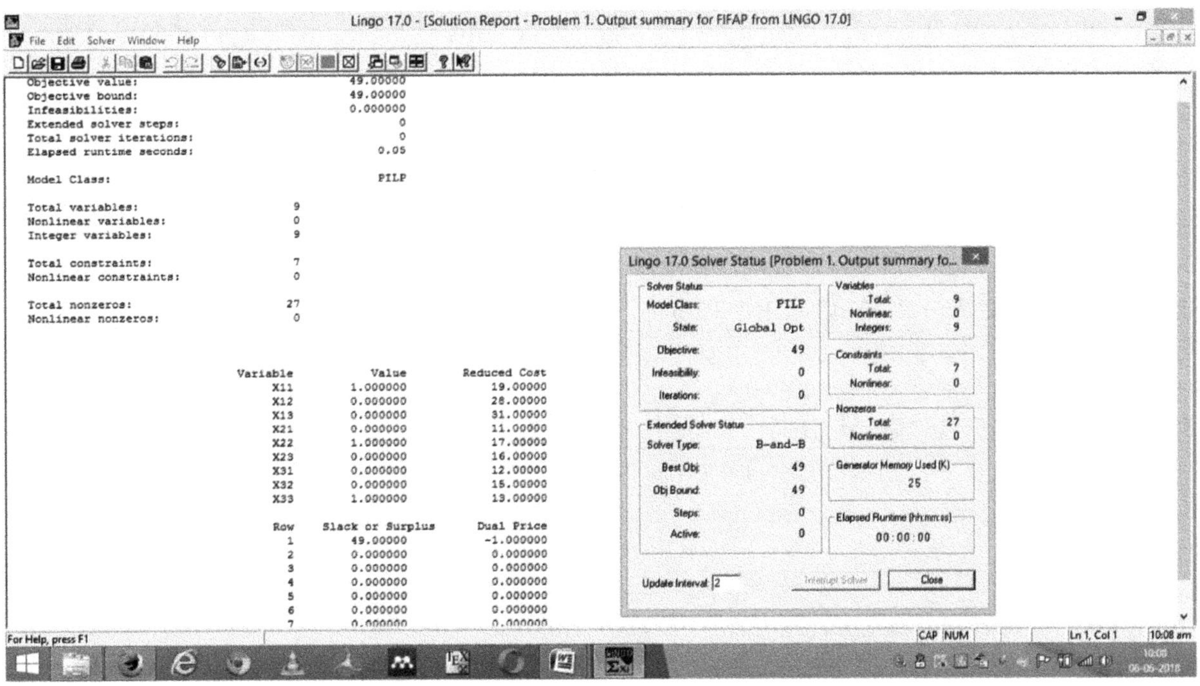

Figure 4. Lingo matrix picture for the crisp AP corresponding to the given FIFAP

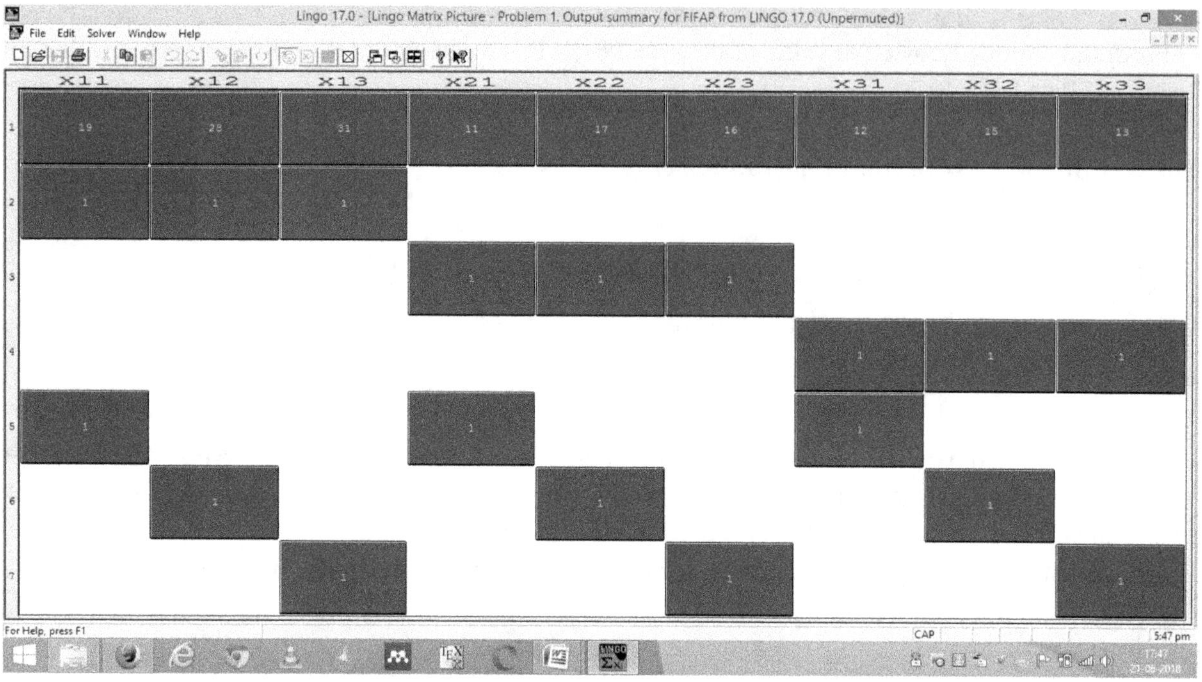

The optimal solution and the total assignment time are:

$x_{11} = x_{22} = x_{33} = 1,\ x_{12} = x_{13} = x_{21} = x_{23} = x_{31} = x_{32} = 0$ and Min Z = 49 (in hours)

From the obtained solution, we can write the optimal objective value for the given FIFAP as follows:

Min $\tilde{Z}^I = (15, 49, 83)(4, 49, 94)$

From the obtained objective value of the given FIFAP, we can write the optimal objective value for the crisp AP as follows:

Min Z = Min $\Re\left(\tilde{Z}^I\right) = \Re(15, 49, 83)(4, 49, 94)$

$$= \frac{1}{3}\left[\frac{(94-4)(49-2(94)-2(4)) + (83-15)(15+49+83) + 3(94^2-4^2)}{94-4+83-15}\right]$$

$$= 49$$

Figure 5 shows the optimal solution and optimal objective value of the given FIFAP and its crisp AP. From Figure 5, the optimal solution and optimal objective value of the given FIFAP and its crisp AP have been verified by using both the proposed method and the existing method.

Note: Prabakaran and Ganesan got the intuitionistic fuzzy optimal assignment for the above problem (Example 1) is $M_1 \rightarrow J_2$, $M_2 \rightarrow J_3$, $M_3 \rightarrow J_1$ and the intuitionistic fuzzy assignment cost is (if r=0) $\tilde{Z}$=(30,43,80)(36,43,84). We know that, if $\left(a_1, a_2, a_3\right)\left(a_1^{'}, a_2, a_3^{'}\right)$ is a TIFN then it satisfies the condition $a_1^{'} \leq a_1 \leq a_2 \leq a_3 \leq a_3^{'}$ and $\mu_A\left(x\right), \vartheta_A\left(x\right) \leq 0.5$ for $\mu_A\left(x\right) = \vartheta_A\left(x\right)$ $\forall x \in R$. But, $36 \nleq 30 \leq 43 \leq 80 \leq 84$ does not satisfy the condition of TIFN. Hence Prabakaran and Ganesan's approach does not fit in all cases. Therefore, the proposed PSK method is better than most of the other existing methods.

Example 2

Let us consider an IFAP with rows representing 4 machines M_1, M_2, M_3, M_4 and columns representing the 4 jobs J_1, J_2, J_3, J_4. The profit matrix $\left[\tilde{c}_{ij}^{I}\right]_{4\times4}$ is given in Table **7** and whose elements are TIFN.

The problem is to find the optimal assignment so that the total profit of job assignment becomes maximum.

Solution

Let x_{11}, x_{12}, x_{13}, x_{14}, x_{21}, x_{22}, x_{23}, x_{24}, x_{31}, x_{32}, x_{33}, x_{34}, x_{41}, x_{42}, x_{43}, x_{44} be the decision variables. To find out the values of x_{11}, x_{12}, x_{13}, x_{14}, x_{21}, x_{22}, x_{23}, x_{24}, x_{31}, x_{32}, x_{33}, x_{34}, x_{41}, x_{42}, x_{43}, x_{44}.

Figure 5. Output summary for FIFAP and its crisp AP: IPP approach (TORA)

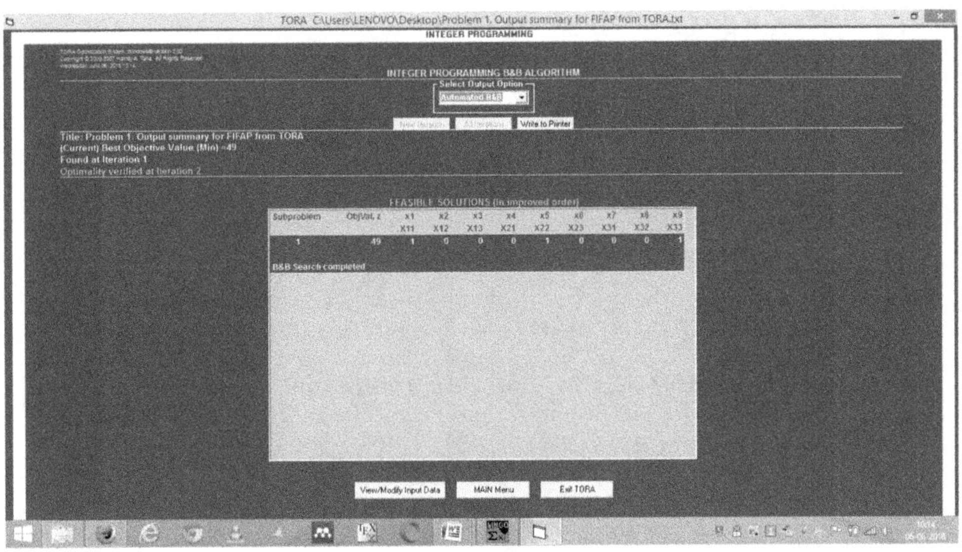

Table 7. IFAP (Example 2)

	J_1	J_2	J_3	J_4
M_1	(27,50,109)(13,50,123)	(56,67,111)(40,67,127)	(8,22,120)(4,22,124)	(75,100,128)(62,100,141)
M_2	(52,68,93)(44,68,101)	(43,90,119)(35,90,127)	(34,56,93)(18,56,109)	(60,70,89)(50,70,99)
M_3	(72,80,109)(58,80,123)	(78,90,108)(65,90,121)	(85,98,150)(76,98,159)	(52,68,93)(44,68,101)
M_4	(23,40,81)(17,40,87)	(44,58,90)(38,58,96)	(63,89,109)(49,89,123)	(64,72,95)(51,72,108)

In conformation to Model (2), an intuitionistic fuzzy assignment problem can be formulated in the following mathematical programming form:

Max $\tilde{Z}^I = \Re(27,50,109)(13,50,123)\, x_{11} + \Re(56,67,111)(40,67,127)\, x_{12}$

$+\Re(8,22,120)(4,22,124)\, x_{13} + \Re(75,100,128)(62,100,141)\, x_{14}$

$+\Re(52,68,93)(44,68,101)\, x_{21} + \Re(43,90,119)(35,90,127)\, x_{22}$

$+\Re(34,56,93)(18,56,109)\, x_{23} + \Re(60,70,89)(50,70,99)\, x_{24}$

$+\Re(72,80,109)(58,80,123)\, x_{31} + \Re(78,90,108)(65,90,121)\, x_{32}$

$+\Re(85,98,150)(76,98,159)\, x_{33} + \Re(52,68,93)(44,68,101)\, x_{34}$

$+\Re(23,40,81)(17,40,87)\, x_{41} + \Re(44,58,90)(38,58,96)\, x_{42}$

$+\Re(63,89,109)(49,89,123)\, x_{43} + \Re(64,72,95)(51,72,108)\, x_{44}$ (objective function)

Subject to the constraints

$x_{11} + x_{12} + x_{13} + x_{14} = 1,$

$x_{21} + x_{22} + x_{23} + x_{24} = 1,$ Machines (M_1, M_2, M_3, M_4) constraint

$x_{31} + x_{32} + x_{33} + x_{34} = 1,$

$x_{41} + x_{42} + x_{43} + x_{44} = 1,$

$x_{11} + x_{21} + x_{31} + x_{41} = 1,$

$x_{12} + x_{22} + x_{32} + x_{42} = 1,$ Jobs (J_1, J_2, J_3, J_4) constraint

$x_{13} + x_{23} + x_{33} + x_{43} = 1,$

$x_{14} + x_{24} + x_{34} + x_{44} = 1,$

$x_{ij} \in \{0,1\}$. That is, $x_{ij} = 0$ if i^{th} machine is not assigned to j^{th} job, $x_{ij} = 1$ if i^{th} machine is assigned to j^{th} job.

Using the ranking method of Varghese and Kuriakose (2012), the above problem can be transformed into the crisp version of the assignment problem is presented in Table 8.

Max Z= Max $\Re\left(\tilde{Z}^I\right) = 62x_{11} + 78x_{12} + 50x_{13} + 101x_{14} + 71x_{21} + 84x_{22}$

$+61x_{23} + 73x_{24} + 87x_{31} + 92x_{32} . +111x_{33} + 71x_{34} + 48x_{41} + 64x_{42} + 87x_{43} + 77x_{44}$

Subject to the constraints

$x_{11} + x_{12} + x_{13} + x_{14} = 1,$

$x_{11} + x_{21} + x_{31} + x_{41} = 1,$

Table 8. Crisp version of IFAP (Example 2)

	J_1	J_2	J_3	J_4
M_1	62	78	50	101
M_2	71	85	61	73
M_3	87	92	111	71
M_4	48	64	87	77

$x_{21} + x_{22} + x_{23} + x_{24} = 1,$

$x_{12} + x_{22} + x_{32} + x_{42} = 1,$

$x_{31} + x_{32} + x_{33} + x_{34} = 1,$

$x_{13} + x_{23} + x_{33} + x_{43} = 1,$

$x_{41} + x_{42} + x_{43} + x_{44} = 1,$

$x_{14} + x_{24} + x_{34} + x_{44} = 1,$

$x_{ij} \in \{0,1\}.$

This problem is solved by the Hungarian Method.
The optimal solution is

$x_{14} = x_{22} = x_{31} = x_{43} = 1,$

$x_{11} = x_{12} = x_{13} = x_{21} = x_{23} = x_{24} = x_{32} = x_{33} = x_{34} = x_{41} = x_{42} = x_{44} = 0,$

With the optimal objective value $\Re\left(\tilde{Z}^I\right) = Rs.359$ which represents the optimal total profit. In other words, the optimal assignment is

$M_1 \rightarrow J_4$, $M_2 \rightarrow J_2$, $M_3 \rightarrow J_1$, $M_4 \rightarrow J_3$

The intuitionistic fuzzy maximum total profit is calculated as

$\tilde{c}^I_{14} + \tilde{c}^I_{22} + \tilde{c}^I_{31} + \tilde{c}^I_{33} = (75,100,128)(62,100,141) + (43,90,119)(35,90,127) + (72,80,109)$

$(58,80,123) +$ (63,89,109)(49,89,123)

Max $\tilde{Z}^I$ =(253,359,465)(204,359,514)

Also we find that

$$\Re\left(\tilde{Z}^I\right) = \Re\left(253, 359, 465\right)\left(204, 359, 514\right) = \text{Rs.}359$$

We can write the LINGO 17.0 computer code to this problem. Additionally, we are able to solve this problem by using software packages (e.g., LINGO 17.0 and TORA).

Example 3

Minimize the following unbalanced intuitionistic fuzzy assignment problem (UBIFAP).

Table 9 shows the UBIFAP.

Solution

Let x_{11}, x_{12}, x_{13}, x_{21}, x_{22}, x_{23}, x_{31}, x_{32}, x_{33} be the decision variables. To find out the values of x_{11}, x_{12}, x_{13}, x_{21}, x_{22}, x_{23}, x_{31}, x_{32}, x_{33}.

By using the proposed method, we get the following optimal solution and optimal objective value for the given UBIFAP.

The optimal solution is

$$x_{12} = x_{21} = x_{33} = 1,\ x_{11} = x_{13} = x_{22} = x_{23} = x_{31} = x_{32} = 0,$$

and Min Z=25.

In other words, the optimal assignment is $M_1 \rightarrow J_2$, $M_2 \rightarrow J_1$, $M_3 \rightarrow J_3$

Minimum intuitionistic fuzzy objective value is

$$\tilde{c}^I_{11} + \tilde{c}^I_{22} + \tilde{c}^I_{33} = \left(5, 9, 22\right)\left(2, 9, 25\right) + \left(4, 16, 19\right)\left(1, 16, 22\right) + 0$$

Min $\tilde{Z}^I = \left(9, 25, 41\right)\left(3, 25, 47\right)$(minimum intuitionistic fuzzy objective value)

In addition, we find that

Table 9. UBIFAP(Example 3)

	J_1	J_2
M_1	(12,25,56)(8,25,60)	(5,9,22)(2,9,25)
M_2	(4,16,19)(1,16,22)	(8,9,16)(2,9,22)
M_3	(6,14,28)(3,14,31)	(7,21,29)(2,21,34)

$\Re\left(\tilde{Z}^{I}\right) = \Re\left(9,25,41\right)\left(3,25,47\right) = 25$ (minimum crisp objective value)

Solution by LINGO 17.0

Now, by applying the ranking method to the given UBIFAP, then we get the following crisp AP (see Table 10).

The balanced assignment problem corresponding to Table 10 is given in Table 11.

We can write the above problem (see Table 11) as a pure integer linear programming (PILP), which is as follows:

Min Z=31 x_{11} +12 x_{12} +0 x_{13} +13 x_{21} +11 x_{22} +0 x_{23} +16 x_{31} +19 x_{32} +0 x_{33} (objective function)

Subject to the constraints

$x_{11} + x_{12} + x_{13} = 1,$

$x_{21} + x_{22} + x_{23} = 1,$ Machines (M_1, M_2, M_3) constraint

Table 10. Crisp version of UBIFAP (Example 3)

	J_1	J_2
M_1	31	12
M_2	13	11
M_3	16	19

Table 11. Crisp version of balanced IFAP (Example 3)

	J_1	J_2	J_3
M_1	31	12	0
M_2	13	11	0
M_3	16	19	0

$x_{31} + x_{32} + x_{33} = 1,$

$x_{11} + x_{21} + x_{31} = 1,$

$x_{12} + x_{22} + x_{32} = 1,$ Jobs (J_1, J_2, J_3) constraint

$x_{13} + x_{23} + x_{33} = 1,$ (dummy job J_3 constraint)

$x_{ij} \in \{0,1\}.$

We can write the computer code for the above PILP in LINGO 17.0 tool, which is as follows:

```
!Objective function;
Min = 31 * x11 + 12 * x12 + 0 * x13 + 13 * x21 + 11 * x22 + 0 * x23 + 16 * x31
+ 19 * x32 + 0 * x33;
!Subject to the constraints;
@BIN(x11);
@BIN(x12);
@BIN(x13);
@BIN(x21);
@BIN(x22);
@BIN(x23);
@BIN(x31);
@BIN(x32);
@BIN(x33);
x11 + x12 + x13 = 1;
x21 + x22 + x23 = 1;
x31 + x32 + x33 = 1;
x11 + x21 + x31 = 1;
x12 + x22 + x32 = 1;
x13 + x23 + x33 = 1;
```

Using the above code in LINGO 17.0 tool, we get the following optimal solution and optimal objective value, to the reduced problem in Table 11.

The optimal solution and the minimum total assignment value are:

$x_{12} = x_{21} = x_{33} = 1,\ x_{11} = x_{13} = x_{22} = x_{23} = x_{31} = x_{32} = 0,$ and Min Z = 25.

From the obtained solution, we can write the optimal objective value for the given UBIFAP as follows:

Min $\tilde{Z}^I = (9,25,41)(3,25,47)$

From the obtained objective value of the given UBIFAP, we can write the optimal objective value for the crisp AP as follows:

$$\text{Min Z} = \Re\left(9,25,41\right)\left(3,25,47\right)$$

$$= \frac{1}{3}\left[\frac{\left(47-3\right)\left(25-2\left(47\right)-2\left(3\right)\right)+\left(41-9\right)\left(9+25+41\right)+3\left(47^2-3^2\right)}{47-3+41-9}\right]$$

$$= 25$$

Figure 6 shows the optimal solution and optimal objective value of the given UBIFAP and its crisp AP. From Figure 6, the optimal solution and optimal objective value of the given UBIFAP and its crisp AP have been verified by using both the proposed method and the existing method.

Figure 7 shows the lingo matrix picture for the crisp AP corresponding to the given UBIFAP.

Solution by TORA

Consider the above integer programming problem (IPP). By applying TORA software to this problem (see Table 11), we get the following optimal solution and optimal objective value.

Figure 6. Output summary for UBIFAP and its crisp AP: PILP approach (LINGO 17.0)

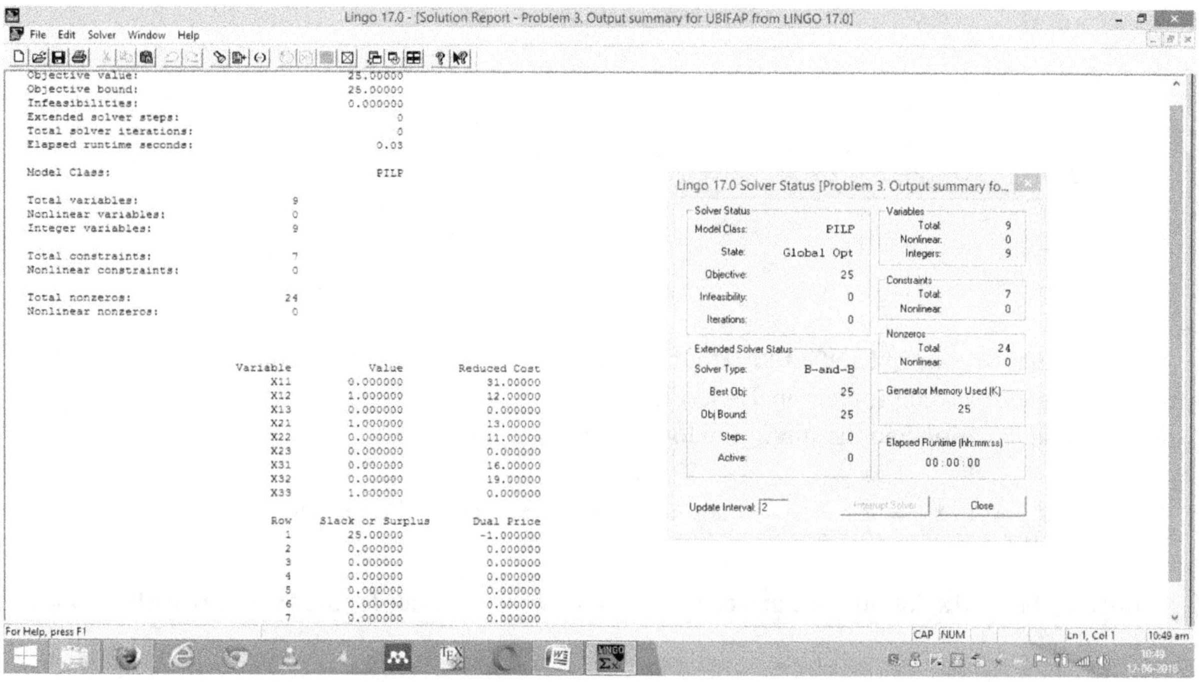

Figure 7. Lingo matrix picture for the crisp AP corresponding to the given UBIFAP

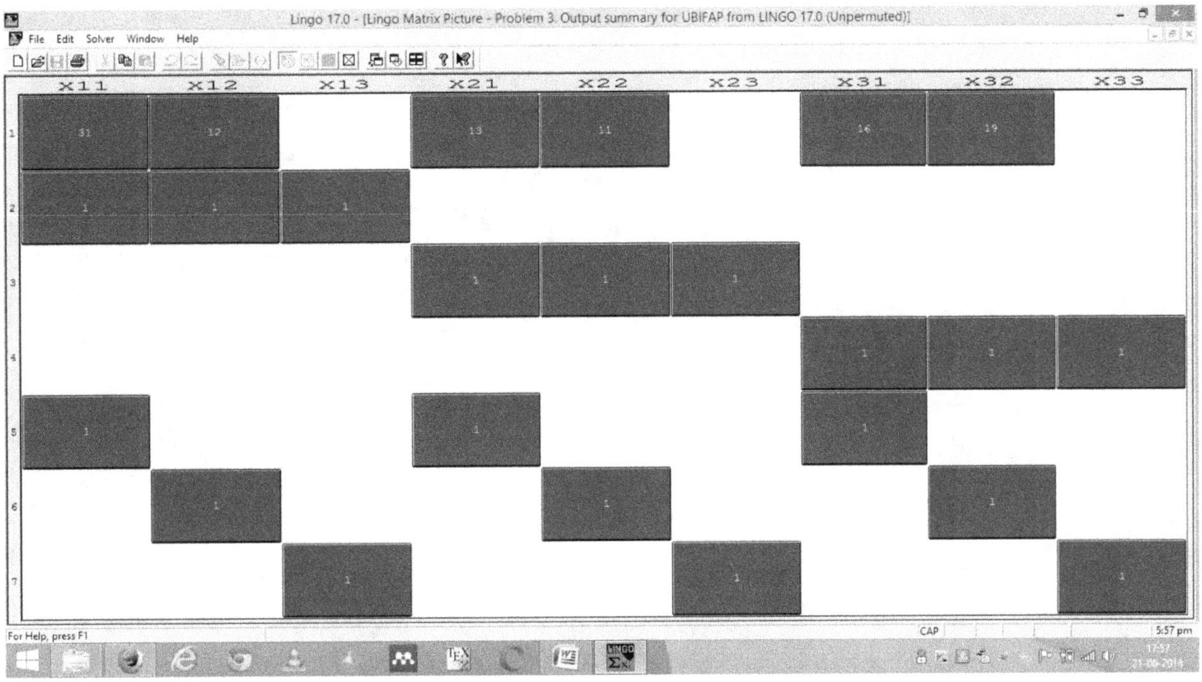

The optimal solution and the minimum total assignment value are:

$x_{12} = x_{21} = x_{33} = 1,\ x_{11} = x_{13} = x_{22} = x_{23} = x_{31} = x_{32} = 0,$ and Min Z = 25.

From the obtained solution, we can write the optimal objective value for the given UBIFAP as follows:

Min $\tilde{Z}^I$ = (9,25,41)(3,25,47) (minimum intuitionistic fuzzy objective value)

From the obtained objective value of the given UBIFAP, we can write the optimal objective value for the crisp AP as follows:

Min Z = Min $\Re\left(\tilde{Z}\right) = \Re\left(9,25,41\right)\left(3,25,47\right)$

$$= \frac{1}{3}\left[\frac{\left(47-3\right)\left(25-2\left(47\right)-2\left(3\right)\right)+\left(41-9\right)\left(9+25+41\right)+3\left(47^2-3^2\right)}{47-3+41-9}\right]$$

$$= 25$$

Figure 8 shows the optimal solution and optimal objective value of the given UBIFAP and its crisp AP. From Figure 8, the optimal solution and optimal objective value of the given UBIFAP and its crisp AP have been verified by using both the proposed method and the existing method.

Figure 8. Output summary for UBIFAP and its crisp AP: IPP approach (TORA)

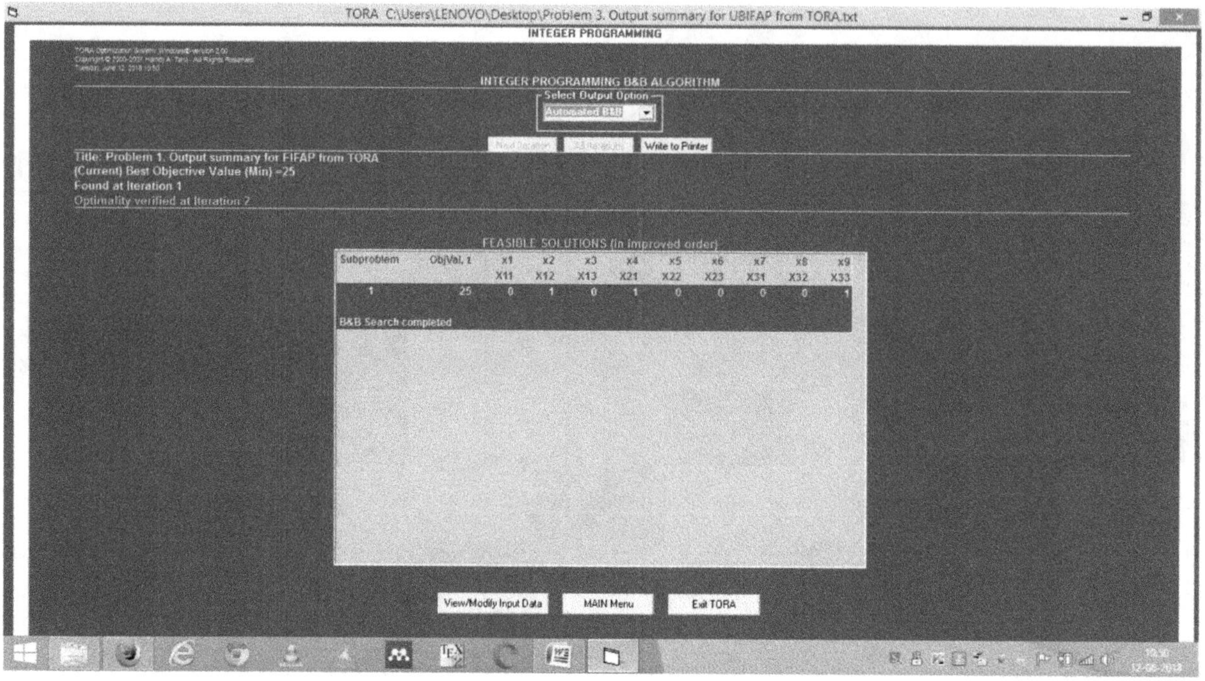

Example 4

Maximize the following UBIFAP.

Table 12 shows the UBIFAP.

Solution

Let x_{11}, x_{12}, x_{13}, x_{14}, x_{21}, x_{22}, x_{23}, x_{24}, x_{31}, x_{32}, x_{33} ., x_{34}, x_{41}, x_{42}, x_{43}, x_{44} be the decision variables. To find out the values of x_{11}, x_{12}, x_{13}, x_{14}, x_{21}, x_{22}, x_{23}, x_{24}, x_{31}, x_{32}, x_{33}, x_{34}, x_{41}, x_{42}, x_{43}, x_{44}.

By using the proposed method, we get the following optimal solution and optimal objective value.

The optimal solution is

Table 12. UBIFAP (Example 4)

	T_1	T_2	T_3	T_4
W_1	(64,72,95)(51,72,108)	(63,89,109)(49,89,123)	(44,58,90)(38,58,96)	(23,40,81)(17,40,87)
W_2	(52,68,93)(44,68,101)	(75,100,128)(62,100,141)	(78,90,108)(65,90,121)	(72,80,109)(58,80,123)
W_3	(60,70,89)(50,70,99)	(34,56,93)(18,56,109)	(43,90,119)(35,90,127)	(52,68,93)(44,68,101)

$$x_{11} = x_{22} = x_{33} = x_{44} = 1,$$

$$x_{12} = x_{13} = x_{14} = x_{21} = x_{23} = x_{24} = x_{31} = x_{32} = x_{34} = x_{41} = x_{42} = x_{43} = 0,$$

and Max Z=263

In other words, the optimum schedule is

$$T_1 \rightarrow W_1,\ T_2 \rightarrow W_2, T_3 \rightarrow W_3,\ T_4 \rightarrow W_4$$

Maximum intuitionistic fuzzy objective value is

$$\tilde{c}^I_{14} + \tilde{c}^I_{22} + \tilde{c}^I_{31} + \tilde{c}^I_{33} = (64,\ 72,\ 95)(51,72,108) + (75,100,128)(62,100,141) + (43,\ 90,119)(35,\ 90,127) + 0$$

(64, 72, 95)(51,72,108)+(75,100,128)(62,100,141)+(43, 90,119)(35, 90,127)+0

Max $\tilde{Z}^I$ =(182,262,342)(148,262,376) (maximum intuitionistic fuzzy objective value)

We can write the LINGO 17.0 computer code to this problem. Also, we are able to solve this problem by using software packages (e.g. LINGO 17.0 and TORA).

Results and Discussion

A comparative study between the proposed method and the existing software approach is given in Table 13. From Table 13, the author concludes that the optimal solution obtained by the PSK method is same as that of the optimal solution obtained by existing software approach. Graphical representation of triangular intuitionistic fuzzy assignment time (TIFAT) is shown in Figure 9.

From equation (7), the minimum total intuitionistic fuzzy assignment time is:

$$\text{Min } \tilde{Z}^I = (15, 49, 83)\ (4, 49, 94) \tag{7}$$

The result in (7) can be explained (Refer to Figure 9) as follows:

The degree of acceptance of the performing time for the DM increases if the time increases from 4 hours to15 hours, while it decreases if the time increases from 4 hours to 49 hours. Beyond (4, 49), the level of acceptance or the level of satisfaction for the DM is zero. The DM is totally satisfied or the performing time is totally acceptable if the performing time is 49 hours. The degree of non-acceptance of the performing time for the DM decreases if the time increases from 4 hours to 49 hours while it increases if the time increases from 49 hours to 94 hours. Beyond (4, 94), the time is totally un-acceptable (Figure 9).

Table 13. Comparative Analysis

Ranking Method	Problem Number	Solution Method			
		Intuitionistic Fuzzy Hungarian Method	PSK Method	LINGO 17.0	TORA
Varghese and Kuriakose	1	(15, 49, 83) (4, 49, 94) 49 (in hours)	(15, 49, 83) (4, 49, 94) 49 (in hours)	(15, 49, 83) (4, 49, 94) 49 (in hours)	(15, 49, 83) (4, 49, 94) 49 (in hours)
	2	(253,359,465) (204,359,514) Rs.359	(253,359,465) (204,359,514) Rs.359	(253,359,465) (204,359,514) Rs.359	(253,359,465) (204,359,514) Rs.359
	3	(9,25,41) (3,25,47) 25	(9,25,41) (3,25,47) 25	(9,25,41) (3,25,47) 25	(9,25,41) (3,25,47) 25
	4	(182,262,342) (148,262,376) 262	(182,262,342) (148,262,376) 262	(182,262,342) (148,262,376) 262	(182,262,342) (148,262,376) 262

Figure 9. Graphical Representation of TIFAT.

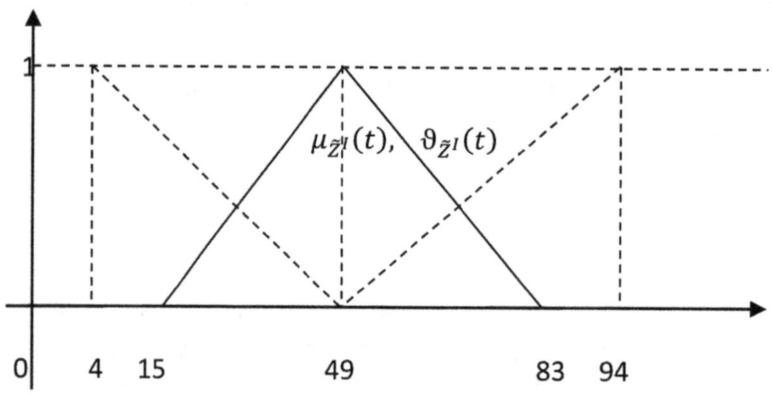

Assuming that $\mu_{\tilde{Z}^I}(t)$ is membership value (degree of acceptance) and $\vartheta_{\tilde{Z}^I}(t)$ is non-membership value (degree of non-acceptance) of performing time *t* (in hours). Then the degree of acceptance of the performing time *t* is $100\ \mu_{\tilde{Z}^I}(t)\%$ for the DM and the degree of non-acceptance is $100\vartheta_{\tilde{Z}^I}(t)\%$ for the DM. DM is not sure by $100\left(1-\mu_{\tilde{Z}^I}(t)-\vartheta_{\tilde{Z}^I}(t)\right)\%$ that he/she should accept the performing time *t* or not.

Values of $\mu_{\tilde{Z}^I}(t)$ and $\vartheta_{\tilde{Z}^I}(t)$ at different values of *t* can be determined by using the following equations (8) and (9).

$$\mu_{\tilde{Z}^I}(t) = \begin{cases} 0, & for\, t < 15 \\ \dfrac{t-15}{34}, & for\, 15 \le t \le 49 \\ 1, & for\, t = 49 \\ \dfrac{83-t}{34}, & for\, 49 \le t \le 83 \\ 0, & for\, t > 83 \end{cases} \tag{8}$$

$$\vartheta_{\tilde{Z}^I}(t) = \begin{cases} 1, & for\, t < 4 \\ \dfrac{49-t}{45}, & for\, 4 \le t \le 49 \\ 0, & for\, t = 49 \\ \dfrac{t-49}{45}, & for\, 49 \le t \le 94 \\ 1, & for\, t > 94 \end{cases} \tag{9}$$

Advantages of the Proposed PSK Method

By using the PSK method, a DM has the following advantages:

1. The proposed method (i.e., PSK method) in this chapter is computationally very simple and easy to understand.
2. The proposed method always gives the optimal solution/assignment. In addition, the PSK method gives the opportunity to the DM to solve all the types of IFAP.
3. The PSK method proposes the alternative ideas to solve the variety of intuitionistic fuzzy optimization problems (IFOPs).
4. The proposed PSK method reduces the computation time of the DM.
5. Both the minimization and maximization IFAP can be solved easily by using PSK method.
6. It is a systematic approach.
7. The solution obtained by the proposed method is always reliable and efficient. In general, the solution obtained by the PSK method is optimal.
8. The PSK method has very less number of steps. Therefore, it is also called the student-friendly approach.
9. It is helpful to solve real-life related assignment issues.
10. From the computational point of view, it has significantly fewer calculations when compared to the existing methods.

11. The DM can easily verify that whether the obtained solution is optimal or not because the proposed method depends on the crisp Hungarian method or software packages such as LINGO, TORA, and so forth.
12. Unbalanced IFAP also can be solved by using the PSK method.
13. If the interested researchers, advanced students, and practitioners are studied to the PSK method then they will get a good amount of knowledge in intuitionistic fuzzy concept.
14. Those who are want to solve the problems that related to management science and operations research can study the PSK method.
15. This proposed method is the backbone for studying intuitionistic fuzzy solid assignment problem (extension of intuitionistic fuzzy assignment problem is called intuitionistic fuzzy solid assignment problem).

Disadvantages of the PSK Method

1. Basically, the PSK method depending on the crisp Hungarian method or software packages like LINGO, TORA, and so forth. Without the assistance of the above-mentioned method or software tool, we are not able to proceed with the PSK method.
2. If software packages are corrupted or not working in that situation, we are not able to solve IFAP by using the PSK method.
3. Before we studying the PSK method, either we should aware of the Hungarian method or software packages (e.g., LINGO, TORA).
4. The solution (or assignment) obtained by the PSK method is efficient (or optimal) only if the corresponding software tool is efficient.

The chapter is concerned with the AP, a well-researched area in the management science and operations research fields. The chapter provides a good introduction, starts with the background to the problem before moving on to review prior literature. The review covers earlier work on linear programming, the (dual) simplex method, flags up the limitations of these methods for dealing with the assignment of tasks and reminds the reader of some of the challenges posed by more realistic settings.

This takes the review into fuzzy set theory and how this development has been used in AP and LLP, including recent developments in fuzzy assignment and transportation problems, and reference is made to the PSK method, which is the main focus of the chapter. The introduction provides quite an extensive review of recent work on the development of algorithms for optimizing fuzzy assignments. Much of the recent work reviewed in the chapter has been developed by a group of academics working in Indian universities and perhaps the chapter is an opportunity to make this work more widely available.

The chapter does provide sufficient background information and literature review regarding its topic. The chapter provides a logical structure by taking the reader through the PSK approach to the AP, provides four fully worked examples with screenshots of output summaries from the software used in the computations. The chapter is well-written and reads as being quite comprehensive, it includes the most recent publications in peer-reviewed journals and given its main purpose is to demonstrate the strength of the PSK method in solving intuitionistic fuzzy assignment problems.

This chapter will help researchers, advanced students, and practitioners interested in knowing more about recent work in this area. The information in this chapter does quite clearly illustrate the issues, problems, and trends related to the theme of this proposed book. The authors believe that the proposed statements and conclusions are all clear and validated. The issues and problems described in this chapter are relevant. In this chapter, the authors are focused on all manifestations of fully intuitionistic fuzzy assignment problems.

- **Weaknesses of This Chapter:** An important part of every study is to use an instrument with high reliability and validity. If such instruments are not used, little faith can be put in the results.
- **Strengths of This Chapter:** There are many mathematic equations, theorems, examples, and figures and so on.

Strengths relate to the application of some very recent developments in the development of algorithms for optimizing fuzzy assignments, and in particular, the PSK method. Four examples are provided to illustrate the proposed method in slightly different settings. Hence, the author would like to share their ideas with the researchers, advanced students, and practitioners interested in this aspect of operations research, through the proposed chapter. Since it will help to learn about some recent developments in this field.

CONCLUSION AND FUTURE STUDY

The chapter is concerned with the application of the PSK as a method of optimizing intuitional fuzzy APs. The chapter provides a good review of prior research related to assignment tasks, and in particular, the chapter provides a competent review of more recent developments such as the application of fuzzy sets, intuitionistic fuzzy sets and the PSK method. Fuzzy set theory is well motivated and the idea of the intuitionistic fuzzy number is introduced and its application to the intuitionistic fuzzy assignment problem is then explained prior to introducing the PSK method, the PSK Theorem and its Corollary is quite thorough. The four examples given in Section 6 are useful.

In this chapter, a new method called the PSK method has been proposed to find the optimal assignment and optimal objective value in FIFAP. This new method gives provision to find the optimal objective value directly. That is, the use of intuitionistic fuzzy Hungarian method is not required. Hence, the PSK method is computationally very simple and easy to understand. Several theorems which are related to FIFAP is proposed and it has been proved.

With the help of the proposed PSK method, the real-life related fully intuitionistic fuzzy assignment problems are solved. With the help of LINGO 17.0 and TORA software packages, the proposed results has been verified. The comparative study between the proposed study and the existing method is presented. Results and discussion and the advantages of the PSK method is also given. Furthermore, it can be concluded that the FIFAP and MIFAP which can be solved by the existing methods ((Kumar and Hussain (2014), Dinagar and Thiripurasundari (2014)) can also be solved by the PSK method. My future research will extend the proposed method (i.e., the PSK method) here to deal with the solid assignment problems under intuitionistic fuzzy environment. Moreover, the author would like to develop the software tool for solving intuitionistic fuzzy assignment problems by using PSK method.

ACKNOWLEDGMENT

The authors sincerely thank the anonymous reviewers and Editors Professor Bryan Christiansen and Dr. Fatima Shuwaikh for their careful reading, constructive comments and fruitful suggestions. The author would also like to acknowledge Dr.S.Ismail Mohideen, Principal, My Guide and Associate Professor Dr.R.Jahir Hussain, Dr.A.Nagoor Gani, Associate Professor, Dr.K.Ramanaiah, Associate Professor (retired), Mr.N.Shamsudeen, Associate Professor (retired), Jamal Mohamed College (Autonomous), Tiruchirappalli, Tamil Nadu, India for their motivation and kind support.

REFERENCES

Aggarwal, S., & Gupta, C. (2014). *Algorithm for solving intuitionistic fuzzy transportation problem with generalized trapezoidal intuitionistic fuzzy number via new ranking method.* arXiv preprint arXiv:1401.3353

Antony, R. J. P., Savarimuthu, S. J., & Pathinathan, T. (2014). Method for solving the transportation problem using triangular intuitionistic fuzzy number. *International Journal of Computing Algorithm, 3*, 590–605.

Atanassov, K. (1983). *Intuitionistic fuzzy sets, VII ITKR's Session, Sofia, June 1983.* Deposed in Central Sci. - Techn. Library of Bulg. Acad. of Sci., 1697/84. (in Bulgarian)

Atanassov, K. (1999). *Intuitionistic fuzzy sets: theory and applications.* New York: Springer.

Avis, D., & Devroye, L. (1985). An analysis of a decomposition heuristic for the assignment problem. *Operations Research Letters, 3*(6), 279–283.

Balinski, M. L. (1986). A competitive (dual) simplex method for the assignment problem. *Mathematical Programming, 34*(2), 125–141.

Ban, A. (2008). Trapezoidal approximations of intuitionistic fuzzy numbers expressed by value, ambiguity, width and weighted expected value. *Notes on Intuitionistic Fuzzy Sets, 14*(1), 38–47.

Barr, R. S., Glover, F., & Klingman, D. (1977). The alternating basis algorithm for assignment problems. *Mathematical Programming, 13*(1), 1–13.

Bellman, R. E., & Zadeh, L. A. (1970). Decision-making in a fuzzy environment. *Management Science, 17*(B) 141-164.

Burillo, P., Bustince, H., & Mohedano, V. (1994). Some definitions of intuitionistic fuzzy number-first properties. *Proceedings of the First Workshop on Fuzzy Based Expert System*, 53-55.

Chakraborty, D., Jana, D. K., & Roy, T. K. (2015). A new approach to solve multi-objective multi-choice multi-item Atanassov's intuitionistic fuzzy transportation problem using chance operator. *Journal of Intelligent & Fuzzy Systems, 28*(2), 843–865.

Das, S., & Guha, D. (2013). Ranking of intuitionistic fuzzy number by centroid point. *Journal of Industrial and Intelligent Information, 1*(2), 107–110.

De, P. K., & Yadav, B. (2012). A general approach for solving assignment problems involving with fuzzy cost coefficients. *Modern Applied Science*, *6*(3), 2.

Dinagar, D. S., & Thiripurasundari, K. (2014). A new method for finding the cost of fuzzy assignment problem using genetic algorithm of artificial intelligence. *International Electronic Journal of Pure and Applied Mathematics, 8*(4).

Dinagar, D. S., & Thiripurasundari, K. (2014). A navel method for solving fuzzy transportation problem involving intuitionistic trapezoidal fuzzy numbers. *International Journal of Current Research*, *6*(6), 7038–7041.

Ebrahimnejad, A., Nasseri, S. H., & Mansourzadeh, S. M. (2011). Bounded Primal Simplex Algorithm for Bounded Linear Programming with Fuzzy Cost Coefficients. *International Journal of Operations Research and Information Systems*, *2*(1), 96–120. doi:10.4018/joris.2011010105

Gani, A. N., & Abbas, S. (2012). Intuitionistic fuzzy transportation problem. *Proceedings of the Heber International Conference on Applications of Mathematics and Statistics (HICAMS)*, 528-535.

Gotmare, A. D., & Khot, P. G. (2016). Solution of a fuzzy assignment problem by using Branch-and-Bound technique with application of linguistic variable. *International Journal of Computers and Technology*, *15*(4), 6649–6653.

Grzegorzewski, P. (2003). Distance and orderings in a family of intuitionistic fuzzy numbers. *Proceedings of the Third Conference of the European Society for Fuzzy Logic and Technology*, 223-227.

Guha, D., & Chakraborty, D. (2010). A theoretical development of distance measure for intuitionistic fuzzy numbers. International Journal of Mathematics and Mathematical Sciences.

Habib, M. (2018). *Handbook of Research on Investigations in Artificial Life Research and Development*. Hershey, PA: IGI Global. doi:10.4018/978-1-5225-5396-0

Hussain, R. J., & Kumar, P. S. (2012a). The transportation problem in an intuitionistic fuzzy environment. *International Journal of Mathematics Research*, *4*(4), 411–420.

Hussain, R. J., & Kumar, P. S. (2012b). Algorithmic approach for solving intuitionistic fuzzy transportation problem. *Applied Mathematical Sciences*, *6*(80), 3981–3989.

Hussain, R. J., & Kumar, P. S. (2012c). The transportation problem with the aid of triangular intuitionistic fuzzy numbers. In *Proceedings in International Conference on Mathematical Modeling and Applied Soft Computing (MMASC-2012)*. Coimbatore Institute of Technology.

Hussain, R. J., & Kumar, P. S. (2013). An optimal more-for-less solution of mixed constraints intuitionistic fuzzy transportation problems. *International Journal of Contemporary Mathematical Sciences*, *8*(12), 565–576. doi:10.12988/ijcms.2013.13056

Jinshuai, Y., Jin, L., Yi, W., Tong, W., & Zhanqiang, L. (2017). Optimization of weapon-target assignment problem by intuitionistic fuzzy genetic algorithm. In *MATEC Web of Conferences* (Vol. 128, p. 02004). EDP Sciences. DOI: 10.1051/matecconf/201712802004

Jose, S., & Kuriakose, S. (2013). Algorithm for solving an assignment model in intuitionistic fuzzy context. *International Journal of Fuzzy Mathematics and Systems*, *3*(5), 345–349.

Kuhn, H. W. (1955). The Hungarian method for the assignment problem. *Naval Research Logistics Quarterly*, *2*(1-2), 83–97.

Kumar, A., & Gupta, A. (2012). Assignment and travelling salesman problems with coefficients as LR fuzzy parameters. *International Journal of Applied Science and Engineering*, *10*(3), 155–170.

Kumar, A., Gupta, A., & Kaur, A. (2009). Method for solving fully fuzzy assignment problems using triangular fuzzy numbers. *International Journal of Computer and Information Engineering*, *3*, 231–234.

Kumar, A., & Kaur, A. (2011). Methods for solving fully fuzzy transportation problems based on classical transportation methods. *International Journal of Operations Research and Information Systems*, *2*(4), 52–71. doi:10.4018/joris.2011100104

Kumar, A., & Kaur, M. (2013). A ranking approach for intuitionistic fuzzy numbers and its application. *Journal of Applied Research and Technology*, *11*(3), 381–396.

Kumar, G., & Bajaj, R. K. (2014). On Solution of Interval Valued Intuitionistic Fuzzy Assignment Problem Using Similarity Measure and Score Function. *International Journal of Mathematical, Computational. Physical and Quantum Engineering*, *8*(4), 713–718.

Kumar, N., & Shukla, D. (2016, March). Resource management through fuzzy assignment problem in cloud computing environment. In *Proceedings of the Second International Conference on Information and Communication Technology for Competitive Strategies* (p. 87). ACM.

Kumar, P. S. (2016a). A simple method for solving type-2 and type-4 fuzzy transportation problems. *International Journal of Fuzzy Logic and Intelligent Systems*, *16*(4), 225–237. doi:10.5391/IJFIS.2016.16.4.225

Kumar, P. S. (2016b). PSK method for solving type-1 and type-3 fuzzy transportation problems. *International Journal of Fuzzy System Applications*, *5*(4), 121–146. doi:10.4018/IJFSA.2016100106

Kumar, P. S. (2017a). *Algorithmic approach for solving allocation problems under intuitionistic fuzzy environment* (Unpublished doctoral dissertation). Jamal Mohamed College (Autonomous), Tiruchirappalli, India. Retrieved from http://hdl.handle.net/10603/209151

Kumar, P. S. (2017b). PSK method for solving type-1 and type-3 fuzzy transportation problems. In Fuzzy Systems: Concepts, Methodologies, Tools, and Applications (pp. 367-392). Hershey, PA: IGI Global. doi:10.4018/978-1-5225-1908-9.ch017

Kumar, P. S. (2018a). Search for an optimal solution to vague traffic problems using the PSK method. In M. Habib (Ed.), *Handbook of Research on Investigations in Artificial Life Research and Development* (pp. 219–257). Hershey, PA: IGI Global; doi:10.4018/978-1-5225-5396-0.ch011

Kumar, P. S. (2018b). Linear programming approach for solving balanced and unbalanced intuitionistic fuzzy transportation problems. *International Journal of Operations Research and Information Systems*, *9*(2), 73–100. doi:10.4018/IJORIS.2018040104

Kumar, P. S. (2018c). A simple and efficient algorithm for solving type-1 intuitionistic fuzzy solid transportation problems. *International Journal of Operations Research and Information Systems*, *9*(3), 90–122. doi:10.4018/IJORIS.2018070105

Kumar, P. S. (2018d). A note on 'a new approach for solving intuitionistic fuzzy transportation problem of type-2'. *International Journal of Logistics Systems and Management*, *29*(1), 102–129. doi:10.1504/IJLSM.2018.10009204

Kumar, P. S. (2018e). Intuitionistic fuzzy zero point method for solving type-2 intuitionistic fuzzy transportation problem. *International Journal of Operational Research*. (in press)

Kumar, P. S. (2018f). PSK method for solving intuitionistic fuzzy solid transportation problems. *International Journal of Fuzzy System Applications*, *7*(4), 62–99. doi:10.4018/ijfsa.2018100104

Kumar, P. S. (2018g). Algorithms for solving the optimization problems using fuzzy and intuitionistic fuzzy set. *International Journal of System Assurance Engineering and Management*. (submitted)

Kumar, P. S. (2018h). Intuitionistic fuzzy solid assignment problems: A software-based approach. *International Journal of System Assurance Engineering and Management*. (submitted)

Kumar, P. S. (2019a). PSK method for solving mixed and type-4 intuitionistic fuzzy solid transportation problems. *International Journal of Operations Research and Information Systems*. (in press)

Kumar, P. S. (2019b). Linear Programming Method for Solving Solid and Intuitionistic Fuzzy Solid Transportation Problems. *International Journal of Uncertainty, Fuzziness and Knowledge-based Systems*. (submitted)

Kumar, P. S. (2019c). Integer Programming Approach for solving solid and Intuitionistic Fuzzy Solid Assignment Problems. *International Journal of Logistics Systems and Management*. (submitted)

Kumar, P. S. (2019d). Computationally Simple and Efficient Method for Solving Real-Life Mixed Intuitionistic Fuzzy Solid Assignment Problems. *International Journal of Fuzzy System Applications*. (submitted)

Kumar, P. S. (2019e). Software-based approach for solving intuitionistic fuzzy solid transportation problems. *International Journal of Applied Management Science*. (submitted)

Kumar, P. S. (2019f). Discovery of a new kind of type-2 fuzzy and type-2 intuitionistic fuzzy transportation problems and identification of its optimal solutions. *International Journal of Operations Research and Information Systems*. (submitted)

Kumar, P. S. (2020). Developing a New Approach to Solve Solid Assignment Problems Under Intuitionistic Fuzzy Environment. *International Journal of Fuzzy System Applications*, *9*(1), 1.

Kumar, P. S., & Hussain, R. J. (2014a). *New algorithm for solving mixed intuitionistic fuzzy assignment problem. In Elixir Applied Mathematics* (pp. 25971–25977). Salem, Tamilnadu, India: Elixir publishers.

Kumar, P. S., & Hussain, R. J. (2014b). A systematic approach for solving mixed intuitionistic fuzzy transportation problems. *International Journal of Pure and Applied Mathematics*, *92*(2), 181–190.

Kumar, P. S., & Hussain, R. J. (2014c) A method for finding an optimal solution of an assignment problem under mixed intuitionistic fuzzy environment. *Proceedings in International Conference on Mathematical Sciences (ICMS-2014)* Elsevier.

Kumar, P. S., & Hussain, R. J. (2014d). A method for solving balanced intuitionistic fuzzy assignment problem. *International Journal of Engineering Research and Applications*, *4*(3), 897–903.

Kumar, P. S., & Hussain, R. J. (2015). A method for solving unbalanced intuitionistic fuzzy transportation problems. *Notes on Intuitionistic Fuzzy Sets*, *21*(3), 54–65.

Kumar, P. S., & Hussain, R. J. (2016a). An algorithm for solving unbalanced intuitionistic fuzzy assignment problem using triangular intuitionistic fuzzy number. *The Journal of Fuzzy Mathematics*, *24*(2), 289–302.

Kumar, P. S., & Hussain, R. J. (2016b). Computationally simple approach for solving fully intuitionistic fuzzy real life transportation problems. *International Journal of System Assurance Engineering and Management*, *7*(1), 90–101. doi:10.100713198-014-0334-2

Kumar, P. S., & Hussain, R. J. (2016c). A simple method for solving fully intuitionistic fuzzy real life assignment problem. *International Journal of Operations Research and Information Systems*, *7*(2), 39–61. doi:10.4018/IJORIS.2016040103

Li, D. F., Nan, J. X., & Zhang, M. J. (2010). A ranking method of triangular intuitionistic fuzzy numbers and application to decision making. *International Journal of Computational Intelligence Systems*, *3*(5), 522–530.

Lin, C. J., & Wen, U. P. (2004). A labeling algorithm for the fuzzy assignment problem. *Fuzzy Sets and Systems*, *142*(3), 373–391.

Lone, M. A., Mir, S. A., Ismail, Y., & Majid, R. (2017). Intuitionistic Fuzzy Assignment Problem: An Application in Agriculture. Asian Journal of Agricultural Extension. *Economia e Sociologia (Evora, Portugal)*, *15*(4), 1–6. doi:10.9734/AJAEES/2017/31967

Mahapatra, G. S., & Roy, T. K. (2009). Reliability evaluation using triangular intuitionistic fuzzy numbers, arithmetic operations. *International Scholarly and Scientific Research & Innovation*, *3*(2), 422–429.

Mahapatra, G. S., & Roy, T. K. (2013). Intuitionistic fuzzy number and its arithmetic operation with application on system failure. *Journal of Uncertain Systems*, *7*(2), 92–107.

Malini, P., & Ananthanarayanan, M. (2016). Solving fuzzy assignment problem using ranking of generalized trapezoidal fuzzy numbers. *Indian Journal of Science and Technology*, *9*(20), 1–4. doi:10.17485/ijst/2016/v9i20/88691

Management Association. (2017). Fuzzy Systems: Concepts, Methodologies, Tools, and Applications. Hershey, PA: IGI Global. doi:10.4018/978-1-5225-1908-9

Mitchell, H. B. (2004). Ranking intuitionistic fuzzy numbers. *International Journal of Uncertainty, Fuzziness and Knowledge-based Systems*, *12*(3), 377–386.

Mohideen, S. I., & Kumar, P. S. (2010). A comparative study on transportation problem in fuzzy environment. *International Journal of Mathematics Research*, *2*(1), 151–158.

Mohideen, S. I., & Kumar, P. S. (2010). *A comparative study on transportation problem in fuzzy environment* (Unpublished master's thesis). Jamal Mohamed College (Autonomous), Tiruchirappalli, India.

Mukherjee, S., & Basu, K. (2010). Application of fuzzy ranking method for solving assignment problems with fuzzy costs. *International Journal of Computational and Applied Mathematics*, *5*(3), 359–368.

Mukherjee, S., & Basu, K. (2012). Solution of a class of intuitionistic fuzzy assignment problem by using similarity measures. *Knowledge-Based Systems*, *27*, 170–179.

Muralidaran, C., & Venkateswarlu, B. (2017, November). A method for solving equally spread symmetric fuzzy assignment problems using branch and bound technique. In IOP Conference Series: Materials Science and Engineering (Vol. 263, No. 4, p. 042123). IOP Publishing. doi:10.1088/1757-899X/263/4/042123

Muruganandam, S., & Hema, K. (2017). An optimal solution to fuzzy assignment problem using ones suffix and improved ones suffix method. *International Journal of Scientific Research*, *6*(5), 267–270.

Nagoorgani, A., Kavikumar, J., Mohamed, V. N., & Shamsidah, A. N. (2016, July). A labeling algorithm for solving intuitionistic fuzzy optimal assignment problems. In *Fuzzy Systems (FUZZ-IEEE), 2016 IEEE International Conference on* (pp. 1621-1627). IEEE.

Nasseri, S. H., & Ebrahimnejad, A. (2011). Sensitivity Analysis on Linear Programming Problems with Trapezoidal Fuzzy Variables. *International Journal of Operations Research and Information Systems*, *2*(2), 22–39. doi:10.4018/joris.2011040102

Nayagam, G., Lakshmana, V., Venkateshwari, G., & Sivaraman, G. (2008, June). Ranking of intuitionistic fuzzy numbers. In *Fuzzy Systems, 2008. FUZZ-IEEE 2008. (IEEE World Congress on Computational Intelligence). IEEE International Conference on* (pp. 1971-1974). IEEE.

Nehi, H. M. (2010). A new ranking method for intuitionistic fuzzy numbers. *International Journal of Fuzzy Systems*, *12*(1), 80–86.

Nehi, H. M., & Maleki, H. R. (2005, July). Intuitionistic fuzzy numbers and it's applications in fuzzy optimization problem. In *Proceedings of the Ninth WSEAS International Conference on Systems* (pp. 1-5). WSEAS.

Palanivel, K., Kumar, K. S., Srinivasan, S., & Muralikrishna, P. (2014, May). Fuzzy assignment problem of trapezoidal membership functions within the sort of alpha optimal solution using ranking principle. In *Advances in Engineering and Technology (ICAET), 2014 International Conference on* (pp. 1-7). IEEE.

Paparrizos, K. (1991). An infeasible (exterior point) simplex algorithm for assignment problems. *Mathematical Programming*, *51*(1-3), 45–54.

Pattnaik, M. (2015). Decision making approach to fuzzy linear programming (FLP) problems with post optimal analysis. *International Journal of Operations Research and Information Systems*, *6*(4), 75–90. doi:10.4018/IJORIS.2015100105

Ping, J. I., & Chu, K. F. (2002). A dual-matrix approach to the transportation problem. *Asia-Pacific Journal of Operational Research, 19*(1), 35–45.

Pothiraj, B., & Rajaram, S. (2017). Intuitionistic fuzzy assignment problem with replacement based on intuitionistic fuzzy aggregation. *International Journal of Mathematical Archive, 8*(2), 69–79.

Prabakaran, K., & Ganesan, K. (2014). Fuzzy Hungarian method for solving intuitionistic fuzzy assignment problems. *International Journal of Scientific and Engineering Research, 5*(9), 11–17.

Prabakaran, K., & Ganesan, K. (2018, April). Fuzzy Hungarian method for solving intuitionistic fuzzy travelling salesman problem. Journal of Physics: Conference Series, 1000(1). doi:10.1088/1742-6596/1000/1/012008

Shabani, A., & Jamkhaneh, E. B. (2014). A new generalized intuitionistic fuzzy number. *Journal of Fuzzy Set Valued Analysis, 24*, 1–10.

Shaw, A. K., & Roy, T. K. (2012). Some arithmetic operations on triangular intuitionistic fuzzy number and its application on reliability evaluation. *International Journal of Fuzzy Mathematics and Systems, 2*(4), 363–382.

Singh, S. (2012). Note on assignment algorithm with easy method of drawing lines to cover all zeros. *International Journal of Operations Research and Information Systems, 3*(3), 87–97. doi:10.4018/joris.2012070106

Singh, S. K., & Yadav, S. P. (2014). Efficient approach for solving type-1 intuitionistic fuzzy transportation problem. *International Journal of System Assurance Engineering and Management*, 1-9. doi:. doi:10.100713198-014-0274-x

Srinivas, B., & Ganesan, G. (2015). A method for solving intuitionistic fuzzy assignment problem using Branch and Bound Method, *International Journal of Engineering Technology. Management and Applied Sciences, 3*(2), 227–237.

Srinivas, B., & Ganesan, G. (2015). Optimal solution for intuitionistic fuzzy transportation problem via Revised Distribution Method. *International Journal of Mathematics Trends and Technology, 19*(2), 150–161.

Thompson, G. L. (1981). A recursive method for solving assignment problems. *Journal of Science Direct- North-Holland Mathematics Studies, 59*, 319-343.

Thorani, Y. L. P., & Shankar, N. R. (2013). Fuzzy assignment problem with generalized fuzzy numbers. *Applied Mathematical Sciences, 7*(71), 3511–3537.

Varghese, A., & Kuriakose, S. (2012). Centroid of an intuitionistic fuzzy number. *Notes on Intuitionistic Fuzzy Sets, 18*(1), 19–24.

Zadeh, L. A. (1965). Fuzzy sets. *Information and Control, 8*(3), 338–353.

APPENDIX

Computerized Output Summary for Problem 1 and 3

Table 14. Problem 1. Output summary for FIFAP from LINGO 17.0

Global optimal solution found.			
Objective value:		49.00000	
Objective bound:		49.00000	
Infeasibilities:		0.000000	
Extended solver steps:		0	
Total solver iterations:		0	
Elapsed runtime seconds:		0.03	
Model Class:		PILP	
Total variables:	9		
Nonlinear variables:	0		
Integer variables:	9		
Total constraints:	7		
Nonlinear constraints:	0		
Total nonzeros:	27		
Nonlinear nonzeros:	0		
	Variable	Value	Reduced Cost
	X11	1.000000	19.00000
	X12	0.000000	28.00000
	X13	0.000000	31.00000
	X21	0.000000	11.00000
	X22	1.000000	17.00000
	X23	0.000000	16.00000
	X31	0.000000	12.00000
	X32	0.000000	15.00000
	X33	1.000000	13.00000
	Row	Slack or Surplus	Dual Price
	1	49.00000	-1.000000
	2	0.000000	0.000000
	3	0.000000	0.000000
	4	0.000000	0.000000
	5	0.000000	0.000000
	6	0.000000	0.000000
	7	0.000000	0.000000

Integer Program Program: Original Data

See Table 15

Table 15. Problem 1. Output summary for FIFAP from TORA

	X11	X12	X13	X21	X22	X23
	x1	x2	x3	x4	x5	x6
Minimize	19.00	28.00	31.00	11.00	17.00	16.00
Subject to						
(1)	1.00	1.00	1.00	0.00	0.00	0.00
(2)	0.00	0.00	0.00	1.00	1.00	1.00
(3)	0.00	0.00	0.00	0.00	0.00	0.00
(4)	1.00	0.00	0.00	1.00	0.00	0.00
(5)	0.00	1.00	0.00	0.00	1.00	0.00
(6)	0.00	0.00	1.00	0.00	0.00	1.00
Lower Bound	0.00	0.00	0.00	0.00	0.00	0.00
Upper Bound	infinity	infinity	infinity	infinity	infinity	infinity
Unrestr'd (y/n)?	n	n	n	n	n	n
Integer (y/n)?	y	y	y	y	y	y
	X31	X32	X33			
	x7	x8	x9			
	12.00	15.00	13.00			
(1)	0.00	0.00	0.00	=	1.00	
(2)	0.00	0.00	0.00	=	1.00	
(3)	1.00	1.00	1.00	=	1.00	
(4)	1.00	0.00	0.00	=	1.00	
(5)	0.00	1.00	0.00	=	1.00	
(6)	0.00	0.00	1.00	=	1.00	
Lower Bound	0.00	0.00	0.00			
Upper Bound	infinity	infinity	infinity			
Unrestr'd (y/n)?	n	n	n			
Integer (y/n)?	y	y	y			

Integer Programming B&B Output Summary

See Table 16

Table 16. Problem 1. Output summary for FIFAP from TORA

OPTIMAL SOLUTION:

Objective Value = 49 (MIN)
Optimum solution found at iteration 1
Result verified at iteration 2

x1: X11 = 1
x2: X12 = 0
x3: X13 = 0
x4: X21 = 0
x5: X22 = 1
x6: X23 = 0
x7: X31 = 0
x8: X32 = 0
x9: X33 = 1

Table 17. Problem 3. Output summary for UBIFAP from LINGO 17.0

Global optimal solution found.			
Objective value:		25.00000	
Objective bound:		25.00000	
Infeasibilities:		0.000000	
Extended solver steps:		0	
Total solver iterations:		0	
Elapsed runtime seconds:		0.05	
Model Class:		PILP	
Total variables:	9		
Nonlinear variables:	0		
Integer variables:	9		
Total constraints:	7		
Nonlinear constraints:	0		
Total nonzeros:	24		
Nonlinear nonzeros:	0		
	Variable	Value	Reduced Cost
	X11	0.000000	31.00000
	X12	1.000000	12.00000
	X13	0.000000	0.000000
	X21	1.000000	13.00000
	X22	0.000000	11.00000
	X23	0.000000	0.000000
	X31	0.000000	16.00000
	X32	0.000000	19.00000
	X33	1.000000	0.000000
	Row	Slack or Surplus	Dual Price
	1	25.00000	-1.000000
	2	0.000000	0.000000
	3	0.000000	0.000000
	4	0.000000	0.000000
	5	0.000000	0.000000
	6	0.000000	0.000000
	7	0.000000	0.000000

Integer Program Program: Original Data

See Table 18.

Table 18. Problem 3. Output summary for UBIFAP from TORA

	X11	X12	X13	X21	X22	X23
	x1	x2	x3	x4	x5	x6
Minimize	31.00	12.00	0.00	13.00	11.00	0.00
Subject to						
(1)	1.00	1.00	1.00	0.00	0.00	0.00
(2)	0.00	0.00	0.00	1.00	1.00	1.00
(3)	0.00	0.00	0.00	0.00	0.00	0.00
(4)	1.00	0.00	0.00	1.00	0.00	0.00
(5)	0.00	1.00	0.00	0.00	1.00	0.00
(6)	0.00	0.00	1.00	0.00	0.00	1.00
Lower Bound	0.00	0.00	0.00	0.00	0.00	0.00
Upper Bound	infinity	infinity	infinity	infinity	infinity	infinity
Unrestr'd (y/n)?	n	n	n	n	n	n
Integer (y/n)?	y	y	y	y	y	y
	X31	X32	X33			
	x7	x8	x9			
	16.00	19.00	0.00			
(1)	0.00	0.00	0.00	=	1.00	
(2)	0.00	0.00	0.00	=	1.00	
(3)	1.00	1.00	1.00	=	1.00	
(4)	1.00	0.00	0.00	=	1.00	
(5)	0.00	1.00	0.00	=	1.00	
(6)	0.00	0.00	1.00	=	1.00	
Lower Bound	0.00	0.00	0.00			
Upper Bound	infinity	infinity	infinity			
Unrestr'd (y/n)?	n	n	n			
Integer (y/n)?	y	y	y			

Integer Programming B&B Output Summary

See Table 19.

Table 19.

OPTIMAL SOLUTION:
Objective Value = 25 (MIN) Optimum solution found at iteration 1 Result verified at iteration 2 x1: X11 = 0 x2: X12 = 1 x3: X13 = 0 x4: X21 = 1 x5: X22 = 0 x6: X23 = 0 x7: X31 = 0 x8: X32 = 0 x9: X33 = 1

Chapter 10
The Probability of Default and Its Design of Experiment

Amir Ahmad dar
B. S. Abdur Rahman Crescent Institute of Science and Technology, India

N. Anuradha
B. S. Abdur Rahman Crescent Institute of Science and Technology, India

ABSTRACT

The Merton Model is the critical model for financial economics to measure the default of a firm. It was the first structural model because it uses the market value of the firm for estimating the default of the firm. The firm will be in default only when the values of the firm goes down to a threshold value (the debt of the firm), and if it occurs, the owner will put the firm to the debt holders. The effects of parameters-asset value V, firms debt D, interest rate r, the volatility σ, and period T on the probability of default was investigated. To estimate the probability of default of a firm, the Black Scholes Model for European call options is used. The aim is to determine which parameter effects more or less on the probability of default. The experiment is based on the orthogonal array L27 in which the five factors (parameters) are varied at three levels. The Taguchi L27 orthogonal method, ANOM, and ANOVA are used to examine the effect of these parameters on the probability of default. It also provides the best combination where the probability of default is minimum.

INTRODUCTION

Risk can be characterized as the deviation of the real outcomes from the normal. It can likewise be portrayed as a misfortune because of the way a borrower or counterparty neglects to satisfy its commitments under the concurred terms (since he/she either cannot or does not have any desire to pay). The probability of default is the hazard that an association or individual will neglect to make an installment they have guaranteed. It is for the most part utilized by the organization to evaluate the expected loss and appointed a particular risk measure, per direction, and speaks to the rate anticipated that would default, estimated most as often as possible by surveying past duty. Credit chance is the main source in the monetary foundation to gauge, recognize, screen and control credit chance with the end goal to

DOI: 10.4018/978-1-5225-8458-2.ch010

guarantee they hold satisfactory capital against the default dangers. The credit chance models can be separated into two classes: a) Reduced form models and b) Structural models.

The reduced credit risk models expect that defaults are incited as a matter of course. There is no supposition of a trigger occasion; however, the default force or the default rate may rely on changes in outer factors such as Gross Domestic Product (GDP) development, loan cost, expansion, and so forth, while structural credit risk models accept that a default can be investigated by a particular trigger point. For example, it very well may be caused by expanding the estimation of the obligation or decline the estimation of the benefit esteem. The default will occur when the value of the asset value is below some threshold (that is the value of the debt). The estimation of the benefits itself is displayed as a stochastic procedure.

Structural models, spearheaded by Black, Scholes and Merton, brilliantly utilize current alternative estimating hypothesis in corporate obligation valuation. In 1974, Robert Merton proposed a numerical model for evaluating the Structural credit risk of a firm by displaying an association's value as a European call option of Black Scholes option pricing model for non-dividend paying stocks. It is the structural model since it is uses the company's incentive to illuminate the likelihood of firms default, and it provides the connection between the estimation of the firm and the default risk. Default occurs at whatever point a stochastic variable (process) speaking to some benefit esteem (value of firm) falls beneath a given edge speaking to the liabilities (debt). It has filled in as the foundation for all other basic models. To outline key ideas driving structure models, the creators survey Merton display in detail and brief acquaintance a few expansions with this model.

The target of this chapter is to depict the factor that influences the probability of default. In this part, the authors will examine which input parameter impacts more on the probability of default for a given data set. The probability of default is a basic device in monetary science to quantify the future risk. The impacts of parameters - asset value, firm's debt, interest rate, the volatility and time period T on the probability of default were examined. To gauge the probability of default of a firm, the Black Scholes Model for European call alternative is utilized. The primary point is to decide the best ideal mix (optimal) where the probability of default is least. The investigation depends on the orthogonal array L27 (Taguchi technique which is an outline of a test whose point is to lessen the quantity of trials) in which the five elements (parameters) are differed at three levels. The Taguchi L27 orthogonal method, Analysis of Mean (ANOM), and Analysis of Variance (ANOVA) are utilized to analyze the impact of these parameters on the probability of default and the ideal mix (optimal combination) where the estimation of the probability of default is minimized.

LITERATURE REVIEW

The Taguchi methods are often used in industrial experiments to investigate the effects of several factors. It is used in every field such as education, engineering, physics, chemistry, environmental science, and so forth. The Taguchi method is a methodical proposal for expansion of different factors with considering to performance, cost, and quality. The standard value of a product is estimated by standard characterizes such as larger is better, nominal is the best, smaller is better (Phadke, 1989; Roy, 2001; Phadke, 1998). Chan et al. (2014) investigated the effect of four parameters; catalyst loading, type of catalyst, reaction temperature and the nitrogen gas on liquid yield (bio-oil). The catalyst loading affects more on liquid yield than others. Shravani et al. (2011) used the Taguchi L9 orthogonal array design to measure the optimized formulation of duloxetine hydrochloride.

Rodrigues et al. (2012) used the Taguchi approach to measure the effects of feed cut, speed and the depth of the cut on roughness and cutting force in turning mild steel using high-speed steel cutting tool. Taguchi orthogonal array measures that the cutting speed had a significant effect on surface roughness and the feed rate and cut-rate had a significant effect on roundness error. Rama and Padmanabhan (2012) investigated the factors that affect on metal removal rate (MMR) are voltage, electrolyte concentration and feed rate. The feed rate affects more on MMR approximately 59% by using the Taguchi L9 orthogonal array.

Wang and Fang (2002) developed a forecast model for surface roughness with the help of the Taguchi Orthogonal model. The parameters feed rate, depth of cut, cutting time, material, point angle and spindle speed are used in order to measure which parameter effects more on surface roughness in finishing turning. Cicek at el. (2012) used the Taguchi orthogonal array method and identified that the cutting speed had a significant effect on surface roughness and the feed rate and cut-rate had a significant effect on roundness error.

The specialists are not dealt with the probability of default by utilizing the Taguchi technique. It very well may be utilized in the probability of default to examine the best ideal mix (best combination) with the assistance of some measurable devices (ANOM and ANOVA). The reason for this part is to complete a trial on the probability of default at three levels utilizing Taguchi symmetrical cluster strategy (three levels and five parameters implies that Authors need to complete 27 attempts rather than 243). Finally, the creators actualize ANOM and ANOVA to depict the different properties.

Therefore, the objective of this chapter is to measure which parameter effects more on the probability of default, the best optimal combination where the value of the probability of default is fewer and also the percentage contribution of each factor with the help of statistical tools Taguchi L27 orthogonal array, ANOM, and ANOVA for a given observed data set.

Black Scholes Model

To undersatnd the Black Scholes model, it is necessary to know about options and how it works.

Options

This is a contract between individuals or firms in which one party agrees to buy and another party decides to sell. An option is a contract that gives the right to purchase or sell any underlying asset at a fixed price/exercise/strike price that predetermined price of an underlying asset on a future date.

There are two types of options:

1. **Call Option:** It gives the holder the right but not the obligation to buy an underlying asset at a fixed price on the future date
2. **Put Option:** It gives the holder the right but not the obligation to sell an underlying asset at a fixed price on the future date

Notations

Below are some notations used in this chapter:

t - The current time;
S_t - The underlying share price at time t;
K - The strike/exercise price;
T - The option exercise date;
r - The interest rate;

Payoff

The money realized by the holder of a derivative (an option) at the end of its life. The profit made by the holder at the maturity date is known as a payoff.

A payoff of European call option: Let us consider a call option with S_t is the price of the underlying at time t and fixed strike price K.

At expiry time T, there are two different opportunities:

At expiry time T, if the price of the underlying asset S_T is greater than the strike price. The call option is then exercised i.e. the holder buys the underlying asset at price K and immediately sell it in the market at price S_T, the holder realize the profit.

i.e., $Payoff = S_T - k$

At expiry time T, if a price of the underlying asset S_T is less than the strike price K. The call option then not exercised. The option expires worthless with $payoff = 0$.

Combine the above two cases, at time T. The value of a call option is given by a function.

$$C_u = \max\left(S_T - k, 0\right) \quad [4]$$

Figure 1 shows payoff of a European call option without any premium.

The only difference between an American and a European option is that with the former the holder can exercise the contract early (before the expiry date) and the latter the holder can exercise only on the expiry date.

Black Scholes Formula

The Black Scholes model is a strategy for option price estimating. It is otherwise called the Black Scholes Option Pricing model. It is a scientific model for assessing the estimations of an investment opportunity (call and put). It depends on the underlying asset/stock pursues a stochastic procedure; it implies that the price of underlying asset/stock at time t+1 is free of the price in time t. The price of an underlying asset alluded to as an arbitrary walk.

Figure 1. Payoff of a European call option
Note: In a call option, the holder expects that the price of the underlying asset will increase in the future.

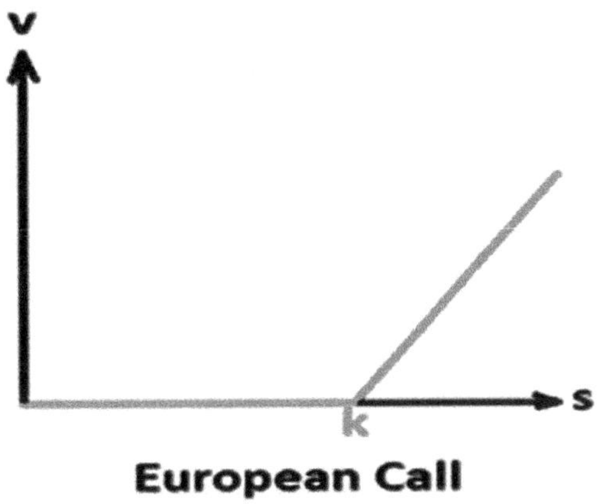

The Black Scholes model is a diagnostic model for European options on non-dividend paying stocks. It is otherwise called the Black-Sholes Merton display since this model obtained the name after its co-makers (Robert Merton, Myron Scholes and Fischer Black). The Black Scholes demonstrate was created in 1973 without dividend-paying stocks. This work, for which its designers obtained the Nobel prize, shapes the foundation of current option estimating hypothesis. The Black Scholes model is a scientific frame, giving an equation into which the determinants of options price are encouraged and the last outcomes on the estimations of the options are inferred. The Black Scholes model is basically a mathematical formula used to estimate the values of the options. It is consists of three parts: the main equation (1), and the two formulas (equation 2 and equation 3) for calculating the parameters.

$$C\left(S,T\right) = S * N\left(d_1\right) - Ke^{-rT} N\left(d_2\right) \quad (1)$$

where

$$d_1 = \frac{\ln\left(\frac{S}{K}\right) + \left(r + \frac{\sigma^2}{2}\right)T}{\sigma\sqrt{T}} \quad (2)$$

$$d_2 = \frac{\ln\left(\frac{S}{K}\right) + \left(r - \frac{\sigma^2}{2}\right)T}{\sigma\sqrt{T}} = d_1 - \sigma\sqrt{T} \quad (3)$$

The equation (1) reveals to us that the price of an European style call choice with development date in time T composed on underlying asset S is equivalent to the price of an underlying asset balanced for the interest rate r, volatility σ and the spread present value of the underlying asset delivery price (or foreordained value/strike value K) likewise balanced for the interest rate r, volatility σ and the spread.

The d1 and d2 are the parameters to the N in the equation (1). N indicates cumulative normal distribution function.

Notations: "S is the present price of the stock, K is the strike price, r is the free risk rate interest, σ is the volatility/variance parameter of the stock and N is the cumulative normal distribution function (CNDF) for a standard normal distribution".

Assumptions of the Black Scholes Model

The assumptions of the Black Scholes Model are divided into four groups:

1. On the basis of the risky underlying asset:
    a. The volatility is constant, the volatility measures how much an underlying asset can be expected to move up or down. It can be constant during a small time period, but at a longer time period it never remains constant. The volatility is known in advance and it is constant as it does not change with time.
    b. No dividends, it is another assumption of the Black Scholes model that the dividends are not paid during the option's life. The Black Scholes model later was modified for dividend payments as well.
    c. Return of an underlying asset follows a normal distribution and the price of an underlying asset follows a lognormal distribution.
    d. Random walk, the price of an underlying asset, cannot be consistently estimated because the direction of the price is unknown. At a future date what will be the price of an underlying asset – It will move either up or down.
2. On the basis of the underlying riskless asset:
    a. The interest rate is constant in the Black Scholes model assuming the interest rate is constant and known and it is same as the volatility.
3. On the basis of the option type: There are two types of style of options
    a. European style options which will expire only on the expiry date.
    b. American options which will expire at any time before the expiry date.
4. On the basis of the market:
    a. There is no transaction cost or tax which means there is no fee to buy or sell the options.
    b. Liquidity which assumes that the market is total perfectly liquid – that means any time it is possible to sell or buy the options.
    c. There are no restrictions for short selling.
    d. It assumes the market is efficient. It also indicated that the price of an underlying asset at time t+1 is independent of the price at time t.

In this chapter, the BSM for call option (European) is used to find the probability default of the firm. The d_2 is very important because it is the idea behind the Merton model and $N(-d_2)$ is the probability of default. See references (Hull, 2009; Dar &Anuradha, 2017a,b).

MERTON MODEL

The Merton model is the principal structural model which estimates the probability of default for firms. This model gauges the probability of default dependent on a straightforward structure of its accounting report. It gives the connection between the default risk and the value of the firm/value of assets (capital) structure of the firm. It accepts that the firm will issue the two obligations D (debt) and value E (equity), and it provides us a chance to accept that the value of assets is V at time t. It will differ over time because of activities by the firm, which does not pay any dividend on the equity or coupon. Firms default when they cannot, or decide not to, meet their money-related commitments.

For simplicity appreciation and articulation, separate the accounting report into two sections: i) equity and debt on one side in light of the fact that both equity and debt holders have a claim on the value of asset; and ii) the value of the asset on the opposite side. The Zero coupon debt is a piece of a firm's entity with ensured reimbursement of sum D at time T. The rest of the firm V at time T will be issued to the shareholders and the firm will be twisted up.

On account of the breeze up the firm, the shareholders rank is underneath the debt holders. In the off chance that the firm will create the great reserve in such a route along these lines, to the point that can pay the debt, at that point the shareholders will get the payoff of (as shown in Figure 2):

$$V - D$$

The firm will default at time T when $V < D$

In the above case, the bondholders will get V rather than D and the shareholders will get nothing. Consider both conditions:

The shareholders will receive the payoff of:

$$\max\left(V - D, 0\right) \tag{5}$$

This is same as the payoff of the European call option as shown in equation (4), with V as an underlying asset price and D as a Strike price. The figure for equity and debt holder in a firm is shown below in Figure 3.

Figure 2.

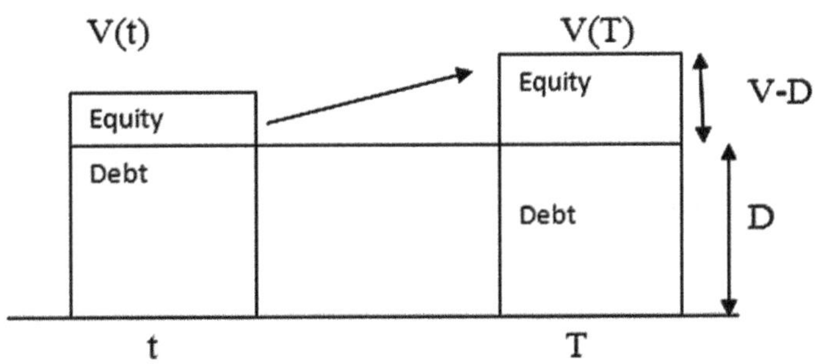

Figure 3. Equity and debt as options

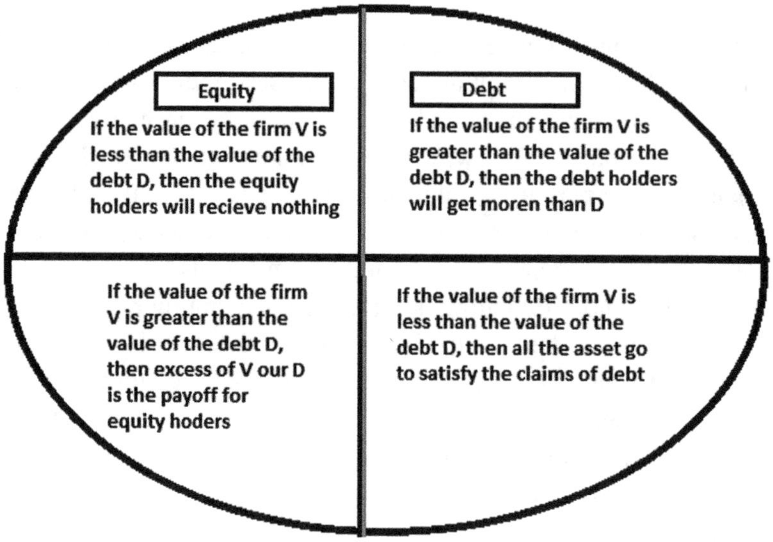

In Merton's model, the company's capital structure is thought to be created by equity and a zero-coupon bond with maturity T and face value of D and can appraise the estimation of the value E by utilizing the Black Scholes recipe for an alternative which is:

$$E = V * N(d_1) - D * e^{-rT} * N(d_2) \tag{6}$$

where:

$$d_1 = \frac{\ln\left(\frac{v}{D}\right) + \left(r + \frac{\sigma^2}{2}\right)T}{\sigma\sqrt{T}}$$

$$d_2 = \frac{\ln\left(\frac{V}{D}\right) + \left(r - \frac{\sigma^2}{2}\right)T}{\sigma\sqrt{T}}$$

$$= d_1 - \sigma\sqrt{T}$$

where: "r is the free risk rate interest, T is the time period, σ is the volatility of the firms value and N is the cumulative standard normal (CDF) function for a standard normal distribution".

Following assumptions would undermine the model efficiency:

1. The firm can default just at time T and not previously

2. The assets of the firm V follow a lognormal distribution.
3. It implies that the the asset value of a firm pursues a geometric Brownian movement/ log-normal distribution, with risk impartial elements given by the stochastic differential condition:

$$\frac{dV}{V} = rdt + \sigma_V dW_t$$

where W_t is a standard Brownian movement under risk unbiased measure, r denotes the continuously risk-free rate of interest, and σ_V is the asset/value of firms return volatility. Likewise require, promote to presumptions: there are no bankruptcy charges, which means the liquidation esteem breaks even with the firm esteem; the debt and equity are frictionless tradable resources

4. The aggregate value of the firm is equivalent to the whole of Equity and additionally debt. From a bookkeeping point of view, the book value of Equity E, Value of a firm V and the Debt D are characterized by a condition:
5. To gauge the distance to default and probability of default the inward price of the Back Scholes recipe for a European call choice i.e. equation (3) is utilized:

Replace:

- The risk-free rate of interest r by the expected continuously compounded return on the value of the firm μ_V.
- The value of the underlying asset S at time t by the value of the asset at time t is V.
- The strike price K by the face value of the debt D.
- The volatility σ by the volatility of the firms value σ_V

The distance to default is given by:

$$d_2 = \frac{\ln\left(\frac{V}{D}\right) + \left(\mu_V - \frac{\sigma_V^{\ 2}}{2}\right)T}{\sigma_V \sqrt{T}} \qquad (7)$$

where μ_V is expected rate of return of the firm's asset and D, is the value of a debt and expected growth of assets is equal to $\left(\mu_V - \frac{\sigma_V^{\ 2}}{2}\right)$.

Equation (7) is really the distance to default; it demonstrates that the distance between expected assets and debt as appeared in Figure 4. It very well may be computed as a total of initial distance and development of that distance inside the period T. In the wake of evaluating the distance to default, the probability of default can be assessed

Figure 4. Probability of default

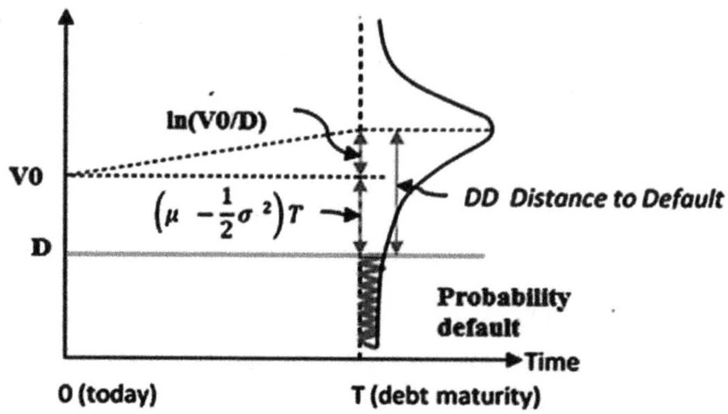

Debt and equity that are considered as options can be esteemed at the option prices by utilizing the Black Scholes Model. The probability of default is a default under option prices are given by $N(-d_2)$, which can be determined with estimation of the debt and equity. The probability of default under the risk nonpartisan measure according to the Black Scholes Merton demonstrate is given by:

$$Probability\,default = N(-d_2) = N\left(-\frac{\ln\left(\frac{V}{D}\right) + \left(\mu_V - \frac{\sigma_V^{\,2}}{2}\right)T}{\sigma_V\sqrt{T}}\right) \tag{8}$$

Or

$$Probability\,default = 1 - N\left(d_2\right)$$

Equation (8) is the probability of default i.e. it is the distance between the value of the firm and the value of the debt (V/D) adjust for the expected growth related to asset volatility $\left(\mu_V - \frac{\sigma_V^{\,2}}{2}\right)$ related to asset volatility.

The equation (8) is the probability of default with 3 unknowns V, σ_V and μ_V. To estimate the probability as per equation (8) the authors need to find the above three unknowns. It is known that the value of the firm V is equal to the sum of the Debt and the Equity of the firm, so Debt D is known and must find Equity E. The equity value E is a continuous time stochastic process that is the Weiner process.

$$E = \mu_E Edt + \sigma_E EdZ \tag{9}$$

where dZ the continuous time is a stochastic process, μ_E is the expected continuously compounded return on E and σ_E is the volatility of the equity value.

By Ito's lemma,

$$\frac{df(\cdot)}{dx}Y_t dZ_t + \left[\frac{df(\cdot)}{dt} + A_t\frac{df(\cdot)}{dx} + 0.5\frac{d^2f(\cdot)}{dx^2}Y_t^2\right]dt$$

We can represent the process for equity E as:

$$dE = \sigma_V V\frac{dE}{dV}dZ + \left[\frac{dE}{dt} + \mu_V V\frac{dE}{dV} + 0.5\left(\sigma_V V\right)^2\frac{d^2E}{dV^2}\right]dt \tag{10}$$

As per the diffusion terms the equation (9) and (10) is equal, so we can write the relation between the two equations as:

$$\sigma_E E = \sigma_V V\frac{dE}{dV} = \sigma_V * N\left(d_1\right) * V \tag{11}$$

Equations (6) and (11) are the two nonlinear simultaneous equations with two unknowns one is σ_V and another is V. We can easily estimate the two parameters by solving the equation (6) and (11). After finding the V and σ_V we need to find the return of the asset that is μ_V.

As per the general definition of return, it is defined as:

$$Return = \frac{today\ price - yesterday\ price}{yesterday\ price}$$

So,

$$\mu_V = \frac{V_t - V_{t-1}}{V_{t-1}} \tag{12}$$

In most extreme cases the return is negative, as it specified in Hillegeist et al. (2004). The normal/expected return can't be a negative and accept that the expected growth is equivalent to the risk free rate of interest. Utilize all the known parameters that include E, r, D, T and σ_E to estimate the three unknown parameters V, σ_V and μ_V, one can evaluate the genuine probability of default by utilizing equation (8).

The general thought of this section is to break down the real impact on probability of default. In the Merton display, default happens when the "astound" term d_2 is sufficiently substantial (ordinarily an extensive negative number). In the numerator, $\ln\left(\frac{V}{D}\right)$ is the real continuously compounded return on the assets that is important to prompt default. On the off chance that $D > V$, this arrival is negative, the asset value must tumble to prompt default. The term $\left(\mu_V - \frac{\sigma^2}{2}\right)T$ is the expected value of the continuously compounded return (generally positive).

Accordingly the numerator is the distinction between the actual continuously compounded rate of return required for default and the expected value of the return, i.e., it is the "shock", or sudden part of the rate of return essential for default. The denominator is the standard deviations of the rate of return. Subsequently, the proportion (again ordinarily negative) measures the quantity of standard deviations of return important to prompt default at time T. The negative of this proportion (a positive number) is known as the distance to-default. Disttance to default is littler (the probability of default - higher) when instability is higher and development is longer (Dar & Anuradha 2017c).

Probability of Default

Credit risk estimation and administration have turned out to be a standout among the most basic themes in money-related financial matters. The term default basically implies an indebted person has not paid an obligation. "Bankruptcy/Insolvency" is a lawful term implying that a borrower cannot pay his/her commitments. A credit is the danger of misfortune because of an account holder's non-instalment of an advance or another credit extension (either the main or intrigue (coupon) or both). It is the hazard because of vulnerability in a counter gathering's (additionally called required or attributes) capacity to meet its commitments.

For instance, an organization cannot reimburse sums anchored by settled or coasting charges over the benefit of the organization; a business which does not pay a representative's wins compensation when due, a wiped out firm will not return assets to an investor. Credit risk demonstrating gauges how much credit is in danger because of a default or changes in credit hazard factors. Likewise, it encourages them to ascertain how much capital they have to set aside to secure against such dangers. In the fund, default happens when an account holder has not met its lawful commitment as per the debt contract. This can occur with all obligation/debt commitments including bonds, home loans, advances, and promissory notes.

Example 1

Let us consider a simple example:

Firm Value (V) = 130, value of Debt (D) = 100, Expected return (mu) = 5%, Time (T) =1 Period, Volatility (σ) = 20%

In order to measure the distance to default DD and the probability of default, we use d_2 to estimate both the measures. The d_2 is the idea behind the Merton model in the credit risk.

So,

$$d_2 = \frac{\ln\left(\frac{S}{K}\right) + \left(r - \frac{\sigma^2}{2}\right)T}{\sigma\sqrt{T}}$$

On the basis of the assumptions we write the above equation in the form of:

$$d_2 = \frac{\ln\left(\frac{V}{D}\right) + \left(\mu_V - \frac{\sigma_V{}^2}{2}\right)T}{\sigma_V\sqrt{T}}$$

Now start at the beginning at time t=0, $\ln\left(V / D\right) = 26.23\%$, it indicates that at the beginning the value of the firm dropped 26.23% before the default. At the end of the expiry time in which time T=1, the expected value of the firm is more than at time t=0 because the expected growth is positive. So, in the above example the value of the firm at time t=1 is V_1=134 as shown in Figure 5. In *equation (6)* we can see $\left(\mu_V - \frac{\sigma^2}{2}\right)$ is the geometric average.

In the Merton model, default occurs when the term d_2 is large enough (typically a large negative number). In the numerator, $\ln\left(\frac{V}{X}\right) = 26.24\%$ (see equation 6) is the actual continuously compounded return on the assets that are necessary to lead to default. If $D > V$, that is the value of the debt is greater than the value of the firm which means that it must fall to lead to default

At the time T=1, $\ln\left(V1 / X\right) = 29.2\%$, this indicates that the firm value at future is 29.2% above the threshold. As per our example, our volatility is 20%, which indicates that our expected future value of the firm will be 1.46 sigma above the threshold of 100. Probability of default = $N\left(-d_2\right) = 7.19\%$.

We estimated the distance to default d_2=1.26 standard deviation or, in other words, 29.2%. The probability of default N(-d_2) is equal to 7.19% which indicates that 7.19% chance that the firm will default. In other words, there is a 7.19% chance that the firm will not pay its debts. In Figure 5, it is seen that the line below the threshold (yellow line below the green line is the probability default) that is probability default.

Example 2

Consider a firm whose equity is Rs 60. The volatility of equity is 80%. The firm's debt is equal to Rs 200 and it must be paid in one year. The risk-free rate of interest on the market is 8% p.a.

Estimate the value: a) V and σ_V and b) what is the probability of default of a firm.

Hint: use equation 11 and 8

Figure 5.

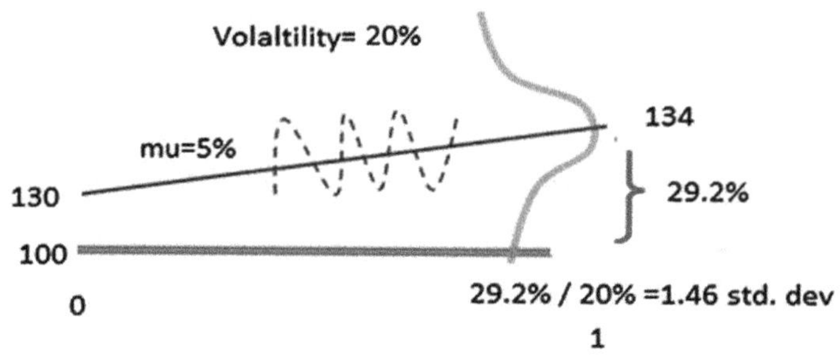

FACTORS AFFECTING PROBABILITY OF DEFAULT

The probability of default affecting various factors that is:

1. Firms value V
2. Value of debt D
3. Mu(r) / μ_V the expected return
4. Time period T
5. Volatility σ

Table 1 demonstrates the estimation of various parameters that are utilized with the end goal to gauge the probability of default of a firm. Here creators are utilizing the accepted information to research the impacts of various factors on reaction variable. Creators transformed one factor (expanded) and others kept consistent in such a manner that they portrayed the components that influencing on the probability of default.

Figure 6 shows the relationship between the factors and the probability of default.

The following conclusions for Figure 6 are given below:

- Figure 6 shows that if the firm value (V) increases then the probability of default will decrease
- Figure 6 shows that if the debt (D) increases then the probability of default will increase
- Figure 6 shows the probability of default decreases when "mu" increases.
- Figure 6 shows the probability of default increases when time increases.

Table 1. The values of parameters/factors

Firm Value(V)	Firm Value Debt (D)	"mu" (r)	Time T	Volatility
130	100	0.05	1	0.2
140	105	0.06	2	0.21
150	110	0.07	3	0.22
160	115	0.08	4	0.23
170	120	0.09	5	0.24
180	125	0.10	6	0.25

Figure 6. Factors vs probability of default

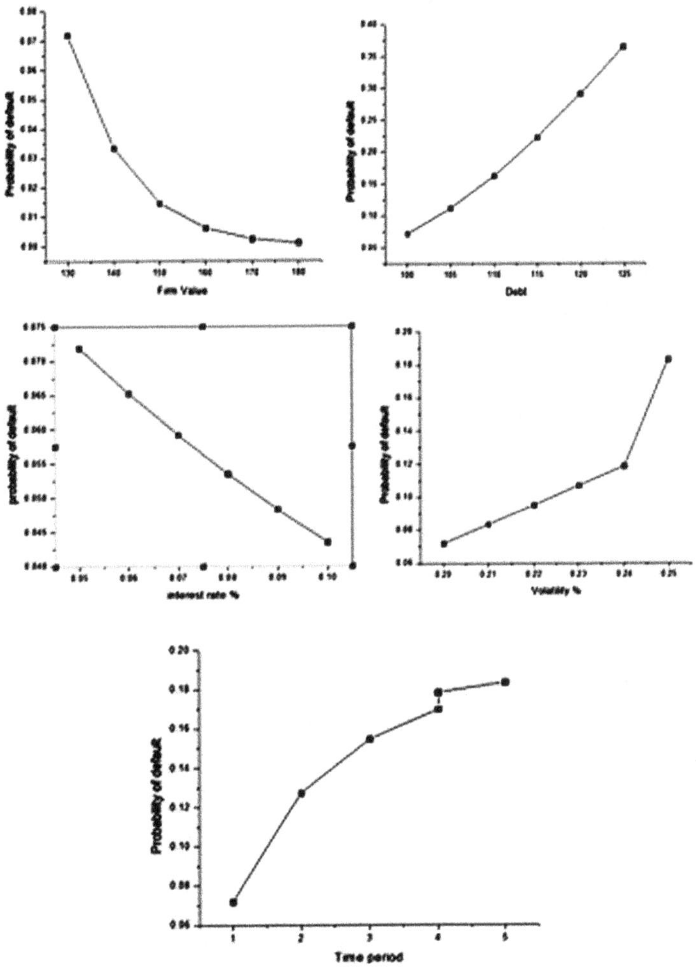

- Figure 6 shows the probability of default increases when time volatility increases

THE TAGUCHI METHOD: A DESIGN OF EXPERIMENT

The design of experiment (DOE) is an offline statistical technique used to achieve best performance of products and processes. It was developed by the English man R. A. Fisher in the 1920s in order to survey the effects of factors simultaneously. It is consists of three components: i) the design of experiment; ii) conduct the experiment; and iii) analyze the data. This technique of laying out the conditions of an experiment involving various factors and this method is known as factorial design. It is a set of experiments whose design consists of more than one parameters each with discrete possible level and whose experiment units takes all possible combinations of all those levels across all such factors.

For example, if there are K factors each at three levels, FFD has 3^K runs. For five factors at three levels, it would take 243 experimental runs. Since most of the industrial experiments usually using the full factorial design for design an experimental studies, it contains a huge number of experiments. So far, within this text the authors have examined experimental designs which have well-defined statistical and analysis structures.

Such designs have illustrated the important of using cost effective and easy to analyze design structures in multi factors investigations. Since the mid 1980s, the search for quality within products and processes has led to increased usage of such methods. One of the forces behind this quality drive has been the work of Dr. Genichi Taguchi, a Japanese engineer. The Taguchi methods represent simple but novel applications of classical experiment designs.

To reduce the number of experiments to a practical level, only a few sets from all the possibilities is selected. The method involves selecting a fewer limited number of experiments. Although this model is well-known, there are no general guidelines for its applications. The Taguchi Method selected a fewer number of experiments which produces the most information. This study is based on the Taguchi orthogonal approach method. Today engineers use the Taguchi Method in order to plan the firm's experiment (Taguchi, 1989). Modern industry demands good products with lower cost.

The Taguchi experiment array design is using to arrange the parameters affecting the process and the levels of which they should be varied. Instead of having all possible experiments like Full Factorial Design (FFD), the Taguchi model provides a minimum number of experiments. In the case of five factors and three levels, it would require 27 experimental runs. The experiments are not randomly generated, but they are based on judgmental sampling. It reduces time, resources, and cost which is why industry employs the Taguchi method in order to reduce time, sources, and cost. The Taguchi experimental array design is using to arrange the parameters affecting the process and the levels which should be varied.

The Taguchi approach is covered in this chapter to identify which parameter effects more on the probability of default. Its aim is to find the relationship between the input and the output variables/factors. The Taguchi approach is a DOE whose aim is to gather all the relevant and efficient information regarding the parameters. The Taguchi orthogonal array is a design matrix that permits the planner of experiments to test combinations of design factors that interact at various levels by carrying out a reduced number of experiments. This method was developed to examine the relationship between the inputs and the output with the fewest number of experiments and it banishes the disadvantages of FFD.

The FFD requires much time, cost, resources because the number of experiments is high. Obviously, if the number of experiments is high, cost, time and resources will increase. The Taguchi Method is very good approach because compared to FFD it reduces the number of experiments, cost and resources. The Taguchi Method is based on the assumption of additive property meaning the individuals or main effects of independent variables on response variable are separable.

The following standard orthogonal arrays are commonly used to design experiments.

- **2-Level Arrays:** L4, L8, L12, L16, L32
- **3-Level Arrays:** L9, L18, L27
- **4-Level Arrays:** L16, L32

This chapter works on the five factors/parameters at three levels. As per the table above, the authors have three choices: L9, L18, and L27. The minimum number of experiments are required are 9 and 81 is maximum as shown above.

The general steps involved in the Taguchi method are as follows

1. Define the target value for a performance measure of the process (i.e., the value of the probability of default.
2. Define the input factors: Before conducting the experiment, the knowledge of the process under investigation is of prime importance for identifying the factors likely to influence the result/outcome. The factors are generally obtained from people involved in the project.
3. Levels for each factor: Once we decided the factors for the experiments, the numbers of levels are to be selected for each factor. If the performance parameter is a linear function of the independent variable, then the number of levels shall be 2 and if it is non-linear then one could go for 3, 4, or higher levels.
4. The orthogonal array: These are used to gather and collect reliable information about the control factors which are considered the design parameters with a minimum number of tests and experiments. The minimum numbers of experiments are required to conduct the Taguchi method can be estimated based on the degree of freedom approach.

$$N = 1 + \sum_{I=1}^{NV} \left(L_I - 1\right)$$

Where N is the minimum number of experiments, L is the number of levels and NV is the number of variables/factors. For example, in case of 4 factors at 3 levels, the minimum number of experiments required based on the above formula is 9:

$$N = 1 + 4\left(3 - 1\right) = 9$$

The number of experiments as per the Taguchi Method is multiple of 2 and 3 because of the balancing property.

5. The result of response variables based on predictors (factors/inputs) assign to each column (to estimate the value of response variable based on the predictors in all combinations).
6. Conduct the experiment and analyse the data: It is to be noted that the test sheets should show only the main factor levels required for each trial. Several methods are available for analysing the data collected from experiment. However, statistical methods should be used to analyse the data so that results and conclusions are objectives. The ANOM is used to identify the best combination and the ANOVA is used to estimate the percentage contribution of each factor on probability of default from given observed data.

Therefore, the Taguchi L27 orthogonal array design, ANOM, and ANOVA are used to conduct the analysis that one can decide which independent variable is not affected more on the probability of default.

Taguchi Orthogonal Array Design

Figure 7 shows the Taguchi orthogonal array selector which shows the orthogonal array for the factors and their levels.

Array Selector

Therefore, the objective of this chapter is to measure which parameter effects more on the probability of default and also the percentage contribution of each factor (V, D, r, σ, and T) with the help of statistical tools Taguchi L27 orthogonal array, ANOM, and ANOVA.

Design of Experimental (Taguchi Method) on Probability of Default

In this study, the five parameters (e.g., Asset value firm, the face value of debt, interest rate, the volatility, and time period) are varied at three levels and we assume the values are fixed; it means we assume that the values remain fixed once they are chosen. The process parameters and the selected levels are presented in Table 2.

This study is based on the probability of default as previously mentioned. “The probability of default is a credit risk which provides an estimate of the likelihood of a borrower who will be unable to meet its debt obligations. In order to estimate the probability of default, Merton uses the inner part of the Black Scholes formula for European call options to measure the probability of default.

The probability of default can be calculated as:

Figure 7. Array selector

Orthogo nal Array	No of experiments	No of factors	Max no of factors at theses levels			
			Level 2	Level 3	Level 4	Level 5
L-4	4	3	3	-	-	-
L-8	8	7	7	-	-	-
L-9	9	4	-	4	-	-
L-12	12	11	11	-	-	-
L-16	16	15	15	-	-	-
L-'16	16	5		-	5	-
L-18	18	8	1	7	-	-
L-25	25	6	-	-	-	6
L-27	27	13	-	13	-	-
L-32	32	31	31	-	-	-
L-'32	32	10	1	-	9	-
L-36	36	23	11	12	-	-
L-'36	36	16	3	13	-	
L-50	50	12	1		-	11
L-54	54	26	1	25	-	-
L-64	64	63	63	-	-	-
L-'64	64	21	-	-	21	-
L-81	81	40	-	40	-	-

Table 2. Selected process parameters and levels

Levels	Parameters	*V*	*D*	*r*	σ	*T*
1		130	100	5%	20%	1
2		140	105	7%	30%	2
3		150	118	9%	40%	3

$$probability\,of\,default = N(-d_2) = N\left(-\left(\ln\left(\frac{V}{D}\right) + \frac{\left(r - \frac{\sigma^2}{2}\right)T}{\sigma\sqrt{T}}\right)\right) \tag{13}$$

where, V = Asset value of firm, X = face value of debt, σ = volatility of asset value, r = interest rate or growth rate, and T = time period.

The authors have five parameters at three levels as shown in Table 2. The orthogonal array is selected as per Taguchi method that is $L27(3^5)$. Only 27 experiments are required instead of 243 as per the factorial method as shown in Table 3.

The data provided in Table 2 is adequate enough to calculate the probability of default by using *equation 12*. The experiment layouts for probability of default process parameters by using the Taguchi L27 approach are shown in Table 2. Only 27 experiments are required as per the Taguchi approach. These experiments are not randomly selected, but they are based on some well-defined procedure or sampling. The Taguchi L27 orthogonal array approach is appropriated for experimentation and the experimental matrix along with result (value of probability of default) is shown in Table 4.

Table 5 is developed by adding the response values corresponding to each level (level 1, level 2 and level 3) of each factor. For example, level 1 total of factors V is the sum of the observations (probability of default) from experiments (runs) 1, 2, 3...9 (Table 4). That is,

$$V_1 = 0.0719 + 0.1272 + 0.15453 + 0.21324 + 0.26722$$
$$+0.28932 + 0.39469 + 0.41818 + 0.42736 = 2.36367$$

Note: V_1 is the value of a response variable at level 1.

Similarly, the level 2 totals of factor X is the sum of response values from experiments 4, 5, 6, 13, 14, 15, 22, 23, and 24. That is:

$$D_2 = 0.21324 + 0.26722 + 0.28932 + 0.03686 + 0.06526$$
$$+0.0754 + 0.20705 + 0.29998 + 0.35015 = 1.8045$$

There are 9 observations in each total.

Table 3. Taguchi orthogonal array L27(3^5). Column number and factor assigned

Experiment No.	Factor 1	Factor 2	Factor 3	Factor 4	Factor 5	Result
1	1	1	1	1	1	**
2	1	1	1	1	2	**
3	1	1	1	1	3	**
4	1	2	2	2	1	**
5	1	2	2	2	2	**
6	1	2	2	2	3	**
7	1	3	3	3	1	**
8	1	3	3	3	2	**
9	1	3	3	3	3	**
10	2	1	2	3	1	**
11	2	1	2	3	2	**
12	2	1	2	3	3	**
13	2	2	3	1	1	**
14	2	2	3	1	2	**
15	2	2	3	1	3	**
16	2	3	1	2	1	**
17	2	3	1	2	2	**
18	2	3	1	2	3	**
19	3	1	3	2	1	**
20	3	1	3	2	2	**
21	3	1	3	2	3	**
22	3	2	1	3	1	**
23	3	2	1	3	2	**
24	3	2	1	3	3	**
25	3	3	2	1	1	**
26	3	3	2	1	2	**
27	3	3	2	1	3	**

Analysis of Mean (ANOM)

The response totals are converted into mean response and given in Table 10. Each total (Table 5) is divided by 9 to calculate the mean of each factors. The range in the mean response of the three levels of each factor is also calculated. This difference (Range=maximum - minimum) represents the effect of the factor. These differences are ranked starting with the highest difference as rank 1, the next highest difference as rank 2, and so forth.

Table 4. Taguchi L27 (3^5) experimental design matrix with result

Experiment #	*V*	*D*	*r*	σ	*T*	Probability of Default
1	130	100	5%	20%	1	0.0719
2	130	100	5%	20%	2	0.1272
3	130	100	5%	20%	3	0.15453
4	130	105	7%	30%	1	0.21324
5	130	105	7%	30%	2	0.26722
6	130	105	7%	30%	3	0.28932
7	130	118	9%	40%	1	0.39469
8	130	118	9%	40%	2	0.41818
9	130	118	9%	40%	3	0.42736
10	140	100	7%	40%	1	0.2072
11	140	100	7%	40%	2	0.28793
12	140	100	7%	40%	3	0.32912
13	140	105	9%	20%	1	0.03686
14	140	105	9%	20%	2	0.06526
15	140	105	9%	20%	3	0.0754
16	140	118	5%	30%	1	0.27876
17	140	118	5%	30%	2	0.33486
18	140	118	5%	30%	3	0.36022
19	150	100	9%	30%	1	0.06661
20	150	100	9%	30%	2	0.12144
21	150	100	9%	30%	3	0.14914
22	150	105	5%	40%	1	0.20705
23	150	105	5%	40%	2	0.29998
24	150	105	5%	40%	3	0.35015
25	150	118	7%	20%	1	0.07356
26	150	118	7%	20%	2	0.1147
27	150	118	7%	20%	3	0.13015

Table 5. Response totals for illustration (Table 4)

Factors	*V*	*D*	*r*	σ	*T*
Level 1	2.36367	1.51506	2.18466	0.84951	1.54989
Level 2	1.97559	1.8045	1.91241	2.0808	2.03679
Level 3	1.51281	2.53251	1.75491	2.92167	2.26539

The mean values (ANOM) of probability of default for each parameter at different levels were calculated. These mean values of probability of default for each independent variable at three levels are given in table 6 by using statistical software Minitab. The procedure for calculating the ANOM of response variables are shown in appendix section.

Range= max. – Min.

Table 6 and Figure 8 indicate that the volatility σ affects more and interest rate r affects less on the probability of default. The selected numbers (**bold**) in Table 6 are the minimum in every column. It is concluded that the best combination is $V3 * X1 * r3 * \sigma 1 * T1$ because the low probability of default is the best that is why the authors choose the ranking from low to high. If the line in Figure 8 is horizontal, then there is no mean effect. However, all the lines are not horizontal which mean each factor affects on the probability of default.

Table 6. ANOM: Response table for mean

Level	*V*	*D*	*r*	Volatility	*T*
1	0.26263	0.16834	0.24274	0.09439	0.17221
2	0.21951	0.2005	0.21249	0.2312	0.22631
3	0.16809	0.28139	0.19499	0.32463	0.25171
Delta	0.09454	0.11305	0.04775	0.23023	0.0795
Rank	3	2	5	1	4

Figure 8. Main effects plot for a mean

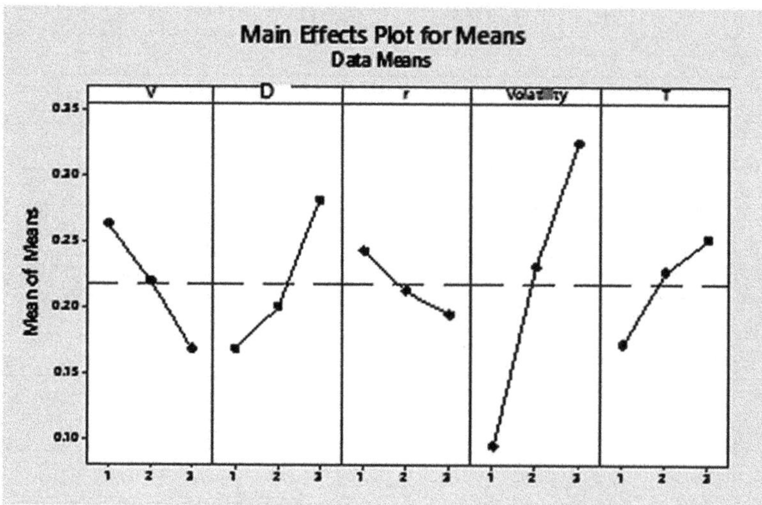

Analysis of Variance (ANOVA)

The ANOVA is used to determine the percentage contribution of each parameter. In other words, it provides the relationship between the inputs and the output. The percentage contribution can be calculated by a formula given below:

$$Percentage\,contribution = \frac{Sum\,of\,squares\left(SS\right)}{Total\,sum\,of\,squares\left(SS\right)}$$

Data Analysis Using ANOVA

First find the correction factor (CF) which is calculated as:

$$CF = \frac{G^2}{N}$$

where G is the total grand sum and N is the total number of observations.

$$CF = \frac{5.85203^2}{27} = 1.26838$$

SS_{Total} is computed using the individual observations (response) data and is calculated as:

$$SS_{Total} = \sum_{i=1}^{N} X_i^{\,2} - CF$$

where X_i = Response value

$$SS_{Total} = 1.656555 - 1.26838 = 0.388176$$

The factor sum of squares is computed using the level totals:

$$SS_V = \frac{V_1^2}{n_{V_1}} + \frac{V_2^2}{n_{V_2}} + \frac{V_3^2}{n_{V_3}} - CF$$

where,

V_1 = level 1 total of factor V

n_{V_1} = number of observations used in V_1

V_2 = level 2 total of factor V

n_{V_2} = number of observations used in V_2

3 = level 3 total of factor V

n_{V_3} = number of observations used in V_3

$$SS_V = \frac{2.36367^2}{9} + \frac{1.97559^2}{9} + \frac{1.51281^2}{9} - 1.26838 = 0.040341$$

Similarly, the sum of squares of all factors are computed

$$SS_D = \frac{X_1^{\,2}}{n_{X_1}} + \frac{X_2^{\,2}}{n_{X_2}} + \frac{X_3^{\,2}}{n_{X_3}} - CF = 0.061091$$

$$SS_V = \frac{r_1^{\,2}}{n_{r_1}} + \frac{r_2^{\,2}}{n_{r_2}} + \frac{r_3^{\,2}}{n_{r_3}} - CF = 0.010482$$

$$SS_\sigma = \frac{\sigma_1^{\,2}}{n_{\sigma_1}} + \frac{\sigma_2^{\,2}}{n_{\sigma_2}} + \frac{\sigma_3^{\,2}}{n_{\sigma_3}} - CF = 0.241348$$

$$SS_T = \frac{T_1^2}{n_{T_1}} + \frac{T_2^{\,2}}{n_{T_2}} + \frac{T_3^{\,2}}{n_{T_3}} - CF = 0.029694$$

The error sum of squares is estimated by subtracting the sum of all factors sums of squares from the total sum of squares:

$$SS_e = SS_{Total} - \left(SS_V - SS_D - SS_r - SS_\sigma - SS_T\right)$$

$$SS_e = 0.388176 - 0.382956 = 0.00522$$

Table 7 shows that a firm's asset value V, firm's debt X, interest rate r, volatility σ and the ime period T effects on the probability of default by 10.39%, 15.73%, 2.70%, 62.17%, and 7.64%, respectively.

Table 7. ANOVA

Source	Sum of Squares	Degree of Freedom	Mean Square	F	%	Rank
V	0.040341	2	0.020171	61.82529	10.39245	3
D	0.061091	2	0.030546	93.62605	15.73796	2
r	0.010482	2	0.005241	16.06437	2.700322	5
Sigma	0.241348	2	0.120674	369.882	62.17489	1
T	0.029694	2	0.014847	45.50805	7.649623	4
Error	0.00522	16	0.000326			
	0.388176	26				

CONCLUSION

Credit risk (probability of default), measurement, and management have become one of the essential components of financial economics. It is necessary for a firm to know which parameter effects more or less on probability of default so a firm will control those parameters. The Taguchi L27 approach, ANOM, and ANOVA was used to identify which parameter effects more on probability of default. The conclusion of this study is:

1. The Taguchi L27 orthogonal array approach was performed to conduct the experiments. Only 27 experiments are required at three levels with five parameters as per the Taguchi Method, but as per the FFD method a total of 243 experiments are required. The Taguchi approach reduces the time and the number of experiments.
2. The ANOM identify that the volatility σ affect more and the interest rate r affects less on probability of default and also it identify the best combination $V3 * X1 * r1 * \sigma 1 * T1$ where the value of probability of default is minimum.
3. The ANOVA measures the percentage contribution of each parameter. The percentage contribution of that firm's asset value V, firm's debt X, interest rate r, volatility σ and time period T effects on probability of default by 10.39%, 15.73%, 2.70%, 62.17%, and 7.64%, respectively. It also identify that the volatility σ affect more and the interest rate r affects less on the probability of default.

Assumption: the percentage contribution or rank of input parameters will change on response variable if the data set will change but the optimal combination will remain same.

REFERENCES

Black, F., & Cox, J. C. (1976). Valuing corporate securities: Some effects of bond indenture provisions. *The Journal of Finance*, *31*(2), 351–367. doi:10.1111/j.1540-6261.1976.tb01891.x

Black, F., & Scholes, M. (1973). The Pricing of Options And Corporate Liabilities. *Journal of Political Economy*, *81*(3), 637–659. doi:10.1086/260062

Chan, Y. H., Dang, K. V., Yusup, S., Lim, M. T., Zain, A. M., & Uemura, Y. (2014). Studies on catalytic pyrolysis of empty fruit bunch (EFB) using Taguchi's L9 Orthogonal Array. *Journal of the Energy Institute*, *87*(3), 227–234. doi:10.1016/j.joei.2014.03.008

Cicek, A., Kıvak, T., & Samtaş, G. (2012). Application of taguchi method for surface roughness and roundness error in drilling of AISI 316 stainless. *Journal of Mechanical Engineering*, *58*(3), 165–174. doi:10.5545v-jme.2011.167

Dar, A. A., & Anuradha, N. (2017a). Option Pricing Using Monte Carlo Simulation. British Journal of Economics. *Finance and Management Sciences*, *13*(2), 52–81.

Dar, A. A., & Anuradha, N. (2017b). One Period Binomial Model: The risk-neutral probability measure assumption and the state price deflator approach. *International Journal of Mathematics Trends and Technology*, *43*(4).

Dar, A. A., & Anuradha, N. (2017c). Probability default in black scholes formula: A qualitative study. *Journal of Business and Economic Development*, *2*(2), 99–106. doi:10.11648/j.jbed.20170202.15

Dar, A. A., & Anuradha, N. (2018). Use of orthogonal arrays and design of experiment via Taguchi L9 method in probability of default. *Accounting*, *4*(3). doi:10.5267/j.ac.2017.11.001

Hillegeist, S. A., Keating, E. K., Cram, D. P., & Lundstedt, K. G. (2004). Assessing the probability of bankruptcy. *Review of Accounting Studies*, *9*(1), 5–34. doi:10.1023/B:RAST.0000013627.90884.b7

Hull, J. C. (2009). Options, Futures And Other Derivatives (7th ed.). Pearson Education.

Merton, R. C. (1974). On the pricing of corporate debt: The risk structure of interest rates. *The Journal of Finance*, *29*(2), 449–470.

Phadke, M. S. (1989). *Quality Engineering Using Robust Design*. Englewood Cliffs, NJ: Prentice-Hall.

Phadke, M. S. (1998). *Quality Engineering Using Design of Experiment, Quality control, Robust Design and Taguchi method*. Thousand Oaks, CA: Warsworth and Books.

Rama, R. S., & Padmanabhan, G. (2012). Application of Taguchi methods and ANOVA in optimization of process parameters for metal removal rate in electrochemical machining of Al/5% SiC composites. *International Journal of Engineering Research and Applications*, *2*(3), 192–197.

Rodrigues, L. L. R., Kantharaj, A. N., Kantharaj, B., Freitas, W. R. C., & Murthy, B. R. N. (2012). Effectin of cutting parameters on surface roughness and cutting force in turning mild steel. *Research Journal of Recent Science*, *1*(10), 19–26.

Roy, R. K. (2001). *Design of experiments using the Taguchi approach: 16 steps to product and process improvement*. New York: John Wiley & Sons.

Shravani, D., Lakshmi, P. K., & Balasubramaniam, J. (2011). Preparation and optimization of various parameters of enteric coated pellets using the Taguchi L9 orthogonal array design and their characterization. *Acta Pharmaceutica Sinica. B*, *1*(1), 56–63. doi:10.1016/j.apsb.2011.04.005

Taguchi, G. (1986). *Orthogonal Arrays and Linear Graph*. Dearborn, MI: American Supplier Institute, Inc.

Wang, X., & Feng, C. X. (2002). Development of empirical models for surface roughness prediction in finish turning. *International Journal of Advanced Manufacturing Technology*, *20*(5), 348–356. doi:10.1007001700200162

APPENDIX

Table 8. Response table for value of a firm

Experiment #	V	D	r	Volatility	T	PD
1	130	100	5%	20%	1	0.0719
2	130	100	5%	20%	2	0.1272
3	130	100	5%	20%	3	0.15453
4	130	105	7%	30%	1	0.21324
5	130	105	7%	30%	2	0.26722
6	130	105	7%	30%	3	0.28932
7	130	118	9%	40%	1	0.39469
8	130	118	9%	40%	2	0.41818
9	130	118	9%	40%	3	0.42736
10	140	100	7%	40%	1	0.2072
11	140	100	7%	40%	2	0.28793
12	140	100	7%	40%	3	0.32912
13	140	105	9%	20%	1	0.03686
14	140	105	9%	20%	2	0.06526
15	140	105	9%	20%	3	0.0754
16	140	118	5%	30%	1	0.27876
17	140	118	5%	30%	2	0.33486
18	140	118	5%	30%	3	0.36022
19	150	100	9%	30%	1	0.06661
20	150	100	9%	30%	2	0.12144
21	150	100	9%	30%	3	0.14914
22	150	105	5%	40%	1	0.20705
23	150	105	5%	40%	2	0.29998
24	150	105	5%	40%	3	0.35015
25	150	118	7%	20%	1	0.07356
26	150	118	7%	20%	2	0.1147
27	150	118	7%	20%	3	0.13015

ANOM: V1 = 0.26263, V2 = 0.21951, V3 = 0.16809.

Note: When the value of a firm is 130, that time what is the value of the response (Probability of default), the average of those responses are the ANOM of V1, similarly for V2 and V3. What is V1? It is the value of the firm at first level that is shown in Table 2.

Table 9. Response table for value of a debt.

Experiment #	*V*	*D*	*r*	Volatility	*T*	PD
1	130	100	5%	20%	1	0.0719
2	130	100	5%	20%	2	0.1272
3	130	100	5%	20%	3	0.15453
4	130	105	7%	30%	1	0.21324
5	130	105	7%	30%	2	0.26722
6	130	105	7%	30%	3	0.28932
7	130	118	9%	40%	1	0.39469
8	130	118	9%	40%	2	0.41818
9	130	118	9%	40%	3	0.42736
10	140	100	7%	40%	1	0.2072
11	140	100	7%	40%	2	0.28793
12	140	100	7%	40%	3	0.32912
13	140	105	9%	20%	1	0.03686
14	140	105	9%	20%	2	0.06526
15	140	105	9%	20%	3	0.0754
16	140	118	5%	30%	1	0.27876
17	140	118	5%	30%	2	0.33486
18	140	118	5%	30%	3	0.36022
19	150	100	9%	30%	1	0.06661
20	150	100	9%	30%	2	0.12144
21	150	100	9%	30%	3	0.14914
22	150	105	5%	40%	1	0.20705
23	150	105	5%	40%	2	0.29998
24	150	105	5%	40%	3	0.35015
25	150	118	7%	20%	1	0.07356
26	150	118	7%	20%	2	0.1147
27	150	118	7%	20%	3	0.13015

ANOM, D1 = 0.16834, D2 = 0.20050, D3 = 0.28139

Table 10. Response table for interest rate

Experiment #	*V*	*D*	*r*	Volatility	*T*	PD
1	130	100	5%	20%	1	0.0719
2	130	100	5%	20%	2	0.1272
3	130	100	5%	20%	3	0.15453
4	130	105	7%	30%	1	0.21324
5	130	105	7%	30%	2	0.26722
6	130	105	7%	30%	3	0.28932
7	130	118	9%	40%	1	0.39469
8	130	118	9%	40%	2	0.41818
9	130	118	9%	40%	3	0.42736
10	140	100	7%	40%	1	0.2072
11	140	100	7%	40%	2	0.28793
12	140	100	7%	40%	3	0.32912
13	140	105	9%	20%	1	0.03686
14	140	105	9%	20%	2	0.06526
15	140	105	9%	20%	3	0.0754
16	140	118	5%	30%	1	0.27876
17	140	118	5%	30%	2	0.33486
18	140	118	5%	30%	3	0.36022
19	150	100	9%	30%	1	0.06661
20	150	100	9%	30%	2	0.12144
21	150	100	9%	30%	3	0.14914
22	150	105	5%	40%	1	0.20705
23	150	105	5%	40%	2	0.29998
24	150	105	5%	40%	3	0.35015
25	150	118	7%	20%	1	0.07356
26	150	118	7%	20%	2	0.1147
27	150	118	7%	20%	3	0.13015

ANOM, r1 = 0.24274, r2 = 0.21249, r3 = 0.19499

Table 11. Response table for volatility

Experiment #	V	D	r	Volatility	T	PD
1	130	100	5%	20%	1	0.0719
2	130	100	5%	20%	2	0.1272
3	130	100	5%	20%	3	0.15453
4	130	105	7%	30%	1	0.21324
5	130	105	7%	30%	2	0.26722
6	130	105	7%	30%	3	0.28932
7	130	118	9%	40%	1	0.39469
8	130	118	9%	40%	2	0.41818
9	130	118	9%	40%	3	0.42736
10	140	100	7%	40%	1	0.2072
11	140	100	7%	40%	2	0.28793
12	140	100	7%	40%	3	0.32912
13	140	105	9%	20%	1	0.03686
14	140	105	9%	20%	2	0.06526
15	140	105	9%	20%	3	0.0754
16	140	118	5%	30%	1	0.27876
17	140	118	5%	30%	2	0.33486
18	140	118	5%	30%	3	0.36022
19	150	100	9%	30%	1	0.06661
20	150	100	9%	30%	2	0.12144
21	150	100	9%	30%	3	0.14914
22	150	105	5%	40%	1	0.20705
23	150	105	5%	40%	2	0.29998
24	150	105	5%	40%	3	0.35015
25	150	118	7%	20%	1	0.07356
26	150	118	7%	20%	2	0.1147
27	150	118	7%	20%	3	0.13015

ANOM, Vol.1 = 0.09439, Vol.2 = 0.23120, Vol.3 = 0.32463

Table 12. Response table for volatility

Experiment #	*V*	*D*	*r*	Volatility	*T*	PD
1	130	100	5%	20%	1	0.0719
2	130	100	5%	20%	2	0.1272
3	130	100	5%	20%	3	0.15453
4	130	105	7%	30%	1	0.21324
5	130	105	7%	30%	2	0.26722
6	130	105	7%	30%	3	0.28932
7	130	118	9%	40%	1	0.39469
8	130	118	9%	40%	2	0.41818
9	130	118	9%	40%	3	0.42736
10	140	100	7%	40%	1	0.2072
11	140	100	7%	40%	2	0.28793
12	140	100	7%	40%	3	0.32912
13	140	105	9%	20%	1	0.03686
14	140	105	9%	20%	2	0.06526
15	140	105	9%	20%	3	0.0754
16	140	118	5%	30%	1	0.27876
17	140	118	5%	30%	2	0.33486
18	140	118	5%	30%	3	0.36022
19	150	100	9%	30%	1	0.06661
20	150	100	9%	30%	2	0.12144
21	150	100	9%	30%	3	0.14914
22	150	105	5%	40%	1	0.20705
23	150	105	5%	40%	2	0.29998
24	150	105	5%	40%	3	0.35015
25	150	118	7%	20%	1	0.07356
26	150	118	7%	20%	2	0.1147
27	150	118	7%	20%	3	0.13015

ANOM, T1 = 0.17221, T2 = 0.22631, T3 = 0.25171

Chapter 11
Real Options and Its Suitability in Assessing International Digital Investment

Jorge Tarifa-Fernández
University of Almería, Spain

Ana María Sánchez-Pérez
University of Almería, Spain

Salvador Cruz-Rambaud
University of Almería, Spain

ABSTRACT

Firms have experienced extreme competition because of changes in technological and global issues. Globalization of manufacturing has arisen through a faster transfer of materials, complex payment systems, and compression of product life cycle. Eventually, firms need the integration of technologies to meet the increasingly sophisticated customers' needs. Among the technologies, artificial intelligence has attracted much of the attention as it has been foreseen to have a major impact on all industries. Real options approach may be applied to make informed decisions concerning digital technologies investments. Therefore, firms could decide to defer the option of investing in artificial intelligence for the sake of finding a more favorable future environment. This chapter provides an adequate tool to reduce uncertainty in deciding whether to implement artificial intelligence in their companies. This tool comprises the strategic perspective of the investment in digital technologies that makes it suitable to be incorporated as a part of the set of strategic tools.

DOI: 10.4018/978-1-5225-8458-2.ch011

INTRODUCTION

Recent developments in computer science have brought about spectacular improvements in the performance of those who make use of this new technology (Szalavetz, 2018). This innovation, when applied to the manufacturing industry, uses its capacity to accumulate and communicate information to achieve greater productivity, higher quality, and lower production costs (Anaya et al., 2015; Tian et al., 2002). This places digital technologies high on the list of possible assets available for the development of business and the improvement of competitiveness. In general terms, the main purpose of digital technologies is to provide sophisticated machines, storage systems, and production facilities which can function autonomously to exchange information, trigger actions and control each other independently (Henning, 2013). The incorporation of this technology in a company will, therefore, enable it to make considerable improvements in what has hitherto been its standard mode of operation.

Although this is already occurring, the future presents high levels of uncertainties, discontinuities, and complexities (Vojak & Chambers, 2004), stimulated by rapid and unprecedented changes in the socio-political, economic and technological status quo (Amadi-Echendu et al., 2011). It is therefore of vital importance for companies to have a reliable prior understanding of the potential of deploying and implementing these technologies. According to Xu et al. (2018), the essence of digital transformation lies in the integration and interoperability of information across production and production support activities and management. As digital technologies are primarily used for the managerial activity, companies are aware that they are true drivers of growth and development, and can, therefore, help to achieve strategic objectives. Therefore, identifying, selecting and implementing the most suitable technologies from among the wide range of available alternatives imply a serious process of decision-making (Amadi-Echendu et al., 2011).

Within the area of digital technology, artificial intelligence (hereinafter, AI) has attracted much of the attention of both practitioners and researchers, as it is expected to have a greater impact on all industries (Ransbotham et al., 2017). As a technology, AI has been applied to provide managerial solutions to business management problems (Shah, 2015) and improve customer experience (Lu et al., 2018). Deciding whether to implement digital technologies is no longer something to be considered at a future date. For most companies, it needs immediate consideration since their implementation is at the core of both strategic and research agendas. Nevertheless, this process requires a detailed analysis of investment potential, since considerable funding is necessary to start (or continue) the digitalization process, especially for those companies of smaller size with limited financial resources and backing. Under these circumstances, they face important investment decisions which present great challenges to the progress of digital application (Zhou et al., 2017).

Despite these difficulties, a reasonable and informed evaluation should facilitate the decisions to be made concerning the possible implementation of digital technologies. Thus, the choice of an appropriate method which accurately assesses risks and rewards becomes compulsory before deciding on the appropriate level of investment. This is of special relevance when dealing with digital technologies because, when compared to other kinds of technology, they may become outdated and superseded due to the rapid improvements and innovations which bring new offers on to the market.

Real options have a valuable part to play in the assessment and justification of investments in technological projects. In essence, real options provide the right, but not the obligation, to take up or reject an investment opportunity in a non-financial or real asset at some time in the future (Mauboussin, 1999). As shown by Lee and Lee (2015), a real-option approach may be applied in order to make informed decisions with respect to digital technology investments. To some extent, this financial assessment tries to foresee the latent strategic value provided by such technologies so that companies are able to set their boundaries and achieve their potential. Companies might, therefore, decide to defer the option of investing in the Internet of Things (IoT) in the hope of finding a more favorable future environment (e.g., less uncertainty or more munificence). This possibility gives managers an extra option when making decisions.

The purpose of this study is to assess AI investments within an international framework. In addition, it aims to raise awareness among managers and directors when making decisions concerning the possible implementation of digital technologies, generally considered to be essential for the future of industrial activity. The main contribution of this study is to provide an adequate tool to reduce managers' uncertainty in deciding whether or not to implement AI in their companies, thereby facilitating the decision-making process. It offers a strategic perspective of the investment in digital technologies, and can, therefore, be incorporated as a part of the set of strategic tools.

The remainder of the study is structured as follows. In the following section, the importance of AI in business management is stressed. Section 3 describes the development of the real options approach from a theoretical point of view, with its corresponding applications. Moreover, in the subsections, the study shows the application of this approach to three different situations in which the decision to defer is a valid option. Finally, Section 4 discusses the principal results and identifies the main implications.

THE IMPORTANCE OF ARTIFICIAL INTELLIGENCE IN BUSINESS MANAGEMENT

According to the *Oxford English Dictionary*, AI is defined as "the theory and development of computer systems able to perform tasks normally requiring human intelligence, such as visual perception, speech recognition, decision-making, and translation between languages." Thus, AI can be considered both the intelligence evident in machines or software, and the field which studies how to create computers and software able to show intelligent behavior (Gadanidis, 2017). Indeed, it is an innovation involving the use of computer systems to execute functions which would normally require human intelligence (Shah, 2015). AI implies a computer program which possesses its own decision-making capability to solve a problem of interest, eventually demonstrating intelligent behavior or expertise (Kumar, 2017). Thus, it can perform different actions such as perception, interpretation, reasoning, learning, communication, and decision-making similar to those of a human being (Kumar, 2017; Tredinnick, 2017).

Consequently, AI, when matching and surpassing human intelligence (artificial intelligence singularity), may be seen as leading to positive technological advances, such as eliminating aging and disease or enhancing space travel (Bostrom & Yudkowsky, 2014). According to Makridakis (2017), AI will bring extensive changes that will result in richly interconnected organizations with decision-making based on the analysis and exploitation of big data. The main applications of AI are widespread and include protocol management, robotics, clinical diagnosis, renewable energy, and environmental analysis to manage agricultural issues such as crop planning, temperature and irrigation control, and harvesting. However, its application has been incorporated into the management of business because of the increasing need for data processing in the decision-making processes (Shah, 2015).

Currently, the industrial revolution is present both in the business models and in the profitability forecasts of the manufacturing industry. Two main drivers can explain it: (a) globalization, which means keen global competition and focuses on basic capabilities, and (b) the digitalized mode of production, that is to say, the transition from an electro-mechanical era into the much more flexible digital age (Kyläheiko & Sandström, 2007). Therefore, the nature of manufacturing is dramatically changing because of the rapid decrease in transactions costs, which in turn is due to the effective use of computers, internet, and telecommunications, and to better use of tools for hedging financial risks related to investment in innovation (Kyläheiko & Sandström, 2007). The more digitalized the manufacturing sector becomes the more new opportunities will be identified for being the first in the field. In effect, for a modern manufacturing company, the optimum timing for an innovation in the market is becoming a crucial issue (Kyläheiko & Sandström, 2007).

In this sense, Gerbert et al. (2017) show that the value of AI lies in two fundamental concepts: (a) it is a non-native intelligence which requires a different kind of input and feedback for its development, and requires access to a considerable amount of information in order to create an algorithm; but its "intelligence" is limited to a specific context; (b) it is a data-to-action process, as data is a source of both action and self-improvement, and allows managers to make decisions based on facts and use them to enhance future decisions.

However, obtaining value from AI becomes a difficult and complex task because of two main reasons. On the one hand, the amount of available data doubles every few years, so finding the proper data which companies need becomes crucial, forcing them to compete in obtaining privileges for accessing data (Ransbotham et al., 2017). On the other hand, deciding whether making or buying AI for business processes requires a variety of human skills such as understanding how to build algorithms, how to collect and integrate relevant data, and how to supervise the training of the algorithm (Baškarada & Koronios, 2017). That is to say, companies deciding to invest in AI are facing greater demands: the quality both of data required and of people with specific skills (see Figure 1).

Figure 1. Implications of Artificial Intelligence for decision-making processes
Source: own elaboration

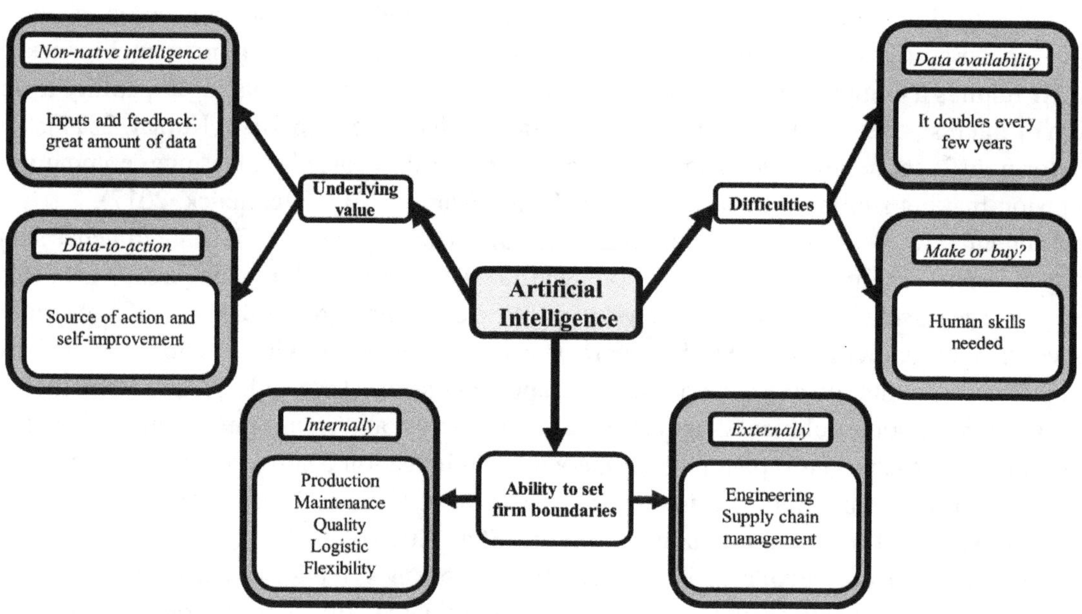

Within a company, AI can be applied to different activities, such as predictive maintenance and technological forecasting. The former activity studies repetitive or high-risk failures by using historical data and detailing occurrences of a machine's operational failures, enabling its maintenance to be conducted during its operation (Basri et al., 2017). Here the AI learning process is based on a trial and error process to determine the optimal result (Abidoye & Chan, 2017). This means that AI must be able to learn from its own experience and to make decisions based on this self-learning process (Gadanidis, 2017). The latter is considered as a prediction of the future characteristics of useful machines, procedures or techniques (Martino, 1993), which includes the provision of information about prioritizing research and development paths, planning new product development or taking strategic decisions (Firat et al., 2008).

According to Küpper et al. (2018), the use of AI can lead to an improvement in productivity as it changes the composition of the workforce and reduces costs because the need for manual activities diminishes in the production process. These authors distinguish between the benefits obtained from outside and inside the factory (see Figure 1). The former cover engineering where, through iterative testing and learning, AI algorithms optimize designs and suggest solutions which may appear unconventional to the human mind. They also include supply chain management where forecasting demand requires considerable attention. Essentially, AI supports forecasting of customer demand by analyzing and learning from data related to product launches and media information.

Benefits obtained inside the factory include production, maintenance, quality, and logistics. With respect to production, AI will reduce cost and increase speed, thus boosting productivity. It also can improve flexibility and cope with the complexity of production (e.g., AI will enable machines to become self-optimized systems which adjust their parameters in real time by continuously analyzing and learning from current and historical data). Regarding maintenance, AI will reduce equipment breakdowns and increase asset utilization. This can be achieved by predictive maintenance as it avoids breakdowns by replacing worn parts based on their calculated condition. In the case of quality, vision systems use image-recognition technology to identify defects and deviations in manufactured products. Moreover, in logistics, AI will enable autonomous movement and efficient supply of materials within the plant, which is essential to manage the growing complexity resulting from multiple product variants and customer-tailored products.

Despite the difficulties that companies may find in its adoption, AI should provide them with comparative advantages and value creation if they know how to act and respond to some key decisions such as the proper moment to invest in digital technology. In this sense, the quality of data and information is crucial as managers face with different sets of them: the first necessary for training the algorithm, the second used for verification and testing (Abidoye & Chan, 2017), and the third as a result of the process.

REAL OPTIONS APPROACH

Favoring the Decision-Making Process

The real-option analytical technique extends financial option theory to options on tangible and intangible real assets of strategic importance for a company (Kyläheiko & Sandström, 2007; Tyler & Chivaka, 2011). Thus, a real option provides the right, but not the obligation, to take up or reject an investment opportunity in a non-financial or real asset at some time in the future (Mauboussin, 1999). It adapts to a world where change and uncertainty are pervasive, and business strategies and investments are continuously re-evaluated (Mun, 2002).

Some of the most valuable applications of real options lie in their importance as inputs to strategy and the capital budgeting process. Therefore, awareness of an asset's options has the potential to prevent loss due to management unknowingly disposing of assets prematurely (Tyler & Chivaka, 2011). The option is valued relative to the underlying asset and therefore has the same value in the actual as in the risk-free world (Schwartz & Trigeorgis, 2004). Thus, this risk neutrality enables all flexibilities to be properly incorporated into the analysis. According to Tyler and Chivaka (2011), the value generated by real options comes from different drivers:

1. The real option is more valuable the longer the time until the option expires;
2. The higher the risk involved in the project, the more valuable the option;
3. The exclusive ownership of an option renders it more valuable than shared ownership;
4. The greater the importance of the uncertain portion of cash flow to the overall value of the project, the greater the option value.

Hence, holding the option provides a company with the opportunity to await a more favorable scenario (e.g., the arrival of additional information, the emergence of new technology, etc.). In doing so, a company is gaining a strategic position as it can anticipate the outcome of an investment decision before making what could be a costly and irreversible mistake. Consequently, the fact of holding the option allows companies to have access to all potential outcomes, which is contrary to conventional financial thinking: "the greater the risk, the lower the value" (Mauboussin, 1999).

A real-option perspective covers different actions as it can be used either to conceptualize and value existing options or to help management to create options within projects which hedge risk, avoid maximum regret or leverage with respect to investment in an option many times over (Mun, 2002). Many strategic investments create subsequent opportunities which may be taken, and so the investment opportunity can be viewed as a stream of cash flow plus a set of strategic options (Kyläheiko & Sandström, 2007). In short, the potential lies in the ability to consider delaying the decision to invest in digital technology until market forces have proven its value.

Theoretical Approach

Although the quantification of real options is analytically robust, it is best understood as a way of thinking (Tyler & Chivaka, 2011). Accordingly, from a managerial decision-making perspective, using real options requires appreciating what types of options exist, how they can be created, how and why option values change, and how to realize their value (Mauboussin, 1999). In this manner, when companies decide to assess whether to make an investment, they should pay more attention to their daily actions (or routines) than their final objectives. Real options deal with both the downside risks as well as those positive opportunities as yet unrealized. Thus, one can often avoid the downside risks by merely waiting for a better moment (deferral option). The risk can also be reduced by staging the investment and waiting, learning and observing until the uncertainty decreases, which eventually reduces the risk of fixed sunk costs (Kyläheiko & Sandström, 2007).

From a strategic point of view, those projects which offer different alternatives and changing scenarios are considered as dynamic since they include real options. In other words, real options allow the assessment of those projects in which strategic decisions may be taken over their lifespan. In this way, AI investment is one example of a project full of business opportunities, so its assessment requires a particular treatment. In this way, before investing in a project, managers need an informed, reasonable and accurate evaluation, in which the implicit uncertainty has a significant role (Schröder, 2011). In this situation, managers are facing the challenge of taking the right investment decision by adapting the traditional models of valuation to a rapidly changing business environment (Schneider & Imai, 2017).

Static methods, as the well-known Net Present Value (NPV), are appropriate to evaluate those investments for which strategic decisions have to be made at the outset without the possibility to be delayed. That is to say, NPV does not allow managerial flexibility which is particularly valuable in risky AI projects. In this context, the implementation of the real option analysis implies a valuable alternative to support investment decision-making by managers. This work focuses on the option to defer as it allows for changes in the future, and, if the circumstances are favorable, the option to be exercised (Van Bekkum et al., 2009), by avoiding possible expensive mistakes if changes are unfavorable. This technique is complementary to NPV as it takes into account that the project value changes constantly. Thus, the main difference between them is that real options adapt the value to change and uncertainty.

To date no research has considered the evaluation of AI projects with real option models. In this study, an approach to value the option to defer the AI projects in a global study worldwide is presented. It is an intuitive model which allows taking into consideration the value of implementing AI projects, which are more than ever both frequent in and relevant to the world of business. Basically, static methods cannot show the real value of a project because they do not take into account the operational flexibility to change its basic conditions; therefore, these methods are not capable of coping with high levels of uncertainty (Boute et al., 2004).

The traditional methodology represented by the static NPV (defined as the difference between the present value of the cash flow and the initial investment) undervalues projects with uncertainty (such as AI projects), for which this work proposes a dynamic version. Mascareñas (1999), Calle Fernandez and Tamayo Bustamante (2009) and Amram and Kulatilaka (1998) are some of the works in which the dynamic NPV has been used. The dynamic NPV includes the possibility to change the original plans, provided that these changes can involve an improvement of the initial situation. Thus, the dynamic NPV is decomposed into two different parts: on the one hand, the static NPV and, on the other hand, the real option value. This method works similarly to the classical one: when the dynamic NPV is greater than zero, the project is feasible:

Dynamic NPV = Static NPV + Real Option Value.

Some managers state that real options may overestimate the value of uncertain projects (Van Putten & MacMillan, 2004). This is because some models employed in real option assessment may imply a certain simplification of risks and opportunities. However, the integration of real options into the assessment reflects both the reality and the project complexity, especially for those uncertain projects with highly promising opportunities. Given that NPV and real options are complementary methods, the influence of uncertainty completes the total (or dynamic) project value.

As a consequence, the importance of uncertainty is twofold. On the one hand, uncertainty reduces NPV but, on the other hand, it generates the real option value. The real option allows covering the negative evolution of cash flow given that the manager may choose not to invest but, simultaneously, he/she may take advantage of the potential benefits (Tyler & Chivaka, 2011). AI projects are subjected to continuous change and are risky by nature. In this way, companies must invest periodically to be updated, meaning that the variable "time" can have a central role when assessing this type of project. This, together with the uncertainty, makes any AI project dependent on a relevant and accurate study before taking the decision of whether or not to invest in it.

ASSESSING AI INVESTMENT

International Application

Real options have been extensively studied from a theoretical point of view, and their importance has been widely recognized. Approaches from a practical point of view are very important (Muñoz Gómez, 2017; Tyler & Chivaka, 2011), especially for those projects which need special treatment in order to analyze their viability, such as AI projects (Zhou et al., 2017; Van Bekkum et al., 2009). This study proposes the binomial option pricing model as an alternative to assess real options and is applied to analyze an investment in AI projects. More specifically, the option to defer allows the flexibility to find the right moment to make the decision to invest. AI projects are characterized by a long-term horizon with high uncertainties, and so their volatility makes necessary the application of methods such as real options, given that traditional methods would systematically undervalue them, and therefore might lead to inappropriate investment decisions.

As a result of the aforementioned, this study focuses on the magnitude of the option value derived from the project value. That is to say, first, the present value of a project is calculated with the option to defer within three, five and ten periods (denoted by $V(D)_0^{(3)}$, $V(D)_0^{(5)}$ and $V(D)_0^{(10)}$, respectively). The analysis will be applied in three stages:

1. The project value is calculated with the NPV method (static NPV)
2. Then, the project value is calculated with the dynamic NPV (static NPV + real option)
3. Finally, the real option value is calculated.

We use the expression of the binomial option pricing model, one of the most usual methods to assess real options together with the Black-Scholes formula. The binomial method has been chosen because it is more intuitive and easier to use for managers and practitioners. As its name indicates, the binomial option pricing model is a method to calculate the option price. To do this, the model works on the assumption that the cash flows of the project value (V_0) may follow a favorable or unfavorable evolution in the following period. These trends are represented by u ($u > 1$) and d ($0 < d < 1$), known as the multiplicative factors to be applied to the cash flows.

Additionally, their probabilities of occurrence are p and q, respectively. The parameter r_f represents the riskless interest rate and I_0 the initial investment which is necessary to carry out the project. Indeed, the value of a project with the option to defer within one period depends on the relative position of the capitalized value of the initial investment, $I_1 := I_0(1 + r_f)$, with respect to the evolution of the value of cash flow: upwards (uVA_0) or downwards (dVA_0). Below, Figure 2 gives the value of the project with the option to be deferred within n periods (Cruz & Sánchez, 2015):

Figure 2.

$$V(D)_0^{(n)} = \begin{cases} 0, & \text{if } I_n \le d^n V_0 \\ \vdots & \vdots \\ \left(\sum_{k=s}^{n} \binom{n}{k} \frac{p^k q^{n-k}}{(1+r_f)^n} - 1 \right) V_0 + \left(1 - \sum_{k=s}^{n} \binom{n}{k} p^k q^{n-k} \right) I_0, & \text{if } d^{n-s+1} u^{s-1} V_0 \le I_n < d^{n-s} u^s V_0 \\ \vdots & \vdots \\ -V_0 + I_0, & \text{if } u^n V_0 \le I_n \end{cases} \quad (1)$$

In order to assess the value of the real option when investing in AI projects, the data has been obtained from the report of "State of Artificial Intelligence for Enterprises" (Teradata, 2017). This report covered 260 interviews in American, European, and Pacific-Asian companies with revenue greater than US$50 million. It deals with various industries including technology and telecommunications, manufacturing and production, retail, distribution and transport, financial services, business and professional services, public sector, private healthcare and services, and other commercial sectors.

The study highlights the optimism for AI, as most respondents (80%) "are already investing in some capacity in related technologies, and 30 percent planning on expanding their investments over the next 36 months". This situation encourages the evaluation and assessment of the option to defer until the market evolution is favorable. Using the information included in the report, some variables have been calculated. The initial investment spend on AI at the present moment is US$19.1 million, and companies' expectations vary according to the three proposed timeframes. Thus, for every dollar invested in AI today, companies expect a Return-on-Investment (ROI) of:

- US$1.23 in the next three years,
- US$1.99 in the next five years, and
- US$2.87 over the next 10 years.

To obtain the probability of success, the report has considered the perception of respondents about the sectors affected by the future growth of AI (Teradata, 2017, p. 12). Hence, on the one hand, "respondents around the world expect to see a positive impact of AI in the following sectors":

- **IT, Technology & Telecoms:** 59%
- **Business & Professional Services:** 43%
- **Consumer Services:** 32%
- **Financial Services:** 32%
- **Manufacturing & Production:** 31%

On the other hand, "respondents around the world expect to see a negative impact of AI in the following sectors":

- **Education:** 37%
- **Media, Leisure & Entertainment:** 37%
- **Government:** 35%
- **Healthcare:** 32%
- **Construction & Property:** 31%

The mean value of the positive impact is 39.4% while the value of the negative impact is 34.4%. Given that both mean values of the studied sectors amount to 73.8%, the relative percentage of the positive expected impact of AI is 53% whereas the negative expected impact is 47%. Therefore, the probability of success (*p*) is 53% whereby, in the binomial model, the probability of failure $(q = 1 - p)$ is 47%.

In order to apply the binomial option pricing method, it is necessary to calculate the risk-free interest rate (r_f). This parameter is typically derived from the return of the government Treasury bond in the market with a lifetime which is symmetrical to the lifetime of the underlying project (Fama & French, 2017; Schneider & Imai, 2017). The risk-free interest rate has been calculated based on the United States 3-, 5- and 10-year bond (consulted on August 28, 2018). In this manner, we may calculate the value of the up and down factors, given that the probability of a favorable scenario is:

$$p = \frac{(1 + r_f) - d}{u - d} \tag{1}$$

(see Copeland et al., 2000) and so the probability of an unfavorable scenario is $q = 1 - p$.

In order to offer a more reasonable description of the possible circumstances, the quantitative information derived from real options is obtained by considering three different situations which cover three different time horizons. Thus, this study provides the value of the option to defer for 3, 5 and 10 years. In doing so, we can see three different scenarios, which are associated with diverse factors which affect the decisions. Here the main idea is to reflect the benefit (or otherwise) of waiting for a better moment to implement (or invest in) AI. However, logic dictates that the longer the time, the lower the uncertainty and, therefore, lower strategic value is expected.

Option to Defer Within Three Years

The value of an AI project during three years without taking into consideration the option to defer may be calculated by employing the static NPV $(NPV = V_0 - I_0)$. In this case, the AI project value is equal to:

$$NPV_0^{(3)} = 21.67255 - 19.1 = \$2.57255 \text{ million.}$$

Parameter values and their corresponding sources are detailed in Table 1.

Table 1 shows that the probability of a favorable scenario of increased cash flow of 19.7% with respect to the previous year is 53%, and so 47% is the probability that the unfavorable scenario reduces the cash flow by 16.5%. Table 2 shows the probability distribution for the next three years, from 2017 to 2020.

Table 1. Parameters to assess the option to defer within 3 years in AI projects (in million dollars)

Parameters	Source
$I_0 = 19.1$	Teradata (2017)
$V_0 = 21.67255$	The present value \$1.23 ROI in the next three years for every dollar invested in AI today (Teradata, 2017)
$r_f = 0.02725$	United States 3-year bond (consulted on August 28, 2018)
$p = 0.53$	Teradata (2017)
$q = 0.47$	$q = 1 - p$
$u = 1.19700$	$p = \dfrac{(1 + r_f) - d}{u - d}$
$d = 0.83542$	$d = 1 / u$

Source: Own elaboration.

Table 2. The distribution of p and q for the next three years by the binomial model

2017	2018	2019	2020
1.00	0.54	0.29	0.16
	0.46	0.50	0.40
		0.21	0.34
			0.10

Source: Own elaboration.

In order to calculate the project value with the option to be deferred after three years, two different methodologies are employed:

1. Figure 2. Given that the value of the initial investment capitalized at moment 3 is equal to:

$$I_3 = I_0(1 + r_f)^3 = 19.1(1 + 0.02725)^3 = \$20.70436 \text{ million},$$

which is in the interval $d^2 u V_0 \geq I_3 > d u^2 V_0$, that is $18.10572 \geq I_3 > 25.94204$, the project value is equal to:

$$V(D)_0^{(3)} = \sum_{k=s}^{n} \binom{n}{k} p^k q^{n-k} \left(\frac{u^k d^{n-k} V_0}{(1 + r_f)^n} - I_0 \right),$$

$$V(D)_0^{(3)} = \sum_{k=2}^{3} \binom{3}{k} p^k q^{3-k} \left(\frac{u^k d^{3-k} 21.67255}{(1+0.02725)^3} - 19.1 \right) = \$4.17514 \text{ million.}$$

This is a direct model to assess the project value with the option to be deferred in three periods.

2. On the other hand, the classical way to calculate the value of the project with the option to defer within *n* periods by the binomial option pricing model is by building the binomial tree, as seen in Tables 3 and 4.

In Table 3, by employing the binomial option pricing model, we can observe the evolution of cash flow value by multiplying the project value at the present moment (V_0) by the up (u) and down (d) factors giving rise to the binomial tree. The methodology is simple:

- The first node is calculated as follows:

$$uV_0 = 1.197 \cdot 21.67255 = \$25.94204 \text{ million.}$$

- The second node is:

$$dV_0 = 0.83542 \cdot 21.67255 = \$18.10572 \text{ million.}$$

- And so forth.

In this way, in Year 3 a total of four possible scenarios have been quantified as follows:

- $u^3V_0 = 1.197^3 \cdot 21.67255 = \$37.16999$ million.
- $u^2dV_0 = 1.197^2 \cdot 0.83542 \cdot 21.67255 = \$25.9420433$ million.
- $u\,d^2V_0 = 1.197 \cdot 0.83542^2 \cdot 21.67255 = \$18.1057233$ million.

Table 3. Evolution of the cash flow value in AI projects of three years' duration (in million dollars)

Year 0	Year 1	Year 2	Year 3
			37.16999
		31.05263	
	25.94204		25.94204
21.67255		21.67255	
	18.10572		18.10572
		15.12592	
			12.63652

Source: Own elaboration.

- $d^3V_0 = 0.83542^3 \cdot 21.67255 = \$\ 12.63652$ million.

By considering these four possible scenarios, managers will choose to carry out the project when the cash flow value at moment 3 is greater than the initial investment capitalized up to this year:

$I_3 = I_0(1+r_f)^3 = 19.1(1+0.02725)^3 = 20.7043$.

In Table 4, the calculation process starts from the project value at year 3 (equal to $\max(V_3 - I_3;0)$), for every case. By following the direction of the arrows, it is necessary to multiply every possible scenario by its probability of occurrence and discount it to arrive at the present moment. This gives the project value at the present moment with the option to be deferred within three years:

$V(D)_0^{(3)} = \$4.17514$ million.

The option value is $O(D)_0^{(3)} = V(D)_0^{(3)} - NPV_0^{(3)}$. So:

$O(D)_0^{(3)} = 4.17514 - 2.57255 = \$1.60258$ million.

Option to Defer Within Five Years

The value of an AI project during five years without taking into consideration the option to defer it may be calculated by employing the static NPV $(NPV = V_0 - I_0)$. In this case, the AI project value is equal to:

$NPV_0^{(5)} = 33.15543 - 19.1 = \$14.05543$ million.

Parameter values and their corresponding sources are detailed in Table 5.

Table 4. Project value with the option to defer within three years (in million dollars)

Year 0	Year 1	Year 2	Year 3
			16.46563
		10.89170	
	6.85587		5.23768
4.17514		2.70233	
	1.39424		0
		0	
			0

Source: Own elaboration.

Table 5. Parameters to assess the option to defer within 5 years in AI projects (in million dollar)

Parameters	Source
$I_0 = 19.1$	Teradata (2017)
$V_0 = 33.15543$	The present value of $1.99 ROI in the next five years for every dollar invested in AI today (Teradata, 2017)
$r_f = 0.0270$	United States 5-year bond (consulted on August 28, 2018)
$p = 0.53$	Teradata (2017)
$q = 0.47$	$q = 1 - p$
$u = 1.20025$	$p = \dfrac{(1 + r_f) - d}{u - d}$
$d = 0.83316$	$d = 1 / u$

Source: Own elaboration.

To calculate the project value with the option to be deferred within five years, two different methodologies are employed:

1. Figure 2. Given that the value of the initial investment capitalized at moment 5:

$$I_5 = I_0(1 + r_f)^5 = 19.1(1 + 0.0277)^5 = \$21.89602\,\text{million}$$

is in the interval $d^4 u V_0 \geq I_5 > d^3 u^2 V_0$, the project value is equal to:

$$V(D)_0^{(5)} = \sum_{k=s}^{5} \binom{5}{k} p^k q^{5-k} \left(\frac{u^k d^{5-k} V_0}{(1 + r_f)^5} - I_0 \right) = \$14.53711\,\text{million.}$$

This is a direct model to assess the project value with the option to defer in five periods.

2. On the other hand, the classical way to calculate the value of the project with the option to defer within five periods by the binomial option pricing model is by building binomial trees, as we can see in Tables 6 and 7.

In Table 5, by employing the binomial option pricing model, we can observe the evolution of the cash flow value by multiplying the project value at the present moment (V_0) by the up (u) and down (d) factors giving rise to the binomial tree. In this way, in year five we have six possible scenarios. With

Table 6. Evolution of the cash flow value in AI projects of five years' duration (in million dollars)

Year 0	Year 1	Year 2	Year 3	Year 4	Year 5
					82.58881
				68.80942	
			57.32903		57.32903
		47.76406		47.76406	
	39.79495		39.79495		39.79495
33.15543		33.15543		33.15543	
	27.62367		27.62367		27.62367
		23.01484		23.01484	
			19.17497		19.17497
				15.97576	
					13.31031

Source: Own elaboration.

these values, managers choose to carry out the project when the cash flow value at moment 5 is greater than the initial investment capitalized up to this year:

$$I_5 = I_0(1 + r_f)^5 = 19.1(1 + 0.0277)^5 = 21.89602\,.$$

In Table 7, the calculation process starts from the project value at year 5 (equal to $\max(V_5 - I_5;0)$), for every case. Then, in order to complete the table, it is necessary to multiply every possible scenario by its probability of occurrence, and discount it to arrive at the present moment. In this way, the project value at the present moment with the option to be deferred within five years is:

Table 7. Project value with the option to defer within five years (in million dollars)

Year 0	Year 1	Year 2	Year 3	Year 4	Year 5
					60.69279
				47.50481	
			36.59951		35.43301
		27.59385		26.45908	
	20.28777		19.06480		17.89893
14.53711		13.24470		11.85018	
	8.90907		7.46219		5.72765
		4.54503		2.95383	
			1.52334		0
				0	
					0

Source: Own elaboration.

Table 8. Parameters to assess the option to defer within ten years in AI projects (in million dollars)

Parameters	Source
$I_0 = 19.1$	Teradata (2017)
$V_0 = 41.25123$	The present value of $2.87 ROI in the next ten years for every dollar invested in AI today (Teradata, 2017)
$r_f = 0.02884$	United States 10-year bond (consulted on August 28, 2018)
$p = 0.53$	Teradata (2017)
$q = 0.47$	$q = 1 - p$
$u = 1.20583$	$p = \dfrac{(1 + r_f) - d}{u - d}$
$d = 0.82930$	$d = 1 / u$

Source: Own elaboration.

$V(D)_0^{(5)} = \$14.53711$ million.

The option value is $O(D)_0^{(5)} = V(D)_0^{(5)} - NPV_0^{(5)}$. So:

$O(D)_0^{(5)} = 14.53711 - 14.05543 = \$0.48168$ million.

Option to Defer Within 10 Years

The value of an AI project during 10 years without taking into consideration the option to defer it may be calculated by employing the static NPV $(NPV = V_0 - I_0)$. In this case, the AI project value is equal to:

$NPV_0^{(10)} = 41.25123 - 19.1 = \$22.15123$ million.

Parameter values and their corresponding sources are detailed in Table 8.

In order to calculate the project value with the option to be deferred within ten years, two different methodologies are employed:

1. Figure 2. Given that the value of the initial investment capitalized at moment 10:

$$I_{10} = I_0(1+r_f)^{10} = 19.1(1+0.02884)^{10} = \$\ 25.38118 \text{ million}$$

is in the interval $d^7u^3V_0 \geq I_0 > d^6u^4V_0$, the project value is equal to:

$$V(D)_0^{(10)} = \sum_{k=8}^{10}\binom{10}{k}p^k q^{10-k}\left(\frac{u^k d^{10-k}V_0}{(1+r_f)^{10}} - I_0\right) = \$22.91103 \text{ million.}$$

This is a direct model to assess the project value with the option to defer in ten periods.

2. On the other hand, the classical way to calculate the value of the project with the option to defer within ten periods by the binomial option pricing model is by building a binomial tree, as we can see in Tables 9 and 10.

Table 9. Evolution of the cash flow value in AI projects of ten years' duration (in million dollars)

Year 0	Year 1	Year 2	Year 3	Year 4	Year 5	Year 6	Year 7	Year 8	Year 9	Year 10
										268.11
									222.34	
								184.39		184.39
							152.91		152.91	
						126.81		126.81		126.81
					105.17		105.17		105.17	
				87.21		87.21		87.21		87.21
			72.33		72.33		72.33		72.33	
		59.98		59.98		59.98		59.98		59.98
	49.74		49.74		49.74		49.74		49.74	
41.25		41.25		41.25		41.25		41.25		41.25
	34.21		34.21		34.21		34.21		34.21	
		28.37		28.37		28.37		28.37		28.37
			23.53		23.53		23.53		23.53	
				19.51		19.51		19.51		19.51
					16.18		16.18		16.18	
						13.42		13.42		13.42
							11.13		11.13	
								9.23		9.23
									7.65	
										6.35

Source: Own elaboration.

Table 10. Project value with the option to defer within ten years (in million dollars)

Year 0	Year 1	Year 2	Year 3	Year 4	Year 5	Year 6	Year 7	Year 8	Year 9	Year 10
										242.73
									197.68	
								160.42		159.01
							129.62		128.25	
						104.17		102.84		101.43
					83.16		81.87		80.50	
				65.83		64.57		63.24		61.83
			51.56		50.32		49.03		47.66	
		39.90		38.64		37.33		36.01		34.60
	30.45		29.19		27.85		26.44		25.07	
22.91		21.67		20.33		18.86		17.27		15.87
	15.81		14.52		13.09		11.47		9.54	
		10.17		8.87		7.39		5.62		2.99
			5.89		4.66		3.26		1.54	
				2.88		1.86		0.79		0.00
					1.06		0.41		0.00	
						0.21		0.00		0.00
							0.00		0.00	
								0.00		0.00
									0.00	
										0.00

Source: Own elaboration.

In Table 9, by employing the binomial option pricing model, we can observe the evolution of the cash flow value by multiplying the project value at the present moment (V_0) by the up (u) and down (d) factors giving rise to the binomial tree. In this way, in year ten there are eleven possible scenarios. With these values, the project will be carried out when the cash flow value at moment 10 is greater than the initial investment capitalized up to this year:

$$I_{10} = I_0(1+r_f)^{10} = 19.1(1+0.02884)^{10} = 25.38118\,.$$

In Table 10, the calculation process starts from the project value at year 10 (equal to $\max(V_{10} - I_{10};0)$), for every case. Then, in order to complete the table, it is necessary to multiply every possible scenario by its probability of occurrence, and discount it to arrive at the present moment. In this way, the project value at the present moment with the option to be deferred within 10 years is:

$$V(D)_0^{(10)} = \$22.9103 \text{ million.}$$

The option value is $O(D)_0^{(10)} = V(D)_0^{(10)} - NPV_0^{(10)}$ so:

$O(D)_0^{(5)} = 22.9103\text{-}22.15123 = \$0.7598$ million.

Main Results of Deferring

The main results obtained in the previous sections have been summarized in Table 11. Three key values have been calculated for the option to defer within 3, 5 and 10 years for AI projects:

- The dynamic project value (NPV + real option),
- the static project value (NPV), and then
- the option value.

As indicated, the project value, whether dynamic or traditional, increases with time. This could lead one to expect the same pattern in the case of the option value. However, the option value, which is always greater than or equal to 0 (Cruz & Sánchez, 2015), does not follow the same trend since it decreases for five years, and then increases for another 5 years, until year 10. On the one hand, when the time horizon considered is three years, the real option value constitutes 38.38 per cent of the dynamic project value. This means that, in the short-term, the option to defer plays a vital role, and it becomes a strategic resource in the making-decision process. On the other hand, considering long-term investment projects (5 and 10 years), the weight of the option value over the total project value is lower: around 3.3 per cent.

DISCUSSION AND CONCLUSION

The real option to defer gives company managers a flexibility of operation, enabling them to calculate the best moment to invest. In this study, the binomial model, based on the NPV definition and parameters, is considered to assess AI projects and the real option to defer them. New investment projects with a high level of uncertainty, such as AI, need new methods of assessment. This paper is one of the first works which relates these two areas, a new type of project and real option assessment, and therefore provides the basis for future research.

Table 11. Option to defer in AI projects (in million dollars)

Time Horizon	Dynamic Project Value	Static project Value	Option Value	Option Value/Dynamic Project Value
3	4.17514	2.57255	1.60258	38.38%
5	14.5371	14.05543	0.48168	3.31%
10	22.91103	22.15123	0.75980	3.32%

Source: Own elaboration.

One of the main concerns of managers is the expectation resulting from AI investments that they may give rise to an increase in revenues or a reduction in costs. However, this expectation varies according to the time-span considered and the degree of involvement in AI developments. Companies more involved in AI mainly expect to deliver revenue in a 5-year temporal horizon whilst only a minority is keen to expect savings in costs. The 5-year option, therefore, comes into play. Most companies, leaving aside other criteria, will prefer to focus on generating revenue rather than cutting costs (Ransbotham et al., 2018).

Increasing the time-frame of the project means a reduction in the significance of the value of the option to defer over the total project value. Thus, in AI projects, the delay of the investment decision for long periods implies "being last in the queue" in the challenge of innovation and change. In this case, the lack of investment in new technologies implies becoming obsolete, and the consequent reduction of future profits, so it does not make sense to defer AI investment projects for a long period.

One of the main questions when dealing with digital technologies is how to manage the global value chain in a market in which most of the production-related and research and development (R&D) processes are becoming more and more commoditized and customized. This means that the choice of the boundaries of a company will be one of the most important strategic decisions (Kyläheiko & Sandström, 2007). Empirical evidence indicates that investment in new technology results in an improvement in expected performance if and only if adequate organizational changes complement this investment, changes in management techniques and an appropriate adaptation of company strategy (Colledani et al., 2014; Tao et al., 2017). Therefore, the windows of opportunity is in part determined by external factors and depends on the acts of rivals, suppliers, complementary capability holders, authorities, and customers (Kyläheiko & Sandström, 2007). Managers must understand that AI is going to lead to better and more accurate decisions than gut instinct. For this reason, every manager should develop an innate understanding of AI and its implications.

Deciding whether to invest depends on whether AI investment represents an opportunity or a risk for the company. Implementing AI requires severe modifications in the business model for most companies (Ransbotham et al., 2017). Although this might constitute a barrier, these changes will probably bring significant improvements and an increase in value. Investing in digital technologies presents a particular characteristic: the process is irreversible. Consequently, companies should react by investing more and more rather than waiting to see other companies obtaining the benefit of being the first.

In essence, the practical implications of investing in AI leads companies to become pioneers and therefore to increase their level of commitment. Otherwise, being a follower lets others experiment and learn from their success and failures and to act in consequence. Any delay, far from being considered an advantage, means allowing other companies to harness the development of AI projects, and results in a loss of competitiveness for themselves.

Real option assessment will provide extra information about what can be expected when investing in AI. In this manner, the value obtained reinforces the idea of becoming leader in digital technologies. The strategic component is fundamental in the first steps of any investment decision, especially in AI where novelty and uncertainty are dominant. These characteristics are precisely the factors which determine whether companies become leaders or followers. Companies need to foresee the strategic position resulting from any investment, and use this as a basis for any decisions affecting future performance, and the best time to implement such decisions bearing in mind their own particular characteristics.

Therefore, real option assessment must be an essential part of the set of strategic tools that a company employs when deciding to invest in AI. Knowing the moment from which the decision of investing in AI is not relevant for a firm becomes essential. This could determine the strategy and, even, the path to follow. Therefore, real options assessment becomes a valid indicator for its incorporation into strategic decision tools such as the balance scorecard.

Notwithstanding the above, this study has its limitations. One of the most important of these is the mathematical rigor and availability of data needed. This may eventually discourage many potential users, even though AI has been pointed out as particularly relevant in recent years. In addition, because it is still in its infancy, there is no historical data available to assess the evolution of investment in AI. The importance of this chapter, its conclusions, and recommendations, lies in its use as a valuable instrument for companies at any stage of considering investment in AI in their strategic planning.

REFERENCES

Abidoye, R. B., & Chan, A. P. (2017). Artificial neural network in property valuation: Application framework and research trend. *Property Management*, *35*(5), 554–571. doi:10.1108/PM-06-2016-0027

Amadi-Echendu, J., Lephauphau, O., Maswanganyi, M., & Mkhize, M. (2011). Case studies of technology roadmapping in mining. *Journal of Engineering and Technology Management*, *28*(1-2), 23–32. doi:10.1016/j.jengtecman.2010.12.002

Amram, M., & Kulatilaka, N. (1998). *Real Options. Managing Strategic Investment in an Uncertain World*. Boston: HBS.

Anaya, L., Dulaimi, M., & Abdallah, S. (2015). An investigation into the role of enterprise information systems in enabling business innovation. *Business Process Management Journal*, *21*(4), 771–790. doi:10.1108/BPMJ-11-2014-0108

Artificial Intelligence. (2018). *Oxford English Dictionary*. Retrieved on September 23, 2018, from: https://en.oxforddictionaries.com/definition/artificial_intelligence

Baškarada, S., & Koronios, A. (2017). Unicorn data scientist: The rarest of breeds. *Program*, *51*(1), 65–74. doi:10.1108/PROG-07-2016-0053

Basri, E. I., Abdul Razak, I. H., Ab-Samat, H., & Kamaruddin, S. (2017). Preventive maintenance (PM) planning: A review. *Journal of Quality in Maintenance Engineering*, *23*(2), 114–143. doi:10.1108/JQME-04-2016-0014

Bostrom, N., & Yudkowsky, E. (2014). The ethics of artificial intelligence. The Cambridge Handbook of Artificial Intelligence, 316–334.

Boute, R., Demeulemeester, E., & Herroelen, W. (2004). A real options approach to project management. *International Journal of Production Research*, *42*(9), 1715–1725. doi:10.1080/00207540310001639946

Calle Fernandez, A., & Tamayo Bustamante, V. M. (2009). Decisiones de inversión a través de opciones. *Estudios Gerenciales*, *25*(111), 107–126. doi:10.1016/S0123-5923(09)70073-7

Colledani, M., Tolio, T., Fischer, A., Iung, B., Lanza, G., Schmitt, R., & Váncza, J. (2014). Design and management of manufacturing systems for production quality. *CIRP Annals-Manufacturing Technology*, *63*(2), 773–796. doi:10.1016/j.cirp.2014.05.002

Copeland, T., Koller, T., & Murrin, J. (2000). *Valuation: Measuring and Managing the Value of Companies* (3rd ed.). New York: Wiley.

Cruz Rambaud, S., & Sánchez Pérez, A. M. (2015). Valoración de la opción de diferimiento en un proyecto de inversión. *XXIX Congreso Internacional de Economía Aplicada*.

Fama, E. F., & French, K. R. (2017). International tests of a five-factor asset pricing model. *Journal of Financial Economics*, *123*(3), 441–463. doi:10.1016/j.jfineco.2016.11.004

Firat, A. K., Woon, W. L., & Madnick, S. (2008). *Technological forecasting–A review. Composite Information Systems Laboratory (CISL)*. Massachusetts Institute of Technology.

Gadanidis, G. (2017). Artificial intelligence, computational thinking, and mathematics education. *The International Journal of Information and Learning Technology*, *34*(2), 133–139. doi:10.1108/IJILT-09-2016-0048

Gerbert, P., Hecker, M., Steinhäuser, S., & Ruwolt, P. (2017). *Putting Artificial Intelligence to Work*. The Boston Consulting Group.

Henning, K. (2013). *Recommendations for implementing the strategic initiative* INDUSTRIE 4.0.

Kumar, S. L. (2017). State of The Art-Intense Review on Artificial Intelligence Systems Application in Process Planning and Manufacturing. *Engineering Applications of Artificial Intelligence*, *65*, 294–329. doi:10.1016/j.engappai.2017.08.005

Küpper, D., Lorenz, M., Kuhlmann, K., Bouffault, O., Heng, L.Y., Van Wyck, J., Köcher, S., & Schlageter, J. (2018). *AI in the Factory of the Future. The Ghost in the Machine*. The Boston Consulting Group.

Kyläheiko, K., & Sandström, J. (2007). Strategic options-based framework for management of dynamic capabilities in manufacturing firms. *Journal of Manufacturing Technology Management*, *18*(8), 966–984. doi:10.1108/17410380710828280

Lee, I., & Lee, K. (2015). The Internet of Things (IoT): Applications, investments, and challenges for enterprises. *Business Horizons*, *58*(4), 431–440. doi:10.1016/j.bushor.2015.03.008

Lu, H. P., & Weng, C. I. (2018). Smart manufacturing technology, market maturity analysis and technology roadmap in the computer and electronic product manufacturing industry. *Technological Forecasting and Social Change*, *133*, 85–94. doi:10.1016/j.techfore.2018.03.005

Makridakis, S. (2017). The forthcoming Artificial Intelligence (AI) revolution: Its impact on society and firms. *Futures*, *90*, 46–60. doi:10.1016/j.futures.2017.03.006

Martino, J. P. (1993). *Technological forecasting for decision making*. McGraw-Hill, Inc.

Mascareñas, J. (1999). *Innovación Financiera: Aplicaciones para la Gestión Empresarial.* Madrid, Spain: McGraw-Hill.

Mauboussin, M. J. (1999). Get real: Using real options in security analysis. *Frontiers of Finance, 10*, 1–30.

Mun, J. (2002). *Real options analysis: Tools and techniques for valuing strategic investments and decisions* (Vol. 137). New York: John Wiley & Sons.

Muñoz Gómez, D. L. (2017). *Decisiones de inversión por medio de opciones reales para el sector de hidrocarburos* (Doctoral dissertation). Universidad Nacional de Colombia-Sede Bogotá.

Ransbotham, S., Gerbert, P., Reeves, M., Kiron, D., & Spira, M. (2018). *Artificial intelligence in business gets real.* MIT Sloan Management Review and The Boston Consulting Group.

Ransbotham, S., Kiron, D., Gerbert, P., & Reeves, M. (2017). Reshaping Business With Artificial Intelligence: Closing the Gap Between Ambition and Action. *MIT Sloan Management Review, 59*(1).

Schneider, R., & Imai, J. (2017). *Valuing Investments in Digital Business Transformation: A Real Options Approach.* Retrieved on April 29, 2018, from: http://realoptions.org/openconf2018/data/papers/162.pdf

Schröder, D. (2011). Investment under ambiguity with the best and worst in mind. *Mathematics and Financial Economics, 4*(2), 107–133. doi:10.100711579-011-0036-3

Schwartz, E. S., & Trigeorgis, L. (Eds.). (2004). Real options and investment under uncertainty: classical readings and recent contributions. MIT Press.

Shah, V. K. (2015). Artificial intelligence management in financial crisis. In *Computational Intelligence and Computing Research (ICCIC), 2015 IEEE International Conference on* (pp. 1-6). IEEE.

Szalavetz, A. (2018). Industry 4.0 and capability development in manufacturing subsidiaries. *Technological Forecasting and Social Change.* doi:10.1016/j.techfore.2018.06.027

Tao, F., Cheng, Y., Zhang, L., & Nee, A. Y. (2017). Advanced manufacturing systems: Socialization characteristics and trends. *Journal of Intelligent Manufacturing, 28*(5), 1079–1094. doi:10.100710845-015-1042-8

Teradata. (2017). *State of artificial intelligence for enterprises.* Teradata.

Tian, G. Y., Yin, G., & Taylor, D. (2002). Internet-based manufacturing: A review and a new infrastructure for distributed intelligent manufacturing. *Journal of Intelligent Manufacturing, 13*(5), 323–338. doi:10.1023/A:1019907906158

Tyler, E., & Chivaka, R. (2011). The use of real options valuation methodology in enhancing the understanding of the impact of climate change on companies. *Business Strategy and the Environment, 20*(1), 55–70. doi:10.1002/bse.668

Van Bekkum, S., Pennings, E., & Smit, H. (2009). A real options perspective on R&D portfolio diversification. *Research Policy, 38*(7), 1150–1158. doi:10.1016/j.respol.2009.03.009

Van Putten, A. B., & MacMillan, I. C. (2004). Making real options really work. *Harvard Business Review, 82*(12), 134–142. PMID:15605572

Vojak, B. A., & Chambers, F. A. (2004). Roadmapping disruptive technical threats and opportunities in complex, technology-based subsystems: The SAILS methodology. *Technological Forecasting and Social Change*, *71*(1-2), 121–139. doi:10.1016/S0040-1625(03)00047-7

Xu, L. D., Xu, E. L., & Li, L. (2018). Industry 4.0: State of the art and future trends. *International Journal of Production Research*, *56*(8), 2941–2962. doi:10.1080/00207543.2018.1444806

Zhou, Z., Liu, X., Pei, J., Pardalos, P. M., Liu, L., & Fu, C. (2017). Real options approach to explore the effect of organizational change on IoT development project. *Optimization Letters*, *11*(5), 995–1011. doi:10.100711590-016-1006-8

Chapter 12
Designing a Neural Network Model for Time Series Forecasting

Paola Andrea Sanchéz Sanchéz
https://orcid.org/0000-0002-3320-016X
Universidad Simon Bolivar, Colombia

José Rafael García González
Universidad Simon Bolivar, Colombia

Carlos Hernán Fajardo-Toro
https://orcid.org/0000-0003-4596-9627
Universidad EAN, Colombia

Paloma María Teresa Martínez Sánchez
Universidad El Bosque, Colombia

ABSTRACT

Artificial neural networks are highly flexible and efficient tools in the approximation of time series patterns. In recent years, more than 5,000 studies oriented to the use of neural networks in time series forecasting have been evidenced in the extant literature. However, the methodology used for its specification and construction still involves a lot of trial and error or is inherited from econometric and statistical procedures that do not fit perfectly to the characteristics of the time series. This is especially true when they present non-linear behavior; moreover, it is not designed for working with neural networks. The objective of this chapter is to present a five-step guide for the specification, design, and validation of a neural network model for forecasting time series.

DOI: 10.4018/978-1-5225-8458-2.ch012

INTRODUCTION

The general objective of the time series forecast is to explain the evolution of the phenomenon in time and, based on this, infer behavior in the future. Although this definition sounds simple, its execution is not since it is closely related to factors such as the structure of the series, the purpose of the prediction, the period of time to be forecasted, among many other aspects. Prediction is an essential input in decision making in the evaluation of future scenarios and, even more, in the very understanding of the series which requires a well-constituted methodological process.

Neural networks have been widely used in the forecast of time series, but also strongly criticized due to the difficulty in the specification and construction of a model, given by the number of parameters that the modeler must select to generate a good forecast. The cost of this flexibility lies in the fact that the modeler must select the correct combination of structural and functional parameters, which involves trial and error since there is no adequate methodology to perform it. The main objective of this chapter is to present a systematic methodological strategy that allows one to specify and build a convergent and replicable neuronal network model for the forecasting time series.

PREVIOUS WORKS

The forecast of time series has been an area of growing interest for many disciplines, and in which many efforts have been devoted to the development of new methods and techniques. Its objective is to provide the modeler with a mathematical representation of a time series, which allows capturing, totally or partially, the most relevant characteristics of the real phenomenon, based on the information contained in the data. Although in the extant literature various models oriented to the representation of time series have been proposed, their usefulness depends on the degree of similarity between the dynamics of the generating process of the series and the mathematical formulation of the model with which it is represented.

In the traditional approaches, the most widespread methodology for the construction of time series models, and therefore the most widely used, is that of Box and Jenkins (1970) which has proved to be useful in the representation of numerous real series and is based on a solid mathematical foundation. However, this methodology is not applicable when the data exhibit non-linear characteristics. For time series with non-linear relationships, there are models that have been developed that attempt to reflect the type of non-linearity present in the data with different functional forms; however, the methodology used for the construction of such models remains Box and Jenkins (Tong, 1990; Granger & Teräsvirta, 1993; Harvey, 1989).

Likewise, models of neural networks have been used motivated by the versatility offered in the recognition of different patterns. In this sense, in the incipient work of Kaastra and Boyd (1996), a guide to build a neural network model for financial time series is presented, but still with the dependence of linear characteristics. A similar work for the case of tourism series is carried out by Palmer, Montaño, and Sesé (2006); in this, the theory that there is no systematic procedure to guide the construction of neural network models for the prediction of time series is supported. Anders and Korn (1999) make an effort that goes beyond representing a single model by presenting a series of procedures oriented to the construction of constructive models, and focusing on the task of selecting the best one.

METHODOLOGY PROPOSED FOR THE CONSTRUCTION OF NEURAL NETWORK MODELS

The strategy proposed in this work is based on a systemic approach oriented to the specification of neural network models for the prediction of time series, highlighting the importance of considering key aspects that have been ignored in the theory and that lead to strong implications in its application, such as the optimization algorithm and the techniques for selecting the best model. Starting from the existence of a time series that is to be modeled and forecasted, the proposed steps for the specification and construction of the neural network model are presented in Figure 1.

Preliminary Exploration

The preliminary exploration phase is oriented to the initial analysis that the modeler makes of the time series, its behavior, characteristics, and aspects related to the environment in which the series develops and the purposes that are intended with the forecast; this exploration can be defined as a process of approximation to the information that is available through subjective analysis and statistical treatment, in order to infer about the hidden structure of the series. The preliminary exploration is not usually considered as an essential process in traditional methodologies, considering itself more an empirical treatment or being merged in other stages of the procedure.

Information About the Series

Each series in particular has its own behavior and characteristics, which makes it difficult to predict its future evolution and therefore demands special treatment.

The information of the series includes the following aspects:

Figure 1. Diagram of proposed steps for the specification and construction of the neural network model
Source. Elaborated by the authors

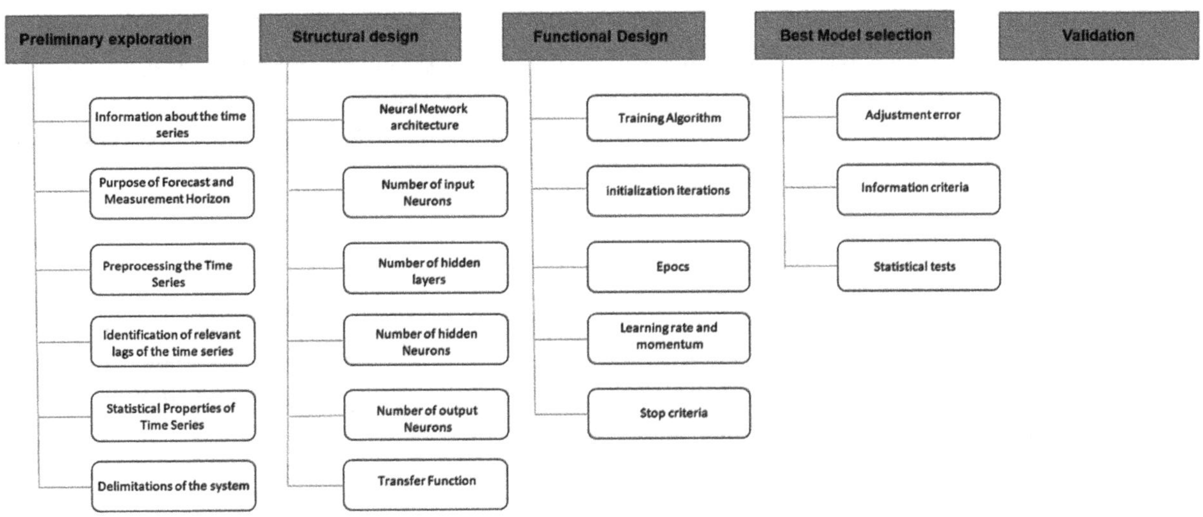

- Presence of regular patterns.
- Stationary behavior vs. Volatility.
- Presence of irregular patterns.
- Influence of causal variables.

Changes in the environment in which the series develops. Each of the highlighted aspects can be evaluated by empirical methods and statistical methods.

Presence of Regular Patterns

The empirical analysis of the regular patterns of a time series is oriented to the visual exploration of the existence of trend components, seasonal and cyclic patterns. In order to guide the visual recognition of such patterns, it is often useful to ask the following questions:

- Does the series show an increasing behavior? decreasing? by sections?
- Does the series present behaviors that are repeated on a regular basis every certain period of time?
- Does the long-term series exhibit behaviors that can be grouped?

Within the statistical treatment for the identification of regular patterns, it is useful to use decomposition techniques in each of the components. As individual techniques for each component, the following can be highlighted:

- In order to detect the presence of tendencies in the series, the most commonly used methods consist of evaluating the degree of adjustment of the tendency to a known functional form (linear, polynomial, exponential, etc.); or soften the behaviors that are detached from the trend, so that its direction can be determined. The most widely used method for this is the moving average.
- In order to detect the frequency and amplitude of seasonal patterns, it is useful to use tools such as frequency or periodogram spectra, autocorrelograms, and wavelets. These elements allow to identify even the presence of different seasonal patterns with different frequencies within the same series. An example of this last case is shown by the series of demand for domestic electrical energy, which has a seasonal intraday, intraweek, and even year-on-year behavior.
- In order to identify long-term cycles, the use of periodograms is equally useful, as well as smoothering the series through filters that minimize the presence of components such as trend and seasonality, and maximize long-term behaviors. One of the best known methods in this field is the Hodrick and Prescott filter.

Stationary Behavior vs. Volatility

The analysis of stationary behavior or the analysis of volatility seeks to determine the frequency and intensity of the variations that occur in the time series. An empirical analysis of the stable or volatile behavior of the time series is also aimed at a visual exploration of the presence of such behaviors, which can be oriented by answering the following questions:

- Does the series present high and low fluctuations that are clearly identifiable in short periods of time?
- Is the behavior of the series approximately stable throughout the measurement period?

Autocorrelation functions, statistical *Q* of Ljung and Box, unit root tests (Dickey-Fuller test being the mostly used), and the Kurtosis statistics and asymmetry coefficient are used for the statistical identification. Slow decreases and significant values, even in very remote lags, in the autocorrelation, values that increase by increasing the lags in the *Q* statistic, and the presence of unitary roots, are signs that indicate the existence of volatility in the time series. Likewise, high values in the Kurtosis are associated with the presence of volatility.

Presence of Irregular Patterns

Irregular patterns in a time series are associated with the presence of atypical behaviors (outliers) and structural changes. The difficulty in not making an early detection of the presence of such irregular patterns in the series is that they can be falsely treated as non-linear behaviors or as volatilities, which would lead to an inadequate specification of their model, manifested by a misrepresentation of the properties of the series and, consequently, results in incorrect conclusions in their interpretation.

The presence of irregular patterns is easily identifiable in the visual inspection of the series, since it reflects such behaviors. Indicative questions to empirically identify the presence of irregular patterns are:

- Does the series present clearly identifiable and infrequent isolated data that do not follow the general behavior?
- Is the series affected by the presence of instantaneous or permanent perturbations in one or more of its regular patterns (changing trend, multiplicative seasonal or cyclical patterns with different periods)?
- The statistical process that is carried out to identify irregular patterns includes:
- The detection of atypical data with statistical methods, for which using Dixon and Grubbs statistics is useful; the first one is based on the distance of a piece of information in relation to the nearest piece of information, while the second is based on the distance of a piece of information with respect to the mean; in both cases, the values that are obtained are compared with critical values to know their significance. Equally useful is the construction of a graph with confidence bands of three times the standard deviation, where the value is considered atypical if it is outside that range.
- For the detection of structural changes, significance tests based on the F statistic are carried out at a known point of change or in a range, information criteria, and visual tools have been developed, such as the CUSUM graphs (cumulative recursive residuals), CUSUMQ (recursive quadratic residuals), and RESIDUAL RECURSIVES, which allow evaluating the possible structural changes that may be affecting the time series based on variations in the behavior of their residuals and the points that cut the significance bands.

There are other irregular patterns associated with calendar events such as Christmas, Easter, dates such as Mother's Day, Thanksgiving, and so forth which can also affect the behavior of some time series. The detection of this type of events is done mostly from the knowledge of their presence.

Influence of Causal Variables

It is well known that the behavior of time series is often affected by the influence of causal variables; the temperature and the rains affect the growth of the crops, the demand influences the offer price of the products, the ingested foods affect the heart rate, and so forth. In this sense, it is important to question whether the behavior of the series under study is influenced by causal variables, and to develop a process aimed at their identification.

The identification of the causal variables allows to expand the knowledge about the past behavior of the series and to infer in some way what the future will be like; however, although the influence of a causal variable in the series is known as a priori, the functional form of this influence and the number of lags of the variable that should be considered in the preliminary models are unknown, at least tentatively. In this manner, the objective of this step is to make a preliminary selection of the causal variables based on a formal reasoning process.

A formal process of identifying the causal variables must involve the following steps:

1. Identify the main physical, economic, biological variables, etc., that affect the behavior of the time series.
2. Collect historical information of the causal variables that are identified.
3. Determine behavior relations of the the causal variables, and their influence on the time series that is being studied, and establish theories.

The steps that have been outlined here require support both from statistical theory and from informed judgment, in such a way that a rational framework is provided for the decision to include or not each causal variable in the model. From statistics, simple and partial cross-correlation functions and the correlation coefficient are often evaluated, however, due to the disadvantages that this practice has demonstrated in series with non-linear relationships, other measures have been proposed in the literature (Granger & Teräsvirta, 1993; Nelson et al., 1999).

Changes in the Environment in Which the Series Develops

The presence of changes in the economy, legislation, climate, environment, business, etc., that occasionally or permanently affect the evolution of the series require a particular analysis. For the identification of the aforementioned changes, it is necessary to investigate in the environment where the studied series is developed. This allows coherent explanation to past events and to foresee the influence of future changes.

Often the changes in the environment in which the time series develops are reflected in the behavior of the series as atypical observations - outliers, or as periods with irregular behavior with respect to the rest of the series, when these are occasional or momentary, or as structural changes when they are permanent (Sánchez & Velásquez, 2005; Sánchez, 2008); therefore, its identification requires the procedures for the identification of the presence of irregular patterns previously mentioned in this section.

Purpose of Forecast and Measurement Horizon

When considering the need to make forecasts of a time series, according to a particular problem, the measurement horizon that will be analyzed must be defined. The horizon of measurement of the forecast has a close relationship with the purpose that is intended:

- **Short Term Forecast**: When instant decision making is required, planning purchases, scheduling work, determining investments and labor levels, assigning work, deciding production levels, analyzing climatic, environmental, economic, short-term changes, etc. Usually, this prediction has a period of up to one year, but it is almost always less than three months.
- **Medium Term Forecast**: When medium-term decisions are required, sales planning, production, analyzing changes in consumption, planning budget execution and cash flow, analyzing various operating scenarios, etc. The time of this forecast can extend between three months and three years.
- **Long-term Forecast**: When it is required to know trends in future behavior, planning new products, capital investments, expansion or relocation of facilities, etc. In general it comprises three or more years.

Medium and long-term forecasts are distinguished from short-term forecasts by three characteristics:

- **First:** The medium and long-term forecasts handle global issues and support, especially, planning tasks, strategic decisions or tactics; the short-term forecast is more oriented to operational decisions.
- **Second:** The short-term forecast usually employs different methodologies. Statistical techniques such as moving averages, exponential smoothing, Box-Jenkins models, decomposition methods, extrapolation of trends and neural networks; while broader and less quantitative methods such as exponential trend models, curve adjustment, and multiple regressions are used in the medium and long term.
- **Third:** Short-term forecasts tend to be more accurate than in the medium and long term; as the time horizon increases, accuracy is more likely to decrease.

Preprocessing the Time Series

The preprocessing of the time series refers to analyzing and transforming the input variables, with the aim of minimizing noise, highlighting important relationships, detecting trends and smoothing the behavior of the series, in such a way that it facilitates the recognition of the hidden patterns.

In the preprocessing of the time series, three types of processes are considered: one aimed at the minimization of noise via transformation of the input data, and elimination of irregular patterns (atypical data, structural changes, among others); the second, tending to the elimination of regular patterns (trends, cycles, and seasonal patterns); and the third, oriented to the escalation of large-scale data.

Transformation of the Time Series and Elimination of Irregular Patterns

Yale (1997) identifies the transformation of input variables as a multistep process that must be included in the construction of the model that represents the series. The transformation seeks to minimize the noise effects that the data may have, through a homogeneous distribution. Transformation is a common preprocessing technique in forecasting (Kaastra & Boyd, 1996), which is useful for correcting the asymmetries that are present in the data, and allows multiplicative order relationships to be converted into additive relationships, simplifying and improving the modeling of the data (Masters, 1993).

In the construction of neural network models, the need to transform or not the time series has been widely debated; some authors claim the universal approximation property that the neural networks possess allows them to obviate a processing via transformation, while those that defend the transformation claim that this procedure allows the neural network to concentrate on the identification of hidden patterns. This is how there is no consensus on its use in neural network models. Some of the most used transformation techniques for time series data in the literature are presented in Table 1.

The treatment of atypical data - "outliers" and structural changes is based on performing procedures for elimination in the first case and fractional modeling (in parts) in the second case. Franses and Van Dijk (2000) perform an approach by using neural networks in the presence of outliers and level changes, but assuming that the series generating process is linear. Sánchez and Velásquez (2005) develop a kind of empirical models that are based on the integration of neural networks and static structural models, for the representation of structural changes. Although, the neural networks have demonstrated the ability to recognize and model atypical behaviors, and structural changes without the need for *a priori* knowledge of the series and without a predefined form of nonlinearity (Tkacz & Hu, 1999), authors such as Hill et al. (1994), report that these models are vulnerable in the presence of outliers, so there is no clarity about the behavior of neural networks against atypical data and structural changes; moreover, there is uncertainty about the signals that lead to the detection of the changes mentioned previously.

Elimination of Regular Patterns

With regard to a pre-processing oriented to the elimination of regular patterns of trends, cycles, and seasonal patterns, the main orientations are via differentiation and seasonal differentiation or through filters; there is a long, and still inconclusive debate about the convenience of modeling trend series and seasonal patterns using original variables or preprocessing them; some authors defend the idea that

Table 1. Functional forms of the main transformations of data

Type of transformation	Functional form
Logarithmic	$\log y_t$ ó $\ln y_t$
Root	$\sqrt{y_t}$
Logistics	$1 / (1 + e^{-y_t})$
Box-Cox	$y_t^\lambda = \begin{cases} (y_t^\lambda - 1)/\lambda & \lambda \neq 0 \\ \ln y_t & \lambda = 0 \end{cases}$

Source. Elaborated by the authors

rational agents decide based on data without prior processing and that removing trend and seasonality implies eliminating information that could be useful for estimating the parameters of a model (Hansen & Sargent, 1993), or that not in all cases the trend components, seasonal and irregular, are independent and separable (Hylleberg, 1994).

Others, on the contrary, support the opposite idea; it is preferable to use preprocessed data, since in the process of adjusting a model to the original data there is a risk of giving too much importance to capturing trends and seasonal effects to the detriment of an effective measurement of the other components of the model; besides, the mentioned movements are predictable, and typically, do not have a direct relationship with the objective of the study and, therefore, it is not necessary to model them explicitly (Gardner & McKenzie, 1989; Sims, 1993). Works that are present in the literature reflect mixed results when evaluating the need to eliminate such components (Faraway & Chatfield, 1998; Franses & Draisma, 1997; Nelson et al., 1999; Qi & Zhang, 2008; Zhang & Qi, 2005).

The defenders of the original data claim that these should be used when:

1. It is required to evaluate the influence of secular components in the series, such as trends and cycles;
2. We want to analyze the propagation of innovations through the model;
3. It is desired to forecast future values of the series.

These assertions are supported by empirical studies (Koopman & Franses, 2002), even to the point of concluding that there is no need for an analysis of adjusted data, and in case of requiring an individual evaluation of the trend and seasonal components, it is always preferable to use unadjusted models instead of mechanical filters such as those used by different adjustment techniques (TRAMO-SEARS, X12 ARIMA). Therefore, there is no clarity about the need of eliminating or not the trend and seasonal components in neural network models.

Some techniques for eliminating regular patterns of time series include:

- Differentiation
- seasonal differentiation
- Moving averages
- Simple and exponential smoothing
- Filter HOLT - WINTERS
- Mechanical filters TRAMO-SEARS, X12 ARIMA

Scaling of Data

The scaling of data aims at having the input variables with an equally significant distribution, so the entries with large absolute value should have the same importance as those with small magnitude (Masters, 1994). Thus, methods of linear scaling and mean scaling, or variance in neural network models have been proposed in the literature (Kaastra & Boyd, 1996). In linear scaling, the observations are linearly scaled in a range of minimum and maximum values, thus reducing the dimensions of the data, however, it is highly susceptible to the presence of atypical data as the uniformity of the distribution does not change; while, in the mean or variance scale, the observations are scaled by adding or subtracting the respective values of mean or variance, creating a more uniform distribution. The scaling is beneficial since it significantly accelerates learning and allows obtaining more consistent results.

Identification of Relevant Lags of the Time Series

The selection of the input lags depends to a large extent on the knowledge that the modeler has about the time series, and it is the task of the latter to decide if it is necessary to include each lag within the model according to some previously fixed criterion. Usually not all potential variables are equally informative since they can be correlated, have noise or not significant relationships with the output variable. The primary importance of making an adequate selection lies in the difficulties of convergence in learning that can result from including irrelevant entries, and the poor performance of the model.

Although there is no systematic way to determine the appropriate set of entries that are accepted by the research community, some of the methodologies that are proposed in the literature are:

- Procedures based on traditional statistical methods, such as autocorrelation functions (Tang & Fishwick, 1993); however, due to the architecture of the neural network, the statistical verification of the significance of each input can be ambiguous, since equal levels of error can be obtained from different configurations, which makes it an inappropriate procedure.
- Heuristic analysis of the importance of each lag (La Rocca & Perna, 2005).
- Statistical tests of non-linear dependence: Multiplicadores de Lagrange (Luukkonen, Saikkonen, & Terasvirta, 1988; Saikkonen & Luukkonen, 1988; Anders & Korn, 1999), Radio de Verosimilitud (Chan & Tong, 1986), and Biespectro (Hinich, 1982).
- Model identification criteria, such as the AIC from Gooijier and Kumar (1992).
- Evolutionary algorithms (Happel & Murre, 1994; Schiffmann, Joost, & Werner, 1993).
- Analysis of sensitivity (Sung, 1998).
- Regularization or constructive algorithms (Reed, 1993).

Statistical Properties of Time Series

Analyzing the statistical properties of the time series and its causal variables is a mechanism that allows us to clearly understand their behavior, identify hidden relationships, and inquire about the interaction between the series and its causal variables. The statistical properties are often related to the distribution that follows the series under study and its structure of dependence in the domain of time and frequency.

Usually the properties that are considered, are grouped as follows:

- Descriptive statistics: Mean, Variance, Kurtosis, Coefficient of asymmetry, Maxima, Minima, Quartiles, etc.
- Simple, Partial Auto-correlograms
- Simple, Partial Cross-correlogram
- Correlation coefficient
- Expectation and conditional variance
- Scatter charts, histograms (Q-Q plot)
- Periodograms
- Linearity tests

Delimitations of the System

Within the limitations of the system, the exact and complete definition of the aspects that will be taken into account in the construction of the model is considered; these aspects are the product of the preliminary analysis of all the components that are included in this section and aspects that are beyond the modeler's control, such as:

- Is the recording of observation of the series appropriate? can there be measuring errors?
- Is the time scale of the data in the series adequate for the forecast horizon that is to be estimated?

The delineation of the system provides a clear orientation of how far you will go with modeling, what will be done and what will not be done. In this definition, the following aspects should be considered:

- **Identification of Regular and Irregular Patterns, and Changes in the Environment in Which the Series is Developed:** Within the limits of the system, one must consider the treatment that will be given to such patterns within the procedure.
- **Identification of the Causal Variables:** it is necessary to determine which causal variables will be considered within the models.
- Purpose of the forecast and measurement horizon: it is necessary to determine the objective that is intended with the forecast and based on this, the time horizon to be predicted.
- **Preprocessing of the Series:** it is necessary to define if the data of the series and their causal variables will have a previous treatment and what type of treatment.
- **Identification of Relevant Lags in the Series:** It is necessary to define the number of lags in the series that will be considered within the models.
- **Statistical Properties:** it is necessary to determine which statistical properties will be evaluated.

Within the limits of the system, it is also necessary to consider other structural characteristics of the series that influence the construction of the neural network, such as:

- Length of the time series (amount of data). For a sufficiently long time series, the neural network can represent any complex structure of the data, which facilitates the task of generalization and forecasting, since patterns that are present in the series are easily identified by the network and can thus learn the characteristics of the series. Nam and Schaefer (1995), empirically show that the size relationship of the series is direct with the performance of the neural network. However, as stated by Kang (1991), the neural network does not necessarily require large sample sizes to perform well.
- Frequency of the observations. Empirical studies such as those developed by Kang (1991) and Hill, O'Connor, and Remus (1996), indicate that the performance of the network is better in monthly and quarterly series than for annual data, perhaps due to the fact that monthly and quarterly data contain more irregularities than annual data (Zhang, Patuwo, & Hu, 1998).
- Training, validation, and test or forecast sets: the training and validation sets are used to build the neural network model and then be evaluated with the test set. The training set is used to estimate the parameters of an alternative number of neural network specifications (networks with different number of inputs and hidden neurons). The generalization capacity of the network is evaluated

with the validation set. The network model that performs best in the validation set is selected as the final model. The validity and utility of the model is then tested using the test set. Often, this last set is used for forecasting purposes, and the network's generalization capacity for unknown data is evaluated. Withal, the criterion of selecting the model based on the best performance of the validation set does not guarantee that the model has a good adjustment in the forecast set, and the selection of the appropriate amount of data in each set can also affect performance. This is how a large training set can lead to over-training. Granger (1993) suggests that at least 20% of the data be used as a test set, yet there is no general guide on how to partition the set of observations, so that optimal results are guaranteed.

Structural Design of Possible Neural Network Models

With the structural design of the network, it is sought to identify the possible neural network models that are adapted to the characteristics of the time series, that is, the appropriate architecture of the network in order to model the series and determine the configuration or network topology to be used. In this step, it is necessary to define the following elements:

- Neural network architecture
- Number of input neurons
- Number of hidden layers
- Number of hidden neurons in each layer
- Number of output neurons
- Transfer or activation function in each layer

These aspects will be addressed in a general way below. (Sánchez & García, 2017) they developed a systemic process that allows the possibility to choose conjuntly the number of input neurons, the number of hidden neurons in each layer, and the estimation and training of the neuronal network parameters.

Neural Network Architecture

Different neural network architectures have been used for the time series forecast. The initial choice of neural network architecture is often associated with the following factors:

- Degree of knowledge of the modeler about the architecture.
- Robustness: some neural network architectures have complex structures, which disadvantage their choice and reduce functionality.
- Availability of software packages or software development.
- Characteristics of the time series: some models are more oriented to the representation of certain characteristics of the series, this is the case of recurrent networks which have been used in time series with highly volatile dynamics (Mishra & Patra, 2009; Sánchez & García, 2018).
- Credibility before the scientific community.
- Trends in implementation: some choices are oriented to the model that is booming or "in fashion", or the very decision to always use the classic models recognized within the scope of the time series; this is how, in finance, the ARNN are regularly used (Franses & Van Dijk, 2000).

Number of Input Neurons

The number of input neurons or input variables is a necessary parameter in the configuration of the neural network. This step involves defining how many and which inputs will be included in the neural network model.

The inputs, in number, must be sufficient to explain the behavior of the series, but not excessive, in such a way that over-training is avoided. Likewise, those input variables whose influence is relevant in the model must be included (Crone & Kourentzes, 2009). In the general case, the inputs correspond to causal variables that influence the evolution of the series, lags of said variables and lags of the series itself; in this work only lagged values of the series are considered as inputs.

Number of Hidden Layers

Regarding the number of hidden layers, theoretically, a neural network with a hidden layer and a sufficient number of neurons can approximate any continuous function defined in a compact domain with some precision (Kaastra & Boyd, 1996). Some authors suggest the use of one hidden layer when the time series is continuous, and of two only if there is some type of discontinuity (Hornik, 1991; Hornik, Stinchicombe, & White, 1989). However, other research has shown that a network with two hidden layers can result in a more compact and highly efficient architecture than networks with only one hidden layer (Srinivasan, Liew, & Chang, 1994; Zhang, 1994; Chester, 1990). The increase in the number of hidden layers only increases the computational time and the danger of overtraining.

Number of Hidden Neurons in Each Layer

Choosing the appropriate number of hidden neurons has been considered a determining parameter in the success or failure of the neural network, since it shows important effects in the level of adjustment of the model to the series. A small number of hidden neurons makes the network unable to properly learn the relationships in the data, while a large number causes the network to memorize the data with poor generalization and little utility for prediction. Some authors propose that the number of hidden neurons should be based on the number of input variables; however, this criterion is, in turn, related to the extension of the time series and the training, validation, and forecast sets.

Usually, ad hoc procedures are followed for the selection of the number of neurons in each hidden layer, where it is sought, under some criterion of error minimization of the and some stopping criterion, to find the appropriate number of neurons; anyhow, this criterion is only mathematical and lacks a conceptual and methodological support, which indicates the convenience of using such a procedure.

Given that the value of the weights in each neuron depends on the degree of error between the desired value and that predicted by the network, the selection of the optimal number of hidden neurons is directly associated with the training process that is used, so it is appropriate to relate both processes.

Number of Output Neurons

Deciding on the number of output neurons is somewhat simpler, since there are compelling reasons to always use a single output neuron (Kaastra & Boyd, 1996). Neural network models with multiple outputs produce lower results than those to which they were compared to with simple outputs. If multiple outlets are served, the network will tend to concentrate its efforts on reducing the largest errors, which often concentrate on some outputs, without producing favorable changes in the other outputs of the network. The solution in this case is to use specialized networks in each output. Likewise, concentrating the work of the network on a single output, will reduce the number of parameters that are necessary to tune up the final model.

In the case of prediction problems, the output of the model is the prediction of the next value in the temporal sequence (forecast one step forward); although, it is possible to generate multiple outputs in the prediction (multistep forecast), these suffer from the aforementioned shortcomings.

Transfer or Activation Function in Each Layer

Different functional forms for the specification of the transfer or activation function $g(u)$ have been proposed in the literature. The classic sigmodia or logistic function has been used successfully by many authors due to its ability to approximate nonlinear and continuous behaviors, characteristics that are common in real series (Cybenko, 1989; Hornik, Stinchicombe, & White, 1989). Other functional forms have also been proposed in the literature, such as the Gaussian function, Hyperbolic Tangent, Lorentzian, Flat wave, and based on wavelets (Zhang et al., 1995). The linear functions are used as a transfer from the hidden layer to the output layer due to the similarity they have with the regression models.

Klimasauskas (1993) suggests that if the behavior of the data is average, the sigmodia function should be used as a transfer from the input layer to the output layer, while if there are deviations from the average behavior, the hyperbolic tangent function presents a better performance. The transfer functions that are based on wavelets can exhibit a more adequate approximation since, due to its properties of scale changes (dilation), they can distinguish the local characteristics of a signal at several scales, and by translation they can cover a wide region of study (Ait Gougam, Tribeche, & Mekideche-Chafa, 2008); however, its application is computationally more complex than other functions.

Functional Design of the Possible Neural Network Models

As has been emphasized throughout this work, the functional design of a neural network, based on the estimation of the adequate parameters and the training of the model, is a determining process in the performance of the neural network, which entails multiple implications in all stages of modeling.

The objective of the functional design of a neural network is to find the set of weights of the parameters that minimize an error function; that is, those weights that make the model have a better adjustment to the time series. Unless the model is overtrained, the set of weights should produce a good generalization.

The training of a neural network is a problem of non-restricted non-linear minimization in which the weights of the network are iteratively modified in order to minimize the error between the desired output and the one that is obtained.

In the functional design it is necessary to define the following elements:

- Training algorithm
- Maximum number of iterations of the algorithm (different starting points) and initialization method
- Maximum number of Epochs (weight training)
- Learning rate and Momentum

- Stop criterion of the algorithm

Training Algorithm

There are several methods that have been proposed in the literature for training the neural network, from which the following are highlighted:

Classical techniques of descending gradient (Bishop, 1995)

- Dynamic adaptive optimization (Pack et al, 1991; Yu, Chen, & Cheng, 1995)
- Quickprop (Falhman, 1989)
- Resilient Backpropagation - Rprop (Riedmiller, 1994), Improved Rprop - iRprop (Igel & Husken, 2003)
- Levenberg-Marquardt (Cottrell et al, 1995)
- Quasi-Newton (Dennis, Schnabel, & Robert, 1983; Battiti, 1992)
- Broyden-Fletcher-Goldfarb-Shanno - BFGS
- Generalized Reduced Gradient - GRG2 (Lasdon & Waren, 1986; Subramanian & Hung, 1993)
- Simulated cooling (Fang & Li, 1990); evolutionary methods (Fogel, Fogel, & Porto, 1990)
- Randomized methods and deterministic searches (Tang & Koehler, 1994)

Maximum Number of Algorithm Iterations (Different Starting Points) and Initialization Method

This parameter measures the number of reboots that are necessary to guarantee that the initial weights of the parameters are valid, which is seen as the possibility of reaching a global optimum. Choosing the number of iterations of the algorithm is often subjective, since there are few studies in the literature that present a systematic way of choosing this parameter; but being very common that the number is chosen more by expert criteria.

Some studies that are based on weight initialization methods guide us about the required number of iterations of the initial weight, which depend on random, deterministic, and heuristic forms, on touring throughout the search space (Lehtokangas, 1999; Cottrell et al., 1995). The commonly used criterion for weight initialization in the literature is to choose random values from a uniform or normal probability distribution.

Maximum Number of Epochs (Training Iterations)

This parameter measures the number of training iterations required in the algorithm to achieve a desired adjustment, therefore, it is directly related to the stopping criteria. A small number of iterations does not allow the algorithm to learn the characteristics of the series; whereas, a large number causes overtraining; that is, the network is dedicated to memorizing particularities that are present in the patterns, thus losing their ability to generalize.

Some authors, such as Shanker, Hu, and Hung (1996), and Chester (1990), propose different functional forms to choose the appropriate number of training iterations, some depending on the number of entries in the model. Just like the number of restarts (see section 0), the number of epochs is often a subjective parameter that is governed by expert criteria, or subject to circumstances (e.g., reaching a level of error, convergence, and so forth).

Learning Rate and Momentum

The learning rate and the momentum in a neural network are parameters that are added to the derived function of the training algorithm in such a way that it is possible to accelerate the adjustment of the weight of the parameters to the model, and to the convergence (Hagan, Demuth, & Beale, 1996). The learning rate is a parameter that allows the modification of the weights in each training iteration, and that makes learning faster or slower, according to the need. The rate assumes values between 0 and 1; if very large values are taken, the algorithm becomes unstable, whereas if very small values are taken, the algorithm takes time to converge.

The momentum can be seen as a low pass filter that allows the network to ignore small features on the surface of the error, and thus overcome local minimums. The moment also assumes values between 0 and 1; although this may vary between epochs.

Algorithm Stopping Criterion

On rare occasions, the characteristics of the time series allow the establishment of an objective function aimed at the approximate identification of global and local optima, being the stopping point of the algorithm a trivial process that is reduced to finding the optimal solution. However, that ideal scenario, in most series does not happen and it is, therefore, difficult to determine when the algorithm should end.

In these cases, either a stopping criterion built according to the characteristics of the series is defined, or the use of one or more of the multiple criteria already available in the literature is used. Table 2 shows a list of the most common stopping criteria used in the literature, and the relationship of their advantages and shortcomings.

The stopping criteria commonly used in neural network models are: stopping when a pre-set value of adjustment error is reached; when a maximum number of epochs or a combination of them is reached. However, none of these guarantees that the global optimum is achieved.

Selection of the Best Model

Throughout this chapter, it has been highlighted the necessity to have an accurate algorithm against the criteria of error reduction as parameters are added, which is a clear indicator of its efficiency, however, sometimes it is equally important to select among the possible models one that balances the level of error and the number of model parameters.

The fact of modifying the number of parameters of a neural network model implies a change in the configuration of the network, that is, different models are generated each time, from which it is necessary to choose the best one. The selection of the best model is given by choosing among the possible models and candidates the one that mostly fulfills a series of characteristics, which allows cataloging it with the “best”. Harvey (1989) defines the following comparative characteristics that a model must meet in order to be selected as the final model:

Table 2. Advantages and disadvantages of the stopping criteria

Criterion	Advantages	Disadvantages
To set a target value of the adjustment error.	The error value that is wanted is reached.	-It can incur in high number of iterations. -It can get stuck in a local optimum. -It involves a fixed configuration of neural network.
To set a maximum number of epochs.	Controlled computer time.	-It can lead to very high adjustment errors. -It involves a fixed configuration of neural network.
The adjustment error increases.	The value of the error that is reached is the minimum of all the evaluated.	-It can incur in high number of iterations. -It involves a fixed configuration of neural network.
Minimal improvement during a certain number of iterations.	The value of the error that is reached is the minimum of all the evaluated.	-It can incur in high number of iterations. -It can get stuck in a local optimum.
In constructive processes: to establish a maximum number of neurons and/or inputs (it is necessary to	Variable network configuration.	-Non-significant inputs and neurons may be included. -It can incur in high number

Source. Elabored by the authors

- **Adjustment:** the adjustment error of the model must be the least compared to other candidate models.
- **Generalization:** The model must have the capacity to provide a good adjustment for the data that is out of the calibration sample, therefore, offer a lower forecast error compared to the error of other candidate models.
- **Parsimony:** The number of parameters of the model (inputs and neurons) is lower compared to other candidate models that exhibit similar performance. In the extant literature, there are different selection criteria that have been proposed for models that meet, to some degree, the previously stated characteristics. Some of the commonly used criteria are:

Selection Based on Error Adjustment

This typology of criteria is based on choosing that model that presents a smaller measure of the error. These criteria require the division of the data sample into at least two sets: adjustment or training, and test or forecast. The training set is used to estimate the appropriate parameters of the model, while the forecast set is used to verify the validity and usefulness of the model. For the training set, a series of error measures have traditionally been used to determine the adjustment of the model to the data of the series. Table 3 shows a compilation of the main ones for all cases.

The comparison based on the accuracy of the forecast set is often made using the respective SSE, MSE, MAE, and MAPE of the forecast set; however, the measures may not coincide, since they highlight aspects that may be favored with some and penalized with others.

Table 3. Error measurements

Sum Squared Error (SSE)	$SSE = \sum_{i=1}^{n} e_i^2$
Mean Squared Error (MSE)	$MSE = \frac{1}{n}\sum_{i=1}^{n} e_i^2$
Root Mean Squared Error (RMSE)	$RMSE = \sqrt{\frac{1}{n}\sum_{i=1}^{n} e_i^2}$
Sum Absolute Error (SAE)	$SAE = \sum_{i=1}^{n} \lvert e_i \rvert$
Mean Absolute Error (MAE)	$MAE = \frac{1}{n}\sum_{i=1}^{n} \lvert e_i \rvert$
Mean Absolute Percentage Error (MAPE)	$MAPE = \frac{1}{n}\sum_{i=1}^{n} \left\lvert \frac{e_i}{y_i} \right\rvert$
Percent Mean Absolute Deviation (PMAD)	$PMAD = \frac{\sum_{i=1}^{n} \lvert e_i \rvert}{\sum_{i=1}^{n} \lvert y_i \rvert}$
Determination Coefficient R^2	$R^2 = \frac{\sum_{i=1}^{n} e_i^2}{\sum_{i=1}^{n} (y_i - \bar{y})^2}$
Maximum Error	$\max e_i$

Source. Elaborated by the authors

Selection Based on Information Criteria

The selection that is based on information criteria seeks to determine the significance of the inclusion of some parameters in the model (an input or a neuron), applying, in turn, a penalty factor to models with many parameters, so it can be considered a benefits to parsimony. The information criteria commonly used in the literature are: the Akaike Information Criterion - AIC (Akaike, 1974), and the Bayesian Information Criterion - BIC (Schwarz, 1978).

Suppose that there are m^* alternative models, where m represents the number of variables that the model M_m has; for all criteria it is a question of choosing that specific value of that minimizes the following expressions:

$$AIC = -2\log\mathscr{L}+2K \tag{1}$$

$$\text{BIC} = -2\log \mathscr{L} + 2k \log n \tag{2}$$

where, is the maximum likelihood function, which is defined as:

$$\mathscr{L} = -\frac{n}{2}\log(2\pi) - \frac{n}{2}\log(\sigma^2) - \frac{1}{2}\sum_{t=1}^{n}\frac{e_t^2}{\sigma^2} \tag{3}$$

In the equations, n corresponds to the number of data in the series, k to the number of model parameters, and to the average of the residuals squared.

The AIC penalizes models according to their deviation from the real data, while BIC penalizes models according to the number of parameters, therefore, this criterion will tend to choose models with few parameters. For both criteria, the best model will be the one that has the smallest value among all the models evaluated, this being the one that shows the best adjustment to the data.

Selection Based on Statistical Tests

It is also possible to make a comparison based on the use of statistical tests such as the Wald test or the contrast of the Likelihood Radio (LR). The likelihood contrast consists of a hypothesis test to assess the performance of a complete model and a restricted model in order to validate the significance within the model of the additional component:

The significance of the test is evaluated with critical values of and the one with the smallest LR is chosen as the best model.

The above leads us to consider the following questions:

- For a consistent algorithm, are the model selection criteria in the capacity of choosing the best model for different network configurations?
- Do all the criteria lead to the same answer?

Validation of Assumptions About Residuals

In the validation, the errors or residuals of the model are analyzed in order to verify if they fulfill the assumptions for normality and randomness. This step, so common in statistical models of time series, is little used in neural network models due to the following reasons:

- The criteria are based on linear characteristics of the series, which are not guaranteed to be met in non-linear series.
- The scientific community is more interested in the functionality that is offered by a low adjustment error than in the stability that it may have.

The diagnosis of the assumptions seeks to verify if the residuals of the selected model meet the following criteria:

1. The residuals of the model follow a normal distribution, with zero mean and constant variance;
2. There is no significant autocorrelation in the residuals;
3. There is no evidence of heterocedastic behavior;
4. There are no atypical observations, or non captured anomalous behaviors.

Failure to comply with any of the criteria set forth in the residuals of the model is a strong evidence of lack of specification in the model; which would lead to a return to previous processes in order to reformulate the model.

Commonly, the inadequate specification of the model involves the following facts:

- The number of entries and/or hidden neurons that are included do not allow to fully explain the behavior of the series, which entails including more inputs and/or neurons.
- The configuration, the shape of the transfer function, or the architecture of the neural network itself, is not sufficient to capture the intrinsic characteristics of the time series.
- There are regular or irregular patterns that are not being received by the neural network.
- Correlated variables are included in the set of inputs.

For the analysis of the assumptions about the stated residuals, visual tools and the calculation of statistics of the residuals of the model are usually used in order to detect inconsistencies that are not easily visible.

In the visual inspection, the graphs of residuals regarding time, standardized residuals, quadratic residuals, among others, are used to validate assumptions about the mean and variance. An analysis of these graphs is useful to detect if the residuals are white noise (zero mean and constant variance), in addition, regions with persistently positive or negative values, or points with low probability of occurrence are of special interest in this analysis.

The validation of the assumption of the uncorrelation of residuals can be done visually by analyzing the simple and partial autocorrelograms of the residuals. Here, we examine if the correlations form a pattern or if they are statistically significant, which would indicate that there is a correlation structure in the residuals, and therefore the hypothesis would be rejected. The values obtained by statistical tests such as Durbin-Watson and Ljung-Box are also considered.

In order to validate the assumption of normality of the residuals, the evolution of the histogram of the standardized residuals is analyzed. This is compared to a standard normal distribution, if its shape is similar, it can be concluded that the residuals are distributed normally. Useful statistical tests for this purpose are Jarque-Bera, and Kurtosis, among others.

The validation of the homoscedasticity assumption of the residuals can be proved by the graphical inspection of the residuals, recursive residuals, and CUSUM and CUSUM2 graphs, or with statistical tests, such as the White test, and that of Golfeld-Quandt. It is said that there is heteroscedasticity when the dispersion or variance of the residuals is not constant and varies with their value. In these cases, it may be necessary to include more inputs and/or neurons in the model.

It is sometimes relevant to evaluate the adjustment of the model that is found in the series. This process can be done by visual inspection of the scatter plot between the series and its calculated model; in this, a good adjustment is reflected in a uniform distribution of the data around a 45° trend line.

Finally, an important point is that the evaluation of the stability of the parameters of the model is often overlooked in the statistical analysis; that is, to contrast the time series mean and variance moments vs the moments that are proper to the model, as well as the statistical properties of the latter. Kaashoek and Van Dijk (2003) explain the utilities of evaluating the stability of model parameters.

CONCLUSION

Throughout this chapter a systematic and complete strategy has been addressed in order to face the task of constructing models of artificial neural networks for time series, considering methodological, conceptual, technical, and practical aspects. The strategy that has bee proposed for the specification and construction of neural network models for time series is based on the sequential development of five steps.

The strength of the specification strategy and model construction of neural network models that has been proposed lies in the following aspects:

1. A preliminary analysis of the time series is formally included, which facilitates the task of specifying the model, and possible configurations. An exhaustive justification of the necessity and way of analyzing each one of the general aspects that influence the preliminary identification is made. This aspect, as highlighted in the text, is usually not considered as an essential process in traditional methodologies, or its need is not sufficiently proven in the literature.
2. The structural and functional design of the possible neural network models is separately addressed, considering, separately, all the aspects that such designs involve.

REFERENCES

Ait Gougam, L., Tribeche, M., & Mekideche-Chafa, F. (2008). A systematic investigation of a neural network for function approximation. *Neural Networks*, *21*(9), 1311–1317. doi:10.1016/j.neunet.2008.06.015 PMID:18662852

Akaike, H. (1974). A new look at statistical model identification. *IEEE Transactions on Automatic Control AC*, *19*(6), 716–723. doi:10.1109/TAC.1974.1100705

Anders, U., & Korn, O. (1999). Model selection in neural networks. *Neural Networks, 12*(2), 309–323. doi:10.1016/S0893-6080(98)00117-8 PMID:12662706

Battiti, R. (1992). First- and second-order methods for learning between steepest descent and Newton's method. *Neural Computation, 4*(2), 141–166. doi:10.1162/neco.1992.4.2.141

Bishop, C. M. (1995). *Neural Networks for Pattern Recognition*. Oxford, UK: Oxford University Press.

Box, G. E. P., & Jenkins, G. M. (1970). *Time Series Analysis: Forecasting and Control*. San Francisco, CA: Holden-Day.

Chan, K. S., & Tong, H. (1986). On estimating thresholds in autoregressive models. *Journal of Time Series Analysis, 7*(3), 178–190. doi:10.1111/j.1467-9892.1986.tb00501.x

Chester, D. L. (1990). Why two hidden layers are better than one? *Proceedings of the International Joint Conference on Neural Networks*, 1265–1268.

Cottrell, M., Girard, B., Girard, Y., Mangeas, M., & Muller, C. (1995). Neural modeling for time series: A statistical stepwise method for weight elimination. *IEEE Transactions on Neural Networks, 6*(6), 1355–1364. doi:10.1109/72.471372 PMID:18263428

Crone, S., & Kourentzes, N. (2009). Input-variable Specification for Neural Networks - An Analysis of Forecasting low and high Time Series Frequency. *Proceedings of the International Joint Conference on Neural Networks, IJCNN'09*. 10.1109/IJCNN.2009.5179046

Cybenko, G. (1989). Approximation by superpositions of a sigmoidal function. *Mathematics of Control, Signals, and Systems, 2*(4), 202–314. doi:10.1007/BF02551274

De Gooijer, I. G., & Kumar, K. (1992). Some Recent Developments in Non- Linear Modelling, Testing, and Forecasting. *International Journal of Forecasting, 8*(2), 135–156. doi:10.1016/0169-2070(92)90115-P

Dennis, J. E., Schnabel, J., & Robert, B. (1983). *Numerical Methods for Unconstrained Optimization and Nonlinear Equations*. New York: Prentice-Hall.

Falhman, S. (1989). Faster-learning variations of back-propagation: An empirical study. *Proceedings of the 1988 Connectionist Models Summer School*, 38–51.

Fang, L., & Li, T. (1990). A globally optimal annealing learning algorithm for multilayer perceptrons with applications. In *AI'90* (pp. 201–206). Perth, Australia: Austrtalian Joint Conf. Artificial Intell.

Faraway, J., & Chatfield, C. (1998). Time series forecasting with neural networks: A comparative study using the airline data. *Journal of the Royal Statistical Society. Series C, Applied Statistics, 47*(2), 231–250. doi:10.1111/1467-9876.00109

Fogel, D. B., Fogel, L. J., & Porto, V. W. (1990). Evolving Neural Networks. *Biological Cybernetics, 63*(6), 487–493. doi:10.1007/BF00199581 PMID:2357472

Franses, P., & Van Dijk, D. (2000). *Non-linear time series models in empirical finance*. Cambridge University Press. doi:10.1017/CBO9780511754067

Franses, P. H., & Draisma, G. (1997). Recognizing changing seasonal patterns using artificial neural networks. *Journal of Econometrics*, *81*(1), 273–280. doi:10.1016/S0304-4076(97)00047-X

Gardner, E. S. Jr, & McKenzie, E. (1989). Seasonal Exponential Smoothing with Damped Trends. *Management Science*, *35*(3), 372–376. doi:10.1287/mnsc.35.3.372

Granger, C. (1993). Strategies for modelling nonlinear time-series relationships. *The Economic Record*, *69*(206), 233–238. doi:10.1111/j.1475-4932.1993.tb02103.x

Granger, C., & Teräsvirta, T. (1993). *Modelling Nonlinear Economic Relationships*. Oxford, UK: Oxford University Press.

Hagan, M. T., Demuth, H. B., & Beale, M. H. (1996). *Neural Network Design*. Boston: PWS Publishing.

Hansen, L. P., & Sargent, T. J. (1993). Recursive Linear Models of Dynamic Economies. *Federal Reserve Bank of San Francisco Proceedings*.

Happel, B. L. M., & Murre, J. M. J. (1994). The design and evolution of modular neural network architectures. *Neural Networks*, *7*(6-7), 985–1004. doi:10.1016/S0893-6080(05)80155-8

Harvey, A. (1989). *Forecasting structural time series models and the kalman filter*. Cambridge, UK: Cambridge University Press.

Hill, T., Marquez, L., O'Connor, M., & Remus, W. (1994). Artificial neural networks for forecasting and decision making. *International Journal of Forecasting*, *10*(1), 5–15. doi:10.1016/0169-2070(94)90045-0

Hill, T., O'Connor, M., & Remus, W. (1996). Neural network models for time series forecasts. *Management Science*, *42*(7), 1082–1092. doi:10.1287/mnsc.42.7.1082

Hinich, M. J. (1982). Testing for Gaussianity and linearity of a statistionary time series. *Journal of Time Series Analysis*, *3*(3), 169–176. doi:10.1111/j.1467-9892.1982.tb00339.x

Hornik, K. (1991). Approximation capability of multilayer feedforward networks. *Neural Networks*, *4*(2), 251–257. doi:10.1016/0893-6080(91)90009-T

Hornik, K., Stinchicombe, M., & White, H. (1989). Multilayer Feedforward Networks are Universal Approximators. *Neural Networks*, *2*(5), 359–366. doi:10.1016/0893-6080(89)90020-8

Hylleberg, S. (1994). Modelling seasonal variation. In *Nonstationary Time Series Analysis and Cointegration* (pp. 153–178). Oxford, UK: Oxford University Press.

Igel, C., & Husken, M. (2003). Empirical evaluation of the improved Rprop learning algorithms. *Neurocomputing*, *50*, 105–123. doi:10.1016/S0925-2312(01)00700-7

Kaashoek, J. F., & Van Dijk, H. K. (2003). Neural Networks: an Econometric Tool. In *Computer-Aided Econometrics* (pp. 351–384). New York: D.E.A. Giles. doi:10.1201/9780203911570.ch12

Kaastra, I., & Boyd, M. (1996). Designing a neural network for forecasting financial and economic series. *Neurocomputing*, *10*(3), 215–236. doi:10.1016/0925-2312(95)00039-9

Kang, S. (1991). *An Investigation of the Use of Feedforward Neural Networks for Forecasting* (Ph.D. Thesis). Kent State University.

Klimasauskas, C. C. (1993). Applying neural networks. In *Neural Networks in Finance and Investing: Using Artificial Intelligence to Improve Real World Performance* (pp. 64–65). Chicago: Probus.

Koopman, S. J., & Franses, P. H. (2002). Constructing seasonally adjusted data with time-varying confidence intervals. *Oxford Bulletin of Economics and Statistics*, *64*(5), 509–526. doi:10.1111/1468-0084.00275

La Rocca, M., & Perna, C. (2005). Variable selection in neural network regression models with dependent data: A subsampling approach. *Computational Statistics & Data Analysis*, *48*(2), 415–429. doi:10.1016/j.csda.2004.01.004

Lasdon, L. S., & Waren, A. D. (1986). *GRG2 User's Guide. Department of General Business Administration*. Austin, TX: The University Texas at Austin.

Lehtokangas, M. (1999). Modelling with constructive backpropagation. *Neural Networks*, *12*(4-5), 707–716. doi:10.1016/S0893-6080(99)00018-0 PMID:12662678

Luukkonen, R., Saikkonen, P., & Terasvirta, T. (1988). Testing linearity in univariate time series models. *Scandinavian Journal of Statistics*, *15*, 161–175.

Masters, T. (1993). *Practical neural network recipes in C*. New York: Academic Press.

Masters, T. (1994). *Signal and image processing with previous neural networks*. John Wiley & Sons, Inc.

Mishra, S., & Patra, S. K. (2009). Short term load forecasting using a novel recurrent neural network. *International Journal of Computational Intelligence: Theory and Practice*, *4*(1), 39–45.

Nam, K., & Schaefer, T. (1995). Forecasting international airline passenger traffic using neural networks. *Logistics and Transportation*, *31*(3), 239–251.

Nelson, M., Hill, T., Remus, T., & O'Connor, M. (1999). Time series forecasting using NNs: Should the data be deseasonalized first? *Journal of Forecasting*, *18*(5), 359–367. doi:10.1002/(SICI)1099-131X(199909)18:5<359::AID-FOR746>3.0.CO;2-P

Pack, D. C., El-Sharkawi, M. A., Marks, R. J. II, & Atlas, L. E. (1991). Electric load forecasting using an artificial neural network. *IEEE Transactions on Power Systems*, *6*(2), 442–449. doi:10.1109/59.76685

Palmer, A., Montaño, J. J., & Sesé, A. (2006). Designing an artificial neural network for forecasting tourism time series. *Tourism Management*, *27*(5), 781–790. doi:10.1016/j.tourman.2005.05.006

Qi, M., & Zhang, P. G. (2008). Trend time-series modeling and forecasting with neural networks. *IEEE Transactions on Neural Networks*, *19*(5), 808–816. doi:10.1109/TNN.2007.912308 PMID:18467210

Reed, R. (1993). Pruning algorithms a survey. *IEEE Transactions on Neural Networks*, *4*(5), 740–747. doi:10.1109/72.248452 PMID:18276504

Riedmiller, M. (1994). Advanced supervised learning in multi-layer perceptrons – from backpropagation to adaptive learning algorithms. *Computer Standards & Interfaces*, *16*(3), 265–278. doi:10.1016/0920-5489(94)90017-5

Saikkonen, P., & Luukkonen, R. (1988). Lagrange multiplier tests for testing non-linearities in time series models. *Scandinavian Journal of Statistics*, *15*, 55–68.

Sánchez, P. (2008). Cambios Estructurales en Series de Tiempo: Una revisión del estado del arte. *Ingenierías*, *7*(12), 115–140.

Sánchez, P. A., & García, J. R. (2017). A New Methodology for Neural Network Training Ensures Error Reduction in Time Series Forecasting. *Journal of Computational Science*, *13*(7), 211–217. doi:10.3844/jcssp.2017.211.217

Sánchez, P. A., & García, J. R. (2018). Autoregressive Moving Average Recurrent Neural Networks Applied to the Modelling of Colombian Exchange Rate. *International Journal of Artificial Intelligence*, *16*(2), 194–207.

Sánchez, P. A., & Velásquez, J. D. (2005). Modelado Estructural No Lineal de Series Temporales. *Avances en Sistemas e Informática*, *2*(2), 27–38.

Schiffmann, W., Joost, M., & Werner, R. (1993). Application of genetic algorithms to the construction of topologies for multilayer perceptron. *Proceedings of the International Conference on Artificial Neural Networks and Genetic Algorithms*, 675–682. 10.1007/978-3-7091-7533-0_98

Schwarz, G. (1978). Estimating the dimension of a model. *Annals of Statistics*, *6*(2), 461–464. doi:10.1214/aos/1176344136

Shanker, M., Hu, M. Y., & Hung, M. S. (1996). Effect of data standardization on neural network training. *Omega*, *24*(4), 385–397. doi:10.1016/0305-0483(96)00010-2

Sims, C. A. (1993). A Variable Probabilistic Macroeconomic Forecasting Model. In Business Cycles, Indicators, and Forecasting (pp. 179-214). University of Chicago Press.

Srinivasan, D., Liew, A. C., & Chang, C. S. (1994). A neural network short-term load forecaster. *Electric Power Systems Research*, *28*(3), 227–234. doi:10.1016/0378-7796(94)90037-X

Subramanian, V., & Hung, M. (1993). A GRG2-based system for training neural networks: Design and computational experience. *ORSA Journal on Computing*, *5*(4), 386–394. doi:10.1287/ijoc.5.4.386

Sung, A. H. (1998). Ranking importance of input parameters of neural networks. *Expert Systems with Applications*, *15*(3-4), 405–411. doi:10.1016/S0957-4174(98)00041-4

Tang, Z., & Fishwick, P. A. (1993). Feedforward neural nets as models for time series forecasting. *ORSA Journal on Computing*, *5*(4), 374–385. doi:10.1287/ijoc.5.4.374

Tang, Z., & Koehler, J. G. (1994). Deterministic global optimal FNN training algorithms. *Neural Networks*, *7*(2), 1405–1412. doi:10.1016/0893-6080(94)90024-8

Tkacz, G., & Hu, S. (1999). *Forecasting GDP growth using artificial neural networks* (Working paper pp. 99-3). Ottawa: Bank of Canada.

Tong, H. (1990). *Nonlinear Time Series: A Dynamical System Approach*. Oxford, UK: Oxford University Press.

Yale, K. (1997). Preparing the right data for training neural networks. *IEEE Spectrum, 34*(3), 64–66. doi:10.1109/6.576011

Yu, X. H., Chen, G. A., & Cheng, S. X. (1995). Dynamic learning rate optimization of the backpropagation algorithm. *IEEE Transactions on Neural Networks, 6*(3), 669–677. doi:10.1109/72.377972 PMID:18263352

Zhang, G. P., Patuwo, B. E., & Hu, M. Y. (1998). Forecasting with artificial neural networks: The state of the art. *International Journal of Forecasting, 14*(1), 35–62. doi:10.1016/S0169-2070(97)00044-7

Zhang, J., Walte, G. G., Miao, Y., & Wayne, W. N. (1995). Wavelet neural networks for function learning. *IEEE Transactions on Signal Processing, 43*(6), 1485–1497. doi:10.1109/78.388860

Zhang, P. G., & Qi, M. (2005). Neural network forecasting for seasonal and trend time series. *European Journal of Operational Research, 160*(2), 501–514. doi:10.1016/j.ejor.2003.08.037

Zhang, X. (1994). Time series analysis and prediction by neural networks. *Optimization Methods & Software, 4*(2), 151–170. doi:10.1080/10556789408805584

Chapter 13
Encryption Techniques for Modern World

Uma Ramachandra Pujeri
MIT – World Peace University, India

Sharmishta Suhas Desai
MIT – World Peace University, India

Amit Savyanavar
https://orcid.org/0000-0001-6092-7017
MIT – World Peace University, India

ABSTRACT

Encryption is the process of converting confidential private data into unreadable form and securing information in the file from unauthorized access using various encryption algorithms. We live in the information age where the exchange of private information has become the integral part of our day-to-day activities. Billions of e-mails and business data are sent throughout the world through internet daily. The success of the information age is to keep private secure data from unauthorized access and key to access the private and secure data for authorized users. Encryption in this information age plays a vital role in the protecting the confidential data from unauthorized access. In the last few decades, the computer network has created a revolution in the use of information. Authorized users access their data or send their private data from anywhere in the world; hence, it has become very important to secure the private data not only where it is stored, but also to maintain high level of confidentiality while transmission of this private data from one machine to another.

DOI: 10.4018/978-1-5225-8458-2.ch013

INTRODUCTION

In today's digital world, billions of emails and pieces of business data are sent across the world via the Internet, which has provided an infrastructure for digital marketing, e-commerce, and online banking that allows money to flow through cyberspace. For example, according to estimates each day half of the world's gross domestic product (GDP) travels through the Society for Worldwide Interbank Financial Telecommunications (SWIFT) network. Because authorized users need to access or send private data from anywhere in the world at any time, it has become crucial to not only secure private data where it is stored, but also to maintain a high level of confidentiality while transmitting such data from one machine to another. In that sense, computer security protects the integrity of information systems. Critically, the success of such activities depends on the ability to protect information as it flows around the world, in a process that relies upon the power of cryptography. By definition, *encryption* is process of converting private, confidential data to unreadable form or concealing private, secure information in the file from unauthorized access by using various encryption algorithms. Today and for the foreseeable future, encryption plays and will play a vital role in protecting confidential data from unauthorized access.

Goals of Information and Data Security

The goals of securing online information and data are threefold: confidentiality, integrity, and availability. Whereas confidentiality is needed in the protection of private data from unauthorized access, integrity is needed in changes made by authorized entities via authorized mechanism. Last, availability is necessary for information created by organizations or users that should be available to authorized entities at anytime and anywhere.

Although computer security ensures the protection of confidential data, computer and network security present major challenges. For one, designing security algorithms is complex as algorithms must consider all possible attacks on security features. To that end, security mechanisms in computer and network systems require constant monitoring. Accordingly, security is an integral to designing algorithms and maintaining them after their implementation. Moreover, managing private data in mobile networks presents the challenge of ensuring the confidentiality of data. Among threats to such confidentiality are internal threats, including when members of organizations inject malware or viruses into local organizational area networks in order to access the confidential data of their organizations.

To ensure the security of private data, cryptography is often used to conceal the contents of messages containing such data by enciphering them. The general aim of this chapter is thus to clarify various encryption and mathematical algorithms that can be applied to prevent unauthorized users (e.g., hackers) from accessing the private data of network users. Once such algorithms are clarified, we present the design of an advanced encryption algorithm using certain mathematical algorithms to facilitate such prevention efforts. In this chapter, we discuss how data encryption plays a vital role in day-to-day life, as well as different mathematical techniques needed to generate ciphertext. Then, we address the design of the Data Encryption Standard (DES) and Advanced Encryption Standard (AES). Afterwards, we explain elliptic curve cryptography (ECC), then we will define and test our hypothesis. Last, we conclude the chapter by addressing the past and future of encryption.

Using Advanced Encryption Algorithms to Transmit Data Online

Encryption makes today's world go round. Every time that someone makes a call from a cellphone, makes a purchase with a credit card in person or online, and accesses cash from ATMs, encryption bestows upon that transaction the confidentiality and security to make it possible. By extension, because most transactions are performed online, data encryption is essential to the effectiveness of any computer security system.

Today, as the Internet continues to revolutionize how people live their lives—more than 50% of the world's population depends on it to perform day-to-day activities—online who parties share confidential, personal information require data security and not only on personal computers. Otherwise, information sent via the Internet without encryption can be viewed by any willing party for whatever purpose. In a typical information-sharing process online, data from a machine are relayed to a local network and, in turn, to Internet service providers, first of the sender and, later, of the receiver, who ultimately may access the data. During that process, since various willing parties could easily obtain supposedly secure information sent online, encryption is vital to protecting confidential data from unauthorized access. As Internet traffic grows exponentially year after year, a total of 40.5% of websites have begun to use encryption by default since July, 2016 versus 21.3% since July, 2015. Unsurprisingly, a total of 97% of surveyed enterprises witnessed an increase in encrypted web traffic, and researchers predict that 75% of all web traffic will be encrypted by 2019.

Background of Cryptographic Algorithms Used in the Banking Sector

A cryptographic algorithm named the Lucifer algorithm was invented in 1970 by Horst Feisted. The Lucifer algorithm was later updated by making changes to the internal function and changing the key size from 112 bits to 56 bits and this new updated algorithm was called Data Encryption Standard (DES) which was published in the Federal Register in 1975. DES became so popular that many well-established financial institutions started using DES algorithms to protect their binary coded data stored in the computer system. However, hackers were able to break this DES algorithm and retrieve some part of resources stored on the system. Hence, a new algorithm which was stronger than DES was proposed which was named 3DES. The 3DES algorithm uses two or three 56 bit DES key and uses original DES algorithm three times to encrypt the data. In 2002, the Advanced Encryption Standard (AES) algorithm was proposed which was also known as the Rijndael algorithm. AES is an iterated block cipher algorithm which uses key length of 128, 192, or 256 bits. The federal government standard announced AES as an effective algorithm on May 20, 2002 after approval by the Secretary of Commerce.

Electronic Banking: Security Using Cryptogyaphy

ATM: Automatic Teller Machine (ATM) [Dixit,2018] is an important technological development which enabled the customer to withdraw their money any time (24 *7) using this ATM machine. ATMs today are well known for their convenience to the customer, effective banking techniques for the bank, and the most secured banking method at anytime and anywhere. To make ATM transactions secure, various encryption algorithms are used to secure online transaction done by the customers. The ATM pin entered by the customer is also encryption for security before sending on to the internet. Biometric Authentication using the AES algorithm is proposed for the ATM to make the system more secure. Finger print details including minor details, and frequency ridges of the customer are stored at the central bank server. During transactions, the finger print of the customer is scanned using high resolution scanner at ATM. This finger print image is encrypted using a private key and sent to the server using a secure channel. At the central server, this finger print image is decrypted using the same key. The AES algorithm uses variable key length and some of its most advanced encryption technologies protect ATM and secures its data.

CARDS (Debit, Credit, Smart): Today in many big malls, shops, and even for online shopping, payment is done using these electronic cards. Each card is associated with four digit PIN for authorization. All the data communication is protected with advanced encryption algorithm making the chip and PIN cards more difficult to hack for hackers.

Online/Mobile Banking – Mobile/Online is a common way used today to do the banking transaction through mobile or through Internet. Customer securely logs in into his banking account using the user ID and password where the customer and perform his/her various banking transactions. For further security, a one time password (OTP) is provided on the customer's registered mobile number. OTP is generated using advanced encryption algorithms which make the online/mobile banking extremely secure.

Mathematical Background of Cryptography and Encryption

Cryptography is based on specific mathematical concepts, including several algorithms, as discussed in this section.

Number Theory

Used since ancient times in arithmetic, numbers are part and parcel of pure mathematics and fundamental to the study of integers. Numbers theory, sometimes also called the "queen of mathematics," is thus the branch of mathematics that encompasses the properties and relationships of numbers, especially positive integers (Katz, 2014; Raji, 2013).

Integer Athematic

Integer arithmetic can be conceived as arithmetic without fractions. The scope of integers, represented by *Z*, contains all integer parts without fractions from negative infinity to positive infinity as shown in Figure 1.

Integers are often split into three subsets: Z^+, Z^-, and 0. Whereas Z^+ contains all positive integers—for example, $Z^+ = \{1, 2, 66, 100, 123, \ldots\}$—$Z^-$ contains all negative integers—for instance, $Z^- = \{\ldots\text{-}100, \text{-}55, \text{-}33, \text{-}5, \text{-}6\}$. Although 0 is excluded from all three of those sets, $Z^{\text{non-negative}}$ contains all positive integers including 0, whereas $Z^{\text{nonpositive}}$ contains all negative integers including 0.

Figure 1. Set of integers

$$Z=\{\ldots\ldots,-3,-2,-1,0,1,2,3,\ldots\ldots\}$$

Within Z, two binary operations—namely, addition (+) and multiplication (×)—can be computed. Those operations satisfy a few basic properties of mathematics, including the communitive property for addition and multiplication, as shown in Equations 1.1 and 1.2, respectively:

$$a + b = b + a \quad 1.1$$

$$a \times b = b \times a \quad 1.2$$

Other such properties include the associative property for addition and multiplication, as shown in Equations 1.3 and 1.4, respectively:

$$(a + b) + c = a + (b + c) \quad 1.3$$

$$(a \times b) \times c = a \times (b \times c) \quad 1.4$$

Another is the distributive property of multiplication over addition as shown in Equation 1.5:

$$a \times (b + c) = a \times b + a \times c \quad 1.5$$

Identity elements 0 and 1 for binary addition and binary multiplication, shown respectively in Equations 1.6 and 1.7, satisfy basic properties when applied within Z:

$$a + 0 = 0 + a = a \quad 1.6$$

$$a \times 1 = 1 \times a = a \quad 1.7$$

Every $a \in Z$.

Set Z allows the additive inverse. For every $a \in Z$, another element exists in Z denoted by $-a$, such that

$$a + (-a) = 0 \quad 1.8$$

Set Z also allows the multiplicative inverse; for every $a \in Z$, another element exists in Z denoted by a^{-1} or $\frac{1}{a}$ such that

$$a \times a^{-1} = 1 \quad 1.9$$

Apart from addition and multiplication, subtraction and division can also be applied within Z. Subtraction is a binary operation, meaning that it can be performed by any two integers in Z. However, division is not, meaning that it can be defined only with specific integers. Subtraction and division are defined as $a - b = a + (-b)$ for every $a, b \in Z$, in which a and b are nonzero integers; a divides b or b is divisible by a only if integer c exists such that $a = b \times c$. In that case, $a \mid b$ or $a \nmid b$. For example, 3,652 is divisible by 2 since 2 × 1,826 = 3,652, for which $a = 2$, $b = 3{,}652$, and $c = 1{,}826$; hence, $2 \mid 3{,}652$.

Divisibility and Division Algorithms

If $b \neq 0$, then b divides a as long as $a = xb$ for x, in which a, b, and x are integers. That is, b divides when there is no remainder following division. Thus, integer $b \neq 0$ divides another integer, a, if $\exists\, x \in Z$, such that $a = x \times b$. In that case, b is a factor or divisor of a. If $b \mid a$, then b divides a.

The positive divisors of 36 are 1, 2, 3, 4, 6, 9, 12, 18, and 24.

$-3 \mid 12$, $13 \mid 182$, $-3 \mid 33$, $12 \mid 144$, $15 \mid 0$, but $5 \nmid 12$.

Simple Properties of Divisibility

Divisibility has several properties as follows:

- If $a \mid 1$, then $a = \pm 1$.
- If $a \mid b$ and $b \mid a$, then $a = \pm b$.
- Any $b \neq 0$ divides 0.
- If $a \mid b$ and $a \mid c$, then $a \mid (b + c)$.
- If $a \mid b$ and $a \mid c$ in which $b > c$, then $a \mid (b - c)$.
- If $a \mid b$ or $a \mid c$, then $a \mid bc$.
- If $a \mid b$ and $b \mid c$, then $a \mid c$.

The Division Algorithm

For division, consider the following example:

$$42 \overline{\big)600}^{\,14} \; r = 12$$

The equation can be rewritten as $600 = 42\,(14) + 12$. For another example, if k is the dividend, d is the divisor, and both are positive integers, then the division of k by d yields quotient q and remainder r, all of which can be written as:

$$d \overline{\big)k}^{\,q} \text{ rem r}$$

Furthermore, since $0 \leq r < d$. We can write the equation in the form

$$k = dq + r \qquad 1.10$$

in which $0 <= r < d$

Division Algorithms for Integers

If k is any number and d is a positive integer, then unique integers q and r exist such that $k = dq + r$, in which $0 \leq r < d$.

In the division algorithm, dividend k is an arbitrary integer. In long division, the case in which $k \geq d$ is familiar, and there are two other cases as well (Davenport, 2008; Day, 2008).

Case 1: Assume $0 <= k < \text{d}$, then set $q = 0$ and $r = k$, such that $k = \text{d}(0) + k$.

Case 2: Assume that the dividend is $-k$ and that k is positive. Since k is positive, we can use long division to obtain integers q and r such that $k = dq + r$. Consequently, $-k = d(-q) - r = d(-q - 1) + (d - r)$. Since $0 \leq r < d$, it follows that $0 < d - r < d$.

Greatest Common Divisors

In cryptography, the greatest common divisor (GCD) is often necessary .Two positive integers—for instance, 80 and 216, written as (80, 216)—can have many common divisors but only one GCD. Whereas common divisors of (80, 216) are 2, 4, 8, and 1, the GCD is 8 (Figure 2).

The GCD of two positive integers (a, b) is largest integer that divides both integers. If their GCD is 1, then both a and b are prime numbers.

Euclidean Algorithm

Among the oldest, most commonly used algorithm to compute the GCD according to a stepwise procedure with well-defined rules, the Euclidean algorithm can be used to reduce fractions to their simplest form and is part of many calculations in number theory and cryptography.

In the Euclidean algorithm, the input is two positive integers a and b, whereas the output is the GCD, or d, of (a, b). The algorithm involves four steps:

Step 1: If $(a < b)$, then swap a and b.
Step 2: Divide a by b to obtain remainder r.
Step 3: If $r = 0$, then report b as the GCD of (a, b).
Step 4: If $a = b$ and $b = r$, then return to Step 2.

Figure 2. Greatest common divisors of two integers

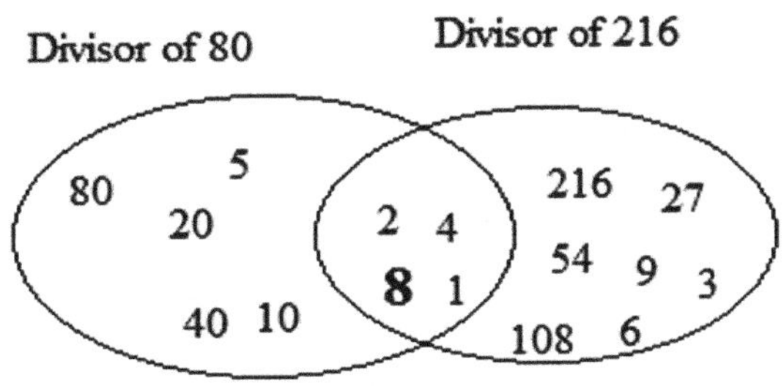

For example, finding the GCD of (1,424, 3,084) with the Euclidean algorithm is performed by following those steps with the equation $3{,}084 = 1{,}424 \times 2 + 236$:

1. $1{,}424 = 236 \times 6 + 8$
2. $236 = 8 \times 29 + 4$
3. $8 = 4 \times 2 + 0$

A breakdown of the various quotients, dividends, divisors, and remainders of the equation appears in Table 1.

When the remainder equals 0, then the remainder of the previous division is the GCD (i.e., 4).

The Extended Euclidean Algorithm

The extended Euclidean algorithm not only computes the GCD of two integers (a, b) but also the coefficients of Bézout's lemma, which are the integers x and y, such that

$ax + by = \text{GCD}(a, b)$ 1.11

A reciprocal of modular exponentiation, the extended Euclidean algorithm facilitates the computation of values for x and y by reversing the steps of the algorithm. To compute those values, the first step is to find the GCD of (a, b), followed by recursively working backward by treating the numbers as variables until obtaining an expression that represents a linear combination of the initial integers.

To clarify how the extended Euclidean algorithm works, assume that $a = 102$ and $b = 38$ to find the GCD of (a, b) and the values of x and y. The previously mentioned steps to determine the GCD are:

1. $102 = 38 \times 2 + 26$
2. $38 = 26 \times 1 + 12$
3. $26 = 12 \times 2 + 2$
4. $12 = 6 \times 2 + 0$

Thus, the GCD of (102, 38) is 2. A breakdown of the various quotients, dividends, divisors, and remainders of the equation appears in Table 2

Next, the values for x and y are computed by reversing the steps of the Euclidean algorithm:

1. $2 = 26 - 2 \times 12$ (refer to Step 3 of the Euclidean algorithm)

Table 1. Greatest common divisor of (1,424, 3,084)

Quotient	Dividend	Divisor	Remainder
2	3,084	1,424	236
6	1,424	236	8
29	236	8	4
2	8	4	0

Table 2. Greatest common divisor of (102, 38)

Quotient	Dividend	Divisor	Remainder
2	102	38	26
1	38	26	12
2	26	12	2
6	12	2	0

2. $12 = 38 - 1 \times 26$ (refer to Step 2 of the Euclidean algorithm)
3. $26 = 102 - 2 \times 38$ (refer to Step 1 of the Euclidean algorithm)

Then, the following computations are performed:

$2 = 26 - 2 \times 12$ (i.e., substitute the value of Step 1 above with that of Step 2 above)

$2 = 26 - 2 \times (38 - 1 \times 26)$

$2 = 26 - 2 \times 38 + 2 \times 26$

$2 = 1 \times 26 - 2 \times 38 + 2 \times 26$

Once like terms are collected, the result is:

$2 = 3 \times 26 - 2 \times 38$

$2 = 3 \times (102 - 2 \times 38) - 2 \times 38$ (i.e., substitute value of Step 3 above with that in Step 4 above)

$2 = 3 \times 102 - 8 \times 38$

Ultimately, x is 3 and y is -8.

Prime Numbers

Prime numbers play a vital role in cryptography [Katz,2014], particularly in cryptographic algorithms such as the Rivest–Shamir–Adleman (RSA) algorithm, the elliptic curve asymmetric algorithm, and the Diffie–Hellman (DH) key exchange algorithm, all of which are based on prime numbers.

A natural number p is a prime number only if $p > 1$. If $p = ab$, then either $a = p$ and $b = 1$ or $a = 1$ and $b = p$. That is, p is prime number only if its factors are 1 and itself.

Factorization

A prime number has no factors other than itself and 1. The prime factors for positive integer p can be defined as the prime numbers that divide the positive integer p with the remainder as 0. The prime factorization of positive integers yields a list of prime factors with their multiplicities. For example:

$864 = 2 \times 2 \times 2 \times 2 \times 2 \times 3 \times 3 \times 3 = 2^5 \times 3^3$

In that example, the prime factors of positive integer 864 are 2 and 3, whereas the multiplicities are 5 and 3.

Fermat's Little Theorem

Fermat's little theorem states that if p is a prime number, then for any integer x, $x^p - x$ is an integer multiple of p.

$x^p \equiv x \pmod{p}$ 1.12

For example, if $x = 3$ and $p = 5$, then $3^5 = 243$ and $243 - 3 = 48 \times 5$ are integer multiples of 5. If x is not divisible by p, then Fermat's little theorem is equivalent to

$x^{p-1} \equiv 1 \pmod{p}$ 1.13

As another example, if $x = 2$ and $p = 7$, then $2^6 = 64$ and $64 - 1 = 63$ are thus multiples of 7. Similarly, with prime number 17, multiply the number 5 by itself within that modulus.

Table 3 shows that all integers from 1 to 17 are hit at least once. Accordingly, the mathematical function works similar to a substitution cipher only if all integers are hit at least once. That concept illustrates the importance of prime numbers in cryptography, in which they can be used to construct large substitution tables simply by raising numbers to exponents.

ENCRYPTION TECHNIQUES

In cryptography, *encryption* refers to the process of encoding confidential messages or private data in such a way that only authorized users can access and read them. In encryption, confidential data and private messages are called *plaintext*, which is encrypted and transformed into unreadable formats, or *ciphertext*, using encryption algorithms. It is impossible to decrypt messages without possessing the key to ciphertext, which only authorized users should possess.

Substitution Methods

Substitution methods are encryption techniques in which letters of plaintext are replaced by other letters or numbers that conceal plaintext by rendering it unreadable.

Table 3. Examples of results of applying Fermat's little theorem to various integers

n	5^n (mod 17)
0	1
1	5
2	8
3	6
4	13
5	14
6	2
7	10
8	16
9	12
10	9
11	11
12	4
13	13
14	15
15	7
16	1
17	5

Caesar Cipher

Caesar cipher [Stallings,2006] an ancient encryption technique used to convert plaintext to ciphertext, uses a simple technique to convert plaintext to unreadable format by replacing each character of plaintext with the character three or *k* (i.e., any number) places to the right or left of the original character. For example, shifting the characters of "Mother India" three places to the right yields "PRWKHU LQGLD." By contrast, shifting the characters three places to the left yields "JLQEBO FKAFX." In both examples, the characters are wrapped—that is, the character following *Z* is *A* and vice versa.

By extension, numerical equivalents may be assigned to each letter (Table 6).

Table 4. Caesar cipher for converting plaintext to ciphertext by right-shifting three characters

Plaintext	a	b	c	d	e	f	g	h	i	j	k	l	m	n	o	p	q	r	s	t	u	v	w	x	y	z
Ciphertext	D	E	F	G	H	I	J	K	L	M	N	O	P	Q	R	S	T	U	V	W	X	Y	Z	A	B	C

Table 5. Caesar cipher for converting plaintext to ciphertext by left-shifting three characters

Plaintext	a	b	c	d	e	f	g	h	i	j	k	l	m	n	o	p	q	r	s	t	u	v	w	x	y	z
Ciphertext	X	Y	Z	A	B	C	D	E	F	G	H	I	J	K	L	M	N	O	P	Q	R	S	T	U	V	W

Table 6. Numerical equivalent of each character

a	b	c	d	e	f	g	h	i	j	k	l	m	n	o
0	1	2	3	4	5	6	7	8	9	10	11	12	13	14
p	q	r	s	t	u	v	w	x	y	z				
15	16	17	18	19	20	21	22	23	24	25				

Algorithm for Caesar Cipher

Let p denote each character from plaintext and C denote each character from ciphertext.

$C = E(3, p) = (p + 3) \bmod 26$ 1.14

Whereas Equation 1.14 shifts the letters by three places to convert plaintext to ciphertext, in the Caesar cipher algorithm characters can be shifted by any amount (k) from 1 to 25 to convert plaintext to ciphertext.

$C = E(k, p) = (p + k) \bmod 26$ 1.15

To convert ciphertext to plaintext, use Equation 1.16:

$P = D(k, C) = (C - k) \bmod 26$ 1.16

in which D represents the decryption algorithm, C represents ciphertext, and k represents the key. However, the Caesar cipher can be solved by intruders for three reasons:

1. Intruders have knowledge of encryption and decryption algorithms;
2. Intruders can easily determine when the Caesar cipher is used, even if they do not know the key value; and
3. There are only 25 keys that intruders can apply to ciphertext to convert it to plaintext.

Thus, solving the Caesar cipher is relatively straightforward. Because there are only 26 possible shifts of characters in the English-language letters, each letter can be tested via brute force attack. One approach to such an attack involves writing a sample of ciphertext in the table of all possible shifts. The example of the ciphertext "lmhhirxviewwyvimrseomwpdrh" appears in Table 7; by applying that strategy to the ciphertext, the plaintext surfaces in the fourth line.

Table 7. Brute force attack on the Caesar cipher

Decryption shift	Ciphertext
0	Lmhhir xviewwyvi mr seo mwpdrh
1	Klgghq wuhdvvxuh lq rdh lvocqg
2	Jkffgp vtgccwtg kp qcm kuncpf
3	Ijeefo usfbttvsf jo pbl jtmboe
4	**Hidden treasure in Oak Island**
5	Ghccdg sqdzrrtqd hg hzj hrkzgc
6	Fgbbcf rpcyqqspc gf gyi gqjxfb
7	Efaabe qobxpprob fe fxh fpixea
8	Dezzad pnawooqna ed ewg eohwdz
9	Cdyyzc omzvnnpmz dc dvf dngvcy
10	Bcxxyb nlyummoly cb cue cmfubx
11	Abwwxa mkxtllnkx ba btd bl etaw
12	Zavvwz ljwskkmjw az asc akdszv

Moreover, with the Caesar cipher, encrypting a text multiple times provides no additional security, because two encryptions of, say, shift A and shift B will be equivalent to a single encryption with shift A + B.

Monoalphabetic Cipher

Since the Caesar cipher can be attacked by brute force using 26 possible keys, to overcome this limitation the keys can be extended with generic substitution or a *monoalphabetic substitution cipher* or *simple substitution cipher*, in which each letter of the alphabet is replaced with fixed proxy of another letter. For example, the letter "a" in the plaintext can be replaced with letter "q" in the ciphertext (Table 8).

The plaintext "home sweet home" can be encrypted to ciphertext using monoalphabetic cipher to "BLDP WEPPG BLDP." To decrypt the ciphertext to plaintext, apply the reverse substitution.

Table 8. Monoalphabetic substitution to encrypt to ciphertext

Plaintext	a	b	c	d	e	f	g	h	i	j	k	l	m	n	o	p	q	r	s	t	U	v	w	x	y	z
Ciphertext	Q	I	K	M	P	R	T	B	U	S	F	Y	D	V	L	Z	A	X	W	G	O	J	E	N	H	C

Table 9. Monoalphabetic substitution to decrypt ciphertext

Ciphertext	Q	I	K	M	P	R	T	B	U	S	F	Y	D	V	L	Z	A	X	W	G	O	J	E	N	H	C
Plaintext	a	b	c	d	e	f	g	h	i	j	k	l	m	n	o	p	q	r	s	t	u	v	w	x	y	z

As a result, the ciphertext "BLDP WEPPG BLDP" is converted to "home sweet home" by using the decryption algorithm.

For another example, the message "Flee at once. We are discovered!" can be enciphered to the ciphertext "SIAA ZQ LKBA. VA ZOA RFPBLUAOAR!" Ciphertext is often written in a block of fixed length (i.e., group) with punctuation, spaces, and special characters omitted. Five-letter groups are common, as a holdover from when messages were transmitted by telegraph. In that approach, the stated ciphertext would be "SIAAZ QLKBA VAZOA RFPBL UAOAR." If the length of the message is not divisible by 5, then it can be padded at the end with so-called "nulls," meaning any characters that decrypt to obvious nonsense so that receivers can easily detect and discard them.

Playfair Cipher

The Playfair cipher, or the *digraph substitution cipher*, encrypts pairs of letters instead of single letters as part of its substitution cipher method. Since the Playfair cipher does not allow frequency analysis, it is more secure than substitution ciphers.

To perform the algorithm, first choose a word as the key, from which punctuation should be removed. Second, generate a 5 × 5 square of letters from the key. For example, if the key is "MITCOE," then the square of letters will appear as shown in Table 10.

The square with key letters is filled, followed by the remaining square with the letters not in the key (i.e., letters in red in Table 1.10).

For example, to encrypt the plaintext "GOLD IS IN LOCKER," pairs of letters should be formed (e.g., "GO LD IS IN LO CK ER"). If an odd number of letters is involved, then add filler letter x at the end. Next, the following rules should be applied to form the ciphertext.

1. If two letters appear in same row of the key table, then choose letters immediately right to them in the same row.
2. If two letters appear in the same column of the key table, then choose letters immediately below them.
3. If letters appear in a different row and different column, then choose letters from the corner of the rectangle formed by those letters.

Thus, "GO LD IS IN LO CK ER" becomes the ciphertext " MN SL QC HO NC LT BP":

```
GO → MN
M  I/JT     C     O
```

Table 10. 5 × 5 square of letters from the key MITCOE

M	I/J	T	C	O
E	A	B	D	F
G	H	K	L	N
P	Q	R	S	U
V	W	X	Y	Z

```
------------------
G  H  K      L      N
------------------

------------------
LD → SL
M  I/JT      C      O
E  A  B      D      F
G  H  K      L      N
P  Q  R      S      U
V  W  X      Y      Z
```

Hill Cipher

Based on linear algebra, the Hill cipher is a polygraphic substitution method that can be used on differently sized blocks. It uses matrices and matrix multiplication to form ciphertext from plaintext. The major feature of the Hill cipher is its use of mathematics in forming ciphertext. The key used in the Hill cipher is a square matrix of any size.

For example, suppose that our key is the 3 × 3 matrix given below.

$$\begin{bmatrix} 3 & 2 & 5 \\ -2 & 4 & 6 \\ 1 & 7 & 3 \end{bmatrix}$$

Break the plaintext "exam paper sealed" into subgroups of three characters (i.e., "exa mpa per sea led") and convert the letters into numbers as a sequence (i.e., 0 for *a*, 1 for *b*, . . . 25 for *z*).

exa → (5, 23, 0) mpa → (12, 15, 0)

To obtain the ciphertext, multiply the key matrix by the plaintext matrix. The ciphertext of exa → (5,23,0) is thus:

To decrypt the ciphertext, multiply the inverse of the key matrix mod 26 with the ciphertext matrix. The plaintext of "JEK" is thus:

$$\begin{bmatrix} 2\ 3 & 2 & 5 \\ -2 & 4 & 6 \\ 1 & 7 & 3 \end{bmatrix} \times \begin{bmatrix} 4 \\ 23 \\ 0 \end{bmatrix} = \begin{bmatrix} 58 \\ 84 \\ 165 \end{bmatrix} \bmod 26$$

$$= \begin{bmatrix} 9 \\ 4 \\ 10 \end{bmatrix} = "JEK"$$

Alphabetic Cipher

In the alphabetic cipher, each letter is not always encrypted by the same letter but by combining mono-alphabetic ciphers. In the method, all letters are written in a 26 × 26 tableau in which 26 ciphertext letters are available:

```
Plaintext: A B C D E F G H I J K L M N O P Q R S T U V W X Y Z
Cipher 1: B D G H K L W M N P Q O V C A S E R F X Z U I T H Y
Cipher 2: D F W T A H J K X Z B C A Q N L M R E W X Z V S Y U
```

For example, the plaintext "Welcome to MIT" is encrypted by encrypting the first letter by using Cipher 1 and the second by using Cipher 2. The ciphertext is thus "IRPNQR FQ QSF."

Autokey Cipher

Also referred to as the *autoclave cipher*, the autokey cipher converts plaintext into a key according to a polyalphabetic substitution cipher related to the Vigenère cipher and with a different method of key generation. For example, the tableau recta (Table 1.11) can be used to convert the plaintext into ciphertext.

To encrypt the plaintext "Hide this in bag" with key "purse," first write the keyword "purse," followed by the plaintext, according to Table 12.

To generate ciphertext, search for the plaintext letter horizontally and the key stream letter vertically in the tableau. A search for 'h' horizontally and 'p' vertically yields 'w'. Thus, the ciphertext for "Hide this in bag" with key "purse" is "wcuw xoqv mg iiy."

One-Time Pads

One-time pads are known as mathematically unbroken cryptosystems, which often use the Vernam cipher or perfect ciphers. In such cryptosystems, plaintext is combined with a random key. To remain unbreakable, one-time pads need to have six properties.

1. The key needs to be as long as the message or text to be encrypted;
2. The key needs to be truly random (i.e., not generated by using normal mathematical functions);
3. The key and plaintext need to be calculated using modulus 10 for digits, modulus 26 for letters, and modulus 2 for binary data;
4. The key needs to be used only once;
5. The key needs to be destroyed by the sender and receiver after its use; and
6. The key needs to be different for the sender as well as the receiver.

For example, if a sender wants to deliver the message "Hide gold," then he or she needs to combine that message with a key. To that end, add values for letters yields 0 for "A" and 1 for "B"; in that way, values are calculated. The addition is converted to Module 26. If the key is "Pune good," then the ciphertext will be XXXXXX, as shown in Table 1.13.

To decrypt the message, the reverse process is applied, as shown in Table 14.

Table 11. Tableau recta

	A	B	C	D	E	F	G	H	I	J	K	L	M	N	O	P	Q	R	S	T	U	V	W	X	Y	Z
A	A	B	C	D	E	F	G	H	I	J	K	L	M	N	O	P	Q	R	S	T	U	V	W	X	Y	Z
B	B	C	D	E	F	G	H	I	J	K	L	M	N	O	P	Q	R	S	T	U	V	W	X	Y	Z	A
C	C	D	E	F	G	H	I	J	K	L	M	N	O	P	Q	R	S	T	U	V	W	X	Y	Z	A	B
D	D	E	F	G	H	I	J	K	L	M	N	O	P	Q	R	S	T	U	V	W	X	Y	Z	A	B	C
E	E	F	G	H	I	J	K	L	M	N	O	P	Q	R	S	T	U	V	W	X	Y	Z	A	B	C	D
F	F	G	H	I	J	K	L	M	N	O	P	Q	R	S	T	U	V	W	X	Y	Z	A	B	C	D	E
G	G	H	I	J	K	L	M	N	O	P	Q	R	S	T	U	V	W	X	Y	Z	A	B	C	D	E	F
H	H	I	J	K	L	M	N	O	P	Q	R	S	T	U	V	W	X	Y	Z	A	B	C	D	E	F	G
I	I	J	K	L	M	N	O	P	Q	R	S	T	U	V	W	X	Y	Z	A	B	C	D	E	F	G	H
J	J	K	L	M	N	O	P	Q	R	S	T	U	V	W	X	Y	Z	A	B	C	D	E	F	G	H	I
K	K	L	M	N	O	P	Q	R	S	T	U	V	W	X	Y	Z	A	B	C	D	E	F	G	H	I	J
L	L	M	N	O	P	Q	R	S	T	U	V	W	X	Y	Z	A	B	C	D	E	F	G	H	I	J	K
M	M	N	O	P	Q	R	S	T	U	V	W	X	Y	Z	A	B	C	D	E	F	G	H	I	J	K	L
N	N	O	P	Q	R	S	T	U	V	W	X	Y	Z	A	B	C	D	E	F	G	H	I	J	K	L	M
O	O	P	Q	R	S	T	U	V	W	X	Y	Z	A	B	C	D	E	F	G	H	I	J	K	L	M	N
P	P	Q	R	S	T	U	V	W	X	Y	Z	A	B	C	D	E	F	G	H	I	J	K	L	M	N	O
Q	Q	R	S	T	U	V	W	X	Y	Z	A	B	C	D	E	F	G	H	I	J	K	L	M	N	O	P
R	R	S	T	U	V	W	X	Y	Z	A	B	C	D	E	F	G	H	I	J	K	L	M	N	O	P	Q
S	S	T	U	V	W	X	Y	Z	A	B	C	D	E	F	G	H	I	J	K	L	M	N	O	P	Q	R
T	T	U	V	W	X	Y	Z	A	B	C	D	E	F	G	H	I	J	K	L	M	N	O	P	Q	R	S
U	U	V	W	X	Y	Z	A	B	C	D	E	F	G	H	I	J	K	L	M	N	O	P	Q	R	S	T
V	V	W	X	Y	Z	A	B	C	D	E	F	G	H	I	J	K	L	M	N	O	P	Q	R	S	T	U
W	W	X	Y	Z	A	B	C	D	E	F	G	H	I	J	K	L	M	N	O	P	Q	R	S	T	U	V
X	X	Y	Z	A	B	C	D	E	F	G	H	I	J	K	L	M	N	O	P	Q	R	S	T	U	V	W
Y	Y	Z	A	B	C	D	E	F	G	H	I	J	K	L	M	N	O	P	Q	R	S	T	U	V	W	Y
Z	Z	A	B	C	D	E	F	G	H	I	J	K	L	M	N	O	P	Q	R	S	T	U	V	W	X	Y

Table 12. Plaintext to key mapping

Plaintext	h	i	d	e	t	h	i	s	i	n	b	a	g
Key stream	p	u	r	s	e	h	i	d	e	t	h	i	s

Transposition Ciphers

Following the literal meaning of *transposition* (i.e., to change or exchange the positions of two entities), cryptography often adopts *transposition ciphers* based on that concept [1,2]. In transposition ciphers, the positions of letters or characters, either as individuals or in groups, in the text are shifted based on

Table 13. Ciphertext generation

Plaintext	H	I	D	E	G	O	L	D
Value 1	7	8	3	4	6	14	11	3
Key	P	U	N	E	G	O	O	D
Value 2	15	20	13	4	6	14	14	3
Addition	22	28	16	8	12	28	25	6
Mod 26	22	2	16	8	12	2	25	6
Ciphertext	W	C	Q	U	P	C	Z	G

Table 14. Ciphertext to plaintext conversion

Ciphertext	W	C	Q	U	P	C	Z	G
Value 1	22	2	16	8	12	2	25	6
Possible key	P	K	N	E	G	Q	O	D
Possible value 2	15	10	13	4	6	16	14	3
Subtraction	7	8	3	4	6	14	11	3
Mod 26	7	8	3	4	6	14	11	3
Plaintext	H	I	D	E	G	O	L	D

a specific logic or function. Consequently, the ciphertext comprises text transposed according to that logic. To decipher the text, conversely, the exact reverse is applied. The logic or function of reordering can be very simple or complex, depending on the desired level of security. Mathematically speaking, transposition ciphers use some type of bijective function. Three types of transposition ciphers—namely, the rail fence cipher, the row transposition cipher, and product ciphers—are elaborated in what follows.

Rail Fence Cipher

The rail fence cipher, also called the *zigzag cipher* [2, 3, 4], is a type of transposition cipher that uses a numeric key referred to as *rails*. The cipher derives its name from the way it is encoded; the plaintext is written first on the rails from top to bottom, second from the bottom to the top, and in that manner until the plaintext is exhausted. In this section, we apply the rail fence cipher with the plaintext "ATTACK FROM SOUTH" and four rails as the key.

Encryption

For the rail fence cipher, a matrix with the size equivalent to the number of rails by the length of plaintext is necessary. In zigzag fashion, the plaintext is written first downward and diagonally on successive rails until the bottommost rail is reached, then diagonally in the upward direction until the topmost rail is reached, and continued until the plaintext is exhausted. Ultimately, the individual rows are combined to obtain the ciphertext "A STKF OTCRMUHAOT."

Table 15. Rail fence cipher encryption matrix

A												S				
	T				K		F						O			
		T		C				R		M				U		H
			A						O						T	

Decryption

To decrypt the message, a matrix of the same size is used. Fill in the topmost left square with the first letter in the ciphertext and move diagonally downward while filling each square until the bottom rail is reached. Next, move diagonally upward while filling each square until the top row is reached. Fill that square with the next letter in the ciphertext and proceed in the same manner.

Repeat the process for the second row.

Repeat the process again for all subsequent rows.

The result of decryption is the plaintext "ATTACK FROM SOUTH."

Table 16. Step 1 of rail fence cipher decryption

A												S				
	-				-		-				-		-			
		-		-				-		-				-		-
			-						-						-	

Table 17. Step 2 of rail fence cipher decryption

A												S				
	T				K		F						O			
		-		-				-		-				-		-
			-						-						-	

Table 18. Step 3 of rail fence cipher decryption

A												S				
	T				K		F						O			
		T		C				R		M				U		H
			-						-						-	

Table 19. Step 4 of rail fence cipher decryption

A												S				
	T				K		F						O			
		T		C				R		M				U		H
			A						O						T	

Discussion

The rail fence cipher is easy to solve, even by manual means, and thus provides no communication security. Nevertheless, when used in combination with other ciphers, it can offer improved resistance.

Row Transposition Cipher

Compared to the rail fence cipher, the row transposition cipher [2,4] is more complex and difficult to break. A key is used to divide the plaintext into rows, the number of which is obtained by dividing the length of the plaintext by the length of the key, which equals the number of columns. In the following example, we use the key "VIGIL" and the plaintext "ATTACK FROM SOUTH."

Encryption

Since the length of the key is 5 and plaintext is 17 characters, four rows and five columns are required. The plaintext is written in the matrix, starting with the first square of the first row until the end of the row is reached. The second row is next used to write the plaintext in a similar way, and spaces are written as blanks. The alphabetical order of the key is used to number the columns of the matrix.

The ciphertext is generated column-wise as "TFS TH ARO COU AKMT" based on the numbering of the columns.

Decryption

To decipher the ciphered text, the number of rows is obtained by dividing the length of the ciphertext by the length of the key, whereas the number of columns equals the length of the key. The ciphertext is written column-wise in the matrix, starting with the column that corresponds to the first letter according to the alphabetical order of the key. Using that key, the plaintext can be retrieved.

Table 20. Row transposition cipher matrix

V	I	G	I	L
5	2	1	3	4
A	T	T	A	C
K		F	R	O
M		S	O	U
T	H			

Discussion

By using a key for ciphering and deciphering, the row transposition cipher boosts the security of communication. The method uses double transposition, first while placing the letters of plaintext in the grid or matrix and second while writing the ciphertext using the alphabetical ordering of the columns of the matrix.

Product Cipher

Although using transposition or substitution provides security for plaintext transmission, those methods are very easily compromised. A more prudent strategy is to make two transpositions or two substitutions instead of a single one. Even more strategically, substitution could be used, followed by transposition or vice versa, which can strengthen the method given the synergy accrued by using both. Current techniques demand such hybrid methods to secure the transmission of confidential data. In that sense, the product cipher can conceived as a bridge from traditional to modern ciphers.

DATA ENCRYPTION STANDARD (DES)

A symmetric key block cipher developed by IBM and published by the National Institute of Science and Technology, the DES is considered to be insecure for some applications given its small key size of only 56 bits. It requires a fixed length of string plaintext and different rounds to convert messages into cipher text.

DES Operation

The DES uses a Feistel cipher with a 16-round structure. Although it employs a 64-bit block size, it uses only 56 of those bits. Its major components are a rounding function, a key generator, initial permutation, and final permutation (Figure 3).

Rounding Function

At the heart of the DES, the rounding function applies a 48-bit key to the rightmost 32 bits to create a 32-bit output. Its chief components include an expansion P-box, an S-box, and a P-box.

Expansion P-Box

Since input to the expansion P-box is 32 bits and the key is 48 bits, the input needs to be expanded into 48 bits (Table 21).

After expansion, XOR is performed with the 48-bit key.

Figure 3. Components of the Data Encryption Standard

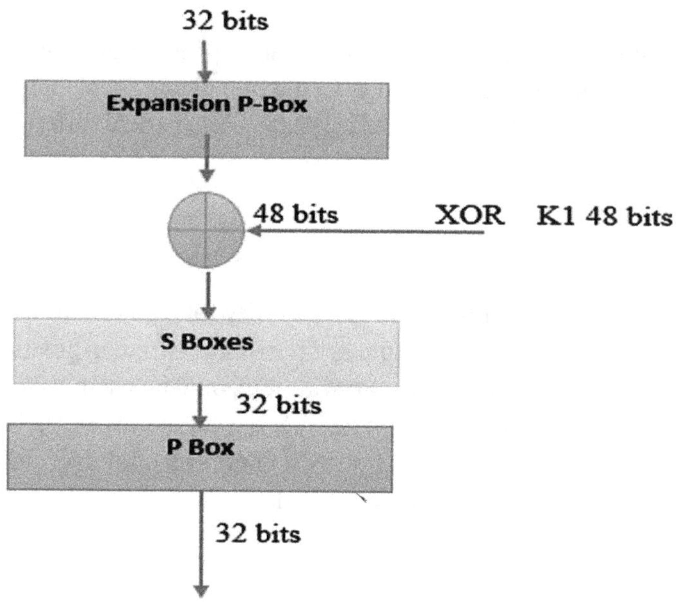

Figure 4. Rounding function of the Data Encryption Standard

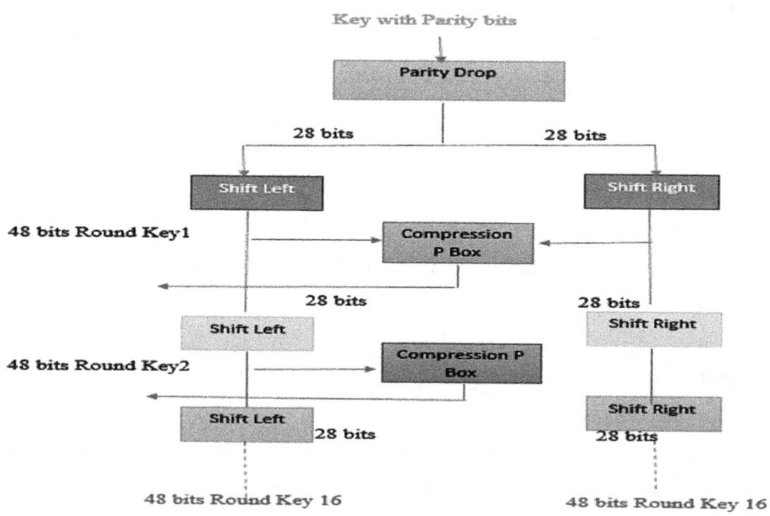

S-Boxes

S-boxes (i.e., substitution boxes) are used for mixing. The DES uses eight S-boxes, each with 6-bit input and 4-bit output. The output of all eight S-boxes is combined into 32-bit output.

Table 21. Expansion P-box

32	01	02	03	04	05
04	05	06	07	08	09
08	09	10	11	12	13
12	13	14	15	16	17
16	17	18	19	20	21
20	21	22	23	24	25
24	25	26	27	28	29
28	29	30	31	32	01

Key Generation

The key generator generates sixteen 48-bit keys from 56-bit keys. In each round, bit shifting is performed by either one or two bits. Whereas only one bit is shifted in Rounds 1, 2, 9, and 16, two are shifted in all other rounds.

Initial and Final Permutation

The initial and final permutations involve straight P-boxes that are inverses of each other. The initial permutation is thus:

```
IP
58    50   42    34    26   18     10    2
60    52   44    36    28   20     12    4
62    54   46    38    30   22     14    6
64    56   48    40    32   24     16    8
```

Figure 5. Key generation

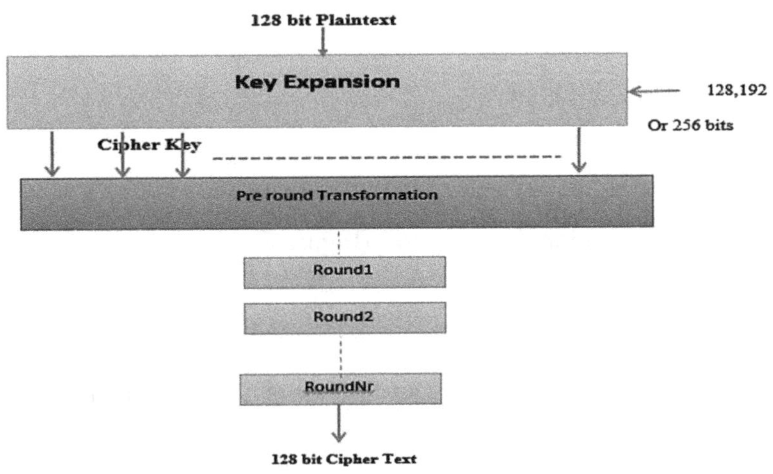

57	49	41	33	25	17	9	1
59	51	43	35	27	19	11	3
61	53	45	37	29	21	13	5
63	55	47	39	31	23	15	7

By some contrast, the final permutation is:

IP-1

40	8	48	16	56	24	64	32
39	7	47	15	55	23	63	31
38	6	46	14	54	22	62	30
37	5	45	13	53	21	61	29
36	4	44	12	52	20	60	28
35	3	43	11	51	19	59	27
34	2	42	10	50	18	58	26
33	1	41	9	49	17	57	25

ADVANCED ENCRYPTION STANDARD (AES)

Developed by the National Institute of Standard and Technology and accepted by the U.S. Government, the AES is a symmetric key algorithm in which the same key is used for encryption and decryption. It is six times faster than triple DES because DES uses a small key size that is vulnerable to attack. Using three types of keys (i.e., 128-,192-, and 256-bit keys) and data with the size of 128 bits, the AES is based on a substitution permutation network. It contains a sequence of substitution tasks (i.e., replacement of input with specific output) and permutation tasks (i.e., shuffling of bits). The algorithm performs operations on bytes instead of bits; it considers 128 bits to be 16 bytes arranged in a 4×4 matrix. The number of rounds in the AES varies depending on the number of bits in the key; it uses 10 rounds for 128-bit keys,12 rounds for 192-bit keys, and 14 rounds for 256-bit keys. Each round uses differently sized key.

AES Operation

The operation of AES appears in Figure 6.

Encryption Subprocesses

Each round consists of four encryption subprocesses (Figure 7).

Byte Substitution

During byte substitution,16 bits of input are replaced by using a fixed table using an S-box.

Figure 6. Operation of the Advanced Encryption Standard

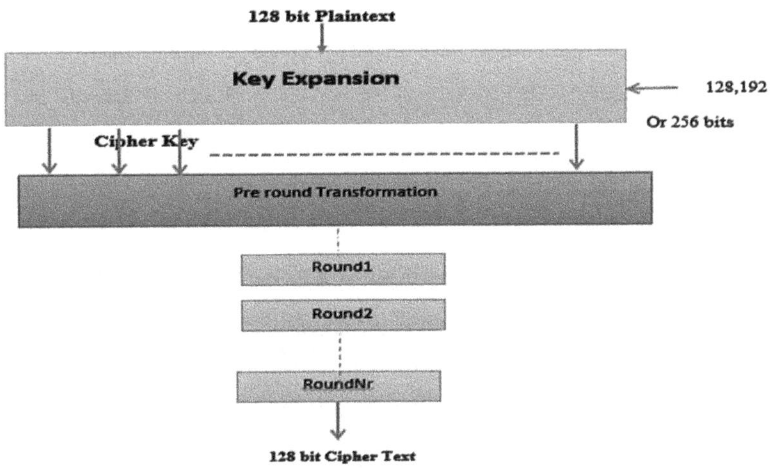

Figure 7. Encryption subprocesses performed each round

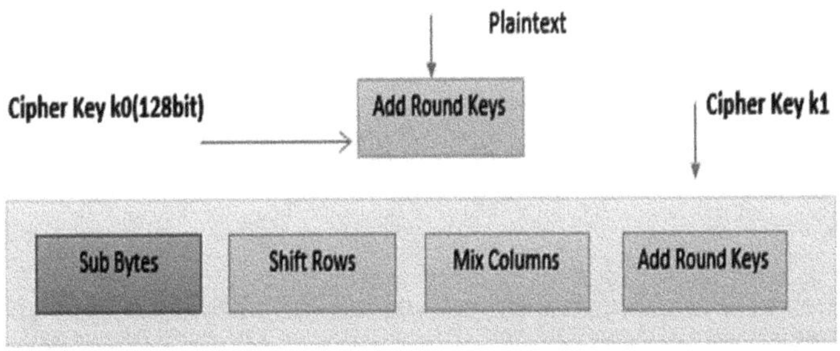

Shift Rows

Each of the four rows is shifted left in a four-step process. First, the first row is kept as is, after which the second row is shifted left by one bit. Third, the third row is shifted left by two bits, and last, the fourth row is shifted left by three positions.

Mix Columns

It applies a mathematical function to convert four bytes of each column into four new bytes for a new 16-byte matrix, although that final step is not performed in last round.

Add Round Keys

The 16 bytes of matrix are considered as 128 bits, and XOR is performed with 128 bits of round key. In the final round, the resulting 128 bits are considered to be ciphertext, whereas in the other rounds they are considered to a 16-byte matrix for further operations.

AES Decryption

AES decryption is identical to encryption except that the steps of encryption are performed in reverse order; round keys are added, columns are mixed, rows are shifted, and bytes are substituted.

ELLIPTIC CURVE CRYPTOGRAPHY (ECC)

ECC is a form of public key cryptography developed by Miller (1986) and Kobitz (1987) in 1990. Because the security of ECC lies in the discrete logarithm problem, it is a full exponential algorithm that can resist brute force attack, as well as timing attacks, side channel attacks, and cryptanalytic attacks. Table 22 compares ECC and the RSA algorithm .

Elliptic Curve Cryptography (ECC) Theory

ECC is used to generate keys using an elliptic curve (Koblitz, 1987), generate digital signatures, and convert plaintext into ciphertext (Stallings, 2011). The elliptic curve over field k is given by Equation 1.17:

$$Y2 = X3 + aX + b \qquad 1.17$$

a, b Є k

By changing the values of a and b, different curves can be obtained, following the constraint $4a3 + 27b2 \neq 0$.

Elliptic curves are defined over the prime field Fp and binary field F (2m) of two fields [36]. The prime field p is given by Equation 1.18:

$$Y2 \bmod p = X3 + aX + b \bmod p \qquad 1.18$$

The elements of the binary field are numbers from 0 to $p - 1$. The equation over the binary field is Equation 1.19:

$$Y2 + XY = X3 + aX + b \qquad 1.19$$

Table 22. Key sizes in bits with equivalent security levels

Time to Break in MIPS Years	ECC	DH, DSA, and RSA	RSA and ECC Key:Size Ratio
10^4	106	512	5:1
10^8	132	768	6:1
10^{11}	160	1,024	7:1
10^{20}	210	2,048	10:1
10^{78}	600	21,000	35:1

The elements of binary field *F* (2m) should be conceived as numbers with maximum *m* bits. In our research, we implemented ECC over binary curves. Two primary operations involved in ECC are point doubling and point tripling.

Converting Plaintext to Ciphertext Using ECC

To convert plaintext into ciphertext in ECC, four steps are executed:

1. Text is converted into ASCII;
2. Points are generated on an elliptic curve;
3. Keys of users are generated;
4. Text is encrypted.

For our work, we modified a model proposed by [Kong, H, et al, 2009] for ECC implementation over field *GF* (2m) for smartphone operating systems (OS). In detail, the ECC algorithm is as follows.

Generating Points on a Curve

```
Algorithm gen_points (a,b,p){
x = 0
while (x < p){
Put values of a, b, and x in the equation y2 + xy = x3 + ax + b
Find roots of the equation y2 + xy = x3 + ax + b
//All values of (x, y) give different points on the elliptic curve.}}
```

Generating Keys for Users

For two users A and B, the algorithm Generate_keys(){ is used to generate keys in three steps. First, User A selects any random number *KA* as a private key. Second, User selects the generator point, *G*, from the curve points so that *G* has small *x* and *y* coordinates. Third, to generate the public key kAp, multiply *KA* by *G* using the point_mult() algorithm. Those same three steps can be followed to generate keys (*kB*, kBp) for User B as well.

Point Multiplication in ECC

To multiply any number *k* by point *p*(*x*, *y*), repeatedly apply point doubling and addition operations.

```
Algorithm Point_mult(){
To double a point (2p), use the formulae:
S = [(3x 2 + a)/2yp] mod p
Then 2p has coordinates (XR, YR) given by
XR = (S2 - 2x) mod p
YR = [S (x - XR) - y] mod p
```

To determine $3P$, we use $p + 2P$ and treat $2P = Q$, in which p has coordinates (x, y) and $Q = 2P$ has coordinates (XQ, yQ).

```
s = [(yQ - y) / (XQ - x)] / mod p
P + Q = -R
XR = (s2 - x - XQ) mod p
YR = (S(x - XR) - y) mod p}
```

Encrypting Text

```
Algorithm Encrypt_Text(){
```

Convert text into its ASCII format.

Select any point *pm* from generated points of an elliptic curve.

Multiply the ASCII value with *pm* to get another point, *pm*1, using the Point_mult algorithm.

The ciphertext will be $\{kG, pm1 + k \times kAp\}\}$.

Decrypting Text

```
Algorithm Decrypt_text (){
```

Take iphertext will be $\{kG, pm1 + k \times kAp\}$

Calculate $pm = pm1 + k \times kAp - kbkG\}$

The above implementation of ECC is alternatively presented in Figures 8 and 9 with use case diagrams. First, the elliptic curve is selected by taking different values of a, b, and m. Second, points and keys are generated. Last, use keys and point texts are converted into ciphertext by using the point multiplication method.

In our implementation of ECC, we experimented by computing coordinates of points as necessary after the point generation of the elliptic curve instead of storing all points of the curve, which spared memory space required for ECC. We considered all integers in terms of polynomials, such that, for example, 7 (111) 2 was $x2 + x + 1$.

Figure 8. Use case diagram for senders

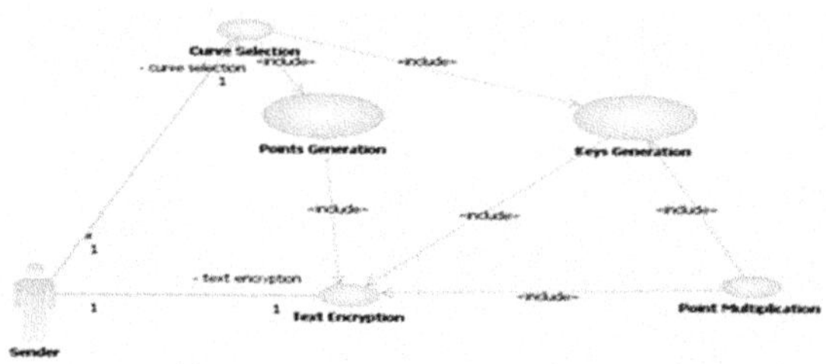

Figure 9. Use case diagram for receivers

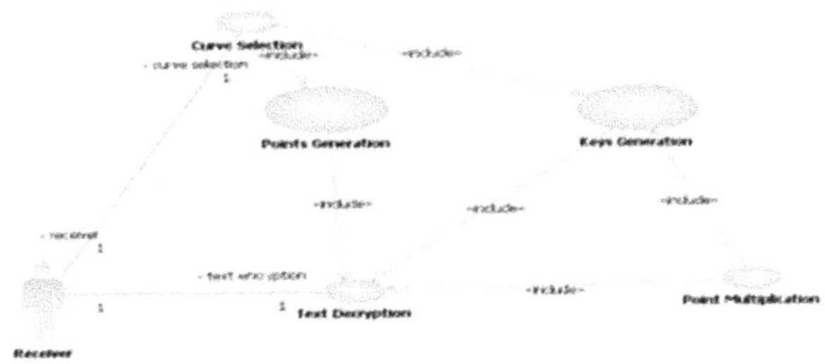

We converted the entire plaintext into ASCII and, in turn, into the point of a curve. The benefit of the method is that it avoids the repetition of ciphertext blocks, which prevents cryptanalytic attack. Furthermore, the size of the ciphertext is reduced, which means a smaller storage space requirement.

ECC has four advantages over the RSA algorithm, all of which were observable in our implementation: less storage space, less processing power required due to the small key size, less bandwidth consumption due to small key size and small ciphertext, and less time required for encryption.

Experimental Results of Elliptic Curve Cryptography with Android

We applied ECC to Android, a popular smartphone OS developed by Google for various mobile devices and notebook computers that supports Java-enabled applications and widely used for banking and financial purposes. In our experiments, we measured the execution time required for ECC as well as the RSA algorithm with varying text and key sizes on Android OS, for results presented in terms of Android SDK Platform version 2.1 with the first update.

Figure 10 illustrates the environment in which we developed our ECC. Regarding machine configurations, we used an Intel Core 2 Duo central processing unit with 1.18 GHz and 0.99 GB of RAM. To develop ECC in Java, we used Eclipse IDE, and both the Java program executed on Android Mobile and the JAD and JAR files for implementing ECC can be executed on Windows Mobile. Although Windows Mobile supports C#, JAD and JAR files can be executed using JBlend.

As shown in Figures 11 and 12, ECC was compared with the RSA algorithm with varying key and data sizes. Figure 11 shows that the RSA algorithm's execution time was less than ECC's when the key size was small. When we increased the key size, however, the RSA algorithm's execution time increased beyond that of ECC's; since larger key sizes mean greater security in the context of security algorithms, key size cannot be compromised. By contrast, Figure 12 presents a comparison of the RSA algorithm's

Figure 10. Environment for developing elliptic curve cryptography

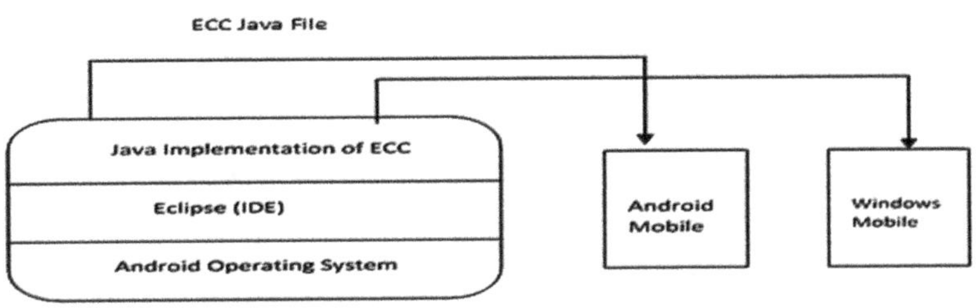

execution time with that of ECC with varying data sizes. No greater effect occurred on the RSA algorithm when we increased the data size.

Figure 13 illustrates the results of ECC when field size was varied. In short, the greater the field size, the longer the execution time and the greater the security.

Figure 14 illustrates the results of key generation time with ECC. In short, the greater the key size, the greater the necessary generation time and execution time.

HYPOTHESIS

We hypothesized that an advanced encryption algorithm designed with proper mathematical algorithms to afford a strong firewall and intrusion prevention system can help to prevent hackers from stealing private data.

Figure 11. Performance of elliptic curve cryptography and the Rivest–Shamir–Adleman algorithm with varying key sizes on Android 2.1

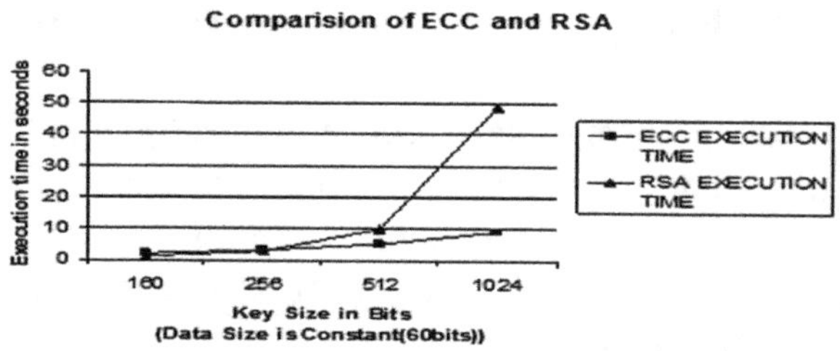

Figure 12. Performance comparison of elliptic curve cryptography with the Rivest–Shamir–Adleman algorithm with varying data sizes on Android 2.1

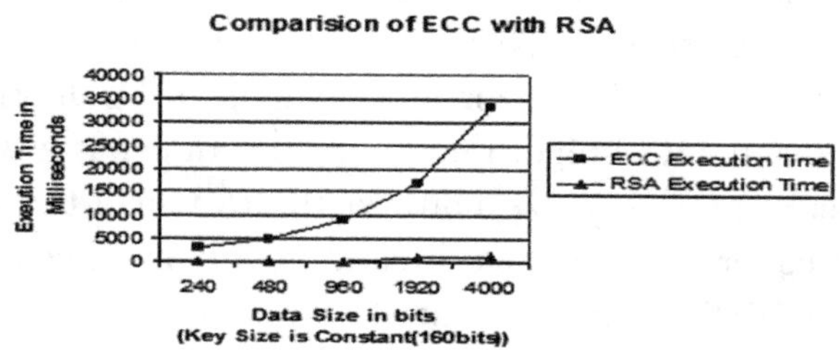

Figure 13. Performance of elliptic curve cryptography with various field sizes on Android 2.1

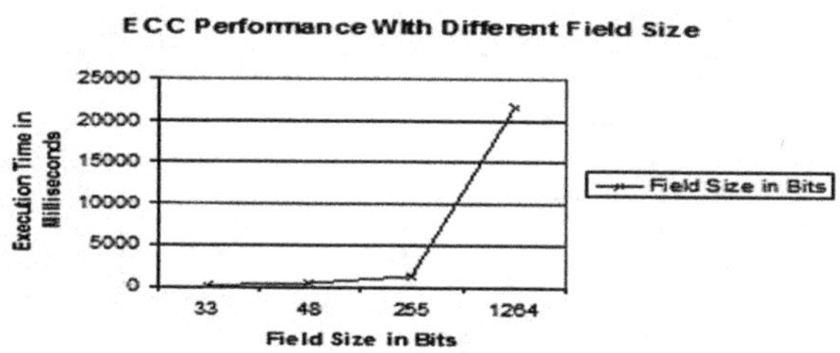

Figure 14. Key generation time with elliptic curve cryptography on Android 2.1

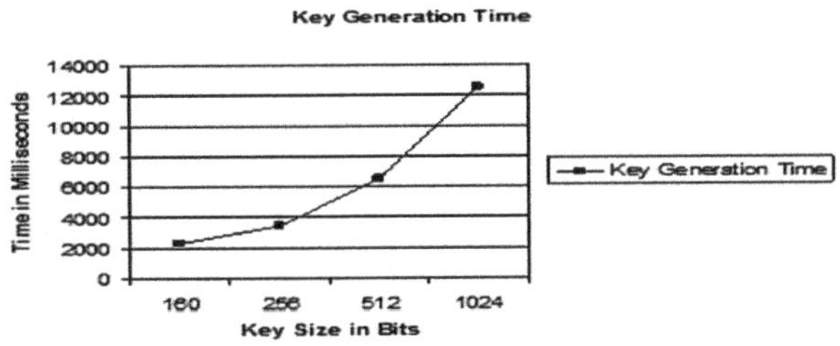

Four kinds of cyberattacks commonly threaten businesses. First, malware is a small piece of code developed with malicious intent that can be used to steal private data and even remove such data from a computer. Second, password attacks occur when third parties try to gain access to or learn passwords to steal private data. Third, man-in-the-middle attacks involve impersonating endpoints in an online information exchange so that third parties may steal data from end users. Fourth and last, Trojan horses allow third parties to access personal data (e.g., banking information, passwords, and IP addresses). To reduce the threat of such cyberattacks, various prevention techniques involving various encryption and mathematical algorithms can be used (Table 23).

Table 23. Three common cyberattacks and aspects of their prevention

Cyber-Attack	Purpose	Prevention Technique	Encryption Algorithm	Mathematical Algorithm	Possibility of Stealing Data (*Easy*, *Difficult*, or *Very Difficult*)
Malware	To steal data and destroy data on computers	Encrypting data stored on computers and storing encrypted copy data securely in another location	Advanced Encryption Standard (AES)	Bit shift operation and XOR operation	Using a 256-bit key with the AES would make solving ciphertext difficult
Password attack	To gain access to or learn passwords to steal private data	Using passwords with at least eight characters, including letters, numbers, and special characters, that are not users' birthdates, names, or partners' names and that are stored in databases in encrypted form and changed every 3 months	Diffie–Hellman key exchange algorithm	Integer arithmetic, modular arithmetic, modular multiplicative inverse, prime numbers	Changing passwords often and storing them in databases in encrypted form make accessing private data difficult, as does exchanging keys in encrypted form
Man-in-the-middle attack	To impersonate endpoints in online information exchange in order to intercept data from end users	Encrypting data by using cryptographic algorithms before transmitting data	Rivest–Shamir–Adleman algorithm	Integer arithmetic, modular arithmetic, modular multiplicative inverse, prime number	Encryption can make stealing data difficult

RECENT INTERNATIONAL CYBERATTACKS

In 2017, three international cyberattacks drew attention to the need for strong encryption and cryptographic technology. In May, the WannaCry ransomware attack targeted computers running Windows OS by encrypting important data and demanding payment in bitcoin for their decryption. The attack affected several large corporations, public utility companies, national health services, and various businesses around the world. In sum, the attackers netted nearly 52 bitcoins, or approximately US$130,000, with their ransomware.

In July, the Equifax data breach involved the theft of the personal data of millions of people worldwide. The breach is ranked among the worst incidents of hacking ever due to the sensitivity of information stolen (e.g., credit card numbers, birthdate information, and Social Security numbers), which can be used for identity theft or misrepresentation.

In October, NotPetya, a fraudulent Ukrainian tax software update, was discovered to have compromised millions of computers worldwide in few days and caused major financial damage. A variant of Petya, the ransomware did not merely encrypt files but also overwrote and encrypted the master boot record. To recover the files, the perpetrators demanded $300 in bitcoins.

We tested our hypothesis against the three cyberattacks (Table 1.24).

Table 24. Results of hypothesis testing with cyberattacks from 2017

Cyberattack	Prevention Techniques	Recommendations According to Hypothesis Testing
WannaCry	1. Use patch file provided by Windows to prevent the cyberattack 2. Deploy a strong firewall and intrusion detection system 3. Use a good network design to halt the spread the ransomware 4. Implement data categorization of rights to access data depending on designation to mitigate damage due to a breach or attack by protecting critical data against exposure	Deploying a strong firewall and intrusion detection system, as well as storing important data in databases in encrypted form using encryption algorithm, can reduce the WannaCry ransomware's capacity to steal data.
Equifax data breach	1. Continuously monitor personal user accounts 2. Change login IDs and passwords regularly 3. Create strong passwords with lower- and uppercase letters, numbers, and special characters 4. Store personal data in databases in encrypted form	Deploying a strong firewall and intrusion detection system, as well as storing important data in databases in encrypted form using encryption algorithm, can reduce the Equifax data breach malware's capacity to steal data.
NotPetya	1. Integrate real-time monitoring tools to issue alerts of cyberattacks and prevent whole-system attacks 2. Back up data regularly 3. Add protection to networks with end-point security tools and intelligent software that detects early infections caused to data by malicious programs and issues alerts when malicious code tries to control networks	Deploying a strong firewall and intrusion detection system, as well as storing important data in databases in encrypted form using encryption algorithm, can reduce the NotPetya ransomware's capacity to steal data.

CONCLUSION

In today's Information Age, encryption and cryptography play a vital role by converting private data into unreadable form via encryption algorithms to protect them from unauthorized access. Encryption techniques were used by ancient Greeks and Romans to send secret messages in unreadable forms; such techniques included the Caesar cipher, in which characters of plaintext are shifted to other characters a certain number of positions distant in the character sequence, and Polybius, in which characters placed in a square are represented by a smaller set of symbols corresponding to their numeric position in the square. By contrast, modern encryption algorithms are either symmetric or asymmetric. Whereas symmetric encryption algorithms use the same secret key for both encryption and decryption, asymmetric ones use public and private keys to encrypt and decrypt plaintext.

Cryptography is based on specific mathematical concepts, especially number theory and algebra. Using those concepts, encryption techniques can be categorized as either substitution ciphers or transposition ciphers. Whereas substitution ciphers involve replacing characters of plaintext with other characters or numbers to make the text unreadable, transposition ciphers involve shifting the position of individual characters or groups of characters according to a specific logic or function.

Developed by IBM, the DES is a symmetric key block cipher that converts the fixed length of strings of plaintext to ciphertext. By contrast, developed by the National Institute of Standard and Technology and accepted by the U.S. Government, the AES is a symmetric key algorithm in which the same key is used for encryption and decryption. It is six times faster than the triple DES, which uses a small key size that is thereby more vulnerable to attack. At the end, it is proved with experimental results that Elliptic curve cryptography performs best as compared with other algorithms like RSA.

FUTURE WORK

Neural networks can be used to construct simple encryption algorithms that computers can mobilize to make encryption algorithms by applying machine learning techniques without being taught specific cryptographic algorithms. Machine learning algorithms used by computers to encrypt data make data theft difficult, can be used to train computers to identify malware, man-in-the-middle attacks, viruses, and spyware, and can protect data from cyberattacks. Although we implemented ECC for Android OS only, in the future researchers can gauge the performance of ECC on different smartphone OSs such as Windows Mobile OS, Blackberry OS, and iOS. Our implementation of ECC is compatible on any machine, OS, or any type of network, and the ECC can be replaced with hyper ECC to obtain the same security with a minimal number of points.

REFERENCES

Allenby, R. B. J. T., & Redfern, E. J. (1989). *Introduction to Number Theory with Computing*. Lincoln, UK: Arnold.

Biham, E., & Shamir, A. (1993). *A Differential Cryptanalysis of the Data Encryption Standard*. New York: Springer. doi:10.1007/978-1-4613-9314-6

Boneh, D., & Shoup, V. (2015). *A Graduate Course on Applied Cryptography*. New York: Author.

Bornemann, F. (2002). PRIMES Is in P: A Breakthrough for "Everyman.". *Notices of the American Mathematical Society*, *10*(4), 545–552. Retrieved from http://www.ams.org/notices/200305/fea-bornemann.pdf

Burn, R. P. (1996). *A Pathway to Number Theory*. Cambridge, UK: Cambridge University Press. doi:10.1017/CBO9780511984051

Cameron, P. J. (2009). *A Course on Number Theory*. Retrieved on April 2, 2018, from: http://www.maths.qmul.ac.uk/~pjc/notes/nt.pdf

Cocks, C. A. (1973). *Note on Non-Secret Encryption* (CESG Report). Retrieved on June 2, 2017, from: https://www.gchq.gov.uk/sites/default/files/document_files/Cliff%20Cocks%20paper%2019731120.pdf

Cormen, T. H., Leiserson, C., & Rivest, R. L. (2009). *Introduction to Algorithms* (3rd ed.). Cambridge, UK: McGraw–Hill.

Cozzens, M., & Miller, S. J. (2013). *The Mathematics of Encryption: An Elementary Introduction*. Providence, RI: American Mathematical Society. doi:10.1090/mawrld/029

Davenport, H. (2008). *The Higher Arithmetic: An Introduction to the Theory of Numbers* (8th ed.). New York: Cambridge University Press. doi:10.1017/CBO9780511818097

Day, M. V. (2008). *An Introduction to Proofs and the Mathematical Vernacular*. Retrieved on November 3, 2017, from: https://www.math.vt.edu/people/day/ProofsBook/IPaMV.pdf

Dixit, U. (2018). Cryptography – Security in E-Banking. *IOSR Journal of Business and Management*, *2*, 33-37. Retrieved on August 19, 2018, from: http://www.iosrjournals.org/iosr-jbm/papers/Conf.17037-2017/Volume-2/6.%2033-37.pdf

Forouzan, B., & Mukhopadhyay, D. (2010). *Cryptography and Network Security*. New York: McGraw–Hill.

Franciscus, Z. (2016, September 21). *What Is Encryption, and How Does It Work?* Retrieved on October 31, 2017, from: https://www.howtogeek.com/howto/33949/htg-explains-what-is-encryption-and-how-does-it-work/

Hoffstein, J., Pipher, J., & Silverman, J. H. (2014). *An Introduction to Mathematical Cryptography*. New York: Springer.

Katz, J., & Lindell, Y. (2014). *Introduction to Modern Cryptography*. Milton Park, UK: Taylor & Francis.

Koblitz, N. (1987). Elliptic Curve Cryptosystems. *Mathematics of Computation*, *48*(177), 203–209. doi:10.1090/S0025-5718-1987-0866109-5

Kong, H., Zeng, Z., Yan, L., Yao, S., & Sheng, N. (2009). Combine Elliptic Curve Cryptography with Digital Watermark for OWL-Based Ontology Encryption. *ACM Digital Library*, *1*, 511–515. doi:10.1109/CIS.2009.99

LeVeque, W. J. (1990). *Elementary Theory of Numbers*. New York: Dover.

Menezes, A. J., Paul, C., & Scott, A. (1996). *Handbook Applied Cryptography*. Boca Raton, FL: CRC Press. doi:10.1201/9781439821916

Miller, V. S. (1986). Use of Elliptic Curves in Cryptography. *Advances in Cryptology*, *85*(218), 417–426.

NSS Labs. (2016, November 9). *NSS Labs Predicts 75% of Web Traffic Will Be Encrypted by 2019.* Retrieved on May 5, 2018, from: https://www.nsslabs.com/company/news/press-releases/nss-labs-predicts-75-of-web-traffic-will-be-encrypted-by-2019/

Paar, C., & Jan, P. (2010). *Understanding Cryptography: A Textbook for Students and Practitioners.* Bochum, Germany: Springer. doi:10.1007/978-3-642-04101-3

Perry, M. L. (2018). *Algorithms.* Retrieved on October 22, 2018, from: https://cryptofundamentals.com/algorithms

Raji, W. (2013). *An Introductory Course in Elementary Number Theory.* Washington, DC: Saylor Foundation.

Schneier, B. (1996). *Applied Cryptography Protocols, Algorithms and Source Code in C.* New York: Wiley.

Stallings, W. (2006). *Cryptography and Network Security Principles and Practice.* London, UK: Pearson Education.

Stallings, W. (2011). *Cryptography and Network Security Principles and Practice.* London, UK: Pearson Education.

Stein, W. (2017). *Elementary Number Theory: Primes, Congruence's, and Secrets.* New York: Springer.

Vigila, S., & Muneeswaran, K. (2010). Implementation of text based cryptosystem using Elliptic Curve Cryptography. *IEEE Xplore Digital Library*, *1*, 82–85. doi:10.1109/ICADVC.2009.5378025

Ward, M. (2013, October 25). *How the modern world depends on encryption.* Retrieved on May 5, 2018, from: http://www.bbc.com/news/technology-24667834

Compilation of References

Aagaard, A. (2019). *Sustainable Business Models: Innovation, Implementation, and Success*. New York: Palgrave Macmillan. doi:10.1007/978-3-319-93275-0

Abdul Talib, A. N., & Md Salleh, M. F. (1997). Firm size and export attitudes of Malaysian exporters. In The Proceedings of Second Asian Academy of Manage. Conference: Towards management excellence in the 21st century Asia (pp. 403-408).

Abdul-Latif, S. A., & Abdul-Talib, A. N. (2017). Consumer racism: A scale modification. *Asia Pacific Journal of Marketing and Logistics*, *29*(3), 616–633. doi:10.1108/APJML-02-2016-0026

Abidoye, R. B., & Chan, A. P. (2017). Artificial neural network in property valuation: Application framework and research trend. *Property Management*, *35*(5), 554–571. doi:10.1108/PM-06-2016-0027

Adler, P. S. (1995). Interdepartmental interdependence and coordination: The case of the design/manufacturing interface. *Organization Science*, *6*(2), 7–16. doi:10.1287/orsc.6.2.147

Afonso, P., Nunes, M., Paisana, A., & Braga, A. (2008). The influence of time-to-market and target costing in the new product development success. *International Journal of Production Economics*, *115*(2), 559–568. doi:10.1016/j.ijpe.2008.07.003

Aggarwal, S., & Gupta, C. (2014). *Algorithm for solving intuitionistic fuzzy transportation problem with generalized trapezoidal intuitionistic fuzzy number via new ranking method.* arXiv preprint arXiv:1401.3353

Aghion, P., Harmgart, H., & Weisshaar, N. (2010). *Fostering growth in CEE countries: a country-tailored approach to growth policy.* European Bank for Reconstruction and Development, Working Paper, No. 118/2010.

Aghion, P., Akcigit, U., Cagé, J., & Kerr, W. R. (2016). Taxation, corruption, and growth. *European Economic Review*, *86*, 24–51. doi:10.1016/j.euroecorev.2016.01.012

Aghion, P., & Howitt, P. (1990). *A model of growth through creative destruction (No. w3223)*. National Bureau of Economic Research. doi:10.3386/w3223

Agosin, M., & French-Davis, R. (1993). La liberalización comercial en América Latina. *Revista de la CEPAL*, *50*, 41–62. doi:10.18356/b4d728f4-en

Aguezzoul, A., & Pires, S. (2016). 3PL performance evaluation and selection: a MCDM method. *Supply Chain Forum: An International Journal*, *17*(2), 87-94.

Aguezzoul, A. (2014). Third-party logistics selection problem: A literature review on criteria and methods. *Omega*, *49*, 69–78. doi:10.1016/j.omega.2014.05.009

Ahmadi, H. B., Petrudi, S. H. H., & Wang, X. (2017). Integrating sustainability into supplier selection with analytical hierarchy process and improved grey relational analysis: A case of telecom industry. *International Journal of Advanced Manufacturing Technology*, *90*(9-12), 2413–2427. doi:10.100700170-016-9518-z

Ait Gougam, L., Tribeche, M., & Mekideche-Chafa, F. (2008). A systematic investigation of a neural network for function approximation. *Neural Networks*, *21*(9), 1311–1317. doi:10.1016/j.neunet.2008.06.015 PMID:18662852

Akaike, H. (1974). A new look at statistical model identification. *IEEE Transactions on Automatic Control AC*, *19*(6), 716–723. doi:10.1109/TAC.1974.1100705

Akbey, F. (2014). Ar-Ge, İnovasyon ve Kalkınma İlişkisine Yönelik Bir Literatür Taraması: Kuramsal Özet. *Maliye Dergisi*, *166*, 1–16.

Alanazi, T. A., Abdul-Talib, A. N., Ashari, H., & Islam, R. (2015). Relationship between teamwork quality and new product development cycle time in Telecom Industry. *Asian Journal of Scientific Research*, *8*(1), 41–53. doi:10.3923/ajsr.2015.41.53

Al-Hawari, M. A. (2011). Do online services contribute to establishing brand equity within the retail banking context? *Journal of Relationship Marketing*, *10*(3), 145–166. doi:10.1080/15332667.2011.596466

Allenby, R. B. J. T., & Redfern, E. J. (1989). *Introduction to Number Theory with Computing*. Lincoln, UK: Arnold.

Altin, O., & Kaya A. (2009). Türkiye'de Ar-Ge Harcamalari Ve Ekonomik Büyüme Arasindaki Nedensel İlişkinin Analizi. *Ege Akademik Bakış*, 250-260.

Amadi-Echendu, J., Lephauphau, O., Maswanganyi, M., & Mkhize, M. (2011). Case studies of technology roadmapping in mining. *Journal of Engineering and Technology Management*, *28*(1-2), 23–32. doi:10.1016/j.jengtecman.2010.12.002

Amram, M., & Kulatilaka, N. (1998). *Real Options. Managing Strategic Investment in an Uncertain World*. Boston: HBS.

Anaya, L., Dulaimi, M., & Abdallah, S. (2015). An investigation into the role of enterprise information systems in enabling business innovation. *Business Process Management Journal*, *21*(4), 771–790. doi:10.1108/BPMJ-11-2014-0108

Anderson, J. (1979). A Theoritical Foundation for the Gravity Equation. *The American Economic Review*, 106–116.

Anderson, J., & Wincoop, V. (2004). Trade Costs. *Journal of Economic Literature*, *42*(3), 691–751. doi:10.1257/0022051042177649

Anders, U., & Korn, O. (1999). Model selection in neural networks. *Neural Networks*, *12*(2), 309–323. doi:10.1016/S0893-6080(98)00117-8 PMID:12662706

Antony, R. J. P., Savarimuthu, S. J., & Pathinathan, T. (2014). Method for solving the transportation problem using triangular intuitionistic fuzzy number. *International Journal of Computing Algorithm*, *3*, 590–605.

Artificial Intelligence. (2018). *Oxford English Dictionary*. Retrieved on September 23, 2018, from: https://en.oxforddictionaries.com/definition/artificial_intelligence

Asako, K. (1979). Environmental pollution in an open economy. *The Economic Record*, *55*(151), 359–367. doi:10.1111/j.1475-4932.1979.tb02241.x

Asano, M. M., Ohya, Y., Tanaka, I., Basieva, I., & Khrennikov, A. (2011). Quantum-like model of brain's functioning: Decision making from decoherence. *Journal of Theoretical Biology*, *281*(1), 56–64. doi:10.1016/j.jtbi.2011.04.022 PMID:21554890

Asano, M., Basieva, I., Khrennikov, A., Ohya, M., Tanaka, Y., & Yamato, I. (2012). Quantum-like Model for the Adaptive Dynamics of the Genetic Regulation of E. Coli's Metabolism of Glucose/Lactose. *Systems and Synthetic Biology*, *6*(1-2), 1–7. doi:10.100711693-012-9091-1 PMID:23730359

Ashari, H., Yusoff, Y. M., Zamani, S. N. M., & Talib, A. N. A. (2018). A Study of the Effect of Market Orientation on Malaysian Automotive Industry Supply Chain Performance. *International Journal of Technology*, *9*(8), 1651–1657. doi:10.14716/ijtech.v9i8.2749

Atanassov, K. (1983). *Intuitionistic fuzzy sets, VII ITKR's Session, Sofia, June 1983*. Deposed in Central Sci. - Techn. Library of Bulg. Acad. of Sci., 1697/84. (in Bulgarian)

Atanassov, K. (1999). *Intuitionistic fuzzy sets: theory and applications*. New York: Springer.

Atuahene-Gima, K. (1995). An Exploratory Analysis of the Impact of Market Orientation on New Product Performance. *Journal of Product Innovation Management*, *12*(4), 275–293. doi:10.1016/0737-6782(95)00027-Q

Aumann, R. J. (1987). Correlated Equilibrium as an Expression of Bayesian Rationality. *Econometrica*, *55*(1), 1–18. doi:10.2307/1911154

Avis, D., & Devroye, L. (1985). An analysis of a decomposition heuristic for the assignment problem. *Operations Research Letters*, *3*(6), 279–283.

Awasthi, A., & Baležentis, T. (2017). A hybrid approach based on BOCR and fuzzy MULTIMOORA for logistics service provider selection. *International Journal of Logistics Systems and Management*, *27*(3), 261–282. doi:10.1504/IJLSM.2017.084466

Baker, D. P., Gustafson, S., Beaubien, J. M., Salas, E., & Barach, P. (2003). *Medical teamwork and patient safety: The evidence-based relation*. Washington, DC: American Institutes for Research.

Bales, R. F. (1958). Task roles and social roles in problem-solving groups. In E. E. Maccoby, T. M. Newcomb, & E. L. Hartley (Eds.), *Social psychology* (3rd ed.; pp. 437–447). New York: Holt, Rinehart and Winston.

Balinski, M. L. (1986). A competitive (dual) simplex method for the assignment problem. *Mathematical Programming*, *34*(2), 125–141.

Bali, Ö., Gümüş, S., & Kaya, I. (2015). A Multi-Period Decision Making Procedure Based on Intuitionistic Fuzzy Sets for Selection Among Third-Party Logistics Providers. *Journal of Multiple-Valued Logic & Soft Computing*, *24*(5).

Ban, A. (2008). Trapezoidal approximations of intuitionistic fuzzy numbers expressed by value, ambiguity, width and weighted expected value. *Notes on Intuitionistic Fuzzy Sets*, *14*(1), 38–47.

Banaeian, N., Mobli, H., Fahimnia, B., Nielsen, I. E., & Omid, M. (2018). Green supplier selection using fuzzy group decision making methods: A case study from the agri-food industry. *Computers & Operations Research*, *89*, 337–347. doi:10.1016/j.cor.2016.02.015

Barclay, M. J., & Smith, C. W. Jr. (2001). The capital structure puzzle: Another look at the evidence. In D. H. Chew (Ed.), *Corporate finance: Where theory meets practice* (3rd ed.; pp. 197–209). Singapore: McGraw-Hill.

Barczak, G., & Wilemon, D. (2003). Team member experiences in new product development: Views from the trenches. *R & D Management*, *33*(5), 463–479. doi:10.1111/1467-9310.00311

Bardhan, P. (1997). Corruption and Development: A Review of Issues. *Journal of Economic Literature*, *35*(3), 1320–1346.

Barney, J. B. (2001). Resource-based theories of competitive advantage: A ten-year retrospective on the resource-based view. *Journal of Management*, *27*(6), 643–650. doi:10.1177/014920630102700602

Barney, J., Wright, M., & Ketchen, D. J. Jr. (2001). The resource-based view of the firm: Ten years after 1991. *Journal of Management*, *27*(6), 625–641. doi:10.1177/014920630102700601

Barro R.J. (1990). Goverment Spending in a Simple Model of Endogenous Growth. *Journal of Political Economy*, *98*(5), 103-125.

Barr, R. S., Glover, F., & Klingman, D. (1977). The alternating basis algorithm for assignment problems. *Mathematical Programming*, *13*(1), 1–13.

Baškarada, S., & Koronios, A. (2017). Unicorn data scientist: The rarest of breeds. *Program*, *51*(1), 65–74. doi:10.1108/PROG-07-2016-0053

Basri, E. I., Abdul Razak, I. H., Ab-Samat, H., & Kamaruddin, S. (2017). Preventive maintenance (PM) planning: A review. *Journal of Quality in Maintenance Engineering*, *23*(2), 114–143. doi:10.1108/JQME-04-2016-0014

Bassanini, A., & Scarpetta, S. (2001). *Does human capital matter for growth in OECD countries? Evidence from pooled mean-group estimates*. Academic Press.

Battiti, R. (1992). First- and second-order methods for learning between steepest descent and Newton's method. *Neural Computation*, *4*(2), 141–166. doi:10.1162/neco.1992.4.2.141

Belasen, A. T., & Toma, R. (2016). *Confronting Corruption in Business. Trusted Leadership, Civic Engagement*. New York: Routledge.

Bellman, R. E., & Zadeh, L. A. (1970). Decision-making in a fuzzy environment. *Management Science*, *17*(B) 141-164.

Bens, D. A., Nagar, V., Skinner, D. J., & Wong, M. H. F. (2003). Employee stock options, EPS dilution, and stock repurchases. *Journal of Accounting and Economics*, *36*(1-3), 51–90. doi:10.1016/j.jacceco.2003.10.006

Bernheim, B., & Whinston, M. (1986). Common agency. *Econometrica*, *54*(4), 923–942. doi:10.2307/1912844

Berry, L. L., & Parasuraman, A. (1991). *Marketing services: Competing through quality*. New York: Free Press.

Bicchieri, C. (2006). *The Grammar of Society: The Nature and Dynamics of Social Norms*. New York: Cambridge University Press.

Biewen, M. (2009). Measuring state dependence in individual poverty histories when there is feedback to employment status and household composition. *Journal of Applied Econometrics*, *24*(7), 1095–1116. doi:10.1002/jae.1081

Biham, E., & Shamir, A. (1993). *A Differential Cryptanalysis of the Data Encryption Standard*. New York: Springer. doi:10.1007/978-1-4613-9314-6

Bingham, B. C., & Eisenhardt, K. M. (2011). Rational heuristics: The 'simple rules' that strategists learn from process experience. *Strategic Management Journal*, *32*(13), 1437–1464. doi:10.1002mj.965

Binici, Y., Senturk, S., & Ozdemir, O. (2015). Selection of the Best Third-Party Logistics (3PL) Company with Fuzzy Analytic Network Process (FANP). *The 4th International Fuzzy Systems Symposium (FUZZYSS'15)*.

Bishop, C. M. (1995). *Neural Networks for Pattern Recognition*. Oxford, UK: Oxford University Press.

Bisin, A., Eleonora, P., Thierry, V., & Yves, Z. (2008). Are Muslim Immigrants Different in Terms of Cultural Integration? *Journal of the European Economic Association*, *6*(2-3), 445–456. doi:10.1162/JEEA.2008.6.2-3.445

Bisin, B., & Topa, G. (2003). Empirical Mode of Cultural Transmission. *Journal of the European Economic Association*, *1*(2-3), 363–375. doi:10.1162/154247603322391008

Black, F., & Cox, J. C. (1976). Valuing corporate securities: Some effects of bond indenture provisions. *The Journal of Finance*, *31*(2), 351–367. doi:10.1111/j.1540-6261.1976.tb01891.x

Black, F., & Scholes, M. (1973). The pricing of options and corporate liabilities. *Journal of Political Economy*, *81*(3), 637–654. doi:10.1086/260062

Black, J. (2009). *A Dictionary of Economics*. Oxford, UK: Oxford University Press. doi:10.1093/acref/9780199237043.001.0001

Boneh, D., & Shoup, V. (2015). *A Graduate Course on Applied Cryptography*. New York: Author.

Bornemann, F. (2002). PRIMES Is in P: A Breakthrough for "Everyman.". *Notices of the American Mathematical Society*, *10*(4), 545–552. Retrieved from http://www.ams.org/notices/200305/fea-bornemann.pdf

Boston Consulting Group. (2006, April 24). The world's most innovative companies. *Business Week*. Retrieved from http://www.businessweek.com/magazine/toc/06_17/B39810617innovation.htm

Bostrom, N., & Yudkowsky, E. (2014). The ethics of artificial intelligence. The Cambridge Handbook of Artificial Intelligence, 316–334.

Bosworth, S. J., Singer, T., & Snower, D. J. (2016). Cooperation, motivation and social balance. *Journal of Economic Behavior & Organization*, *126*, 72–94. doi:10.1016/j.jebo.2015.12.005

Boute, R., Demeulemeester, E., & Herroelen, W. (2004). A real options approach to project management. *International Journal of Production Research*, *42*(9), 1715–1725. doi:10.1080/00207540310001639946

Box, G. E. P., & Jenkins, G. M. (1970). *Time Series Analysis: Forecasting and Control*. San Francisco, CA: Holden-Day.

Boyd, R., & Richerson, P. J. (1982). Cultural Transmission and the Evolution of Cooperative Behaviour. *Human Ecology*, *10*(3), 325–351. doi:10.1007/BF01531189

Boyd, R., & Richerson, P. J. (1985). *Culture and the Evolutionary Process*. Chicago: University of Chicago Press.

Boyd, R., & Richerson, P. J. (2009). Culture and the Evolution of Human Cooperation. *Philosophical Transactions of the Royal Society of London. Series B, Biological Sciences*, *364*(1533), 3281–3288. doi:10.1098/rstb.2009.0134 PMID:19805434

Boyd, R., Richerson, P. J., & Henrich, J. (2011). Rapid cultural adaptation can facilitate the evolution of large-scale cooperation. *Behaviorial Ecology of Social Biology*, *65*(3), 431–444. doi:10.100700265-010-1100-3 PMID:21423337

Brander, J. A., & Spencer, B. J. (1987). Foreign direct investment with unemployment and endogenous taxes and tariffs. *Journal of International Economics*, *22*(3-4), 257–279. doi:10.1016/S0022-1996(87)80023-5

Brav, A., Graham, J., Harvey, C., & Michaely, R. (2005). Payout policy in the 21st century. *Journal of Financial Economics*, *77*(3), 483–527. doi:10.1016/j.jfineco.2004.07.004

Breusch, T. S., & Pagan, A. R. (1980). The Lagrange Multiplier Test and Its Applications to Model Specification in Econometrics. *The Review of Economic Studies*, *47*(1), 239–253. doi:10.2307/2297111

Burillo, P., Bustince, H., & Mohedano, V. (1994). Some definitions of intuitionistic fuzzy number-first properties. *Proceedings of the First Workshop on Fuzzy Based Expert System*, 53-55.

Burn, R. P. (1996). *A Pathway to Number Theory*. Cambridge, UK: Cambridge University Press. doi:10.1017/CBO9780511984051

Büyüközkan, G., & Göçer, F. (2017). Application of a new combined intuitionistic fuzzy MCDM approach based on axiomatic design methodology for the supplier selection problem. *Applied Soft Computing*, *52*, 1222–1238. doi:10.1016/j.asoc.2016.08.051

Calle Fernandez, A., & Tamayo Bustamante, V. M. (2009). Decisiones de inversión a través de opciones. *Estudios Gerenciales*, *25*(111), 107–126. doi:10.1016/S0123-5923(09)70073-7

Cameron, P. J. (2009). *A Course on Number Theory*. Retrieved on April 2, 2018, from: http://www.maths.qmul.ac.uk/~pjc/notes/nt.pdf

Campos, J. E., Lien, D., & Pradhan, S. (1999). The Impact of Corruption on Investment: Predictability Matters. *World Development*, *27*(6), 1059–1067. doi:10.1016/S0305-750X(99)00040-6

Cannon-Bowers, J. A., Tannenbaum, S. I., Salas, E., & Volpe, C. E. (1995). Defining competencies and establishing team training requirements. In *Team effectiveness and decision making in organizations* (pp. 333–380). San Francisco: Jossey-Bass.

Carbonell, P., & Rodríguez-Escudero, A. I. (2009). Relationships among team's organizational context, innovation speed, and technological uncertainty: An empirical analysis. *Journal of Engineering and Technology Management*, *26*(1–2), 28–45. doi:10.1016/j.jengtecman.2009.03.005

CEFTA. (2017). *CEFTA Parties*. Retrieved April 25, 2018, from: http://cefta.int/cefta-parties-2/

Celo, S., & Chacar, A. (2015). International Coherence and MNE Performance. *Journal of International Business Studies*, *46*(5), 620–628. doi:10.1057/jibs.2015.4

Chai, J., Liu, J. N., & Ngai, E. W. (2013). Application of decision-making techniques in supplier selection: A systematic review of literature. *Expert Systems with Applications*, *40*(10), 3872–3885. doi:10.1016/j.eswa.2012.12.040

Chakraborty, D., Jana, D. K., & Roy, T. K. (2015). A new approach to solve multi-objective multi-choice multi-item Atanassov's intuitionistic fuzzy transportation problem using chance operator. *Journal of Intelligent & Fuzzy Systems*, *28*(2), 843–865.

Chang, D. Y. (1996). Applications of the extent analysis method on fuzzy AHP. *European Journal of Operational Research*, *95*(3), 649–655. doi:10.1016/0377-2217(95)00300-2

Chan, K. S., & Tong, H. (1986). On estimating thresholds in autoregressive models. *Journal of Time Series Analysis*, *7*(3), 178–190. doi:10.1111/j.1467-9892.1986.tb00501.x

Chan, Y. H., Dang, K. V., Yusup, S., Lim, M. T., Zain, A. M., & Uemura, Y. (2014). Studies on catalytic pyrolysis of empty fruit bunch (EFB) using Taguchi's L9 Orthogonal Array. *Journal of the Energy Institute*, *87*(3), 227–234. doi:10.1016/j.joei.2014.03.008

Chen, H. M. W., Chou, S. Y., Luu, Q. D., & Yu, T. H. K. (2016). A fuzzy MCDM approach for green supplier selection from the economic and environmental aspects. *Mathematical Problems in Engineering*.

Chen, J., Damanpour, F., & Reilly, R. R. (2010). Understanding antecedents of new product development speed: A meta-analysis. *Journal of Operations Management*, *28*(1), 17–33. doi:10.1016/j.jom.2009.07.001

Chester, D. L. (1990). Why two hidden layers are better than one? *Proceedings of the International Joint Conference on Neural Networks*, 1265–1268.

Chew, D. H. (2001). Introduction: Financial innovation in the 1980s and 1990s. In D. H. Chew (Ed.), *Corporate finance: Where theory meets practice* (3rd ed.; pp. xiii–xxii). Singapore: McGraw-Hill.

Chin, W. W. (1998). The partial least squares approach to structural equation modeling. In G. A. Marcoulides (Ed.), *Modern Methods for Business Research* (pp. 295–336). Mahwah, NJ: Laurence Erlbaum Associates.

Chin, W. W. (2010). How to write up and report PLS analyses. In V. E. Vinzi, W. W. Chin, J. Henseler, & H. Wang (Eds.), *Handbook of partial least squares: Concepts, methods and applications in marketing and related fields* (pp. 655–690). Berlin: Springer. doi:10.1007/978-3-540-32827-8_29

Chow, T., & Cao, D. B. (2008). A survey study of critical success factors in agile software projects. *Journal of Systems and Software*, *81*(6), 961–971. doi:10.1016/j.jss.2007.08.020

Cicek, A., Kıvak, T., & Samtaş, G. (2012). Application of taguchi method for surface roughness and roundness error in drilling of AISI 316 stainless. *Journal of Mechanical Engineering*, *58*(3), 165–174. doi:10.5545v-jme.2011.167

Cocks, C. A. (1973). *Note on Non-Secret Encryption* (CESG Report). Retrieved on June 2, 2017, from: https://www.gchq.gov.uk/sites/default/files/document_files/Cliff%20Cocks%20paper%2019731120.pdf

Colledani, M., Tolio, T., Fischer, A., Iung, B., Lanza, G., Schmitt, R., & Váncza, J. (2014). Design and management of manufacturing systems for production quality. *CIRP Annals-Manufacturing Technology*, *63*(2), 773–796. doi:10.1016/j.cirp.2014.05.002

Collins, C. (2018). Retrieved on April 2018, 23, from: https://www.collinsdictionary.com/dictionary/english/free-trade

Colquitt, J. A., & Zapata-Phelan, C. P. (2007). Trends in Theory Building and Theory Testing: A Five-Decade Study of the Academy of Management Journal. *Academy of Management Journal*, *50*(6), 1281–1303. doi:10.5465/amj.2007.28165855

Comment, R., & Jarrell, G. A. (1991). The relative signalling power of Dutch-Auctionand fixed-price self-tender offers and open-market share repurchases. *The Journal of Finance*, *46*(4), 1243–1271. doi:10.1111/j.1540-6261.1991.tb04617.x

Copeland, T., Koller, T., & Murrin, J. (2000). *Valuation: Measuring and Managing the Value of Companies* (3rd ed.). New York: Wiley.

Cordes, C., Richerson, P. J., McElreath, R. S., & Strimling, P. (2008). A Naturalistic Approach to the Theory of the Firm: The Role of Cooperation and Cultural Evolution. *Journal of Economic Behavior & Organization*, *68*(1), 125–139. doi:10.1016/j.jebo.2008.03.008

Cormen, T. H., Leiserson, C., & Rivest, R. L. (2009). *Introduction to Algorithms* (3rd ed.). Cambridge, UK: McGraw–Hill.

Correa-Cabrera, G. (2013). Violence and FDI in Mexico. The Economic Impact of the "War against Drugs". *Voices of Mexico*, *96*(1), 17–22.

Cortez Yactayo, W. W., & Espinosa Ramirez, R. S. (2011). Reentendiendo la inversión extranjera directa vertical: Una aproximación a la evidencia latinoamericana actual. *Carta Economica Regional*, *107*, 129–144.

Cottrell, M., Girard, B., Girard, Y., Mangeas, M., & Muller, C. (1995). Neural modeling for time series: A statistical stepwise method for weight elimination. *IEEE Transactions on Neural Networks*, *6*(6), 1355–1364. doi:10.1109/72.471372 PMID:18263428

Cozzens, M., & Miller, S. J. (2013). *The Mathematics of Encryption: An Elementary Introduction*. Providence, RI: American Mathematical Society. doi:10.1090/mawrld/029

Crawford, V. P. (1995). Adaptive Dynamics in Coordination Games. *Econometrica*, *63*(1), 103–143. doi:10.2307/2951699

Crone, S., & Kourentzes, N. (2009). Input-variable Specification for Neural Networks - An Analysis of Forecasting low and high Time Series Frequency. *Proceedings of the International Joint Conference on Neural Networks, IJCNN'09*. 10.1109/IJCNN.2009.5179046

Cruz Rambaud, S., & Sánchez Pérez, A. M. (2015). Valoración de la opción de diferimiento en un proyecto de inversión. *XXIX Congreso Internacional de Economía Aplicada.*

Cuervo-Cazurra, A. (2016). Corruption in international business. *Journal of World Business, 51*(1), 35–49. doi:10.1016/j.jwb.2015.08.015

Cunha, F., & Heckman, J. J. (2009). The economics and psychology of inequality and human development. *Journal of the European Economic Association, 7*(2-3), 320–364. doi:10.1162/JEEA.2009.7.2-3.320 PMID:20209045

Cybenko, G. (1989). Approximation by superpositions of a sigmoidal function. *Mathematics of Control, Signals, and Systems, 2*(4), 202–314. doi:10.1007/BF02551274

D'Agostino, G., Dunne, J. P., & Pieroni, L. (2016). Corruption and growth in Africa. *European Journal of Political Economy, 43*, 71–88. doi:10.1016/j.ejpoleco.2016.03.002

Dadkhah, K. (2011). *Foundations of Mathematical and Computational Economics* (2nd ed.). Berlin: Springer-Verlag. doi:10.1007/978-3-642-13748-8

Dam, M. M., & Yıldız, B. (2016). BRICS-TM Ülkelerinde AR-GE ve İnovasyonun Ekonomik Büyüme Üzerine Etkisi: Ekonometrik Bir Analiz. *Akdeniz Üniversitesi İktisadi ve İdari Bilimler Fakültesi Dergisi,* (33), 220-236.

Damodaran, A. (2002). *Investment valuation: Tools and techniques for determining the value of any asset* (2nd ed.). New York: John Wiley and Sons.

Dann, L. Y. (1992). Common stock repurchases: What do they really accomplish? In J. M. Stern & D. H. Chew (Eds.), *The revolution in corporate finance*. Cambridge, MA: Basil Blackwell.

Dar, A. A., & Anuradha, N. (2017b). One Period Binomial Model: The risk-neutral probability measure assumption and the state price deflator approach. *International Journal of Mathematics Trends and Technology, 43*(4).

Dar, A. A., & Anuradha, N. (2017a). Option Pricing Using Monte Carlo Simulation. British Journal of Economics. *Finance and Management Sciences, 13*(2), 52–81.

Dar, A. A., & Anuradha, N. (2017c). Probability default in black scholes formula: A qualitative study. *Journal of Business and Economic Development, 2*(2), 99–106. doi:10.11648/j.jbed.20170202.15

Dar, A. A., & Anuradha, N. (2018). Use of orthogonal arrays and design of experiment via Taguchi L9 method in probability of default. *Accounting, 4*(3). doi:10.5267/j.ac.2017.11.001

Darwin, C. (1859). *On the Origin of the Species by Means of Natural Selection.* London: J. Murray.

Das, S., & Guha, D. (2013). Ranking of intuitionistic fuzzy number by centroid point. *Journal of Industrial and Intelligent Information, 1*(2), 107–110.

Davenport, H. (2008). *The Higher Arithmetic: An Introduction to the Theory of Numbers* (8th ed.). New York: Cambridge University Press. doi:10.1017/CBO9780511818097

Day, M. V. (2008). *An Introduction to Proofs and the Mathematical Vernacular.* Retrieved on November 3, 2017, from: https://www.math.vt.edu/people/day/ProofsBook/IPaMV.pdf

Dayan, M., & Benedetto, C. A. D. (2009). Antecedents and consequences of teamwork quality in new product development projects. *European Journal of Innovation Management, 12*(1), 129–155. doi:10.1108/14601060910928201

Dayan, M., & di Benedetto, C. A. (2010). The impact of structural and contextual factors on trust formation in product development teams. *Industrial Marketing Management, 39*(4), 691–703. doi:10.1016/j.indmarman.2010.01.001

De Gooijer, I. G., & Kumar, K. (1992). Some Recent Developments in Non- Linear Modelling, Testing, and Forecasting. *International Journal of Forecasting*, *8*(2), 135–156. doi:10.1016/0169-2070(92)90115-P

Deal, T. E., & Kennedy, A. A. (2000). *Corporate Cultures*. Boston: Addison- Wesley.

Deardorff, A. (1998). *Determinants of Bilateral Trade: Does Gravity Work in a Neoclassical World?* Chicago: University of Chicago Press.

Delarue, A., Hootegem, G. V., Proctor, S., & Burridge, M. (2008). Team working and organizational performance: A review of survey-based research. *International Journal of Management Reviews*, *10*(2), 127–148. doi:10.1111/j.1468-2370.2007.00227.x

Della Porta, D. (2017). *Corrupt Exchanges. Actors, Resources, and Mechanisms of Political Corruption*. New York: Routledge. doi:10.4324/9781315080284

Della Porta, D., & Vannucci, A. (2016). *The Hidden Order of Corruption. An Institutional Approach*. London: Routledge. doi:10.4324/9781315557267

Denison, D. R., & Mishra, A. K. (1995). Toward a theory of Organizational Culture and effectiveness. *Organization Science*, *6*(2), 204–223. doi:10.1287/orsc.6.2.204

Dennis, J. E., Schnabel, J., & Robert, B. (1983). *Numerical Methods for Unconstrained Optimization and Nonlinear Equations*. New York: Prentice-Hall.

De, P. K., & Yadav, B. (2012). A general approach for solving assignment problems involving with fuzzy cost coefficients. *Modern Applied Science*, *6*(3), 2.

Deshpande, R., & Farley, J. U. (1998). Measuring market orientation: Generalization and synthesis. *Journal of Market Focused Management*, *2*, 231–232.

Deshpande, R., & Webster, F. E. Jr. (1989). Organizational culture and marketing: Defining the research agenda. *Journal of Marketing*, *53*(1), 3–15. doi:10.1177/002224298905300102

DiMaggio, P. (1997). Culture and cognition. *Annual Review of Sociology*, *23*(1), 263–287. doi:10.1146/annurev.soc.23.1.263

DiMaggio, P., & Markus, H. (2010). Culture and social psychology: Converging perspectives. *Social Psychology Quarterly*, *73*(4), 347–452. doi:10.1177/0190272510389010

Dinagar, D. S., & Thiripurasundari, K. (2014). A new method for finding the cost of fuzzy assignment problem using genetic algorithm of artificial intelligence. *International Electronic Journal of Pure and Applied Mathematics*, *8*(4).

Dinagar, D. S., & Thiripurasundari, K. (2014). A navel method for solving fuzzy transportation problem involving intuitionistic trapezoidal fuzzy numbers. *International Journal of Current Research*, *6*(6), 7038–7041.

Dinopoulos, E., & Şener, F. (2003). New Directions in Schumpeterian Growth Theory. *Erişim Tarihi*.

Dixit, U. (2018). Cryptography – Security in E-Banking. *IOSR Journal of Business and Management*, *2*, 33-37. Retrieved on August 19, 2018, from: http://www.iosrjournals.org/iosr-jbm/papers/Conf.17037-2017/Volume-2/6.%2033-37.pdf

Dixit, A. K. (1996). Special-interest Lobbying and endogenous Commodity taxation. *Eastern Economic Journal*, *22*(4), 375–388.

Dixit, A. K., Grossman, G. M., & Helpman, E. (1997). Common agency and coordination: General theory and application to policy making. *Journal of Political Economy*, *105*(4), 752–769. doi:10.1086/262092

Dumitrescu, E., & Hurlin, C. (2012). Testing for Granger Non-causality in Heterogeneous Panels. *Economic Modelling, 29*(4), 1450–1460. doi:10.1016/j.econmod.2012.02.014

Dweiri, F., Kumar, S., Khan, S. A., & Jain, V. (2016). Designing an integrated AHP based decision support system for supplier selection in automotive industry. *Expert Systems with Applications, 62*, 273–283. doi:10.1016/j.eswa.2016.06.030

Dzhumashev, R. (2014). Corruption and growth: The role of governance, public spending, and economic development. *Economic Modelling, 37*, 202–215. doi:10.1016/j.econmod.2013.11.007

Ebrahimnejad, A., Nasseri, S. H., & Mansourzadeh, S. M. (2011). Bounded Primal Simplex Algorithm for Bounded Linear Programming with Fuzzy Cost Coefficients. *International Journal of Operations Research and Information Systems, 2*(1), 96–120. doi:10.4018/joris.2011010105

EC. (2006, April 3). *European Comission: Trade.* Retrieved on April 23, 2018, from: http://trade.ec.europa.eu/doclib/docs/2006/september/tradoc_129992.pdf

Ecer, F. (2018). Third-party logistics (3PLs) provider selection via Fuzzy AHP and EDAS integrated model. *Technological and Economic Development of Economy, 24*(2), 615–634. doi:10.3846/20294913.2016.1213207

ECLAC. (2018). *Foreign Direct Investment in Latin America and the Caribbean 2018.* Retrieved on August 24, 2018, from: https://repositorio.cepal.org/bitstream/handle/11362/43690/7/S1800683_en.pdf

Edelman, G. M. (1989). *The remembered present: A biological theory of consciousness.* New York: Basic Books.

Edelman, G. M. (2006). *Second Nature: Brain Science and Human Knowledge.* New Haven, CT: Yale University Press.

Edge, K. (2010). *Free Trade and Protection: Advantages and Disadvantages of Free Trade.* Cardiff, UK: Cardiff High School.

Eid, A. (2012). Higher education R&D and productivity growth: An empirical study on high-income OECD countries. *Education Economics, 20*(1), 53–68. doi:10.1080/09645291003726855

Eisenhardt, K. M., & Martin, J. A. (2000). Dynamic capabilities: What are they? *Strategic Management Journal, 21*(10-11), 1105–1121. doi:10.1002/1097-0266(200010/11)21:10/11<1105::AID-SMJ133>3.0.CO;2-E

Emirmahmutoğlu, F., & Köse, N. (2011). Testing for Granger Causality in Heterogeneous Mixed Panels. *Economic Modelling, 28*(3), 870–876. doi:10.1016/j.econmod.2010.10.018

Erkiletlioğlu, H. (2013). *Dünyada ve Türkiye'de Ar-Ge Faaliyetleri. Türkiye İş Bankası İktisadi Araştırmalar Bölümü.* Retrieved on August 19, 2018, from: https://ekonomi. isbank. com.tr/UserFiles/pdf/ar_07_2013.pdf

Etgar, M. (1979). Sources and types of intrachannel conflict. *Journal of Retailing, 55*, 61–78.

Fahmi, A., Kahraman, C., & Bilen, Ü. (2016). ELECTRE I method using hesitant linguistic term sets: An application to supplier selection. *International Journal of Computational Intelligence Systems, 9*(1), 153–167. doi:10.1080/18756891.2016.1146532

Falhman, S. (1989). Faster-learning variations of back-propagation: An empirical study. *Proceedings of the 1988 Connectionist Models Summer School*, 38–51.

Fama, E. F. (1978). The effects of a firm's investment and financing decisions on the welfare of its security holders. *The American Economic Review, 68*, 272–284.

Fama, E. F., & French, K. R. (2017). International tests of a five-factor asset pricing model. *Journal of Financial Economics, 123*(3), 441–463. doi:10.1016/j.jfineco.2016.11.004

Fang, L., & Li, T. (1990). A globally optimal annealing learning algorithm for multilayer perceptrons with applications. In *AI'90* (pp. 201–206). Perth, Australia: Austrtalian Joint Conf. Artificial Intell.

Faraj, S., & Sproull, L. (2000). Coordinating expertise in software development teams. *Management Science*, *46*(12), 1554–1568. doi:10.1287/mnsc.46.12.1554.12072

Faraway, J., & Chatfield, C. (1998). Time series forecasting with neural networks: A comparative study using the airline data. *Journal of the Royal Statistical Society. Series C, Applied Statistics*, *47*(2), 231–250. doi:10.1111/1467-9876.00109

Farrag, N. A., & Ezzat, A. M. (2016). The Impact of Corruption on Economic Growth: A Comparative Analysis between Europe and MENA Countries. In M. M. Erdoğdu & B. Christiansen (Eds.), *Handbook of Research on Comparative Economic Development Perspectives on Europe and the MENA Region* (pp. 74–97). Hershey, PA: IGI Global. doi:10.4018/978-1-4666-9548-1.ch005

Findlay, R., & Wellisz, S. (1982). Endogenous tariffs, the political economy of trade restrictions, and welfare. In J. N. Bhagwati (Ed.), *Import competition and response* (pp. 223–234). Chicago: University of Chicago Press.

Firat, A. K., Woon, W. L., & Madnick, S. (2008). *Technological forecasting–A review. Composite Information Systems Laboratory (CISL)*. Massachusetts Institute of Technology.

Fogel, D. B., Fogel, L. J., & Porto, V. W. (1990). Evolving Neural Networks. *Biological Cybernetics*, *63*(6), 487–493. doi:10.1007/BF00199581 PMID:2357472

Fornell, C., & Bookstein, F. L. (1982). Two structural equation models: LISREL and PLS applied to consumer exit-voice theory. *JMR, Journal of Marketing Research*, *19*(4), 440–452. doi:10.1177/002224378201900406

Fornell, C., & Larcker, D. (1981a). Structural equation models with unobservable variables and measurement error: Algebra and statistics. *JMR, Journal of Marketing Research*, *18*(3), 382–388. doi:10.1177/002224378101800313

Fornell, C., & Larcker, D. F. (1981b). Evaluating Structural Equation Models with unobservable variables and measurement error. *JMR, Journal of Marketing Research*, *18*(1), 39–50. doi:10.1177/002224378101800104

Forouzan, B., & Mukhopadhyay, D. (2010). *Cryptography and Network Security*. New York: McGraw–Hill.

Franciscus, Z. (2016, September 21). *What Is Encryption, and How Does It Work?* Retrieved on October 31, 2017, from: https://www.howtogeek.com/howto/33949/htg-explains-what-is-encryption-and-how-does-it-work/

Franses, P. H., & Draisma, G. (1997). Recognizing changing seasonal patterns using artificial neural networks. *Journal of Econometrics*, *81*(1), 273–280. doi:10.1016/S0304-4076(97)00047-X

Franses, P., & Van Dijk, D. (2000). *Non-linear time series models in empirical finance*. Cambridge University Press. doi:10.1017/CBO9780511754067

Freeman, C., & Soete, L. (2003). *Yenilik İktisadı*. Ankara: Tübitak Yayını.

Frishammar, J., & Åke Hörte, S. (2007). The Role of Market Orientation and Entrepreneurial Orientation for New Product Development Performance in Manufacturing Firms. *Technology Analysis and Strategic Management*, *19*(6), 765–788. doi:10.1080/09537320701711231

Gadanidis, G. (2017). Artificial intelligence, computational thinking, and mathematics education. *The International Journal of Information and Learning Technology*, *34*(2), 133–139. doi:10.1108/IJILT-09-2016-0048

Gani, A. N., & Abbas, S. (2012). Intuitionistic fuzzy transportation problem. *Proceedings of the Heber International Conference on Applications of Mathematics and Statistics (HICAMS)*, 528-535.

Gardner, E. S. Jr, & McKenzie, E. (1989). Seasonal Exponential Smoothing with Damped Trends. *Management Science*, *35*(3), 372–376. doi:10.1287/mnsc.35.3.372

Garriga, A. N., & Phillips, B. J. (2015). *Criminal Violence and the Subnational Distribution of Foreign Direct Investment* (Documentos de Trabajo CIDE No. 279). Retrieved from The CIDE website: http://repositorio-digital.cide.edu/handle/11651/1377

Gerbert, P., Hecker, M., Steinhäuser, S., & Ruwolt, P. (2017). *Putting Artificial Intelligence to Work.* The Boston Consulting Group.

Ghobadian, A., Stainer, A., & Kiss, T. (1993). A computerized vendor rating system. In *Proceedings of the first international symposium on logistics*. The University of Nottingham.

Ghorabaee, M. K., Amiri, M., Kazimieras Zavadskas, E., & Antuchevičienė, J. (2017). Assessment of third-party logistics providers using a CRITIC–WASPAS approach with interval type-2 fuzzy sets. *Transport*, *32*(1), 66–78. doi:10.3846/16484142.2017.1282381

Ghorabaee, M. K., Amiri, M., Zavadskas, E. K., & Antucheviciene, J. (2017). Supplier evaluation and selection in fuzzy environments: A review of MADM approaches. *Economic research-. Ekonomska Istrazivanja*, *30*(1), 1073–1118. doi:10.1080/1331677X.2017.1314828

Ghorabaee, M. K., Zavadskas, E. K., Amiri, M., & Turskis, Z. (2016). Extended EDAS method for fuzzy multi-criteria decision-making: An application to supplier selection. *International Journal of Computers, Communications & Control*, *11*(3), 358–371. doi:10.15837/ijccc.2016.3.2557

Gintis, H. (2014). Inclusive Fitness and the Sociobiology of the Genome. *Biology & Philosophy*, *29*(4), 477–515. doi:10.100710539-013-9404-0

Gladstein, D. L. (1984). Groups in context: A model of task group effectiveness. *Administrative Science Quarterly*, *29*(4), 499–517. doi:10.2307/2392936

Gnizy, I., Cadogan, J. W., Oliveira, J. S., & Nizam, A. (2017). The empirical link between export dispersion and export performance: A contingency-based approach. *International Business Review*, *26*(2), 239–249. doi:10.1016/j.ibusrev.2016.07.002

Göçer, İ., & Gerede, A. G. C. (2016). *Dış Ticaretin Enflasyon Üzerindeki Etkileri: Türkiye İçin Zaman İçinde Değişen Birim Kök ve Nedensellik Testler.i* Eskişehir Osmangazi Üniversitesi IIBF Dergisi.

Gotmare, A. D., & Khot, P. G. (2016). Solution of a fuzzy assignment problem by using Branch-and-Bound technique with application of linguistic variable. *International Journal of Computers and Technology*, *15*(4), 6649–6653.

Govindan, K., & Chaudhuri, A. (2016). Interrelationships of risks faced by third party logistics service providers: A DEMATEL based approach. *Transportation Research Part E, Logistics and Transportation Review*, *90*, 177–195. doi:10.1016/j.tre.2015.11.010

Govindan, K., Khodaverdi, R., & Vafadarnikjoo, A. (2016). A grey DEMATEL approach to develop third-party logistics provider selection criteria. *Industrial Management & Data Systems*, *116*(4), 690–722. doi:10.1108/IMDS-05-2015-0180

Granger, C. (1993). Strategies for modelling nonlinear time-series relationships. *The Economic Record*, *69*(206), 233–238. doi:10.1111/j.1475-4932.1993.tb02103.x

Granger, C., & Teräsvirta, T. (1993). *Modelling Nonlinear Economic Relationships*. Oxford, UK: Oxford University Press.

Griffin, A. (1997). The effect of project and process characteristics on product development cycle time. *JMR, Journal of Marketing Research, 34*(1), 24–35. doi:10.1177/002224379703400103

Grossman, G. M., & Elhanan Helpman, E. (1989). *Quality Ladders in the Growth Theory.* NBER Working Paper No. 3099.

Grossman, G. M., & Helpman, E. (1994). Protection for Sale. *The American Economic Review, 84*(4), 833–854.

Grullon, G., & Ikenberry, D. L. (2000). What do we know about stock repurchases? *Journal of Applied Corporate Finance, 13*(1), 31–51. doi:10.1111/j.1745-6622.2000.tb00040.x

Grzegorzewski, P. (2003). Distance and orderings in a family of intuitionistic fuzzy numbers. *Proceedings of the Third Conference of the European Society for Fuzzy Logic and Technology*, 223-227.

Guasch, J. L., Laffont, J.-J., & Straub, S. (2003). *Renegotiation of concession contracts in Latin America.* World Bank Policy Research Working Paper, 3011.

Guasch, J. L., Laffont, J.-J., & Straub, S. (2007). Concessions of infrastructure in Latin America: Government-led renegotiation. *Journal of Applied Econometrics, 22*(7), 1267–1294. doi:10.1002/jae.987

Guha, D., & Chakraborty, D. (2010). A theoretical development of distance measure for intuitionistic fuzzy numbers. International Journal of Mathematics and Mathematical Sciences.

Gülmez, A., & Yardımcıoğlu, F. (2012). OECD Ülkelerinde Ar-Ge Harcamaları ve Ekonomik Büyüme İlişkisi: Panel Eşbütünleşme ve Panel Nedensellik Analizi (1990-2010). *Maliye Dergisi, 163*(1), 335–353.

Guloglu, B., & Tekin, R. B. (2012). A panel causality analysis of the relationship among research and development, innovation, and economic growth in high-income OECD countries. *Eurasian Economic Review, 2*(1), 32–47.

Gürcan, Ö. F., Yazıcı, İ., Beyca, Ö. F., Arslan, Ç. Y., & Eldemir, F. (2016). Third party logistics (3PL) provider selection with AHP application. *Procedia: Social and Behavioral Sciences, 235*, 226–234. doi:10.1016/j.sbspro.2016.11.018

Habib, M. (2018). *Handbook of Research on Investigations in Artificial Life Research and Development.* Hershey, PA: IGI Global. doi:10.4018/978-1-5225-5396-0

Hagan, M. T., Demuth, H. B., & Beale, M. H. (1996). *Neural Network Design.* Boston: PWS Publishing.

Hair, J. F., Hult, G. T. M., Ringle, C. M., & Sarstedt, M. (2014). *A primer on partial least squares structural equation modeling (PLS-SEM).* Thousand Oaks, CA: Sage Publications.

Hair, J. F., Ringle, C. M., & Sarstedt, M. (2011a). PLS-SEM: Indeed a Silver Bullet. *Journal of Marketing Theory and Practice, 18*(2), 139–152. doi:10.2753/MTP1069-6679190202

Hair, J. F., Ringle, C. M., & Sarstedt, M. (2011b). The Use of Partial Least Squares (PLS) to Address Marketing Management Topics: From the Special Issue Guest Editors. *Journal of Marketing Theory and Practice, 18*(2), 135–138. doi:10.1080/10696679.2011.11046435

Hair, J. F., Sarstedt, M., Pieper, T. M., & Ringle, C. M. (2012a). The Use of Partial Least Squares Structural Equation Modeling in Strategic Management Research: A Review of Past Practices and Recommendations for Future Applications. *Long Range Planning, 45*(5–6), 320–340. doi:10.1016/j.lrp.2012.09.008

Hair, J. F., Sarstedt, M., Ringle, C. M., & Mena, J. A. (2012b). An assessment of the use of partial least squares structural equation modeling in marketing research. *Journal of the Academy of Marketing Science, 40*(3), 414–433. doi:10.100711747-011-0261-6

Hannan, M. T., & Freeman, J. (1989). *Organizational Ecology.* Cambridge, MA: Harvard University Press.

Hansen, L. P., & Sargent, T. J. (1993). Recursive Linear Models of Dynamic Economies. *Federal Reserve Bank of San Francisco Proceedings.*

Happel, B. L. M., & Murre, J. M. J. (1994). The design and evolution of modular neural network architectures. *Neural Networks, 7*(6-7), 985–1004. doi:10.1016/S0893-6080(05)80155-8

Harvey, A. (1989). *Forecasting structural time series models and the kalman filter.* Cambridge, UK: Cambridge University Press.

Hashemi, S. H., Karimi, A., & Tavana, M. (2015). An integrated green supplier selection approach with analytic network process and improved Grey relational analysis. *International Journal of Production Economics, 159*, 178–191. doi:10.1016/j.ijpe.2014.09.027

Hauptman, O., & Hirji, K. K. (1996). The influence of process concurrency on project outcomes in product development: An empirical study of cross-functional teams. *IEEE Transactions on Engineering Management, 43*(3), 153–164. doi:10.1109/17.509981

Henning, K. (2013). *Recommendations for implementing the strategic initiative* INDUSTRIE 4.0.

Henrich, J. (2004). Cultural group selection, coevolutionary processes and large-scale cooperation. *Journal of Economic Behavior & Organization, 53*, 127–143. doi:10.1016/S0167-2681(03)00117-3

Henseler, J., & Dijkstra, T. K. (2014). *ADANCO 1.0. Kleve: Composite Modeling.* Retrieved on August 13, 2017, from: http://www.compositemodeling.com

Henseler, J., Ringle, C. M., & Sarstedt, M. (2012). Using Partial Least Squares Path Modeling in International Advertising Research: Basic Concepts and Recent Issues. In S. Okazaki (Ed.), *Handbook of Research in International Advertising* (pp. 252–276). Cheltenham, UK: Edward Elgar Publishing. doi:10.4337/9781781001042.00023

Henseler, J., Ringle, C. M., & Sinkovics, R. R. (2009). The Use of Partial Least Squares Path Modeling in International Marketing. In R. R. Sinkovics & P. N. Ghauri (Eds.), *Advances in International Marketing* (Vol. 20, pp. 277–320). Bingley: Emerald. doi:10.1108/S1474-7979(2009)0000020014

Henseler, J., Wilson, B., Götz, O., & Hautvast, C. (2007). Investigating the moderating role of fit on sports sponsoring and brand equity: A structural model. *International Journal of Sports Marketing & Sponsorship, 8*(4), 321–329. doi:10.1108/IJSMS-08-04-2007-B005

Hernandez, E., & Guillen, M. F. (2018). What's theoretically novel about emerging-market multinationals? *Journal of International Business Studies, 49*(1), 24–33. doi:10.105741267-017-0131-7

Hillegeist, S. A., Keating, E. K., Cram, D. P., & Lundstedt, K. G. (2004). Assessing the probability of bankruptcy. *Review of Accounting Studies, 9*(1), 5–34. doi:10.1023/B:RAST.0000013627.90884.b7

Hill, T., Marquez, L., O'Connor, M., & Remus, W. (1994). Artificial neural networks for forecasting and decision making. *International Journal of Forecasting, 10*(1), 5–15. doi:10.1016/0169-2070(94)90045-0

Hill, T., O'Connor, M., & Remus, W. (1996). Neural network models for time series forecasts. *Management Science, 42*(7), 1082–1092. doi:10.1287/mnsc.42.7.1082

Hinich, M. J. (1982). Testing for Gaussianity and linearity of a statistionary time series. *Journal of Time Series Analysis, 3*(3), 169–176. doi:10.1111/j.1467-9892.1982.tb00339.x

Hirshleifer, J. (1965). Investment decisions under uncertainty: Choice theoretic approaches. *The Quarterly Journal of Economics, 79*(4), 509–536. doi:10.2307/1880650

Hirshleifer, J. (1966). Investment decisions under uncertainty: Applications of the state preference approach. *The Quarterly Journal of Economics*, *80*(2), 611–617. doi:10.2307/1880692

Hoegl, M., Ernst, H., & Proserpio, L. (2007). How teamwork matters more as team member dispersion increases. *Journal of Product Innovation Management*, *24*(2), 156–165. doi:10.1111/j.1540-5885.2007.00240.x

Hoegl, M., & Gemuenden, H. G. (2001). Teamwork quality and the success of innovative projects: A theoretical concept and empirical evidence. *Organization Science*, *12*(4), 435–449. doi:10.1287/orsc.12.4.435.10635

Hoegl, M., & Parboteeah, K. P. (2003). Goal Setting And Team Performance In Innovative Projects: On the Moderating Role of Teamwork Quality. *Small Group Research*, *34*(1), 3–19. doi:10.1177/1046496402239575

Hoff, K., & Stiglitz, J. E. (2016). Striving for balance in economics: Towards a theory of the social determination of behaviour. *Journal of Economic Behavior & Organization*, *126*, 25–57. doi:10.1016/j.jebo.2016.01.005

Hoffstein, J., Pipher, J., & Silverman, J. H. (2014). *An Introduction to Mathematical Cryptography*. New York: Springer.

Hong, Y., Morris, M. W., Chiu, C., & Benet-Martinez, V. (2000). Multicultural minds: A dynamic constructivist approach to culture and cognition. *The American Psychologist*, *55*(7), 709–720. doi:10.1037/0003-066X.55.7.709 PMID:10916861

Hornik, K. (1991). Approximation capability of multilayer feedforward networks. *Neural Networks*, *4*(2), 251–257. doi:10.1016/0893-6080(91)90009-T

Hornik, K., Stinchicombe, M., & White, H. (1989). Multilayer Feedforward Networks are Universal Approximators. *Neural Networks*, *2*(5), 359–366. doi:10.1016/0893-6080(89)90020-8

Ho, W., Xu, X., & Dey, P. K. (2010). Multi-criteria decision making approaches for supplier evaluation and selection: A literature review. *European Journal of Operational Research*, *202*(1), 16–24. doi:10.1016/j.ejor.2009.05.009

Hribar, P., Jenkins, N. T., & Johnson, W. B. (2006). Stock repurchases as an earnings management device. *Journal of Accounting and Economics*, *41*(1-2), 3–27. doi:10.1016/j.jacceco.2005.10.002

Hsu, S., Shih, S., Chiang, J. C., & Liu, Y. (2012). The impact of transactive memory systems on IS development teams' coordination, communication, and performance. *International Journal of Project Management*, *30*(3), 329–340. doi:10.1016/j.ijproman.2011.08.003

Huang, C.-J. (2017). Is corruption bad for economic growth? Evidence from Asia-Pacific countries. *The North American Journal of Economics and Finance*, *35*, 247–256. doi:10.1016/j.najef.2015.10.013

Hull, J. C. (2009). Options, Futures And Other Derivatives (7th ed.). Pearson Education.

Hussain, R. J., & Kumar, P. S. (2012a). The transportation problem in an intuitionistic fuzzy environment. *International Journal of Mathematics Research*, *4*(4), 411–420.

Hussain, R. J., & Kumar, P. S. (2012b). Algorithmic approach for solving intuitionistic fuzzy transportation problem. *Applied Mathematical Sciences*, *6*(80), 3981–3989.

Hussain, R. J., & Kumar, P. S. (2012c). The transportation problem with the aid of triangular intuitionistic fuzzy numbers. In *Proceedings in International Conference on Mathematical Modeling and Applied Soft Computing (MMASC-2012)*. Coimbatore Institute of Technology.

Hussain, R. J., & Kumar, P. S. (2013). An optimal more-for-less solution of mixed constraints intuitionistic fuzzy transportation problems. *International Journal of Contemporary Mathematical Sciences*, *8*(12), 565–576. doi:10.12988/ijcms.2013.13056

Hylleberg, S. (1994). Modelling seasonal variation. In *Nonstationary Time Series Analysis and Cointegration* (pp. 153–178). Oxford, UK: Oxford University Press.

Igel, C., & Husken, M. (2003). Empirical evaluation of the improved Rprop learning algorithms. *Neurocomputing, 50*, 105–123. doi:10.1016/S0925-2312(01)00700-7

Ikenberry, D., Lakonishok, J., & Vermaelen, T. (1995). Market underreaction to open market share repurchases. *Journal of Financial Economics, 39*(2-3), 161–180. doi:10.1016/0304-405X(95)00826-Z

INSTAT. (2017). *Institute of Statistics: International Trade*. Retrieved on April 25, 2018, from: http://instat.gov.al/en/themes/international-trade/international-trade-in-goods

Isard, W. (1975). A Simple Rationale for Gravity-Model-Type Behavior. *Papers in Regional Science, 35*(1), 25–30. doi:10.1007/BF01947465

Jain, V., Sangaiah, A. K., Sakhuja, S., Thoduka, N., & Aggarwal, R. (2018). Supplier selection using fuzzy AHP and TOPSIS: A case study in the Indian automotive industry. *Neural Computing & Applications, 29*(7), 555–564. doi:10.100700521-016-2533-z

Jaworski, B. J., & Kohli, A. K. (1993). Market orientation: Antecedents and consequences. *Journal of Marketing, 57*(3), 53–70. doi:10.1177/002224299305700304

Jeffcott, S. A., & Mackenzie, C. F. (2008). Measuring team performance in healthcare: Review of research and implications for patient safety. *Journal of Critical Care, 23*(2), 188–196. doi:10.1016/j.jcrc.2007.12.005 PMID:18538211

Jinshuai, Y., Jin, L., Yi, W., Tong, W., & Zhanqiang, L. (2017). Optimization of weapon-target assignment problem by intuitionistic fuzzy genetic algorithm. In *MATEC Web of Conferences* (Vol. 128, p. 02004). EDP Sciences. DOI: 10.1051/matecconf/201712802004

Johlke, M. C., & Duhan, D. F. (2000). Testing competing models of sales force communication. *Journal of Personal Selling & Sales Management, 21*(4), 265–277.

Johnsona, D. P., Michael, E. P., & Van Vugt, M. (2013). Darwin's invisible hand: Market competition, evolution and the firm. *Journal of Economic Behavior & Organization, 90*, 128–140. doi:10.1016/j.jebo.2012.12.016

Joseph, M., McClure, C., & Joseph, B. (1999). Service quality in the banking sector: The impact of technology on service delivery. *International Journal of Bank Marketing, 17*(4), 182–193. doi:10.1108/02652329910278879

Jose, S., & Kuriakose, S. (2013). Algorithm for solving an assignment model in intuitionistic fuzzy context. *International Journal of Fuzzy Mathematics and Systems, 3*(5), 345–349.

Jude, C., & Levieuge, G. (2017). Growth Effect of Foreign Direct Investment in Developing Economies: The Role of Institutional Quality. *World Economy, 40*(4), 715–742. doi:10.1111/twec.12402

Kaashoek, J. F., & Van Dijk, H. K. (2003). Neural Networks: an Econometric Tool. In *Computer-Aided Econometrics* (pp. 351–384). New York: D.E.A. Giles. doi:10.1201/9780203911570.ch12

Kaastra, I., & Boyd, M. (1996). Designing a neural network for forecasting financial and economic series. *Neurocomputing, 10*(3), 215–236. doi:10.1016/0925-2312(95)00039-9

Kang, S. (1991). *An Investigation of the Use of Feedforward Neural Networks for Forecasting* (Ph.D. Thesis). Kent State University.

Kannan, D., Govindan, K., & Rajendran, S. (2015). Fuzzy Axiomatic Design approach based green supplier selection: A case study from Singapore. *Journal of Cleaner Production, 96*, 194–208. doi:10.1016/j.jclepro.2013.12.076

Karlamova, G., & Vertelieva, O. (2013). The International Competitiveness of Countries: Economic-Mathematical Approach. *Economia e Sociologia (Evora, Portugal)*, *6*(2), 39–52.

Karlgren, B. (1923). Analytic Dictionary of Chinese and Sino-Japanese. Taipei: CH'ENG-WEN Publishing Company.

Kastrati, P. (2015, September 25). *University of Tirana*. Retrieved on May 4, 2018, from: http://www.doktoratura.unitir.edu.al/2015/09/doktoratura-pranvera-kastrati-fakulteti-ekonomik-departamenti-i-manaxhimit/

Katz, R., & Allen, T. J. (1988). Investigating the not invented here (NIH) syndrome: a look at the performance, tenure, and communication patterns of 50 R&D project groups. In L. Michael, W. L. Tushman, & Moore (Eds.), Readings in the management of innovations (pp. 293–309). Cambridge, MA: Ballinger Publishing.

Katzenbach, J. R., & Smith, D. K. (2003). *The wisdom of teams*. New York: Harper Collins Publishers.

Katz, J., & Lindell, Y. (2014). *Introduction to Modern Cryptography*. Milton Park, UK: Taylor & Francis.

Keller, R. T. (1994). Technology-information processing fit and the performance of R&D project groups: A test of contingency theory. *Academy of Management Journal*, *37*(1), 167–179.

Keppel, G., Saufley, W. H., & Tokunaga, H. (1992). *Introduction to design and analysis: A students handbook* (2nd ed.). New York: W.H. Freeman & Company.

Keršuliene, V., Zavadskas, E. K., & Turskis, Z. (2010). Selection of rational dispute resolution method by applying new step-wise weight assessment ratio analysis (SWARA). *Journal of business economics and management*, *11*(2), 243–258. doi:10.3846/jbem.2010.12

Kessler, E. H., & Chakrabarti, A. K. (1996). Innovation speed: A conceptual model of context, antecedents, and outcomes. *Academy of Management Review*, *21*(4), 1143–1191. doi:10.5465/amr.1996.9704071866

Kessler, E. H., & Chakrabarti, A. K. (1999). Speeding up the pace of new product development. *Journal of Product Innovation Management*, *16*(3), 231–247. doi:10.1016/S0737-6782(98)00048-4

Ketchen, D. J., Hult, G. T. M., & Slater, S. F. (2007). Toward greater understanding of market orientation and the resource-based view. *Strategic Management Journal*, *28*(9), 961–964. doi:10.1002mj.620

Kiprop, J. (2018, February 6). *Economics: What is CEFTA*. Retrieved on April 25, 2018, from: https://www.worldatlas.com/articles/what-is-the-central-european-free-trade-agreement.html

Klarner, P., Sarstedt, M., Hoeck, M., & Ringle, C. M. (2013). Disentangling the Effects of Team Competences, Team Adaptability, and Client Communication on the Performance of Management Consulting Teams. *Long Range Planning*, *46*(3), 258–286. doi:10.1016/j.lrp.2013.03.001

Kleijnen, M., Wetzels, M., & De Ruyter, K. (2004). Consumer acceptance of wireless finance. *Journal of Financial Services Marketing*, *8*(3), 206–217. doi:10.1057/palgrave.fsm.4770120

Klimasauskas, C. C. (1993). Applying neural networks. In *Neural Networks in Finance and Investing: Using Artificial Intelligence to Improve Real World Performance* (pp. 64–65). Chicago: Probus.

Koblitz, N. (1987). Elliptic Curve Cryptosystems. *Mathematics of Computation*, *48*(177), 203–209. doi:10.1090/S0025-5718-1987-0866109-5

Kohli, A. K., & Jaworski, B. J. (1990). Market orientation: The construct, research propositions, and managerial implications. *Journal of Marketing*, *54*(2), 1–18. doi:10.1177/002224299005400201

Kong, H., Zeng, Z., Yan, L., Yao, S., & Sheng, N. (2009). Combine Elliptic Curve Cryptography with Digital Watermark for OWL-Based Ontology Encryption. *ACM Digital Library*, *1*, 511–515. doi:10.1109/CIS.2009.99

Koopman, S. J., & Franses, P. H. (2002). Constructing seasonally adjusted data with time-varying confidence intervals. *Oxford Bulletin of Economics and Statistics*, *64*(5), 509–526. doi:10.1111/1468-0084.00275

Kraimer, M. L., Shaffer, M. A., Harrison, D. A., & Ren, H. (2012). No place like home? An identity strain perspective on repatriate turnover. *Academy of Management Journal*, *55*(2), 399–420. doi:10.5465/amj.2009.0644

Kraja, I., & Sejdini, A. (2014). International Trade of Albania. Gravity model. *European Journal of Social Sciences Education and Research*, 219-227.

Krugman, P., Obstfeld, M., & Melitz, M. (2012). *International Economics*. Boston: Pearson Education.

Kuhn, H. W. (1955). The Hungarian method for the assignment problem. *Naval Research Logistics Quarterly*, *2*(1-2), 83–97.

Kumar, P. S. (2017a). *Algorithmic approach for solving allocation problems under intuitionistic fuzzy environment* (Unpublished doctoral dissertation). Jamal Mohamed College (Autonomous), Tiruchirappalli, India. Retrieved from http://hdl.handle.net/10603/209151

Kumar, P. S. (2017b). PSK method for solving type-1 and type-3 fuzzy transportation problems. In Fuzzy Systems: Concepts, Methodologies, Tools, and Applications (pp. 367-392). Hershey, PA: IGI Global. doi:10.4018/978-1-5225-1908-9.ch017

Kumar, P. S., & Hussain, R. J. (2014c) A method for finding an optimal solution of an assignment problem under mixed intuitionistic fuzzy environment. *Proceedings in International Conference on Mathematical Sciences (ICMS-2014)* Elsevier.

Kumar, A., & Gupta, A. (2012). Assignment and travelling salesman problems with coefficients as LR fuzzy parameters. *International Journal of Applied Science and Engineering*, *10*(3), 155–170.

Kumar, A., Gupta, A., & Kaur, A. (2009). Method for solving fully fuzzy assignment problems using triangular fuzzy numbers. *International Journal of Computer and Information Engineering*, *3*, 231–234.

Kumar, A., & Kaur, A. (2011). Methods for solving fully fuzzy transportation problems based on classical transportation methods. *International Journal of Operations Research and Information Systems*, *2*(4), 52–71. doi:10.4018/joris.2011100104

Kumar, A., & Kaur, M. (2013). A ranking approach for intuitionistic fuzzy numbers and its application. *Journal of Applied Research and Technology*, *11*(3), 381–396.

Kumar, G., & Bajaj, R. K. (2014). On Solution of Interval Valued Intuitionistic Fuzzy Assignment Problem Using Similarity Measure and Score Function. *International Journal of Mathematical, Computational. Physical and Quantum Engineering*, *8*(4), 713–718.

Kumar, N., & Shukla, D. (2016, March). Resource management through fuzzy assignment problem in cloud computing environment. In *Proceedings of the Second International Conference on Information and Communication Technology for Competitive Strategies* (p. 87). ACM.

Kumar, P. S. (2016a). A simple method for solving type-2 and type-4 fuzzy transportation problems. *International Journal of Fuzzy Logic and Intelligent Systems*, *16*(4), 225–237. doi:10.5391/IJFIS.2016.16.4.225

Kumar, P. S. (2016b). PSK method for solving type-1 and type-3 fuzzy transportation problems. *International Journal of Fuzzy System Applications*, *5*(4), 121–146. doi:10.4018/IJFSA.2016100106

Kumar, P. S. (2018a). Search for an optimal solution to vague traffic problems using the PSK method. In M. Habib (Ed.), *Handbook of Research on Investigations in Artificial Life Research and Development* (pp. 219–257). Hershey, PA: IGI Global; doi:10.4018/978-1-5225-5396-0.ch011

Kumar, P. S. (2018b). Linear programming approach for solving balanced and unbalanced intuitionistic fuzzy transportation problems. *International Journal of Operations Research and Information Systems*, *9*(2), 73–100. doi:10.4018/IJORIS.2018040104

Kumar, P. S. (2018c). A simple and efficient algorithm for solving type-1 intuitionistic fuzzy solid transportation problems. *International Journal of Operations Research and Information Systems*, *9*(3), 90–122. doi:10.4018/IJORIS.2018070105

Kumar, P. S. (2018d). A note on 'a new approach for solving intuitionistic fuzzy transportation problem of type-2'. *International Journal of Logistics Systems and Management*, *29*(1), 102–129. doi:10.1504/IJLSM.2018.10009204

Kumar, P. S. (2018e). Intuitionistic fuzzy zero point method for solving type-2 intuitionistic fuzzy transportation problem. *International Journal of Operational Research*. (in press)

Kumar, P. S. (2018f). PSK method for solving intuitionistic fuzzy solid transportation problems. *International Journal of Fuzzy System Applications*, *7*(4), 62–99. doi:10.4018/ijfsa.2018100104

Kumar, P. S. (2018g). Algorithms for solving the optimization problems using fuzzy and intuitionistic fuzzy set. *International Journal of System Assurance Engineering and Management*. (submitted)

Kumar, P. S. (2018h). Intuitionistic fuzzy solid assignment problems: A software-based approach. *International Journal of System Assurance Engineering and Management*. (submitted)

Kumar, P. S. (2019a). PSK method for solving mixed and type-4 intuitionistic fuzzy solid transportation problems. *International Journal of Operations Research and Information Systems*. (in press)

Kumar, P. S. (2019b). Linear Programming Method for Solving Solid and Intuitionistic Fuzzy Solid Transportation Problems. *International Journal of Uncertainty, Fuzziness and Knowledge-based Systems*. (submitted)

Kumar, P. S. (2019c). Integer Programming Approach for solving solid and Intuitionistic Fuzzy Solid Assignment Problems. *International Journal of Logistics Systems and Management*. (submitted)

Kumar, P. S. (2019d). Computationally Simple and Efficient Method for Solving Real-Life Mixed Intuitionistic Fuzzy Solid Assignment Problems. *International Journal of Fuzzy System Applications*. (submitted)

Kumar, P. S. (2019e). Software-based approach for solving intuitionistic fuzzy solid transportation problems. *International Journal of Applied Management Science*. (submitted)

Kumar, P. S. (2019f). Discovery of a new kind of type-2 fuzzy and type-2 intuitionistic fuzzy transportation problems and identification of its optimal solutions. *International Journal of Operations Research and Information Systems*. (submitted)

Kumar, P. S. (2020). Developing a New Approach to Solve Solid Assignment Problems Under Intuitionistic Fuzzy Environment. *International Journal of Fuzzy System Applications*, *9*(1), 1.

Kumar, P. S., & Hussain, R. J. (2014a). *New algorithm for solving mixed intuitionistic fuzzy assignment problem. In Elixir Applied Mathematics* (pp. 25971–25977). Salem, Tamilnadu, India: Elixir publishers.

Kumar, P. S., & Hussain, R. J. (2014b). A systematic approach for solving mixed intuitionistic fuzzy transportation problems. *International Journal of Pure and Applied Mathematics*, *92*(2), 181–190.

Kumar, P. S., & Hussain, R. J. (2014d). A method for solving balanced intuitionistic fuzzy assignment problem. *International Journal of Engineering Research and Applications*, *4*(3), 897–903.

Kumar, P. S., & Hussain, R. J. (2015). A method for solving unbalanced intuitionistic fuzzy transportation problems. *Notes on Intuitionistic Fuzzy Sets*, *21*(3), 54–65.

Kumar, P. S., & Hussain, R. J. (2016a). An algorithm for solving unbalanced intuitionistic fuzzy assignment problem using triangular intuitionistic fuzzy number. *The Journal of Fuzzy Mathematics*, *24*(2), 289–302.

Kumar, P. S., & Hussain, R. J. (2016b). Computationally simple approach for solving fully intuitionistic fuzzy real life transportation problems. *International Journal of System Assurance Engineering and Management*, *7*(1), 90–101. doi:10.100713198-014-0334-2

Kumar, P. S., & Hussain, R. J. (2016c). A simple method for solving fully intuitionistic fuzzy real life assignment problem. *International Journal of Operations Research and Information Systems*, *7*(2), 39–61. doi:10.4018/IJORIS.2016040103

Kumar, S. L. (2017). State of The Art-Intense Review on Artificial Intelligence Systems Application in Process Planning and Manufacturing. *Engineering Applications of Artificial Intelligence*, *65*, 294–329. doi:10.1016/j.engappai.2017.08.005

Küpper, D., Lorenz, M., Kuhlmann, K., Bouffault, O., Heng, L.Y., Van Wyck, J., Köcher, S., & Schlageter, J. (2018). *AI in the Factory of the Future. The Ghost in the Machine.* The Boston Consulting Group.

Kura, K. M. (2016). Environmentally-specific transformational leadership and green behaviour at work: Exploring the mediating role of environmental concern. *Global Business Review*, *17*(6), 1S–14S. doi:10.1177/0972150916631069

Kyläheiko, K., & Sandström, J. (2007). Strategic options-based framework for management of dynamic capabilities in manufacturing firms. *Journal of Manufacturing Technology Management*, *18*(8), 966–984. doi:10.1108/17410380710828280

La Rocca, M., & Perna, C. (2005). Variable selection in neural network regression models with dependent data: A subsampling approach. *Computational Statistics & Data Analysis*, *48*(2), 415–429. doi:10.1016/j.csda.2004.01.004

Lancaster, G., & Van Der Velden, H. (2004). The influence of employee characteristics on market orientation. *International Journal of Bank Marketing*, *22*(5), 343–365. doi:10.1108/02652320410549656

Landesmann, M., & Pfaffermayr, M. (1997). Technological competition and trade performance. *Applied Economics*, *29*(2), 179–196. doi:10.1080/000368497327254

Lasdon, L. S., & Waren, A. D. (1986). *GRG2 User's Guide. Department of General Business Administration.* Austin, TX: The University Texas at Austin.

Lattimore, R. (2009). *OECD.* Retrieved on January 2018, from: Free, Fair and Open: http://www.oecd.org/

Lee, I., & Lee, K. (2015). The Internet of Things (IoT): Applications, investments, and challenges for enterprises. *Business Horizons*, *58*(4), 431–440. doi:10.1016/j.bushor.2015.03.008

Leff, N. H. (1964). Economic development through bureaucratic corruption. *The American Behavioral Scientist*, *8*(3), 8–14. doi:10.1177/000276426400800303

Lehtokangas, M. (1999). Modelling with constructive backpropagation. *Neural Networks*, *12*(4-5), 707–716. doi:10.1016/S0893-6080(99)00018-0 PMID:12662678

Leung, K., & Morris, M. W. (2015). Values, schemas, and norms in the culture–behavior nexus: A situated dynamics framework. *Journal of International Business Studies*, *46*(9), 1028–1050. doi:10.1057/jibs.2014.66

LeVeque, W. J. (1990). *Elementary Theory of Numbers.* New York: Dover.

Levinthal, D. A. (2017). Mendel in the C-Suite: Design and the Evolution of Strategies. *Strategy Science*, *2*(4), 282–287. doi:10.1287tsc.2017.0047

Levinthal, D. A., & March, J. G. (1981). A model of adaptive organizational search. *Journal of Economic Behavior & Organization*, *2*(4), 307–333. doi:10.1016/0167-2681(81)90012-3

Liao, C. N., & Kao, H. P. (2010). Supplier selection model using Taguchi loss function, analytical hierarchy process and multi-choice goal programming. *Computers & Industrial Engineering*, *58*(4), 571–577. doi:10.1016/j.cie.2009.12.004

Lichtenberg, F. R. (1992). *R&D investment and international productivity differences (No. w4161)*. National Bureau of Economic Research.

Li, D. F., Nan, J. X., & Zhang, M. J. (2010). A ranking method of triangular intuitionistic fuzzy numbers and application to decision making. *International Journal of Computational Intelligence Systems*, *3*(5), 522–530.

Li, F., Li, L., Jin, C., Wang, R., Wang, H., & Yang, L. (2012). A 3PL supplier selection model based on fuzzy sets. *Computers & Operations Research*, *39*(8), 1879–1884. doi:10.1016/j.cor.2011.06.022

Lin, C. J., & Wen, U. P. (2004). A labeling algorithm for the fuzzy assignment problem. *Fuzzy Sets and Systems*, *142*(3), 373–391.

Linnemann, H. (1966). *An Econometric Study of International Trade Flows*. Amsterdam: North-Holland.

Li, Y., Liu, Y., & Zhao, Y. (2006). The role of market and entrepreneurship orientation and internal control in the new product development activities of Chinese firms. *Industrial Marketing Management*, *35*(3), 336–347. doi:10.1016/j.indmarman.2005.05.016

Lone, M. A., Mir, S. A., Ismail, Y., & Majid, R. (2017). Intuitionistic Fuzzy Assignment Problem: An Application in Agriculture. Asian Journal of Agricultural Extension. *Economia e Sociologia (Evora, Portugal)*, *15*(4), 1–6. doi:10.9734/AJAEES/2017/31967

Lonergan, W. (2000). *The valuation of businesses, shares and other equity* (3rd ed.). Warriewood, NSW, Australia: Business and Professional Publishing.

Loret de Mola, C. (2001). *El Negocio: LA Economía De México Atrapada Por El Narcotráfico*. DF, Mexico: Grijalbo Mondadori.

Lucas, R. E. Jr. (1988). On The Mechanics of Economic Development. *Journal of Monetary Economics*, *22*(1), 25–50. doi:10.1016/0304-3932(88)90168-7

Lu, H. P., & Weng, C. I. (2018). Smart manufacturing technology, market maturity analysis and technology roadmap in the computer and electronic product manufacturing industry. *Technological Forecasting and Social Change*, *133*, 85–94. doi:10.1016/j.techfore.2018.03.005

Luukkonen, R., Saikkonen, P., & Terasvirta, T. (1988). Testing linearity in univariate time series models. *Scandinavian Journal of Statistics*, *15*, 161–175.

Magee, S. P., Brock, W. A., & Young, L. (1989). *Black hole tariffs and endogenous policy theory*. Cambridge, UK: Cambridge University Press.

Mahapatra, G. S., & Roy, T. K. (2009). Reliability evaluation using triangular intuitionistic fuzzy numbers, arithmetic operations. *International Scholarly and Scientific Research & Innovation*, *3*(2), 422–429.

Mahapatra, G. S., & Roy, T. K. (2013). Intuitionistic fuzzy number and its arithmetic operation with application on system failure. *Journal of Uncertain Systems*, *7*(2), 92–107.

Makridakis, S. (2017). The forthcoming Artificial Intelligence (AI) revolution: Its impact on society and firms. *Futures*, *90*, 46–60. doi:10.1016/j.futures.2017.03.006

Malini, P., & Ananthanarayanan, M. (2016). Solving fuzzy assignment problem using ranking of generalized trapezoidal fuzzy numbers. *Indian Journal of Science and Technology*, *9*(20), 1–4. doi:10.17485/ijst/2016/v9i20/88691

Management Association. (2017). Fuzzy Systems: Concepts, Methodologies, Tools, and Applications. Hershey, PA: IGI Global. doi:10.4018/978-1-5225-1908-9

Martino, J. P. (1993). *Technological forecasting for decision making*. McGraw-Hill, Inc.

Mascareñas, J. (1999). *Innovación Financiera: Aplicaciones para la Gestión Empresarial*. Madrid, Spain: McGraw-Hill.

Masters, T. (1993). *Practical neural network recipes in C*. New York: Academic Press.

Masters, T. (1994). *Signal and image processing with previous neural networks*. John Wiley & Sons, Inc.

Mauboussin, M. J. (1999). Get real: Using real options in security analysis. *Frontiers of Finance*, *10*, 1–30.

Mavi, R. K., Goh, M., & Zarbakhshnia, N. (2017). Sustainable third-party reverse logistic provider selection with fuzzy SWARA and fuzzy MOORA in plastic industry. *International Journal of Advanced Manufacturing Technology*, *91*(5-8), 2401–2418. doi:10.100700170-016-9880-x

Mayer, W. (1984). Endogenous tariff formation. *The American Economic Review*, *74*(5), 970–985.

Mayr, E. (1997). The objects of selection. *Proceedings of the National Academy of Sciences of the United States of America*, *94*(6), 2091–2094. doi:10.1073/pnas.94.6.2091 PMID:9122151

McElreath, R., Boyd, R., & Richerson, P. J. (2003). Shared norms and the evolution of ethnic markers. *Current Anthropology*, *44*(1), 122–129. doi:10.1086/345689

McNally, R. C., Akdeniz, M. B., & Calantone, R. J. (2011). New Product Development Processes and New Product Profitability: Exploring the Mediating Role of Speed to Market and Product Quality. *Journal of Product Innovation Management*, *28*(s1), 63–77. doi:10.1111/j.1540-5885.2011.00861.x

Melnikas, B. (2008). Transformation Processes in Central and Eastern Europe: Liberalization Integral Cultural Space and Social Environment for Economic Development. *Ekonomika (Nis)*, 63–80.

Menezes, A. J., Paul, C., & Scott, A. (1996). *Handbook Applied Cryptography*. Boca Raton, FL: CRC Press. doi:10.1201/9781439821916

Mengel, F. (2008). Matching structure and the cultural transmission of social norms. *Journal of Economic Behavior & Organization*, *67*(3-4), 608–623. doi:10.1016/j.jebo.2008.01.001

Merton, R. C. (1974). On the pricing of corporate debt: The risk structure of interest rates. *The Journal of Finance*, *29*(2), 449–470.

Mesoudi, A. (2009). How cultural evolutionary theory can inform social psychology, and vice versa. *Psychological Review*, *116*(4), 929–952. doi:10.1037/a0017062 PMID:19839691

Miller, M. H. (2001). The Modigliani-Miller propositions after thirty years. In D. H. Chew (Ed.), *Corporate finance: Where theory meets practice* (3rd ed.; pp. 184–196). Singapore: McGraw-Hill.

Miller, V. S. (1986). Use of Elliptic Curves in Cryptography. *Advances in Cryptology*, *85*(218), 417–426.

Ming-Hsien, Y., & Chih-She, W.U. (2015). Revisit Export and GDP Nexus in China and Taiwan: A Rolling Window Granger Causality Test. *Theoretical & Applied Economics*, *22*(3).

Ming-Sung Cheng, J., Shih-Tse Wang, E., Ying-Chao Lin, J., & Vivek, S. D. (2009). Why do customers utilize the internet as a retailing platform? A view from consumer perceived value. *Asia Pacific Journal of Marketing and Logistics, 21*(1), 144–160. doi:10.1108/13555850910926290

Mishra, S., & Patra, S. K. (2009). Short term load forecasting using a novel recurrent neural network. *International Journal of Computational Intelligence: Theory and Practice, 4*(1), 39–45.

Mitaj, A., & Osmani, M. (2017). Trade Creation and Trade Diversion Effects for Albania. *International Journal of Economics, Commerce and Management*, 569-588.

Mitchell, H. B. (2004). Ranking intuitionistic fuzzy numbers. *International Journal of Uncertainty, Fuzziness and Knowledge-based Systems, 12*(3), 377–386.

Modigliani, F., & Miller, M. H. (1958, June). The cost of capital, corporation finance, and the theory of investment. *The American Economic Review*, 261–297.

Mohideen, S. I., & Kumar, P. S. (2010). *A comparative study on transportation problem in fuzzy environment* (Unpublished master's thesis). Jamal Mohamed College (Autonomous), Tiruchirappalli, India.

Mohideen, S. I., & Kumar, P. S. (2010). A comparative study on transportation problem in fuzzy environment. *International Journal of Mathematics Research, 2*(1), 151–158.

Mukherjee, S., & Basu, K. (2010). Application of fuzzy ranking method for solving assignment problems with fuzzy costs. *International Journal of Computational and Applied Mathematics, 5*(3), 359–368.

Mukherjee, S., & Basu, K. (2012). Solution of a class of intuitionistic fuzzy assignment problem by using similarity measures. *Knowledge-Based Systems, 27*, 170–179.

Mun, J. (2002). *Real options analysis: Tools and techniques for valuing strategic investments and decisions* (Vol. 137). New York: John Wiley & Sons.

Muñoz Gómez, D. L. (2017). *Decisiones de inversión por medio de opciones reales para el sector de hidrocarburos* (Doctoral dissertation). Universidad Nacional de Colombia-Sede Bogotá.

Muralidaran, C., & Venkateswarlu, B. (2017, November). A method for solving equally spread symmetric fuzzy assignment problems using branch and bound technique. In IOP Conference Series: Materials Science and Engineering (Vol. 263, No. 4, p. 042123). IOP Publishing. doi:10.1088/1757-899X/263/4/042123

Muruganandam, S., & Hema, K. (2017). An optimal solution to fuzzy assignment problem using ones suffix and improved ones suffix method. *International Journal of Scientific Research, 6*(5), 267–270.

Nagoorgani, A., Kavikumar, J., Mohamed, V. N., & Shamsidah, A. N. (2016, July). A labeling algorithm for solving intuitionistic fuzzy optimal assignment problems. In *Fuzzy Systems (FUZZ-IEEE), 2016 IEEE International Conference on* (pp. 1621-1627). IEEE.

Nakata, C., & Im, S. (2010). Spurring cross-functional integration for higher new product performance: A group effectiveness perspective. *Journal of Product Innovation Management, 27*(4), 554–571. doi:10.1111/j.1540-5885.2010.00735.x

Nam, K., & Schaefer, T. (1995). Forecasting international airline passenger traffic using neural networks. *Logistics and Transportation, 31*(3), 239–251.

Nasseri, S. H., & Ebrahimnejad, A. (2011). Sensitivity Analysis on Linear Programming Problems with Trapezoidal Fuzzy Variables. *International Journal of Operations Research and Information Systems, 2*(2), 22–39. doi:10.4018/joris.2011040102

Nayagam, G., Lakshmana, V., Venkateshwari, G., & Sivaraman, G. (2008, June). Ranking of intuitionistic fuzzy numbers. In *Fuzzy Systems, 2008. FUZZ-IEEE 2008. (IEEE World Congress on Computational Intelligence). IEEE International Conference on* (pp. 1971-1974). IEEE.

Nehi, H. M. (2010). A new ranking method for intuitionistic fuzzy numbers. *International Journal of Fuzzy Systems, 12*(1), 80–86.

Nehi, H. M., & Maleki, H. R. (2005, July). Intuitionistic fuzzy numbers and it's applications in fuzzy optimization problem. In *Proceedings of the Ninth WSEAS International Conference on Systems* (pp. 1-5). WSEAS.

Nekrasova, I., Karnaukhova, O., & Christiansen, B. (2018). *Fractal Approaches for Modeling Financial Assets and Predicting Crises*. Hershey, PA: IGI Global. doi:10.4018/978-1-5225-3767-0

Nelson, M., Hill, T., Remus, T., & O'Connor, M. (1999). Time series forecasting using NNs: Should the data be deseasonalized first? *Journal of Forecasting, 18*(5), 359–367. doi:10.1002/(SICI)1099-131X(199909)18:5<359::AID-FOR746>3.0.CO;2-P

Newton, I. (1687). *Principia*. London: Pepys Press.

NSS Labs. (2016, November 9). *NSS Labs Predicts 75% of Web Traffic Will Be Encrypted by 2019*. Retrieved on May 5, 2018, from: https://www.nsslabs.com/company/news/press-releases/nss-labs-predicts-75-of-web-traffic-will-be-encrypted-by-2019/

Nunkoo, R., Ramkissoon, H., & Gursoy, D. (2013). Use of Structural Equation Modeling in Tourism Research: Past, Present, and Future. *Journal of Travel Research, 52*(6), 759–771. doi:10.1177/0047287513478503

OEC. (2016). *The Observatory of Economic Complexity: Albania Indicators*. Retrieved on April 22, 2017, from: https://atlas.media.mit.edu/en/profile/country/alb/

OECD. (2007). *Innovations and growth: Rational for an innovation strategy*. OECD.

OECD. (2016). *OECD Science, Technology and Innovation Outlook 2016*. Paris: OECD Publishing.

Olivier, J., Thoenig, M., & Verdier, T. (2008). Globalization and the Dynamics of Cultural Identity. *Journal of International Economics, 76*(2), 356–370. doi:10.1016/j.jinteco.2008.06.009

ONDCP. (2012). *National Control Drug Strategy*. Retrieved on April 22, 2018, from: https://obamawhitehouse.archives.gov/sites/default/files/ondcp/2012_ndcs.pdf

ONDCP. (2016). *2016 National Control Drug Strategy*. Retrieved on April 22, 2018, from: https://obamawhitehouse.archives.gov/sites/default/files/ondcp/policy-and-research/2016_ndcs_final_report.pdf

O'Reilly, C., & Roberts, K. (1976). *Relationships among components of credibility and communication*. Academic Press.

Ostrom, E. (2000). Collective action and the evolution of social norms. *The Journal of Economic Perspectives, 14*(3), 137–158. doi:10.1257/jep.14.3.137

Özcan, B., & Arı, A. (2014). Araştırma-Geliştirme Harcamaları ve Ekonomik Büyüme İlişkisi: *Panel Veri Analizi. Maliye Dergisi, 166*(1), 39–55.

Paar, C., & Jan, P. (2010). *Understanding Cryptography: A Textbook for Students and Practitioners*. Bochum, Germany: Springer. doi:10.1007/978-3-642-04101-3

Pack, D. C., El-Sharkawi, M. A., Marks, R. J. II, & Atlas, L. E. (1991). Electric load forecasting using an artificial neural network. *IEEE Transactions on Power Systems, 6*(2), 442–449. doi:10.1109/59.76685

Palanivel, K., Kumar, K. S., Srinivasan, S., & Muralikrishna, P. (2014, May). Fuzzy assignment problem of trapezoidal membership functions within the sort of alpha optimal solution using ranking principle. In *Advances in Engineering and Technology (ICAET), 2014 International Conference on* (pp. 1-7). IEEE.

Palmer, A., Montaño, J. J., & Sesé, A. (2006). Designing an artificial neural network for forecasting tourism time series. *Tourism Management*, *27*(5), 781–790. doi:10.1016/j.tourman.2005.05.006

Paparrizos, K. (1991). An infeasible (exterior point) simplex algorithm for assignment problems. *Mathematical Programming*, *51*(1-3), 45–54.

Parumasur, S. B., & Govender, P. (2013). The Importance of Teamwork, Continuous Top Management Support and Training in Bringing About TQM. *Journal of Economics and Behavioral Studies*, *9*(5), 639–651.

Pattnaik, M. (2015). Decision making approach to fuzzy linear programming (FLP) problems with post optimal analysis. *International Journal of Operations Research and Information Systems*, *6*(4), 75–90. doi:10.4018/IJORIS.2015100105

Payne, A. F. (1988). Developing a marketing-oriented organization. *Business Horizons*, *31*(3), 46–53. doi:10.1016/0007-6813(88)90008-0

Peng, D. X., & Lai, F. (2012). Using partial least squares in operations management research: A practical guideline and summary of past research. *Journal of Operations Management*, *30*(6), 467–480. doi:10.1016/j.jom.2012.06.002

Perry, M. L. (2018). *Algorithms*. Retrieved on October 22, 2018, from: https://cryptofundamentals.com/algorithms

Pesaran, M. H. (2004). *General Diagnostic Tests for Cross Section Dependence in Panels*. Cambridge Working Papers in Economics, No: 0435. Retrieved on June 2, 2018, from: http://www.econ.cam.ac.uk/dae/repec/cam/pdf/cwpe0435.pdf

Pesaran, M. H. (2007). A Simple Panel Unit Root Test in the Presence of Cross-Section Dependence. *Journal of Applied Econometrics*, *22*(2), 265–312. doi:10.1002/jae.951

Pesaran, M. H., & Yamagata, T. (2008). Testing Slope Homogeneity in Large Panels. *Journal of Econometrics*, *142*(1), 50–93. doi:10.1016/j.jeconom.2007.05.010

Pessoa, A. (2007). *Innovation and Economic Growth: What is the actual importance of R&D?* University of Porto, FEP Working Papers, no. 254.

Peysakhovich, A., & Rand, D. G. (2016). Habits of virtue: Creating norms of cooperation and defection in the laboratory. *Management Science*, *62*(3), 631–647. doi:10.1287/mnsc.2015.2168

Phadke, M. S. (1989). *Quality Engineering Using Robust Design*. Englewood Cliffs, NJ: Prentice-Hall.

Phadke, M. S. (1998). *Quality Engineering Using Design of Experiment, Quality control, Robust Design and Taguchi method*. Thousand Oaks, CA: Warsworth and Books.

Pilar, C., & Ana, I. R. E. (2010). The effect of market orientation on innovation speed and new product performance. *Journal of Business and Industrial Marketing*, *25*(7), 501–513. doi:10.1108/08858621011077736

Ping, J. I., & Chu, K. F. (2002). A dual-matrix approach to the transportation problem. *Asia-Pacific Journal of Operational Research*, *19*(1), 35–45.

Pinto, J. E., Henry, E., Robinson, T. R., & Stowe, J. D. (2010). *Equity asset valuation* (2nd ed.). Hoboken, NJ: John Wiley & Sons.

Pinto, M. B., & Pinto, J. K. (1990). Project Team Communication and Cross-Functional Cooperation in New Program Development. *Journal of Product Innovation Management*, *7*(3), 200–212. doi:10.1016/0737-6782(90)90004-X

Pllaha, A. (2012). *Free Trade Agreements and Trade Integration among South Eastern European Countries: Gravity Model Estimations*. Tirana: Bank of Albania.

Pothiraj, B., & Rajaram, S. (2017). Intuitionistic fuzzy assignment problem with replacement based on intuitionistic fuzzy aggregation. *International Journal of Mathematical Archive*, *8*(2), 69–79.

Prabakaran, K., & Ganesan, K. (2018, April). Fuzzy Hungarian method for solving intuitionistic fuzzy travelling salesman problem. Journal of Physics: Conference Series, 1000(1). doi:10.1088/1742-6596/1000/1/012008

Prabakaran, K., & Ganesan, K. (2014). Fuzzy Hungarian method for solving intuitionistic fuzzy assignment problems. *International Journal of Scientific and Engineering Research*, *5*(9), 11–17.

Prakash, C., & Barua, M. K. (2016). A combined MCDM approach for evaluation and selection of third-party reverse logistics partner for Indian electronics industry. *Sustainable Production and Consumption*, *7*, 66–78. doi:10.1016/j.spc.2016.04.001

Preacher, K. J., & Hayes, A. (2008). Asymptotic and resampling strategies for assessing and comparing indirect effects in multiple mediator models. *Behavior Research Methods*, *40*(3), 879–891. doi:10.3758/BRM.40.3.879 PMID:18697684

Preacher, K. J., & Hayes, A. F. (2004). SPSS and SAS procedures for estimating indirect effects in simple mediation models. *Behavior Research Methods, Instruments, & Computers*, *36*(4), 717–731. doi:10.3758/BF03206553 PMID:15641418

Price, J., & Mueller, C. (1986). *Handbook of organizational measurement*. Marshfield, MA: Pitman Publishing.

Pudney, S. (2004). Keeping off the Grass? An econometric model of cannabis consumption in Britain. *Journal of Applied Econometrics*, *19*(4), 435–453. doi:10.1002/jae.746

Qi, M., & Zhang, P. G. (2008). Trend time-series modeling and forecasting with neural networks. *IEEE Transactions on Neural Networks*, *19*(5), 808–816. doi:10.1109/TNN.2007.912308 PMID:18467210

Qin, J., Liu, X., & Pedrycz, W. (2017). An extended TODIM multi-criteria group decision making method for green supplier selection in interval type-2 fuzzy environment. *European Journal of Operational Research*, *258*(2), 626–638. doi:10.1016/j.ejor.2016.09.059

Radović, D., Stević, Ž., Pamučar, D., Zavadskas, E., Badi, I., Antuchevičiene, J., & Turskis, Z. (2018). Measuring performance in transportation companies in developing countries: A novel rough ARAS model. *Symmetry*, *10*(10), 434. doi:10.3390ym10100434

Rajesh, R., & Ravi, V. (2015). Supplier selection in resilient supply chains: A grey relational analysis approach. *Journal of Cleaner Production*, *86*, 343–359. doi:10.1016/j.jclepro.2014.08.054

Raji, W. (2013). *An Introductory Course in Elementary Number Theory*. Washington, DC: Saylor Foundation.

Rama, R. S., & Padmanabhan, G. (2012). Application of Taguchi methods and ANOVA in optimization of process parameters for metal removal rate in electrochemical machining of Al/5% SiC composites. *International Journal of Engineering Research and Applications*, *2*(3), 192–197.

Ramos, R., & Suriñach, J. (2013). *A Gravity Model of Migration Between ENC and EU*. Barcelona: Research Institute of Applied Economics.

Rand, D. G., & Nowak, M. A. (2013). Human cooperation. *Trends in Cognitive Sciences*, *17*(8), 413–425. doi:10.1016/j.tics.2013.06.003 PMID:23856025

Ransbotham, S., Gerbert, P., Reeves, M., Kiron, D., & Spira, M. (2018). *Artificial intelligence in business gets real*. MIT Sloan Management Review and The Boston Consulting Group.

Ransbotham, S., Kiron, D., Gerbert, P., & Reeves, M. (2017). Reshaping Business With Artificial Intelligence: Closing the Gap Between Ambition and Action. *MIT Sloan Management Review*, *59*(1).

Rebelo, S. T. (1991). Long-Run Policy Analysis and Long-Run Growth. *Journal of Political Economy*, *99*(3), 500–521. doi:10.1086/261764

Reed, R. (1993). Pruning algorithms a survey. *IEEE Transactions on Neural Networks*, *4*(5), 740–747. doi:10.1109/72.248452 PMID:18276504

Ricardo, D. (1817). *On the Principles of Political Economy and Taxation*. London: John Murrey.

Riedmiller, M. (1994). Advanced supervised learning in multi-layer perceptrons – from backpropagation to adaptive learning algorithms. *Computer Standards & Interfaces*, *16*(3), 265–278. doi:10.1016/0920-5489(94)90017-5

Rodrigues, L. L. R., Kantharaj, A. N., Kantharaj, B., Freitas, W. R. C., & Murthy, B. R. N. (2012). Effectin of cutting parameters on surface roughness and cutting force in turning mild steel. *Research Journal of Recent Science*, *1*(10), 19–26.

Romer, P.M. (1990). Endogenous Technical Change. *Journal of Political Economy*, *98*(5).

Romer, P. M. (1986). Increasing Returns and Long-Run Growth. *Journal of Political Economy*, *94*(5), 1002–1037. doi:10.1086/261420

Ross, S. (1976). Return, risk and arbitrage. In I. Friend & J. Bicksler (Eds.), *Risk and return in finance* (Vol. 1, pp. 189–219). Cambridge, MA: Ballinger.

Roy, R. K. (2001). *Design of experiments using the Taguchi approach: 16 steps to product and process improvement*. New York: John Wiley & Sons.

Sahu, N. K., Datta, S., & Mahapatra, S. S. (2015). Fuzzy based appraisement module for 3PL evaluation and selection. *Benchmarking: An International Journal*, *22*(3), 354–392. doi:10.1108/BIJ-01-2013-0002

Saikkonen, P., & Luukkonen, R. (1988). Lagrange multiplier tests for testing non-linearities in time series models. *Scandinavian Journal of Statistics*, *15*, 55–68.

Salacuse, J. W. (2017). BIT by BIT: The Growth of Bilateral Investment Treaties and Their Impact on Foreign Investment in Developing Countries. In F. Beveridge (Ed.), *Globalization and International Investment* (pp. 655–676). London: Routledge.

Salas, E., Stagle, K. C., Burke, C. S., & Goodwin, G. F. (2007). Fostering team effectiveness in organizations: Toward an integrative theoretical framework of team performance. In R. A. Dienstbier, J. W. Shuart, W. Spaulding, & J. Poland (Eds.), Modeling complex systems: Motivation, cognition and social processes. Academic Press.

Salas, E., Bowers, C. A., & Cannon-Bowers, J. A. (1995). Military team research: 10 years of progress. *Military Psychology*, *7*(2), 55–75. doi:10.120715327876mp0702_2

Salas, E., Sims, D. E., & Burke, C. S. (2005). Is there a "Big Five" in teamwork? *Small Group Research*, *36*(5), 555–599. doi:10.1177/1046496405277134

Sánchez, P. (2008). Cambios Estructurales en Series de Tiempo: Una revisión del estado del arte. *Ingenierías*, *7*(12), 115–140.

Sánchez, P. A., & García, J. R. (2017). A New Methodology for Neural Network Training Ensures Error Reduction in Time Series Forecasting. *Journal of Computational Science*, *13*(7), 211–217. doi:10.3844/jcssp.2017.211.217

Sánchez, P. A., & García, J. R. (2018). Autoregressive Moving Average Recurrent Neural Networks Applied to the Modelling of Colombian Exchange Rate. *International Journal of Artificial Intelligence*, *16*(2), 194–207.

Sánchez, P. A., & Velásquez, J. D. (2005). Modelado Estructural No Lineal de Series Temporales. *Avances en Sistemas e Informática*, *2*(2), 27–38.

Sang, X., & Liu, X. (2016). An interval type-2 fuzzy sets-based TODIM method and its application to green supplier selection. *The Journal of the Operational Research Society*, *67*(5), 722–734. doi:10.1057/jors.2015.86

Sasser, E. W., & Arbeit, S. P. (1976). Selling jobs in the services sector. *Business Horizons*, *19*(3), 61–65. doi:10.1016/0007-6813(76)90053-7

Schiffmann, W., Joost, M., & Werner, R. (1993). Application of genetic algorithms to the construction of topologies for multilayer perceptron. *Proceedings of the International Conference on Artificial Neural Networks and Genetic Algorithms*, 675–682. 10.1007/978-3-7091-7533-0_98

Schneider, R., & Imai, J. (2017). *Valuing Investments in Digital Business Transformation: A Real Options Approach.* Retrieved on April 29, 2018, from: http://realoptions.org/openconf2018/data/papers/162.pdf

Schneier, B. (1996). *Applied Cryptography Protocols, Algorithms and Source Code in C.* New York: Wiley.

Schröder, D. (2011). Investment under ambiguity with the best and worst in mind. *Mathematics and Financial Economics*, *4*(2), 107–133. doi:10.100711579-011-0036-3

Schwartz, E. S., & Trigeorgis, L. (Eds.). (2004). Real options and investment under uncertainty: classical readings and recent contributions. MIT Press.

Schwarz, G. (1978). Estimating the dimension of a model. *Annals of Statistics*, *6*(2), 461–464. doi:10.1214/aos/1176344136

Seers, A. (1989). Team-member exchange quality: A new construct for role-making research. *Organizational Behavior and Human Decision Processes*, *43*(1), 118–135. doi:10.1016/0749-5978(89)90060-5

Senturk, S., Erginel, N., & Binici, Y. (2017). Interval Type-2 Fuzzy Analytic Network Process for Modelling a Third-party Logistics (3PL) Company. *Journal of Multiple-Valued Logic & Soft Computing, 28.*

Sezgin, F. H. (2017, October). AR-GE Harcamalarının Büyüme ile İlişkisinin Analizi: Gelişmiş ve Gelişmekte Ülkeler Karşılaştırması. *3rd International Conference on Economic and Social Impacts of Globalization*, 69.

Shabani, A., & Jamkhaneh, E. B. (2014). A new generalized intuitionistic fuzzy number. *Journal of Fuzzy Set Valued Analysis*, *24*, 1–10.

Shah, V. K. (2015). Artificial intelligence management in financial crisis. In *Computational Intelligence and Computing Research (ICCIC), 2015 IEEE International Conference on* (pp. 1-6). IEEE.

Shanker, M., Hu, M. Y., & Hung, M. S. (1996). Effect of data standardization on neural network training. *Omega*, *24*(4), 385–397. doi:10.1016/0305-0483(96)00010-2

Shaw, A. K., & Roy, T. K. (2012). Some arithmetic operations on triangular intuitionistic fuzzy number and its application on reliability evaluation. *International Journal of Fuzzy Mathematics and Systems*, *2*(4), 363–382.

Shi, W., Sun, S. L., Yan, D., & Zhu, Z. (2017). Institutional fragility and outward foreign direct investment from China. *Journal of International Business Studies*, *48*(4), 452–476. doi:10.105741267-016-0050-z

Shravani, D., Lakshmi, P. K., & Balasubramaniam, J. (2011). Preparation and optimization of various parameters of enteric coated pellets using the Taguchi L9 orthogonal array design and their characterization. *Acta Pharmaceutica Sinica. B*, *1*(1), 56–63. doi:10.1016/j.apsb.2011.04.005

Siau, K., Tan, X., & Sheng, H. (2010). Important characteristics of software development team members: An empirical investigation using Repertory Grid. *Information Systems Journal*, *20*(6), 563–580. doi:10.1111/j.1365-2575.2007.00254.x

Sims, C. A. (1993). A Variable Probabilistic Macroeconomic Forecasting Model. In Business Cycles, Indicators, and Forecasting (pp. 179-214). University of Chicago Press.

Singh, H., & Jun, K. W. (1995). *Some New Evidence on Determinants of Foreign Direct Investment in Developing Countries* (Policy Research Working Paper No. WPS 1531). Retrieved on September 22, 2017, from: https://elibrary.worldbank.org/doi/abs/10.1596/1813-9450-1531

Singh, S. K., & Yadav, S. P. (2014). Efficient approach for solving type-1 intuitionistic fuzzy transportation problem. *International Journal of System Assurance Engineering and Management*, 1-9. doi:. doi:10.100713198-014-0274-x

Singh, R. K., Gunasekaran, A., & Kumar, P. (2017). Third party logistics (3PL) selection for cold chain management: A fuzzy AHP and fuzzy TOPSIS approach. *Annals of Operations Research*, 1–23.

Singh, S. (2012). Note on assignment algorithm with easy method of drawing lines to cover all zeros. *International Journal of Operations Research and Information Systems*, *3*(3), 87–97. doi:10.4018/joris.2012070106

Smidts, A., Pruyn, A. T. H., & van Riel, C. B. M. (2001). The impact of employee communication and perceived external prestige on organizational identification. *Academy of Management Journal*, *44*, 1051–1062.

Smith, A. (1776). *The Wealth of Nations*. London: Methuen and Co., Ltd.

Smith, C. W. Jr. (1990). The theory of corporate finance: A historical overview. In C. W. Smith Jr., (Ed.), *The modern theory of corporate finance* (2nd ed.; pp. 3–24). New York: McGraw-Hill.

Smith, M., & Thomas, E. (2017). Exploring the Social Impact of Foreign Direct Investment on Institutional Change: The case of Russia. In M. A. Khan (Ed.), *Multinational Enterprise Management Strategies in Developing Countries* (pp. 198–214). Hershey, PA: IGI Global.

Soltis, J., Boyd, R., & Richerson, P. J. (1995). Can Group-Functional Behaviors Evolve by Cultural Group Selection? An Empirical Test. *Current Anthropology*, *63*(3), 473–494. doi:10.1086/204381

Srinivasan, D., Liew, A. C., & Chang, C. S. (1994). A neural network short-term load forecaster. *Electric Power Systems Research*, *28*(3), 227–234. doi:10.1016/0378-7796(94)90037-X

Srinivas, B., & Ganesan, G. (2015). A method for solving intuitionistic fuzzy assignment problem using Branch and Bound Method, *International Journal of Engineering Technology. Management and Applied Sciences*, *3*(2), 227–237.

Srinivas, B., & Ganesan, G. (2015). Optimal solution for intuitionistic fuzzy transportation problem via Revised Distribution Method. *International Journal of Mathematics Trends and Technology*, *19*(2), 150–161.

Stallings, W. (2006). *Cryptography and Network Security Principles and Practice*. London, UK: Pearson Education.

Stauss, V. B., & Schultze, H. S. (1990). Internet marketing. *Journal of Marketing*, *3*(3), 149–158.

Stein, W. (2017). *Elementary Number Theory: Primes, Congruence's, and Secrets*. New York: Springer.

Stephens, C. P., & Weisbach, M. S. (1998). Actual share reacquisitions in open-market repurchase programs. *The Journal of Finance*, *53*(1), 313–333. doi:10.1111/0022-1082.115194

Stević, Ž., Pamučar, D., Kazimieras Zavadskas, E., Ćirović, G., & Prentkovskis, O. (2017b). The selection of wagons for the internal transport of a logistics company: A novel approach based on rough BWM and rough SAW methods. *Symmetry*, *9*(11), 264. doi:10.3390ym9110264

Stević, Ž., Pamučar, D., Vasiljević, M., Stojić, G., & Korica, S. (2017a). Novel Integrated Multi-Criteria Model for Supplier Selection: Case Study Construction Company. *Symmetry*, *9*(11), 279. doi:10.3390ym9110279

Stiglitz, J. (1974, December). On the irrelevance of corporate financial policy. *The American Economic Review*, 851–866.

Subramanian, R., & Gopalakrishna, P. (2001). The market orientation-performance relationship in the context of a developing economy: An empirical analysis. *Journal of Business Research*, *53*(1), 1–13. doi:10.1016/S0148-2963(99)00109-5

Subramanian, V., & Hung, M. (1993). A GRG2-based system for training neural networks: Design and computational experience. *ORSA Journal on Computing*, *5*(4), 386–394. doi:10.1287/ijoc.5.4.386

Sung, A. H. (1998). Ranking importance of input parameters of neural networks. *Expert Systems with Applications*, *15*(3-4), 405–411. doi:10.1016/S0957-4174(98)00041-4

Sun, H., Zhao, Y., & Yau, H. K. (2009). The relationship between quality management and the speed of new product development. *The TQM Journal*, *21*(6), 576–588. doi:10.1108/17542730910995855

Sussman, N. M. (2000). The dynamic nature of cultural identity throughout cultural transitions: Why home is not so sweet. *Personality and Social Psychology Review*, *4*(4), 355–373. doi:10.1207/S15327957PSPR0404_5

Sussman, N. M. (2002). Testing the cultural identity model of the cultural transition cycle: Sojourners return home. *International Journal of Intercultural Relations*, *26*(4), 391–408. doi:10.1016/S0147-1767(02)00013-5

Szalavetz, A. (2018). Industry 4.0 and capability development in manufacturing subsidiaries. *Technological Forecasting and Social Change*. doi:10.1016/j.techfore.2018.06.027

Taguchi, G. (1986). *Orthogonal Arrays and Linear Graph*. Dearborn, MI: American Supplier Institute, Inc.

Tang, Z., & Fishwick, P. A. (1993). Feedforward neural nets as models for time series forecasting. *ORSA Journal on Computing*, *5*(4), 374–385. doi:10.1287/ijoc.5.4.374

Tang, Z., & Koehler, J. G. (1994). Deterministic global optimal FNN training algorithms. *Neural Networks*, *7*(2), 1405–1412. doi:10.1016/0893-6080(94)90024-8

Tao, F., Cheng, Y., Zhang, L., & Nee, A. Y. (2017). Advanced manufacturing systems: Socialization characteristics and trends. *Journal of Intelligent Manufacturing*, *28*(5), 1079–1094. doi:10.100710845-015-1042-8

Teece, D. J. (2007). Explicating dynamic capabilities: The nature and microfoundations of (sustainable) enterprise performance. *Strategic Management Journal*, *28*(13), 1319–1350. doi:10.1002mj.640

Teece, D. J., Pisano, G. P., & Shuen, A. (1997). Dynamic capabilities and strategic management. *Strategic Management Journal*, *18*(7), 119–142. doi:10.1002/(SICI)1097-0266(199708)18:7<509::AID-SMJ882>3.0.CO;2-Z

Teradata. (2017). *State of artificial intelligence for enterprises*. Teradata.

Thompson, G. L. (1981). A recursive method for solving assignment problems. *Journal of Science Direct- North-Holland Mathematics Studies, 59*, 319-343.

Thorani, Y. L. P., & Shankar, N. R. (2013). Fuzzy assignment problem with generalized fuzzy numbers. *Applied Mathematical Sciences*, *7*(71), 3511–3537.

Tian, G. Y., Yin, G., & Taylor, D. (2002). Internet-based manufacturing: A review and a new infrastructure for distributed intelligent manufacturing. *Journal of Intelligent Manufacturing*, *13*(5), 323–338. doi:10.1023/A:1019907906158

Tinbergen, J. (1962). *Shaping the World Economy; Suggestions for an International Economic Policy*. New York: Twentieth Century Fund.

Tkacz, G., & Hu, S. (1999). *Forecasting GDP growth using artificial neural networks* (Working paper pp. 99-3). Ottawa: Bank of Canada.

Tokarczyk, J., Hansen, E., Green, M., & Down, J. (2007). A Resource-Based View and Market Orientation Theory Examination of the Role of "Familiness" in Family Business Success. *Family Business Review*, *20*(1), 17–31. doi:10.1111/j.1741-6248.2007.00081.x

Tong, H. (1990). *Nonlinear Time Series: A Dynamical System Approach*. Oxford, UK: Oxford University Press.

Tyler, E., & Chivaka, R. (2011). The use of real options valuation methodology in enhancing the understanding of the impact of climate change on companies. *Business Strategy and the Environment*, *20*(1), 55–70. doi:10.1002/bse.668

Ulku, H. (2004). R&D, innovation, and Economic Growth: An Empirical Analysis (No. 4-185). International Monetary Fund.

Ulutas, A., Shukla, N., Kiridena, S., & Gibson, P. (2016). A utility-driven approach to supplier evaluation and selection: Empirical validation of an integrated solution framework. *International Journal of Production Research*, *54*(5), 1554–1567. doi:10.1080/00207543.2015.1098787

UNCTAD. (2018). *World Investment Report 2015*. Retrieved on April 22, 2018, from: https://unctad.org/en/PublicationsLibrary/wir2018_en.pdf

UNODC. (2018). *2018 World Drug Report*. Retrieved on April 22, 2018, from: https://www.unodc.org/wdr2018/

Van Bekkum, S., Pennings, E., & Smit, H. (2009). A real options perspective on R&D portfolio diversification. *Research Policy*, *38*(7), 1150–1158. doi:10.1016/j.respol.2009.03.009

Van Laarhoven, P. J. M., & Pedrycz, W. (1983). A fuzzy extension of Saaty's priority theory. *Fuzzy Sets and Systems*, *11*(1-3), 229–241. doi:10.1016/S0165-0114(83)80082-7

Van Putten, A. B., & MacMillan, I. C. (2004). Making real options really work. *Harvard Business Review*, *82*(12), 134–142. PMID:15605572

Varghese, A., & Kuriakose, S. (2012). Centroid of an intuitionistic fuzzy number. *Notes on Intuitionistic Fuzzy Sets*, *18*(1), 19–24.

Vasiljević, M., Fazlollahtabar, H., Stević, Ž., & Vesković, S. (2018). A rough multicriteria approach for evaluation of supplier criteria in automotive industry. *Decision Making: Applications in Management and Engineering*, *1*(1), 82–96.

Vermaelen, T. (1981). Common stock repurchases and market signalling: An empirical study. *Journal of Financial Economics*, *9*(2), 139–183. doi:10.1016/0304-405X(81)90011-8

Vigila, S., & Muneeswaran, K. (2010). Implementation of text based cryptosystem using Elliptic Curve Cryptography. *IEEE Xplore Digital Library*, *1*, 82–85. doi:10.1109/ICADVC.2009.5378025

Vojak, B. A., & Chambers, F. A. (2004). Roadmapping disruptive technical threats and opportunities in complex, technology-based subsystems: The SAILS methodology. *Technological Forecasting and Social Change*, *71*(1-2), 121–139. doi:10.1016/S0040-1625(03)00047-7

Wang, T. C., & Tsai, S. Y. (2018). Solar panel supplier selection for the photovoltaic system design by using fuzzy multi-criteria decision making (MCDM) approaches. *Energies*, *11*(8), 1989. doi:10.3390/en11081989

Wang, T. K., Zhang, Q., Chong, H. Y., & Wang, X. (2017). Integrated supplier selection framework in a resilient construction supply chain: An approach via analytic hierarchy process (AHP) and grey relational analysis (GRA). *Sustainability*, *9*(2), 289. doi:10.3390u9020289

Wang, X., & Feng, C. X. (2002). Development of empirical models for surface roughness prediction in finish turning. *International Journal of Advanced Manufacturing Technology*, *20*(5), 348–356. doi:10.1007001700200162

Wan, S. P., Xu, G. L., & Dong, J. Y. (2017). Supplier selection using ANP and ELECTRE II in interval 2-tuple linguistic environment. *Information Sciences*, *385*, 19–38. doi:10.1016/j.ins.2016.12.032

Ward, M. (2013, October 25). *How the modern world depends on encryption*. Retrieved on May 5, 2018, from: http://www.bbc.com/news/technology-24667834

Witt, U. (2000). Changing cognitive frames --Changing organizational forms: An entrepreneurial theory of organizational development. *Industrial and Corporate Change*, *9*(4), 733–745. doi:10.1093/icc/9.4.733

Wolf, S. (2016). Drugs, Violence, and Corruption: Perspectives from Mexico and Central America. *Latin American Politics and Society*, *58*(1), 146–155. doi:10.1111/j.1548-2456.2016.00298.x

World Data Bank. (2018). Retrieved on July 8, 2018, from: http://databank.worldbank.org/data/source/world-development-indicators

Wren, B. M., Souder, W. E., & Berkowitz, D. (2000). Market Orientation and New Product Development in Global Industrial Firms. *Industrial Marketing Management*, *29*(6), 601–611. doi:10.1016/S0019-8501(00)00120-6

Wu, Y., Chen, K., Zeng, B., Xu, H., & Yang, Y. (2016). Supplier selection in nuclear power industry with extended VIKOR method under linguistic information. *Applied Soft Computing*, *48*, 444–457. doi:10.1016/j.asoc.2016.07.023

Wu, Y., Zhou, L., & Li, J. X. (2007). Cointegration and causality between R&D expenditure and economic growth in China: 1953-2004. *International Conference on Public Administration*, 76.

Xhepa, S., & Agolli, M. (2003). *Albania's Foreign Trade Through a Gravity Model*. Tirana: Trade and Economic Integration of the Western Balkan Countries in the European Union.

Xu, L. D., Xu, E. L., & Li, L. (2018). Industry 4.0: State of the art and future trends. *International Journal of Production Research*, *56*(8), 2941–2962. doi:10.1080/00207543.2018.1444806

Yale, K. (1997). Preparing the right data for training neural networks. *IEEE Spectrum*, *34*(3), 64–66. doi:10.1109/6.576011

Yayla, A. Y., Oztekin, A., Gumus, A. T., & Gunasekaran, A. (2015). A hybrid data analytic methodology for 3PL transportation provider evaluation using fuzzy multi-criteria decision making. *International Journal of Production Research*, *53*(20), 6097–6113. doi:10.1080/00207543.2015.1022266

Yıldırım, D. Ç., & Kantarcı, T. (2014). Araştırma Geliştirme Harcamaları ve Ekonomik Büyüme İlişkisi Üzerine Bir Panel Veri Analizi. *Anemon Muş Alparslan Üniversitesi Sosyal Bilimler Dergisi*, *6*(5), 661–670.

You, X. Y., You, J. X., Liu, H. C., & Zhen, L. (2015). Group multi-criteria supplier selection using an extended VIKOR method with interval 2-tuple linguistic information. *Expert Systems with Applications*, *42*(4), 1906–1916. doi:10.1016/j.eswa.2014.10.004

Yu, X. H., Chen, G. A., & Cheng, S. X. (1995). Dynamic learning rate optimization of the backpropagation algorithm. *IEEE Transactions on Neural Networks*, *6*(3), 669–677. doi:10.1109/72.377972 PMID:18263352

Zadeh, L. A. (1965). Fuzzy sets. *Information and Control*, *8*(3), 338–353.

Zadeh, L. A. (1965). Fuzzy sets. *Information and Control*, *8*(3), 338–353. doi:10.1016/S0019-9958(65)90241-X

Zamani, S. N. M., Abdul-Talib, A. N., & Ashari, H. (2016). Strategic orientations and new product success: The mediating impact of innovation speed. International Information Institute (Tokyo) Information, 19(7B), 2785.

Zamani, M., Rabbani, A., Yazdani-Chamzini, A., & Turskis, Z. (2014). An integrated model for extending brand based on fuzzy ARAS and ANP methods. *Journal of Business Economics and Management*, *15*(3), 403–423. doi:10.3846/16111699.2014.923929

Zarbakhshnia, N., Soleimani, H., & Ghaderi, H. (2018). Sustainable third-party reverse logistics provider evaluation and selection using fuzzy SWARA and developed fuzzy COPRAS in the presence of risk criteria. *Applied Soft Computing*, *65*, 307–319. doi:10.1016/j.asoc.2018.01.023

Zavadskas, E. K., Stević, Ž., Tanackov, I., & Prentkovskis, O. (2018). A Novel Multicriteria Approach–Rough Step-Wise Weight Assessment Ratio Analysis Method (R-SWARA) and Its Application in Logistics. *Studies in Informatics and Control*, *27*(1), 97–106. doi:10.24846/v27i1y201810

Zerenler, M., Türker, N., & Şahin, E. (2007). Küresel Teknoloji, Araştırma-Geliştirme (Ar-Ge) Ve Yenilik İlişkisi. *Selçuk Üniversitesi Sosyal Bilimler Enstitüsü Dergisi*, *1*(17), 653–667.

Zhang, G. P., Patuwo, B. E., & Hu, M. Y. (1998). Forecasting with artificial neural networks: The state of the art. *International Journal of Forecasting*, *14*(1), 35–62. doi:10.1016/S0169-2070(97)00044-7

Zhang, J., Walte, G. G., Miao, Y., & Wayne, W. N. (1995). Wavelet neural networks for function learning. *IEEE Transactions on Signal Processing*, *43*(6), 1485–1497. doi:10.1109/78.388860

Zhang, P. G., & Qi, M. (2005). Neural network forecasting for seasonal and trend time series. *European Journal of Operational Research*, *160*(2), 501–514. doi:10.1016/j.ejor.2003.08.037

Zhang, S., & Li, X. (2015). A hybrid performance evaluation model of TPL providers in agricultural products based on fuzzy ANP-TOPSIS. *Custos E Agronegocio On Line*, *11*(3), 144–165.

Zhang, X. (1994). Time series analysis and prediction by neural networks. *Optimization Methods & Software*, *4*(2), 151–170. doi:10.1080/10556789408805584

Zhou, Z., Liu, X., Pei, J., Pardalos, P. M., Liu, L., & Fu, C. (2017). Real options approach to explore the effect of organizational change on IoT development project. *Optimization Letters*, *11*(5), 995–1011. doi:10.100711590-016-1006-8

About the Contributors

Bryan Christiansen is the Chief Executive Officer of Global Research Society, LLC in Michigan, USA. A former business lecturer at universities in Russia, Turkey, and the USA, he has traveled to 41 countries where he has conducted international business since 1985 in multiple languages and various industries with Global 500 firms and smaller. Christiansen received his Bachelor of Science degree in Marketing at the University of the State of New York in 1996 and his MBA degree at Capella University in 2003. The author of 22 Scopus-indexed Reference books on business, cultural studies, economics, and psychology, he is fluent in Chinese, Japanese, Spanish, and Turkish. Christiansen is currently working with a Russian theoretical mathematician on a new economic model for developing nations.

* * *

Asmat Abdul-Talib teaches international business and international marketing at the Universiti Utara Malaysia. He received his PhD in International Marketing from Aston Business School, Aston University, UK, his MBA in International Business from Cardiff University, UK, and a Bachelors Degree in Economics from Concordia University, Canada. At current, his academic research has received financial support or support in kind from various institutions. His research interests lie primarily in international marketing and strategic marketing, especially in export market intelligence, and the use of export market intelligence in the firm's export decision process.

Turki Abdullah Alanazi is a senior manager at Saudi Telekom Company, Saudi Arabia.

Hasbullah Ashari is an Associate Professor at Faculty of Science and Information Technology, Universiti Teknologi Petronas, Malaysia.

Salvador Cruz Rambaud was born in Cádiz, Spain, in 1957. He received the degree in Mathematics from the University of Granada, Spain, in 1981; later, he received the degree in Economics and the Ph. D. degree in Economics and Business from the Open University, Madrid, Spain, in 1991 and 1994, respectively. In 1992, he joined the Department Accounting and Finance, University of Almería, as a lecturer, where he became an Associate Professor in 1996, and a Full Professor in 2010. His current research interests include anomalies in intertemporal choice, mathematical analysis of financial operations and elicitation of new statistical distributions in Finance. Professor Cruz Rambaud has acted as reviewer of many important journals: International Journal of Uncertainty and Knowledge-Based Systems, Physica A, European Journal of Operational Research, among others.

Amir Ahmad Dar is the Research Scholar in Department of Mathematics and Actuarial Science at B S Abdur Rahman Crescent University Chennai. He received his BSc in Actuarial and Financial Mathematics from Islamic University of Science and Technology Kashmir and his MSc in Actuarial Science from B S Abdur Rahman Crescent University Chennai. He passed the India Actuarial Common Entrance Test (ACET) in the year 2014. He did Eight weeks Internship at Cluster innovation center the University of Delhi in the year 2014 and Six weeks Internship at Jammu and Kashmir Bank in year 2016. The area of interest: Financial mathematics, financial economics, statistics and business mathematics.

Sharmishta Desai has completed Ph.D in computer Engineering from Pune University, India. Her area of research is machine learning, Big Data and cyber security. She has received different research grants and published papers in SCOPUS index journals, IEEE, Springer Conferences.

Carlos Hernán Fajardo-Toro received a PhD degree in Computer Science (Tools for developing intelligent software) and the degree of MSc in Management and Logistics and Supply Chain of the University of Vigo (Spain). He serves currently as a full-time teacher at the School of Business Administration - EAN (Bogota, Colombia).

Nerajda Feruni is graduated from Economics Department of Epoka University. She is interested in international trade and the reasons behind it.

Eglantina Hysa is a Lecturer of Economics at the Epoka University where she teaches International Economy, Development and Growth, and Microeconomics courses. Eglantina Hysa's research focuses on International Trade, Development and Econometric Models. She has been part of some training programs related to the Public Interior Auditing and International/National Standards of Accounting. Her recent papers examine characteristics that cover the economical aspects such as the pension system, demographic change, corruption, inequality, human development and the foreign direct investment in Western Balkans and with a particular focus in Albania. She is part of national networks by being either the founder or active member in associations related to economics and sociology. Actually she is head of Economics Department at Epoka University. At the same time, she is engaged as an External Expert on behalf of Public Accreditation Agency for Higher Education, Republic of Albania.

Gökhan Karahan received his master's degree (2011) and doctorate degree (2016) at İnönü University in Turkey. He currently works as assistant professor at Batman University. He writes on macroeconomics and econometric analysis.

P. Senthil Kumar is an Associate Professor (Mathematics) in Department of Humanities and Sciences at Navodaya Institute of Technology, Raichur, Karnataka, India. He has eight years (approximately) of teaching experience. He received his BSc, MSc and MPhil from Jamal Mohamed College, Tiruchirappalli in 2006, 2008, 2010 respectively. He completed his BEd in Jamal Mohamed College of Teacher Education in 2009. He completed PGDCA in 2011 in the Bharathidasan University and PGDAOR in 2012 in the Annamalai University, Tamil Nadu, India. He has done his Ph.D titled "Algorithmic approach for solving allocation problems under intuitionistic fuzzy environment" at Jamal Mohamed College in 2017. He has published many research papers in referred national and international journals like Springer, Korean Institute of Intelligent Systems, IGI Global, Inderscience, etc. He has published two book chapters in IGI Global publication. He also presented his research paper in Elsevier Conference Proceedings (ICMS-2014), MMASC-2012, etc. His areas of research interest include fuzzy optimization, intuitionistic fuzzy optimization, operations research, numerical analysis and graph theory, etc.

Siti Norhasmaedayu Mohd Zamani is a senior lecturer at College of Business, Universiti Utara Malaysia.

Anuradha N. is the Associate Professor in the Department of Management Studies at B S Abdur Rahman Crescent University Chennai. She received her BSc in Physics from Madurai Kamaraj University, Chennai and her MBA in Finance from Madurai Kamaraj University, Chennai. Also she received the Doctorate in Financial System from Anna University, Chennai.

Uma R. Pujeri was born in Sangli, India, in 1981. She has received M.Tech degree from PSG Tech college of Engineering Coimbatore in 2008. She has received doctorate degree from Anna University Chennai in May 2017. Her research area is computer network congestion control algorithm. She has worked as a Assistant Professor in Adithya College of Engineering Coimbatore for six years. Currently she is working as a Associate Professor in MIT College Of Engineering Pune Maharashtra as Associate Professor. She has total ten years of teaching experience. She is a Life Member of the Indian Society for Technical Education (ISTE). She has total 10 publications in International journal.

Ana Sánchez Pérez works in the area of knowledge of Financial Economy and Accounting of the Department of Economy and Business of the University of Almería (Spain). Her main line of research focuses on the analysis and management of risk in financial-random operations; as well as the study of the valuation methods of financial assets and real options.

Rafael Espinosa Ramirez has a Ph.D. in Economics (University of Essex); M.Sc. in Economics (Center for Research and Teaching in Economics, CIDE); B.A. in Economics (University of Guadalajara). Rafael is head of the Center for Social and Economic Research (CISE), Professor at the Department of Economics, University of Guadalajara. Research Interest: International Economics, Institutional Economics, Crime Economics, Industrial Organization and Economics and Psychology.

Paola Sanchez-Sanchez received the Bs. degree in industrial engineering in 2001, the MS degree in Systems Engineering in 2006, and the PhD degree in Engineering in 2012, all of them from the Universidad Nacional de Colombia, Medellin, Colombia. Since 2005 she has worked in education as a teacher in different universities. At present, she is associate professor of the engineering faculty in the Simón Bolívar University, Barranquilla, Colombia. Her current interests are in develop and understanding of methods of computational intelligence in modeling and forecasting of time series; quantitative optimization; application of knowledge extraction techniques in databases using computational intelligence; develop of intelligent systems with learning machine.

Amit Savyanavar received M.E. degree in Computer Science and Engineering from Shivaji University, Kolhapur. He is pursuing his PhD in Computer Science and Engineering from Shivaji University, Kolhapur. Currently, he is working in Department of Computer Engineering at MIT's college of Engineering, Pune. He has a total teaching experience of 16 years. His research interests are mobile computing, operating systems and distributed systems. He has published his research work in various reputed journals and books.

Jorge Tarifa-Fernández is Research Fellow in the Department of Economics and Business at the The University of Almería. He received the MBA Degree in 2012 from the University of Almería and the Ph.D. in 2017 also in the University of Almería. His research interests include supply chain management, environmental management, and strategy.

Alptekin Ulutaş is assistant professor in International Trade and Logistics Dept. at Cumhuriyet University in Sivas, Turkey. He has taken a PhD degree from University of Wollongong in February 2016. He has been serving as assistant professor at the Faculty of Economics and Administrative Sciences at Cumhuriyet University since June 2017. So far, he has written 7 articles and 11 conference papers in total. His research area is optimization and multi-criteria decision making, fuzzy and stochastic programming.

Index

M

N

O

P

R

S

T

U

V

www.ingramcontent.com/pod-product-compliance
Lightning Source LLC
LaVergne TN
LVHW062122300926
849161LV00010B/2522